Negro Social
and Political
THOUGHT
1850-1920

Negro Social and Political THOUGHT

1850-1920

Representative Texts

EDITED BY

HOWARD BROTZ

Basic Books, Inc., Publishers

NEW YORK : LONDON

Preface

The purpose of this anthology is to bring together the most serious thought of Negroes about the future of their race in this country. In organizing the materials, I have been guided by the tension, explicit or implicit, between the two poles of this thought. These are, on the one hand, those voices which clearly projected civic assimilation as the goal of Negro aspiration and which thought through what this aim would entail, and on the other hand, those nationalist or separatist voices which despaired of ever having a dignified future in a bi-racial society. Given the fact that a dialectic between these two positions is concerned with the most fundamental question that any minority group can face, it is not surprising to find raised within the framework of this dialectic many, if not almost all, the questions which still arise today. The period of time comprehended by these selections is from about 1850, when emigration first emerged as an issue within Negro thought, until the first decades of this century, when nationalism, cultural and political, briefly re-emerged as a dissent to the policy of assimilation—the latter having become unquestionably dominant since the abolition of slavery. Since the anthology is limited to social and political thought in as strict a sense as possible, theological disputations of the sort that appeared in the anti-slavery controversy and in popular mythology have been excluded.

In the preparation of this anthology, I should like to acknowledge the great help given me by Mrs. Emma Kaplan and Miss Patricia Delks, reference librarians at Smith College, in locating and bringing together materials. I have benefited much from unpublished papers of Mr. Herbert Storing and Mr. Hollis Lynch, on Frederick Douglass and Negro nationalism respectively, and look forward to their publication. I should like to thank the staff of the Schomburg Collection of the New York Public Library for their help. Mrs. Elsie Gilardino rendered invaluable secretarial assistance. Smith College kindly provided funds toward the preparation of the manuscript. I should like to thank Mrs. Alice Gloster Green for her research assistance and also for our many stimulating discussions about problems of Negro thought. Finally, I should like to thank Mr. Werner J. Dannhauser, who read the manuscript and made many helpful suggestions.

HOWARD BROTZ

New York City
March 1966

Contents

Negro Social and Political THOUGHT

1850-1920

INTRODUCTION

A GUIDE TO THE MATERIALS

> The question is: Can the white and colored people of this country be blended into a common nationality, and enjoy together, in the same country, under the same flag, the inestimable blessings of life, liberty, and the pursuit of happiness, as neighborly citizens of a common country? I answer most unhesitatingly, I believe they can.
>
> —FREDERICK DOUGLASS, "The Present and Future of the Colored Race in America," May 1863

> The problem is how to make these millions of Negroes self-supporting, intelligent, economical, and valuable citizens, as well as how to bring about proper relations between them and the white citizens among whom they live.
>
> —BOOKER T. WASHINGTON, *The Future of the American Negro*, p. 5

What are the main questions with which Negro social and political thought has been concerned? As we shall see, there has been one overarching question, whose comprehensive character has affected all the others, and that question is whether the Negro could look forward to a future as a citizen of this republic. Was color prejudice of such a magnitude and of such a fixed character that the Negro was not assimilable? This question, dealing with the end, had to be settled, as indeed it was, in a dispute that was to take place not merely between Negro and white opinion, but within Negro thought as well. After the Negro's destiny as an equal citizen had been affirmed, two further questions arose. The first concerned the meaning of assimilation. Would the Negro disappear? Would one have to be concerned with this as a problem? Second, there arose a question as to the political and social means necessary to achieve the end of equal citizenship.

EMIGRATION

The first issue to arise within Negro opinion concerned emigration. Throughout the first decades of the nineteenth century, the opinion of free Negroes was opposed, as was antislavery opinion in general, to the aims of the American Colonization Society to resettle freed Negroes in Af-

rica.[1] Such a program was regarded as merely a scheme by which to
perpetuate slavery. By the 1850's, however, a small but vocal number of
Negroes decided that there was no future for the colored man in the
United States. This judgment was a reaction to the growing voice of the
slave interest in national affairs, the consequent deterioration of the civil
position of the free Negro in the North, and above all the passage of the
Fugitive Slave Law of 1850 which endangered his very security.[2]

Martin Delany, in his *The Condition, Elevation, Emigration, and Destiny of the Colored People of the United States*, "Politically Considered"
—the most thoughtful treatise of this segment of Negro opinion—has two
broad objectives. The first is "to understand our true position," to articu-
late theoretically the causes and the cure of the Negro's condition. The
second is rhetorically to awaken in the Negro a manliness that will induce
him to act upon these principles. As to the first, Delany's argument is that
color prejudice is so deep that the Negro is not and can never be politically included in the body politic. This prejudice could be removed only
by the complete destruction of the identity of the colored man. Even if this
were desirable, which he doubts, it would take ages to effect. Thus, to
remain in America is to remain in vassalage. Having diagnosed the true
condition, he proposes the remedy: emigration to a country where there is
no color prejudice, where the colored people "can become worthy citizens"
and elevate themselves above the condition of a race of servants. Block-
ing them from this awareness is their religion, which, he contends, they
carry too far. They do not know that God works through fixed laws of
nature which are His means for every end. They believe that their degraded condition is due to God's displeasure toward them for their unfaithfulness to Him rather than to the fact that they are consumers and
not producers. Their religion thus leads them to expect Him to do for
them what it is necessary for them to do for themselves. He exhorts the
colored people to become pioneers as the whites in the United States had
been. He criticizes them for preferring to be servants in cities built by
others. He shames them by saying, "We cling to our oppressors as the
objects of our love." [3]

In the main part of his treatise Delany rejects Liberia as a tool of slavery
and argues the merits of Central and South America as emigration sites.
The people there would receive the free colored population of the United
States with open arms and as equals. In the appendix he shifts his ground
in two respects: he extends his political aims beyond mere emigration to
project the establishment of a nation as a necessary basis of respect, and

[1] James Forten and Russell Perrott, "An Address to the Humane and Benevolent
Inhabitants of the City and Country of Philadelphia," August 10, 1817, in Carter Woodson, ed., *Negro Orators and Their Orations* (Washington, D.C.: The Associated Publishers, 1925), pp. 52–55. See also page 47.

[2] See Leon Litwack, *North of Slavery: The Negro in the Free States, 1790–1860*
(Chicago: Phoenix Books, 1965), pp. 247–262.

[3] See pages 39, 50–54, 84, 86 f., 93, 96.

he turns to East Africa as the site. He does this without any sentimental considerations whatsoever. In his matter-of-fact way of considering a variety of sites, he reminds one of those Jewish Zionists who were quite prepared to accept Uganda as the Jewish homeland. Nothing matters but that the colored people should have a place somewhere to build for themselves a self-respecting nation. Only later, in his *Official Report of the Niger Valley Exploring Party,* does he speak of Africa as "our fatherland" and state that "our policy must be *Africa for the African race, and black men to rule them.*" He defined black men as "men of African descent who claim an identity with the race." [4] Delany's later views thus resembled somewhat those of his younger contemporary Edward Blyden, who was among the first of what might be called pan-African nationalists. To Blyden, the Negro in this country, whom he often calls African, was in exile. In the attainment of a nationality, Blyden saw not a mere means of relieving degradation, but rather the completion of human nature itself. "Nationality is an ordinance of Nature. The heart of every true Negro yearns after a distinct and separate nationality." [5] Related to this was his view that in each separate race, as in each separate man, something of the absolute is incarnated. "Therefore we cannot extinguish any race either by conflict or amalgamation without serious responsibility." [6]

In the regeneration of Africa, which Blyden regards as the duty of the African in exile to undertake, he sees the solution of the "African problem."

We need some African power, some great center of the race where our physical, pecuniary, and intellectual strength may be collected. We need some spot where such an influence may go forth in behalf of the race as shall be felt by the nations. We are now so scattered and divided that we can do nothing.[7]

On the other hand, Africa, and particularly Liberia, of which Blyden was a supporter, "appeals to the colored men of this country for assistance. . . ." It is of interest to note that Blyden dismissed the objection to the unfavorable climate of Africa as unworthy of pioneers. Moreover, he regarded as a providential interposition the fact that Africa, "while the owners of the soil have been abroad, though entirely unprotected, has lain uninvaded." In his view, it was a providential call to Africans everywhere to "go up and possess the land." [8]

Another writer in this group, whom we briefly note, was James T. Holly, who urged emigration to Haiti. His most important work is *A Vindication of the Capacity of the Negro Race for Self-Government and Civ-*

4 See pages 73–80, 83 f., 98, 100 f., 103, 110.
5 See page 117.
6 See page 138.
7 See page 116.
8 See pages 115, 119 f., 124.

ilized Progress as Demonstrated by Historical Events of the Haitian Revolution. According to Holly, there were two reasons that induced him to undertake this work. The first was to refute, "by the undoubted facts of history . . . the impious dogma of our natural and inherent inferiority." [9] The second was to effect a change in the spirit of the Negro people themselves:

> I wish to do all in my power to inflame the latent embers of self-respect, that the cruelty and injustice of our oppressors have nearly extinguished in our bosoms during the midnight chill of centuries that we have clanked the galling chains of slavery. [10]

In looking at the whole body of nationalist thought, one is struck by the grandeur of the ideals and aspirations which these men projected for the Negro people. All of them stood for political freedom; all of them stood for a manly elevation in the attainment of a high level of civilized achievement which they thought the Negro had no opportunity to pursue in this country. But one is equally bound to note the cynicism inherent in their outlook and the peculiar effect it had in constricting their estimates of what was politically possible. Delany, for example, commenting on the uselessness of contending against the Fugitive Slave Law, writes as follows:

> This is the law of the land and must be obeyed; and we candidly advise that it is useless for us to contend against it. To suppose its repeal is to anticipate an overthrow of the Confederative Union; and we must be allowed an expression of opinion, when we say, that candidly we believe, the existence of the Fugitive Slave Law *necessary* to the continuance of the National Compact. This Law is the foundation of the Compromise—remove it and the consequences are easily determined. We say necessary to the continuance of the National Compact: certainly we will not be understood as meaning that the enactment of such a Law was *really* necessary, or as favoring in the least this political monstrosity of the Thirty-First Congress of the United States of America; but we speak logically and politically, leaving morality and right out of the question—taking our position on the acknowledged popular basis of American Policy; arguing from premise to conclusion. We must abandon all vague theory, and look at *facts* as they really are; viewing ourselves in our true political position in the body politic. To imagine ourselves to be included in the body politic, except by express legislation, is at war with common sense and contrary to fact. [11]

Similarly, Blyden, in expounding his thesis, states, "It ought to be clear to every thinking and impartial mind that there can never occur in this country an equality, social or political, between whites and blacks." [12] As

[9] See page 142.
[10] *Loc. cit.*
[11] See pages 71 f.
[12] See page 114.

late as 1890, he quotes in support of this same point Jefferson's famous phrase:

Nothing is more clearly written in the Book of Destiny than the emancipation of the blacks; and it is equally certain that the two races can never live in a state of equal freedom under the same Government, so insurmountable are the barriers which nature, habit, and opinion have established between them.[13]

What is more, Blyden denies that the above is a prejudiced and anti-Christian conception. He further contends that as the Negroes rise in education and culture, and therefore in love and pride of race, they will welcome this truth as "indispensable to the preservation and prosperity of both races, and as pointing to the regeneration of the African Fatherland." [14]

Thus their moral stance—which to themselves was a tough-minded willingness to face the facts of color prejudice—in fact induced them to look on the status quo as inevitable, permanent, and natural. They absolutized the present, ruled out the possibility of politically improving it, and fled from it in thought. Thus their orientation toward politics, emphasizing as it did what could *not* be done, stimulated the theoretical quest for the "final solution" in emigration.

ASSIMILATION

Frederick Douglass

Frederick Douglass stood in the strongest opposition to these emigrationists. Douglass was not only the most famous Negro abolitionist; he was also a lifelong enemy of colonization schemes, both white and Negro, and these two concerns of his were not unconnected.

No one idea has given rise to more oppression and persecution toward the colored people of this country than that which makes Africa, not America their home. It is that wolfish idea that elbows us off the sidewalk and denies us the rights of citizenship.[15]

As a "solution" to slavery, emigrationism, in his view, was simply an evasion of the problem; for one should strike at an injustice in the place where it existed.

The abolition of American slavery, and the moral, mental, and social improvement of our people, are objects of immediate, pressing, and transcendent importance, involving a direct and positive issue with the pride and selfishness of the American people. The prosecution of this grand issue against all the principalities and powers of church and state furnishes ample occu-

---

[13] See page 131.
[14] *Ibid.*
[15] See page 264; see also pages 243, 269, 328 ff.

pation for all our time and talents; and we instinctively shrink from any movement which involves *a substitution of a doubtful and indirect issue, for one which is direct and certain,* for we believe that the demand for the abolition of slavery now made in the name of humanity, and according to the law of the Living God, though long delayed, will, if faithfully pressed, certainly triumph. The African Civilization Society proposes to plant its guns too far from the battlements of slavery for us. Its doctrines and measures are those of doubt and retreat, and it must land just where the American Colonization movement, upon the lying assumption that white and black people can never live in the same land on terms of equality. Detesting this heresy as we do and believing it to be full of all "deceivableness" of unrighteousness, we shun the paths that lead to it, no matter what taking names they bear, or how excellent the men who bid us to walk in them.[16]

His refusal to compromise with slavery wherever it existed self-evidently prevented him from imprisoning himself within the horizon of the present. Thus he plunged into an attack against slavery, at first joining the ranks of the Garrisonians who—holding that the Constitution was proslavery—advocated the dissolution of the Union. Later on, however, in his judgment of the evil against which he set himself in combat, he became aware that public opinion about the Negro had deteriorated from the period immediately following the Constitutional Convention during which colored men had voted in eleven of the thirteen original states. He saw that colored men had lost rights in the free states, let alone the slave states, as a result of national deference to the rising demands of the slave power for national security and national status for slave property.[17] In his reflections about this change in public opinion, he came to the conclusion that the Constitution, for all its compromises, had not been a proslavery document. On this point, he broke with the Garrisonians, and, in so doing, he broke with that moral absolutism which transcended all considerations of politics. Douglass could indeed wonder what future there would be for the slaves in the South if the Union were dissolved.[18] The obverse of his politic judgment about the past was his sensitivity to those changes in opinion that were beginning to take place in the opposite direction. Douglass saw in the protest against the extension of slavery a political response to the growing arrogance of the slave power which, though short of his demands for immediate emancipation, could not help but affect the future of the Negro. Overarching his work and his hopes lay an understanding of the crisis which slavery posed not simply for the Negro, but for the nation as a whole. In 1855 he wrote:

We behold [the doom of the Black Power] written in unmistakable characters, by the great Republican Movement, which is sweeping like a whirlwind over the Free States. We rejoice in this demonstration. It evinces the fact of a

---

[16] See page 264; italics mine—H.B. See also pages 191 ff.
[17] See pages 261, 273; see also Litwack, *op. cit.,* pp. 30–63.
[18] See pages 254 f.

growing determination on the part of the North to redeem *itself* from bondage.[19]

Just as Douglass refused to see slavery as permanent, so he refused to accept the fact of color prejudice in general as natural and, hence, permanent:

I know this is false, from my own experience in this country. I remember that, but a few years ago, upon the railroads from New Bedford and Salem . . . colored men and women were subjected to all manner of indignity in the use of those conveyances. Anti-slavery men, however . . . went abroad, exposing this proscription in the light of justice. What is the result? Not a single railroad can be found in any part of Massachusetts, where a colored man is treated and esteemed in any other light than that of a man and a traveller. Prejudice has given way and must give way.[20]

Moreover, at a time when most of the Negroes in this country were still slaves, he boldly declared that the Negro could be politically assimilated and, indeed, would have to be if the republic were not to destroy its principles.

I shall advocate for the Negro, his most full and complete adoption into the great national family of America. I shall demand for him the most perfect civil and political equality, and that he shall enjoy all the rights, privileges and immunities enjoyed by any other members of the body politic. I weigh my words and I mean all I say, when I contend as I do contend, that this is the *only solid, and final* solution of the problem before us. It is demanded not less by the terrible exigencies of the nation, than by the Negro himself for the Negro and the nation are to rise or fall, be killed or cured, saved or lost together. Save the Negro and you save the nation, destroy the Negro and you destroy the nation, and to save both you must have but one great law of Liberty, Equality, and Fraternity for all Americans without respect to color.[21]

In all this he refused to become trapped by the snare that caught so many of the colonizers, both white and Negro, that is, the assumption that justice for the Negro or his political assimilation requires his biological amalgamation.[22] Where black men and white men face each other as large masses one might reason *either* that political equality would lead to biological fusion *or else* that the failure of the whites to absorb the blacks

[19] See page 246.
[20] See page 214.
[21] See page 268.
[22] It may be useful to emphasize that throughout this analysis assimilation is regarded as different from amalgamation. Assimilation can include this, it can lead to it, and it may be facilitated by it. But, insofar as assimilation is essentially the acquisition of cultural, moral, and political standards and habits, it is a learning, not a biological process. As with an individual, a group as a whole can acquire new standards without disappearing as an entity, whether it wants to disappear or not. In these terms, one can speak of the assimilation of the group. See Nathan Glazer and Daniel Moynihan, *Beyond the Melting Pot* (Cambridge: M.I.T. Press and Harvard University Press, 1964), pp. 1–24.

would leave the latter with feelings of being despised, and hence a potentially inimical bloc—should they ever acquire the freedom to act politically in concert. On the basis of such an assumption, one could therefore argue that, if there is a powerful prejudice, unchangeable by law, against socially sanctioned absorption, that is, against intermarriage, it "proves" the political nonassimilability of the Negro. One is then justified in withholding any semblance of political justice from the Negro, any semblance of equality whatsoever; the demands of self-preservation are the sufficient grounds. Fusion *or* race war, the theoretically conceivable "all" in the here and now *or* nothing—these are the alternatives seen by this mode of reasoning.[23] Douglass, on the contrary, looked at the whole question of racial intermarriage from two different perspectives: theoretically and practically. In a theoretical reflection he thought, as did Henry Highland Garnet,[24] that the Negro would ultimately be absorbed.

Of course this result will not be reached by any hurried or forced process. It will not arise out of any theory of the wisdom of such blending of the two races. If it comes at all, it will come without shock or noise or violence of any kind, and only in the fullness of time, and it will be so adjusted to surrounding conditions as hardly to be observed. I would not be understood as advocating intermarriage between the two races. I am not a propagandist, but a prophet. . . . While I would not be understood as advocating the desirability of such a result, I would not be understood as deprecating it.[25]

Theoretically, then, he thought that the Negro would be absorbed if and when opinion on this question changed. Practically, however, as these last remarks also suggest, his goal was to affirm the irrelevance to public policy of such theoretical reflections about the future:

The question is not can there be social equality? That does not exist anywhere. . . . The real question, the all-commanding question, is whether American justice, American liberty, American civilization, American law, and American Christianity can be made to include and protect alike and forever all American citizens in the rights which, in a generous moment in the nation's life, have been guaranteed to them by the organic and fundamental law of the land.[26]

By these rights Douglass meant the civic rights of the public sphere: the right to vote, to have a voice in the representation of one's interests, to walk through the land without stigma and insult. He made it perfectly clear, for example, that the right to stop at a hotel was a civil right and not

---

[23] Cf. Tocqueville's view that the only alternatives for the whites in the South (before the Civil War) were "either to emancipate the Negroes and to intermingle with them, or, remaining isolated from them, to keep them in slavery as long as possible." *Democracy in America,* ed. Phillips Bradley (New York: Knopf, 1945), Vol. I, p. 379.

[24] See page 200.

[25] See page 310.

[26] See pages 271, 314.

a "social" right to enter into social relations with anyone, and he ridiculed the use of this argument to deprive Negroes of elementary civilities.[27]

Thus in opposition to those who would cite the color prejudice of the present as proof of the eternal nonassimilability of the Negro, Douglass single-mindedly projected the goal of the future and used it as a spark to change the present. Prejudice existed, but it could be changed by both word and deed. Throughout his long career of public agitation, which began when there was slavery and which continued through the vicissitudes of post-Civil War America, he demanded justice for the Negro. But at the same time Douglass, with what one may call a sociological perspective, understood that assimilation was not simply a matter of legal or political justice but entailed the elevation of the Negro. It was this goal which was the core of Douglass' policy of assimilation; and his hostility to emigrationism was founded as much on the conviction that the opportunities to improve oneself were greater in America than in Africa as it was on the legal claim to stay in the country of one's birth.

It was in relation to this end of elevation that Douglass looked upon the political status of the Negro. Injustice had kept the Negro down and in the process had necessarily impoverished the whole community.[28] Where there was justice, there was no conflict of interests between black and white, and the elevation of the one made for the elevation of the other.

Some of your old citizens, no doubt, continue to regret the change which has taken place in the relations of the people of Tennessee. In the loss of slavery the State, in their estimation, has parted with the source of its happiness and prosperity. To my mind it would be hard to find a greater mistake than this. Emancipation in this State was not only a triumph of justice, but a triumph of agricultural industry.

I put to the common sense of all who hear me: what possible motive had the slave for a careful, successful cultivation of the soil? What concern could he have for increasing the wealth of the master, or for improving or beautifying the land? [29]

But his demands were not solely on the political environment; they extended to the colored people themselves. He did not see a disjunction between these two things because, in his view, elevation required efforts that went beyond changes in political conditions.

We must get character for ourselves, as a people. A change in our political condition would do very little for us without this.[30]

The key to this was independence, of the kind which is created by skills and education.

---

[27] See page 306.
[28] See page 268.
[29] See page 291.
[30] See page 207.

Every blow of the sledge hammer, wielded by a sable arm, is a powerful blow in support of our cause. Every colored mechanic is, by virtue of circumstances, an elevator of his race. Every house built by black men is a strong tower against the allied hosts of prejudice. It is impossible for us to attach too much importance to this aspect of the subject. Trades are important. Wherever a man may be thrown by misfortune, if he has in his hands a useful trade, he is useful to his fellow man, and will be esteemed accordingly; and of all men in the world who need trades we are the most needy. Understand this, that independence is an essential condition of respectability. To be dependent, is to be degraded. Man may indeed pity us, but they cannot respect us. We do not mean that we can become entirely independent of all men; that would be absurd and impossible, in the social state. But we mean that we must become equally independent with other members of the community. That other members of the community shall be as dependent upon us, as we upon them.[31]

In his 1848 article, "What Are the Colored People Doing for Themselves," he asserted a thesis that later became the basis of a controversy between Booker T. Washington and W. E. B. Du Bois. The question was whether the elevation of the Negro would take place through the creation of a distinguished elite or whether it required general change in the people as a whole. Douglass opted for the latter alternative with great rhetorical emphasis, pointing out that so long as the elite are seen as exceptions, "their talents can do little to give us character in the eyes of the world." In the same article, he asserts that, as the Negro experienced a *general* elevation, prejudice, or, to be more precise, contempt, would weaken. At the basis of this judgment is the assumption that, unless prejudice was armed with the kind of total power it possessed under the slave regime, which enabled it to keep the Negro in a categorically depressed condition, it was changeable. This was so because prejudice, to justify itself, could not help but appeal to facts as to what the Negro had achieved. Hence, so long as the Negro had that minimal degree of freedom, even within a milieu marked by social prejudice, to demonstrate those facts which controverted prejudice, he would shock it and ultimately change it.

There are certain great elements of character in us which may be hated but never despised. Industry, sobriety, honesty, combined with intelligence and a due self-respect, find them where you will, among black or white, must be looked up to—can never be looked down upon. In their presence, prejudice is abashed, confused, and mortified.[32]

While Douglass was the most honored and revered Negro of his time, he did experience a minor degree of criticism from Negroes. First, he was accused of not having race pride, meaning pride in his color. He regarded

31 See page 211.
32 See page 207.

this as a form of counter-racism that was no more defensible than feelings of racial superiority among whites and spoke out against it:

> Our race and color are not of our own choosing. The only excuse for pride in individuals or races is in the fact of their achievements. Our color is the gift of the Almighty. We should neither be proud of it nor ashamed of it.[33]

In contemporary terms he rejected the turning of color into a mystique as a basis of identification.

Yet he was also accused of advocating something akin to segregation because he urged colored people to form colored associations in order to voice and protect their interests. He emphatically stated, "Never refuse to act with a white society or institution because it is white, or a black one because it is black." [34] At the same time, he pointed out that "we shall undoubtedly for many years be compelled to have institutions of a complexional character in order to attain this very idea of human brotherhood." [35]

His stand between these two poles of radically self-conscious self-enclosure and its opposite was the moderate, commonsensical one of a practical man. Today one might ask how Douglass would have answered the question, "Why should I be a Negro?" While it is true that he would have regarded the form of the question as curiously academic and doctrinaire, he did, in fact, answer it—and in the plainest language:

> We are one people—one in general complexion, one in a common degradation, one in popular estimation. As one rises, all must rise, and as one falls, all must fall.[36]

This answer was not only the key to his common-sensical stand on the above questions. It was also the key to his whole assimilationist policy. As he saw it the Negro would remain a socially defined entity within American society for many years. To him this was a completely neutral datum. The fact that white people defined Negroes as Negroes (and vice versa) in no way offended him because it was essentially irrelevant to the most important practical goal: the assimilation on an elevated level of the Negro into American life. Speculations concerning the possibility of the Negro's ultimate disappearance were no more than theoretical distractions to Douglass. One may call the solution envisioned by Douglass the pluralism of privately organized groups within a framework of nationally common civic standards. That Douglass thought the Negro could and would be assimilated in this way, that the Negro like the Jew would rise in the social scale was his answer to the emigrationists.[37] It has remained the dominant point of view in Negro thought from then until the present day.

[33] See page 316.
[34] See page 211.
[35] Loc. cit.
[36] See page 210.
[37] See page 308.

Booker T. Washington

Douglass' most important successor was Booker T. Washington, whose broad theoretical understanding of the nature and solution of the race problem was identical with that of his predecessor. That is, he thought that the race problem would be solved by the elevation of the Negro, by his assimilation of the best standards of citizenship and family life. Even without regard to the Negro's rank, elevation, as he understood it, constituted the Negro's true human interest.[38] But, as Washington saw, the destiny of the two races was linked together. "We rise as you rise; when we fall, you fall." "You can only keep the Negro in the ditch by staying down there with him." And just as he saw that the future health of the South depended on the elevation of the Negro, so he saw that the health of the North and, indeed, of the whole country, depended on the elevation of the South. In his dedication to his work for the Negro he always maintained a truly national perspective of the scope of the common good.[39]

Washington became a controversial figure in his own lifetime and was accused of being a compromiser or an accommodationist, a view that we shall discuss in the following section. At present, we need only point out one factor that may have contributed to this view, which has not been seen clearly enough. This is that Washington was more than fifty years ahead of his time. Today, as the last vestiges of legal inequality are being cleared away, it is becoming a common view that the fundamental problems of the Negro are "beyond civil rights." One thereby simply acknowledges the visibility of the fact that while the Negro as a whole will have legal equality, he still will not be equal in a number of important social and economic respects. Legal equality, to be sure, will positively affect the whole atmosphere in which the remaining inequalities are considered as problems, but it will hardly cause them to disappear. Among these inequalities is the Negro's smaller capacity to earn a good living, which is productive of so many deleterious consequences. Today the highest councils of the land are beginning to appreciate the problem of the Negro's inequality as one that must be attacked in ways over and above mere legal equalization.

Washington saw the problem as early as 1880. He understood that slavery had left the Negro ill prepared to take care of himself. Having been worked, the Negro had not learned how to work. Washington thought that it was a serious mistake to confuse these two things. Having been worked for someone else's advantage, the Negro had come to despise labor as such. He lacked the skills that awakened intelligence and energy.[40]

Washington looked at the legacy of slavery without resentment. The question was what to do here and now. In Washington's estimate the Ne-

[38] See pages 379–382.
[39] See pages 361, 370, 460.
[40] See page 409.

gro was a progressive force, open to education and eager for it. What he needed was not well-meaning lectures on the necessity for pulling oneself up by one's own bootstraps, lectures that by themselves could only be offensive. What was needed, rather, was knowledge of *how,* of how to manage, how to improve and perfect the arts of economy and domestic economy, beginning with the most elementary considerations of hygiene and diet. Washington regarded this as the means of independence, the means of escape from a degraded condition, and, hence, the foundation of everything else.[41]

Tuskegee Institute, which he founded in the heart of the Black Belt of Alabama, was intended to correct the legacy of slavery. The curriculum of the school consisted of what he called "industrial education," although a more precise term would be training in industriousness. This included the acquisition of a skill, with a strong emphasis on agriculture, but it also included education in a frame of habits for the utilization of any skill in a methodical, progressive, and energetic way. Moreover, Tuskegee was to radiate an influence far beyond its confines. Its demonstrators would go into farm and home throughout a wide area, and the Negro farmers were involved with it through a series of annual conferences among other things. Its success can be gauged from the way in which it revitalized an area which had been a depressed relic of the plantation system.

Washington's fundamental tenet was that only through an essential education could the Negro elevate himself, that it would involve struggle, and that there were no short cuts. Even if the Negro were a privileged ward of the nation, or if the Negro were on a self-governing island such as Haiti, the case would be the same. As he saw it, this program was valid not simply for Southern Negroes in 1880 but for people of any race in a similar stage of development. He thought that his work would be just as valuable for poor whites as for poor Negroes, and, indeed, many of his methods were subsequently adopted in agricultural extension services in the Southern states. As for the struggle involved, Washington again held that what was involved was not a unique disability of the Negro race, but, rather, something that all people who have changed themselves in a progressive direction have had to undergo.[42]

He thus conceived of his program as one of social education the case for which did not depend in its most important respects on the character of the political context. But nothing that a Negro leader proposed for his people could be irrelevant to that context, and Washington, indeed, thought that the diffusion of his program would help to bring about a harmonious and just pattern of racial relations. He saw that the Negro had been a pawn in someone else's struggles and that, after the antagonists had made peace with each other, the Negro had been left to bear the brunt of resentments. The result was that black and white in the South

[41] See page 355.
[42] See page 445.

were divided into two parties, each suspecting the other of wanting some form of revenge. The problem was how to eliminate this racial-political tension. The obvious solution, in principle, which not only Washington but such of his contemporaries as Fortune saw, was to bring into being a community of interests between black and white that would crosscut racial lines. How could this community be brought into being? In part, there was a need for prudence on the part of the Negro in the way he used his vote. Simply voting yes because whites voted no, as many Negro leaders pointed out, did not bring about interracial trust.[43] But of more basic importance was the emergence among Negroes themselves of a substantial class of yeomanry, of independent farmers, artisans, and businessmen. So long as the Negro was primarily a proletarian or economically dependent element, he was politically a danger to himself and, paradoxically, to the whole society, even if he did nothing but remain a mute bystander. This was because as a depressed element he could not help becoming a football in the conflicts among other interests. To exaggerate somewhat for purposes of explanation, the rich would seek him as an ally against the white poor. The white poor would seek him as an ally against the rich. Or the North would seek him as an ally against the South. Any of these alliances, real or seeming, would invite the racial question into politics; and his mere mute presence would permit it to be dragged in by demagogues to the disadvantage of—again—the Negro. The only alternative would be for the Negro to be in a position to ally himself with the predominant middle-class interest of the society, not as a football, a dependent retainer whose right to give this support would be attacked, but, rather, as a social and economic equal, standing on his own feet. In that case his right to assert himself as a member of the broad coalition that constituted the middle class could not be questioned without questioning the rights of all others in that coalition.[44]

But of course one could argue that, if the Negro were poor and without unambiguous political power, he would be the object of political injustice that would keep him poor. Washington was certainly not so naïve as not to know that there were powerful interests in the society that wanted to keep the Negro depressed so that he could provide a source of cheap labor. Among these interests, for example, were those seeking to employ convict labor and who thus had an interest in a high crime rate or at least a high rate of imprisonment among Negroes. Such an interest was opposed not merely to industrial education, but to any education whatsoever for the Negro.[45] Then, too, there was the bigotry and prejudice of the failures, who, without a direct economic interest in the depression of the Negro, felt threatened by and resented the spectacle of Negro success.

[43] See pages 343 f., 353.
[44] See pages 366, 372, 383, 404, 406 f.
[45] See pages 457 f.

But, as Washington thought, to argue from such facts to a doctrinaire "chicken or the egg" formulation of "politics before economics" would be as fatal for action as the equally doctrinaire formulation of the reverse. Short of the extreme situation—such as was chattel slavery, where the only way in which a slave could improve himself was to escape—politics and economics had to go together. Within a practical orientation the crucial thing was to grasp at any opportunity for elevation that existed. Here Washington was aware of the way in which Negroes, as is true of all minorities subject to discrimination, might be induced to blame discrimination for all their woes; and his optimism sought to encourage the Negro, to persuade him from giving up in advance, and to make clear that one could discover the true force of an obstacle only by making some effort to overcome it.[46] Furthermore, he was aware of the heterogeneity of white opinion in the South on racial relations, and he knew that not all whites thought it advantageous to have a high Negro crime rate. There was an interest, in other words, that saw and welcomed the educated Negro as an asset to the community. It was with such addressees in mind that Washington could speak out within the South—with force—on lynching, on the unequal education the Negro was receiving, on the situation with regard to convict labor.[47] But in speaking in behalf of the interests of his race, he never projected racial claims in a spirit of race conflict, in a way that presumed a categorical political division into black and white. He was also a Southerner, speaking to other Southerners about the common good of their region. To attack the South as the "white South," as an outsider, as though every white Southerner were a natural enemy, would not only be inexpedient but inaccurate and unfair.[48]

Washington's program rested on the premise that as the Negro became elevated he would receive more respect, and by this he meant not simply civic and political rights, but also that status enjoyed by a person who is not conscious of any disabilities. In a crucial sense, he was let down—regionally as well as nationally. At the very time when he achieved national recognition for the work he was doing at Tuskegee, the Southern states effectively disfranchised the Negro and the Supreme Court upheld the constitutionality of segregation, thus sanctioning the rapid increase of segregation ordinances in the South.[49] In his letter to the Louisiana State Constitutional Convention, Washington tried to avert what was in effect a racial disfranchisement with a stand for a qualified, nonracial franchise. He admitted the necessity for voting qualifications impartially applied to both races, but he also insisted on the necessity for the best education for

[46] See pages 380, 430.
[47] See pages 454 f., 457 f., 459 f.
[48] See pages 353 f., 428.
[49] For a description of this development see C. Vann Woodward's *The Strange Career of Jim Crow* (New York: Oxford University Press, 1957).

both races.[50] He did not succeed in Louisiana; and though his firm stand here had an effect later on in delaying a similar proposal in Georgia,[51] the process of disfranchisement was finally completed throughout the South. Among Negro radicals, as we note in the next section, Washington was accused of indirectly contributing to this result. This, however, overlooks the possibility that it was he, a Negro, who may well have been the *de facto* leader of the opinion in the South, white as well as black, which opposed disfranchisement and which knew the corroding effect this would have upon race relations. Be that as it may, Washington, though he continued to speak and to act for re-enfranchisement,[52] did not think that disfranchisement was a catastrophe equal to slavery. He thought that it would not stop the progress which the Negro in his condition of partial freedom had made since emancipation and would continue to make.[53] As the center of gravity, socially and economically, rose upward among Negroes, they would recover their rights and on a firmer foundation than they had ever before possessed them. He predicted that the process would take about fifty years.

A major problem would remain, however. Given a color-blind legal context, given the continued presence of Negroes with superior energy and skill—of the kind who had been able to make a mark not only during segregation, but during slavery as well—one cannot overlook the fact that the Negro was forced to make a historical shift from a system where efficiency was punitive to one where inefficiency was disastrous. Washington, with his Spencerian terminology, saw the place of rational, skilled labor in the "industrial society" of the modern world and the difficulty which unskilled labor would have in competing with machines.[54] In the Social Darwinist framework of that period, many writers stated that the Negro would have to sink or swim. Indeed, some Negroes themselves thought the Negro had a right to ask for no more than his freedom to sink or swim.

Washington rejected the harshness in this approach as well as the fuzziness of the other pole which, in seeing the Negro exclusively as a victim of discrimination, obscured the tremendous progress that the Negro had already made in his condition. Standing between and above these two poles, he saw that the Negro was faced with a major need for education that was in principle analogous to that of the immigrants though radically different in detail. He also saw that this was not specifically a "Southern" problem, that intertwined with the differential between the quality of Negro and white education in the poorest states of the South was the differential between this index in the South and the North. Implied in his views

[50] See pages 373 ff.
[51] See pages 376–379.
[52] See pages 458 f. Washington supplied funds for the legal attack in the courts upon the constitutionality of the grandfather clause.
[53] See pages 396–401, 421–423; see also page 308.
[54] See pages 361, 371, 405, 409.

was a call for national recognition of what was truly a national problem and a demand for appropriate support from the entire nation. But this presupposed a revolution in thinking, not simply about race relations, but also about social welfare and the role of government in attaining it. The underlying cause of group tension and conflict would thus be eliminated by channeling activity into training for development on a nonracial basis. Washington also knew that, in spite of existing obstructions to the workings of the merit principle—such as job discrimination by employers or by unions, against which he protested throughout his whole life—the drift of an expanding industrial economy was toward an increasing demand for skill and highly specialized services.[55] As such the logic of the economy would not only invite, but would require, a continual upgrading of Negro employment and hence would nullify the problems arising from a fear of "racial competition."

In sum, his views were that the nation could ill afford *not* to pull the Negro up or, more precisely, to help him pull himself up. A modern, egalitarian democracy would be dragged down by a depressed stratum. Over and above the freedom from punitive discrimination that would enable one to do one's proper work and to get one's proper reward was the necessity for an education that would give the Negro a fair chance and correct the legacy of the past. As we have attempted to show, Washington was totally free of shallow sentimentalism. He was not motivated by resentment, nor did he wish to stimulate people to become suffused with guilt about the "Negro problem" in a way that would lead them to put more emphasis upon words and feelings than upon constructive action. His stand was a tough, public-spirited one, which saw the needs of the Negro in the light of the whole as posing an urgent task, but not a gloomy "problem." This stand was a mixture of toughness in the maintenance of high standards with the friendship of the stronger for the weaker, which he held up to the nation as a whole as the only basis of getting rid of *its* problem.

There is no defense or security for any of us except in the highest intelligence and development of all. If anywhere there are efforts tending to curtail the fullest growth of the Negro, let these efforts be turned into stimulating, encouraging, and making him the most useful and intelligent citizen. Effort or means so invested will pay a thousand per cent interest. These efforts will be twice blessed—"Blessing him that gives and him that takes."

There is no escape through law of man or God from the inevitable. . . . Nearly sixteen millions of hands will aid you in pulling the load upward, or they will pull, against you, the load downward. We shall constitute one-third and more of the ignorance and crime of the South, or one-third its intelligence and progress; we shall contribute one-third to the business and indus-

[55] See Seymour Martin Lipset and Reinhard Bendix, *Social Mobility in Industrial Society* (Berkeley and Los Angeles: University of California Press, 1959), pp. 83–85, for statistical documentation of this process of the contraction of unskilled positions and the expansion of skilled ones in the United States, 1850–1935.

trial prosperity of the South, or we shall prove a veritable body of death, stagnating, depressing, retarding every effort to advance the body politic.[56]

The longer I live and the more I study the question, the more I am convinced that it is not so much a problem as to what you will do with the Negro as what the Negro will do with you and your civilization.[57]

As for the social question, that is the problem of "social separation" or "social equality," Washington was prepared to dismiss this with even more pointedness than Douglass. In the rhetoric of the time "social equality" meant intermarriage or intimate private contact bordering on it. Since it was the irrelevant slogan that could always enter into public discussion and serve as a cover and excuse for political injustice, Washington had no hesitation in categorically rejecting it. In his Atlanta speech he stated:

In all things that are purely social we can be as separate as the fingers, yet one as the hand in all things essential to mutual progress.[58]

Did this conceivably mean caste or segregation by law? Washington stated in "Is the Negro Having a Fair Chance?" that what the Negro objected to on the railroads was not the separation but the fact that he had to pay the same fare as the white man for inferior accommodations.[59] As is well known, the whole history of the *legal* challenge to the "separate but equal" doctrine began precisely by forcing the states practicing segregation to conform to the doctrine with respect to equality. In this same article, he points out, as did Douglass, that in most parts of the United States civil and legal privileges are confused with social intermingling.

The fact that two men ride in the same railway coach does not mean in any country in the world that they are socially equal.[60]

From his undeviating stand on the injustice of unequal laws, including anti-miscegenation laws under the protection of which whites could disavow the obligations of paternity, it is clear that by "social separation" or "social equality" he was concerned only with private "social circles." [61] Washington did not look upon the formation of these among Negroes as a concession to or even particularly as a product of segregation. On the contrary, he looked upon them as things which would naturally evolve as an internally differentiated Negro society emerged, in which private social groups would arise on the basis of common education, life style, and common interests. Whether one private circle was superior to another, whether such circles in their private social life ultimately overlapped with one another with regard to religion, race, occupation, sex,

[56] See page 358.
[57] See page 367.
[58] See page 358.
[59] See page 453.
[60] See page 447; see also page 306.
[61] See pages 447, 460 ff.

were questions that Washington thought beyond the considerations of public deliberation.[62]

CULTURAL NATIONALISM

W. E. B. Du Bois

The two most important successors of Booker T. Washington were W. E. B. Du Bois and Marcus Garvey; and in the thinking of both there is evidence of a partial break with the assimilationist policy of Washington. In the case of Du Bois the break is manifestly suggested by his attack on Washington's leadership. In his essay, "Of Mr. Washington and Others," he criticized Washington as a compromiser, attacking the program of industrial education as a preparation for a subordinate status. Such a charge bears examination, but first it must be emphasized that the focal point of Du Bois's attack on assimilationism lay elsewhere. Washington stressed rights and qualifications. Du Bois, in a more radical spirit, though he also spoke about duties, put the primary stress upon rights. But these rights were the same for both. In the more radical statement of demands for these rights, such as in the Resolutions of the Niagara Movement which Du Bois wrote, there was no break with the goal of equal citizenship as projected by Douglass or Washington. Du Bois's break with assimilationism had other implications and other roots; unlike Washington, he was preoccupied with race.

At the time when Du Bois came to maturity, racism was very much a feature of the intellectual milieu, on both a popular and an academic level. Writers and politicians were openly preaching the doctrine that the Negro was an inferior and debased race.[63] Moreover, racialism was buttressed by historical-evolutionary theories which judged the Negro as inferior on the grounds that he had contributed nothing to civilization. Implicit in these theories was the assumption that race and culture were in some way connected so that one could speak of the *distinctive* culture or spirit of different racial groups.

Now the inclination of such practical men as Douglass and Washington, so far as these academic doctrines are concerned, was to ignore them. Douglass did, to be sure, write an essay affirming that the Negro was a man. From a "scientific" point of view his reasoning may appear primitive, but on a deeper level it shows his utter indifference to the very terms of such a doctrinal argument.

A very recondite author says, that man "is distinguished from all other animals, in that he resists as well as adapts himself to his circumstances." He does not take things as he finds them, but goes to work to improve them.

---

[62] See Emmett J. Scott and Lyman Beecher Stowe, *Booker T. Washington: Builder of a Civilization* (New York: Doubleday, 1917), pp. 34 f.

[63] See Woodward, *op. cit.,* p. 78. See also page 312, this volume.

Tried by this test, too, the Negro is a man. You may see him yoke the oxen, harness the horse, and hold the plow. He can swim the river; but he prefers to fling over it a bridge. The horse bears him on his back—admits his mastery and dominion. The barnyard fowl know his step, and flock around to receive their morning meal from his sable hand. The dog dances when he comes home, and whines piteously when he is absent. All these know that the Negro is a MAN. Now, presuming that what is evident to beast and to bird, cannot need elaborate argument to be made plain to men, I assume, with this brief statement, that the Negro is a man.[64]

Thus he refused to be bound by the terms of doctrinal disputations which a priori depreciated the status of what was evident to his human eyes. Along the same lines, Washington, to the best of my knowledge, mentions the very term "racial difference" but once in the entire corpus of his writings. In pointing out that there is a difference in behavior between Negroes and whites, he states that this is not a racial one, "but a difference growing out of unequal opportunities in the past." [65]

Thus neither of these men was preoccupied with current doctrine about racial inferiority; and its conceptions, from their point of view, were totally irrelevant to their work. As practical men, they looked forward, not backward. Thus the question of origins was of no interest, except, perhaps, as a base line from which to estimate present and future progress. Then, too, these men were uninterested in historical theories that predicated a connection between race and culture. From their simple practical point of view, just as a poor white person could improve himself by education, so could a poor Negro. In other words they thought of morality and civilization having the universality of mathematics, and this underpinned their assimilationist policy. When a Negro learned something worth while from a white person, they saw this as the acquisition not of "white" civilization but, rather, of civilization simply. Their view of the universality of morality and civilization gave them a platform from which to judge not merely Negroes but whites as well. It made it possible for them to see the acquisition of civilization, which accidentally may have been "carried" by certain whites, not as slavish imitation of whites because they had power. They saw it, rather, as the acquisition of something valuable in its own right and defensible in universal terms. Though Washington could frequently speak of the stage of development of the Negro, he did not thereby refer either to a determinate historical-evolutionary process or to race. In these respects he spoke very much as would a contemporary sociologist.

All this is in the sharpest opposition to the standpoint of Du Bois. To begin with, Du Bois was an academic man who would understandably have a professional interest in doctrines or theories. In many ways he was

[64] See page 229.
[65] Booker T. Washington, *The Future of the American Negro* (Boston: Small, Maynard & Co., 1902), pp. 31 f.

a true son of the Enlightenment who thought that the most important things in social and political life were doctrines. To Du Bois, for example, a primary cause of slavery or of disfranchisement was a doctrine or an "ism" postulating the inferiority of the Negro.[66] Hence, to change the power pattern one had to change the doctrine by disseminating a counter doctrine. Much of his scholarly work was rooted precisely in his expectations of the benign effect that scientific studies of the Negro might have upon public opinion. To Douglass, on the other hand, the primary cause of slavery was not a doctrine, but greed. He saw that the doctrines of the time that sought to justify slavery on the grounds of racial inferiority had emerged historically as an ideology with which to conceal the underlying impulse. Thus to attack slavery one had to attack *it* and its underlying injustice and not the ideological superstructure, except in so far as to unmask the latter in order to focus attention back upon the true cause.

Then, too, for personal reasons Du Bois was much more humiliated by racialist theories than either of his two great predecessors. Perhaps because they had both come "up from slavery," Douglass and Washington had inner resources which made them much more independent than Du Bois of white opinion or any opinion. They both, to be sure, were prudentially concerned about the use which demagogues could make of vulgar racialism to inflame public opinion (as in newspapers).[67] So was Du Bois. But there is no question that neither vulgar racialism nor academic racialism ever had the slightest effect upon their estimate of their own excellence. Du Bois, on the other hand, moved in a world in which, to exaggerate only somewhat, he felt that every white person regarded him as inferior because of his Negro "blood." Reacting to this with resentment, he plunged into an attack on racialism. But, as is often the case, he became imprisoned by the assumptions of the very people he was attacking. This is strikingly illustrated in his essay "The Conservation of Races." Faced with the academic view that the Negro was inferior because he had contributed nothing to civilization, he sought to establish a theoretical basis for the equality of the Negro, but, curiously, within a framework that completely accepted the idea of the racial basis of culture. The core of his argument is that the history of the world is the history not of individuals, nor of nations, but of races. He then notes that the peoples of the world are divided into eight distinct races: Among these eight race groups are the English of Great Britain and America, the Teutons of middle Europe, the Mongolians of eastern Asia, and the Negroes of Africa and America. He then postulates the particularity of the culture or spirit of each racial group:

At the same time the spiritual and physical differences of race groups became deep and decisive. The English nation stood for constitutional liberty and commercial freedom; the German nation for science and philosophy; the

---

[66] See page 543.

[67] See Ray Stannard Baker's description of the way in which the press fomented a race riot in Atlanta in *Following the Color Line* (New York: Harper & Row, 1964).

Romance nations stood for literature and art, and the other race groups are striving, each in its own way, to develop for civilization its particular message, its particular ideal, which shall help to guide the world nearer and nearer that perfection of human life for which we all long. . . .[68]

While it is true that he does speak of civilization as something unified that would embrace particular contributions, the emphasis is nonetheless wholly on the particularity of the contribution. To Douglass and Washington civilization comprehended standards and ways of universal validity; for Du Bois the emphasis shifted not only to particularity but to originality. According to Du Bois, not unlike the contemporary proponents of Negritude, the problem was that Negroes, in order to validate themselves as a civilized race, had to contribute an original message to the world.[69] This problem tortured his soul throughout his whole life, leading him into the most curious theoretical and practical points of view. As he looked toward the future, he advocated a positive development of race organizations, Negro colleges, newspapers, and business organizations to develop the special spiritual ideals of the race. While there was nothing unusual in the goal of organizations as such for self-help, the peculiarity of the motivations which he imparted to these schemes is apparent in the fact that later on he advocated even a self-segregated economy.[70] (Although he took up the cause of Pan-Africanism or anti-colonialism, he stopped short of any interest in mass emigration or in a political formation of a "nation within a nation.") On the other hand, as he looked backward in time, he sought to establish for the Negro something akin to a Golden Age, on the basis of which he could say that the Negro race had already contributed part of its message to the world. This led him to seize upon such information as that the first person to discover iron was a Negro, that the ancient Egyptians were Negro (or Negroid), etc.[71] It is interesting to compare the tone of Du Bois with that of Douglass on this very question:

And what if the Negro may not be able to prove his relationship to Nubians, Abyssinians, and Egyptians? What if ingenious men are able to find plausible objections to all arguments maintaining the oneness of the human race? What, after all, if they are able to show very good reasons for believing the Negro to have been created precisely as we find him on the Gold Coast— along the Senegal and the Niger—I say, what of all this?—*"A man's a man for a' that."* [72]

It is in the absence of precisely this detachment that one sees the workings of resentment. While in one context Du Bois was able to praise the contri-

[68] See page 487.

[69] The best critique of Negritude and, indirectly, of the parallel assumptions present in Du Bois's thought is Ezekiel Mphahlele's essay, "What Price 'Negritude'?" in his *The African Image* (New York: Praeger, 1962), pp. 25–40.

[70] See Francis L. Broderick, *W. E. B. Du Bois: Negro Leader in Time of Crisis* (Stanford: Stanford University Press, 1959), p. 168.

[71] See page 487.

[72] See page 242.

butions of the English "race," his racialist perspective also gave him a platform from which he could express his contempt for "white" America. In an early address before an audience of Boston Negroes, he stated, "No Negro can afford to stoop to an Anglo-Saxon standard of morality." [73]

In so far as he injected this spirit of resentment into his domestic political agitation, he ultimately broke not merely with white America but also with the N.A.A.C.P., which rejected his advocacy of a positive program of self-segregation.[74] Much of his work as editor of the *Crisis*, however, was a straightforward and eloquent defense of the Negro's rights and an exposé of injustices, uncomplicated by his historicist-racialist preoccupations. The same was true of his sociological studies of the condition of the Negro and the effects of discrimination.[75] It is on the basis of such work that he occupies a distinguished position in Negro life. But where the preoccupation with race entered into his judgment, it could, and did, lead to confusion. For example, in his famous attack on Booker T. Washington he denounced Washington's program of industrial education as tantamount to the acceptance of the inferior status of Negroes, and hence an accommodation to white supremacy.[76] Further, he charged Washington with acquiescing in the racist view that the Negro was unable to learn from books, even though Washington had written on the issue as follows:

> Perhaps there were too many institutions started at that time for teaching Greek and Latin, considering that the foundations had not yet been laid in a good common-school system. It should be remembered, however, that the people who started these schools had a somewhat different purpose from that for which schools ordinarily exist today. They believed that it was necessary to complete the emancipation of the Negro by demonstrating to the world that the black man was just as able to learn from books as the white man, a thing that had been frequently denied during the long anti-slavery controversy. *I think it is safe to say that that has now been demonstrated.* What remains to be shown is that the Negro can go as far as the white man in using his education, of whatever kind it may be, to make himself a more useful and valuable member of society.[77]

This still leaves open the question of whether Washington's program was as valid for elevating the condition of poor whites or poor Mexicans as of poor Negroes. One would then have to raise in objective, color-blind terms the question of whether any of these socioeconomic groups would be elevated primarily by the creation of a small, literarily educated elite or by the general diffusion of more practical arts.[78] From the standpoint of

[73] Broderick, *op. cit.*, p. 20.
[74] *Ibid.*, pp. 169–175.
[75] See pages 492–508.
[76] See page 513.
[77] See page 440, italics mine—H.B.
[78] See "The Talented Tenth," pages 518–533. On page 518, Du Bois states: "The Negro race, like all races, is going to be saved by its exceptional men." Then the question arises: Are poor whites a race separate from the exceptional whites who already exist?

this racially neutral question Du Bois might then have been more aware of Washington's interest in the creation of a Negro professional class and the support he gave, in these respects, both to individuals and institutions. One would also have to consider in these respects the crisp view of T. T. Fortune:

> Should one then not have some scholars, men learned in all that higher education gives? Of course; and we should have them. Men fitted by nature for special pursuits in life will make preparation for that work. Water will find its level. . . . *Genius will take care of itself;* . . . It is therefore that I plead that the masses of the colored race should receive such preparation for the fierce competition of everyday life that the odds shall not be against them.[79]

Similarly, Du Bois saw in Washington's view that citizenship presupposes qualifications an abject surrender to the disfranchisement of the Negro. Once again he seems to have overlooked the point that what Washington had in mind was a wholly nonracial standard, applicable to whites and Negroes alike. On the basis of this standard a more radical expression of protest against disfranchisement than was possible for any Southern Negro leader at that time needed to be, and could have been, formulated from a Northern center, but one which in no way questioned the value of a curriculum for economic independence. Substantially this took place shortly before Washington's death and is taking place with greater clarity now.

POLITICAL NATIONALISM

Marcus Garvey

Marcus Garvey revived political nationalism among American Negroes and gave it a popular expression that it had never before possessed. This has much to do with the changed context. Whereas Delany and the pre-

---

In this interesting and important essay, Du Bois, to be sure, insisted that he was arguing, not against the necessity of the industrial and common school, but only for a recognition of the primacy of higher education. Among other things, he contended that the industrial school depended on the university for its supply of teachers. In a broad way Washington agreed with Du Bois on this point. But beyond this administrative technicality, the deeper question to which this polemic points is the means of elevation of a people, or how good habits are brought into being. In this respect, the issue between Washington and Du Bois then concerns the question of whether good habits or morals are *formed,* primarily by demonstration, or whether they are *taught,* by indoctrination or exposure to the intellectual life. At the least, one would have to note that Washington, who was primarily a practical man, was much more mindful of the debasement and fraudulence that could arise in the sphere of the intellectual life without the integrity acquired in the realm of morals. The net result, then, of trying to transform the habits of an underdeveloped people by mass high culture is that their habits would not be changed and their education would be spurious. Washington was painfully aware of the one-man Negro "colleges" in the South run by sincere men, offering everything from Hebrew to telegraphy. See pages 437 f.

[79] See pages 334 f., italics mine—H.B.

Civil War emigrationists lived and worked in an atmosphere in which the free Negro in the North was small in number with very much the status of an outlaw, Garvey entered the scene in post-World War I Harlem. To the urban masses, many of them new migrants from the South and newly possessed of a vote, Garvey exuberantly preached the doctrine of "Africa for the Africans" and the redemption of Africa. His impact on these people is to be seen as much as, if not more, in the race pride he projected than in any practical activities he fostered.

Garvey founded a newspaper, the *Negro World,* which became the vehicle for his views, which may be summarized as follows. First, race assimilation, which to Garvey meant amalgamation, is impossible because the white man feels that by assimilation he will be committing racial suicide.[80] Therefore, the Negro is doomed to remain a permanent minority whom white color prejudice will keep in an inferior position. As the Negro strives to better himself, "racial competition" will arise and further inflame such color prejudice. In the ensuing conflict the Negro, who is outnumbered, is at a disadvantage. The results of this can only be catastrophic for the Negro, a terrible race war in which the Negro would suffer the fate of the American Indian:

Prejudice we shall always have between black and white, so long as the latter believes that the former is intruding upon their rights. So long as white laborers believe that black laborers are taking and holding their jobs . . . so long as white political leaders and statesmen believe that black politicians and statesmen are seeking the same positions in the nation's government; so long as white men believe that black men want to associate with, and marry, white women, then we will ever have prejudice, and not only prejudice but riots, lynchings, burnings, and God to tell what next will follow. It is this danger that drives me mad. It must be prevented.[81]

Garvey, to be sure, thought that just whites might open the door of opportunity to educated, ambitious, and politically assertive Negroes who would demand the high positions for which they were capable. However, these just whites would not be able to control the mob:

But, ladies and gentlemen, what about the mob, that starving crowd of your own race? Will they stand by, suffer and starve, and allow an opposite, competitive race to prosper in the midst of their distress? If you can conjure these things up in your mind, then you have the vision of the race problem of the future in America.[82]

Garvey's thesis was that the Negro should not delude himself with the aim of "social equality," that is, amalgamation. This was imprudent, productive only of hate and discord from which the Negro would suffer. But he also asserted that it was undignified. He maintained that the desire for

[80] See page 553.
[81] See pages 556 f.
[82] See page 558.

race purity was legitimate and valid for all races. The Negro, thus, instead
of wanting to be amalgamated, should be proud of his own racial purity:

I believe that white men should be white, yellow men should be yellow,
and black men should be black. . . .[83]

If amalgamation is, then, something that the Negro himself ought to
reject (even apart from the prejudices of whites), the only solution is the
national one of having a country of one's own. This is the Negro's right,
"to have an outlet for Negro energy, ambition, and passion, away from the
attractions of white opportunity." It is also the Negro's duty, for he can
only be truly respected when he has emancipated himself:

No Negro . . . shall be truly respected until the race as a whole has
emancipated itself, through self-achievement and progress, from universal
prejudice. The Negro will have to build his own government, industry, art,
science, literature and culture, before the world will stop to consider him.
Until then, Negroes are but wards of a superior race and civilization and the
outcasts of a standard social system.[84]

In his program the locale for the Negro's auto-emancipation was to be
in Africa, and his image of the future was of a modern Africa that would
bestow the blessings of democracy upon all mankind. He appealed to the
soul of the rich white race to help lift the poor and backward black race to
"the common standard of progress and civilization." [85]

Friends, white cannot prosper to the disadvantage of black.[86]

But, as one notes in the above, he also spoke of racial cultures:

Jewish culture is different from Irish culture. . . . Why should the Negro
be lost among the other races and nations of the world and to himself? [87]

Garvey was accused of wanting to lead a mass exodus back to Africa.
(In fact, only a few actually emigrated under his auspices.) He denied
this, contending among other things that he was interested only in the
industrious and adventurous of the Negro population:

The Negro who is wrangling about and fighting for social equality will
naturally pass away in fifty years, and yield his place to the progressive Negro
who wants a society and country of his own.[88]

More interesting, however, is the fact that as he was pressed either by such
criticism or by the actual circumstances of Negro life in America, he was
capable of a switch, from doctrinaire theory to a more practical orientation. The former, his apartheid theory, partakes of all the classical features

[83] See page 553.
[84] See page 564.
[85] See page 559.
[86] See page 560.
[87] See page 573.
[88] See page 576.

of a rigid simplification of alternatives. These are, as he saw it, *either* total assimilation (meaning amalgamation) *or* total separation. With his orientation toward this "final solution," he could foresee nothing in between these two extremes except oppression or the extinction of the Negro. (He also thought that mass unemployment would be chronic.) On the level of such "theoretical" prognostications, it would almost seem that Garvey simply did not believe that the Negro could ever get any rights in the United States.

The fact is that he did. As soon as he turned to the here and now, he disencumbered himself from the "final solution" and spoke in different terms. In what is perhaps the clearest statement of his real view, he states:

> To fight for African redemption does not mean that we must give up our domestic fights for political justice and industrial rights. It does not mean that we must become disloyal to any government or to any country wherein we were born. . . . We can be as loyal American citizens or British subjects as the Irishman or the Jew, and yet fight for the redemption of Africa, a complete emancipation of the race. Fighting for the establishment of Palestine does not make the American Jew disloyal; fighting for the independence of Ireland does not make the Irish-American a bad citizen. Why should fighting for the freedom of Africa make the Afro-American disloyal or a bad citizen? [89]

In this mode of expression of pan-Negro sentiment there is certainly no radical break—if indeed there is any break at all—with the assimilationist tradition.

CONCLUSION: BEYOND THE "FINAL SOLUTION"

It will be recalled that the core of the emigrationist standpoint consisted of two assumptions about the race problem. The first was that color prejudice was so deep that the Negro would never get political or social equality. Implicit in this assumption is the notion that equality is something that is one and indivisible. Within the perspective created by this theoretical view of the indivisibility of equality, any form whatsoever of color prejudice—or even, perhaps, of the mere awareness of color—could only be seen as an abridgment of perfect equality. The same view fortified the conviction that it was useless to think of the Negro's becoming a citizen, since he was looked on as a member of a despised caste.

The second point in the emigrationist thesis is that without power there will be no respect and that in a world of nation states true power for any people logically entails their acquisition of national sovereignty. Anything less than true political independence would thus be inadequate. But this is only one possible inference drawn from the more general thesis that equality rests upon equal power and that equalization for the Negro must

[89] See page 568.

take place essentially via a change in power relations. As we see today, such a view need not necessarily be attached to nationalist sentiments.

The elements in the emigrationist position, then, are a combination of utopianism on the one hand and Machiavellianism on the other. One may well suspect that this is not a stable combination.

Now the initial impulse of such assimilationists as Douglass and Washington was not to take issue with emigrationism on theoretical grounds. As we shall see, however, they did. To deal first with Douglass, his immediate reaction (to paraphrase his views somewhat) was to raise the following question: Assuming that a few thousand emigrants attain perfect freedom from color prejudice, if not perfect equality and justice, will three and a half million slaves be liberated thereby? When they eyed the emergence of a Negro republic, would the slaveholders have a new respect for the Negro that would dissolve their "race prejudice," induce them to look on their slaves as equals and free them? Douglass saw the slavocracy casting eyes upon Mexico and Cuba as likely sites for the expansion of slavery. He knew that, if an expansionist policy of this sort became dominant in the nation, it would seek to extinguish any symbolic threat to slavery posed by the existence of an independent Negro republic. And as for a military threat which an infant Negro republic might pose to American slavery, Douglass would not even waste time with such considerations. He rejected all emigrationism as a textbook "solution" that left the most urgent problem—namely, slavery—untouched, let alone solved.

In Washington's lifetime Negro emigrationism had more or less expired but there was still a stratum of white opinion, some of it well meaning, that thought that the "Negro problem" could be solved only by the deportation of the Negroes (or, derivatively, their dispersion throughout the whole country with each state getting its proportionate share). Apart from perceiving the aberration of "solving" a problem by wishing it out of existence, Washington knew that the economy of the South depended upon Negro labor for which there was no practical substitute. Thus regardless of the respectability of deportation in Southern rhetoric, those who had a direct interest in the use of this Negro labor would oppose and even obstruct the loss of their labor supply.[90] Emigrationism was thus the same fraud it had been under the slave regime, a textbook solution that, by declaring the Negro to be a transient, evaded the real problems of assimilation and adjustment in the place where he was. Knowing this, Washington could authoritatively say that the Negro is here and here to stay. This is a frequent theme in his writings and speeches aimed at silencing the rumbling noises of the advocates of deportation.

Both men, then, gave the highest priority to the most urgent tasks within a concrete political situation. Whether these tasks be the destruction of slavery or the problems of construction after freedom, they had to

[90] Vernon Lane Wharton, *The Negro in Mississippi, 1865–1890* (New York: Harper Torchbooks, 1947), pp. 97–105. See also pages 323 and 397 in this volume.

be looked at in their own light, which is the light by which an acting man in a political situation sees what is going on, what has to be done, and what can be done. They would permit nothing—theoretical maxims, history, myth—to deflect them from their grasp of these tasks. Whether respect was based on power, or whether power was based on respect, slavery had to be destroyed, the Negro needed an education, the Negro was not leaving because his labor was needed. They would allow nothing of a theoretical nature to obscure the tasks and the facts of the situation.

The problem posed by these two different political styles is that of the proper relationship between theory and practice. In the case of the "final solutionists," we see a type of reasoning *from* a fixed theory *to* the situation, consuming itself in solutions which bypass the most urgent tasks. Indifferent to the facts, the theory imposes a "solution" upon the situation. It runs away from the facts, from reality. The precise term for this aberrant relationship between theory and practice is doctrinairism.

Now the reason that Douglass and Washington were able to avoid doctrinairism is not that they were antitheoretical. Primarily, to be sure, they were both practical men engaged in the practical pursuit of providing leadership for their race. Nonetheless, they were both extraordinarily reflective men who thought with detachment about social and political life in general and race relations in particular. It is, of course, true that their theoretical insights and generalizations are not codified in any treatise, but rather emerged from their practical concerns; yet one can learn a great deal from these men about the characteristics of prejudice, the nature of public opinion and the possibility of changing it, the problems of a modern democracy. Indeed, it is precisely because their theoretical reflections emerge from their practical concerns that they have a distinctive style. Instead of imposing a theory on the situation, both Douglass and Washington begin with the agenda, never losing sight of them, but rather reasoning from them toward general considerations that enable them to see the same agenda with greater clarity than one can in the heat of political controversy. No "theoretical" doctrine could persuade Douglass that he was not a man if for no other reason than that only a man could understand such a doctrine. By the same token, no doctrine could make him forget that slavery was the most urgent problem not only for the Negro, but for the nation as a whole. Given the place of practical tasks in his framework, he could see that any theory denying this fact was simply fortifying slavery.

When one confronts the emigrationist position as a whole with the position of Douglass and Washington, one sees that the difference between them is not that one emphasizes power while the other stresses principle. Both positions are concerned with both. Douglass and Washington were as much concerned with power as were Delany and Blyden and as ardent in their defense of principle. Thus the difference in the two positions is not the same as the difference between doctrinairism or ideology, on the one hand, and a movement "back to pragmatism," on the other. While such a distinction points out the style of the "final solution" (and parallel "isms"), it renders the moderate stance of Douglass and Washington as devoid of an orientation to principle. Hence, it distorts it. The fact is that the second position corrects both the utopianism and the Machiavellianism of the first position. It does so by relating both considerations of power and considerations of principle to the tasks of the political situation.

To take power first, Douglass, in one of the most illuminating of his many theoretical aperçus, drawing on his own experience as a slave, wrote the following:

A man without force is without the essential dignity of humanity. Human nature is so constituted that it cannot honor a helpless man, though it can pity him, and even this it cannot do long, if signs of power do not arise; you can put a man so far beneath the level of his kind that he loses all just ideals of his natural position.[91]

Certainly Douglass would have agreed with the nationalist contention that without at least *some* power there can be no respect, as the extreme situation of chattel slavery makes manifestly clear. And one might add as a corollary, without some self-assertion in the defense of one's rights, one will be subjected to exploitation by some people. In the present situation, Douglass and Washington (who places great importance on this passage in his quotation of it) would have seen the tremendous importance of the Negro's own self-assertion through legal challenges and other modes of *commanding* respect for bringing about a change in his status. But to draw from this an inference to the effect that every gain made by the Negro must be the result solely of increasing power, and legal power at that, would be regarded by them as a doctrinaire simplification of the processes of social and political life. They would never have looked upon power so legalistically. They would never have looked upon it as something solely directed toward or over others, in a framework of conflict or competition. When Douglass spoke of force he meant not merely legal rights, but also something that must exist within a man, lest he be helpless. The failure to take this inner aspect of force into account obscures the importance of the social and educational changes within the Negro himself in enabling him to stand up and assert his rights. These changes in part explain why he was able to do this in the 1950's with an effectiveness that he did not have in 1900 when Negroes in a number of southern cities attempted to annul Jim Crow laws through boycotting of the newly segregated streetcars.[92] But this does not negate the fact either that he had to stand up to command respect in order to complete and secure these changes.

[91] Booker T. Washington, *Frederick Douglass* (Philadelphia: George W. Jacobs & Co., 1907), p. 98.

[92] August Meier, *Negro Thought in America, 1880–1915* (Ann Arbor: The University of Michigan Press, 1963), p. 175.

It is also of interest to note that Negro settlements abroad were the objects of serious interest and concern to both Douglass and Washington. Douglass was in fact the United States Minister to Haiti from 1889 to 1891. Washington was interested in the emergence of "Tuskegees" not only in the United States, but in Haiti and Liberia as well. He saw that the people there did not know how to develop their resources, which made both republics economically dependent upon other nations and races.[93]

As for equality, the nub of the assimilationist view, as contrasted with that of the theoretical radicals, is its denial of the indivisibility of equality. Douglass might well have asked Blyden how the Negro could seriously concern himself about the absence of social equality when he did not as yet have civic and political rights. Implicit in this question is the understanding that there is a hierarchy of different kinds of equality and that equality in public life is more serious because more strategic than the equality conferred within private life. The very boundaries of what is permissible in private are defined by the public context. The acquisition of public equality thus constituted the most urgent goal for the Negro as seen by these men. As stated earlier, this public status included not only legal rights, but also those social qualifications which give a person public respect in the society.[94] Within the political perspective in which the public status is seen as the primary practical goal, considerations about ulterior equalities, either now or in the far-off future, become politically irrelevent.

But does not this focusing on the immediate actually obscure an understanding of the situation in theoretical respects? If the Negro cannot be amalgamated en masse in the practical future, does this not constitute an abridgment of perfect racial equality? Granted that the Negro by and large may not have any desire to be so absorbed. Granted that the Negro may be perfectly content with the degree of public equality in the comprehensive sense of this term, which he will acquire but which he does not yet possess. The theoretical question still remains as to whether the mere fact that he is a minority group, which means a group socially defined as a separate entity, does not constitute an inequality. That this has some consequences for individual rights or opportunities even in the public sphere is seen, for example, in the fact that the occupancy of the highest political offices by members of minority groups cannot help but be politically noticeable. No one raises the question, "Can a white man be president?" Thus from a strict theoretical standpoint there is some inequality in being a member of a minority. The practical question would then seem to be not whether one can achieve perfect equality but, rather, whether one can live well with this residual inequality. Can the Negro achieve happiness as a Negro in a predominantly non-Negro society?

[93] Basil Mathews, *Booker T. Washington* (Cambridge: Harvard University Press, 1948), p. 251.

[94] For a more detailed theoretical treatment of public status in these terms, see Howard Brotz, "Social Stratification and the Political Order," *The American Journal of Sociology*, 64 (May 1959), 571–578.

Is he to be compelled to try to run away from himself in order to be equal in a practically satisfying way? That the inequality of being a member of a minority group can be pleasantly concealed by the absence of any serious public obstructions on the *individual's* life chances would seem to be the crucial fact that would make this a viable arrangement. This is precisely the experience of other minorities in America. Douglass, in one reference, uses the term "final solution" to mean complete civic and political equality.[95] Strictly speaking, however, the "final solution," or perfect justice, is no more, and no less, than an ultimate standard to guide and perfect social and political life, and the awareness of this is not without relevance to policy. In this respect, the race problem is simply a particular instance of the political problem in general.

SUGGESTED READINGS

General Background

Franklin, John Hope. *From Slavery to Freedom* (2nd ed., rev. and enl.; New York: Knopf, 1956).

Logan, Rayford. *The Negro in the United States* (Princeton, N.J.: Van Nostrand Co., 1957).

Loggins, Vernon. *The Negro Author* (New York: Columbia University Press, 1931).

Washington, Booker T. *The Story of the Negro* (New York: Doubleday, 1909).

Colonization, Emigration, Nationalism

Bell, Howard H. "Negro Nationalism: A Factor in Emigration Projects, 1858–1861," *Journal of Negro History,* XLVII (January 1962), No. 1, 42–53.

Cromwell, John W. "The Early Negro Convention Movement," *Occasional Papers,* No. 9 (Washington, D.C.: The American Negro Academy, 1904).

Fox, Early Lee. *The American Colonization Society, 1817–1840* (Balti-

more: Johns Hopkins University Press, 1919).

Litwack, Leon. *North of Slavery,* "The Negro in the Free States, 1790–1860" (Chicago: Phoenix Books, 1960).

Mehlinger, Louis R. "The Attitude of the Free Negro toward Colonization," *Journal of Negro History,* I (1916), No. 3.

Meier, August. "The Emergence of Negro Nationalism," *Midwest Journal,* IV (Winter 1951–1952), No. 1.

Woodson, Carter G. *The Mind of the Negro as Reflected in Letters Written during the Crisis, 1800–1860* (Washington, D.C.: The Association for the Study of Negro Life and History, Inc., 1926).

Frederick Douglass

Charnwood, Lord. *Abraham Lincoln* (London: Constable & Co., 1919).

Foner, Philip S. *The Life and Writings of Frederick Douglass* (New York: International Publishers, 1950), 4 vols.

Holland, Frederic May. *Frederick Douglass,* "The Colored Orator" (New York: Funk & Wagnalls Co., 1891).

95 See page 268.

Washington, Booker T. *Frederick Douglass* (Philadelphia: George W. Jacobs & Co., 1907).

Booker T. Washington

Mathews, Basil. *Booker T. Washington, Educator and Interracial Interpreter"* (Cambridge: Harvard University Press, 1948).

Meier, August. *Negro Thought in America, 1800–1915,* "Racial Ideologies in the Age of Booker T. Washington" (Ann Arbor: University of Michigan, 1963).

Scott, Emmett J., and Stowe, Lyman Beecher. *Booker T. Washington,* "Builder of a Civilization" (Garden City, N.J.: Doubleday, 1917).

Spencer, Samuel R., Jr. *Booker T. Washington and the Negro's Place in American Life* (Boston: Little, Brown, 1955).

Storing, Herbert. "The School of Slavery: A Reconsideration of Booker T. Washington," in Robert A. Goldwin, ed., *100 Years of Emancipation* (Chicago: Rand McNally, 1964).

Woodward, C. Vann. *The Origins of the New South, 1877–1913* (Baton Rouge: Louisiana State University Press, 1951).

Woodward, C. Vann. *The Strange Career of Jim Crow* (New York: Oxford University Press, 1957).

W. E. B. Du Bois

Broderick, Francis, L. *W. E. B. Du Bois,* "Negro Leader in a Time of Crisis" (Stanford, Calif.: Stanford University Press, 1959).

Gossett, Thomas F. *Race: The History of an Idea in America* (Dallas: Southern Methodist University Press, 1963).

Rudwick, Elliott M. *W. E. B. Du Bois,* "A Study in Minority Group Leadership" (Philadelphia: University of Wisconsin Press, 1960).

Marcus Garvey

Cronon, Edmund D. *Black Moses,* "The Story of Marcus Garvey and the Universal Negro Improvement Association" (Madison: University of Wisconsin Press, 1955).

Garvey, A. Jacques. *Garvey and Garveyism* (Kingston, Jamaica: Privately printed, 1963).

PART I

Emigration

MARTIN R. DELANY

(1812–1883)

Associated with Frederick Douglass on The North Star *from 1847–1849, Martin Delany subsequently became interested in colonization, publishing his book* The Condition, Elevation, Emigration, and Destiny of the Colored People of the United States, "Politically Considered" *in 1852. His interest in this book was in emigration to Nicaragua and New Grenada (in the northern part of South America). Later on, he became interested in the possibilities of Africa for settlement and development and organized a party to explore the Niger Valley. His* Official Report of the Niger Valley Exploring Party *was published in 1861. With the outbreak of Civil War, however, he was active in the recruitment of Negro soldiers and was commissioned as a medical officer with the rank of major. After the Civil War, he served in the Freedmen's Bureau and held other offices during the Reconstruction period.*

THE CONDITION, ELEVATION, EMIGRATION, AND DESTINY OF THE COLORED PEOPLE OF THE UNITED STATES

I. CONDITION OF MANY CLASSES IN EUROPE CONSIDERED

That there have been in all ages and in all countries, in every quarter of the habitable globe, especially among those nations laying the greatest claim to civilization and enlightenment, classes of people who have been deprived of equal privileges, political, religious and social, cannot be denied, and that this deprivation on the part of the ruling classes is cruel and unjust, is also equally true. Such classes have ever been looked upon as inferior to their oppressors, and have ever been mainly the domestics and menials of society, doing the low offices and drudgery of those among whom they lived, moving about and existing by mere sufferance, having no rights nor privileges but those conceded by the common consent of their political superiors. These are historical facts that cannot be controverted, and therefore proclaim in tones more eloquently than thunder, the listful attention of every oppressed man, woman, and child under the government of the people of the United States of America.

In past ages there were many such classes, as the Israelites in Egypt, the

Gladiators in Rome, and similar classes in Greece; and in the present age, the Gipsies in Italy and Greece, the Cossacs in Russia and Turkey, the Sclaves and Croats in the Germanic States, and the Welsh and Irish among the British, to say nothing of various other classes among other nations.

That there have in all ages, in almost every nation, existed a nation within a nation—a people who although forming a part and parcel of the population, yet were from force of circumstances, known by the peculiar position they occupied, forming in fact, by the deprivation of political equality with others, no part, and if any, but a restricted part of the body politic of such nations, is also true.

Such then are the Poles in Russia, the Hungarians in Austria, the Scotch, Irish, and Welsh in the United Kingdom, and such also are the Jews, scattered throughout not only the length and breadth of Europe, but almost the habitable globe, maintaining their national characteristics, and looking forward in high hopes of seeing the day when they may return to their former national position of self-government and independence, let that be in whatever part of the habitable world it may. This is the lot of these various classes of people in Europe, and it is not our intention here, to discuss the justice or injustice of the causes that have contributed to their degradation, but simply to set forth the undeniable facts, which are as glaring as the rays of a noon-day's sun, thereby to impress them indelibly on the mind of every reader of this pamphlet.

It is not enough, that these people are deprived of equal privileges by their rulers, but, the more effectually to succeed, the equality of these classes must be denied, and their inferiority by nature as distinct races, actually asserted. This policy is necessary to appease the opposition that might be interposed in their behalf. Wherever there is arbitrary rule, there must of necessity, on the part of the dominant classes, superiority be assumed. To assume superiority, is to deny the equality of others, and to deny their equality, is to premise their incapacity of self-government. Let this once be conceded, and there will be little or no sympathy for the oppressed, the oppressor being left to prescribe whatever terms at discretion for their government, suits his own purpose.

Such then is the condition of various classes in Europe; yes, nations, for centuries within nations, even without the hope of redemption among those who oppress them. And however unfavorable their condition, there is none more so than that of the colored people of the United States.

II. COMPARATIVE CONDITION OF THE COLORED
PEOPLE OF THE UNITED STATES

The United States, untrue to her trust and unfaithful to her professed principles of republican equality, has also pursued a policy of political degradation to a large portion of her native born countrymen, and that class is the Colored People. Denied an equality not only of political, but of natural rights, in common with the rest of our fellow citizens, there is no species of degradation to which we are not subject.

Reduced to abject slavery is not enough, the very thought of which should awaken every sensibility of our common nature; but those of their descendants who are freemen even in the non-slaveholding States, occupy the very same position politically, religiously, civilly and socially, (with but few exceptions,) as the bondman occupies in the slave States.

In those States, the bondman is disfranchised, and for the most part so are we. He is denied all civil, religious, and social privileges, except such as he gets by mere sufferance, and so are we. They have no part nor lot in the government of the country, neither have we. They are ruled and governed without representation, existing as mere nonentities among the citizens, and excrescences on the body politic—a mere dreg in community, and so are we. Where then is our political superiority to the enslaved? None, neither are we superior in any other relation to society, except that we are defacto masters of ourselves and joint rulers of our own domestic household, while the bondman's self is claimed by another, and his relation to his family denied him. What the unfortunate classes are in Europe, such are we in the United States, which is folly to deny, insanity not to understand, blindness not to see, and surely now full time that our eyes were opened to these startling truths, which for ages have stared us full in the face.

It is time that we had become politicians, we mean, to understand the political economy and domestic policy of nations; that we had become as well as moral theorists, also the practical demonstrators of equal rights and self-government. Except we do, it is idle to talk about rights, it is mere chattering for the sake of being seen and heard—like the slave, saying something because his so called "master" said it, and saying just what he told him to say. Have we got now sufficient intelligence among us to understand our true position, to realise our actual condition, and determine for ourselves what is best to be done? If we have not now, we never shall have, and should at once cease prating about our equality, capacity, and all that.

Twenty years ago, when the writer was a youth, his young and yet uncultivated mind was aroused, and his tender heart made to leap with anxiety in anticipation of the promises then held out by the prime movers in the cause of our elevation.

In 1830 the most intelligent and leading spirits among the colored men in the United States, such as James Forten, Robert Douglass, I. Bowers, A. D. Shadd, John Peck, Joseph Cassey, and John B. Vashon of Pennsylvania; John T. Hilton, Nathaniel and Thomas Paul, and James G. Barbadoes of Massachusetts; Henry Sipkins, Thomas Hamilton, Thomas L. Jennings, Thomas Downing, Samuel E. Cornish, and others of New York; R. Cooley and others of Maryland, and representatives from other States

which cannot now be recollected, the data not being at hand, assembled in
the city of Philadelphia, in the capacity of a National Convention, to "devise ways and means for the bettering of our condition." These Conventions determined to assemble annually, much talent, ability, and energy of
character being displayed; when in 1831 at a sitting of the Convention in
September, from their previous pamphlet reports, much interest having
been created throughout the country, they were favored by the presence of
a number of whites, some of whom were able and distinguished men, such
as Rev. R. R. Gurley, Arthur Tappan, Elliot Cresson, John Rankin, Sim-
eon Jocelyn and others, among them William Lloyd Garrison, then quite
a young man, all of whom were staunch and ardent Colonizationists,
young Garrison at that time, doing his mightiest in his favorite work.

Among other great projects of interest brought before the convention at
a previous sitting, was that of the expediency of a general emigration, as
far as it was practicable, of the colored people to the British Provinces of
North America. Another was that of raising sufficient means for the establishment and erection of a College for the proper education of the colored
youth. These gentlemen long accustomed to observation and reflection on
the condition of their people, saw at once, that there must necessarily be
means used adequate to the end to be attained—that end being an unqualified equality with the ruling class of their fellow citizens. They saw
that as a class, the colored people of the country were ignorant, degraded
and oppressed, by far the greater portion of them being abject slaves in the
South, the very condition of whom was almost enough, under the circumstances, to blast the remotest hope of success, and those who were freemen, whether in the South or North, occupied a subservient, servile, and
menial position, considering it a favor to get into the service of the whites,
and do their degrading offices. That the difference between the whites and
themselves, consisted in the superior advantages of the one over the other,
in point of attainments. That if a knowledge of the arts and sciences, the
mechanical occupations, the industrial occupations, as farming, commerce,
and all the various business enterprises, and learned professions were necessary for the superior position occupied by their rulers, it was also necessary for them. And very reasonably too, the first suggestion which occurred to them was, the advantages of a location, then the necessity of a
qualification. They reasoned with themselves, that all distinctive differences made among men on account of their origin, is wicked, unrighteous,
and cruel, and never shall receive countenance in any shape from us, therefore, the first act of the measures entered into by them, was to protest,
solemnly protest, against every unjust measure and policy in the country,
having for its object the proscription of the colored people, whether state,
national, municipal, social, civil, or religious.

But being far-sighted, reflecting, discerning men, they took a political
view of the subject, and determined for the good of their people to be
governed in their policy according to the facts as they presented them-

selves. In taking a glance at Europe, they discovered there, however unjustly, as we have shown in another part of this pamphlet, that there are
and have been numerous classes proscribed and oppressed, and it was not
for them to cut short their wise deliberations, and arrest their proceedings
in contention, as to the cause, whether on account of language, the color
of eyes, hair, skin, or their origin of country—because all this is contrary
to reason, a contradiction to common sense, at war with nature herself,
and at variance with facts as they stare us every day in the face, among all
nations, in every country—this being made the pretext as a matter of *policy* alone—a fact worthy of observation, that wherever the objects of
oppression are the most easily distinguished by any peculiar or general
characteristics, these people are the more easily oppressed, because the war
of oppression is the more easily waged against them. This is the case with
the modern Jews and many other people who have strongly-marked, peculiar, or distinguishing characteristics. This arises in this wise. The policy of
all those who proscribe any people, induces them to select as the objects of
proscription, those who differed as much as possible, in some particulars,
from themselves. This is to ensure the greater success, because it engen-
ders the greater prejudice, or in other words, elicits less interest on the part
of the oppressing class, in their favor. This fact is well understood in national conflicts, as the soldier or civilian, who is distinguished by his dress,
mustache, or any other peculiar appendage, would certainly prove himself
a madman, if he did not take the precaution to change his dress, remove
his mustache, and conceal as much as possible his peculiar characteristics,
to give him access among the repelling party. This is mere policy, nature
having nothing to do with it. Still, it is a fact, a great truth well worthy of
remark, and as such we adduce it for the benefit of those of our readers,
unaccustomed to an enquiry into the policy of nations.

In view of these truths, our fathers and leaders in our elevation, discovered that as a policy, we the colored people were selected as the subordinate class in this country, not on account of any actual or supposed inferiority on their part, but simply because, in view of all the circumstances of
the case, they were the very best class that could be selected. They would
have as readily had any other class as subordinates in the country, as the
colored people, but the condition of society *at the time,* would not admit
of it. In the struggle for American Independence, there were among those
who performed the most distinguished parts, the most common-place
peasantry of the Provinces. English, Danish, Irish, Scotch, and others, were
among those whose names blazoned forth as heroes in the American Revolution. But a single reflection will convince us, that no course of policy
could have induced the proscription of the parentage and relatives of such
men as Benjamin Franklin the printer, Roger Sherman the cobbler, the
tinkers, and others of the signers of the Declaration of Independence. But
as they were determined to have a subservient class, it will readily be
conceived, that according to the state of society at the time, the better

policy on their part was, to select some class, who from their political position—however much they may have contributed their aid as we certainly did, in the general struggle for liberty by force of arms—who had the least claims upon them, or who had the *least chance,* or was the *least potent* in urging their claims. This class of course was the colored people and Indians.

The Indians who in the early settlement of the continent, before an African captive had ever been introduced thereon, were reduced to the most abject slavery, toiling day and night in the mines, under the relentless hands of heartless Spanish taskmasters, but being a race of people raised to the sports of fishing, the chase, and of war, were wholly unaccustomed to labor, and therefore sunk under the insupportable weight, two millions and a half having fallen victims to the cruelty of oppression and toil suddenly placed upon their shoulders. And it was only this that prevented their farther enslavement as a class, after the provinces were absolved from the British Crown. It is true that their general enslavement took place on the islands and in the mining districts of South America, where indeed, the Europeans continued to enslave them, until a comparatively recent period; still, the design, the feeling, and inclination from policy, was the same to do so here, in this section of the continent.

Nor was it until their influence became too great, by the political position occupied by their brethren in the new republic, that the German and Irish peasantry ceased to be sold as slaves for a term of years fixed by law, for the repayment of their passage-money, the descendants of these classes of people for a long time being held as inferiors, in the estimation of the ruling class, and it was not until they assumed the rights and privileges guaranteed to them by the established policy of the country, among the leading spirits of whom were their relatives, that the policy towards them was discovered to be a bad one, and accordingly changed. Nor was it, as is frequently very erroneously asserted, by colored as well as white persons, that it was on account of hatred to the African, or in other words, on account of hatred to his color, that the African was selected as the subject of oppression in this country. This is sheer nonsense; being based on policy and nothing else, as shown in another place. The Indians, who being the most foreign to the sympathies of the Europeans on this continent, were selected in the first place, who, being unable to withstand the hardships, gave way before them.

But the African race had long been known to Europeans, in all ages of the world's history, as a long-lived, hardy race, subject to toil and labor of various kinds, subsisting mainly by traffic, trade, and industry, and consequently being as foreign to the sympathies of the invaders of the continent as the Indians, they were selected, captured, brought here as a laboring class, and as a matter of policy held as such. Nor was the absurd idea of natural inferiority of the African ever dreamed of, until recently adduced by the slave-holders and their abettors, in justification of their policy. This, with contemptuous indignation, we fling back into their face, as a scorpion to a vulture. And so did our patriots and leaders in the cause of regeneration know better, and never for a moment yielded to the base doctrine. But they had discovered the great fact, that a cruel policy was pursued towards our people, and that they possessed distinctive characteristics which made them the objects of proscription. These characteristics being strongly marked in the colored people, as in the Indians, by color, character of hair and so on, made them the more easily distinguished from other Americans, and the policies more effectually urged against us. For this reason they introduced the subject of emigration to Canada, and a proper institution for the education of the youth.

At this important juncture of their proceedings, the afore named white gentlemen were introduced to the notice of the Convention, and after gaining permission to speak, expressed their gratification and surprise at the qualification and talent manifested by different members of the Convention, all expressing their determination to give the cause of the colored people more serious reflection. Mr. Garrison, the youngest of them all, and none the less honest on account of his youthfulness, being but 26 years of age at the time, (1831) expressed his determination to change his course of policy at once, and espouse the cause of the elevation of the colored people here in their own country. We are not at present well advised upon this point, it now having escaped our memory, but we are under the impression that Mr. Jocelyn also, at once changed his policy.

During the winter of 1832, Mr. Garrison issued his "Thoughts on African Colonization," and near about the same time or shortly after, issued the first number of the "Liberator," in both of which, his full convictions of the enormity of American slavery, and the wickedness of their policy towards the colored people, were fully expressed. At the sitting of the Convention in this year, a number, perhaps all of these gentlemen were present, and those who had denounced the Colonization scheme, and espoused the cause of the elevation of the colored people in this country, or the Anti-Slavery cause, as it was now termed, expressed themselves openly and without reserve.

Sensible of the high-handed injustice done to the colored people in the United States, and the mischief likely to emanate from the unchristian proceedings of the deceptious Colonization scheme, like all honest-hearted penitents, with the ardor only known to new converts, they entreated the Convention, whatever they did, not to entertain for a moment, the idea of recommending emigration to their people, nor the establishment of separate institutions of learning. They earnestly contended, and doubtless honestly meaning what they said, that they (the whites) had been our oppressors and injurers, they had obstructed our progress to the high positions of civilization, and now, it was their bounden duty to make full amends for the injuries thus inflicted on an unoffending people. They exhorted the Convention to cease; as they had laid on the burden, they would also take it off; as they had obstructed our pathway, they would remove the hindrance. In a word, as they had oppressed and trampled down the colored people, they would now elevate them. These suggestions and promises, good enough to be sure, after they were made, were accepted by the Convention—though some gentlemen were still in favor of the first project as the best policy, Mr. A. D. Shadd of West Chester, Pa., as we learn from himself, being one among that number—ran through the country like wild-fire, no one thinking, and if he thought, daring to speak above his breath of going any where out of certain prescribed limits, or of sending a child to school, if it should but have the name of "colored" attached to it, without the risk of being termed a "traitor" to the cause of his people, or an enemy to the Anti-Slavery cause.

At this important point in the history of our efforts, the colored men stopped suddenly, and with their hands thrust deep in their breeches-pockets, and their mouths gaping open, stood gazing with astonishment, wonder, and surprise, at the stupendous moral colossal statues of our Anti-Slavery friends and brethren, who in the heat and zeal of honest hearts, from a desire to make atonement for the many wrongs inflicted, promised a great deal more than they have ever been able half to fulfill, in thrice the period in which they expected it. And in this, we have no fault to find with our Anti-Slavery friends, and here wish it to be understood, that we are not laying any thing to their charge as blame, neither do we desire for a moment to reflect on them, because we heartily believe that all that they did at the time, they did with the purest and best of motives, and further believe that they now are, as they then were, the truest friends we have among the whites in this country. And hope, and desire, and request, that our people should always look upon *true* Anti-Slavery people, Abolitionists we mean, as their friends, until they have just cause for acting otherwise. It is true, that the Anti-Slavery, like all good causes has produced some recreants, but the cause itself is no more to be blamed for that, than Christianity is for the malconduct of any professing hypocrite, nor the society of Friends, for the conduct of a broad-brimmed hat and shad-belly coated horsethief, because he spoke *thee* and *thou* before stealing the horse. But what is our condition even amidst our Anti-Slavery friends? And here, as our sole intention is to contribute to the elevation of our people, we must be permitted to express our opinion freely, without being thought uncharitable.

In the first place, we should look at the objects for which the Anti-Slavery cause was commenced, and the promises or inducements it held out at the commencement. It should be borne in mind, that Anti-Slavery took its rise among *colored men*, just at the time they were introducing their greatest projects for their own elevation, and that our Anti-Slavery brethren were converts of the colored men, in behalf of their elevation. Of course, it would be expected that being baptized into the new doctrines, their faith would induce them to embrace the principles therein contained, with the strictest possible adherence.

The cause of dissatisfaction with our former condition, was, that we were proscribed, debarred, and shut out from every respectable position, occupying the places of inferiors and menials.

It was expected that Anti-Slavery, according to its professions, would extend to colored persons, as far as in the power of its adherents, those advantages nowhere else to be obtained among white men. That colored boys would get situations in their shops and stores, and every other advantage tending to elevate them as far as possible, would be extended to them. At least, it was expected, that in Anti-Slavery establishments, colored men would have the preference. Because, there was no other ostensible object in view, in the commencement of the Anti-Slavery enterprise, than the *elevation* of the *colored man,* by facilitating his efforts in attaining to equality with the white man. It was urged, and it was true, that the colored people were susceptible of all that the whites were, and all that was required was to give them a fair opportunity, and they would prove their capacity. That it was unjust, wicked, and cruel, the result of an unnatural prejudice, that debarred them from places of respectability, and that public opinion could and should be corrected upon this subject. That it was only necessary to make a sacrifice of feeling, and an innovation on the customs of society, to establish a different order of things,—that as Anti-Slavery men, they were willing to make these sacrifices, and determined to take the colored man by the hand, making common cause with him in affliction, and bear a part of the odium heaped upon him. That his cause was the cause of God—that "In as much as ye did it not unto the least of these my little ones, ye did it not unto me," and that as Anti-Slavery men, they would "do right if the heavens fell." Thus, was the cause espoused, and thus did we expect much. But in all this, we were doomed to disappointment, sad, sad disappointment. Instead of realising what we had hoped for, we find ourselves occupying the very same position in relation to our Anti-Slavery friends, as we do in relation to the Pro-Slavery part of the community—a mere secondary, underling position, in all our relations to them, and any thing more than this, is not a matter of course affair—it comes not by established Anti-Slavery custom or right, but like that which emanates from the Pro-Slavery portion of the community, by mere sufferance.

It is true, that the "Liberator" office, in Boston, has got Elijah Smith, a colored youth, at the cases—the "Standard," in New York, a young colored man, and the "Freeman," in Philadelphia, William Still, another, in the publication office, as "packing clerk"; yet these are but three out of the hosts that fill these offices in their various departments, all occupying places that could have been, and as we once thought, would have been, easily enough, occupied by colored men. Indeed, we can have no other idea about Anti-Slavery in this country, than that the legitimate persons to fill any and every position about an Anti-Slavery establishment are colored persons. Nor will it do to argue in extenuation, that white men are as justly entitled to them as colored men; because white men do not from *necessity* become Anti-Slavery men in order to get situations; they being white men, may occupy any position they are capable of filling—in a word, their chances are endless, every avenue in the country being opened to them. They do not therefore become abolitionists, for the sake of employment—at least, it is not the song that Anti-Slavery sung, in the first love of the new faith, proclaimed by its disciples.

And if it be urged that colored men are incapable as yet to fill these positions, all that we have to say is, that the cause has fallen far short; almost equivalent to a failure, of a tithe, of what it promised to do in half the period of its existence, to this time, if it has not as yet, now a period of twenty years, raised up colored men enough, to fill the offices within its patronage. We think it is not unkind to say, if it had been half as faithful to itself, as it should have been—its professed principles we mean; it could have reared and tutored from childhood, colored men enough by this time, for its own especial purpose. These we know could have been easily obtained, because colored people in general, are favorable to the Anti-Slavery cause, and wherever there is an adverse manifestation, it arises from sheer ignorance; and we have now but comparatively few such among us. There is one thing certain, that no colored person, except such as would reject education altogether, would be adverse to putting their child with an Anti-Slavery person, for educational advantages. This then, could have been done. But it has not been done, and let the cause of it be whatever it may, and let whoever may be to blame, we are willing to let all that pass, and extend to our Anti-Slavery brethren the right-hand of fellowship, bidding them God-speed in the propagation of good and wholesome sentiments—for whether they are practically carried out or not, the professions are in themselves all right and good. Like Christianity, the principles are holy and of divine origin. And we believe, if ever a man started right, with pure and holy motives, Mr. Garrison did; and that, had he the power of making the cause what it should be, it would all be right, and there never would have been any cause for the remarks we have made, though in kindness, and with the purest of motives. We are nevertheless, still occupying a miserable position in the community, wherever we live; and what we most desire is, to draw the attention of our people to this fact, and point out what, in our opinion, we conceive to be a proper remedy.

III. AMERICAN COLONIZATION

When we speak of colonization, we wish distinctly to be understood, as speaking of the "American Colonization Society"—or that which is under its influence—commenced in Richmond, Virginia, in 1817, under the influence of Mr. Henry Clay of Ky., Judge Bushrod Washington of Va., and other Southern slaveholders, having for their express object, as their speeches and doings all justify us in asserting in good faith, the removal of the free colored people from the land of their birth, for the security of the slaves, as property to the slave propagandists.

This scheme had no sooner been propagated, than the old and leading colored men of Philadelphia, Pa., with Richard Allen, James Forten, and others at their head, true to their trust and the cause of their brethren, summoned the colored people together, and then and there, in language and with voices pointed and loud, protested against the scheme as an outrage, having no other object in view, than the benefit of the slave-holding interests of the country, and that as freemen, they would never prove recreant to the cause of their brethren in bondage, by leaving them without hope of redemption from their chains. This determination of the colored patriots of Philadelphia was published in full, authentically, and circulated throughout the length and breadth of the country by the papers of the day. The colored people every where received the news, and at once endorsed with heart and soul, the doings of the Anti-Colonization Meeting of colored freemen. From that time forth, the colored people generally have had no sympathy with the colonization scheme, nor confidence in its leaders, looking upon them all, as arrant hypocrites, seeking every opportunity to deceive them. In a word, the monster was crippled in its infancy, and has never as yet recovered from the stroke. It is true, that like its ancient sire, that was "more subtile than all the beasts of the field," it has inherited a large portion of his most prominent characteristic—an idiosyncrasy with the animal—that enables him to entwine himself into the greater part of the Church and other institutions of the country, which having once entered there, leaves his venom, which put such a spell on the conductors of those institutions, that it is only on condition that a colored person consents to go to the neighborhood of his kindred brother monster the boa, that he may find admission in the one or the other. We look upon the American Colonization Society as one of the most arrant enemies of the colored man, ever seeking to discomfit him, and envying him of every privilege that he may enjoy. We believe it to be anti-Christian in its character, and misanthropic in its pretended sympathies. Because if this were not the case, men could not be found professing morality and Christianity —as to our astonishment we have found them—who unhesitatingly say, "I know it is right"—that is in itself—"to do" so and so, "and I am willing and ready to do it, but only on condition, that you go to Africa." Indeed, a highly talented clergyman, informed us in November last (three months ago) in the city of Philadelphia, that he was present when the Rev. Doctor J. P. Durbin, late President of Dickinson College, called on Rev. Mr. P. of B., to consult him about going to Liberia, to take charge of the literary department of an University in contemplation, when the following conversation ensued: Mr. P.—"Doctor, I have as much and more than

I can do here, in educating the youth of our own country, and preparing them for usefulness here at home." Dr. D—"Yes, but do as you may, you can never be elevated here." Mr. P.—"Doctor, do you not believe that the religion of our blessed Redeemer Jesus Christ, has morality, humanity, philanthropy, and justice enough in it to elevate us, and enable us to obtain our rights in this our own country?" Dr. D.—"No, indeed, sir, I do not, and if you depend upon that, your hopes are vain!" Mr. P.—Turning to Doctor Durbin, looking him solemnly, though affectionately in the face, remarked—"Well, Doctor Durbin, we both profess to be ministers of Christ; but dearly as I love the cause of my Redeemer, if for a moment, I could entertain the opinion you do about Christianity, I would not serve him another hour!" We do not know, as we were not advised, that the Rev. doctor added in fine,—"Well, you may quit now, for all your serving him will not avail against the power of the god (hydra) of Colonization." Will any one doubt for a single moment, the justice of our strictures on colonization, after reading the conversation between the Rev. Dr. Durbin and the colored clergyman? Surely not. We can therefore make no account of it, but that of setting it down as being the worst enemy of the colored people.

Recently, there has been a strained effort in the city of New York on the part of the Rev. J. B. Pinney and others, of the leading white colonizationists, to get up a movement among some poor pitiable colored men—we say pitiable, for certainly the colored persons who are at this period capable of loaning themselves to the enemies of their race, against the best interest of all that we hold sacred to that race, are pitiable in the lowest extreme, far beneath the dignity of an enemy, and therefore, we pass them by with the simple remark, that this is the hobby that colonization is riding all over the country, as the "tremendous" access of colored people to their cause within the last twelve months. We should make another remark here perhaps, in justification of Governor Pinney's New York allies —that is, report says, that in the short space of some three or five months, one of his confidants, benefited himself to the "reckoning" of from eleven to fifteen hundred dollars, or "such a matter," while others were benefited in sums "pretty considerable" but of a less "reckoning." Well, we do not know after all, that they may not have quite as good a right, to pocket part of the spoils of this "grab game," as any body else. However, they are of little consequence, as the ever watchful eye of those excellent gentleman and faithful guardians of their people's rights—the *Committee of Thirteen,* consisting of Messrs. John J. Zuille, *Chairman,* T. Joiner White, Philip A. Bell, *Secretaries,* Robert Hamilton, George T. Downing, Jeremiah Powers, John T. Raymond, Wm. Burnett, James McCuen Smith, Ezekiel Dias, Junius C. Morel, Thomas Downing, and Wm. J. Wilson, have properly chastised this pet-slave of Mr. Pinney, and made it "know its place," by keeping within the bounds of its master's enclosure.

In expressing our honest conviction of the designedly injurious character of the Colonization Society, we should do violence to our own sense of individual justice, if we did not express the belief that there are some honest hearted men, who not having seen things in the proper light, favor that scheme, simply as a means of elevating the colored people. Such persons, so soon as they become convinced of their error, immediately change their policy, and advocate the elevation of the colored people, anywhere and everywhere, in common with other men. Of such were the early abolitionists as before stated; and the great and good Dr. F. J. Lemoyne, Gerrit Smith, and Rev. Charles Avery, and a host of others, who were Colonizationists, before espousing the cause of our elevation, here at home, and nothing but an honorable sense of justice, induces us to make these exceptions, as there are many good persons within our knowledge, whom we believe to be well wishers of the colored people, who may favor colonization.* But the animal itself is the same "hydra-headed monster," let whomsoever may fancy to pet it. A serpent is a serpent, and none the less a viper, because nestled in the bosom of an honest hearted man. This the colored people must bear in mind, and keep clear of the hideous thing, lest its venom may be tost upon them. But why deem any argument necessary to show the unrighteousness of colonization? Its very origin as before shown—the source from whence it sprung, being the offspring of slavery —is in itself, sufficient to blast it in the estimation of every colored person in the United States, who has sufficient intelligence to comprehend it.

We dismiss this part of the subject, and proceed to consider the mode and means of our elevation in the United States.

IV. OUR ELEVATION IN THE UNITED STATES

That very little comparatively as yet has been done, to attain a respectable position as a class in this country, will not be denied, and that the successful accomplishment of this end is also possible, must also be admitted; but in what manner, and by what means, has long been, and is even now, by the best thinking minds among the colored people themselves, a matter of difference of opinion.

We believe in the universal equality of man, and believe in that declaration of God's word, in which it is there positively said, that "God has

* Benjamin Coates, Esq., a merchant of Philadelphia, we believe to be an honest hearted man, and real friend of the colored people, and a true, though as yet, rather undecided philanthropist. Mr. Coates, to our knowledge, has supported three or four papers published by colored men, for the elevation of colored people in the United States, and given, as he continues to do, considerable sums to their support. We have recently learned from himself, that, though he still advocates Colonization, simply as a means of elevating the colored race of the United States, that he has *left* the Colonization Society, and prefers seeing colored people located on this continent, to going to Liberia, or elsewhere off of it—though his zeal for the enlightenment of Africa, is unabated, as every good man's should be; and we are satisfied, that Mr. Coates is neither well understood, nor rightly appreciated by the friends of our cause. One thing we do know, that he left the Colonization Society, because he could not conscientiously subscribe to its measures.

made of one blood all the nations that dwell on the face of the earth."
Now of "the nations that dwell on the face of the earth," that is, all the
people—there are one thousand millions of souls, and of this vast number
of human beings, two-thirds are colored, from black, tending in complexion to the olive or that of the Chinese, with all the intermediate and ad-
mixtures of black and white, with the various "crosses" as they are physio-
logically, but erroneously termed, to white. We are thus explicit in stating
these points, because we are determined to be understood by all. We have
then, two colored to one white person throughout the earth, and yet, singular as it may appear, according to the present geographical and political
history of the world, the white race predominates over the colored; or in
other words, wherever there is one white person, that one rules and gov-
erns two colored persons. This is a living undeniable truth, to which we
call the especial attention of the colored reader in particular. Now there is
a cause for this, as there is no effect without a cause, a comprehensible
remediable cause. We all believe in the justice of God, that he is impartial, "looking upon his children with an eye of care," dealing out to them
all, the measure of his goodness; yet, how can we reconcile ourselves to
the difference that exists between the colored and the white races, as they
truthfully present themselves before our eyes? To solve this problem, is to
know the remedy; and to know it, is but necessary, in order successfully to
apply it. And we shall but take the colored people of the United States, as
a fair sample of the colored races everywhere of the present age, as the
arguments that apply to the one, will apply to the other, whether Christians, Mahommedans, or pagans.

The colored races are highly susceptible of religion; it is a constituent
principle of their nature, and an excellent trait in their character. But
unfortunately for them, they carry it too far. Their hope is largely developed, and consequently, they usually stand still—hope in God, and really
expect Him to do that for them, which it is necessary they should do themselves. This is their great mistake, and arises from a misconception of the
character and ways of Deity. We must know God, that is understand His
nature and purposes, in order to serve Him; and to serve Him well, is but
to know him rightly. To depend for assistance upon God, is a *duty* and
right; but to know when, how and in what manner to obtain it, is the key
to this great Bulwark of Strength, and Depository of Aid.

God himself is perfect; perfect in all his works and ways. He has means
for every end; and every means used must be adequate to the end to be
gained. God's means are laws—fixed laws of nature, a part of His own
being, and as immutable, as unchangeable as Himself. Nothing can be
accomplished but through the medium of, and comformable to these laws.

They are *three*—and like God himself, represented in the three persons
in the God-head—the *Spiritual, Moral* and *Physical* Laws.

That which is Spiritual, can only be accomplished through the medium
of the Spiritual law; that which is Moral, through the medium of the

Moral law; and that which is Physical, through the medium of the Physical law. Otherwise than this, it is useless to expect any thing. Does a person want a spiritual blessing, he must apply through the medium of the spiritual law—*pray* for it in order to obtain it. If they desire to do a moral good, they must apply through the medium of the moral law—exercise their sense and feeling of *right* and *justice,* in order to effect it. Do they want to attain a physical end, they can only do so through the medium of the physical law—go to *work* with muscles, hands, limbs, might and strength, and this, and nothing else will attain it.

The argument that man must pray for what he receives, is a mistake, and one that is doing the colored people especially, incalculable injury. That man must pray in order to get to Heaven, every Christian will admit —but a great truth we have yet got to learn, that he can live on earth whether he is religious or not, so that he conforms to the great law of God, regulating the things of earth; the great physical laws. It is only necessary, in order to convince our people of their error and palpable mistake in this matter, to call their attention to the fact, that there are no people more religious in this Country, than the colored people, and none so poor and miserable as they. That prosperity and wealth, smiles upon the efforts of wicked white men, whom we know to utter the name of God with curses, instead of praises. That among the slaves, there are thousands of them religious, continually raising their voices, sending up their prayers to God, invoking His aid in their behalf, asking for a speedy deliverance; but they are still in chains, although they have thrice suffered out their three score years and ten. That "God sendeth rain upon the just and unjust," should be sufficient to convince us that our success in life, does not depend upon our religious character, but that the physical laws governing all earthly and temporary affairs, benefit equally the just and the unjust. Any other doctrine than this, is downright delusion, unworthy of a free people, and only intended for slaves. That all men and women, should be moral, upright, good and religious—we mean *Christians*—we would not utter a word against, and could only wish that it were so; but, what we here desire to do is, to correct the long standing error among a large body of the colored people in this country, that the cause of our oppression and degradation, is the displeasure of God towards us, because of our unfaithfulness to Him. This is not true; because if God is just—and he is—there could be no justice in prospering white men with his fostering care, for more than two thousand years, in all their wickedness, while dealing out to the colored people, the measure of his displeasure, for not half the wickedness as that of the whites. Here then is our mistake, and let it forever henceforth be corrected. We are no longer slaves, believing any interpretation that our oppressors may give the word of God, for the purpose of deluding us to the more easy subjugation; but freemen, comprising some of the first minds of intelligence and rudimental qualifications, in the country. What then is the remedy, for our degradation and oppression? This appears now to be the only remaining question—the means of successful elevation in this our own native land? This depends entirely upon the application of the means of Elevation.

V. MEANS OF ELEVATION

Moral theories have long been resorted to by us, as a means of effecting the redemption of our brethren in bonds, and the elevation of the free colored people in this country. Experience has taught us, that speculations are not enough; that the *practical* application of principles adduced, the thing carried out, is the only true and proper course to pursue.

We have speculated and moralised much about equality—claiming to be as good as our neighbors, and every body else—all of which, may do very well in ethics—but not in politics. We live in society among men, conducted by men, governed by rules and regulations. However arbitrary, there are certain policies that regulate all well organized institutions and corporate bodies. We do not intend here to speak of the legal political relations of society, for those are treated on elsewhere. The business and social, or voluntary and mutual policies, are those that now claim our attention. Society regulates itself—being governed by mind, which like water, finds its own level. "Like seeks like," is a principle in the laws of matter, as well as of mind. There is such a thing as inferiority of things, and positions; at least society has made them so; and while we continue to live among men, we must agree to all *just* measures—all those we mean, that do not necessarily infringe on the rights of others. By the regulations of society, there is no equality of persons, where there is not an equality of attainments. By this, we do not wish to be understood as advocating the actual equal attainments of every individual; but we mean to say, that if these attainments be necessary for the elevation of the white man, they are necessary for the elevation of the colored man. That some colored men and women, in a like proportion to the whites, should be qualified in all the attainments possessed by them. It is one of the regulations of society the world over, and we shall have to conform to it, or be discarded as unworthy of the associations of our fellows.

Cast our eyes about us and reflect for a moment, and what do we behold! every thing that presents to view gives evidence of the skill of the white man. Should we purchase a pound of groceries, a yard of linen, a vessel of crockeryware, a piece of furniture, the very provisions that we eat,—all, all are the products of the white man, purchased by us from the white man, consequently, our earnings and means, are all given to the white man.

Pass along the avenues of any city or town, in which you live—behold the trading shops—the manufactories—see the operations of the various machinery—see the stage-coaches coming in, bringing the mails of intelligence—look at the railroads interlining every section, bearing upon them their mighty trains, flying with the velocity of the swallow, ushering in the hundreds of industrious, enterprising travelers. Cast again your eyes widespread over the ocean—see the vessels in every direction with their white sheets spread to the winds of heaven, freighted with the commerce, merchandise and wealth of many nations. Look as you pass along through the cities, at the great and massive buildings—the beautiful and extensive structures of architecture—behold the ten thousand cupolas, with their spires all reared up towards heaven, intersecting the territory of the clouds —all standing as mighty living monuments, of the industry, enterprise, and intelligence of the white man. And yet, with all these living truths, rebuking us with scorn, we strut about, place our hands akimbo, straighten up ourselves to our greatest height, and talk loudly about being "as good as any body." How do we compare with them? Our fathers are their coachmen, our brothers their cookmen, and ourselves their waiting-men. Our mothers their nurse-women, our sisters their scrub-women, our daughters their maid-women, and our wives their washer-women. Until colored men, attain to a position above permitting their mothers, sisters, wives, and daughters, to do the drudgery and menial offices of other men's wives and daughters; it is useless, it is nonsense, it is pitiable mockery, to talk about equality and elevation in society. The world is looking upon us, with feelings of commiseration, sorrow, and contempt. We scarcely deserve sympathy, if we peremptorily refuse advice, bearing upon our elevation.

We will suppose a case for argument: In this city reside, two colored families, of three sons and three daughters each. At the head of each family, there is an old father and mother. The opportunities of these families, may or may not be the same for educational advantages—be that as it may, the children of the one go to school, and become qualified for the duties of life. One daughter becomes school-teacher, another a mantua-maker, and a third a fancy shop-keeper; while one son becomes a farmer, another a merchant, and a third a mechanic. All enter into business with fine prospects, marry respectably, and settle down in domestic comfort— while the six sons and daughters of the other family, grow up without educational and business qualifications, and the highest aim they have, is to apply to the sons and daughters of the first named family, to hire for domestics! Would there be an equality here between the children of these two families? Certainly not. This, then, is precisely the position of the colored people generally in the United States, compared with the whites. What is necessary to be done, in order to attain an equality, is to change the condition, and the person is at once changed. If, as before stated, a knowledge of all the various business enterprises, trades, professions, and sciences, is necessary for the elevation of the white, a knowledge of them also is necessary for the elevation of the colored man; and he cannot be elevated without them.

White men are producers—we are consumers. They build houses, and we rent them. They raise produce, and we consume it. They manufacture clothes and wares, and we garnish ourselves with them. They build coaches, vessels, cars, hotels, saloons, and other vehicles and places of accommodation, and we deliberately wait until they have got them in readiness, then walk in, and contend with as much assurance for a "right," as though the whole thing was bought by, paid for, and belonged to us. By their literary attainments, they are the contributors to, authors and teachers of, literature, science, religion, law, medicine, and all other useful attainments that the world now makes use of. We have no reference to ancient times—we speak of modern things.

These are the means by which God intended man to succeed: and this discloses the secret of the white man's success with all of his wickedness, over the head of the colored man, with all of his religion. We have been pointed and plain, on this part of the subject, because we desire our readers to see persons and things in their true position. Until we are determined to change the condition of things, and raise ourselves above the position in which we are now prostrated, we must hang our heads in sorrow, and hide our faces in shame. It is enough to know that these things are so; the causes we care little about. Those we have been examining, complaining about, and moralising over, all our life time. This we are weary of. What we desire to learn now is, how to effect a *remedy;* this we have endeavored to point out. Our elevation must be the result of *self-efforts,* and work of our *own hands.* No other human power can accomplish it. If we but determine it shall be so, it will be so. Let each one make the case his own, and endeavor to rival his neighbor, in honorable competition.

These are the proper and only means of elevating ourselves and attaining equality in this country or any other, and it is useless, utterly futile, to think about going any where, except we are determined to use these as the necessary means of developing our manhood. The means are at hand, within our reach. Are we willing to try them? Are we willing to raise ourselves superior to the condition of slaves, or continue the meanest underlings, subject to the beck and call of every creature bearing a pale complexion? If we are, we had as well remained in the South, as to have come to the North in search of more freedom. What was the object of our parents in leaving the South, if it were not for the purpose of attaining equality in common with others of their fellow citizens, by giving their children access to all the advantages enjoyed by others? Surely this was their object. They heard of liberty and equality here, and they hastened on to enjoy it, and no people are more astonished and disappointed than they, who for the first time, on beholding the position we occupy here in the free North—what is called, and what they expect to find, the free States. They at once tell us, that they have as much liberty in the South as we have in the North—that there as free people, they are protected in their rights—that we have nothing more—that in other respects they have the same opportunity, indeed the preferred opportunity, of being their maids, servants, cooks, waiters, and menials in general, there, as we have here—that had they known for a moment, before leaving, that such was to be the only position they occupied here, they would have remained where they were, and never left. Indeed, such is the disappointment in many cases, that they immediately return back again, completely insulted at the idea, of having us here at the north, assume ourselves to be their superiors. Indeed, if our superior advantages of the free States, do not induce and stimulate us to the higher attainments in life, what in the name of degraded humanity will do it? Nothing, surely nothing. If, in fine, the advantages of free schools in Massachusetts, New York, Pennsylvania, Ohio, Michigan, and wherever else we may have them, do not give us advantages and pursuits superior to our slave brethren, then are the unjust assertions of Messrs. Henry Clay, John C. Calhoun, Theodore Frelinghuysen, late Governor Poindexter of Mississippi, George McDuffy, Governor Hammond of South Carolina, Extra Billy (present Governor) Smith, of Virginia, and the host of our oppressors, slave-holders and others true, that we are insusceptible and incapable of elevation to the more respectable, honorable, and higher attainments among white men. But this we do not believe—neither do you, although our whole life and course of policy in this country are such, that it would seem to prove otherwise. The degradation of the slave parent has been entailed upon the child, induced by the subtle policy of the oppressor, in regular succession handed down from father to son—a system of regular submission and servitude, menialism and dependence, until it has become almost a physiological function of our system, an actual condition of our nature. Let this no longer be so, but let us determine to equal the whites among whom we live, not by declarations and unexpressed self-opinion, for we have always had enough of that, but by actual proof in acting, doing, and carrying out practically, the measures of equality. Here is our nativity, and here have we the natural right to abide and be elevated through the measures of our own efforts.

VI. THE UNITED STATES OUR COUNTRY

Our common country is the United States. Here were we born, here raised and educated; here are the scenes of childhood; the pleasant associations of our school going days; the loved enjoyments of our domestic and fireside relations, and the sacred graves of our departed fathers and mothers, and from here will we not be driven by any policy that may be schemed against us.

We are Americans, having a birthright citizenship—natural claims upon the country—claims common to all others of our fellow citizens—natural rights, which may, by virtue of unjust laws, be obstructed, but never can be annulled. Upon these do we place ourselves, as immovably fixed as the decrees of the living God. But according to the economy that regulates the policy of nations, upon which rests the basis of justifiable claims to all freemen's rights, it may be necessary to take another view of, and enquire into the political claims of colored men.

VII. CLAIMS OF COLORED MEN AS CITIZENS
OF THE UNITED STATES

The political basis upon which rests the establishment of all free nations, as the first act in their organization, is the security by constitutional provisions, of the fundamental claims of citizenship.

The legitimate requirement, politically considered, necessary to the justifiable claims for protection and full enjoyment of all the rights and privileges of an unqualified freeman, in all democratic countries is, that each person so endowed, shall have made contributions and investments in the country. Where there is no investment there can be but little interest; hence an adopted citizen is required to reside a sufficient length of time, to form an attachment and establish some interest in the country of his adoption, before he can rightfully lay any claims to citizenship. The pioneer who leads in the discovery or settlement of a country, as the first act to establish a right therein, erects a building of whatever dimensions, and seizes upon a portion of the soil. The soldier, who braves the dangers of the battle-field, in defence of his country's rights, and the toiling laborer and husbandman, who cuts down and removes the forest, levels and constructs post-roads and other public highways—the mechanic, who constructs and builds up houses, villages, towns, and cities, for the conveniency of inhabitants—the farmer, who cultivates the soil for the production of bread-stuffs and forage, as food and feed for man and beast—all of these are among the first people of a democratic state, whose claims are legitimate as freemen of the commonwealth. A freeman in a political sense, is a citizen of unrestricted rights in the state, being eligible to the highest position known to their civil code. They are the preferred persons in whom may be invested the highest privileges, and to whom may be entrusted fundamentally the most sacred rights of the country; because, having made the greatest investments, they necessarily have the greatest interests; and consequently, are the safest hands into which to place so high and sacred a trust. Their interest being the country's, and the interest of the country being the interest of the people; therefore, the protection of their own interests necessarily protects the interests of the whole country and people. It is this simple but great principle of primitive rights, that forms the fundamental basis of citizenship in all free countries, and it is upon this principle, that the rights of the colored man in this country to citizenship are fixed.

The object of this volume is, to enlighten the minds of a large class of readers upon a subject with which they are unacquainted, expressed in comprehensible language, therefore we have studiously avoided using political and legal phrases, that would serve more to perplex than inform them. To talk about the barons, King John, and the Magna Charta, would be foreign to a work like this, and only destroy the interest that otherwise might be elicited in the subject. Our desire is, to arrest the attention of the American people in general, and the colored people in particular, to great truths as heretofore but little thought of. What claims then have colored men, based upon the principles set forth, as fundamentally entitled to citizenship? Let the living records of history answer the enquiry.

When Christopher Columbus, in 1492, discovered America, natives were found to pay little or no attention to cultivation, being accustomed by hereditary pursuit, to war, fishing, and the sports of the chase. The Spaniards and Portuguese, as well as other Europeans who ventured here, came as mineral speculators, and not for the purpose of improving the country.

As the first objects of speculation are the developements of the mineral wealth of every newly discovered country, so was it with this. Those who came to the new world, were not of the common people, seeking in a distant land the means of livelihood, but moneyed capitalists, the grandees and nobles, who reduced the natives to servitude by confining them to the mines. To have brought large numbers of the peasantry at that early period, from the monarchies of Europe, to the wilds of America, far distant from the civil and military powers of the home governments, would have been to place the means of self-control into their own hands, and invite them to rebellion against the crowns. The capitalist miners were few, compared to the number of laborers required; and the difficulty at that time of the transportation of suitable provisions for their sustenance, conduced much to the objection of bringing them here. The natives were numerous, then easily approached by the wily seductions of the Europeans, easily yoked and supported, having the means of sustenance at hand, the wild fruits and game of the forest, the fish of the waters and birds of the country. All these as naturally enough, European adventurers would be cautious against introducing into common use among hundreds of thousands of laborers, under all the influences incident to a foreign climate in a foreign country, in its primitive natural state. The Indians were then preferred for many reasons, as the common laborers on the continent, where nothing but the mining interests were thought of or carried on. This noble race of Aborigines, continued as the common slaves of the new world, to bear the yoke of foreign oppression, until necessity induced a substitute for them. They sunk by scores under the heavy weight of oppression, and were fast passing from the shores of time. At this, the foreigners grew alarmed, and of necessity, devised ways and means to obtain an adequate substitute. A few European laborers were brought into the country, but the influence of climate and mode of living, operated entirely against them. They were as inadequate to stand the climate, as the nobles were themselves.

From the earliest period of the history of nations, the African race had been known as an industrious people, cultivators of the soil. The grain fields of Ethiopia and Egypt were the themes of the poet, and their garners, the subject of the historian. Like the present American, all the world went to Africa, to get a supply of commodities. Their massive piles of masonry, their skillful architecture, their subterranean vaults their deep and mysterious wells, their extensive artificial channels, their mighty sculptured solid rocks, and provinces of stone quarries; gave indisputable evidence, of the hardihood of that race of people.

Nor was Africa then, without the evidence of industry, as history will testify. All travelers who had penetrated towards the interior of the continent, have been surprised at the seeming state of civilization and evidences of industry among the inhabitants of that vast country. These facts were familiar to Europeans, who were continually trading on the coast of Africa, as it was then the most important part of adventure and research, known to the world. In later periods still, the history of African travelers, confirm all the former accounts concerning the industry of the people.

John and Richard Lander, two young English noblemen, in 1828, under the patronage of the English government, sailed to the western coast of Africa, on an expedition of research. In their voyage up the river Niger, their description of the scenes is extravagant. They represent the country on each side of the river, for several hundred miles up the valley, as being not only beautiful and picturesque, but the fields as in a high state of cultivation, clothed in the verdure of husbandry, waving before the gentle breezes, with the rich products of industry—maize, oats, rye, millet, and wheat, being among the fruits of cultivation. The fences were of various descriptions: hedge, wicker, some few pannel, and the old fashioned zig-zag, known as the "Virginia worm fence"—the hedge and worm fence being the most common. Their cattle were fine and in good order, looking in every particular, except perhaps in size, as well as European cattle on the best managed farms. The fruit groves were delightful to the eye of the beholder. Every variety common to the country, were there to be seen in a high state of cultivation. Their roads and public highways were in good condition, and well laid out, as by the direction of skillful supervising surveyors. The villages, towns, and cities, many of them, being a credit to the people. Their cities were well laid out, and presented evidence of educated minds and mechanical ingenuity. In many of the workshops in which they went, they found skillful workmen, in iron, copper, brass, steel, and gold; and their implements of husbandry and war, were as well manufactured by African sons of toil, as any in the English manufactures, save that they had not quite so fine a finish, garnish and embellishment. This is a description, given of the industry and adaptedness of the people of Africa, to labor and toil of every kind. As it was very evident, that where there were manufactories of various metals, the people must of necessity be inured to mining operations, so it was also very evident, that this people must be a very hardy and enduring people.

In 1442, fifty years previous to the sailing of Columbus in search of a new world, Anthony Gonzales, Portuguese, took from the Gold Coast of Guinea, ten Africans and a quantity of gold dust, which he carried back to Lisbon with him. These Africans were set immediately to work in the gardens of the emperor, which so pleased his queen, that the number were much augmented, all of whom were found to be skillful and industrious in agriculture.

In 1481, eleven years prior to the discovery by Columbus, the Portuguese built a fort on the Gold Coast, and there commenced mining in search of gold. During this time until the year 1502, a period of ten years, had there been no other evidence, there was sufficient time and opportunity, to give full practical demonstrations of the capacity of this people to endure toil, especially in the mining operations, and for this cause and this alone, were they selected in preference to any other race of men, to do the labor of the New World. They had proven themselves physically superior either to the European or American races—in fact, superior physically to any living race of men—enduring fatigue, hunger and thirst—enduring change of climate, habits, manners and customs, with infinitely far less injury to their physical and mental system, than any other people on the face of God's earth. . . .

From 1492, the discovery of Hispaniola, to 1502, the short space of but four years, such was the mortality among the natives, that the Spaniards then holding rule there, "began to employ a few" Africans in the mines of the Island. The experiment was effective—a successful one. The Indian and African were enslaved together, when the Indian sunk, and the African stood. It was not until June the 24th of the year 1498, that the Continent was discovered by John Cabot, a Venetian, who sailed in August of the previous year 1497, from Bristol, under the patronage of Henry VII., King of England, with two vessels "freighted by the merchants of London and Bristol, with articles of traffic," his son Sebastian, and 300 men. In 1517, but the short period of thirteen years from the date of their first introduction, Carolus V., King of Spain, by the right of a patent, granted permission to a number of persons, annually, to supply to the Islands of Hispaniola, (St. Domingo,) Cuba, Jamaica, and Porto Rico, natives of Africa, to the number of four thousand annually. John Hawkins, an unprincipled Englishman—whose name should be branded with infamy—was the first person known to have engaged in so inhuman a traffic, and that living monster his mistress, Queen Elizabeth, engaged with him and shared in the profits.

The natives of Africa, on their introduction into a foreign country, soon discovered the loss of their accustomed food, and mode and manner of living. The Aborigines subsisted mainly by game and fish, with a few patches of maize or Indian corn near their wigwams, which were generally attended by the women, while the men were absent. The grains and fruits, such as they had been accustomed to, were not to be had among the Aborigines of the country, and this first induced the African to cultivate patches of ground in the neighborhood of the mines, for the raising of food for his own sustenance. This trait in their character was observed, and regarded by the Spaniards with considerable interest; and when on contracting with the English slave-dealer, Captain Hawkins, and others for new supplies of slaves, they were careful to request them to secure a quantity of the seeds and different products of the country, to bring with them to the New World. Many of these were cultivated to some extent, while those indigenous to America, were cultivated by them with considerable success. And up to this day, it is a custom on many of the slave plantations of the South, to allow the slave his "patch," and Saturday afternoon or Sabbath day, to cultivate it.

Shortly after the commencement of the shameful traffic in the blood and bones of men—the destiny and chastity of women by Captain Hawkins, and what was termed England's "Virgin Queen;" Elizabeth gave a license to Sir Walter Raleigh, to search for uninhabited lands, and seize upon all uninhabited by Christians. Sir Walter discovered the coast of North Carolina and Virginia, assigning the name of "Virginia" to the whole coast now composing the old state. A feeble colony was settled here, which did not avail, and it was not until the month of April, 1607, that the first permanent settlement was made in Virginia, under the patronage of letters patent from James I., King of England, to Thomas Gates and his associates.

This was the first settling of North America, and thirteen years anterior to the landing of the Pilgrims.

"No permanent settlement was effected in what is now called the United States, till the reign of James the First."—Ramsay's Hist. U. S., vol. I., p. 38.

"The month of April, 1607, is the epoch of the first permanent settlement on the coast of Virginia; the name then given to all that extent of country which forms thirteen States."—*Ib.*, p. 39. The whole coast of the country was now explored, not for the purpose of trade and agriculture—because there were no products in the country—the natives not producing sufficient provisions to supply present wants, and, consequently, nothing to trade for; but like the speculations of their Spanish and Portuguese predecessors, on the islands and in South America, but for that of mining gold. Trade and the cultivation of the soil was foreign to their designs and intention on coming to the continent of the new world, and they were consequently, disappointed when failing of success. "At a time when the precious metals were conceived to be the peculiar and only valuable productions of the new world, when every mountain was supposed to contain a treasure, and every rivulet was searched for its golden sands, this appearance was fondly considered as an infallible indication of the mine. Every hand was eager to dig."   *   *   *

"There was now," says Smith, "no talk, no hope, no work; but dig gold, wash gold, refine gold. With this imaginary wealth, the first vessel returning to England was loaded, while the *culture of the land,* and every useful occupation was *totally neglected."*   *   *   *

The colonists, thus left, were in miserable circumstances for want of provisions. The remainder of what they had brought with them, was so small in quantity, as to be soon expended—so damaged in the course of a long voyage, as to be a source of disease.   *   *   *   In their expectation of getting gold, the people were disappointed, the glittering substance they had sent to England, proving to be a valueless mineral. "Smith, on his return to Jamestown, found the colony reduced to thirty-eight persons, who, in despair, were preparing to abandon the country. He employed caresses, threats, and even violence, in order to prevent them from executing this fatal resolution." *Ibid.,* pp. 45–6. In November, 1620, the Pilgrims or Puritans made the harbor of Cape Cod, and after solemn vows and organization previous to setting foot on shore, they landed safely on "Plymouth Rock," December the 20th, about one month after. They were one hundred and one in number, and from the toils and hardships consequent to a severe season, in a strange country, in less than six months after their arrival, "forty-four persons, nearly one-half of their original number," had died.

    *   *   *   "In 1618, in the reign of James I., the British government established a regular trade on the coast of Africa. In the year 1620, Negro slaves began to be imported into Virginia: a Dutch ship bringing twenty of them for sale."—Sampson's Hist. Dict., p. 348. The Dutch ship landed her cargo at New Bedford, (now Massachusetts,) as it will be remembered, that the whole coast, now comprising the "Old Thirteen," and original United States, was then called Virginia, so named by Sir Walter Raleigh, in honor of his royal Mistress and patron, Elizabeth, the Virgin Queen, under whom he received his royal patent commission of adventure and expedition.

Beginning their preparation in the slave-trade in 1618, just two years previous, giving time for successfully carrying out the project against the landing of the first emigrant settlers, it will be observed that the African captain, and the "Puritan" emigrants, landed upon the same section of the continent at the same time, 1620—the Pilgrims at Plymouth, and the captives at New Bedford, but a few miles comparatively south.

The country at this period, was one vast wilderness. "The continent of North America was then one continued forest."   *   *   *
There were no horses, cattle, sheep, hogs, or tame beasts of any kind.
    *   *   *   There were no domestic poultry.   *   *

    *   There were no gardens, orchards, public roads, meadows, or cultivated fields.   *   *   *   They "often burned the woods that they could advantageously plant their corn."   *   *   * They had neither spice, salt, bread, butter, cheese, nor milk.   *   *

    *   They had no set meals, but eat when they were hungry, and could find any thing to satisfy the cravings of nature.   *   *   *

Very little of their food was derived from the earth, except what it spontaneously produced.   *   *   *   The ground was both their seat and table.   *   *   *   Their best bed was a skin.
    *   *   *   They had neither steel, iron, nor any metallic instruments.   *   *   *—Ramsay's Hist., pp. 39–40.

We adduce not these historical extracts to disparage our brother the Indian—far be it: whatever he may think of our race, according to the manner in which he has been instructed to look upon it, by our mutual oppressor the American nation; we admire his, for the many deeds of noble daring, for which the short history of his liberty-loving people are replete: we sympathise with them, because our brethren are the successors of their fathers in the degradation of American bondage—but we adduce them in evidence against the many aspersions charged against the African race, that their inferiority to the other races caused them to be reduced to servitude. For the purpose of proving that their superiority, and not inferiority, alone was the cause which first suggested to Europeans the substitution of Africans for that of aboriginal or Indian laborers in the mines; and that their superior skill and industry, first suggested to the colonists, the propriety of turning their attention to agricultural and other industrial pursuits, than that of mining.

It is very evident, from what has been adduced, the settlement of Captain John Smith, being in the course of a few months, reduced to thirty-eight, and that of Plymouth, from one hundred and one, to that of fifty-seven in six months—it is evident, that the whites nor the Indians were equal to the hard and almost insurmountable difficulties, that now stood wide-spread before them.

An endless forest, the impenetrable earth; the one to be removed, and the other to be excavated. Towns and cities to be built, and farms to be cultivated—all these presented difficulties too arduous for the European then here, and unknown to the Indian.

It is very evident, that at a period such as this, when the natives themselves had fallen victims to tasks imposed upon them by their usurpers, and the Europeans were sinking beneath the weight of climate and hardships; when food could not be had nor the common conveniences of life procured—when arduous duties of life were to be performed and none capable of doing them, but those who had previously by their labors, not only in their native country, but in the new, so proven themselves—as the most natural consequence, the Africans were resorted to, for the performance of every duty common to domestic life.

There were no laborers known to the colonists from Cape Cod to Cape Look Out, than those of the African race. They entered at once into the mines, extracting therefrom, the rich treasures that for a thousand ages lay hidden in the earth. And from their knowledge of cultivation, the farming interests in the North, and planting in the South, were commenced with a prospect never dreamed of before the introduction of this most extraordinary, hardy race of men: though pagans, yet skilled in all the useful duties of life. Farmers, herdsmen, and laborers in their own country, they required not to be taught to work, and how to do it—but it was only necessary to tell them to go to work, and they at once knew what to do, and how it should be done.

It is notorious, that in the planting States, the blacks themselves are the only skillful cultivators—the proprietor knowing little or nothing about the art, save that which he learns from the African husbandman, while his ignorant white overseer, who is merely there to see that the work is attended to, knows a great deal less. Tobacco, cotton, rice, hemp, Indigo, the improvement in Indian corn, and many other important products, are all the result of African skill and labor in this country. And the introduction of the zigzag, or "Virginia Worm Fence," is purely of African origin. Nor was their skill as herdsmen inferior to their other attainments, being among the most accomplished trainers and horsemen in the world. Indeed, to this class of men may be indebted the entire country for the improvement South in the breed of horses. And any one who has travelled South, could not fail to have observed, that all of the leading trainers, jockies, and judges of horses, as well as riders, are men of African descent.

In speaking of the Bornouese, a people from among whom a great many natives have been enslaved by Arabian traders, and sold into foreign bondage, and of course many into this country, "It is said that Bornou can muster 15,000 Shonaas in the field mounted. They are the greatest breeders of cattle in the country, and annually supply Soudan with from two to three thousand horses."   *   *   *   "Our road lying along one of them, gave me an excellent view of beautiful villages all round, and herds of cattle grazing in the open country."   *   *   *

"Plantations of cotton or indigo now occupy the place where the houses formerly stood."   *   *   *   "The Souga market is well supplied with every necessary and luxury in request among the people of the interior." "The country still open and well cultivated, and the villages numerous. We met crowds of people coming from Karro with goods. Some carried them on their heads, others had asses or bullocks, according to their wealth."   *   *   *   "The country still highly cultivated."   *   *   *   "We also passed several walled towns, quite deserted, the inhabitants having been sold by their conquerors, the Felatohs." "Women sat spinning cotton by the roadside, offering for sale to the passing caravans, gussub water, roast-meat, sweet potatoes, coshen nuts," &c. (Dunham and Clapperton's Travels and Dis-

coveries in North and Central Africa. Vol. 2, pp. 140. 230. 332, 333.
353.)

The forests gave way before them, and extensive verdant fields, richly
clothed with produce, rose up as by magic before these hardy sons of toil.
In the place of the unskillful and ill-constructed wigwam, houses, villages,
towns and cities quickly were reared up in their stead. Being farmers,
mechanics, laborers and traders in their own country, they required little
or no instruction in these various pursuits. They were in fact, then, to the
whole continent, what they are in truth now to the whole Southern section
of the Union—the bone and sinews of the country. And even now, the
existence of the white man, South, depends entirely on the labor of the
black man—the idleness of the one, is sustained by the industry of the
other. Public roads and highways are the result of their labor, as are also
the first public works, as wharves, docks, forts, and all such improvements.
Are not these legitimate investments in the common stock of the nation,
which should command a proportionate interest?

We shall next proceed to review the contributions of colored men to
other departments of the nation, and as among the most notorious and
historical, we refer to colored American warriors.

[Chapters VIII to XV, which are deleted, constitute this review of colored achievement as warriors, businessmen and mechanics, literary and
professional men and women, farmers and herdsmen. Chapter XV concludes as follows—H.B.] If such evidence of industry and interest, as has
been exhibited in the various chapters on the different pursuits and engagements of colored Americans, do not entitle them to equal rights and
privileges in our common country, then indeed, is there nothing to justify
the claims of any portion of the American people to the common inheritance of Liberty. We proceed to another view of our condition in the
United States.

XVI. NATIONAL DISFRANCHISEMENT OF
COLORED PEOPLE

We give below the Act of Congress, known as the "Fugitive Slave Law,"
for the benefit of the reader, as there are thousands of the American people of all classes, who have never read the provisions of this enactment;
and consequently, have no conception of its enormity. We had originally
intended, also, to have inserted here, the Act of Congress of 1793, but
since this Bill includes all the provisions of that Act, in fact, although
called a "supplement," is a substitute, *de facto,* it would be superfluous;
therefore, we insert the Bill alone, with explanations following:—

AN ACT

To Amend, and Supplementary to the Act, entitled, "An Act respecting Fugitives from justice, and persons escaping from the service of their masters," approved February 12, 1793.

Be it enacted by the Senate and House of Representatives of the United States of America in Congress assembled, That the persons who have been, or may hereafter be, appointed commissioners, in virtue of any act of Congress, by the circuit courts of the United States, and who, in consequence of such appointment, are authorized to exercise the powers that any justice of the peace or other magistrate of any of the United States may exercise in respect to offenders for any crime or offence against the United States, by arresting, imprisoning, or bailing the same under and by virtue of the thirty-third section of the act of the twenty-fourth of September, seventeen hundred and eighty-nine, entitled "An act to establish the judicial courts of the United States," shall be, and are hereby authorized and required to exercise and discharge all the powers and duties conferred by this act.

Sec. 2. *And be it further enacted,* That the superior court of each organized territory of the United States shall have the same power to appoint commissioners to take acknowledgements of bail and affidavit, and to take depositions of witnesses in civil causes, which is now possessed by the circuit courts of the United States; and all commissioners who shall hereafter be appointed for such purposes by the superior court of any organized territory of the United States shall possess all the powers and exercise all the duties conferred by law upon the commissioners appointed by the circuit courts of the United States for similar purposes, and shall moreover exercise and discharge all the powers and duties conferred by this act.

Sec. 3. *And be it further enacted,* That the circuit courts of the United States, and the superior courts of each organized territory of the United States, shall from time to time enlarge the number of commissioners, with a view to afford reasonable facilities to reclaim fugitives from labor, and to the prompt discharge of the duties imposed by this act.

Sec. 4. *And be it further enacted,* That the commissioners above named shall have concurrent jurisdiction with the judges of the circuit and district courts of the United States, in their respective circuits and districts within the several States, and the judges of the superior courts of the Territories, severally and collectively, in term time and vacation; and shall grant certificates to such claimants, upon satisfactory proof being made, with authority to make and remove such fugitives from service or labor, under the restrictions herein contained to the State or territory from which such persons may have escaped or fled.

Sec. 5. *And be it further enacted,* That it shall be the duty of all marshals and deputy marshals to obey and execute all warrants and precepts issued under the provisions of this act, when to them directed; and should any marshal or deputy refuse to receive such warrant or other process, when tendered, or to use all proper means diligently to execute the same, he shall, on conviction thereof, be fined in the sum of one thousand dollars to the use of such claimant, on the motion of such claimant, by the circuit or district court for the district of such marshal; and after arrest of such fugitive by such marshal or his deputy, or whilst at any time in his custody, under the provisions of this act, should such fugitive escape, whether with or without the assent of such marshal or his deputy, such marshal shall be liable, on his official bond, to be prosecuted, for the benefit of such claimant for the full value of the service or labor of said fugitive in the State, Territory, or district whence he escaped; and the better to enable the said commissioners, when thus appointed, to execute their duties faithfully and efficiently, in conformity with the requirements of the constitution of the United States and of this act, they are hereby authorized and empowered, within their counties respectively, to appoint in writing under their hands, any one or more suitable persons, from time to time, to execute all such warrants and other process as may be issued by them in the lawful performance of their respective duties; with an authority to such commissioners, or the persons to be appointed by them, to execute process as aforesaid, to summon and call to their aid the bystanders or *posse comitatus* of the proper county, when necessary to insure a faithful observance of the clause of the constitution referred to, in conformity with the provisions of this act: and all good citizens are hereby commanded to aid and assist in the prompt and efficient execution of this law, whenever their services may be required, as aforesaid, for that person; and said warrants shall run and be executed by said officers anywhere in the State within which they are issued.

SEC. 6. *And be it further enacted,* That when a person held to service or labor in any State or Territory of the United States has heretofore or shall hereafter escape into another State or Territory of the United States, the person or persons to whom such service or labor may be due, or his, her, or their agent or attorney, duly authorized, by power of attorney, in writing, acknowledged and certified under the seal of some legal office or court of the State or Territory in which the same may be executed, may pursue and reclaim such fugitive person, either by procuring a warrant from some one of the courts, judges, or commissioners aforesaid, of the proper circuit, district or county, for the apprehension of such fugitive from service or labor, or by seizing and arresting such fugitive, where the same can be done without process, and by taking and causing such person to be taken forthwith before such court, judge or commissioner, whose duty it shall be to hear and determine the case of such claimant in a summary manner; and upon satisfactory proof being made, by deposition or affidavit, in writing, to be taken and certified by such court, judge, or commissioner, or by other satisfactory testimony, duly taken and certified by some court, magistrate, justice of the peace, or other legal officer authorized to administer an oath, and take depositions under the laws of the State or Territory from which such person owing service or labor may have escaped, with a certificate of such magistracy or other authority, as aforesaid, with the seal of the proper court or officer thereto attached, which seal shall be sufficient to establish the competency of the proof, and with proof, also by affidavit, of the identity of the person whose service or labor is claimed to be due as aforesaid, that the person so arrested does in fact owe service or labor to the person or persons claiming him or her, in the State or Territory from which such fugitive may have escaped as aforesaid, and that said person escaped, to make out and deliver to such claimant, his or her agent or attorney, a certificate setting forth the substantial facts as to the service or labor due from such fugitive to the claimant, and of his or her escape from the State or Territory in which such service or labor was due to the State or Territory in which he or she was arrested, with authority to such claimant, or his or her agent or attorney to use such reasonable force and restraint as may be necessary under the circumstances of the case, to take and remove such fugitive person back to the State or Territory from whence he or she may have escaped as aforesaid. In no trial or hearing under this act shall the testimony of such alleged fugitive be admitted in evidence; and the certificates in this and the first section mentioned shall be conclusive of the right of the person or persons in whose favor granted to remove such fugitive to the State or Territory from which he escaped, and shall prevent all molestation of said person or persons by any process issued by any court, judge, magistrate, or other person whomsoever.

SEC. 7. *And be it further enacted,* That any person who shall knowingly and willingly obstruct, hinder, or prevent such claimant, his agent or attorney, or any person or persons, lawfully assisting him, her, or them, from arresting such a fugitive from service or labor, either with or without process as aforesaid; or shall rescue, or attempt to rescue such fugitive from service or labor, from the custody of such claimant, his or her agent or attorney or other person or persons lawfully assisting as aforesaid, when so arrested, pursuant to the authority herein given and declared: or shall aid, abet, or assist such person, so owing service or labor as aforesaid, directly or indirectly, to escape from such claimant, his agent or attorney, or other person or persons, legally authorized as aforesaid; or shall harbor or conceal such fugitive, so as to prevent the discovery and arrest of such person, after notice or knowledge of the fact that such person was a fugitive from service or labor as aforesaid, shall, for either of said offences, be subject to a fine not exceeding one thousand dollars, and imprisonment not exceeding six months, by indictment and conviction before the district court of the United States for the district in which such offence may have been committed, or before the proper court of criminal jurisdiction, if committed within any one of the organized territories of the United States; and shall moreover forfeit and pay, by way of civil damages to the party injured by such illegal conduct, the sum of one thousand dollars for each fugitive so lost as aforesaid, to be recovered by action of debt in any of the district or territorial courts aforesaid, within whose jurisdiction the said offence may have been committed.

SEC. 8. *And be it further enacted,* That the marshals, their deputies, and the clerks of the said district and territorial courts, shall be paid for their services the like fees as may be allowed to them for similar services in other cases; and where such services are rendered exclusively in the arrest, custody, and delivery of the fugitive to the claimant, his or her agent or attorney, or where such supposed fugitive may be discharged out of custody for the want of sufficient proof as aforesaid, then such fees are to be paid in the whole by such claimant, his agent or attorney; and in all cases where the proceedings are before a commissioner, he shall be entitled to a fee of ten dollars in full for his services in each case, upon delivery of the said certificate to the claimant, his or her agent or attorney; or a fee of five dollars in cases where the proof shall not, in the opinion of such commissioner, warrant such certificate and delivery, inclusive of all services incident to such arrest and examination, to be paid in either case, by the claimant, his or her agent or attorney. The person or persons authorized to execute the process to be issued by such commissioners for the arrest and detention of fugitives from service or labor as aforesaid, shall also be entitled to a fee of five dollars each for each person he or they may arrest and take before any such commissioner as aforesaid at the instance and request of such claimant, with such other fees as may be deemed reasonable by such commissioner for such other additional services as may be necessarily performed by him or them: such as attending to the examination, keeping the fugitive in custody, and providing him with food and lodging during his detention, and until the final determination of such commissioner; and in general for performing such other duties as may be required by such claimant, his or her attorney or agent, or commissioner in the premises; such fees to be made up in conformity with the fees usually charged by the officers of the courts of justice within the proper district or county, as near as may be practicable, and paid by such claimants, their agents or attorneys, whether such supposed fugitive from service or labor be ordered to be delivered to such claimants by the final determination of such commissioners or not.

SEC. 9. *And be it further enacted,* That upon affidavit made by the claimant of such fugitive, his agent or attorney, after such certificate has been issued, that he has reason to apprehend that such fugitive will be rescued by force from his or their possession before he can be taken beyond the limits of the State in which the arrest is made, it shall be the duty of the officer making the arrest to retain such fugitive in his custody, and to remove him to the State whence he fled, and there to deliver him to said claimant, his agent or attorney. And to this end the officer aforesaid is hereby authorized and required to employ so many persons as he may deem necessary, to overcome such force, and to retain them in his service so long as circumstances may require; the said officer and his assistants, while so employed, to receive the same compensation, and to be allowed the same expenses as are now allowed by law for the transportation of criminals, to be certified by the judge of the district within which the arrest is made, and paid out of the treasury of the United States.

SEC. 10. *And be it further enacted,* That when any person held to service or labor in any State or Territory, or in the District of Columbia, shall escape therefrom, the party to whom such service or labor shall be due, his, her, or their agent or attorney may apply to any court of record therein, or judge thereof, in vacation, and make satisfactory proof to such court, or judge, in vacation, of the escape aforesaid, and that the person escaping owed service or labor to such party. Whereupon the court shall cause a record to be made of the matters so proved, and also a general description of the person so escaping, with such convenient certainty as may be; and a transcript of such record authenticated by the attestation of the clerk, and of the seal of the said court, being produced in any other State, Territory, or District in which the person so escaping may be found, and being exhibited to any judge, commissioner, or other officer, authorized by the law of the United States to cause persons escaping from service or labor to be delivered up, shall be held and taken to be full and conclusive evidence of the fact of escape, and that the service or labor of the person escaping is due to the party in such record mentioned. And upon the production by the said party of other and further evidence, if necessary, either oral or by affidavit, in addition to what is contained in the said record of the identity of the person escaping, he or she shall be delivered up to the claimant. And the said court, commissioner, judge or other person authorized by this act to grant certificates to claimants of fugitives, shall, upon the production of the record and other evidences aforesaid, grant to such claimant a certificate of his right to take any such person identified and proved to be owing service or labor as aforesaid, which certificate shall authorize such claimant to seize or arrest and transport such person to the State or Territory from which he escaped: *Provided,* That nothing herein contained shall be construed as requiring the production of a transcript of such record as evidence as aforesaid; but in its absence, the claim shall be heard and determined upon other satisfactory proofs competent in law.

> HOWELL COBB,
> *Speaker of the House of Representatives.*
> WILLIAM R. KING,
> *President of the Senate, pro tempore.*

Approved September 18, 1850.

> MILLARD FILLMORE.

The most prominent provisions of the Constitution of the United States, and those which form the fundamental basis of personal security, are they which provide, that every person shall be secure in their person and property: that no person may be deprived of liberty without due process of law, and that for crime or misdemeanor; that there may be no process of law that shall work corruption of blood. By corruption of blood is meant, that process, by which a person is *degraded* and deprived of rights common to the enfranchised citizen—of the rights of an elector, and of eligibility to the office of a representative of the people; in a word, that no person nor their posterity, may ever be debased beneath the level of the recognised basis of American citizenship. This debasement and degradation is "corruption of blood;" politically understood—a legal acknowledgement of inferiority of birth.

Heretofore, it ever has been denied, that the United States recognised or knew any difference between the people—that the Constitution makes no distinction, but includes in its provisions, all the people alike. This is not true, and certainly is blind absurdity in us at least, who have suffered the dread consequences of this delusion, not now to see it.

By the provisions of this bill, the colored people of the United States are positively degraded beneath the level of the whites—are made liable at any time, in any place, and under all circumstances, to be arrested—and upon the claim of any white person, without the privilege, even of making a defence, sent into endless bondage. Let no visionary nonsense about *habeas corpus,* or a *fair trial,* deceive us; there are no such rights granted in this bill, and except where the commissioner is too ignorant to understand when reading it, or too stupid to enforce it when he does understand, there is no earthly chance—no hope under heaven for the colored person who is brought before one of these officers of the law. Any leniency that may be expected, must proceed from the whims or caprice of the magistrate—in fact, it is optional with them; and *our* rights and liberty entirely at their disposal.

We are slaves in the midst of freedom, waiting patiently, and unconcernedly—indifferently, and stupidly, for masters to come and lay claim to us, trusting to their generosity whether or not they will own us and carry us into endless bondage.

The slave is more secure than we; he knows who holds the heel upon his bosom—we know not the wretch who may grasp us by the throat. His master may be a man of some conscientious scruples; ours may be unmerciful. Good or bad, mild or harsh, easy or hard, lenient or severe, saint or satan—whenever that master demands any one of us—even our affectionate wives and darling little children, *we must go into slavery*—there is *no alternative.* The *will* of the man who sits in judgment on our liberty, is the law. To him is given *all power* to say, whether or not we have a right to enjoy freedom. This is the power over the slave in the South—this is now extended to the North. The will of the man who sits in judgment over us is the law; because it is explicitly provided that the *decision* of the commissioner shall be final, from which there can be no appeal.

The freed man of the South is even more secure than the freeborn of the North; because such persons usually have their records in the slave states, bringing their "papers" with them; and the slaveholders will be faithful to their own acts. The Northern freeman knows no records; he despises the "papers."

Depend upon no promised protection of citizens in any quarter. Their own property and liberty are jeopardised, and they will not sacrifice them for us. This we may not expect them to do.

Besides, there are no people who ever lived, love their country and obey their laws as the Americans.

Their country is their Heaven—their Laws their Scriptures—and the decrees of their Magistrates obeyed as the fiat of God. It is the most consummate delusion and misdirected confidence to depend upon them for protection; and for a moment suppose even our children safe while walking in the streets among them.

A people capable of originating and sustaining such a law as this, are not the people to whom we are willing to entrust our liberty at discretion.

What can we do?—What shall we do? This is the great and important question:—Shall we submit to be dragged like brutes before heartless men, and sent into degradation and bondage?—Shall we fly, or shall we resist? Ponder well and reflect.

A learned jurist in the United States, (Chief Justice John Gibson of Pennsylvania,) lays down this as a fundamental right in the United States: that "Every man's house is his castle, and he has the right to defend it unto the taking of life, against any attempt to enter it against his will, except for crime," by well authenticated process.

But we have no such right. It was not intended for us, any more than any other provision of the law, intended for the protection of Americans. The policy is against us—it is useless to contend against it.

This is the law of the land and must be obeyed; and we candidly advise that it is useless for us to contend against it. To suppose its repeal, is to anticipate an overthrow of the Confederate Union; and we must be allowed an expression of opinion, when we say, that candidly we believe, the existence of the Fugitive Slave Law *necessary* to the continuance of the National Compact. This Law is the foundation of the Compromise—remove it, and the consequences are easily determined. We say necessary to the continuance of the National Compact: certainly we will not be understood as meaning that the enactment of such a Law was *really* necessary, or as favoring in the least this political monstrosity of the THIRTY-FIRST CONGRESS of the UNITED STATES of AMERICA—surely not at all; but we speak logically and politically, leaving morality and right out of the question—taking our position on the acknowledged popular basis of American Policy; arguing from premise to conclusion. We must abandon all vague theory, and look at *facts* as they really are; viewing ourselves in our true political position in the body politic. To imagine ourselves to be included in the body politic, except by express legislation, is at war with common sense, and contrary to fact. Legislation, the administration of the laws of the country, and the exercise of rights by the people, all prove to the contrary. We are politically, not of them, but aliens to the laws and political privileges of the country. These are truths—fixed facts, that quaint theory and exhausted moralising, are impregnable to, and fall harmlessly before.

It is useless to talk about our rights in individual States: we can have no rights there as citizens, not recognised in our common country; as the citizens of one State, are entitled to all the rights and privileges of an American citizen in all the States—the nullity of the one necessarily implying the nullity of the other. These provisions then do not include the colored people of the United States; since there is no power left in them, whereby they may protect us as their own citizens. Our descent, by the laws of the country, stamps us with inferiority—upon us has this law worked *corruption of blood*. We are in the hands of the General Government, and no State can rescue us. The Army and Navy stand at the service of our enslavers, the whole force of which, may at any moment—even in the dead of night, as has been done—when sunk in the depth of slumber, be called out for the purpose of forcing our mothers, sisters, wives, and children, or ourselves, into hopeless servitude, there to weary out a miserable life, a relief from which, death would be hailed with joy. Heaven and earth—God and Humanity!—are not these sufficient to arouse the most worthless among mankind, of whatever descent, to a sense of their true position? These laws apply to us—shall we not be aroused?

What then shall we do?—what is the remedy—is the important question to be answered?

This important inquiry we shall answer, and find a remedy in when treating of the emigration of the colored people.

XVII. EMIGRATION OF THE COLORED PEOPLE OF THE UNITED STATES

That there have been people in all ages under certain circumstances, that may be benefited by emigration, will be admitted; and that there are circumstances under which emigration is absolutely necessary to their political elevation, cannot be disputed.

This we see in the Exodus of the Jews from Egypt to the land of Judea; in the expedition of Dido and her followers from Tyre to Mauritania; and not to dwell upon hundreds of modern European examples—also in the ever memorable emigration of the Puritans, in 1620, from Great Britain, the land of their birth, to the wilderness of the New World, at which may be fixed the beginning of emigration to this continent as a permanent residence.

This may be acknowledged; but to advocate the emigration of the colored people of the United States from their native homes, is a new feature in our history, and at first view, may be considered objectionable, as pernicious to our interests. This objection is at once removed, when reflecting on our condition as incontrovertibly shown in a foregoing part of this work. And we shall proceed at once to give the advantages to be derived from emigration, to us as a people, in preference to any other policy that we may adopt. This granted, the question will then be, Where shall we go? This we conceive to be all-important—of paramount consideration, and shall endeavor to show the most advantageous locality; and premise the recommendation, with the strictest advice against any countenance whatever, to the emigration scheme of the so called Republic of Liberia.

XVIII. "REPUBLIC OF LIBERIA"

That we desire the civilization and enlightenment of Africa—the high and elevated position of Liberia among the nations of the earth, may not be doubted, as the writer was among the first, seven or eight years ago, to make the suggestion and call upon the Liberians to hold up their heads like men; take courage, having confidence in their own capacity to govern themselves, and come out from their disparaging position, by formally declaring their Independence.

As our desire is to impart information, and enlighten the minds of our readers on the various subjects herein contained, we present below a large extract from the "First Annual Report of the Trustees of Donations for Education in Liberia." This Extract will make a convenient statistic reference for matters concerning Liberia. We could only wish that many of our readers possessed more historical and geographical information of the world, and there could be little fears of their going anywhere that might be incongenial and unfavorable to their success. We certainly do intend to deal fairly with Liberia, and give the reader every information that may tend to enlighten them. What the colored people most need, is *intelligence;* give them this, and there is no danger of them being duped into anything they do not desire. This Board was incorporated by the Legislature of Massachusetts, March 19th, 1850—Ensign H. Kellogg, Speaker of the House, Marshall P. Wilder, President of the Senate. Trustees of the Board—Hon. George N. Briggs, LL.D., Hon. Simon Greenleaf, LL.D., Hon. Stephen Fairbanks, Hon. William J. Hubbard, Hon. Joel Giles, Hon. Albert Fearing, Amos A. Lawrence, Esq. Officers of the Board— Hon. G. N. Briggs, President; Hon. S. Fairbanks, Treasurer; Rev. J. Tracy, Secretary. The conclusion of the Report says:—"In view of such considerations, the Trustees cannot doubt the patrons of learning will sustain them in their attempt to plant the FIRST COLLEGE on the *only* continent which yet remains *without* one." In this, the learned Trustees have fallen into a statistical and geographical error, which we design to correct. The *continent* is *not without* a College. There are now in Egypt, erected under the patronage of that singularly wonderful man, Mehemet Ali, four colleges conducted on the European principle—Scientific, Medical, Legal, and Military.* These are in successful operation; the Military College having an average of eleven hundred students annually. The continent of Africa then, is not without a college, but though benighted enough, even to an apparent hopeless degeneration, she is still the seat of learning, and must some day rise, in the majesty of ancient grandeur, and vindicate the rights and claims of her own children, against the incalculable wrongs perpetrated through the period of sixty ages by professedly enlightened Christians, against them.

A glance at the map will show a sharp bend in this coast at Cape Palmas, from which it extends, on the one side, about 1,100 miles northwest and north, and on the other, about 1,200 or 1,300 almost directly east. In this bend is the Maryland Colony of Cape Palmas, with a jurisdiction extending nearly 100 miles eastward. This Colony is bounded on the north-west by the Republic of Liberia, which extends along the coast about 400 miles to Sherbro. These two governments will ultimately be united in one Republic, and may be considered as one, for all the purposes of this inquiry. The extent of their united sea-coast is about 520 miles. The jurisdiction of the Republic over the four hundred miles or more which it claims, has been formally acknowledged by several of the leading powers of Europe, and is questioned by none. To almost the whole of it, the native title has been extinguished; the natives, however, still occupying, as citizens, such portions of it as they need.

The civilized population of these governments, judging from the census of 1843, and other information, is some 7,000 or 8,000. Of the heathen population, no census has ever been taken; but it probably exceeds 300,000.

The grade of Liberian civilization may be estimated from the fact, that the people have formed a republican government, and so administer it, as to secure the confidence of European governments in its stability. The native tribes who have merged themselves in the Republic, have all bound themselves to receive and encourage teachers; and some of them have insisted on the insertion, in their treaties of annexation, of pledges that teachers and other means of civilization shall be furnished.

Our accounts of churches, clergy and schools are defective, but show the following significant facts:

The clergy of the Methodist Episcopal Church in Liberia are nearly all Liberian citizens, serving as missionaries of the Methodist Missionary Society

---

* It may be, that the Medical and Legal Schools, are adjunct departments of the Scientific College, which would make the number of Colleges in Egypt but two: as we are certain that the Military is separate entirely from the Scientific School, and spoken of by travelers as a splendid College.

in the United States. The last Report of that Society gives the names of fifteen missionaries, having in charge nine circuits, in which are 882 members in full communion, and 235 probationers; total, 1,117. They have 20 Sabbath Schools, with 114 officers and teachers, 810 scholars, and 507 volumes in their libraries. They have a Manual Labor School and Female Academy. The number of Day Schools is not reported; but seven of the missionaries are reported as superintendents of schools, and the same number have under their charge several "native towns," in some of which there are schools. The late superintendent of the missions writes:—

"It appears plain to my mind, that nothing can now retard the progress of our missions in this land, unless it be the want of a good high school, in which to rear up an abundant supply of well qualified teachers, to supply, as they shall rapidly increase in number, all your schools."

The Baptists are next in number to the Methodists. The Northern Baptist Board, having its seat in Boston, has in Liberia one mission, two out-stations, one boarding-school, and two day schools, with about twenty scholars each, one native preacher, and four native assistants. The whole mission is in the hands of converted natives. The Southern Board operates more extensively. More than a year since, the Rev. John Day, its principal agent there, reported to the Rev. R. R. Gurley, United States Commissioner to Liberia, as follows:

"In our schools are taught, say, 330 children, 92 of whom are natives. To more than 10,000 natives, the Word of Life is statedly preached; and in every settlement in these colonies, we have a church, to whom the means of grace are administered; and in every village we have an interesting Sunday school, where natives as well as colonists are taught the truths of God's word. Say, in our Sunday schools, are taught 400 colonists, and 200 natives. * * * We have this year baptized 18 natives and 7 colonists, besides what have been baptized by Messrs. Murray and Drayton, from whom I have had no report."

The missionaries are all, or nearly all, Liberian citizens.

The Board of Missions of the Presbyterian Church in the United States has five missionaries at four stations in Liberia. The first is at Monrovia, under the care of the Rev. Harrison W. Ellis, well known as "the Learned Black Blacksmith." While a slave in Alabama, and working at his trade as a blacksmith, he acquired all the education, in English, Latin, Greek, Hebrew, and Theology, which is required for ordination as a Presbyterian minister. The Presbyterians of that region then bought him, and sent him out as a missionary. His assistant, Mr. B. V. R. James, a colored man, was for some years a printer in the service of the American Board at their mission at Cape Palmas and the Gaboon River. He first went to Liberia as a teacher, supported by a society of ladies in New York. In the Presbyterian church under the care of Mr. Ellis are 39 communicants. During the year, 24 had been added, and 8 had been dismissed to form a new church in another place. Mr. Ellis also has charge of the "Alexander High School," which is intended mainly for teaching the rudiments of a classical education. This institution has an excellent iron school-house, given by a wealthy citizen of New York, at the cost of one thousand dollars, and a library and philosophical apparatus, which cost six hundred dollars, given by a gentleman in one of the southern States. The library contains a supply of classical works, probably equal to the wants of the school for some years. The land needed for the accommodation of the school was given by the government of Liberia. The number of scholars appears to be between twenty and thirty, a part of whom support themselves by their daily labor. The English High School under the care of Mr. James, had, according to the last Annual Report, 52 scholars. At a later date, the number in both schools was 78. Mr. James has also a large Sabbath school; but the number of pupils is not given.

The school station is at the new settlement of Kentucky, on the right or north bank of the St. Paul's, about fifteen miles from Monrovia, and six miles below Millsburgh. The missionary is a Liberian, Mr. H. W. Erskine. On a lot of ten acres, given by the government, buildings on an economical scale have been erected, in which is a school of twenty scholars. A church was organized in November, 1849, with eight members from the church in Monrovia. They have since increased to fourteen. Here, too, is a flourishing Sabbath school. The citizens, and especially the poor natives in the neighbourhood, are extremely anxious that a boarding school should be established. To this the Committee having charge of this mission objects, as the expense for buildings and for the support of pupils would be great, and would absorb funds that can be more profitably expended on day schools.

The third station is on the Sinou river, 150 miles down the coast from Monrovia, where, at the mouth of the river, is the town of Greenville, and a few miles higher up, the newer settlements of Readville and Rossville. It is under the care of the Rev. James M. Priest. The number of communicants, at the latest date, was thirty, and the field of labor was rapidly enlarging by immigration. The station is new, and it does not appear that any mission school had yet been organized.

The fourth station is at Settra Kroo, where there are five or six miles of coast, to which the native title has not yet been extinguished. This station has been maintained for some years, at a lamentable expense of the lives and health of white missionaries. About 200 boys and a few girls have been taught to read. The station is now under the care of Mr. Washington McDonogh, formerly a slave of the late John McDonogh, of Louisiana, so well known for the immense estate which he has bequeathed to benevolent purposes. He was well educated, and with more than eighty others, sent out some years since at his master's expense. He has a school of fifteen scholars, with the prospect of a large increase.

The mission of the Protestant Episcopal Church is located in the Maryland Colony at Cape Palmas. Its last Report specifies seven schools, and alludes to several others, in actual operation; all containing from 200 to 300 scholars, of whom about 100 are in one Sabbath school. Five other schools had been projected, and have probably gone into operation since that time. The greater part of the pupils are from native families. The Report states the number of communicants at sixty-seven, of whom forty are natives. A High school was opened January 1, 1850.

The laws of the Republic of Liberia provide for a common school in every town. It is supposed, however, that where there is a mission school, accessible to all children of suitable age, no other school exists; so that, in fact, nearly all the common schools in Liberia are connected with the different missions, the missionaries have the superintendence of their studies, and the Missionary

Societies defray a large portion of the expense. Yet is must be remembered that a large majority of the missionaries were citizens of the Republic, and some of them native Africans; so that the immediate control of the schools is not generally in foreign hands. A portion, also, of the missionary funds, is contributed in Liberia; and something is paid by parents for the tuition of their children. Yet the Republic evidently needs an educational system more independent of missionary aid and control; and for that purpose, needs a supply of teachers who are not raised up in mission schools. And we have it in testimony, that the missions themselves might be more efficient for good, if well supplied with teachers of higher qualifications.

Here, then, we have a Republic of some 300,000 inhabitants, of whom 7,000 or 8,000 may be regarded as civilized, and the remainder as having a right to expect, and a large part of them actually expecting and demanding the means of civilization and Christianity. We have—supplying as well as we can by estimate, the numbers not definitely given—more than 2,000 communicants in Christian churches, and more than 1,500 children in Sabbath Schools; some 40 day schools containing, exclusive of the Methodists, who are the most numerous, and of whose numbers in school we have no report, about 635 scholars. The whole number in day schools, therefore, is probably not less than 1,200. We have the Alexander High School at Monrovia, where instruction is given to some extent in the classics; the English High School, at the same place, under Mr. James; the Methodist Manual Labor School and Female Academy at Millsburg; the Baptist Boarding School at Bexley; and the Protestant Episcopal High School at Cape Palmas. These institutions must furnish some students for a higher seminary, such as we propose to establish; and such a population must need their labors when educated.

However foreign to the designs of the writer of ever making that country or any other out of America, his home; had this been done, and honorably maintained, the Republic of Liberia would have met with words of encouragement, not only from himself, an humble individual, but we dare assert, from the leading spirits among, if not from the whole colored population of the United States. Because they would have been willing to overlook the circumstances under which they went there, so that in the end, they were willing to take their stand as men, and thereby throw off the degradation of slaves, still under the control of American slaveholders, and American slave-ships. But in this, we were disappointed—grievously disappointed, and proceed to show in short, our objections to Liberia.

Its geographical position, in the first place, is objectionable, being located in the *sixth degree* of latitude North of the equator, in a district signally unhealthy, rendering it objectionable as a place of destination for the colored people of the United States. We shall say nothing about other parts of the African coast, and the reasons for its location where it is: it is enough for us to know the facts as they are, to justify an unqualified objection to Liberia.

In the second place, it originated in a deep laid scheme of the slave-holders of the country, to *exterminate* the free colored of the American continent; the origin being sufficient to justify us in impugning the motives.

Thirdly and lastly—Liberia is not an Independent Republic: in fact, *it is not* an independent nation at all; but a poor *miserable mockery*—a *burlesque* on a government—a pitiful dependency on the American Colonizationists, the Colonization Board at Washington city, in the District of Columbia, being the Executive and Government, and the principal man, called President, in Liberia, being the echo—a mere parrot of Rev. Robert R. Gurley, Elliot Cresson, Esq., Governor Pinney, and other leaders of the Colonization scheme—to do as they bid, and say what they tell him. This we see in all of his doings.

Does he go to France and England, and enter into solemn treaties of an honorable recognition of the independence of his country; before his own nation has any knowledge of the result, this man called President, dispatches an official report to the Colonizationists of the United States, asking their gracious approval? Does king Grando, or a party of fishermen besiege a village and murder some of the inhabitants, this same "President," dispatches an official report to the American Colonization Board, asking for instructions—who call an Executive Session of the Board, and immediately decide that war must be waged against the enemy, placing ten thousand dollars at his disposal—and war *actually declared in Liberia,* by virtue of the *instructions* of the *American Colonization Society.* A mockery of a government—a disgrace to the office pretended to be held—a parody on the position assumed. Liberia in Africa, is a mere dependency of Southern slaveholders, and American Colonizationists, and unworthy of any respectful consideration from us.

What would be thought of the people of Hayti, and their heads of government, if their instructions emanated from the American Anti-Slavery Society, or the British Foreign Missionary Board? Should they be respected at all as a nation? Would they be worthy of it? Certainly not. We do not expect Liberia to be all that Hayti is; but we ask and expect of her, to have a decent respect for herself—to endeavor to be freemen instead of voluntary slaves. Liberia is no place for the colored freemen of the United States; and we dismiss the subject with a single remark of caution against any advice contained in a pamphlet, which we have not seen, written by Hon. James. G. Birney, in favor of Liberian emigration. Mr. Birney is like the generality of white Americans, who suppose that we are too ignorant to understand what we want; whenever they wish to get rid of us, would drive us any where, so that we left them. Don't adhere to a word therein contained; we will think for ourselves. Let Mr. Birney go his way, and we will go ours. This is one of those confounded gratuities that is forced in our faces at every turn we make. We dismiss it without further comment—and with it Colonization *in toto*—and Mr. Birney *de facto.*

But to return to emigration: Where shall we go? We must not leave this continent; America is our destination and our home.

That the continent of America seems to have been designed by Providence as an asylum for all the various nations of the earth, is very apparent. From the earliest discovery, various nations sent a representation here, either as adventurers and speculators, or employed seamen and soldiers, hired to do the work of their employers. And among the earliest and most numerous class who found their way to the New World, were those of the African race. And it is now ascertained to our mind, beyond a peradventure, that when the continent was discovered, there were found in Central America, a tribe of the black race, of fine looking people, having characteristics of color and hair, identifying them originally of the African race —no doubt being a remnant of the Africans who, with the Carthaginian expedition, were adventitiously cast upon this continent, in their memorable excursion to the "Great Island," after sailing many miles distant to the West of the Pillars of Hercules.

We are not inclined to be superstitious, but say, that we can see the "finger of God" in all this; and if the European race may with propriety, boast and claim, that this continent is better adapted to their development, than their own father-land; surely, it does not necessarily detract from our father-land, to claim the superior advantages to the African race, to be derived from this continent. But be that as it may, the world belongs to mankind—his common Father created it for his common good—his temporal destiny is here; and our present warfare, is not upon European rights, nor for European countries; but for the common rights of man, based upon the great principles of common humanity—taking our chance in the world of rights, and claiming to have originally more right to this continent, than the European race. And had we no other claims than those set forth in a former part of this work, they are sufficient to cause every colored man on the continent, to stand upon the soil unshaken and unmoved. The aboriginee of the continent, is more closely allied to us by consanguinity, than to the European—being descended from the Asiatic, whose alliance in matrimony with the African is very common—therefore, we have even greater claims to this continent on that account, and should unite and make common cause in elevation, with our similarly oppressed brother, the Indian.

The advantages of this continent are superior, because it presents every variety of climate, soil, and production of the earth, with every variety of mineral production, with all kinds of water privileges, and ocean coast on all sides, presenting every commercial advantage. Upon the American continent we are determined to stay, in spite of every odds against us. What part of the great continent shall our destination be—shall we emigrate to the North or South?

XX. THE CANADAS

This is one of the most beautiful portions of North America. Canada East, formerly known as Lower Canada, is not quite so favorable, the climate being cold and severe in winter, the springs being late, the summers rather short, and the soil not so productive. But Canada West, formerly called Upper Canada, is equal to any portion of the Northern States. The climate being milder than that of the Northern portions of New York, Ohio, Michigan, Indiana, Illinois, or any of the States bordering on the lakes, the soil is prolific in productions of every description. Grains, vegetables, fruits, and cattle, are of the very best kind; from a short tour by the writer, in that country in the fall, 1851, one year ago, he prefers Canada West to any part of North America, as a destination for the colored people. But there is a serious objection to the Canadas—a political objection. The Canadians are descended from the same common parentage as the Americans on this side of the Lakes—and there is a manifest tendency on the part of the Canadians generally, to Americanism. That the Americans are determined to, and will have the Canadas, to a close observer, there is not a shadow of doubt; and our brethren should know this in time. This there would be no fear of, were not the Canadian people in favor of the project, neither would the Americans attempt an attack upon the provinces, without the move being favored by the people of those places.

Every act of the Americans, ostensibly as courtesy and friendship, tend to that end. This is seen in the policy pursued during the last two or three years, in the continual invitations, frequently reciprocated, that pass from the Americans to their "Canadian brethren"—always couched in affectionate language—to join them in their various celebrations, in different parts of the States. They have got them as far as Boston, and we may expect to hear of them going to New York, Philadelphia, Baltimore—and instead of the merrymaking over the beginning or ending of internal improvements, we may expect to see them ere long, wending their way to the seat of the federal government—it may be with William McKenzie, the memorable *patriot* and present member of the Colonial parliament, bearing in his hand the stars and stripes as their ensign—there to blend their voices in the loud shout of jubilee, in honor of the "bloodless victory," of Canadian annexation. This we forewarn the colored people, in time, is the inevitable and not far distant destiny of the Canadas. And let them come into the American Republic when they may, the fate of the colored man, however free before, is doomed, doomed, forever doomed. Disfranchisement, degradation, and a delivery up to slave catchers and kidnappers, are their only fate, let Canadian annexation take place when it will. The odious infamous fugitive slave law, will then be in full force with all of its terrors; and we have no doubt that fully in anticipation of this event, was the despicable law created.

Let not colored people be deceived and gulled by any visionary argument about original rights, or those of the people remaining the same as they were previous to cecession of the territory. The people can claim no rights than such as are known to exist previous to their annexation. This is manifestly the case with a large class of the former inhabitants of Mexico, who though citizens before, in the full exercise of their rights as such, so soon as the cecession of the territory took place, lost them entirely, as they could claim only such as were enjoyed by the people of a similar class, in the country to which they made their union. The laudatories heaped upon the Americans, within the hearing of the writer, while traveling the provinces the last fall, by one of the Canadian officiaries, in comparing their superior intelligence to what he termed the "stupid aristocracy," then returning from the Boston celebration, where there was a fair opportunity of comparing the intellect of their chief magistrate, his excellency, Lord Elgin, governor-general of the Canadas, and Sir Allen Napier McNab, knight baronet with that of some of the "plain republicans" who were present on the occasion, were extravagant. The Canadians generally were perfectly carried away with delight at their reception. They reminded us of some of our poor brethren, who had just made their escape from Southern bondage, and for the first time in their life, had been taken by the hand by a white man, who acknowledged them as equals. They don't know when to stop talking about it, they really annoy one with extravagant praises of them. This was the way with those gentlemen; and we dare predict, that from what we heard on that occasion, that Mr. McKenzie nor Big Bill Johnson, hero of the Forty Islands, are no greater *patriots* than these Canadian visitors to the Boston husa! We are satisfied that the Canadas are no place of safety for the colored people of the United States; otherwise we should have no objection to them.

But to the fugitive—our enslaved brethren flying from Southern despotism—we say, until we have a more preferable place—go on to Canada. Freedom, always; liberty any place and ever—before slavery. Continue to fly to the Canadas, and swell the number of the twenty-five thousand already there. Surely the British cannot, they will not look with indifference upon such a powerful auxiliary as these brave, bold, daring men—the very flower of the South, who have hazarded every consequence, many of whom have come from Arkansas and Florida in search of freedom. Worthy surely to be free, when gained at such a venture. Go on to the North, till the South is ready to receive you—for surely, he who can make his way from Arkansas to Canada, can find his way from Kentucky to Mexico. The moment his foot touches this land South, he is free. Let the bondman but be assured that he can find the same freedom South that there is in the North; the same liberty in Mexico, as in Canada, and he will prefer going South to going North. His risk is no greater in getting there. Go either way, and he in the majority of instances must run the gauntlet of the slave states.

XXI. CENTRAL AND SOUTH AMERICA
AND THE WEST INDIES

Central and South America, are evidently the ultimate destination and future home of the colored race on this continent; the advantages of which in preference to all others, will be apparent when once pointed out.*

Geographically, from the Northern extremity of Yucatan, down through Central and South America, to Cape Horn, there is a variation of climate from the twenty-second degree of North latitude, passing through the equatorial region; nowhere as warm as it is in the same latitude in Africa; to the *fifty-fifth degree* of South latitude, including a climate as cold as that of the Hudson Bay country in British America, colder than that of Maine, or any part known to the United States of North America; so that there is every variety of climate in South, as well as North America.

In the productions of grains, fruits, and vegetables, Central and South America are also prolific; and the best of herds are here raised. Indeed, the finest Merino sheep, as well as the principal trade in rice, sugar, cotton, and wheat, which is now preferred in California to any produced in the United States—the Chilian flour—might be carried on by the people of this most favored portion of God's legacy to man. The mineral productions excel all other parts of this continent; the rivers present the greatest internal advantages, and the commercial prospects, are without a parallel on the coast of the new world.

The advantages to the colored people of the United States, to be derived from emigration to Central, South America, and the West Indies, are incomparably greater than that of any other parts of the world at present.

In the first place, there never have existed in the policy of any of the nations of Central or South America, an inequality on account of race or color, and any prohibition of rights, has generally been to the white, and not to the colored races.† To the whites, not because they were white, not

---

* The native language of these countries, as well as the greater part of South America, is *Spanish,* which is the easiest of all foreign languages to learn. It is very remarkable and worthy of note, that with a view of going to Mexico or South America, the writer several years ago paid some attention to the Spanish language; and now, a most singular coincidence, without preunderstanding, in almost every town, where there is any intelligence among them, there are some *colored persons* of both sexes, who are studying the Spanish language. Even the Methodist and other clergymen, among them. And we earnestly entreat all colored persons who can, to study, and have their children taught Spanish. No foreign language will be of such *import* to colored people, in a very short time, as the Spanish. Mexico, Central and South America, importune us to speak their language; and if nothing else, the silent indications of Cuba, urge us to learn the Spanish tongue.

† The Brazilians have formed a Colonization Society, for the purpose of colonizing

on account of their color, but because of the policy pursued by them towards the people of other races than themselves. The population of Central and South America, consist of fifteen millions two hundred and forty thousand, adding the ten millions of Mexico; twenty-five millions two hundred and forty thousand, of which vast population, but *one-seventh* are whites, or the pure European race. Allowing a deduction of one-seventh of this population for the European race that may chance to be in those countries, and we have in South and Central America alone, the vast colored population of *thirteen millions one hundred and seventy-seven thousand;* and including Mexico, a *colored* population on this glorious continent of *twenty-one millions, six hundred and forty thousand.*

This vast number of people, our brethren—because they are precisely the same people as ourselves and share the same fate with us, as the case of numbers of them have proven, who have been adventitiously thrown among us—stand ready and willing to take us by the hand—nay, are anxiously waiting, and earnestly importuning us to come, that they may make common cause with us, and we all share the same fate. There is nothing under heaven in our way—the people stand with open arms ready to receive us. The climate, soil, and productions—the vast rivers and beautiful sea-coast—the scenery of the landscape, and beauty of the starry heavens above—the song of the birds—the voice of the people say come—and God our Father bids us go.—Will we go? Go we must, and go we will, as there is no alternative. To remain here in North America, and be crushed to the earth in vassalage and degradation, we never will.

Talk not about religious biases—we have but one reply to make. We had rather be a Heathen *freeman,* than a Christian *slave.*

There need be no fear of annexation in these countries—the prejudices of the people are all against it, and with our influences infused among

---

free blacks to Africa. The Brazilians are Portuguese, the only nation that can be termed white, and the only one that is a real slave holding nation in South America. Even the black and colored men have equal privileges with whites; and the action of this society will probably extend only to the sending back of such captives as may be taken from piratical slavers.

Colonization in Brazil, has doubtless been got up under the influence of United States slave holders and their abettors, such as the consuls and envoys, who are sent out to South America, by the government. Chevalier Niteroi, *charge de affaires* from Brazil near the government of Liberia, received by the President on the 28th of last January, is also charged with the mission of establishing a colony of free blacks in Liberia. The Chevalier was once a Captain in the Brazilian navy on the coast of Africa; and no doubt is conversant with the sentiments of Roberts, who was charged with the slave trade at one time. The scheme of United States slaveholders and President J. J. Roberts, their agent of Liberia, will not succeed, in establishing prejudice against the *black* race; not even in slaveholding Brazil.

We have no confidence in President Roberts of Liberia, believing him to be wholly without principle—seeking only self-aggrandizement; even should it be done, over the ruined prospects of his staggering infant country. The people of Liberia, should beware of this man. His *privy councillors* are to be found among *slaveholders* in the United States.

them, the aversion would be ten-fold greater. Neither need there be any fears of an attempt on the part of the United States, at a subjugation of these countries. Policy is against it, because the United States has too many colored slaves in their midst, to desire to bring under their government, twenty-one millions of disfranchised people, whom it would cost them more to keep under subjection, than ten-fold the worth of the countries they gained. Besides, let us go to whatever parts of Central and South America we may, we shall make common cause with the people, and shall hope, by one judicious and signal effort, to assemble one day—and a glorious day it will be—in a great representative convention, and form a glorious union of South American States, "inseparably connected one and forever."

This can be done, easily done, if the proper course be pursued, and necessity will hold them together as it holds together the United States of North America—self-preservation. As the British nation serves to keep in check the Americans; so would the United States serve to keep in Union the South American States.

We should also enter into solemn treaties with Great Britain, and like other free and independent nations, take our chance, and risk consequences. Talk not of consequences; we are now in chains; shall we shake them off and go to a land of liberty? shall our wives and children be protected, secure, and affectionately cherished, or shall they be debased and degraded as our mothers and fathers were? By the light of heaven, no! By the instincts of nature, no!

Talk not about consequences. White men seek responsibilities; shall we shun them? They brave dangers and risk consequences; shall we shrink from them? What are consequences, compared in the scale of value, with liberty and freedom; the rights and privileges of our wives and children? In defence of our liberty—the rights of my wife and children; had we the power, we would command the vault of a volcano, charged with the wrath of heaven, and blast out of existence, every thing that dared obstruct our way.

The time has now fully arrived, when the colored race is called upon by all the ties of common humanity, and all the claims of consummate justice, to go forward and take their position, and do battle in the struggle now being made for the redemption of the world. Our cause is a just one; the greatest at present that elicits the attention of the world. For if there is a remedy; that remedy is now at hand. God himself as assuredly as he rules the destinies of nations, and entereth measures into the "hearts of men," has presented these measures to us. Our race is to be redeemed; it is a great and glorious work, and we are the instrumentalities by which it is to be done. But we must go from among our oppressors; it never can be done by staying among them. God has, as certain as he has ever designed any thing, has designed this great portion of the New World, for us, the colored races; and as certain as we stubborn our hearts, and stiffen our necks against it, his protecting arm and fostering care will be withdrawn from us.

Shall we be told that we can live nowhere, but under the will of our North American oppressors; that this (the United States,) is the country most favorable to our improvement and progress? Are we incapable of self-government, and making such improvements for ourselves as we delight to enjoy after American white men have made them for themselves? No, it is not true. Neither is it true that the United States is the best country for our improvement. That country is the best, in which our manhood can be best developed; and that is Central and South America, and the West Indies—all belonging to this glorious Continent.

Whatever may be our pretended objections to any place, whenever and wherever our oppressors go, there will our people be found in proportionate numbers. Even now could they get possession of the equatorial region of South America, there would colored men be found living on their boats and in their houses to do their menial services; but talk to them about going there and becoming men, and a thousand excuses and objections are at once raised against the climate or whatever else.

The writer, within the past few years, and as early as seventeen years ago, then being quite young, and flushed with geographical and historical speculations, introduced in a Literary Institution of Young Men, the subject of Mexican, Californian, and South American Emigration. He was always hooted at, and various objections raised: one on account of distance, and another that of climate.

He has since seen some of the same persons engage themselves to their white American oppressors—officers in the war against Mexico, exposing themselves to the chances of the heat of day and the damp of night—risking the dangers of the battle-field, in the capacity of servants. And had the Americans taken Mexico, no people would have flocked there faster than the colored people from the United States. The same is observed of California.

In conversation, in the city of New York, a few weeks ago, with a colored lady of intelligence, one of the "first families," the conversation being the elevation of the colored people, we introduced emigration as a remedy, and Central America as the place. We were somewhat surprised, and certainly unprepared to receive the rebuking reply—"Do you suppose that I would go in the woods to live for the sake of freedom? no, indeed! If you wish to do so, go and do it. I am free enough here!" Remarking at the same time, that her husband was in San Francisco, and she was going to him, as she learned that that city was quite a large and handsome place.

We reminded her, that the industry of white men and women, in four years' time, had made San Francisco what it is. That in 1846, before the

American emigration, the city contained about seven hundred people, surrounded by a dense wilderness; and that we regretted to contrast her conduct or disposition with that of the lady of Col. Fremont, a daughter of Senator Benton, who tenderly and indulgently raised, in the spring after his arduous adventure across the mountains, and almost miraculous escape, while the country was yet a wilderness, left her comfortable home in Missouri, and braved the dangers of the ocean, to join her husband and settle in the wilderness. That she was going now to San Francisco, because it was a populous and "fine city"—that Mrs. Fremont went, when it was a wilderness, to help to *make* a populous and fine city.

About two hours previous to the writing of the following fact, two respectable colored ladies in conversation, pleasantly disputing about the superiority of the two places, Philadelphia and New York, when one spoke of the uniform cleanliness of the streets of Philadelphia, and the dirtiness of those of New York; when the other triumphantly replied.— "The reason that our streets are so dirty is, that we do more business in one day, than you do in a month." The other acknowledged the fact with some degree of reluctance, and explained, with many "buts" as an excuse in extenuation. Here was a seeming appreciation of business and enterprise; but the query flashed through our mind in an instant, as to whether they thought for a moment, of the fact, that *they* had no interest in either city, nor its *business*. It brought forcibly to our mind, the scene of two of our oppressed brethren South, fighting each other, to prove his *master* the greatest gentleman of the two.

Let no objections be made to emigration on the ground of the difficulty of the fugitive slave, in reaching us; it is only necessary for him to know, that he has safety South, and he will find means of reaching the South, as easily as he now does the North. Have no fears about that—his redemption draws nigh, the nearer we draw to him. Central and South America, *must be our future homes.* Our oppressors will not want us to go there. They will move heaven and earth to prevent us—they will talk about us getting our rights, and offer us a territory here, and all that. It is of no use. They have pressed us to the last retreat—the die is cast—the Rubicon must be crossed—go we will, in defiance of all the slave-power in the Union. And we shall not go there, to be idle—passive spectators to an invasion of South American rights. No—go when we will, and where we may, we shall hold ourselves amenable to defend and protect the country that embraces us. We are fully able to defend ourselves, once concentrated, against any odds—and by the help of God, we will do it. We do not go, without counting the cost, cost what it may; all that it may cost, it is worth to be free.

In going, let us have but one object—to become elevated men and women, worthy of freedom—the worthy citizens of an adopted country. What to us will be adopted—to our children will be legitimate. Go not with an anxiety of political aspirations; but go with the fixed intention—as Europeans come to the United States—of cultivating the soil, entering into the mechanical operations, keeping the shops, carrying on merchandise, trading on land and water, improving property—in a word, to become the producers of the country, instead of the consumers.

Let young men who go, have a high object in view; and not go with a view of becoming servants to wealthy gentlemen there; for be assured, that they place themselves beneath all respectful consideration.

XXII. NICARAGUA AND NEW GRENADA

As it is not reasonable to suppose, that all who read this volume—especially those whom it is intended most to benefit—understand geography; it is deemed advisable, to name some particular places, as locality of destination.

We consequently, to begin with, select NICARAGUA, in Central America, North, and NEW GRENADA, the Northern part of South America, South of Nicaragua, as the most favorable points at present, in every particular, for us to emigrate to.

In the first place, they are the nearest points to be reached, and countries at which the California adventurers are now touching, on their route to that distant land, and not half the distance of California.

In the second place, the advantages for all kinds of enterprise, are equal if not superior, to almost any other points—the climate being healthy and highly favorable.

In the third place, and by no means the least point of importance, the British nation is bound by solemn treaty, to protect both of those nations from foreign imposition, until they are able to stand alone.

Then there is nothing in the way, but everything in favor, and opportunities for us to rise to the full stature of manhood. Remember this fact, that in these countries, colored men now fill the highest places in the country: and colored people have the same chances there, that white people have in the United States. All that is necessary to do, is to go, and the moment your foot touches the soil, you have all the opportunities for elevating yourselves as the highest, according to your industry and merits.

Nicaragua and New Grenada, are both Republics, having a President, Senate, and Representatives of the people. The municipal affairs are well conducted; and remember, however much the customs of the country may differ, and appear strange to those you have left behind—remember that you are free; and that many who, at first sight, might think that they could not become reconciled to the new order of things, should recollect, that they were once in a situation in the United States, (in *slavery,*) where they were compelled to be content with customs infinitely more averse to their feelings and desires. And that customs become modified, just in proportion as people of different customs from different parts, settle in the same communities together. All we ask is Liberty—the rest follows as a matter of course.

XXIII. THINGS AS THEY ARE

"And if thou boast TRUTH to utter,
SPEAK, and leave the rest to God."

In presenting this work, we have but a single object in view, and that is, to inform the minds of the colored people at large, upon many things pertaining to their elevation, that but few among us are acquainted with. Unfortunately for us, as a body, we have been taught to believe, that we must have some person to think for us, instead of thinking for ourselves. So accustomed are we to submission and this kind of training, that it is with difficulty, even among the most intelligent of the colored people, an audience may be elicited for any purpose whatever, if the expounder is to be a colored person; and the introduction of any subject is treated with indifference, if not contempt, when the originator is a colored person. Indeed, the most ordinary white person, is almost revered, while the most qualified colored person is totally neglected. Nothing from them is appreciated.

We have been standing comparatively still for years, following in the footsteps of our friends, believing that what they promise us can be accomplished, just because they say so, although our own knowledge should long since, have satisfied us to the contrary. Because even were it possible, with the present hate and jealousy that the whites have towards us in this country, for us to gain equality of rights with them; we never could have an equality of the exercise and enjoyment of those rights—because, the great odds of numbers are against us. We might indeed, as some at present, have the right of the elective franchise—nay, it is not the elective franchise, because the *elective franchise* makes the enfranchised, *eligible* to any position attainable; but we may exercise the right of *voting* only, which to us, is but poor satisfaction; and we by no means care to cherish the privilege of voting somebody into office, to help to make laws to degrade us.

In religion—because they are both *translators* and *commentators,* we must believe nothing, however absurd, but what our oppressors tell us. In Politics, nothing but such as they promulge; in Anti-Slavery, nothing but what our white brethren and friends say we must; in the mode and manner of our elevation, we must do nothing, but that which may be laid down to be done by our white brethren from some quarter or other; and now, even in the subject of emigration, there are some colored people to be found, so lost to their own interest and self-respect, as to be gulled by slave owners and colonizationists, who are led to believe there is no other place in which they can become elevated, but Liberia, a government of American slave-holders, as we have shown—simply, because white men have told them so.

Upon the possibility, means, mode and manner, of our Elevation in the United States—Our Original Rights and Claims as Citizens—Our Determination not to be Driven from our Native Country—the Difficulties in the Way of our Elevation—Our Position in Relation to our Anti-Slavery Brethren—the Wicked Design and Injurious Tendency of the American Colonization Society—Objections to Liberia—Objections to Canada—Preferences to South America, &c., &c., all of which we have treated without reserve; expressing our mind freely, and with candor, as we are determined that as far as we can at present do so, the minds of our readers shall be enlightened. The custom of concealing information upon vital and important subjects, in which the interest of the people is involved, we do not agree with, nor favor in the least; we have therefore, laid this cursory treatise before our readers, with the hope that it may prove instrumental in directing the attention of our people in the right way, that leads to their Elevation. Go or stay—of course each is free to do as he pleases—one thing is certain; our Elevation is the work of our own hands. And Mexico, Central America, the West Indies, and South America, all present now, opportunities for the individual enterprise of our young men, who prefer to remain in the United States, in preference to going where they can enjoy real freedom, and equality of rights. Freedom of Religion, as well as of politics, being tolerated in all of these places.

Let our young men and women, prepare themselves for usefulness and business; that the men may enter into merchandise, trading, and other things of importance; the young women may become teachers of various kinds, and otherwise fill places of usefulness. Parents must turn their attention more to the education of their children. We mean, to educate them for useful practical business purposes. Educate them for the Store and the Counting House—to do every-day practical business. Consult the children's propensities, and direct their education according to their inclinations. It may be, that there is too great a desire on the part of parents, to give their children a professional education, before the body of the people, are ready for it. A people must be a business people, and have more to depend upon than mere help in people's houses and Hotels, before they are either able to support, or capable of properly appreciating the services of professional men among them. This has been one of our great mistakes—we have gone in advance of ourselves. We have commenced at the superstructure of the building, instead of the foundation—at the top instead of the bottom. We should first be mechanics and common tradesmen, and professions as a matter of course would grow out of the wealth made thereby. Young men and women, must now prepare for usefulness—the day of our Elevation is at hand—all the world now gazes at us—and Central and South America, and the West Indies, bid us come and be men and women, protected, secure, beloved and Free.

The branches of Education most desirable for the preparation of youth, for practical useful every-day life, are Arithmetic and good Penmanship, in order to be Accountants; and a good rudimental knowledge of Geography—which has ever been neglected, and underestimated—and of Political Economy; which without the knowledge of the first, no people can ever become adventurous—nor of the second, never will be an enterprising people. Geography, teaches a knowledge of the world, and Political Economy, a knowledge of the wealth of nations; or how to make money. These are not abstruse sciences, or learning not easily acquired or understood; but simply, common School Primer learning, that every body may get. And, although it is the very Key to prosperity and success in common life, but few know anything about it. Unfortunately for our people, so soon as their children learn to read a Chapter in the New Testament, and scribble a miserable hand, they are pronounced to have "Learning enough"; and taken away from School, no use to themselves, nor community. This is apparent in our Public Meetings, and Official Church Meetings; of the great number of men present, there are but few capable of filling a Secretaryship. Some of the large cities may be an exception to this. Of the multitudes of Merchants, and Business men throughout this country, Europe, and the world, few are qualified, beyond the branches here laid down by us as necessary for business. What did John Jacob Astor, Stephen Girard, or do the millionaires and the greater part of the merchant princes, and mariners, know about Latin and Greek, and the Classics? Precious few of them know any thing. In proof of this, in 1841, during the Administration of President Tyler, when the mutiny was detected on board of the American Man of War Brig Somers, the names of the Mutineers, were recorded by young S—a Midshipman in Greek. Captain Alexander Slidell McKenzie, Commanding, was unable to read them; and in his despatches to the Government, in justification of his policy in executing the criminals, said that he "discovered some curious characters which he was unable to read," &c.; showing thereby, that that high functionary, did not understand even the Greek Alphabet, which was only necessary, to have been able to read proper names written in Greek.

What we most need then, is a good business practical Education; because, the Classical and Professional education of so many of our young men, before their parents are able to support them, and community ready to patronize them, only serves to lull their energy, and cripple the otherwise, praiseworthy efforts they would make in life. A Classical education, is only suited to the wealthy, or those who have a prospect of gaining a livelihood by it. The writer does not wish to be understood, as underrating a Classical and Professional education; this is not his intention; he fully appreciates them, having had some such advantages himself; but he desires to give a proper guide, and put a check to the extravagant idea that is fast obtaining, among our people especially, that a Classical, or as it is termed, a "finished education," is necessary to prepare one for usefulness in life. Let us have an education, that shall practically develop our thinking faculties and manhood; and then, and not until then, shall we be able to vie with our oppressors, go where we may. We as heretofore, have been on the extreme; either no qualification at all, or a Collegiate education. We jumped too far; taking a leap from the deepest abyss to the highest summit; rising from the ridiculous to the sublime; without medium or intermission.

Let our young women have an education; let their minds be well informed; well stored with useful information and practical proficiency, rather than the light superficial acquirements, popularly and fashionably called accomplishments. We desire accomplishments, but they must be *useful*.

Our females must be qualified, because they are to be the mothers of our children. As mothers are the first nurses and instructors of children; from them children consequently, get their first impressions, which being always the most lasting, should be the most correct. Raise the mothers above the level of degradation, and the offspring is elevated with them. In a word, instead of our young men, transcribing in their blank books, recipes for *Cooking;* we desire to see them making the transfer of *Invoices of Merchandise.* Come to our aid then; the *morning* of our *Redemption* from degradation, adorns the horizon.

In our selection of individuals, it will be observed, that we have confined ourself entirely to those who occupy or have occupied positions among the whites, consequently having a more general bearing as useful contributors to society at large. While we do not pretend to give all such worthy cases, we gave such as we possessed information of, and desire it to be understood, that a large number of our most intelligent and worthy men and women, have not been named, because from their more private position in community, it was foreign to the object and design of this work. If we have said aught to offend, "take the will for the deed," and be assured, that it was given with the purest of motives, and best intention, from a true hearted man and brother; deeply lamenting the sad fate of his race in this country, and sincerely desiring the elevation of man, and submitted to the serious consideration of all, who favor the promotion of the cause of God and humanity.

XXIV. A GLANCE AT OURSELVES—CONCLUSION

With broken hopes—sad devastation;
A race *resigned* to DEGRADATION!

We have said much to our young men and women, about their vocation and calling; we have dwelt much upon the menial position of our people in this country. Upon this point we cannot say too much, because there is a seeming satisfaction and seeking after such positions manifested on their part, unknown to any other people. There appears to be, a want of a sense of propriety or *self-respect,* although inexplicable; because young men and women among us, many of whom have good trades and homes, adequate to their support, voluntarily leave them, and seek positions, such as servants, waiting maids, coachmen, nurses, cooks in gentlemen's kitchen, or such like occupations, when they can gain a livelihood at something more respectable, or elevating in character. And the worse part of the whole matter is, that they have become so accustomed to it, it has become so "fashionable," that it seems to have become second nature, and they really become offended, when it is spoken against.

Among the German, Irish, and other European peasantry who come to this country, it matters not what they were employed at before and after they come; just so soon as they can better their condition by keeping shops, cultivating the soil, the young men and women going to night-schools, qualifying themselves for usefulness, and learning trades—they do so. Their first and last care, object and aim is, to better their condition by raising themselves above the condition that necessity places them in. We do not say too much, when we say, as an evidence of the deep degradation of our race, in the United States, that there are those among us, the wives and daughters, some of the *first ladies,* (and who dare say they are not the "first," because they belong to the "first class" and associate where any body among us can?) whose husbands are industrious, able and willing to support them, who voluntarily leave home, and become chambermaids, and stewardesses, upon vessels and steamboats, in all probability, to enable them to obtain some more fine or costly article of dress or furniture.

We have nothing to say against those whom *necessity* compels to do these things, those who can do no better; we have only to do with those who can, and will not, or do not do better. The whites are always in the advance, and we either standing still or retrograding; as that which does not go forward, must either stand in one place or go back. The father in all probability is a farmer, mechanic, or man of some independent business; and the wife, sons and daughters, are chamber-maids, on vessels, nurses and waiting-maids, or coachmen and cooks in families. This is retrogradation. The wife, sons, and daughters should be elevated above this condition as a necessary consequence.

If we did not love our race superior to others, we would not concern ourself about their degradation; for the greatest desire of our heart is, to see them stand on a level with the most elevated of mankind. No people are ever elevated above the condition of their *females;* hence, the condition of the *mother* determines the condition of the child. To know the position of a people, it is only necessary to know the *condition* of their *females;* and despite themselves, they cannot rise above their level. Then what is our condition? Our *best ladies* being washerwomen, chambermaids, children's traveling nurses, and common house servants, and menials, we are all a degraded, miserable people, inferior to any other people as a whole, on the face of the globe.

These great truths, however unpleasant, must be brought before the minds of our people in its true and proper light, as we have been too delicate about them, and too long concealed them for fear of giving offence. It would have been infinitely better for our race, if these facts had been presented before us half a century ago—we would have been now proportionably benefitted by it.

As an evidence of the degradation to which we have been reduced, we dare premise, that this chapter will give offence to many, very many, and why? Because they may say, "He dared to say that the occupation of a *servant* is a degradation." It is not necessarily degrading; it would not be, to one or a few people of a kind; but a *whole race of servants* are a degradation to that people.

Efforts made by men of qualifications for the toiling and degraded millions among the whites, neither gives offence to that class, nor is it taken unkindly by them; but received with manifestations of gratitude; to know that they are thought to be, equally worthy of, and entitled to stand on a level with the elevated classes; and they have only got to be informed of the way to raise themselves, to make the effort and do so as far as they can. But how different with us. Speak of our position in society, and it at once gives insult. Though we are servants; among ourselves we claim to be *ladies* and *gentlemen,* equal in standing, and as the popular expression goes, "Just as good as any body"—and so believing, we make no efforts to raise above the common level of menials; because the *best* being in that capacity, all are content with the position. We cannot at the same time, be domestic and lady; servant and gentleman. We must be the one or the other. Sad, sad indeed, is the thought, that hangs drooping in our mind, when contemplating the picture drawn before us. Young men and women, "we write these things unto you, because ye are strong," because the writer, a few years ago, gave unpardonable offence to many of the young people of Philadelphia and other places, because he dared tell them, that he thought too much of them, to be content with seeing them the servants of other people. Surely, she that could be the mistress, would not be the maid; neither would he that could be the master, be content with being the servant; then why be offended, when we point out to you, the way that leads from the menial to the mistress or the master. All this we seem to reject with fixed determination, repelling with anger, every effort on the part of our intelligent men and women to elevate us, with true Israelitish degradation, in reply to any suggestion or proposition that may be offered, "Who made thee a ruler and judge?"

The writer is no "Public Man," in the sense in which this is understood among our people, but simply an humble individual, endeavoring to seek a livelihood by a profession obtained entirely by his own efforts, without relatives and friends able to assist him; except such friends as he gained by the merit of his course and conduct, which he here gratefully acknowledges; and whatever he has accomplished, other young men may, by making corresponding efforts, also accomplish.

We have advised an emigration to Central and South America, and even to Mexico and the West Indies, to those who prefer either of the last named places, all of which are free countries, Brazil being the only real slave-holding State in South America—there being nominal slavery in Dutch Guiana, Peru, Buenos Ayres, Paraguay, and Uraguay, in all of which places colored people have equality in social, civil, political, and religious privileges; Brazil making it punishable with death to import slaves into the empire.

Our oppressors, when urging us to go to Africa, tell us that we are better adapted to the climate than they—that the physical condition of the constitution of colored people better endures the heat of warm climates than that of the whites; this we are willing to *admit,* without argument, without adducing the physiological reason why, that colored people can and do stand warm climates better than whites; and find an answer fully to the point in the fact, that they also stand *all other* climates, cold, temperate, and modified, that white people can stand; therefore, according to our oppressors' own showing, we are a *superior race,* being endowed with properties fitting us for *all parts* of the earth, while they are only adapted to *certain* parts. Of course, this proves our right and duty to live wherever we may *choose;* while the white race may only live where they *can.* We are content with the fact, and have ever claimed it. Upon this rock, they and we shall ever agree.

Of the West India Islands, Santa Cruz, belonging to Denmark; Porto Rico, and Cuba with its little adjuncts, belonging to Spain, are the only slave-holding Islands among them—three-fifths of the whole population of Cuba being colored people, who cannot and will not much longer endure the burden and the yoke. They only want intelligent leaders of their own color, when they are ready at any moment to charge to the conflict—to liberty or death. The remembrance of the noble mulatto, PLACIDO, the gentleman, scholar, poet, and intended Chief Engineer of the Army of Liberty and Freedom in Cuba; and the equally noble black, CHARLES BLAIR, who was to have been Commander-in-Chief, who were shamefully put to death in 1844, by that living monster, Captain General O'Donnell, is still fresh and indelible to the mind of every bondman of Cuba.

In our own country, the United States, there are *three million five hundred thousand slaves;* and we, the nominally free colored people, are *six hundred thousand* in number; estimating one-sixth to be men, we have *one hundred thousand* able bodied freemen, which will make a powerful auxiliary in any country to which we may become adopted—an ally not to be despised by any power on earth. We love our country, dearly love her, but she doesn't love us—she despises us, and bids us begone, driving us from her embraces; but we shall not go where she desires us; but when we do go, whatever love we have for her, we shall love the country none the less that receives us as her adopted children.

For the want of business habits and training, our energies have become paralyzed; our young men never think of business, any more than if they were so many bondmen, without the right to pursue any calling they may think most advisable. With our people in this country, dress and good appearances have been made the only test of gentleman and ladyship, and that vocation which offers the best opportunity to dress and appear well, has generally been preferred, however menial and degrading, by our young people, without even, in the majority of cases, an effort to do better; indeed, in many instances, refusing situations equally lucrative, and superior in position; but which would not allow as much display of dress and personal appearance. This, if we ever expect to rise, must be discarded from among us, and a high and respectable position assumed.

One of our great temporal curses is our consummate poverty. We are the poorest people, as a class, in the world of civilized mankind—abjectly, miserably poor, no one scarcely being able to assist the other. To this, of course, there are noble exceptions; but that which is common to, and the very process by which white men exist, and succeed in life, is unknown to colored men in general. In any and every considerable community may be found, some one of our white fellow-citizens, who is worth more than all the colored people in that community put together. We consequently have little or no efficiency. We must have means to be practically efficient in all the undertakings of life; and to obtain them, it is necessary that we should be engaged in lucrative pursuits, trades, and general business transactions. In order to be thus engaged, it is necessary that we should occupy positions that afford the facilities for such pursuits. To compete now with the mighty odds of wealth, social and religious preferences, and political influences of this country, at this advanced stage of its national existence, we never may expect. A new country, and new beginning, is the only true, rational, politic remedy for our disadvantageous position; and that country we have already pointed out, with triple golden advantages, all things considered, to that of any country to which it has been the province of man to embark.

Every other than we, have at various periods of necessity, been a migratory people; and all when oppressed, shown a greater abhorrence of oppression, if not a greater love of liberty, than we. We cling to our oppressors as the objects of our love. It is true that our enslaved brethren are here, and we have been led to believe that it is necessary for us to remain, on that account. Is it true, that all should remain in degradation, because a part are degraded? We believe no such thing. We believe it to be the duty of the Free, to elevate themselves in the most speedy and effective manner possible; as the redemption of the bondman depends entirely upon the elevation of the freeman; therefore, to elevate the free colored people of America, anywhere upon this continent; forebodes the speedy redemption of the slaves. We shall hope to hear no more of so fallacious a doctrine— the necessity of the free remaining in degradation, for the sake of the oppressed. Let us apply, first, the lever to ourselves; and the force that elevates us to the position of manhood's considerations and honors, will cleft the manacle of every slave in the land.

When such great worth and talents—for want of a better sphere—of men like Rev. Jonathan Robinson, Robert Douglass, Frederick A. Hinton, and a hundred others that might be named, were permitted to expire in a barber-shop; and such living men as may be found in Boston, New York, Philadelphia, Baltimore, Richmond, Washington City, Charleston, (S.C.) New Orleans, Cincinnati, Louisville, St. Louis, Pittsburg, Buffalo, Rochester, Albany, Utica, Cleveland, Detroit, Milwaukee, Chicago, Columbus, Zanesville, Wheeling, and a hundred other places, confining themselves to barber-shops and waiterships in Hotels; certainly the necessity of such a course as we have pointed out, must be cordially acknowledged; appreciated by every brother and sister of oppression; and not rejected as heretofore, as though they preferred inferiority to equality. These minds must become "unfettered," and have "space to rise." This cannot be in their present positions. A continuance in any position, becomes what is termed "Second Nature"; it begets an *adaptation,* and *reconciliation* of *mind* to such condition. It changes the whole physiological condition of the system, and adapts man and woman to a higher or lower sphere in the pursuits of life. The offsprings of slaves and peasantry, have the general characteristics of their parents; and nothing but a different course of training and education, will change the character.

The slave may become a lover of his master, and learn to forgive him for continual deeds of maltreatment and abuse; just as the Spaniel would couch and fondle at the feet that kick him; because he has been taught to reverence them, and consequntly, becomes adapted in body and mind to his condition. Even the shrubbery-loving Canary, and lofty-soaring Eagle, may be tamed to the cage, and learn to love it from habit of confinement. It has been so with us in our position among our oppressors; we have been so prone to such positions, that we have learned to love them. When reflecting upon this all important, and to us, all absorbing subject; we feel in the agony and anxiety of the moment, as though we could cry out in the language of a Prophet of old: "Oh that my head were waters, and mine eyes a fountain of tears, that I might weep day and night for the" degradation "of my people! Oh that I had in the wilderness a lodging place of wayfaring men; that I might leave my people, and go from them!"

The Irishman and German in the United States, are very different persons to what they were when in Ireland and Germany, the countries of their nativity. There their spirits were depressed and downcast; but the instant they set their foot upon unrestricted soil; free to act and untrammelled to move; their physical condition undergoes a change, which in time becomes physiological, which is transmitted to the offspring, who when born under such circumstances, is a decidedly different being to what it would have been, had it been born under different circumstances.

A child born under oppression, has all the elements of servility in its constitution; who when born under favorable circumstances, has to the contrary, all the elements of freedom and independence of feeling. Our children then, may not be expected, to maintain that position and manly bearing; born under the unfavorable circumstances with which we are surrounded in this country; that we so much desire. To use the language of the talented Mr. Whipper, "they cannot be raised in this country, without being stoop shouldered." Heaven's pathway stands unobstructed, which will lead us into a Paradise of bliss. Let us go on and possess the land, and the God of Israel will be our God.

The lessons of every school book, the pages of every history, and columns of every newspaper, are so replete with stimuli to nerve us on to manly aspirations, that those of our young people, who will now refuse to enter upon this great theatre of Polynesian adventure, and take their position on the stage of Central and South America, where a brilliant engagement, of certain and most triumphant success, in the drama of human equality awaits them; then, with the blood of *slaves,* write upon the lintel of every door in sterling Capitals, to be gazed and hissed at by every passer by—

> Doomed by the Creator
> To servility and degradation;
> The SERVANT of the *white man,*
> And despised of every nation!

APPENDIX. A PROJECT FOR AN EXPEDITION OF ADVENTURE TO THE EASTERN COAST OF AFRICA

Every people should be the originators of their own designs, the projector of their own schemes, and creators of the events that lead to their destiny—the consummation of their desires.

Situated as we are, in the United States, many, and almost insurmountable obstacles present themselves. We are four-and-a-half millions in numbers, free and bond; six hundred thousand free, and three-and-a-half millions bond.

We have native hearts and virtues, just as other nations; which in their pristine purity are noble, potent, and worthy of example. We are a nation within a nation;—as the Poles in Russia, the Hungarians in Austria, the Welsh, Irish, and Scotch in the British dominions.

But we have been, by our oppressors, despoiled of our purity, and corrupted in our native characteristics, so that we have inherited their vices, and but few of their virtues, leaving us in character, really a *broken people*.

Being distinguished by complexion, we are still singled out—although having merged in the habits and customs of our oppressors—as a distinct nation of people; as the Poles, Hungarians, Irish, and others, who still retain their native peculiarities, of language, habits, and various other traits. The claims of no people, according to established policy and usage, are respected by any nation, until they are presented in a national capacity.

To accomplish so great and desirable an end, there should be held, a great representative gathering of the colored people of the United States; not what is termed a National Convention, represented en masse, such as have been, for the last few years, held at various times and places; but a true representation of the intelligence and wisdom of the colored freemen; because it will be futile and an utter failure, to attempt such a project without the highest grade of intelligence.

No great project was ever devised without the consultation of the most mature intelligence, and discreet discernment and precaution.

To effect this, and prevent intrusion and improper representation, there should be a CONFIDENTIAL COUNCIL held; and circulars issued, only to such persons as shall be *known* to the projectors to be equal to the desired object.

The authority from whence the call should originate, to be in this wise: —The originator of the scheme, to impart the contemplated Confidential Council, to a limited number of known, worthy gentlemen, who agreeing with the project, endorse at once the scheme, when becoming joint proprietors in interest, issue a *Confidential Circular,* leaving blanks for *date, time,* and *place* of *holding* the Council; sending them to trusty, worthy, and suitable colored freemen, in all parts of the United States, and the Canadas, inviting them to attend; who when met in Council, have the right to project any scheme they may think proper for the general good of the whole people—provided, that the project is laid before them after its maturity.

By this Council to be appointed, a Board of Commissioners, to consist of three, five, or such reasonable number as may be decided upon, one of whom shall be chosen as Principal or Conductor of the Board, whose duty and business shall be, to go on an expedition to the EASTERN COAST OF AFRICA, to make researches for a suitable location on that section of the coast, for the settlement of colored adventurers from the United States, and elsewhere. Their mission should be to all such places as might meet the approbation of the people; as South America, Mexico, the West Indies, &c.

The Commissioners all to be men of decided qualifications; to embody among them, the qualifications of physician, botanist, chemist, geologist, geographer, and surveyor,—having a sufficient knowledge of these sciences, for practical purposes.

Their business shall be, to make a topographical, geographical, geological, and botanical examination, into such part or parts as they may select, with all other useful information that may be obtained; to be recorded in a journal kept for that purpose.

The Council shall appoint a permanent Board of Directors, to manage and supervise the doings of the Commissioners, and to whom they shall be amenable for their doings, who shall hold their office until successors shall be appointed.

A National Confidential Council, to be held once in three years; and sooner, if necessity or emergency should demand it; the Board of Directors giving at least three months' notice, by circulars and newspapers. And should they fail to perform their duty, twenty-five of the representatives from any six States, of the former Council, may issue a call, authentically bearing their names, as sufficient authority for such a call. But when the Council is held for the reception of the report of the Commissioners, a general mass convention should then take place, by popular representation.

Manner of Raising Funds

The National Council shall appoint one or two Special Commissioners, to England and France, to solicit, in the name of the Representatives of a Broken Nation, of four-and-a-half millions, the necessary outfit and support, for any period not exceeding three years, of such an expedition. Certainly, what England and France would do, for a little nation—mere nominal nation, of five thousand civilized Liberians, they would be willing and ready to do, for five millions; if they be but authentically represented, in a national capacity. What was due to Greece, enveloped by Turkey, should be due to US, enveloped by the United States; and we believe would be respected, if properly presented. To England and France, we should look for sustenance, and the people of those two nations—as they would have every thing to gain from such an adventure and eventual settlement on the EASTERN COAST OF AFRICA—the opening of an immense trade being the consequence. The whole Continent is rich in minerals, and the most precious metals, as but a superficial notice of the topographical and geological reports from that country, plainly show to any mind versed in the least, in the science of the earth.

The Eastern Coast of Africa has long been neglected, and never but little known, even to the ancients; but has ever been our choice part of the Continent. Bounded by the Red Sea, Arabian Sea, and Indian Ocean, it presents the greatest facilities for an immense trade, with China, Japan,

Siam, Hindoostan, in short, all the East Indies—of any other country in the world. With a settlement of enlightened freemen, who with the immense facilities, must soon grow into a powerful nation. In the Province of Berbera, south of the Strait of Babelmandel, or the great pass, from the Arabian to the Red Sea, the whole commerce of the East must touch this point.

Also, a great rail road could be constructed from here, running with the Mountains of the Moon, clearing them entirely, except making one mountain pass, at the western extremity of the Mountains of the Moon, and the southeastern terminus of the Kong Mountains; entering the Province of Dahomey, and terminating on the Atlantic Ocean West; which would make the GREAT THOROUGHFARE for all the trade with the East Indies and Eastern Coast of Africa, and the Continent of America. All the world would pass through Africa upon this rail road, which would yield a revenue infinitely greater than any other investment in the world.

The means for prosecuting such a project—as stupendous as it may appear—will be fully realised in the prosecution of the work. Every mile of the road, will thrice pay for itself, in the development of the rich treasures that now lie hidden in the bowels of the earth. There is no doubt, that in some one section of twenty-five miles, the developments of gold would more than pay the expenses of any one thousand miles of the work. This calculation may, to those who have never given this subject a thought, appear extravagant, and visionary; but to one who has had his attention in this direction for years, it is clear enough. But a few years will witness a development of gold, precious metals, and minerals in Eastern Africa, the Moon and Kong Mountains, ten-fold greater than all the rich productions of California.

There is one great physiological fact in regard to the colored race—which, while it may not apply to all colored persons, is true of those having black skins—that they can bear *more different* climates than the white race. They bear *all* the temperates and extremes, while the other can only bear the temperates and *one* of the extremes. The black race is endowed with natural properties, that adapt and fit them for temperate, cold, and hot climates; while the white race is only endowed with properties that adapt them to temperate and cold climates; being unable to stand the warmer climates; in them, the white race cannot work, but become perfectly indolent, requiring somebody to work for them—and these, are always people of the black race.

The black race may be found, inhabiting in healthful improvement, every part of the globe where the white race reside; while there are parts of the globe where the black race reside, that the white race cannot live in health.

What part of mankind is the "denizen of every soil, and the lord of terrestrial creation," if it be not the black race? The Creator has indisputably adapted us for the "denizens of *every soil*," all that is left for us to do, is to *make* ourselves the *"lords* of terrestrial creation." The land is ours—there it lies with inexhaustible resources; let us go and possess it. In Eastern Africa must rise up a nation, to whom all the world must pay commercial tribute.

We must MAKE an ISSUE, CREATE an EVENT, and ESTABLISH a NATIONAL POSITION for OURSELVES; and never may expect to be respected as men and women, until we have undertaken, some fearless, bold, and adventurous deeds of daring—contending against every odds—regardless of every consequence.

OFFICIAL REPORT OF THE NIGER VALLEY EXPLORING PARTY

WHAT AFRICA NOW REQUIRES

From the foregoing, it is very evident that missionary duty has reached its *ultimatum.* By this, I mean that the native has received all that the missionary was sent to teach, and is now really ready for more than he can or may receive. He sees and knows that the white man, who first carried him the Gospel, which he has learned to a great extent to believe a reality, is of an entirely different race to himself; and has learned to look upon everything which he has, knows and does, which has not yet been imparted to him (especially when he is told by the missionaries, which frequently must be the case, to relieve themselves of the endless teasing enquiries which persons in their position are subject to concerning all and every temporal and secular matter, law, government, commerce, military, and other matters foreign to the teachings of the gospel; that these things he is not sent to teach, but simply the gospel) as peculiarly adapted and belonging to the white man. Of course, there are exceptions to this. Hence, having reached what he conceives to be the *maximum* of the black man's or African's attainments, there must be a re-action in some direction, and if not progressive it will be retrogressive.

The missionary has informed him that the white man's country is great. He builds and resides in great houses; lives in great towns and cities, with great churches and palaver-houses (public and legislative halls); rides in great carriages; manufactures great and beautiful things; has great ships, which go to sea, to all parts of the world, instead of little canoes such as he has paddling up and down the rivers and on the coast; that the wisdom, power, strength, courage, and wealth of the white man and his country are as much greater than him and his, as the big ships are larger and stronger than the little frail canoes; all of which he is made sensible of, either by the exhibition of pictures or the reality.

He at once comes to a stand. "Of what use is the white man's religion and 'book knowledge' to me, since it does not give me the knowledge and wisdom nor the wealth and power of the white man, as all these things belong only to him? Our young men and women learn their book, and talk on paper (write), and talk to God like white man (worship), but God no hear 'em like He hear white man! Dis religion no use to black man." And so the African *reasonably* reasons when he sees that despite his having yielded up old-established customs, the laws of his fathers, and almost his entire social authority, and the rule of his household to the care and guardianship of the missionary, for the sake of acquiring his knowledge and power—when, after having learned all that his children can, he is doomed to see them sink right back into their old habits, the country continue in the same condition, without the beautiful improvements of the white man—and if a change take place at all, he is doomed to witness what he never expected to see and dies regretting—himself and people entangled in the meshes of the government of a people foreign in kith, kin, and sympathy, when he and his are entirely shoved aside and compelled to take subordinate and inferior positions, if not, indeed, reduced to menialism and bondage. I am justified in asserting that this state of things has brought missionary efforts to their *maximum* and native progress to a pause.

Religion has done its work, and now requires temporal and secular aid to give it another impulse. The improved arts of civilized life must now be brought to bear, and go hand in hand in aid of the missionary efforts which are purely religious in character and teaching. I would not have the standard of religion lowered a single stratum of the common breeze of heaven. No, let it rather be raised, if, indeed, higher it can be. Christianity certainly is the most advanced civilization that man ever attained to, and wherever propagated in its purity, to be effective, law and government must be brought in harmony with it—otherwise it becomes corrupted, and a corresponding degeneracy ensues, placing its votaries even in a worse condition than the primitive. This was exemplified by the Author of our faith, who, so soon as he began to teach, commenced by admonishing the people to a modification of their laws—or rather himself to condemn them. But it is very evident that the social must keep pace with the religious, and the political with the social relations of society, to carry out the great measures of the higher civilization.

Of what avail, then, is advanced intelligence to the African without improved social relations—acquirements and refinement without an opportunity of a practical application of them—society in which they are appreciated? It requires not the most astute reformer and political philosopher to see.

The native sees at once that all the higher social relations are the legitimate result and requirements of a higher intelligence, and naturally enough expects, that when he has attained it, to enjoy the same privileges and blessings. But how sadly mistaken—what dire disappointment!

The habits, manners, and customs of his people, and the social relations all around him are the same; improvements of towns, cities, roads, and methods of travel are the same; implements of husbandry and industry are the same; the methods of conveyance and price of produce (with comparative trifling variation) are the same. All seem dark and gloomy for the future, and he has his doubts and fears as to whether or not he has committed a fatal error in leaving his native social relations for those of foreigners whom he cannot hope to emulate, and who, he thinks, will not assimilate themselves to him.

It is clear, then, that essential to the success of civilization, is the establishment of all those social relations and organizations, without which enlightened communities cannot exist. To be successful, these must be carried out by proper agencies, and these agencies must be a *new element* introduced into their midst, possessing all the attainments, socially and politically, morally and religiously, adequate to so important an end. This element must be *homogenous* in all the *natural* characteristics, claims, sentiments, and sympathies—the *descendants of Africa* being the only element that can effect it. To this end, then, a part of the most enlightened of that race in America design to carry out these most desirable measures by the establishment of social and industrial settlements among them, in order at once to introduce, in an effective manner, all the well-regulated pursuits of civilized life.

That no mis-step be taken and fatal error committed at the commencement, we have determined that the persons to compose this new element to be introduced into Africa, shall be well and most carefully selected in regard to moral integrity, intelligence, acquired attainments, fitness, adaptation, and, as far as practicable, religious sentiments and professions. We are serious in this; and, so far as we are concerned as an individual, it shall be restricted to the letter, and we will most strenuously oppose and set our face against any attempt from any quarter to infringe upon this arrangement and design. Africa is our fatherland and we its legitimate descendants, and we will never agree nor consent to see this—the first voluntary step that has ever been taken for her regeneration by her own descendants—blasted by a disinterested or renegade set, whose only object might be in the one case to get rid of a portion of the colored population, and in the other, make money, though it be done upon the destruction of every hope entertained and measure introduced for the accomplishment of this great and prospectively glorious undertaking. We cannot and will not permit or agree that the result of years of labor and anxiety shall be blasted at one reckless blow, by those who have never spent a day in the cause of our race, or know nothing about our wants and requirements. The descendants of Africa in North America will doubtless, by the census of 1860, reach five millions; those of Africa may number two hundred millions. I have outgrown, long since, the boundaries of North America, and with them have also outgrown the boundaries of their claims. I, therefore, cannot consent to sacrifice the prospects of two hundred millions, that a fraction of five millions may be benefitted, especially since the measures adopted for the many must necessarily benefit the few.

Africa, to become regenerated, must have a national character, and her position among the existing nations of the earth will depend mainly upon the high standard she may gain compared with them in all her relations, morally, religiously, socially, politically, and commercially.

I have determined to leave to my children the inheritance of a country, the possession of territorial domain, the blessings of a national education, and the indisputable right of self-government; that they may not succeed to the servility and degradation bequeathed to us by our fathers. If we have not been born to fortunes, we should impart the seeds which shall germinate and give birth to fortunes for them.

TO DIRECT LEGITIMATE COMMERCE

As the first great national step in political economy, the selection and security of a location to direct and command commerce legitimately carried on, as an export and import metropolis, is essentially necessary. The facilities for a metropolis should be adequate—a rich, fertile, and productive country surrounding it, with some great staple (which the world requires as a commodity) of exportation. A convenient harbor as an outlet and inlet, and natural facilities for improvement, are among the necessary requirements for such a location.

The basis of great nationality depends upon three elementary principles: first, territory; second, population; third, a great staple production either natural or artificial, or both, as a permanent source of wealth; and Africa comprises these to an almost unlimited extent. The continent is five thousand miles from Cape Bon (north) to the Cape of Good Hope (south), and four thousand at its greatest breadth, from Cape Guardifui (east) to Cape de Verde (west), with an average breadth of two thousand five hundred miles, any three thousand of which within the tropics north and south, including the entire longitude, will produce the staple cotton, also sugar cane, coffee, rice, and all the tropical staples, with two hundred millions of *natives* as an industrial element to work this immense domain. The world is challenged to produce the semblance of a parallel to this. It has no rival in fact.

Lagos, at the mouth of the Ogun river in the Bight of Benin, Gulf of Guinea, 6 deg. 31 min. west coast of Africa, 120 miles north-west of the

Nun (one of the mouths of the great river Niger) is the place of our location. This was once the greatest slave-trading post on the west coast of Africa, and in possession of the Portuguese—the slavers entering Ako Bay, at the mouth of the Ogun river, lying quite inland, covered behind the island till a favorable opportunity ensued to escape with their cargoes of human beings for America. Wydah, the great slave-port of Dahomi, is but 70 or 80 miles west of Lagos. This city is most favorably located at the mouth of a river which during eight months in the year is a great thoroughfare for native produce, which is now brought down and carried up by native canoes and boats, and quite navigable up to Aro the port of Abbeokuta, a distance of eighty or a hundred miles, for light-draught steamers, such as at no distant day we shall have there. Ako Bay is an arm of the gulf, extending quite inland for three and a half miles, where it spreads out into a great sea, extending north ten or fifteen miles, taking a curve east and south, passing on in a narrow strip for two or three hundred miles, till it joins the Niger at the mouth of the Nun. It is the real harbor of Lagos, and navigable for light-draught vessels, as the Baltimore clippers and all other such slavers, formerly put into it; and Her Majesty's war-steamer Medusa has been in, and H. M.'s cruiser Brun lies continually in the bay opposite the Consulate.

This is the great outlet of the rich valley of the Niger by land, and the only point of the ocean upon which the intelligent and advanced Yorubas are settled. The commerce of this part is very great, being now estimated at ten million pounds sterling. Besides all the rich products, as enumerated in another section, palm oil* and ivory are among the great staple products of this rich country. But as every nation, to be potent must have some great source of wealth—which if not natural must be artificial—so Africa has that without which the workshops of Great Britain would become deserted, and the general commerce of the world materially reduced; and Lagos must not only become the outlet and point at which all this commodity must centre, but the great metropolis of this quarter of the world.

The trade of this port now amounts to more than two millions of pounds sterling, or ten millions of dollars, there having been at times as many as sixty vessels in the roadstead.

The merchants and business men of Lagos are principally native black gentlemen, there being but ten white houses in the place—English, German, French, Portuguese, and Sardinian—and all of the clerks are native blacks.

Buoys in the roadstead, lighthouses (two) and wharf improvements at the city in the bay, with steam-tugs or tenders to tow vessels over the Ogun bar-mouth or inlet, are all that we require to make Lagos a desirable

---

* Nine-tenths of all the Palm Oil of commerce goes from this point.

seaport, with one of the safest harbors in the world for light-draught vessels.

The fish in these waters are very fine, and Ako is one of the finest natural oyster bays in the world. The shell-fish are generally of good size, frequently large, and finely flavored.

As a religious means, such a position must most largely contribute, by not only giving security to the Missionary cause, but by the actual infusion of a religious social element permanently among the natives of the country; and as a philanthropic, by a permanent check to the slave-trade, and also by its reflex influence on American slavery—not only thus far cutting off the supply, but also by superseding slavery in the growth and supply of those articles which comprise its great staple and source of wealth— thereby rendering slave labor *unprofitable and worthless,* as the succeeding section will show.

As to the possibility of putting a stop to the slave-trade, I have only to say that we do not leave America and go to Africa to be passive spectators of such a policy as traffic in the flesh and blood of our kindred, nor any other species of the human race—more we might say—that we will not live there and permit it. "Self-preservation is the first law of nature," and we go to Africa to be *self-sustaining;* otherwise we have no business there, or anywhere else, in my opinion. We will bide our time; *but the Slave-trade shall not continue!*

Another important point of attention: that is, the slave-trade ceases in Africa, wherever enlightened Christian civilization gains an influence. And as to the strength and power necessary, we have only to add, that Liberia, with a coast frontier of seven hundred miles, and a sparse population, which at the present only numbers fifteen thousand settlers, has been effective in putting a stop to that infamous traffic along her entire coast. And I here record with pleasure, and state what I know to be the fact, and but simple justice to as noble-hearted antagonists to slavery as live, that the Liberians are uncompromising in their opposition to oppression and the enslavement of their race, or any other part of the human family. I speak of them as a nation or people and ignore entirely their Iscariots, if any there be. What they have accomplished with less means, we, by the help of Providence, may reasonably expect to effect with more—what they did with little, we may do with much. And I speak with confidence when I assert, that if we in this new position but do and act as we are fondly looked to and expected—as I most fondly hope and pray God that, by a prudent, discretionate and well-directed course, dependant upon Him, we may, nay, I am certain we will do—I am sure that there is nothing that may be required to aid in the prosecution and accomplishment of this important and long-desired end, that may not be obtained from the greatest and most potent Christian people and nation that ever graced the world. There is no aid that might be wanted, which may not be obtained through a responsible, just, and equitable negotiation.

There is some talk by Christians and philanthropists in Great Britain of subsidizing the King of Dahomi. I hope for the sake of humanity, our race, and the cause of progressive civilization, this most injurious measure of compensation for wrong, never will be resorted to nor attempted.

To make such an offering just at a time when we are about to establish a policy of self-regeneration in Africa, which may, by example and precept, effectually check forever the nefarious system, and reform the character of these people, would be to offer inducements to that monster to continue, and a license to other petty chiefs to commence the traffic in human beings, to get a reward of subsidy.

COTTON STAPLE

Cotton grows profusely in all this part of Africa, and is not only produced naturally, but extensively cultivated throughout the Yoruba country. The soil, climate, and the people are the three natural elements combined to produce this indispensible commodity, and with these three natural agencies, no other part of the world can compete.

In India there is a difficulty and great expense and outlay of capital required to obtain it. In Australia it is an experiment; and though it may eventually be obtained, it must also involve an immense outlay of capital, and a long time before an adequate supply can be had, as it must be admitted, however reluctantly by those desirous it should be otherwise, that the African, as has been justly said by a Manchester merchant, has in all ages, in all parts of the world, been sought to raise cotton wherever it has been produced.

In America there are several serious contingencies which must always render a supply of cotton from that quarter problematical and doubtful, and always expensive and subject to sudden, unexpected and unjust advances in prices. In the first place, the land is purchased at large prices; secondly, the people to work it; thirdly, the expense of supporting the people, with the contingencies of sickness and death; fourthly, the uncertainty of climate and contingencies of frost, and a backward season and consequent late or unmatured crop; fifthly, insubordination on the part of the slaves, which is not improbable at any time; sixthly, suspension of friendly relations between the United States and Great Britain; and lastly, a rupture between the American States themselves, which I think no one will be disposed now to consider impossible. All, or any of these circumstances combined, render it impossible for America to compete with Africa in the growth and sale of cotton, for the following reasons:

Firstly, landed tenure in Africa is free, the occupant selecting as much as he can cultivate, holding it so long as he uses it, but cannot convey it to another; secondly, the people all being free, can be hired at a price less than the *interest* of the capital invested in land and people to work it— they finding their own food, which is the custom of the country; thirdly, there are no contingencies of frost or irregular weather to mar or blight the crop; and fourthly, we have two regular crops a year, or rather one continuous crop, as while the trees are full of pods of ripe cotton, they are at the same time blooming with fresh flowers. And African cotton is planted only every seven years, whilst the American is replanted every season. Lastly, the average product per acre on the best Mississippi and Louisiana cotton plantations in America, is three hundred and fifty pounds; the average per acre in Africa, a hundred per cent. more, or seven hundred pounds. As the African soil produces two crops a year to one in America, then we in Africa produce fourteen hundred pounds to three hundred and fifty in America; the cost of labor a hand being one dollar or four shillings a day to produce it; whilst in Africa at present it is nine hundred per cent. less, being only ten cents or five pence a day for adult labor. At this price the native lives better on the abundance of produce in the country, and has more money left at the end of a week than the European or free American laborer at one dollar a day.

Cotton, as before stated, is the great commodity of the world, entering intimately into, being corporated with almost every kind of fabric of wearing apparel. All kinds of woollen goods—cloths, flannels, alpacas, merinoes, and even silks, linen, nankin, ginghams, calicoes, muslins, cordages, ship sails, carpeting, hats, hose, gloves, threads, waddings, paddings, tickings, every description of book and newspaper, writing paper, candle wicks, and what not, all depend upon the article cotton.

By this it will be seen and admitted that the African occupies a much more important place in the social and political element of the world than that which has heretofore been assigned him—holding the balance of commercial power, the source of the wealth of nations in his hands. This is indisputably true—undeniable, that cotton cannot be produced without Negro labor and skill in raising it.

Great Britain alone has directly engaged in the manufacture of pure fabrics from the raw material, five millions of persons; two-thirds more of the population depend upon this commodity indirectly for a livelihood. The population (I include in this calculation Ireland) being estimated at 30,000,000, we have then 25,000,000 of people, or five-sixths of the population of this great nation, depending upon the article cotton alone for subsistence, and the black man is the producer of the raw material, and the source from whence it comes. What an important fact to impart to the heretofore despised and under-rated Negro race, to say nothing of all the other great nations of Europe, as France, for instance, with her extensive manufactures of muslin delaines—which simply mean *cotton and wool*—more or less engaged in the manufacture and consumption of cotton.

If the Negro race—as slaves—can produce cotton as an *exotic* in foreign climes to enrich white men who oppress them, they can, they must, they will, they shall, produce it as an *indigene* in their own-loved native

Africa to enrich themselves, and regenerate their race; if a faithful reliance upon the beneficence and promise of God, and an humble submission to his will, as the feeble instruments in his hands through which the work is commenced, shall be available to this end.

The Liberians must as a policy as much as possible, patronise home manufactured, and home produced articles. Instead of using foreign, they should prefer their own sugar, molasses, and coffee, which is equal to that produced in any other country; and if not, it is the only way to encourage the farmers and maufacturers to improve them. The coffee of Liberia, is equal to any in the world, and I have drunk some of the native article, superior in strength and flavor to Java or Mocca, and I rather solicit competition in judgment of the article of coffee. And singular as it may appear, they are even supplied from abroad with spices and condiments, although their own country as also all Africa, is prolific in the production of all other articles, as allspice, ginger, pepper black and red, mustard and everything else.

They must also turn their attention to supplying the Coast settlements with sugar and molasses, and everything else of their own production which may be in demand. Lagos and the Missionary stations in the interior, now consume much of these articles, the greater part of which— sugar and molasses—are imported from England and America. This trade they might secure in a short time without successful competition, because many of the Liberia merchants now own vessels, and the firm of Johnson, Turpin and Dunbar, own a fine little coasting steamer, and soon they would be able to undersell the foreigners; whilst at present their trade of these articles in America is a mere *favor* through the benevolence of some good hearted gentlemen, personal *friends* of theirs, who receive and dispose of them—sugar and molasses—at a price much above the market value, to encourage them. This can only last while these friends continue, when it must then cease. To succeed as a state or nation, we must become self-reliant, and thereby able to create our own ways and means; and a trade created *in* Africa *by* civilized Africans, would be a national rock of "everlasting ages."

The domestic trade among the natives in the interior of our part of Africa—Yoruba—is very great. Corn meal, Guinea corn flour very fine, and a fine flour made of yams is plentiful in every market, and cooked food can always be had in great abundance from the women at refreshment stands kept in every town and along the highway every few miles when traveling.

Molasses candy or "taffy," is carried about and sold by young girls, made from the syrup of sugar cane, which does not differ in appearance and flavor from that of civilized countries.

Hard and soft soap are for sale in every market for domestic uses, made from lye by percolation or dripping of water through ashes in large earthern vessels or "hoppers."

Coloring and dying is carried on very generally, every woman seeming to understand it as almost a domestic necessity; also the manufacturing of indigo, the favorite and most common color of the country. Red comes next to this which is mostly obtained of camwood, another domestic employment of the women. Yellow is the next favorite color. Hence, blue, red, and yellow may be designated as the colors of Yoruba or Central Africa.

The manufactory of cotton cloth is carried on quite extensively among them; and in a ride of an hour through the city of Illorin, we counted one hundred and fifty-seven looms in operation in several different establishments. Beautiful and excellent leather is also manufactured, from which is made sandals, shoes, boots, bridles, saddles, harness-caparisons for horses, and other ornaments and uses. They all wear clothes of their own manufacture. The inhabitants of Abbeokuta are called Egbas, and those of all the other parts of Yoruba are called Yorubas—all speaking the Egba language.

Our policy must be—and I hazard nothing in promulging it; nay, without this design and feeling, there would be a great deficiency of self-respect, pride of race, and love of country, and we might never expect to challenge the respect of nations—*Africa for the African race, and black men to rule them.* By black men I mean, men of African descent who claim an identity with the race.

So contrary to old geographical notions, Africa abounds with handsome navigable rivers, which during six or eight months in the year, would carry steamers suitably built. Of such are the Gallinos, St. Paul, Junk, and Kavalla of Liberia; the Ogun, Ossa, the great Niger and others of and contiguous to Yoruba; the Gambia, Senegambia, Orange, Zambesi and others of other parts. The Kavalla is a beautiful stream which for one hundred miles is scarcely inferior to the Hudson of New York, in any particular; and all of them equal the rivers of the Southern States of America generally which pour out by steamers the rich wealth of the planting States into the Mississippi. With such prospects as these; with such a people as the Yorubas and others of the best type, as a constituent industrial, social, and political element upon which to establish a national edifice, what is there to prevent success? Nothing in the world.

The Governments in this part are generally Patriarchial, the Kings being elective from ancient Royal families by the Council of Elders, which consists of men chosen for life by the people, for their age, wisdom, experience, and service among them. They are a deliberative body, and all cases of great importance; of state, life and death, must be brought before them. The King as well as either of themselves, is subject to trial and punishment for misdemeanor in office, before the Council of Elders.

Lagos is the place of the family residence of that excellent gentleman Aji, or the Rev. Samuel Crowther, the native Missionary; and also his son-in-law Rev. T. B. Macaulay, who has an excellent school, assisted by his wife an educated native lady.

"Princes shall come out of Egypt; Ethiopia shall soon stretch out her hands unto God."—Ps. lxviii. 31. With the fullest reliance upon this blessed promise, I humbly go forward in—I may repeat—the grandest prospect for the regeneration of a people that ever was presented in the history of the world. The disease has long since been known; we have found and shall apply the remedy. I am indebted to Rev. H. H. Garnet, an eminent black clergyman and scholar, for the construction, that "soon," in the Scriptural passage quoted, "has reference to the period ensuing *from the time of beginning.*" With faith in the promise, and hope from this version, surely there is nothing to doubt or fear.

EDWARD W. BLYDEN

(1832–1912)

*Born in St. Thomas, West Indies, Blyden came to the United States in 1850;
he later emigrated to Liberia. A highly learned man, he spent a lifetime in
educational and missionary work in Liberia and in the encouragement of emigration to Liberia. In 1880, he became president of Liberia College. His works
include* Liberia's Offering, *1862;* The Negro in Ancient History, *1869;* Liberia: Past, Present and Future, *1869;* From West Africa to Palestine, *1873;*
Christianity, Islam and the Negro Race, *1887.*

THE CALL OF PROVIDENCE TO THE
DESCENDANTS OF AFRICA IN AMERICA

> "BEHOLD, the Lord thy God hath set
> the land before thee: go up and possess
> it, as the Lord God of thy fathers hath
> said unto thee; fear not, neither be dis-
> couraged."
> —DEUTERONOMY 1 : 21.

Among the descendants of Africa in this country the persuasion seems to
prevail, though not now to the same extent as formerly, that they owe no
special duty to the land of their forefathers; that their ancestors having
been brought to this country against their will, and themselves having
been born in the land, they are in duty bound to remain here and give
their attention exclusively to the acquiring for themselves, and perpetuating to their posterity, social and political rights, notwithstanding the urgency of the call which their fatherland, by its forlorn and degraded moral
condition, makes upon them for their assistance.

All other people feel a pride in their ancestral land, and do everything
in their power to create for it, if it has not already, an honorable name.
But many of the descendants of Africa, on the contrary, speak disparag-
ingly of their country; are ashamed to acknowledge any connection with
that land, and would turn indignantly upon any who would bid them go
up and take possession of the land of their fathers.

It is a sad feature in the residence of Africans in this country, that it has
begotten in them a forgetfulness of Africa—a want of sympathy with her
in her moral and intellectual desolation, and a clinging to the land which
for centuries has been the scene of their thralldom. A shrewd European

observer* of American society, says of the Negro in this country, that he "makes a thousand fruitless efforts to insinuate himself among men who repulse him; he conforms to the taste of his oppressors, adopts their opinions, and hopes by imitating them to form a part of their community. Having been told from infancy that his race is naturally inferior to that of the whites, he assents to the proposition, and is ashamed of his own nature. In each of his features he discovers a trace of slavery, and, if it were in his power, he would willingly rid himself of everything that makes him what he is."

It can not be denied that some very important advantages have accrued to the black man from his deportation to this land, but it has been at the expense of his manhood. Our nature in this country is not the same as it appears among the lordly natives of the interior of Africa, who have never felt the trammels of a foreign yoke. We have been dragged into depths of degradation. We have been taught a cringing servility. We have been drilled into contentment with the most undignified circumstances. Our finer sensibilities have been blunted. There has been an almost utter extinction of all that delicacy of feeling and sentiment which adorns character. The temperament of our souls has become harder or coarser, so that we can walk forth here, in this land of indignities, in ease and in complacency, while our complexion furnishes ground for every species of social insult which an intolerant prejudice may choose to inflict.

But a change is coming over us. The tendency of events is directing the attention of the colored people to some other scene, and Africa is beginning to receive the attention, which has so long been turned away from her; and as she throws open her portals and shows the inexhaustible means of comfort and independence within, the black man begins to feel dissatisfied with the annoyances by which he is here surrounded, and looks with longing eyes to his fatherland. I venture to predict that, within a very brief period, that down-trodden land instead of being regarded with prejudice and distaste, will largely attract the attention and engage the warmest interest of every man of color. A few have always sympathized with Africa, but it has been an indolent and unmeaning sympathy—a sympathy which put forth no effort, made no sacrifices, endured no self-denial, braved no obloquy for the sake of advancing African interests. But the scale is turning, and Africa is becoming the all-absorbing topic.

It is my desire, on the present occasion, to endeavor to set before you the work which, it is becoming more and more apparent, devolves upon the black men of the United States; and to guide my thoughts, I have chosen the words of the text: "Behold, the Lord thy God hath set the land before thee: go up and possess it, as the Lord God of thy fathers hath said unto thee; fear not, neither be discouraged."

You will at once perceive that I do not believe that the work to be done by black men is in this country. I believe that their field of operation is in

* De Tocqueville, *Democracy in America* [Vol. I, p. 346].

some other and distant scene. Their work is far nobler and loftier than that which they are now doing in this country. It is theirs to betake themselves to injured Africa, and bless those outraged shores, and quiet those distracted families with the blessings of Christianity and civilization. It is theirs to bear with them to that land the arts of industry and peace, and counteract the influence of those horrid abominations which an inhuman avarice has introduced—to roll back the appalling cloud of ignorance and superstition which overspreads the land, and to rear on the those shores an asylum of liberty for the down-trodden sons of Africa wherever found. This is the work to which Providence is obviously calling the black men of this country.

I am aware that some, against all experience, are hoping for the day when they will enjoy equal social and political rights in this land. We do not blame them for so believing and trusting. But we would remind them that there is a faith against reason, against experience, which consists in believing or pretending to believe very important propositions upon very slender proofs, and in maintaining opinions without any proper grounds. It ought to be clear to every thinking and impartial mind, that there can never occur in this country an equality, social or political, between whites and blacks. The whites have for a long time had the advantage. All the affairs of the country are in their hands. They make and administer the laws; they teach the schools; here, in the North, they ply all the trades, they own all the stores, they have possession of all the banks, they own all the ships and navigate them; they are the printers, proprietors, and editors of the leading newspapers, and they shape public opinion. Having always had the lead, they have acquired an ascendency they will ever maintain. The blacks have very few or no agencies in operation to counteract the ascendant influence of the Europeans. And instead of employing what little they have by a unity of effort to alleviate their condition, they turn all their power against themselves by their endless jealousies, and rivalries, and competition; everyone who is able to "pass" being emulous of a place among Europeans or Indians. This is the effect of their circumstances. It is the influence of the dominant class upon them. It argues no essential inferiority in them—no more than the disadvantages of the Israelites in Egypt argued their essential inferiority to the Egyptians. They are the weaker class overshadowed and depressed by the stronger. They are the feeble oak dwarfed by the overspreadings of a large tree, having not the advantage of rain, and sunshine, and fertilizing dews.

Before the weaker people God has set the land of their forefathers, and bids them go up and possess it without fear or discouragement. Before the tender plant he sets an open field, where, in the unobstructed air and sunshine, it may grow and flourish in all its native luxuriance.

There are two ways in which God speaks to men: one is by his word and the other by his providence. He has not sent any Moses, with signs and wonders, to cause an exodus of the descendants of Africa to their fatherland, yet he has loudly spoken to them as to their duty in the matter. He has spoken by his providence. First; By suffering them to be brought here and placed in circumstances where they could receive a training fitting them for the work of civilizing and evangelizing the land whence they were torn, and by preserving them under the severest trials and afflictions. Secondly; By allowing them, notwithstanding all the services they have rendered to this country, to be treated as strangers and aliens, so as to cause them to have anguish of spirit, as was the case with the Jews in Egypt, and to make them long for some refuge from their social and civil deprivations. Thirdly; By bearing a portion of them across the tempestuous seas back to Africa, by preserving them through the process of acclimation, and by establishing them in the land, despite the attempts of misguided men to drive them away. Fourthly; By keeping their fatherland in reserve for them in their absence.

The manner in which Africa has been kept from invasion is truly astounding. Known for ages, it is yet unknown. For centuries its inhabitants have been the victims of the cupidity of foreigners. The country has been rifled of its population. It has been left in some portions almost wholly unoccupied, but it has remained unmolested by foreigners. It has been very near the crowded countries of the world, yet none has relieved itself to any great extent of its overflowing population by seizing upon its domains. Europe, from the North, looks wishfully and with longing eyes across the narrow straits of Gilbraltar. Asia, with its teeming millions, is connected with us by an isthmus wide enough to admit of her throwing thousands into the country. But, notwithstanding the known wealth of the resources of the land, of which the report has gone into all the earth, there is still a terrible veil between us and our neighbors, the all-conquering Europeans, which they are only now essaying to lift; while the teeming millions of Asia have not even attempted to leave their boundaries to penetrate our borders. Neither alluring visions of glorious conquests, nor brilliant hopes of rapid enrichment, could induce them to invade the country. It has been preserved alike from the boastful civilization of Europe, and the effete and barbarous institutions of Asia. We call it, then, a Providential interposition, that while the owners of the soil have been abroad, passing through the fearful ordeal of a most grinding oppression, the land, though entirely unprotected, has lain uninvaded. We regard it as a providential call to Africans every where, to "go up and possess the land"; so that in a sense that is not merely constructive and figurative, but truly literal, God says to the black men of this country, with reference to Africa: "Behold, I set the land before you, go up and possess it."

Of course it can not be expected that this subject of the duty of colored men to go up and take possession of their fatherland, will be at once clear to every mind. Men look at objects from different points of view, and form their opinions according to the points from which they look, and are guided in their actions according to the opinions they form. As I have already said, the majority of exiled Africans do not seem to appreciate the great privilege of going and taking possession of the land. They seem to have lost all interest in that land, and to prefer living in subordinate and inferior positions in a strange land among oppressors, to encountering the risks involved in emigrating to a distant country. As I walk the streets of these cities, visit the hotels, go on board the steamboats, I am grieved to notice how much intelligence, how much strength and energy is frittered away in those trifling employments, which, if thrown into Africa, might elevate the millions of that land from their degradation, tribes at a time, and create an African power which would command the respect of the world, and place in the possession of Africans, its rightful owners, the wealth which is now diverted to other quarters. Most of the wealth that could be drawn from that land, during the last six centuries, has passed into the hands of Europeans, while many of Africa's own sons, sufficiently intelligent to control those immense resources, are sitting down in poverty and dependence in the land of strangers—exiles when they have so rich a domain from which they have never been expatriated, but which is willing, nay, anxious to welcome them home again.

We need some African power, some great center of the race where our physical, pecuniary, and intellectual strength may be collected. We need some spot whence such an influence may go forth in behalf of the race as shall be felt by the nations. We are now so scattered and divided that we can do nothing. The imposition begun last year by a foreign power upon Hayti, and which is still persisted in, fills every black man who has heard of it with indignation, but we are not strong enough to speak out effectually for that land. When the same power attempted an outrage upon the Liberians, there was no African power strong enough to interpose. So long as we remain thus divided, we may expect impositions. So long as we live simply by the sufferance of the nations, we must expect to be subject to their caprices.

Among the free portion of the descendants of Africa, numbering about four or five millions, there is enough talent, wealth, and enterprise, to form a respectable nationality on the continent of Africa. For nigh three hundred years their skill and industry have been expended in building up the southern countries of the New World, the poor, frail constitution of the Caucasian not allowing him to endure the fatigue and toil involved in such labors. Africans and their descendants have been the laborers, and the mechanics, and the artisans in the greater portion of this hemisphere. By the results of their labor the European countries have been sustained and enriched. All the cotton, coffee, indigo, sugar, tobacco, etc., which have formed the most important articles of European commerce, have been raised and prepared for market by the labor of the black man. Dr. Palmer of New-Orleans, bears the same testimony.* And all this labor

* In the famous sermon of this distinguished divine on *Slavery a Divine Trust*, he says: "The enriching commerce which has built the splendid cities and marble palaces

they have done, for the most part not only without compensation, but with abuse, and contempt, and insult, as their reward.

Now, while Europeans are looking to our fatherland with such eagerness of desire, and are hastening to explore and take away its riches, ought not Africans in the Western hemisphere to turn their regards thither also? We need to collect the scattered forces of the race, and there is no rallying-ground more favorable than Africa. There

> "No pent-up Utica contracts our powers,
> The whole boundless continent is ours."

Ours as a gift from the Almighty when he drove asunder the nations and assigned them their boundaries; and ours by peculiar physical adaptation.

An African nationality is our great need, and God tells us by his providence that he has set the land before us, and bids us go up and possess it. We shall never receive the respect of other races until we establish a powerful nationality. We should not content ourselves with living among other races, simply by their permission or their endurance, as Africans live in this country. We must build up Negro states; we must establish and maintain the various institutions; we must make and administer laws, erect and preserve churches, and support the worship of God; we must have governments; we must have legislation of our own; we must build ships and navigate them; we must ply the trades, instruct the schools, control the press, and thus aid in shaping the opinions and guiding the destinies of mankind. Nationality is an ordinance of Nature. The heart of every true Negro yearns after a distinct and separate nationality.

Impoverished, feeble, and alone, Liberia is striving to establish and build up such a nationality in the home of the race. Can any descendant of Africa turn contemptuously upon a scene where such efforts are making? Would not every right-thinking Negro rather lift up his voice and direct the attention of his brethren to that land? Liberia, with outstretched arms, earnestly invites all to come. We call them forth out of all nations; we bid them take up their all and leave the countries of their exile, as of old the Israelites went forth from Egypt, taking with them their trades and their treasures, their intelligence, their mastery of arts, their knowledge of the sciences, their practical wisdom, and every thing that will render them useful in building up a nationality. We summon them from these States, from the Canadas, from the East and West-Indies, from South-America, from every where, to come and take part with us in our great work.

But those whom we call are under the influence of various opinions, having different and conflicting views of their relations and duty to Africa,

---

of England as well as of America, has been largely established upon the products of Southern soil; and the blooms upon Southern fields, gathered by black hands, have fed the spindles and looms of Manchester and Birmingham not less than of Lawrence and Lowell."

according to the different stand-points they occupy. So it was with another people who, like ourselves, were suffering from the effects of protracted thralldom, when on the borders of the land to which God was leading them. When Moses sent out spies to search the land of Canaan, every man, on his return, seemed to be influenced in his report by his peculiar temperament, previous habits of thought, by the degree of his physical courage, or by something peculiar in his point of observation. All agreed, indeed, that it was an exceedingly rich land, "flowing with milk and honey," for they carried with them on their return, a proof of its amazing fertility. But a part, and a larger part, too, saw only giants and walled towns, and barbarians and cannibals. "Surely," said they, "it floweth with milk and honey. Nevertheless the people be strong that dwell in the land, and the cities are walled, and very great; and moreover we saw the children of Anak there. The land through which we have gone to search it, is a land that eateth up the inhabitants thereof; and all the people that we saw in it are men of a great stature. And there we saw the giants, the sons of Anak, which come of the giants: and we were in our own sight as grasshoppers, and so we were in their sight." It was only a small minority of that company that saw things in a more favorable light. "Caleb stilled the people before Moses, and said, Let us go up at once and possess it; for we be well able to overcome it." (Numbers 13.)

In like manner there is division among the colored people of this country with regard to Africa, that land which the providence of God is bidding them go up and possess. Spies sent from different sections of this country by the colored people—and many a spy not commissioned—have gone to that land, and have returned and reported. Like the Hebrew spies, they have put forth diverse views. Most believe Africa to be a fertile and rich country, and an African nationality a desirable thing. But some affirm that the land is not fit to dwell in, for "it is a land that eateth up the inhabitants thereof," notwithstanding the millions of strong and vigorous aborigines who throng all parts of the country, and the thousands of colonists who are settled along the coast; some see in the inhabitants incorrigible barbarism, degradation, and superstition, and insuperable hostility to civilization; others suggest that the dangers and risks to be encountered, and the self-denial to be endured, are too great for the slender advantages which, as it appears to them, will accrue from immigration. A few only report that the land is open to us on every hand—that "every prospect pleases," and that the natives are so tractable that it would be a comparatively easy matter for civilized and Christianized black men to secure all the land to Christian law, liberty, and civilization.

I come to-day to defend the report of the minority. The thousands of our own race, emigrants from this country, settled for more than forty years in that land, agree with the minority report. Dr. Barth, and other travelers to the east and south-east of Liberia, indorse the sentiment of the minority, and testify to the beauty, and healthfulness, and productiveness of the country, and to the mildness and hospitality of its inhabitants. In Liberia we hear from natives, who are constantly coming to our settlements from the far interior, of land exuberantly fertile, of large, numerous, and wealthy tribes, athletic and industrious; not the descendants of Europeans —according to Bowen's insane theory—but *black* men, pure Negroes, who live in large towns, cultivate the soil, and carry on extensive traffic, maintaining amicable relations with each other and with men from a distance.

The ideas that formerly prevailed of the interior of Africa, which suited the purposes of poetry and sensation writing, have been proved entirely erroneous. Poets may no longer sing with impunity of Africa:

> "A region of drought, where no river glides,
> Nor rippling brook with osiered sides;
> Where sedgy pool, nor bubbling fount,
> Nor tree, nor cloud, nor misty mount,
> Appears to refresh the aching eye,
> But barren earth and the burning sky,
> And the blank horizon round and round."

No; missionary and scientific enterprises have disproved such fallacies. The land possesses every possible inducement. That extensive and beauteous domain which God has given us appeals to us and to black men every where, by its many blissful and benigant aspects; by its flowery landscapes, its beautiful rivers, its serene and peaceful skies; by all that attractive and perennial verdure which overspreads the hills and valleys; by its every prospect lighted up by delightful sunshine; by all its natural charms, it calls upon us to rescue it from the grasp of remorseless superstition, and introduce the blessings of the Gospel.

But there are some among the intelligent colored people of this country who, while they profess to have great love for Africa, and tell us that their souls are kindled when they hear of their fatherland, yet object to going themselves, because, as they affirm, the black man has a work to accomplish in this land—he has a destiny to fulfill. He, the representative of Africa, like the representatives from various parts of Europe, must act his part in building up this great composite nation. It is not difficult to see what the work of the black man is in this land. The most inexperienced observer may at once read his destiny. Look at the various departments of society here in the *free* North; look at the different branches of industry, and see how the black man is aiding to build up this nation. Look at the hotels, the saloons, the steamboats, the barbershops, and see how successfully he is carrying out his destiny! And there is an extreme likelihood that such are forever to be the exploits which he is destined to achieve in this country until he merges his African peculiarities in the Caucasian.

Others object to the *climate* of Africa, first, that it is unhealthy, and secondly, that it is not favorable to intellectual progress. To the first, we reply that it is not more insalubrious than other new countries. Persons going to Africa, who have not been broken down as to their constitutions in this country, stand as fair a chance of successful acclimation as in any other country of large, unbroken forests and extensively uncleared lands. In all new countries there are sufferings and privations. All those countries which have grown up during the last two centuries, in this hemisphere, have had as a foundation the groans, and tears, and blood of the pioneers. But what are the sufferings of pioneers, compared with the greatness of the results they accomplish for succeeding generations? Scarcely any great step in human progress is made without multitudes of victims. Every revolution that has been effected, every nationality that has been established, every country that has been rescued from the abominations of savagism, every colony that has been planted, has involved perplexities and sufferings to the generation who undertook it. In the evangelization of Africa, in the erection of African nationalities, we can expect no exceptions. The man, then, who is not able to suffer and to die for his fellows when necessity requires it, is not fit to be a pioneer in this great work.

We believe, as we have said, that the establishment of an African nationality in Africa is the great need of the African race; and the men who have gone, or may hereafter go to assist in laying the foundations of empire, so far from being dupes, or cowards, or traitors, as some have ignorantly called them, are the truest heroes of the race. They are the soldiers rushing first into the breach—physicians who at the risk of their own lives are first to explore an infectious disease. How much more nobly do they act than those who have held for years that it is nobler to sit here and patiently suffer with our brethren! Such sentimental inactivity finds no respect in these days of rapid movement. The world sees no merit in mere innocence. The man who contents himself to sit down and exemplify the virtue of patience and endurance will find no sympathy from the busy, restless crowd that rush by him. Even the "sick man" must get out of the way when he hears the tramp of the approaching host, or be crushed by the heedless and massive car of progress. Blind Bartimeuses are silenced by the crowd. The world requires active service; it respects only productive workers. The days of hermits and monks have passed away. Action—work, work—is the order of the day. Heroes in the strife and struggle of humanity are the demand of the age.

"They who would be free, *themselves* must *strike* the blow."

With regard to the objection founded upon the unfavorableness of the climate to intellectual progress, I have only to say, that proper moral agencies, when set in operation, can not be overborne by physical causes. "We continually behold lower laws held in restraint by higher; mechanic by dynamic; chemical by vital; physical by moral."* It has not yet been proved that with the proper influences, the tropics will not produce men

* Dean Trench, quoted by Baden Powell in *Essays and Reviews,* 1861.

of "cerebral activity." Those races which have degenerated by a removal from the North to the tropics did not possess the proper moral power. They had in themselves the seed of degeneracy, and would have degenerated any where. It was not Anglo-Saxon blood, nor a temperate climate, that kept the first emigrants to this land from falling into the same indolence and inefficiency which have overtaken the European settlers in South-America, but the Anglo-Saxon Bible—the principles contained in that book, are the great conservative and elevating power. Man is the same, and the human mind is the same, whether existing beneath African suns or Arctic frosts. I can conceive of no difference. It is the moral influences brought to bear upon the man that make the difference in his progress.

"High degrees of moral sentiment," says a distinguished American writer,* "control the unfavorable influences of climate; and some of our grandest examples of men and of races come from the equatorial regions." Man is elevated by taking hold of that which is higher than himself. Unless this is done, climate, color, race, will avail nothing.

> "—unless above himself he can
> Erect himself, how poor a thing is man!"

For my own part, I believe that the brilliant world of the tropics, with its marvels of nature, must of necessity give to mankind a new career of letters, and new forms in the various arts, whenever the millions of men at present uncultivated shall enjoy the advantages of civilization.

Africa will furnish a development of civilization which the world has never yet witnessed. Its great peculiarity will be its moral element. The Gospel is to achieve some of its most beautiful triumphs in that land. "God shall enlarge Japheth, and he shall dwell in the tents of Shem," was the blessing upon the European and Asiatic races. Wonderfully have these predictions been fulfilled. The all-conquering descendants of Japheth have gone to every clime, and have planted themselves on almost every shore. By means fair and unfair, they have spread themselves, have grown wealthy and powerful. They have been truly "enlarged." God has "dwelt in the tents of Shem," for so some understand the passage. The Messiah— God manifest in the flesh—was of the tribe of Judah. He was born and dwelt in the tents of Shem. The promise to Ethiopia, or Ham, is like that to Shem, of a spiritual kind. It refers not to physical strength, not to large and extensive domains, not to foreign conquests, not to wide-spread domination, but to the possession of spiritual qualities, to the elevation of the soul heavenward, to spiritual aspirations and divine communications. "Ethiopia shall stretch forth her hands unto God." Blessed, glorious promise! Our trust is not to be in chariots or horses, not in our own skill or power, but our help is to be in the name of the Lord. And surely, in

* R. W. Emerson, in the *Atlantic Monthly*, April, 1862.

reviewing our history as a people, whether we consider our preservation in the lands of our exile, or the preservation of our fatherland from invasion, we are compelled to exclaim: "Hitherto hath the Lord helped us!" Let us, then, fear not the influences of climate. Let us go forth stretching out our hands to God, and if it be as hot as Nebuchadnezzar's furnace, there will be one in the midst like unto the Son of God, counteracting its deleterious influences.

Behold, then, the Lord our God has set the land before us, with its burning climate, with its privations, with its moral, intellectual, and political needs, and by his providence he bids us go up and possess it without fear or discouragement. Shall we go up at his bidding? If the black men of this country, through unbelief or indolence, or for any other cause, fail to lay hold of the blessings which God is proffering to them, and neglect to accomplish the work which devolves upon them, the work will be done, but others will be brought in to do it, and to take possession of the country.

For while the colored people here are tossed about by various and conflicting opinions as to their duty to that land, men are going thither from other quarters of the globe. They are entering the land from various quarters with various motives and designs, and may eventually so preöccupy the land as to cut us off from the fair inheritance which lies before us, unless we go forth without further delay and establish ourselves.

The enterprise and energy manifested by white men who, with uncongenial constitutions, go from a distance to endeavor to open up that land to the world, are far from creditable to the civilized and enlightened colored men of the United States, when contrasted with their indifference in the matter. A noble army of self-expatriated evangelists have gone to that land from Europe and America; and, while anxious to extend the blessings of true religion, they have in no slight degree promoted the cause of science and commerce. Many have fallen, either from the effects of the climate or by the hands of violence;* still the interest in the land is by no means diminished. The enamored worshiper of science, and the Christian philanthropist, are still laboring to solve the problem of African geography, and to elevate its benighted tribes. They are not only disclosing to the world the mysteries of regions hitherto unexplored, but tribes whose very existence had not before been known to the civilized world have been

* The names of John Ledyard, Frederick Horneman, Dr. Walter Oudney, Captain Clapperton, Major Denman, John Richardson, and Dr. Overweg occur in the list of those who have fallen victims either to the climate of the hardships of their pilgrimage. But a more melancholy enumeration may be made. Major Houghton perished, or was murdered, in the basin of the Gambia. The truly admirable Mungo Park was killed in an attack of the natives, at a difficult passage of the Niger. The same fate befell Richard Lander in the lower course of the river. Major Laing was foully slain in his tent at a halting-place in the Sahara. John Davidson was assassinated soon after passing the fringe of the desert. Dr. Cowan and Captain Donovan disappeared in the wilds of South-Africa. Dr. Vogel was assassinated in the country about Lake Chad.—*Leisure Hour.*

brought, through their instrumentality, into contact with civilization and Christianity. They have discovered in the distant portions of that land countries as productive as any in Europe and America. They have informed the world of bold and lofty mountains, extensive lakes, noble rivers, falls rivaling Niagara, so that, as a result of their arduous, difficult, and philanthropic labors of exploration, the cause of Christianity, ethnology, geography, and commerce has been, in a very important degree, subserved.

Dr. Livingstone, the indefatigable African explorer, who, it is estimated, has passed over not less than eleven thousand miles of African ground, speaking of the motives which led him to those shores, and still keep him there in spite of privations and severe afflictions, says:

"I expect to find for myself no large fortune in that country; nor do I expect to explore any large portions of a new country; but I do hope to find a pathway, by means of the river Zambesi, which may lead to highlands, where Europeans may form a settlement, and where, by opening up communication and establishing commercial intercourse with the natives of Africa, they may slowly, but not the less surely, impart to the people of that country the knowledge and inestimable blessings of Christianity."

The recently formed Oxford, Cambridge, and Dublin Missionary Society state their object to be to spread Christianity among the untaught people of Central Africa, "so to operate among them as by mere teaching and influence to help *to build up native Christian states.*" The idea of building up "native Christian states" is a very important one, and is exactly such an idea as would be carried out if there were a large influx of civilized blacks from abroad.

I am sorry to find that among some in this country, the opinion prevails that in Liberia a distinction is maintained between the colonists and the aborigines, so that the latter are shut out from the social and political privileges of the former. No candid person who has read the laws of Liberia, or who has visited that country, can affirm or believe such a thing. The idea no doubt arises from the fact that the aborigines of a country generally suffer from the settling of colonists among them. But the work of Liberia is somewhat different from that of other colonies which have been planted on foreign shores. The work achieved by other emigrants has usually been —the enhancement of their own immediate interests; the increase of their physical comforts and conveniences; the enlargement of their borders by the most speedy and available methods, without regard to the effect such a course might have upon the aborigines. Their interests sometimes coming into direct contact with those of the owners of the soil, they have not unfrequently, by their superior skill and power, reduced the poor native to servitude or complete annihilation. The Israelites could live in peace in the land of Canaan only by exterminating the indigenous inhabitants. The colony that went out from Phenicia, and that laid the foundations of empire on the northern shores of Africa, at first paid a yearly tax to the natives; with the increasing wealth and power of Carthage, however, the respective conditions of the Carthaginians and the natives were changed, and the Phenician adventurers assumed and maintained a dominion over the Lybians. The colonies from Europe which landed at Plymouth Rock, at Boston, and at Jamestown—which took possession of the West-India islands and of Mexico, treated the aborigines in the same manner. The natives of India, Australia, and New-Zealand are experiencing a similar treatment under the overpowering and domineering rule of the Anglo-Saxons. Eagerness for gain and the passion for territorial aggrandisement have appeared to the colonists necessary to their growth and progress.

The work of Liberia, as I have said, is different and far nobler. We, on the borders of our fatherland, can not, as the framers of our Constitution wisely intimated, allow ourselves to be influenced by "avaricious speculations," or by desires for "territorial aggrandisement." Our work there is moral and intellectual as well as physical. We have to work upon the *people*, as well as upon the *land*—upon *mind* as well as upon *matter*. Our prosperity depends as much upon the wholesome and elevating influence we exert upon the native population, as upon the progress we make in agriculture, commerce, and manufacture. Indeed the conviction prevails in Liberia among the thinking people that we can make no important progress in these things without the coöperation of the aborigines. We believe that no policy can be more suicidal in Liberia than that which would keep aloof from the natives around us. We believe that our life and strength will be to elevate and incorporate them among us as speedily as possible.

And, then, the aborigines are not a race alien from the colonists. We are a part of them. When alien and hostile races have come together, as we have just seen, one has had to succumb to the other; but when different peoples of the same family have been brought together, there has invariably been a fusion, and the result has been an improved and powerful class. When three branches of the great Teutonic family met on the soil of England, they united. It is true that at first there was a distinction of caste among them in consequence of the superiority in every respect of the great Norman people; but, as the others came up to their level, the distinctions were quietly effaced, and Norman, Saxon, and Dane easily amalgamated. Thus, "a people inferior to none existing in the world was formed by the mixture of three branches of the great Teutonic family with each other and the aboriginal Britons." *

In America we see how readily persons from all parts of Europe assimilate; but what great difficulty the Negro, the Chinese, and the Indian experience! We find here representatives from all the nations of Europe easily blending with each other. But we find elements that will not assimilate. The Negro, the Indian, and the Chinese, who do not belong to the same family, repel each other, and are repelled by the Europeans. "The

* Macaulay's History of England, vol. i. chap. i.

antagonistic elements are in contact, but refuse to unite, and as yet no agent has been found sufficiently potent to reduce them to unity."

But the case with Americo-Liberians and the aborigines is quite different. We are all descendants of Africa. In Liberia there may be found persons of almost every tribe in West-Africa, from Senegal to Congo. And not only do we and the natives belong to the same race, but we are also of the same family. The two peoples can no more be kept from assimilating and blending than water can be kept from mingling with its kindred elements. The policy of Liberia is to diffuse among them as rapidly as possible the principles of Christianity and civilization, to prepare them to take an active part in the duties of the nationality which we are endeavoring to erect. Whence, then, comes the slander which represents Liberians as "maintaining a distance from the aborigines—a constant and uniform separation"?

To take part in the noble work in which they are engaged on that coast, the government and people of Liberia earnestly invite the descendants of Africa in this country.* In all our feebleness, we have already accomplished something; but very little in comparison of what has to be done. A beginning has been made, however—a great deal of preparatory work accomplished. And if the intelligent and enterprising colored people of this country would emigrate in large numbers, an important work would be done in a short time. And we know exactly the kind of work that would be done. We know that where now stand unbroken forests would spring up towns and villages, with their schools and churches—that the natives would be taught the arts of civilization—that their energies would be properly directed—that their prejudices would disappear—that there would be a rapid and important revulsion from the practices of heathenism, and a radical change in their social condition—that the glorious principles of a Christian civilization would diffuse themselves throughout those benighted communities. Oh! that our people would take this matter into serious consideration, and think of the great privilege of kindling in the depths of the moral and spiritual gloom of Africa a glorious light—of causing the wilderness and the solitary place to be glad—the desert to bloom and blossom as the rose—and the whole land to be converted into a garden of the Lord.

Liberia, then, appeals to the colored men of this country for assistance in the noble work which she has begun. She appeals to those who believe that the descendants of Africa live in the serious neglect of their duty if they fail to help to raise the land of their forefathers from her degradation. She appeals to those who believe that a well-established African na-

* The Legislature of Liberia, at its last session, 1861–62, passed an Act authorizing the appointment of Commissioners to "itinerate among and lecture to the people of color in the United States of North-America, to present to them the claims of Liberia, and its superior advantages as a desirable home for persons of African descent." The President appointed for this work, Professors Crummell and Blyden and J. D. Johnson, Esq.

tionality is the most direct and efficient means of securing respectability and independence for the African race. She appeals to those who believe that a rich and fertile country, like Africa, which has lain so long under the cheerless gloom of ignorance, should not be left any longer without the influence of Christian civilization—to those who deem it a far more glorious work to save extensive tracts of country from barbarism and continued degradation than to amass for themselves the means of individual comfort and aggrandizement—to those who believe that there was a providence in the deportation of our forefathers from the land of their birth, and that that same providence now points to a work in Africa to be done by us their descendants. Finally, Liberia appeals to all African patriots and Christians—to all lovers of order and refinement—to lovers of industry and enterprise—of peace, comfort, and happiness—to those who having felt the power of the Gospel in opening up to them life and immortality, are desirous that their benighted kindred should share in the same blessings. "Behold, the Lord thy God hath set the land before thee: go up and possess it, as the Lord God of thy fathers hath said unto thee; fear not, neither be discouraged"—1862.

THE AFRICAN PROBLEM AND
THE METHOD OF ITS SOLUTION

I am seriously impressed with a sense of the responsibility of my position to-night. I stand in the presence of the representatives of that great organization which seems first of all the associations in this country to have distinctly recognized the hand of God in the history of the Negro race in America—to have caught something of the meaning of the Divine purpose in permitting their exile to and bondage in this land. I stand also in the presence of what, for the time being at least, must be considered the foremost congregation of the land—the religious home of the President of the United States. There are present, also, I learn, on this occasion, some of the statesmen and lawmakers of the land.

My position, then, is one of honor as well as of responsibility, and the message I have to deliver, I venture to think, concerns directly or indirectly the whole human race. I come from that ancient country, the home of one of the great original races, occupied by the descendants of one of the three sons to whom, according to Biblical history, the whole world was assigned—a country which is now engaging the active attention of all Europe. I come, also, from the ancestral home of at least five millions in this land. Two hundred millions of people have sent me on an errand of invitation to their blood relations here. Their cry is, "Come over and help us." And I find among hundreds of thousands of the invited an eager and enthusiastic response. They tell me to wave the answer across the deep to the anxious and expectant hearts, which, during the long and weary night of separation, have been constantly watching and praying for the return—to the Rachels weeping for their children, and refusing to be comforted because they are not—they tell me, "Wave the answer back to our brethren to hold the fort for we are coming." They have for the last seventy years been returning through the agency of the Society whose anniversary we celebrate to-night. Some have gone every year during that period, but they have been few compared to the vast necessity. They have gone as they have been able to go, and are making an impression for good upon that continent. My subject to-night will be, THE AFRICAN PROBLEM AND THE METHOD OF ITS SOLUTION.

This is no new problem. It is nearly as old as recorded history. It has interested thinking men in Europe and Asia in all ages. The imagination of the ancients peopled the interior of that country with a race of beings shut out from and needing no intercourse with the rest of mankind lifted by their purity and simplicity of character above the necessity of intercourse with other mortals—leading a blameless and protracted existence and producing in their sequestered, beautiful, and fertile home, from which flowed the wonderful Nile, the food of the Gods. Not milk and honey but nectar and ambrosia were supposed to abound there. The Greeks especially had very high conceptions of the sanctity and spirituality of the interior Africans. The greatest of their poets picture the Gods as vacating Olympus every year and proceeding to Ethiopia to be feasted by its inhabitants. Indeed, the religion of some portion of Greece is supposed to have been introduced from Africa. But leaving the region of mythology, we know that the three highest religions known to mankind—if they had not their origin in Africa—were domiciled there in the days of their feeble beginnings, Judaism, Christianity, and Mohammedanism.

A sacred mystery hung over that continent, and many were the aspirations of philosophers and poets for some definite knowledge of what was beyond the narrow fringe they saw. Julius Caesar, fascinated while listening to a tale of the Nile, lost the vision of military glory. The philosopher overcame the soldier and he declared himself ready to abandon for a time the alluring fields of politics in order to trace out the sources of that mysterious river which gave to mankind Egypt with her magnificent conceptions and splendid achievements.

The mystery still remains. The problem continues unsolved. The conquering races of the world stand perplexed and worried before the difficulties which beset their enterprise of reducing that continent to subjection. They have overcome the whole of the Western Hemisphere. From Behring Straits to Cape Horn America has submitted to their sway. The native races have almost disappeared from the mainland and the islands of the sea. Europe has extended her conquests to Australia, New Zealand, and the Archipelagos of the Pacific. But, for hundreds of years, their ships have passed by those tempting regions, where "Afric's sunny fountains roll down their golden sands," and though touching at different points on the coast, they have been able to acquire no extensive foothold in that country. Notwithstanding the reports we receive on every breeze that blows from the East, of vast "spheres of influence" and large European possessions, the points actually occupied by white men in the boundless equatorial regions of that immense continent may be accurately represented on the map only by microscopic dots. I wish that the announcements we receive from time to time with such a flourish of trumpets, that a genuine civilization is being carried into the heart of the Dark Continent, were true. But the fact is, that the bulk of Central Africa is being rapidly subjected to Mohammedanism. That system will soon be—or rather is now—knitting together the conquerors and the conquered into a harmonious whole; and unless Europe gets a thorough understanding of the situation, the gates of missionary enterprise will be closed; because, from all we can learn of the proceedings of some, especially in East Africa, the industrial *régime* is being stamped out to foster the militant. The current number of the *Fortnightly*, near the close of an interesting article on "Stanley's Expedition," has this striking sentence: "Stanley has triumphed, but Central Africa is darker than ever!"

It would appear that the world outside of Africa has not yet stopped to consider the peculiar conditions which lift that continent out of the range of the ordinary agencies by which Europe has been able to occupy other countries and subjugate or exterminate their inhabitants.

They have not stopped to ponder the providential lessons on this subject scattered through the pages of history, both past and contemporary.

First. Let us take the most obvious lesson as indicated in the climatic conditions. Perhaps in no country in the world is it so necessary (as in Africa) that the stranger or new comer should possess the *mens sana in corpore sano*—the sound mind in sound body; for the climate is most searching, bringing to the surface any and every latent physical or mental defect. If a man has any chronic or hereditary disease it is sure to be developed, and if wrong medical treatment is applied it is very apt to be exaggerated and often to prove fatal to the patient. And as with the body so with the mind. Persons of weak minds, either inherited or brought on by excessive mental application or troubles of any kind, are almost sure to develop an impatience or irritability, to the surprise and annoyance of their friends who knew them at home. The Negro immigrant from a temperate region sometimes suffers from these climatic inconveniences, only in his case, after a brief process of acclimatization, he becomes himself again, while the white man never regains his soundness in that climate, and can retain his mental equilibrium only by periodical visits to his native climate. The regulation of the British Government for West Africa is that their officials are allowed six months' leave of absence to return to Europe after fifteen month's residence at Sierra Leone and twelve months on the Gold Coast or Lagos; and for every three days during which they are kept on the coast after the time for their leave arrives, they are allowed one day in Europe. The neglect of this regulation is often attended with most serious consequences.

Second. When we come into the moral and intellectual world it would seem as if the Almighty several times attempted to introduce the foreigner and a foreign civilization into Africa and then changed his purpose. The Scriptures seem to warrant the idea that in some way inexplicable to us, and incompatible with our conception of the character of the Sovereign of the Universe, the unchangeable Being sometimes reverses His apparent plans. We read that, "it repented God," &c. For thousands of years the northeastern portion of Africa witnessed a wonderful development of civilization. The arts and sciences flourished in Egypt for generations, and that country was the centre of almost universal influence; but there was no effect produced upon the interior of Africa. So North Africa became the seat of a great military and commercial power which flourished for 700 years. After this the Roman Catholic Church constructed a mighty influence in the same region, but the interior of the continent received no impression from it.

In the fifteenth century the Congo country, of which we now hear so much, was the scene of extensive operations of the Roman Catholic Church. Just a little before the discovery of America thousands of the natives of the Congo, including the most influential families, were baptized by Catholic missionaries; and the Portuguese, for a hundred years, devoted themselves to the work of African evangelization and exploration. It would appear that they knew just as much of interior Africa as is known now after the great exploits of Speke and Grant and Livingstone, Baker and Cameron and Stanley. It is said that there is a map in the Vatican, three hundred years old, which gives all the general physical relief and the river and lake systems of Africa with more or less accuracy; but the Arab geographers of a century before had described the mountain system, the great lakes, and the course of the Nile.

Just about the time that Portugal was on the way to establish a great empire on that continent, based upon the religious system of Rome, America was discovered, and, instead of the Congo, the Amazon became the seat of Portuguese power. Neither Egyptian, Carthaginian, Persian, or Roman influence was allowed to establish itself on that continent. It would seem that in the providential purpose no solution of the African problem was to come from alien sources. Africans were not doomed to share the fate of some other dark races who have come in contact with the aggressive European. Europe was diverted to the Western Hemisphere. The energies of that conquering race, it was decreed, should be spent in building up a home for themselves on this side. Africa followed in chains.

The Negro race was to be preserved for a special and important work in the future. Of the precise nature of that work no one can form any definite conception. It is probable that if foreign races had been allowed to enter

their country they would have been destroyed. So they were brought over
to be helpers in this country and at the same time to be preserved. It was
not the first time in the history of the world that a people have been
preserved by subjection to another people. We know that God promised
Abraham that his seed should inherit the land of Canaan; but when He
saw that in their numerically weak condition they would have been destroyed in conflicts with the indigenous inhabitants, he took them down to
Egypt and kept them there in bondage four hundred years that they might
be fitted, both by discipline and numerical increase, for the work that
would devolve upon them. Slavery would seem to be a strange school in
which to preserve a people; but God has a way of salting as well as purify-
ing by fire.

The Europeans, who were fleeing from their own country in search of
wider areas of freedom and larger scope for development, found here an
aboriginal race unable to co-operate with them in the labors required for
the construction of the material framework of the new civilization. The
Indians would not work, and they have suffered the consequences of that
indisposition. They have passed away. To take their place as accessories in
the work to be done God suffered the African to be brought hither, who
could work and would work, and could endure the climatic conditions of a
new southern country, which Europeans could not. Two currents set across
the Atlantic towards the west for nigh three hundred years—the one from
Europe, the other from Africa. The one from Africa had a crimson color.
From that stream of human beings millions fell victims to the cruelties of
the middle passage, and otherwise suffered from the brutal instincts of
their kidnappers and enslavers. I do not know whether Africa has been
invited to the celebration of the fourth centenary of the discovery of
America; but she has quite as much reason, if not as much right, to participate in the demonstration of that occasion as the European nations. Englishman, Hollander, and Huguenot, Nigritian and Congo came together.
If Europe brought the head, Africa furnished the hands for a great portion
of the work which has been achieved here, though it was the opinion of an
African chief that the man who discovered America ought to have been
imprisoned for having uncovered one people for destruction and opened a
field for the oppression and suffering of another.

But when the new continent was opened Africa was closed. The veil,
which was being drawn aside, was replaced, and darkness once more enveloped the land, for then not the *country* but the *people* were needed.
They were to do a work elsewhere, and meanwhile their country was to be
shut out from the view of the outside world.

The first Africans landed in this country in the State of Virginia in the
year 1619. Then began the first phase of what is called the Negro problem. These people did not come hither of their own accord. Theirs was not
a voluntary but a compulsory expatriation. The problem, then, on their
arrival in this country, which confronted the white people was how to

reduce to effective and profitable servitude an alien race which it was neither possible nor desirable to assimilate. This gave birth to that peculiar institution, established in a country whose *raison d'être* was that all men might enjoy the "right to life, liberty, and the pursuit of happiness." Laws had to be enacted by Puritans, Cavaliers, and Roundheads for slaves, and every contrivance had to be devised for the safety of the institution. It was a difficult problem, in the effort to solve which both master and slave suffered.

It would seem, however, that in the first years of African slavery in this country, the masters upon many of whom the relationship was forced, understood its providential origin and purpose, until after a while, avarice and greed darkened their perceptions, and they began to invent reasons, drawn even from the Word of God, to justify their holding these people in perpetual bondage for the advantage of themselves and their children forever. But even after a blinding cupidity had captured the generality by its bewitching spell, there were those (far-sighted men, especially after the yoke of Great Britain had been thrown off) who saw that the abnormal relation could not be permanent under the democratic conditions established by the fundamental law of the land. It was Thomas Jefferson, the writer of the Declaration of Independence, who made the celebrated utterance: "Nothing is more clearly written in the Book of Destiny than the emancipation of the blacks; and it is equally certain that the two races will never live in a state of equal freedom under the same Government, so insurmountable are the barriers which nature, habit, and opinion have established between them."

For many years, especially in the long and weary period of the anti-slavery conflict, the latter part of this dictum of Jefferson was denounced by many good and earnest men. The most intelligent of the colored people resented it as a prejudiced and anti-Christian conception. But as the years go by and the Negroes rise in education and culture, and therefore in love and pride of race, and in proper conception of race gifts, race work and race destiny, the latter clause of that famous sentence is not only being shorn of its obscurity and repulsiveness, but is being welcomed as embodying a truth indispensable to the preservation and prosperity of both races, and as pointing to the regeneration of the African Fatherland. There are some others of the race who, recognizing Jefferson's principle, would make the races one by amalgamation.

It was under the conviction of the truth expressed by that statesman that certain gentlemen of all political shades and differing religious views, met together in this city in the winter of 1816–'17, and organized the American Colonization Society. Though friendly to the anti-slavery idea, and anxious for the extinction of the abnormal institution, these men did not make their views on that subject prominent in their published utterances. They were not Abolitionists in the political or technical sense of that phrase. But their labors furnished an outlet and encouragement for persons desiring to free their slaves, giving them the assurance that their freedmen would be returned to their Fatherland, carrying thither what light of Christianity and civilization they had received. It seems a pity that this humane, philanthropic, and far-seeing work should have met with organized opposition from another band of philanthropists, who, anxious for a speedy deliverance of the captives, thought they saw in the Colonization Society an agency for riveting instead of breaking the fetters of the slave, and they denounced it with all the earnestness and eloquence they could command, and they commanded, both among whites and blacks, some of the finest orators the country has ever produced. And they did a grand work, both directly and indirectly, for the Negro and for Africa. They did their work and dissolved their organization. But when their work was done the work of the Colonization Society really began.

In the development of the Negro question in this country the colonizationists might be called the prophets and philosophers; the abolitionists, the warriors and politicians. Colonizationists saw what was coming and patiently prepared for its advent. Abolitionists attacked the first phase of the Negro problem and labored for its immediate solution; colonizationists looked to the last phase of the problem and labored to get both the whites and blacks ready for it. They labored on two continents, in America and in Africa. Had they not begun as early as they did to take up lands in Africa for the exiles, had they waited for the abolition of slavery, it would now have been impossible to obtain a foothold in their fatherland for the returning hosts. The colonizationist, as prophet, looked at the State as it would be; the abolitionist, as politician, looked at the State as it was. The politician sees the present and is possessed by it. The prophet sees the future and gathers inspiration from it. The politician may influence legislation; the prophet, although exercising great moral influence, seldom has any legislative power. The agitation of the politician may soon culminate in legal enactments; the teachings of the prophet may require generations before they find embodiment in action. The politician has to-day; the prophet, to-morrow. The politician deals with facts, the prophet with ideas, and ideas take root very slowly. Though nearly three generations have passed away since Jefferson made his utterance, and more than two since the organization of the Colonization Society, yet the conceptions they put forward can scarcely be said to have gained maturity, much less currency, in the public mind. But the recent discussions in the halls of Congress show that the teachings of the prophet are now beginning to take hold of the politician. It may take many years yet before the people come up to these views, and, therefore, before legislation upon them may be possible, but there is evidently movement in that direction.

The first phase of the Negro problem was solved at Appomattox, after the battle of the warrior, with confused noise and garments rolled in blood. The institution of slavery, for which so many sacrifices had been made, so many of the principles of humanity had been violated, so many of the finer sentiments of the heart had been stifled, was at last destroyed by violence.

Now the nation confronts the second phase, the educational, and millions are being poured out by State governments and by individual philanthropy for the education of the freedmen, preparing them for the third and last phase of the problem, viz: EMIGRATION.

In this second phase, we have that organization, which might be called the successor of the old Anti-Slavery Society, taking most active and effective part. I mean the American Missionary Association. I have watched with constant gratitude and admiration the course and operations of that Society, especially when I remember that, organized in the dark days of slavery, twenty years before emancipation, it held aloft courageously the banner on which was inscribed freedom for the Negro and no fellowship with his oppressors. And they, among the first, went South to lift the freedmen from the mental thraldom and moral degradation in which slavery had left him. They triumphed largely over the spirit of their opponents. They braved the dislike, the contempt, the apprehension with which their work was at first regarded, until they succeeded by demonstrating the advantages of knowledge over ignorance, to bring about that state of things to which Mr. Henry Grady, in his last utterances, was able to refer with such satisfaction, viz., that since the war the South has spent $122,000,000 in the cause of public education, and this year it is pledged to spend $37,000,000, in the benefits of which the Negro is a large participant.

It is not surprising that some of those who, after having been engaged in the noble labors of solving the first phase of the problem—in the great anti-slavery war—and are now confronting the second phase, should be unable to receive with patience the suggestion of the third, which is the emigration phase, when the Negro, freed in body and in mind, shall bid farewell to these scenes of his bondage and discipline and betake himself to the land of his fathers, the scene of larger opportunities and loftier achievements. I say it is not surprising that the veterans of the past and the present should be unable to give much enthusiasm to the work of the future. It is not often given to man to labor successfully in the land of Egypt, in the wilderness and across the Jordan. Some of the most effective workers, must often, with eyes undimmed and natural force unabated, lie down and die on the borders of full freedom, and if they live, life to them is like a dream. The young must take up the work. To old men the indications of the future are like a dream. Old men are like them that dream. Young men see visions. They catch the spirit of the future and are able to place themselves in accord with it.

But things are not yet ready for the solution of the third and last phase of the problem. Things are not ready in this country among whites or blacks. The industrial condition of the South is not prepared for it. Things are not yet ready in Africa for a complete exodus. Europe is not yet ready;

she still thinks that she can take and utilize Africa for her own purposes. She does not yet understand that Africa is to be for the African or for nobody. Therefore she is taking up with renewed vigor, and confronting again, with determination, the African problem. Englishmen, Germans, Italians, Belgians, are taking up territory and trying to wring from the grey-haired mother of civilization the secret of the ages. Nothing has come down from Egypt so grand and impressive as the Sphinxes that look at you with calm and emotionless faces, guarding their secret to-day as they formerly guarded the holy temples. They are a symbol of Africa. She will not be forced. She only can reveal her secret. Her children trained in the house of bondage will show it to the world. Some have already returned and have constructed an independent nation as a beginning of this work on her western borders.

It is a significant fact that Africa was completely shut up until the time arrived for the emancipation of her children in the Western World. When Jefferson and Washington and Hamilton and Patrick Henry were predicting and urging the freedom of the slave, Mungo Park was beginning that series of explorations by English enterprise which has just ended in the expedition of Stanley. Just about the time that England proclaimed freedom throughout her colonies, the brothers Lander made the great discovery of the mouth of the Niger; and when Lincoln issued the immortal proclamation, Livingstone was unfolding to the world that wonderful region which Stanley has more fully revealed and which is becoming now the scene of the secular and religious activities of Christendom. The King of the Belgians has expended fortunes recently in opening the Congo and in introducing the appliances of civilization, and by a singular coincidence a bill has been brought forward in the U. S. Senate to assist the emigration of Negroes to the Fatherland just at the time when that philanthropic monarch has despatched an agent to this country to invite the co-operation in his great work of qualified freedmen. This is significant.

What the King of the Belgians has just done is an indication of what other European Powers will do when they have exhausted themselves in costly experiments to utilize white men as colonists in Africa. They will then understand the purpose of the Almighty in having permitted the exile and bondage of the Africans, and they will see that for Africa's redemption the Negro is the chosen instrument. They will encourage the establishment and building up of such States as Liberia. They will recognize the scheme of the Colonization Society as the providential one.

The little nation which has grown up on that coast as a result of the efforts of this Society, is now taking hold upon that continent in a manner which, owing to inexperience, it could not do in the past. The Liberians have introduced a new article into the commerce of the world—the Liberian coffee. They are pushing to the interior, clearing up the forests, extending the culture of coffee, sugar, cocoa, and other tropical articles, and are training the aborigines in the arts of civilization and in the principles of Christianity. The Republic occupies five hundred miles of coast with an elastic interior. It has a growing commerce with various countries of Europe and America. No one who has visited that country and has seen the farms on the banks of the rivers and in the interior, the workshops, the schools, the churches, and other elements and instruments of progress will say that the United States, through Liberia, is not making a wholesome impression upon Africa—an impression which, if the members of the American Congress understood, they would not begrudge the money required to assist a few hundred thousand to carry on in that country the work so well begun. They would gladly spare them from the laboring element of this great nation to push forward the enterprises of civilization in their Fatherland, and to build themselves up on the basis of their race manhood.

If there is an intelligent Negro here to-night I will say to him, let me take you with me in imagination to witness the new creation or development on that distant shore; I will not paint you an imaginary picture, but will describe an historical fact; I will tell you of reality. Going from the coast, through those depressing alluvial plains which fringe the eastern and western borders of the continent, you reach, after a few miles' travel, the first high or undulating country, which, rising abruptly from the swamps, enchants you with its solidity, its fertility, its verdure, its refreshing and healthful breezes. You go further, and you stand upon a higher elevation where the wind sings more freshly in your ears, and your heart beats fast as you survey the continuous and unbroken forests that stretch away from your feet to the distant horizon. The melancholy cooing of the pigeons in some unseen retreat or the more entrancing music of livelier and picturesque songsters alone disturb the solemn and almost oppressive solitude. You hear no human sound and see the traces of no human presence. You decline to pursue your adventurous journey. You refuse to penetrate the lonely forest that confronts you. You return to the coast, thinking of the long ages which have elapsed, the seasons which, in their onward course, have come and gone, leaving those solitudes undisturbed. You wonder when and how are those vast wildernesses to be made the scene of human activity and to contribute to human wants and happiness. Finding no answer to your perplexing question you drop the subject from your thoughts. After a few years—a very few it may be—you return to those scenes. To your surprise and gratification your progress is no longer interrupted by the inconvenience of bridle-paths and tangled vines. The roads are open and clear. You miss the troublesome creeks and drains which, on your previous journey, harassed and fatigued you. Bridges have been constructed, and without any of the former weariness you find yourself again on the summit, where in loneliness you had stood sometime before. What do you now see? The gigantic trees have disappeared, houses have sprung up on every side. As far as the eye can see the roofs of com-

fortable and homelike cottages peep through the wood. The waving corn
and rice and sugar-cane, the graceful and fragrant coffee tree, the un-
brageous cocoa, orange, and mango plum have taken the place of the
former sturdy denizens of the forest. What has brought about the change?
The Negro emigrant has arrived from America, and, slender though his
facilities have been, has produced these wonderful revolutions. You look
beyond and take in the forests that now appear on the distant horizon.
You catch glimpses of native villages embowered in plantain trees, and
you say these also shall be brought under civilized influences, and you feel
yourself lifted into manhood, the spirit of the teacher and guide and missionary comes upon you, and you say, "There, below me and beyond lies
the world into which I must go. There must I cast my lot. I feel I have a
message to it, or a work in it"; and the sense that there are thousands
dwelling there, some of whom you may touch, some of whom you may
influence, some of whom may love you or be loved by you, thrills you with
a strange joy and expectation, and it is a thrill which you can never forget;
for ever and anon it comes upon you with increased intensity. In that hour
you are born again. You hear forevermore the call ringing in your ears,
"Come over and help us."

These are the visions that rise before the Liberian settler who has
turned away from the coast. This is the view that exercises such an influence upon his imagination, and gives such tone to his character, making
him an independent and productive man on the continent of his fathers.

As I have said, this is no imaginary picture, but the embodiment of
sober history. Liberia, then, is a fact, an aggressive and progressive fact,
with a great deal in its past and everything in its future that is inspiring
and uplifting.

It occupies one of the most charming countries in the western portion
of that continent. It has been called by qualified judges the garden spot of
West Africa. I love to dwell upon the memories of scenes which I have
passed through in the interior of that land. I have read of countries which
I have not visited—the grandeur of the Rocky Mountains and the charms
of the Yosemite Valley, and my imagination adds to the written description and becomes a gallery of delightful pictures. But of African scenes
my memory is a treasure-house in which I delight to revel. I have distinctly before me the days and dates when I came into contact with their
inexhaustible beauties. Leaving the coast line, the seat of malaria, and
where are often seen the remains of the slaver's barracoons, which always
give an impression of the deepest melancholy, I come to the high table-
lands with their mountain scenery and lovely valleys, their meadow
streams and mountain rivulets, and there amid the glories of a changeless
and unchanging nature, I have taken off my shoes and on that consecrated
ground adored the God and Father of the Africans.

This is the country and this is the work to which the American Negro is
invited. This is the opening for him which, through the labors of the

American Colonization Society, has been effected. This organization is more than a *colonization* society, more than an emigration society. It might with equal propriety and perhaps with greater accuracy be called the African *Repatriation* Society; or since the idea of planting towns and introducing extensive cultivation of the soil is included in its work, it might be called the African Repatriation and Colonization Society, for then you bring in a somewhat higher idea than mere colonization—the mere settling of a new country by strangers—you bring in the idea of restoration, of compensation to a race and country much and long wronged.

Colonizationists, notwithstanding all that has been said against them, have always recognized the manhood of the Negro and been willing to trust him to take care of himself. They have always recognized the inscrutable providence by which the African was brought to these shores. They have always taught that he was brought hither to be trained out of his sense of irresponsibility to a knowledge of his place as a factor in the great work of humanity; and that after having been thus trained he could find his proper sphere of action only in the land of his origin to make a way for himself. They have believed that it has not been given to the white man to fix the intellectual or spiritual status of this race. They have recognized that the universe is wide enough and God's gifts are varied enough to allow the man of Africa to find out a path of his own within the circle of genuine human interests, and to contribute from the field of his particular enterprise to the resources—material, intellectual, and moral—of the great human family.

But will the Negro go to do this work?

Is he willing to separate himself from a settled civilization which he has helped to build up to betake himself to the wilderness of his ancestral home and begin anew a career on his own responsibility?

I believe that he is. And if suitable provision were made for their departure to-morrow hundreds of thousands would avail themselves of it. The African question, or the Negro problem, is upon the country, and it can no more be ignored than any other vital interest. The chief reason, it appears to me, why it is not more seriously dealt with is because the pressure of commercial and political exigencies does not allow time and leisure to the stronger and richer elements of the nation to study it. It is not a question of color simply—that is a superficial accident. It lies deeper than color. It is a question of race, which is the outcome not only of climate, but of generations subjected to environments which have formed the mental and moral constitution.

It is a question in which two distinct races are concerned. This is not a question then purely of reason. It is a question also of instinct. Races feel; observers theorize.

The work to be done beyond the seas is not to be a reproduction of what we see in this country. It requires, therefore, distinct race perception and entire race devotion. It is not to be the healing up of an old sore, but the unfolding of a new bud, an evolution; the development of a new side of God's character and a new phase of humanity. God said to Moses, "I am that I am"; or, more exactly, "I shall be that I shall be." Each race sees from its own standpoint a different side of the Almighty. The Hebrews could not see or serve God in the land of the Egyptians; no more can the Negro under the Anglo-Saxon. He can serve *man* here. He can furnish the labor of the country, but to the inspiration of the country he must ever be an alien.

In that wonderful sermon of St. Paul on Mars Hill in which he declared that God hath made of one blood all nations of men to dwell on all the face of the earth and hath determined the bounds of their habitation, he also said, "In Him we live and move and have our being." Now it cannot be supposed that in the types and races which have already displayed themselves God has exhausted himself. It is by God in us, where we have freedom to act out ourselves, that we do each our several work and live out into action, through our work, whatever we have within us of noble and wise and true. What we do is, if we are able to be true to our nature, the representation of some phase of the Infinite Being. If we live and move and have our being in Him, God also lives, and moves and has His being in us. This is why slavery of any kind is an outrage. It spoils the image of God as it strives to express itself through the individual or the race. As in the Kingdom of Nature, we see in her great organic types of being, in the movement, changes, and order of the elements, those vast thoughts of God, so in the great types of man, in the various races of the world, as distinct in character as in work, in the great divisions of character, we see the will and character and consciousness of God disclosed to us. According to this truth a distinct phase of God's character is set forth to be wrought out into perfection in every separate character. As in every form of the inorganic universe we see some noble variation of God's thought and beauty, so in each separate man, in each separate race, something of the absolute is incarnated. The whole of mankind is a vast representation of the Deity. Therefore we cannot extinguish any race either by conflict or amalgamation without serious responsibility.

You can easily see then why one race overshadowed by another should long to express itself—should yearn for the opportunity to let out the divinity that stirs within it. This is why the Hebrews cried to God from the depths of their affliction in Egypt, and this is why thousands and thousands of Negroes in the South are longing to go to the land of their fathers. They are not content to remain where everything has been done on the line of another race. They long for the scenes where everything is to be done under the influence of a new racial spirit, under the impulse of new skies and the inspiration of a fresh development. Only those are fit for this new work who believe in the race—have faith in its future—a prophetic insight into its destiny from a consciousness of its possibilities. The inspiration of the race is in the race.

Only one race has furnished the prophets for humanity—the Hebrew race; and before they were qualified to do this they had to go down to the depths of servile degradation. Only to them were revealed those broad and pregnant principles upon which every race can stand and work and grow; but for the special work of each race the prophets arise among the people themselves.

What is pathetic about the situation is, that numbers among whites and blacks are disposed to ignore the seriousness and importance of the question. They seem to think it a question for political manipulation and to be dealt with by partisan statesmanship, not recognizing the fact that the whole country is concerned. I freely admit the fact, to which attention has been recently called, that there are many Afro-Americans who have no more to do with Africa than with Iceland, but this does not destroy the truth that there are millions whose life is bound up with that continent. It is to them that the message comes from their brethren across the deep, "Come over and help us"—1890.

JAMES T. HOLLY

(1829–1911)

A clergyman, James T. Holly was the most vocal advocate in the decade before the Civil War of emigration to Haiti. His tract, A Vindication of the Capacity of the Negro Race as Demonstrated by Historical Events of the Haitian Revolution, *was published in 1857. He later settled in Haiti.*

A VINDICATION OF THE CAPACITY
OF THE NEGRO RACE FOR
SELF-GOVERNMENT AND CIVILIZED PROGRESS

DEDICATION
TO REV. WILLIAM C. MUNROE,
RECTOR OF ST. MATTHEW'S CHURCH
DETROIT, MICHIGAN

Permit me the honor of inscribing this work to you. It is a lecture that I prepared and delivered before a Literary Society of Colored Young Men, in the City of New Haven, Ct., after my return from Hayti, in the autumn of 1855; and subsequently repeated in Ohio, Michigan, and Canada West, during the summer of 1856.

I have permitted it to be published at the request of the Afric-American Printing Company, an association for the publication of Negro literature, organized in connection with the Board of Publication, which forms a constituent part of the National Emigration Convention, over which you so ably presided, at its sessions, held in Cleveland, Ohio, in the years 1854–6.

I dedicate this work to you, in token of my appreciation of the life-long services you have so sacredly devoted to the cause of our oppressed race; the ardor of which devotion has not yet abated, although the evening of your life has far advanced in the deepening shadows of the approaching night of physical death.

And as the ground-work of this skeleton treatise is based in the events of Haytian History, it becomes peculiarly appropriate that I should thus dedicate it to one who has spent three of the most valuable years of his life as a missionary of the cross in that island; who there deposited the slumbering ashes of his own bosom companion a willing sacrifice to her constancy and devotion; and who yet desires to consume the remainder of his own flickering lamp of life by the resumption of those labors in that island, under more favorable and better auspices, in the service of Christ and his church.

Finally, I dedicate this work to you as a filial token of gratitude, for that guidance which under God, I have received from your fatherly teachings; by which I have been awakened to higher inspirations, of our most holy religion; aroused to deeper emotions of human liberty and quicker pulsations of the universal brotherhood of man; and thereby animated with a more consecrated devotion to the service of my suffering race than might otherwise have fallen to my lot.

Deign, therefore, I beseech you, to accept this dedication as the spontaneous offering of a grateful and dutiful heart.

LECTURE

The task that I propose to myself in the present lecture, is an earnest attempt to defend the inherent capabilities of the Negro race, for self-government and civilized progress. For this purpose, I will examine the events of Haytian History, from the commencement of their revolution down to the present period, so far as the same may contribute to illustrate the points I propose to prove and defend. Permit me, however, to add, in extenuation of this last comprehensive proposition, that I must, necessarily, review these events hastily, in order to crowd them within the compass of an ordinary lecture.

Reasons for Assuming Such a Task

Notwithstanding the remarkable progress of philanthropic ideas and humanitarian feelings, during the last half century, among almost every nation and people throughout the habitable globe; yet the great mass of the Caucasian race still deem the Negro as entirely destitute of those qualities, on which they selfishly predicate their own superiority.

And we may add to this overwhelming class that cherish such self-complacent ideas of themselves, to the great prejudice of the Negro, a large quota also of that small portion of the white race, who profess to believe the truths, "That God is no respecter of persons;" and that "He has made of one blood, all the nations that dwell upon the face of the earth." Yes, I say, we may add a large number of the noisy agitators of the present day, who would persuade themselves and the world, that they are really christian philanthropists, to that overwhelming crowd who openly traduce the Negro; because too many of those pseudo-humanitarians have lurking in their heart of hearts, a secret infidelity in regard to the real equality of the black man, which is ever ready to manifest its concealed sting, when the full and unequivocal recognition of the Negro, in all respects, is pressed home upon their hearts.

Hence, between this downright prejudice against this long abused race, which is flauntingly maintained by myriads of their oppressors on the one hand; and this woeful distrust of his natural equality, among those who claim to be his friends, on the other; no earnest and fearless efforts are put forth to vindicate their character, by even the few who may really acknowledge this equality of the races. They are overawed by the overpowering influence of the contrary sentiment. This sentiment unnerves their hands and palsies their tongue; and no pen is wielded or voice heard, among that race of men, which fearlessly and boldly places the Negro side by side with the white man, as his equal in all respects. But to the contrary, every thing is done by the enemies of the Negro race to vilify and debase them. And the result is, that many of the race themselves, are almost persuaded that they are a brood of inferior beings.

It is then, to attempt a fearless but truthful vindication of this race with which I am identified—however feeble and immature that effort may be —that I now proceed to set forth the following address:

I wish, by the undoubted facts of history, to cast back the vile aspersions and foul calumnies that have been heaped upon my race for the last four centuries, by our unprincipled oppressors; whose base interest, at the expense of our blood and our bones, have made them reiterate, from generation to generation, during the long march of ages, every thing that would prop up the impious dogma of our natural and inherent inferiority.

An Additional Reason for the Present Task

But this is not all. I wish hereby to contribute my influence—however small that influence—to effect a grander and dearer object to our race than even this truthful vindication of them before the world. I wish to do all in my power to inflame the latent embers of self-respect, that the cruelty and injustice of our oppressors, have nearly extinguished in our bosoms, during the midnight chill of centuries, that we have clanked the galling chains of slavery. To this end, I wish to remind my oppressed brethren, that dark and dismal as this horrid night has been, and sorrowful as the general reflections are, in regard to our race; yet, notwithstanding these discouraging considerations, there are still some proud historic recollections, linked indissolubly with the most important events of the past and present century, which break the general monotony, and remove some of the gloom that hang over the dark historic period of African slavery, and the accursed traffic in which it was cradled.

The Revolutionary History of Hayti
THE BASIS OF THIS ARGUMENT

These recollections are to be found in the history of the heroic events of the Revolution of Hayti.

This revolution is one of the noblest, grandest, and most justifiable outbursts against tyrannical oppression that is recorded on the pages of the world's history.

A race of almost dehumanized men—made so by an oppressive slavery of three centuries—arose from their slumber of ages, and redressed their own unparalled wrongs with a terrible hand in the name of God and humanity.

In this terrible struggle for liberty, the Lord of Hosts directed their arms to be the instruments of His judgment on their oppressors, as the recompense of His violated law of love between man and his fellow, which these tyrants of the new world had been guilty of, in the centuries of blood, wrong, and oppression, which they had perpetrated on the Negro race in that isle of the Carribean Sea.

But aside from this great providential and religious view of this great movement, that we are always bound to seek for, in all human affairs, to see how they square with the mind of God, more especially if they relate to the destinies of nations and people;—the Haytian Revolution is also the grandest political event of this or any other age. In weighty causes, and wondrous and momentous features, it surpasses the American revolution, in an incomparable degree. The revolution of this country was only the revolt of a people already comparatively free, independent, and highly enlightened. Their greatest grievance was the imposition of three pence per pound tax on tea, by the mother country, without their consent. But the Haytian revolution was a revolt of an uneducated and menial class of slaves, against their tyrannical oppressors, who not only imposed an absolute tax on their unrequited labor, but also usurped their very bodies; and who would have been prompted by the brazen infidelity of the age then rampant, to dispute with the Almighty, the possession of the souls of these poor creatures, could such brazen effrontery have been of any avail, to have wrung more ill-gotten gain out of their victims to add to their worldly goods.

These oppressors, against whom the Negro insurgents of Hayti had to contend, were not only the government of a far distant mother country, as in the case of the American revolution; but unlike and more fearful than this revolt, the colonial government of Hayti was also thrown in the balance against the Negro revolters. The American revolters had their colonial government in their own hands, as well as their individual liberty at the commencement of the revolution. The black insurgents of Hayti had yet to grasp both their personal liberty and the control of their colonial government, by the might of their own right hands, when their heroic struggle began.

The obstacles to surmount, and the difficulties to contend against, in the American revolution, when compared to those of the Haytian, were, (to use a homely but classic phrase,) but a "tempest in a teapot," compared to the dark and lurid thunder storm of the dissolving heavens.

Never before, in all the annals of the world's history, did a nation of abject and chattel slaves arise in the terrific might of their resuscitated manhood, and regenerate, redeem, and disenthral themselves: by taking their station at one gigantic bound, as an independent nation, among the sovereignties of the world.

It is, therefore, the unparallelled incidents that led to this wonderful event, that I now intend to review rapidly, in order to demonstrate thereby, the capacity of the Negro race for self-government and civilized progress, to the fullest extent and in the highest sense of these terms.

Preliminary Incidents of the Revolution

I shall proceed to develop the first evidence of the competency of the Negro race for self-government, amid the historical incidents that preceded their terrible and bloody revolution; and in the events of that heroic struggle itself.

When the cosmopolitan ideas of "Liberty, Fraternity, and Equality," which swayed the mighty minds of France, toward the close of the 18th century, reached the colony of St. Domingo, through the Massaic club, composed of wealthy colonial planters, organized in the French capital; all classes in that island, except the black slave and the free colored man, were instantly wrought up to the greatest effervescence, and swayed with the deepest emotions, by the startling doctrines of the equal political rights of all men, which were than so boldly enunciated in the face of the tyrannical despotisms and the immemorial assumptions of the feudal aristocracies of the old world.

The colonial dignitaries, the military officers, and other agents of the government of France, then resident in St. Domingo, the rich planters and the poor whites, (these latter called in the parlance of that colony "Les petits blancs,) were all from first to last, swayed with the intensest and the most indescribable feelings, at the promulgation of these bold and radical theories.

All were in a perfect fever to realize and enjoy the priceless boon of political and social privileges that these revolutionary ideas held out before them. And in their impatience to grasp these precious prerogatives, they momentarily forgot their colonial dependance on France, and spontaneously came together in a general assembly, at a small town of St. Domingo, called St. Marc; and proceeded to deliberate seriously about taking upon themselves all the attributes of national sovereignty and independence.

And when they had deliberately matured plans to suit themselves, they did not hesitate to send representatives to propose them to the national government of France, for its acknowledgment and acquiescence in their desires.

Such was the radical consequence to which the various classes of white colonists in St. Domingo seized upon, and carried the cosmopolitan theories of the French philosophers and political agitators of the last century.

But from all this excitement and enthusiasm, I have already excepted the black and colored inhabitants of that island.

The white colonists of St. Domingo, like our *liberty loving* and *democratic* fellow citizens of the United States, never meant to include this despised race, in their glowing dreams of "Liberty, Equality, and Fraternity."

Like our *model Republicans,* they looked upon this hated race of beings, as placed so far down the scale of humanity, that when the "Rights of man" were spoken of, they did not imagine that the most distant reference was thereby made to the Negro; or any one through whose veins his tainted blood sent its crimsoned tide.

And so blind were they to the fact that the "Rights of Man" could be so construed as to recognise the humanity of that oppressed race; that when the National assembly of France, swayed by the just representations of the "Friends of the Blacks" was led to extend equal political rights to the free men of color in St. Domingo, at the same time that this National body ratified the doings of the General Colonial assembly of St. Marc: these same colonists who had been so loud in their hurrahs for the *Rights of Man,* now ceased their clamors for liberty in the face of this just national decree, and sullenly resolved "To die rather than share equal political rights with a bastard race." Such was the insulting term that this colonial assembly then applied to the free men of color, in whose veins coursed the blood of the proud planter, commingled with that of the lowly Negress.

The Self-Possession of the Blacks
AN EVIDENCE OF THEIR CAPACITY FOR SELF-GOVERNMENT

The exceptional part which the blacks played in the moving drama that was then being enacted in St. Domingo, by their stern self-possession amid the furious excitement of the whites, is one of the strongest proofs that can be adduced to substantiate the capabilities of the Negro race for self-government.

The *careless reserve* of the seemingly dehumanized black slave, who continued to toil and delve on, in the monotonous round of planatation labor, under a cruel task master, in a manner so entirely heedless of the furious hurrahs for freedom and independence; the planting of Liberty poles, surmounted by the cap of Liberty; and the erection of statues to the goddess of Liberty, which was going on around him: this apparent indifference and carelessness to the surging waves of freedom that were then awakening the despotisms of earth from their slumber of ages, showed that the slave understood and appreciated the difficulties of his position. He felt that the hour of destiny, appointed by the Almighty, had not yet tolled its summons for him to arise, and avenge the wrong of ages.

He therefore remained heedless of the effervescence of liberty that bubbled over in the bosom of the white man; and continued at his sullen labors, biding his time for deliverance. And in this judicious reserve on the part of the blacks, we have one of the strongest traits of self-government.

When we look upon this characteristic of cool, self-possession, we cannot but regard it as almost a miracle under the circumstances. We cannot see what magic power could keep such a warm blooded race of men in such an ice bound spell of cold indifference, when every other class of men in that colony was flush with the excitement of *liberty;* and the whole island was rocked to its center, with the deafening surges of EQUALITY, that echoed from ten thousand throats.

One would have supposed, that at the very first sound of freedom, the 500,000 bondmen in that island, whose ancestry for three centuries had worn the yoke of slavery; would have raised up, at once, in their overwhelming numerical power and physical stalwartness, and cried out LIBERTY! with a voice so powerful as to have cleft asunder the bowels of the earth, and buried slavery and every Negro hater and oppressor who might dare oppose their just rights, in one common grave.

But as I have said, they did no such thing; they had a conscious faith in the ultimate designs of God; and they silently waited, trusting to the workings of His over-ruling Providence to bring about the final day of their deliverance. In doing so, I claim they have given an evidence of their ability to govern themselves, that ought to silence all pro-slavery calumniators of my race at once, and forever, by its powerful and undying refutation of their slanders.

And let no one dare to rob them of this glorious trait of character, either by alleging that they remained thus indifferent, because they were too ignorant to appreciate the blessings of liberty; or by saying, that if they understood the import of these clamors for the "Rights of Man," they were thus quiet, because they were too cowardly to strike for their disenthralment.

The charge that they were thus ignorant of the priceless boon of freedom, is *refuted* by the antecedent history of the servile insurrections, which never ceased to rack that island from 1522 down to the era of Negro independence. The Negro insurgents, Polydore, Macandel, and Padrejan, who had at various times, led on their enslaved brethren to daring deeds, in order to regain their God-given liberty, brand that assertion as a libel on the Negro character, that says, he was too cowardly to strike for the inheritance of its precious boon.

And the desperate resolution to be free, that the Maroon Negroes of the island maintained for 85 years, by their valorous struggles, in their wild mountain fastnesses, against the concentrated and combined operations of the French and Spanish authorities then in that colony; and which finally compelled these authorities to conclude a treaty with the intrepid Maroon chief, Santiago, and thereby acknowledge their freedom forever thereafter: this fact I say, proves him to be a base calumniator, who shall dare to say that a keen appreciation of liberty existed not in the bosom of the Negroes of St. Domingo.

But again, as to the plea of cowardice, in order to account for the fact of their cool self-possession amidst the first convulsive throes of Revolutionary liberty, permit me to add in refutation of this fallacy, that if the daring incidents of antecedent insurrections do not sufficiently refute this correlative charge also; then the daring deeds of dreadless heroism performed by a Toussaint, a Dessalines, a Rigaud, and a Christophe, in the subsequent terrible, but necessary revolution of the Negroes; in which black troops gathered from the plantations of slavery, met the best appointed armies of France, and at various times, those of England and Spain also: and proved their equal valor and prowess with these best disciplined armies of Europe —this dreadless heroism, evinced by the blacks, I say, is sufficient to nail the infamous imputation of cowardice to the wall, at once and forever.

Hence nothing shall rob them of the immaculate glory of exhibiting a stern self-possession, in that feverish hour of excitement, when every body around them were crying out Liberty. And in this judicious self-control at this critical juncture, when their destiny hung on the decision of the hour, we have a brilliant illustration of the capacity of the race for self-government.

Similar Evidence on the Part of the Free Men of Color

But additional and still stronger evidence of this fact crowd upon us, when we see that the free men of color remained entirely passive during the first stage of this revolutionary effervescence. This class of men, as a general thing, was educated and wealthy; and they were burthened with duties by the State, without being invested with corresponding political privileges. From such unjust exactions they had every reason to seek a speedy deliverance. And this great tumult that now swept over the island, offered them a propitious opportunity to agitate with the rest of the free men of the colony for the removal of their political disabilities.

They had greater cause to agitate than the whites, because they suffered under heavier burdens than that class. Nevertheless, in the first great outbreak of the water-floods of liberty—tempting as the occasion was, and difficult as restraint must have been; yet the free men of color also possessed their souls in patience and awaited a more propitious opportunity. Certainly no one will attempt to stigmatise the calm judgment of these men in this awful crisis of suspense, as the result of ignorance of the blessings of freedom, when it is known that many of this class were educated in the seminaries of France, under her most brilliant professors; and that they were also patrons of that prodigy of literature, the Encyclopedia of France.

Neither can they stigmatise this class of men as cowards, as it is also known that they were the voluntary compeers of the Revolutionary heroes of the United States; and who, under the banners of France, mingled their sable blood with the Saxon and the French in the heroic battle of Savannah.

Then this calm indifference of the men of color in this crisis, notwithstanding the blood of three excitable races mingled in their veins with that of the African, viz: that of the French, the Spanish, and the Indian; and notwithstanding, they had glorious recollections of their services in the cause of American Independence, inciting them on—this calm indifference, on their part, I say, notwithstanding these exciting causes, is another grand and striking illustration of the conservative characteristics of the Negro race, that demonstrate their capacity for self-government.

The Opportune Movement of the Free Colored Men

The tumultuous events of this excitement among the white colonists rolled onward, and brought the auspicious hour of Negro destiny in that island nearer and nearer, when Providence designed that he should play his part in the great drama of freedom that was then being enacted. Of course the propitious moment for the free men of color to begin to move would present itself prior to that for the movement of the Negro slaves.

The opportunity for the men of color presented itself when the general colonial assembly of St. Marc's (already referred to) sent deputies to France, to present the result of its deliberations to the National Assembly; and to ask that august body to confer on the colony the right of self-government.

At this time, therefore, when the affairs of the colony were about to undergo examination in the supreme legislature of the mother country, the free men of color seized upon the occasion to send deputies to France also, men of their own caste, to represent their grievances and make their wishes known to the National Assembly. This discreet discernment of such an opportune moment to make such a movement divested of every other consideration, shows a people who understand themselves, what they want, and how to seek it.

But when we proceed to consider the most approved manner in which the representations were made to the National Assembly, by the colored delegates in behalf of their caste, in the colony of St. Domingo, and the influences they brought to bear upon that body, as exhibited hereafter: we shall perceive thereby that they showed such an intimate acquaintance with the secret springs of governmental machinery, as demonstrated at once their capacity to govern themselves.

This deputation first drew up a statement in behalf of their caste in the colony, of such a stirring nature as would be certain to command the national sympathy in their cause, when presented to the National Assembly. But previously to presenting it to that assembly, they took the wise precaution to wait upon the honorable president of that august body, in order to enlist and commit him in their favor, as the first stepping stone to secure the success of their object before the Supreme Legislature.

They prevailed in their mission to the President of the Assembly; and succeeded in obtaining this very emphatic assurance from him: "No part of the nation shall vainly reclaim their rights before the assembly of the representatives of the French people."

Having accomplished this important step, the colored deputies next began to operate through the Abolition Society of Paris, called "Les Amis des Noirs," upon such of the members of the assembly as were affiliated with this society, and thus already indirectly pledged to favor such a project as theirs, asking simple justice for their race. They were again successful, and Charles De Lameth, one of the zealous patrons of that society, and an active member of the National Assembly, was engaged to argue their cause before the Supreme Legislature of the nation, although strange to say, he was himself a colonial slaveholder at that time.

And at the appointed moment in the National Assembly, this remarkable man felt prompted to utter these astounding words in behalf of this oppressed and disfranchised class of the colony: "I am one of the greatest proprietors of St. Domingo; yet I declare to you, that sooner than lose sight of principles so sacred to justice and humanity, I would prefer to lose all that I possess. I declare myself in favor of admitting the men of color to the rights of citizenship; and in favor of the freedom of the blacks."

Now let us for a moment stop and reflect on the measures resorted to by the colored deputies of St. Domingo, in Paris, who, by their wise stratagems, had brought their cause step by step to such an eventful and auspicious crisis as this.

Could there have been surer measures concocted for the success of their plans, than thus committing the president of the assembly to their cause in the first place; and afterwards pressing a liberty-loving slaveholder into their service, to thunder their measures through the National Assembly, by such a bold declaration?

Who among the old fogies of Tammany Hall—that junta of scheming politicians who govern this country by pulling the wires of party, and thereby making every official of the nation, from the President of the United States down to the Commissioners for Street Sweeping in the City of New York, dance as so many puppets at their bidding—I repeat it— who among these all powerful but venal politicians of old Tammany, could have surpassed these tactics of those much abused men of color, who thus swayed the secret springs of the National Assembly of France? And who, after this convincing proof to the contrary, shall dare to say that the Negro race is not capable of self-government?

But to return to the thread of our narrative. When the secret springs had been thus secured in their behalf, they had nothing to fear from the popular heart of the nation, already keenly alive to the sentiments of Liberty, Equality, and Fraternity; because the simple justice of their demands would commend them to the people as soon as they were publicly made known in France.

In order to make the very best impression on the popular heart of the nation, their petition demanding simple justice to their caste was accompanied with a statement very carefully drawn up.

In this statement they showed that their caste in the colony of St. Domingo possessed one-third of the real estate, and one-fourth of the personal effects of the island. They also set forth the advantages of their position in the political and social affairs of St. Domingo, as a balance of power in the hand of the imperial government of France, against the high pretensions of the haughty planters on the one hand, and the seditious spirit of the poor whites on the other. And, as an additional consideration, by way of capping the climax, they offered in the name, and in behalf of the free men of color in the colony, six millions of francs as a loyal contribution to the wants and financial exigencies of the National Treasury, to be employed in liquidating the debt of their common country.

Thus, if neither their wire-working maneuvers, the justice of their cause, or the conservative influence which their position gave them in the colony, had not been enough to secure the end which they sought; then the tempting glitter of so much cash, could not be resisted, when its ponderous weight was also thrown in the scale of justice. They succeeded, as a matter of course, in accomplishing their purpose; and the National Assembly of France promulgated a decree on the 8th of March, 1790, securing equal political rights to the men of color.

The very success of this movement, and the means by which its success was effected, the opportune moment when it was commenced, and the immense odds that were against those that sought its accomplishment— all these things must hereafter be emblazoned on the historic page as an everlasting tribute to the genius of the Negro race, and remain an ineffaceable evidence of their capacity for self-government; that may be triumphantly adduced and proudly pointed at in this and every succeeding generation of the world, until the latest syllable of recorded time.

The Crisis Produced in the Colony by This Decree
THE MEN OF COLOR ON THE SIDE OF LIBERTY, LAW, AND ORDER

It was when this decree was made known in the colony of St. Domingo, that the General Assembly of the colony, then sitting at St. Marc's, expressed the malignant sentiments of the white colonists, in a resolution that I have already quoted, viz: they resolved that they would "Rather die, than share equal political rights with a bastard race."

Vincent Oje, a man of color, and one of the delegates to Paris, in behalf of his caste, anticipated a venomous feeling of this kind against his race, on the part of the white colonists, when these decrees should be made known to them. He however, resolved to do whatever was within his power, to allay this rancorous feeling. He did not therefore hasten home to the colony immediately after the decree was promulgated. He delayed, in order to allow time for their momentary excitement as expressed in the resolution above, to cool off, by a more calm reflection on their sober second thought. He also tarried in France, to secure a higher political end, by which he would be personally prepared to return to St. Domingo, to make the most favorable impression in behalf of his race, and the objects of that decree, on the minds of the white colonists.

To this end he succeeds in getting the appointment of Commissioner of France, from the French government, to superintend the execution of the decree of the 8th of March, 1790, in the island of St. Domingo.

Certainly, he might hope, that being invested with the sacred dignity of France, his person, his race, (thus honored through him by that imperial government,) and the National decree itself, with which he was charged, would now be respected.

But not content with accumulating the national honors of France; fearing lest the pro-Slavery colonists would disregard these high prerogatives, by looking upon them as having been obtained through the *fanatical* "Friends of the Blacks" at Paris, by those partisans exerting an undue influence on the National Government: he further proceeds to gather additional honors, by ingratiating himself into the favor of a potentate of Holland—the Prince of Limbourg; from whom he received the rank of Lieutenant Colonel, and the order of the Lion. Thus he wished to demonstrate to the infatuated colonists, who regarded his race as beneath their consideration, that he could not only obtain titles and reputation in France, by means of ardent friends, but that over and above these, and beyond the boundaries of France, he could also command an European celebrity.

This was indeed a splendid course of conduct on his part; and by thus gathering around him and centering within himself these commanding prestiges of respect, he demonstrated his thorough knowledge of one of the most important secrets in the art of governing; and so far made another noble vindication of the capacity of the Negro race for self-government.

But as we proceed to consider the manner that he afterwards undertook to prosecute his high National Commission in promulgating in St. Domingo, the decree of the 8th of March, 1790, we shall see additional evidence of the same master skill crowd upon us.

He had now delayed his return from Europe in order to allow time for the allaying of hasty excitement, and for the purpose of making the most favorable advent to the island.

He comes a commissioned envoy of the French nation, and an honored chevalier of Europe. Nevertheless, with that prudent foresight which anticipates all possible emergencies, he landed in St. Domingo in a cautious and unostentatious manner, so as not to provoke any forcible demonstration against him. Having landed, he gathered around him a suite of 200 men for his personal escort, which his station justified him in having as his cortege; and which might also serve the very convenient purpose of a body guard to defend him against any attempt at a cowardly assassination from any lawless or ruthless desperadoes of oppression in the colony.

At the head of this body of men, he at once proceeded to place himself in communication with the Colonial Assembly, then in session; to inform it officially of his commission and the national decree which he bore; and to require that assembly, as the legislative authority of the island, to enforce its observance, by enacting an ordinance in accordance with the same.

In this communication of Oje, being aware of their pro-slavery prejudices, he endeavored to conciliate them by a peace offering. That peace offering was the sanctioning of Negro Slavery; for he stated to the assembly that the decree did not refer to the blacks in servitude; neither did the men of color, said he, desire to acknowledge their equality.

This specific assurance on the part of Oje, although it does not speak much for his high sense of justice, when abstractly considered; yet it shows as much wisdom and tact in the science of government, as is evinced by the sapient or *sap* headed legislators of this country, who make similar compromises as a peace offering to the prejudice and injustice of the oligarchic despots of this nation.

Oje, however, failed to make the desired impression on the infatuated colonists, either by his National and European dignities, or by his peace offering of 500,000 of his blacker brethren. He fell beneath the malignant hate of the slaveholding colonists, after defending himself with his little band of followers, against the overwhelming odds of these sanguinary tigers, with a manly heroism, only equalled by the Spartans at the pass of Thermopylae, and thus has cut for himself an enduring niche among the heroes in the temple of fame.

He was captured; and after a mock trial, illustrative of pro-slavery justice; something similar, for instance, to our Fugitive Slave Law trials in Boston, Philadelphia, and Cincinnati—(though more merciful in its penalty than these)—this mock court of St. Domingo condemned Vincent Oje and his brave lieutenant, Jean Chevanne, with their surviving compatriots, to be broken alive on the wheel.

We forget the error of the head committed by this right hearted, noble, and generous man, towards his more unfortunate brethren, in order to weep over his ignoble and unworthy fate, received at the hands of those monsters of cruelty in St. Domingo.

I cannot better close this notice of Oje, than by repeating the concluding lines from a Poem dedicated to him, by that distinguished man of color, our own fellow countryman, Prof. George B. Vashon, of McGrawville College:

Sad was your fate, heroic band,
Yet mourn we not, for yours the stand
Which will secure to you a fame,
That never dieth, and a name
That will, in coming ages be
A signal word for Liberty.
Upon the Slave's o'erclouded sky,
    Your gallant actions traced the bow,
Which whispered of deliverance nigh—
    The need of one decisive blow.
Thy coming fame, Oje! is sure;
Thy name with that of L'Ouverture,
And the noble souls that stood
With both of you, in times of blood,
Will live to be the tyrant's fear—
Will live, the sinking soul to cheer!

The Hour of Destiny for the Blacks

This untimely death of the great leader of the men of color, served only to develop how plentifully the race was supplied with sagacious characers, capable of performing daring deeds—it served to show how well the race was supplied with the material out of which great leaders are made, at any moment, and for any exigency.

Now came the hour for the patient, delving black slave to begin to move. He has manfully bided his time, whilst the white colonists were rampant in pursuit of high political prerogatives; and he has remained quiet, whilst his brother—the freed man of color, has carried his cause demanding equal political rights, triumphantly through the National Assembly of France.

But most intolerable of all, he has been perfectly still, whilst his more fortunate brethren have offered even to strike hands with the vile oppressor in keeping the iron yoke on his neck.

Nevertheless, he has lived to see both of these classes foiled by the overruling hand of Providence, from interpreting the words "Liberty, Equality, and Fraternity," to suit their own selfish and narrow notions. He finds these two parties now at open hostilities with one another. He sees, on one hand, the despicable colonists inviting foreign aid into the island, to resist the execution of the National decree and to prop up their unhallowed cause by the dread alternative of treason and rebellion. Whilst on the other hand, he beholds the men of color fighting on the side of the nation, law, and order, against the white colonists. Amid this general commotion his pulsations grow quick, and he feels that the hour of destiny is coming for *even* him to strike.

Yet he still possesses his soul in patience until the destined moment. At last he hears that France now vacillates in carrying out the tardy measure of justice that her National Legislature had enacted. The mother country, that had so nobly commenced the work of justice, by the national decree, enfranchising the free men of color, now begins to recede from the high position she had assumed in order to favor the frenzied prejudice of the infatuated colonists. The Negro slave had hoped that by this national act of justice to the free man of color, that a permanent step had been taken towards universal emancipation, and consequently his own eventual disenthralment. With this hope he was willing to continue quietly to wear his galling chains, rejoicing in the newly acquired boon of his more fortunate brethren, as the earnest and pledge of his own future deliverance, by a similar act of national justice. Thus the way seemed already paved for a peaceful termination of his servitude.

But, I repeat it again, the toiling black slave at last hears that the National Government of France vacillates in her judgment, quails before the storm of pro-slavery invectives, hurled by the insensate bigots of St. Domingo against the men of color, and finally, she recedes from her high position by the National Assembly repealing the decree of the 8th of March, 1790. Thus the slaves' dawning ray of hope and liberty is extinguished, and there is nothing ahead but the impenetrable gloom of eternal slavery.

This, then, is the ominous moment reserved for the chained bondmen to strike; and he rises now from his slumber of degradation in the terrific power of brute force. Bouckman, (called by a Haytian historian the Spartacus of his race,) was raised up as the leader of the insurgents, who directed their fury in the desperate struggle for liberty and revenge, until the work of devastation and death was spread throughout the island to the most frightful extent. He continued to ride on the storm of revolution in its hurricane march, with a fury that became intensified as it progressed, until the colonists, by some fortuitous circumstances, were enabled to wreak their vengeance on this Negro hero.

But when this first hero of the slaves was captured and executed by their oppressors, like Oje, the first hero of the free men of color; the capacity of the race to furnish leaders equal to any emergency, was again demonstrated.

A triumvirate of Negro and mulatto chieftains now succeeded these two martyred heroes.

Jean François, Biassou, and Jeannot, now appeared upon the stage of action, and directed the arms of the exasperated insurgents against a faithless nation, the cruel colonists and their English allies, whose aid these colonists had invited, in their treasonable resistance to the National decree, which Oje came from France to promulgate in the name of the nation.

In order to contend against such overwhelming odds effectually, and for the purpose of obtaining the necessary supply of arms and ammunition, the insurgents went over, for a time, to the service of Spain. This government had always regarded the French as usurpers in the island; and the Spaniards were therefore glad of any prospect of expelling the French colonists entirely from St. Domingo. Hence they gladly accepted the proffered service of the blacks as a means to effect this end.

However, we have no reason to regard the Spanish government as being more favorably disposed towards the blacks than that of France. We may rather conclude that Spain was willing to use the blacks to subserve her end, and afterwards would doubtless have endeavored to reduce them to a state of slavery again.

Nevertheless the black slaves and free men of color went over to the cause of Spain, and used her to subserve their purpose in driving France not only to re-enact her previous decree in relation to the men of color; but also to proclaim the immediate emancipation of the blacks, and to invest them with equal political rights. For this purpose, three National Commissioners of France were sent to the island, bearing these decrees of the Supreme Government.

When this glorious result was thus triumphantly effected, they left the service of Spain and returned to the cause of France again.

During the struggles that took place while the insurgents were in the cause of Spain, the three leaders who headed them when they united with the Spaniards, were shifted, by the fortunes of war, from their chieftainship, and replaced by Toussaint and Rigaud—one a black, and the other a mulatto, when they returned to the service of France.

These two leaders, at the head of their respective castes in the service of France, fighting on the side of liberty, law, and order, compelled the turbulent and treasonable colonists to respect these last national decrees; drove their English allies from the *colony,* and extinguished the Spanish dominion therein, and thus reduced the whole island to the subjection of France.

When we duly consider this shrewd movement of the blacks in thus pressing Spain in their service at that critical moment, when every thing depended upon the decision of the hour, by which they were enabled to accomplish such a glorious result, we have thereby presented another strong and convincing proof of the capacity of the Negro to adopt suitable means to accomplish great ends; and it therefore demonstrates in the most powerful manner, his ability for self-government.

The Auspicious Dawn of Negro Rule

Toussaint, by his acute genius and daring prowess, made himself the most efficient instrument in accomplishing these important results, contemplated by the three French commissioners, who brought the last decrees of the National Assembly of France, proclaiming liberty throughout the island to all the inhabitants thereof; and thus, like another Washington, proved himself the regenerator and savior of his country.

On this account, therefore, he was solemnly invested with the executive authority of the colony; and their labors having been thus brought to such a satisfactory and auspicious result, two of the Commissioners returned home to France.

No man was more competent to sway the civil destinies of these enfranchised bondmen than he who had preserved such an unbounded control over them as their military chieftain, and led them on to glorious deeds amid the fortunes of warfare recently waged in that island. And no one else could hold that responsible position of an official mediator between them and the government of France, with so great a surety and pledge of their continued freedom, as Toussaint L'Ouverture. And there was no other man, in fine, that these rightfully jealous freemen would have permitted to carry out such stringent measures in the island, so nearly verging to serfdom, which were so necessary at that time in order to restore industry, but one of their own caste whose unreserved devotion to the cause of their freedom, placed him beyond the suspicion of any treacherous design to re-enslave them.

Hence, by these eminent characteristics possessed by Toussaint in a super excellent degree, he was the very man for the hour; and the only one fitted for the governorship of the colony calculated to preserve the interests of all concerned.

The leading Commissioners of France, then in the island, duly recognized this fact, and did not dispute with him the claim to this responsible position. Thus had the genius of Toussaint developed itself to meet an emergency that no other man in the world was so peculiarly prepared to fulfil; and thereby he has added another inextinguishable proof of the capacity of the Negro for self-government.

But if the combination of causes, which thus pointed him out as the only man that could safely undertake the fulfillment of the gubernatorial duties, are such manifest proofs of Negro capacity; then the manner in which we shall see that he afterwards discharged the duties of that official station, goes still further to magnify the self-evident fact of Negro capability.

The means that he adapted to heal the internecine dissensions that threatened civil turmoil; and the manner that he successfully counteracted the machinations of the ambitious General Hedouville, a French Commissioner that remained in the colony, who desired to overthrow Toussaint, showed that the Negro chieftain was no tyro in the secret of government.

He also established commercial relations between that island and foreign nations; and he is said to be the first statesman of modern times, who promulgated the doctrine of free trade and reduced it to practice. He also desired to secure a constitutional government to St. Domingo, and for this purpose he assembled around him a select council of the most eminent men in the colony, who drew up a form of constitution under his supervision and approval, and which he transmitted, with a commendatory letter to Napoleon Bonaparte, then First Consul of France, in order to obtain the sanction of the imperial government.

But that great bad man did not even acknowledge its receipt to Toussaint; but in his mad ambition he silently meditated when he should safely dislodge the Negro chief from his responsible position, as the necessary prelude to the re-enslavement of his sable brethren, whose freedom was secure against his nefarious designs, so long as Toussaint stood at the helm of affairs in the colony.

But decidedly the crowning act of Toussaint L'Ouverture's statesmanship, was the enactment of the Rural Code, by the operation of which, he was successful in restoring industrial prosperity to the island, which had been sadly ruined by the late events of sanguinary warfare. He effectually solved the problem of immediate emancipation and unimpaired industry, by having the emancipated slaves produce thereafter, as much of the usual staple productions of the country, as was produced under the horrible regime of slavery; nevertheless, the lash was entirely abolished, and a system of wages adopted, instead of the uncompensated toil of the lacerated and delving bondman.

In fact, the island reached the highest degree of prosperity that it ever attained, under the Negro governorship of Toussaint.

The rural code, by which so much was accomplished, instead of being the horrible nightmare of despotism—worse than slavery, that some of the pro-slavery calumniators of Negro freedom and rule would have us believe; was, in fact, nothing more than a prudent government regulation of labor—a regulation which made labor the first necessity of a people in a state of freedom,—a regulation which struck a death blow at idleness, the parent of poverty and all the vices—a regulation, in fine, which might be adopted with advantage in every civilized country in the world, and thereby extinguish two-thirds of the pauperism, vagrancy, and crime, that curse these nations of the earth; and thus lessen the need for poor-houses, police officers, and prisons, that are now sustained at such an enormous expense, for the relief of the poor and the correction of felons.

This Haytian Code compelled every vagabond or loafer about the towns and cities, who had no visible means of an honest livelihood, to find an employer and work to do in the rural districts. And if no private employer could be found, then the government employed such on its rural estates, until they had found a private employer. The hours and days of labor were prescribed by this code, and the terms of agreement and compensation between employer and employed were also determined by its provisions. Thus, there could be no private imposition on the laborers; and, as a further security against such a spirit, the government maintained rural magistrates and a rural police, whose duty it was to see to the faithful execution of the law on both sides.

By the arrangement of this excellent and celebrated code, every body in the commonwealth was sure of work and compensation for the same, either from private employers or from the government. No body need fear being starved for want of work to support themselves, as is often the case among the laborers of Europe, and is fast coming to pass in the densely populated communities of this country, where labor is left to take care of itself under the private exploitation of mercenary capitalists. Under this code nobody need fear being exploited on by such unprincipled and usurious men, who willingly take advantage of the poor to pay them starvation prices for their labor; because, against such, the law of Toussaint secured to each laborer a living compensation.

By the operation of this code, towns and cities were cleared of all those idle persons who calculate to live by their wits, and who commit nine-tenths of all the crimes that afflict civilized society. All such were compelled to be engaged at active industrial labors, and thus rendered a help to themselves and a blessing to the community at large.

By this industrial regulation, every thing flourished in the island in an unprecedented degree; and the Negro genius of Toussaint, by a bold and straight-forward provision for the regulation and protection of his emancipated brethren, affected that high degree of prosperity in Hayti, which all the wisdom of the British nation has not been able to accomplish in her emancipated West India colonies, in consequence of her miserable shuffling in establishing Coolie and Chinese apprenticeship—that semi-system of slavery—in order to gratify the prejudices of her pro-slavery colonial planters; and because of the baneful influence of absentee land-lordism, which seems to be an inseparable incident of the British system of property.

Thus did the Negro government of St. Domingo, show more paternal solicitude for the well being of her free citizens, than they ever could have enjoyed under the capricious despotism of individual masters who might pretend to care for them; and thus did it more truly subserve the purposes of a government than any or all of the similar organizations of civilization, whose only care and object seem to be the protection of the feudal rights of property in the hands of the wealthy few; leaving the honest labor of the many unprotected, and the poor laborer left to starve, or to become a criminal, to be punished either by incarceration in the jails, prisons and dungeons provided for common felons; or executed on the gallows as the greatest of malefactors.

The genius of Toussaint by towering so far above the common ideas of this age in relation to the true purposes of government; and by carrying out his bold problem with such eminent success, has thereby emblazoned on the historic page of the world's statemanship a fame more enduring than Pitt, who laid the foundation of a perpetual fund to liquidate the national debt of England.

I say Toussaint has carved for himself a more enduring fame, because his scheme was more useful to mankind. The Negro statesman devised a plan that comprehended in its scope the well being of the masses of humanity. But Pitt only laid a scheme whereby the few hereditary paupers pensioned on a whole nation, with the absurd right to govern it, might still continue to plunge their country deeper and deeper into debt, to subserve their own extravagant purposes; and then provide for the payment of the same out of the blood and sweat, and bones of the delving operatives and colliers of Great Britain. Thus, then Toussaint by the evident superiority of his statesmanship, has left on the pages of the world's statute book, an enduring and irrefutable testimony of the capacity of the Negro for self-government, and the loftiest achievements in national statesmanship.

And Toussaint showed that he had not mistaken his position by proving himself equal to that trying emergency when that demigod of the historian Abbott, Napoleon Bonaparte, first Consul of France, conceived the infernal design of reenslaving the heroic blacks of St. Domingo; and who for the execution of this nefarious purpose sent the flower of the French Army, and a naval fleet of fifty-six vessels under command of General Leclerc, the husband of Pauline, the voluptuous and abandoned sister of Napoleon.

When this formidable expedition arrived on the coast of St. Domingo, the Commander found Toussaint and his heroic compeers ready to defend their God given liberty against even the terrors of the godless First Consul of France. Wheresoever these minions of slavery and despotism made their sacrilegous advances, devastation and death reigned under the exasperated genius of Toussaint.

He made that bold resolution and unalterable determination, which, in ancient times, would have entitled him to be deified among the gods; that resolution was to reduce the fair eden-like Isle of Hispaniola to a desolate waste like Sahara; and suffer every black to be immolated in a manly defense of his liberty, rather than the infernal and accursed system of Negro slavery should again be established on that soil. He considered it far better, that his sable countrymen should be DEAD FREEMEN than LIVING SLAVES.

The French veterans grew pale at the terrible manner that the blacks set to work to execute this resolution. Leclerc found it impossible to execute his design by force; and he was only able to win the reconciliation of the exasperated blacks to the government of France, by abandoning his hostilities and pledging himself to respect their freedom thereafter. It was then that the brave Negro Generals of Toussaint went over in the service of Leclerc; and it was then, that the Negro Chieftain himself, resigned his post to the Governor General appointed by Napoleon, and went into the shades of domestic retirement, at his home in Ennery.

Thus did Toussaint, by his firm resolution to execute his purpose, by his devotion to liberty and the cause of his race, so consistently maintained under all circumstances, more than deify himself; he proved himself more than a patriot; he showed himself to be the unswerving friend and servant of God and humanity.

Now, with the illustrious traits of character of this brilliant Negro before us, who will dare to say that the race who can thus produce such a noble specimen of a hero and statesman, is incapable of self-government. Let such a vile slanderer, if there any longer remains such, hide his diminutive head in the presence of his illustrious Negro superior!

I know it may be said that, after all Toussaint was found wanting in the necessary qualities to meet, and triumph in, the last emergency, when he was finally beguiled, and sent to perish in the dungeons of France, a victim of the perfidious machinations of the heartless Napoleon.

On this point I will frankly own that Toussaint was deficient in those qualities by which his antagonist finally succeeded in getting him in his power.

So long as manly skill and shrewdness—so long as bold and open tactics and honorable stratagems were resorted to, the black had proved himself, in every respect, the equal of the white man. But the Negro's heart had not yet descended to that infamous depth of subtle depravity, that could justify him in solemnly and publicly taking an oath, with the concealed, jesuitical purpose, of thereby gaining an opportunity to deliberately violate the same. He had no conception, therefore, that the white man from whom he had learned all that he knew of true—religion I repeat it—he had no conception that the white man, bad as he was, slaveholder as he was—that *even* HE was really so debased, vile, and depraved, as to be capable of such a double-dyed act of villainy, as breaking an oath solemnly sealed by invoking the name of the Eternal God of Ages.

Hence, when the Captain General, Leclerc, said to Toussaint, in presence of the French and Black Generals, uplifting his hand and jewelled sword to heaven: "I swear before the face of the Supreme Being, to respect the liberty of the people of St. Domingo." Toussaint believed in the sincerity of this solemn oath of the white man. He threw down his arms, and went to end the remainder of his days in the bosom of his family. This was, indeed, a sad mistake for him, to place so much confidence in the word of the white man. As the result of this first error, he easily fell into another equally treacherous. He was invited by General Brunet, another minion of Napoleon, in St. Domingo, to partake of the social hospitalities of his home; but, Toussaint, instead of finding the domestic civilities that he expected, was bound in chains, sent on board the Hero, a vessel already held in readiness for the consummation of the vile deed, in which he was carried a prisoner to France.

The magnanimous man bitterly repented at his leisure, his too great confidence in the word of the white man, in the cold dark dungeons of the castle of Joux. And the depth of his repentance was intensified by a compulsory fast ordered by that would-be great and magnanimous man, Napoleon Bonaparte, who denied him food, and starved him to death.

Great God! how the blood runs chill, in contemplating the ignoble end of the illustrious Negro chieftain and statesman, by such base and perfidious means!

A Bloody Interlude Finally Establishes Negro Sovereignty

But if the godlike Toussaint had thus proved himself deficient in those mean and unhallowed qualities that proved his sad overthrow, nevertheless, the race again proved itself equal to the emergency, by producing other leaders to fill up the gap now left open.

The Negro generals, who had gone over to the service of France, on the solemn assurances and protestations of Leclerc, soon learned to imitate this new lesson of treachery, and accordingly deserted his cause, and took up arms against France again.

And, if afterwards, the heroic but sanguinary black chief, Dessalines, who had previously massacred 500 innocent whites (if any of these treacherous colonists can be called innocent) at Mirebalais; 700 more at Verettes, and several hundred others at La Riviere—I say again, if we now see him resume his work of slaughter and death, and hang 500 French prisoners on gibbets erected in sight of the very camp of General Rochambeau, we may see in this the bitter fruit of the treachery of the whites, in this dreadful reaction of the blacks.* These were the roots springing up, which Toussaint spoke of so sorrowfully on the ship's deck, as he was borne away a prisoner to France, from the coast of St. Domingo. The captive hero, on this occasion, compared himself to a tree, saying: "They have cut down in me the trunk of the tree; but the roots are many and deep." The furious Dessalines was therefore, one of the foremost and firmest of these roots left in St. Domingo by the fallen chief, Toussaint, who soon sprung up into a verdant and luxurious growth of sanguinary deeds, by which the independence of his Island home was baptized in a Sea of Blood.

Finally, if we see Dessalines with red hot shot, prepared to sink the squadron of general Rochambeau, as it departed for France, although the Negro chief had solemnly stipulated to allow it to sail from the harbor unmolested, we find in this determination of the blood-thirsty man, how well he had learned the lesson of treachery and perfidy from the example of the white man.

Thus, if shocking depravity in perfidiousness and covenant breaking, is needed as another evidence of the Negro's equality with the white man, in order to prove his ability to govern himself, then the implacable black chief, Dessalines, furnishes us with that proof.

I think, however, we may thank God, that the last act of destruction contemplated by Dessalines was not consummated, in consequence of an English fleet taking Rochambeau and his squadron as prisoners of war in

---

* General Leclerc had now fallen a victim to the ravages of yellow fever, and Rochambeau had succeeded to the supreme command of the invading forces.

the harbor of Port-au-Prince; and thus, by this providential interposition, saved the race from a stigma on the pages of history, as foul as that which darkens the moral character of their antagonists.

Having now arrived at the epoch when the banners of Negro independence waved triumphantly over the Queen of the Antilles; if we look back at the trials and tribulations through which they came up to this point of National regeneration, we have presented to us, in the hardy endurance and perseverance manifested by them, in the steady pursuit of Liberty and Independence, the overwhelming evidence of their ability to govern themselves. For fourteen long and soul-trying years—twice the period of the revolutionary struggle of this country—they battled manfully for freedom. It was on the 8th of March, 1790, as we have seen, that the immortal man of color, Vincent Oje, obtained a decree from the National Assembly guaranteeing equal political privileges to the free men of color in the island. And, after a continued sanguinary struggle dating from that time, the never-to-be-forgotten self-emancipated black slave, Jean Jacque Dessalines, on the 1st of January, 1804, proclaimed Negro freedom and independence throughout the island of St. Domingo.

That freedom and independence are written in the world's history in the ineffaceable characters of blood; and its crimsoned letters will ever testify of the determination and of the ability of the Negro to be free, throughout the everlasting succession of ages.

Evidences of Self-Government since 1804

I will now proceed to give a hasty synopsis of the evidences that the Haytians have continued to manifest since their independence in demonstration of the Negroes' ability to govern themselves.

Dessalines the Liberator of his country was chosen as a matter of course the first Ruler of Hayti. During his administration, the efficient organization of an army of 60,000 men to defend the country against invaders—the erection of immense fortifications, and the effort to unite and consolidate the Spanish part of the Island in one government with the French portion over which he presided, showed that he understood the precautionary measures necessary to preserve the freedom and independence of his country; and so far he kept up the character of the race for capacity in self-government.

In the succeeding administrations of the rival chiefs, Christophe and Petion, we have indeed the sorrowful evidence of division, between the blacks and the men of color or mulatoes, the seeds of which was planted in the days of slavery. Nevertheless in that mutual good understanding that existed between them by which it was agreed to unite together whenever a foreign foe invaded the island; and in the contemptuous manner that both chiefs rejected the perfidious overtures of Bonaparte, we have still the evidence of that conservative good sense which fully exhibits the Negroes ability to take care of himself.

In the next administration of Boyer where we find these divisions in the French part of the island happily healed; and the Spanish colony also united in one government with the French, as Dessalines ardently desired in his time; we have the most astonishing evidence of the perfection the Black race could make in the art of self-government, during the short period of twenty years independence.

After Boyer's administration there were some slight manifestations of disorder, arising from the smouldering feud between the blacks and men of color that the ancient regime of slavery had created among them; the baneful influence of which the work of freedom and independence has not yet had time to entirely efface. In this disorder we find the Spanish part of the island secede and set up a separate nationality.—But we find every thing in the French part soon settling down into order again, under the vigorous sceptre of the present ruler, Faustin I.

And in his known sentiments to harmonize all classes of his people, and to unite the whole island under one strong government, to secure which end he has exerted every influence within his power, we have the continued evidence of those large and extended views of national policy among the rulers of Hayti, that proves their ability to govern themselves in a manner that will compare favorably with the statesmanship of any existing government of modern civilization.

Here we shall rest the evidence in proof of the competency of the Negro race for self-government which we have drawn out to rather a protracted length for the space assigned to a single Lecture; and turn our attention now to some of the evidences of civilized progress evinced by that people. We shall be brief in the elucidation of this point, because as their ample competency to govern themselves, has now been firmly established from the highest point of view, this fact of itself demonstrates that the soundest elements of civilized progress are inherent among such a people. Nevertheless it will be well to particularize some of the proofs on this point also.

Evidences of Civilized Progress
NATIONAL ENTERPRISE

Under the administration of Dessalines aside from the Military preparations we have noticed; he continued the Code Rural of Toussaint as the law of the land, thereby demonstrating that the Negro in independence could carry forward measures of industry for his own benefit as well as for the whites when he governed for and in the name of France; for such was the case during the Governor Generalship of Toussaint. He also established schools in nearly every district of his dominions, and the people seeing what advantage was possessed by those who had received instruction, attached great importance to its acquisition; and as the result in a short time there were but few who did not learn to read and write.

In the constitution that he promulgated, it was declared that he who was not a good father, a good husband, and above all a good soldier, was unworthy to be called a Haytian citizen. It was not permitted fathers to disinherit their children; and every person was required by law to exercise some mechanical art or handicraft.

Thus fundamental measures were taken to make education, well regulated families and the mechanic arts, those three pillars of civilization, the basis of Haytian Society.—And in this fact where such high necessities were recognized and appreciated, we have the most undoubted evidence of civilized progress.

The overthrow of the government of Dessalines, by the spontaneous uprising of the people in their majesty, when it had become a merciless and tyrannical despotism, may also be noted here as another evidence of progress in political freedom of thought that made the race scorn to be tyrannized over by an oppressive master, whether that master was a cruel white tyrant, or a merciless Negro despot.

Passing on to the two-fold government of Petion and Christophe, we not only discover the same military vigilance kept up by the construction of the tremendous fortification called the Citadel Henry that was erected by Christophe, under the direction of European Engineers, mounting 300 cannons;—but we also find both of these chiefs introducing teachers from Europe in their respective dominions; and establishing the Lancasterian system of schools.

We discover also during their administration, Protestant Missionaries availing themselves of the tolerant provision in regard to religious worship that had been maintained in the fundamental laws of the country since the days of Dessalines. These Missionaries commenced their work of evangelization with the approbation of the Negro and mulatto chieftains; —and Christophe went so far as to import a cargo of Bibles for gratuitous distribution among his people.

Thus do we find that progress continued to make its steady steps of advancement among these people, notwithstanding the political divisions that had now taken place among them.

The succeeding administration of General Jean Pierre Boyer, under whom these divisions were happily healed, was fraught with stupendous projects of advancement.

The whole of the laws of the island were codified and made simple, under six different heads, viz: The Code Rural, the Civil Code, the Commercial Code, the Criminal Code, and the Code of Civil and Criminal procedure, regulating the practice in the several courts of the island. Thus, by this codification of her laws, did Hayti execute over thirty years ago, that which the States of this Union are just arousing to the necessity of doing. Boyer also set on foot a project of emigration, for the purpose of inducing the colored people of the United States to remove to Hayti, in order to replenish and accelerate the growth of the Haytian population.

This project resulted in the removal of 6,000 colored people to that island from this country.

In addition to this important movement, various enterprises were undertaken by men of public spirit, during this administration, to promote industry among the people of Hayti.

A company was formed to carry on a mahogany saw mill, which expended $20,000 in the purchase of the necessary machinery from France. The mill was erected at St. Marc's. Judge Lespinasse, chief justice of the Court of Cassation, was President of the Company; and it was under the special patronage of General Boyer, the President of the Republic.

Another company was also formed, under the presidency of Senator Jorge, for tanning purposes, and expended $10,000 in preparations for carrying on the business. A saw mill was also erected at Port-au-Prince, by a private individual, at the cost of $15,000.

Thus were the most vigorous efforts of progress manifested during the administration of Boyer.

In the subsequent administration of Guerrier, Pierrot, and Riviere, which followed each other in quick and rather chaotic succession, the work of industrial progress did not abate. Two steamers were purchased by the government, a model agricultural farm was established under a scientific director from France; and English architects, carpenters, and stone masons were hired to come in the country to improve the style of building.

Finally, we also discover the same evidences of gradual progress, when we come down to the present administration of Faustin I. A navy of about twenty armed vessels has been created. Thirteen steam sugar mills have been erected. The system of education improved and extended. And a house of industry erected at Port-au-Prince, for the purpose of instructing boys in the mechanic arts.

And here let me add, that during the whole period of these successive administrations, that we have thus summarily passed under review, a thrifty commercial trade has been maintained between that island and the maritime nations of Europe and America, amounting in the aggregate, to several millions of dollars per annum.

Hence, these evidences of educational and industrial development, expanding continually as years roll onward, we regard as the most irrefragable proof of true civilized progress on the part of the Haytian people.

Stability of the Government

But in addition to these facts, we may adduce the general stability of the government they have maintained, as another evidence of civilized progress. There have been but eight rulers in Hayti since 1804, counting separately, Christophe and Petion, who ruled cotemporaneously. This is a period of fifty-three years down to the present time. And in the United

States, since 1809, there have been ten different chief magistrates—a period of forty-eight years. Thus, this country has had two more rulers than Hayti, within a period five years less than the Haytian sovereignty.

The fact is, there is no nation in North America, but the United States, nor any in South America, except Brazil, that can pretend to compare with Hayti, in respect to general stability of government. The Spanish Republics of America will have as many different rulers in eight years as Hayti has had in a half century.

And the colonial dependencies of European nations change governors at least three times as often as that Negro nation has done. This political stability, therefore, on the part of the Haytians, indicates a vast remove from Barbarism. It is far ahead of the anarchy of some so-called civilized nations. And it therefore indicates a high degree of civilization and progress.

Some exceptions might be taken, by the over scrupulous partizan of popular institutions, at the tendency manifested to vacillate between a Republican and Monarchial form of government, that has constantly been exhibited in Hayti, since the days of Dessalines.

The desire for Republican institutions has its rise in the Cosmopolitan ideas and example of France, at the time of the Haytian Revolution. The proximate example of the United States may also influence this desire for republicanism to some extent.

On the other hand, Monarchy is an ancient traditionary predilection of the race derived from Africa, which ancient continent maintains that form of government in common with the rest of the old world. The gorgeous splendor and august prestige of aristocratic rank and title, always attendant on this form of government, hold an imperious sway over the minds of this race of men who have such a keen appreciation of the beautiful. With these monarchical instincts on the one hand, and those powerful republican influences on the other, Hayti has continually oscillated between a republican and a monarchial form of government. But be it ever remembered to her credit, this oscillation has not unsettled the permanent stability of her national administration, as the facts previously adduced, abundantly prove.

Permit me, however, to urge with due deference to the republican ideas which surround me, that it matters not in the eternal principles of morality, what the form of government may be, so long as the ruling powers of a nation maintain the inviolability of personal liberty, exact justice and political equality among all of its honest citizens and subjects. If these things are not so maintained, a republic is as great, nay a greater despotism that an autocracy.

If there is but one despot to oppress the people, then there is but one neck to be severed in order to rid the earth of such a loathesome pest. But if the petty despots are numbered by the millions; then woe to that prescribed class that may fall under their tyranny, for it will need more axes and more executioners than can be supplied, in order to get this countless brood out of the way.

A popular despotism therefore, whose rulers are composed of political gamblers for the spoils of office and burglarious plunderers of the public treasury that tyrannizes over any class of its citizens and subject, is less tolerable than a monarchical or an aristocratic despotism, even though its rulers are a hereditary class of blood-titled paupers pensioned from generation to generation, on the public bounty of the nation. Among this latter class of rulers there is not to be found such a desperate and reckless set of lawless adventurers as will be found among the former. And should such monsters present themselves, they are in a more tangible shape to be got at and disposed of in a government of the few, than in that of the many. Hence the sacred purposes of government in securing the welfare of the whole people will always be more nearly arrived at in the one than in the other.

The Haytian people when governed by the crowned and imperial Dessalines testified their love of liberty, by destroying the tyrant when he violated the constitution and overstepped the laws of his country.

The American people under a republican form of government manifest their want of a love of true liberty, when they permit a vagabond set of politicians, whose character for rowdyism disgraces the nation, to enact such an odious law as the Fugitive Slave bill, violating the writ of *Habeas Corpus,* and other sacred guarantees of the Constitution;—and then tamely submit to this high handed outrage, because such unprincipled scoundrels voted in their insane revelry, that it must be the Supreme law of the land.

If there was one-half of the real love of liberty among even the people of the professedly free northern states, as there is among the Negroes of Hayti, every one of their national representatives who voted for that infamous bill, or who would not vote instantaneously for its repeal, would be tried for his life, condemned and publicly executed as accessory to man stealing. Thus would a free people, determined to preserve their liberties, rid themselves of a brood of petty tyrants who seek to impose their unhallowed partizan caprices upon the country, as the supreme law of the land, over-riding even the Higher Law of God. And thus in time would they exhibit an equally jealous regard for their rights, as the Haytians did, when they rid themselves of the tyrant Dessalines.

If such was the real love of liberty among the northern people of this vain-glorious Republic, we should soon annihilate that morally spineless class of politicians, who need decision of character, when they get to Washington, to legislate for freedom. All such as were thus morally destitute of spinal vertebrae to resist the aggressions of the slave power, in the National Halls of legislation, would also soon be physically deficient in their cervical vertebrae, when they returned home, to meet the extreme penalty of an outraged and indignant constituency.

But such a determined spirit of liberty does not exist here, and honest men must submit therefore with lamb-like patience to this republican despotism of irresponsible political partizans who violate every just principle of law, because these unrighteous decrees are perpetrated in the name of the sovereign people.

Hence there is far more security for personal liberty and the general welfare of the governed, among the monarchical Negroes of Hayti where the rulers are held individually responsible for their public acts, than exists in this bastard democracy.

The single necked despot is soon reached by the keen avenging axe of liberty, for any acts of despotism among the Haytian blacks; but here its dull and blunted edge lays useless; for it might be hurled in vain and fall powerless among a nameless crowd of millions.

Conclusion

But our historical investigations are at an end, and we must hasten to bring our reflections to a conclusion. I have now fulfilled my design in vindicating the capacity of the Negro race for self-government and civilized progress against the unjust aspersions of our unprincipled oppressors, by boldly examining the facts of Haytian history and deducing legitimate conclusions therefrom. I have summoned the sable heroes and statesmen of that independent isle of the Caribbean Sea, and tried them by the high standard of modern civilization, fearlessly comparing them with the most illustrious men of the most enlightened nations of the earth;—and in this examination and comparison the Negro race has not fell one whit behind their contemporaries. And in this investigation I have made no allowance for the Negroes just emerging from a barbarous condition and out of the brutish ignorance of West Indian slavery. I have been careful not to make such an allowance, for fear that instead of proving Negro equality only, I should prove Negro superiority. I shun the point of making this allowance to the Negro, as it might reverse the case of the question entirely, that I have been combatting and instead of disproving his alleged inferiority only, would on the other hand, go farther, and establish his superiority. Therefore as it is my design to banish the words "superiority" and "inferiority" from the vocabulary of the world, when applied to the natural capacity of races of men, I claim no allowance for them on the score of their condition and circumstances.

Having now presented the preceding array of facts and arguments to establish, before the world, the Negro's equality with the white man in carrying forward the great principles of self-government and civilized progress; I would now have these facts exert their legitimate influence over the minds of my race, in this country, in producing that most desirable object of arousing them to a full consciousness of their own inherent dignity; and thereby increasing among them that self-respect which shall urge them on to the performance of those great deeds which the age and the race now demand at their hands.

Our brethren of Hayti, who stand in the vanguard of the race, have already made a name, and a fame for us, that is as imperishable as the world's history. They exercise sovereign authority over an island, that in natural advantages is the Eden of America, and the garden spot of the world. Her rich resources invite the capacity of 10,000,000 human beings to adequately use them. It becomes then an important question for the Negro race in America to well consider the weighty responsibility that the present exigency devolves upon them, to contribute to the continued advancement of this Negro nationality of the New World until its glory and renown shall overspread and cover the whole earth, and redeem and regenerate by its influence in the future, the benighted Fatherland of the race in Africa.

Here in this black nationality of the New World, erected under such glorious auspices, is the stand point that must be occupied, and the lever that must be exerted, to regenerate and disenthrall the oppression and ignorance of the race, throughout the world. We must not overlook this practical vantage ground which Providence has raised up for us out of the depths of the sea, for any man-made and utopian scheme that is prematurely forced upon us, to send us across the ocean, to rummage the graves of our ancestors, in fruitless, and ill-directed efforts at the wrong end of human progress. Civilization and Christianity is passing from the East to the West; and its pristine splendor will only be rekindled in the ancient nations of the Old World, after it has belted the globe in its westward course, and revisited the Orient again. The Serpentine trial of civilization and Christianity, like the ancient philosophic symbol of eternity, must coil backward to its fountain head. God, therefore in permitting the accursed slave traffic to transplant so many millions of the race, to the New World, and educing therefrom such a Negro nationality as Hayti, indicates thereby, that we have a work now to do here in the Western World, which in his own good time shall shed its orient beams upon the Fatherland of the race. Let us see to it, that we meet the exigency now imposed upon us, as nobly on our part at this time as the Haytians met theirs at the opening of the present century. And in seeking to perform this duty, it may well be a question with us, whether it is not our duty, to go and identify our destiny with our heroic brethren in that independent isle of the Carribean Sea, carrying with us such of the arts, sciences and genius of modern civilization, as we may gain from this hardy and enterprising Anglo-American race, in order to add to Haytian advancement; rather than to indolently remain here, asking for political rights, which, if granted a social proscription stronger than conventional legislation will ever render nugatory and of no avail for the manly elevation and general well-being of the race. If one powerful and civilized Negro sovereignty can be developed to the summit of national grandeur in the West Indies, where the keys to the commerce of both hemispheres can be held; this fact will solve all questions respecting the Negro, whether they be those of slavery, prejudice or proscription, and wheresoever on the face of the globe such questions shall present themselves for a satisfactory solution.

A concentration and combination of the Negro race, of the Western Hemisphere in Hayti, can produce just such a national development. The duty to do so, is therefore incumbent on them. And the responsibility of leading off in this gigantic enterprise Providence seems to have made our peculiar task by the eligibility of our situation in this country, as a point for gaining an easy access to that island. Then let us boldly enlist in this high pathway of duty, while the watchwords that shall cheer and inspire us in our noble and glorious undertaking, shall be the soul-stirring anthem of GOD and HUMANITY.

ALEXANDER CRUMMELL

(1819–1898)

A clergyman, Alexander Crummell went to England where he took a degree at Queen's College, Cambridge. From there he went to Africa, where he spent the next twenty years of his life in missionary and educational work in Liberia and Sierra Leone. In 1862, he visited the United States together with Edward Blyden as an official representative of the Liberian government to encourage emigration to Liberia. In 1873, he returned permanently to the United States to become pastor of a church in Washington. While he continued to be interested in the welfare of Liberia and of Africa, he was as much concerned with the domestic problems of the American Negro. He was one of the founders of the American Negro Academy. His works include The Future of Africa, 1862, *and* Africa and America, Addresses and Discourses, *1891.*

THE RELATIONS AND DUTIES OF FREE COLORED MEN IN AMERICA TO AFRICA

"It is in Africa that this evil must be rooted out—by African hands and African exertions chiefly that it can be destroyed."
—McQUEEN, *View of Northern Central Africa.*

"We may live to behold the nations of Africa engaged in the calm occupations of industry, and in the pursuit of a just and legitimate commerce; we may behold the beams of science and philosophy breaking in upon their land, which at some happier period, in still later times, may blaze with full lustre, and joining their influence to that of PURE RELIGION, may illuminate and invigorate the most distant extremities of that immense continent."
—WM. PITT.

LETTER

It is now many months since I received a letter from you, just as you were about sailing from our shores for your home. In that note you requested me to address you a letter setting forth my views concerning Liberia, suggesting, at the same time, that such a letter might prove interesting to many of our old friends and schoolmates in New York. I have not forgotten your request, although I have not heretofore complied with it. Though convinced of the need and possible usefulness of such a letter as you asked from me, I have shrunk from a compliance with your request. Not to mention other grounds of reluctance, let me say here that I have felt it a venturesome thing to address four hundred thousand men; albeit it be indirectly through you. Neither my name, position, nor any personal qualities give me authority thus to do. The only excuse I have is the depth and solemnity of all questions connected with Africa. I see that no one else of our race has done it; perhaps I may be pardoned for assuming so great a task.

I may add here that I address the "Free Colored Men of America," because I am identified with them; and not because I feel that *they,* especially, and above all the other sons of Africa, in distant lands, are called upon for zeal and interest in her behalf. It is the exaggeration of the relation of *American* black men to Africa, which has turned the hearts of many of her own children from her. Your duties, in this respect, are no greater than those of our West Indian, Haytian, and eventually our Brazilian brethren. Whatever in this letter applies to our brethren in the United States, applies in an equal degree to them. But I am not the man to address them. I fear I *presume* even in writing this letter to American black men, and have only just now concluded to do so by the encouragement I have received in two pleasant interviews with Mr. Campbell and Dr. Delany.

And even now it is with doubt and diffidence that I conclude to send you this communication. My reluctancy has arisen chiefly from a consideration of the claim put forth by leading colored men in the United States, to the effect "that it is unjust to disturb their residence in the land of their birth by a continual call to go to Africa." This claim is, in my opinion, a most just one. Three centuries' residence in a country seems clearly to give any people a right to their nationality therein without disturbance. Our brethren in America have other claims besides this; they have made large contributions to the clearing of their country; they have contributed by sweat and toil to the wealth thereof; and by their prowess and their blood they have participated in the achievement of its liberties. But their master right lies in the fact that they are Christians; and one will have to find some new page and appendage to the Bible, to get the warrant for Christians to repel and expatriate Christians, on account of blood, or race, or color. In fact, it seems to me a most serious thing to wantonly trench upon rights thus solemnly and providentially guaranteed a people, that is, by a constant, ceaseless, fretting iteration of a repelling sentiment.

Of course I do not intend any thing akin to this in my letter. I would not insult the intellect and conscience of any colored man who thinks it his duty to labor for his race on American soil, by telling him that it is his duty to come to Africa. If he is educated up to the ideas of responsibility and obligation, he knows his duty better than I do. And, indeed, generally, it is best to leave individuals to themselves as to the *details* of obligation and responsibility.

"The primal duties shine aloft like stars";—and it is only when men *will* not see them, that we are bound to repeat and re-utter them, until the souls of men are aroused, and they are moved to moral resolution and to noble actions. But as to the *mode, form,* and *manner* of meeting their duties, let the common sense of every man decide it for himself.

My object in writing this letter is not to vex any of our brethren by the iteration of the falsehood that America is not their home, nor by the misty theory "that they will all yet have to come to Liberia." I do not even intend to invite any one to Liberia, glad as I would be to see around me many of the wise and sterling men I know in the United States, who would be real acquisitions to this nation, and as much as I covet their society. I am not putting in a plea for colonization. My object is quite different; in fact it is not a strict compliance with the terms of your letter, for I shall have but little to say about Liberia. But believing that *all* men hold some relation to the land of their fathers, I wish to call the attention of the sons of Africa in America to their "RELATIONS AND DUTY TO THE LAND OF THEIR FATHERS."

And even on such a theme I know I must prepare myself for the rebuff from many—"Why talk to *us* of fatherland? What have *we* to do with Africa? *We* are not Africans; we are Americans. You ask no peculiar interest on the part of Germans, Englishmen, the Scotch, the Irish, the Dutch, in the land of their fathers, why then do you ask it of us?"

Alas for us, as a race! so deeply harmed have we been by oppression that we have lost the force of strong, native principles, and prime natural affections. Because exaggerated contempt has been poured upon us, we too become apt pupils in the school of scorn and contumely. Because repudiation of the black man has been for centuries the wont of civilized nations, black men themselves get shame at their origin and shrink from the terms which indicate it.

Sad as this is, it is not to be wondered at. "Oppression" not only "makes a wise man mad," it robs him also of his self-respect. And this is our loss; but having emerged from slavery, it is our duty to cast off its grave-clothes and resist its deadly influences.

Our ancestors were unfortunate, miserable, and benighted; but nothing more. Their history was a history, not of ignominy and disgrace, but of heathenism and benightedness. And even in that state they exhibited a nobleness of native character, they cherished such virtues, and manifested so much manliness and bravery, that the civilized world is now magnanimous enough to recognize such traits; and its greatest men are free to render their warm eulogies.*

* For a most able and discriminating article upon this topic, see "WESTMINSTER REVIEW," January 7, 1842, Art., Dr. Arnold. Also, those humane and truthful Essays of Mr. HEAPS—"FRIENDS IN COUNCIL," vol. 2.

When then colored men question the duty of interest in Africa, because they are not Africans, I beg to remind them of the kindred duty of self-respect. And my reply to such queries as I have mentioned above is this: 1. That there is no need of asking the interest of Englishmen, Germans, Dutchmen and others in the land of their fathers, because they have this interest, and are always proud to cherish it. And 2d. I remark that the abject state of Africa is a most real and touching appeal to *any* heart for sympathy and aid. It is an appeal, however, which comes with a double force to every civilized man who has Negro blood flowing in his veins.

Africa lies low and is wretched. She is the maimed and crippled arm of humanity. Her great powers are wasted. Dislocation and anguish have reached every joint. Her condition in every point calls for succor—moral, social, domestic, political; commercial, and intellectual. Whence shall flow aid, mercy, advantage to her? Here arises the call of duty and obligation to colored men. Other people may, if they choose, forget the homes of their sires; for almost every European nation is now reaping the fruits of a thousand years' civilization. Every one of them can spare thousands and even millions of their sons to build up civilization in Australia, Canada, New Zealand, South Africa, or Victoria. But Africa is the victim of her heterogeneous idolatries. Africa is wasting away beneath the accretions of civil and moral miseries. Darkness covers the land, and gross darkness the people. Great social evils universally prevail. Confidence and security are destroyed. Licentiousness abounds everywhere. Moloch rules and reigns throughout the whole continent, and by the ordeal of Sassywood, Fetiches, human sacrifices, and devil-worship, is devouring men, women, and little children. They have not the Gospel. They are living without God. The Cross has never met their gaze, and its consolations have never entered their hearts, not its everlasting truths cheered their deaths.

And all this only epitomizes the miseries of Africa, for it would take a volume to detail and enumerate them. But this is sufficient to convince any son of Africa that the land of our fathers is in great spiritual need, and that those of her sons who haply have ability to aid in her restoration will show mercy to her, and perform an act of filial love and tenderness which is but their "reasonable service."

I have two objects in view in addressing you this letter: *one* relates to the temporal, material interests of adventurous, enterprising colored men; and the *other* pertains to the best and most abiding interests of the million masses of heathen on this continent—I mean their evangelization.

First, I am to speak with reference to the temporal and material interests of adventurous, enterprising and aspiring men in the United States of America. I wish to bring before such persons reasons why they should feel interest in Africa. These reasons are not, I am free to confess, directly and distinctively philanthropic; although I do, indeed, aim at human well-being through their force and influence. But I appeal now more especially to the hopes, desires, ambition, and aspirations of such men. I am referring to that sentiment of self-regard which prompts to noble exertions for support and superiority. I am aiming at that principle of SELF-LOVE which spurs men on to self-advantage and self-aggrandizement—a principle which, in its normal state and in its due degree, to use the words of BUTLER, "is as just and morally good as any affection whatever." In fine, I address myself to all that class of sentiments in the human heart which creates a thirst for wealth, position, honor, and power. I desire the auxiliary aid of this class of persons, and this class of motives, for it is such influences and agencies which are calculated to advance the material growth of Africa. She needs skill, enterprise, energy, *worldly* talent, to raise her; and these applied here to her needs and circumstances, will prove the handmaid of religion, and will serve the great purposes of civilization and enlightenment through all her borders.

There seems to me to be a natural call upon the children of Africa in foreign lands to come and participate in the opening treasures of the land of their fathers. Though these treasures are the manifest gift of God to the Negro race, yet that race reaps but the most partial measure of their good and advantage. It has always been thus in the past, and now as the resources of Africa are being more and more developed, the extent of *our* interest therein is becoming more and more diminutive. The slave-trade is interdicted throughout Christendom; the chief powers of earth have put a lien upon the system of slavery; interest and research in Africa have reached a state of intensity; mystery has been banished from some of her most secret quarters; sunlight, after ages of darkness, has burst in upon the charmed regions of her wealth and value; and yet the Negro, on his native soil, is but "a hewer of wood and drawer of water"; and the sons of Africa in foreign lands, inane and blinded, suffer the adventurous foreigner, with greed and glut, to jostle them aside, and to seize with skill and effect upon their own rightful inheritance.

For three centuries and upwards, the civilized nations of the earth have been engaged in African commerce. Traffic on the coast of Africa anticipated the discoveries of Columbus. From Africa the purest gold got its characteristic three hundred years ago. From Africa dyes of the greatest value have been carried to the great manufacturing marts of the world. From Africa palm oil is exported by thousands of tons; and now, as the observant eye of commerce is becoming more and more fastened upon this continent, grain, gums, oils of divers kinds, valuable woods, copper and other ore, are being borne from the soil to meet the clamorous demands of distant marts.

The chief item of commerce in this continent has been the "slave-trade." The coast of Africa has been more noted for this than for any thing else. Ever since 1600, the civilized nations of the earth have been transporting in deadly holds, in poisonous and pestilential cabins, in "perfidious barks," millions of our race to foreign lands. This trade is now almost universally regarded as criminal; but in the light of commercial prudence and pecuniary advantage, the slave-trade was as great a piece of folly as it was a crime; for almost beneath their eyes, yea, doubtless, often immediately in their sight, were lying treasures, rivalling far the market value of the flesh and blood they had been so eager to crowd beneath their hatches.

Africa is as rich in resources as India is; not as yet as valuable in products, because she is more unenlightened and has a less skilful population. But so far as it respects mineral and vegetable capacity, there seems to me but little, if any, doubt that Africa more than rivals the most productive lands on the globe. . . .

I am not blind to difficulties. I know some of the trials of emigration. I have been called to some of the difficulties, not to say severities, of missionary life. And therefore I shall be free, I trust, from the charge of flippancy. So likewise I am aware of the peculiar obstacles in the way of our brethren in the States. I, too am an American black man. I, too, have an acquaintance with obstructive idiosyncrasies in them. If you speak of hindrances and difficulties specially theirs, I know all about them.

But I say it deliberately, that the difficulties in the way of our brethren doing a goodly work for Africa, are more subjective than objective. *One of these hindrances is a want of missionary zeal.* This is a marked characteristic of *American* black Christians. I say *American,* for from all I hear, it does not characterize our West Indian brethren; and the infant church of Sierra Leone is already, in sixty years from its birth, a mother of missions. *This* is our radical defect. *Our* religion is not diffusive, but rather introversive. It does not flow out, but rather inward. As a people we like religion —we like religious services. Our people like to go to church, to prayer-meetings, to revivals. But we go to get enjoyment. We like to be made happy by sermons, singing, and pious talk. All this is indeed correct so far as it goes; but it is only *one* side of religion. It shows only that phase of piety which may be termed the *"piety of self-satisfaction."* But if we are true disciples, we should not only seek a comforting piety, but we should also exhibit an effective and expansive one. We should let our godliness exhale like the odor of flowers. We should live for the good of our kind, and strive for the salvation of the world.

Another of these hindrances is what the phrenologists term *"inhabitativeness,"*—the stolid inhabitativeness of our race. As a people, we cling with an almost deadly fixity to locality. I see this on both sides of the Atlantic. Messrs. Douglass and Watkins assail Messrs. Horace Greeley and Gerrit Smith for pointing out this peculiarity of character in our people. But without doubt they tell the truth of us. We are not "given to change." The death of a master, the break-up of a family, may cast a few black men from the farm to the city, but they go no further. We lack speculation. Man has been called a creature,

Looking before and after——

But not so we. We look where we stand, and but few beyond.

So here, on this side of the water. The colonization ship brings a few hundred freed men to this west coast of Africa. They gather together in the city of Monrovia, or the town of Greenville, and there they sit, yea, and would sit forever, if it were not for some strong *external* influence which now and then scatters a few, and a precious few, here and there along the coast.

Here then you see, in this same people, on both sides of the waters, an exaggeration of the "home feeling," which is so exceedingly opposite to Anglo-Saxon influences that I wonder that we, who have been trained for centuries under them, have not ere this outgrown it. Sixteen years from the settlement of Plymouth, sixty families started from Boston and cut their way to Windsor, on the Connecticut.* We in Liberia have never yet had a *spontaneous* movement of old settlers in a body and with a purpose to a new location. The colored people of Rochester, N. Y., in 1853, I hear, were mostly fugitive slaves. The "Fugitive Slave Law" prompted them to emigrate to Canada; but proximity determined their choice of a home rather than any large principle. We read in the Acts of the Apostles, that when those who at Stephen's death were persecuted, were scattered abroad, "they went everywhere, preaching the word." So when our brethren felt constrained to leave the United States, it was meet, it seems to me, that *some* of them should have thought of Africa and her needs. On the other hand, if Liberians had been duly awake to the welfare of our race, we should have shown our brotherly feeling by inviting the wanderers to our shores.

These *two* hindrances, that is, a lack of missionary zeal and a tenacious hold on locality, will doubtless prevent active efforts for the regeneration of Africa. So, too, they will serve to check commercial enterprise. But as a people, we shall have to rise above these things. The colored churches of America will find, by and by, they can retain no spiritual vitality unless they rise above the range of selfish observation, to broad, general, humane ideas and endeavors. Self-preservation, self-sustentation, are only single items in the large and comprehensive category of human duties and obligations.

> Unless above himself, he can erect himself,
> How poor a thing is man.

And this is equally true with regard to Liberian black Christians. Do not think that I pretend to say that we in Africa stand on such a high vantage-ground that we can point invidiously at our brethren in America. I have no hesitation in saying, as my own opinion, that in both the respects referred to above, we are more blameworthy than you.

* Bancroft's History of America, ch. ix.

A *third* hindrance may be mentioned here. There will be a reluctance on the part of even some good and zealous Christians to engage in the propagation of the Gospel in Africa on the ground "that its ultimate tendency must be to subserve the objectionable scheme of African colonization." But surely any one can see that such an objection is wicked. The Gospel *must* be reached in all the world. The Master commands it. The history of the Church shows that it does not necessarily, if generally, carry colonization with it. But even if in this particular case it does so, no Christian has a right to shrink from his duty. And that man must be demented who cannot see God's beneficent providence in colonization,—that man blind who does not recognize good and mercy in its work, civil and religious, on the coast of Africa! The duties of our present state are not to be determined by imaginary results or prospective issues. They always grow out of the positive commands of the Bible, or manifest human relations; and *both* fasten the duty upon us to care for the heathen in general, and for our heathen kin in particular.

I have no doubt, however, that every effort that is henceforth made to spread the Gospel in Africa, will bring many, from the impulse of emigration, to Africa. Up to a certain future, but I hope not distant, point in American sentiment, there will be, I feel quite certain, a large exodus of the better, more cultivated, and hence more sensitive minds, partly to Africa, Hayti, Brazil, and the British colonies. Those who "having done all," still STAND, must bear with those who leave. Hayti *needs a* PROTESTANT, Anglo-African element of the stamp Mr. Holly will give her. Jamaica is blessed by the advent in her midst of such a strong-minded, open-eyed, energetic spirit, as my old school-mate and friend SAMUAL R. WARD. And Liberia's wants in this respect are stronger than either of the above. You should learn willingly to give, even of your best, to save, and regenerate, and build up the RACE in distant quarters.* You should study to rise above the niggard spirit which grudgingly and pettishly yields its grasp upon a fellow laborer. You should claim in regard to this continent that "THIS IS OUR AFRICA," in all her gifts, and in her budding grace and glory. And you should remember, too, with regard to emigrants, the words of that great man, EDMUND BURKE,—"the poorest being that crawls on earth, contending to save itself from injustice and oppression, is an object respectable in the eyes of God and man."

But it is time that I should draw to a close, for I have fallen into a too common fault: I have made too long a "palaver." My letter has run out to a greater length than I intended. And now I shall weary you no longer.

For nigh three centuries the Negro race, in exile and servitude, has been grovelling in lowly places, in deep degradation. Circumstance and position alike have divorced us from the pursuits which give nobleness and gran-

* The 2d article of the Constitution of African Civilization Society sets forth my views in better language than my own: "The Evangelization and Civilization of Africa and the descendants of African ancestors, *wherever dispersed.*"

deur to life. In our time of trials we have shown, it is true, a matchless patience, and a quenchless hope: the one prophetic of victory, and the other the germ of a high Christian character, now developing. These better qualities, however, have been disproportioned, and the life of the race, in general, has been alien from ennobling and aspiring effort.

But the days of passivity should now come to an end. The active, creative, and saving powers of the race should begin to show themselves. The power of the Negro, if he has such power, to tell upon human interests, and to help shape human destinies, should, at an early day, make full demonstration of itself. We owe it to ourselves, to our race, and to our generous defenders and benefactors, both in Europe and America, to show that we are capable "of receiving the seed of present history into a kindly yet a vigorous soil, and [that we can] reproduce it, the same, and yet new, for a future period"* in all the homes of this traduced yet vital and progressive race.

Surely the work herein suggested is fitted to just such ends, and is fully worthy the noblest faculties and the highest ambition. If I were aiming but to startle the fancy, to kindle the imagination, and thereby to incite to brave and gallant deeds, I know no theme equal to this in interest and commanding influence. And just this *is* the influence it is now exerting upon passionate and romantic minds, in England and the United States, in France and Germany, in Austria and Sardinia. These civilized States are sending out their adventurous travellers to question, on the spot, the mysterious spell which seems to shut out Africa from the world and its civilization. These enterprising spirits are entering every possible avenue to the heart of Africa, anxious to assure the inner tribes of the continent that the enlightened populations of Europe would fain salute them as brethren, and share with them the culture and enlightenment which, during the ages, have raised *them* from rudeness and degradation; if they can only induce them to throw aside the exclusiveness of paganism and the repulsiveness of barbarism.

But the enlightened sons of Africa, in distant lands, are called to a far higher work than even this; a work which as much transcends mere civilization as the abiding interests of eternity outvie the transient concerns of time. To wrest a continent from ruin; to bless and animate millions of torpid and benighted souls; to destroy the power of the devil in his strongholds, and to usher therein light, knowledge, blessedness, inspiring hope, holy faith, and abiding glory, is, without doubt, a work which not only commands the powers of the noblest men, but is worthy the presence and the zeal of angels. It is just this work which now claims and calls for the interest and the activity of the sons of Africa. Its plainest statement and its simplest aspect are sufficient, it seems to me, to move these men in every quarter of the world to profound sensibility, to deep resolve, to burning ardor. Such a grand and awful necessity, covering a vast continent, touch-

* Dr. Arnold. Inaugural Lecture.

ing the best hopes and the endless destiny of millions of men, ought, I
think, to stir the soul of many a self-sacrificing spirit, and quicken it to
lofty purposes and noble deeds. And when one considers that never before
in human history has such a grand and noble work been laid out in the
Divine Providence, before the Negro race, and that it rises up before them
in its full magnitude now, at the very time when they are best fitted for its
needs and requirements, it seems difficult to doubt that many a generous
and godly soul will hasten to find its proper place in this great work of
God and man, whether it be by the personal and painful endeavors of a
laborer in the field of duty, or by the generous benefactions and the cheering incitements which serve to sustain and stimulate distant and tried
workers in their toils and trials. "A benefaction of this kind seems to enlarge the very being of a man, extending it to distant places and to future
times, inasmuch as unseen countries and after ages may feel the effects of
his bounty, while he himself reaps the reward in the blessed society of all
those who 'having turned many to righteousness, shine as the stars forever
and ever'" *—September 1, 1860.

THE RACE PROBLEM IN AMERICA

ADDRESS

The residence of various races of men in the same national community, is
a fact which has occurred in every period of time and in every quarter of
the globe. So well known is this fact of history that the mention of a few
special instances will be sufficient for this occasion.

It took place in earliest times on the plains of Babylon. It was seen on
the banks of the Nile, in the land of the Pharaohs. The same fact occurred
again when the barbarian hosts of the North fell upon effete Roman society, and changed the fate of Europe. Once more we witness the like fact
when the Moors swept along the banks of the Mediterranean, and seated
themselves in might and majesty on the hills of Granada and along the
fertile slopes of Arragon and Castile. And now, in the 19th century, we
have the largest illustration of the same fact in our own Republic, where
are gathered together, in one national community, sixty millions of people
of every race and kindred under the sun. It might be supposed that an
historical fact so large and multiform would furnish a solution of the great
race-problem, which now invites attention in American society. We read
the future by the past. And without doubt there are certain principles of
population which are invariable in their working and universal in their
results. Such principles are inductions from definite conditions, and may be
called the laws of population. They are, too, both historical and predictive.

* Bp. Berkley: "Proposal for supplying churches."

One cannot only ascertain through them the past condition of States and peoples, but they give a light which opens up with clearness the future of great commonwealths.

But, singular as it may seem, there is no fixed law of history by which to determine the probabilities of the race-problem in the United States. We can find nowhere such invariability of result as to set a principle or determine what may be called an historical axiom.

Observe just here the inevitable confusion which is sure to follow the aim after historical precedent in this problem.

The descendants of Nimrod and Assur, people of two different stocks, settled in Babylon; and the result was amalgamation.*

The Jews and the Egyptians under the Pharaohs inhabited the same country 400 years; but antagonism was the result, and expulsion the final issue.

The Tartars overran China in the tenth century, and the result has been amalgamation.

The Goths and Vandals poured into Italy like a flood, and the result has been absorption.

The Celts and Scandinavians clustered like bees from the fourth to the sixth centuries in the British Isles, and the result has been absorption.

The Northmen and Gauls have lived side by side in Normandy since the tenth century, and the result has been absorption.

The Moors and Spaniards came into the closest contact in the sixth century, and it resulted in constant antagonism and in final expulsion.

The Caucasian and the Indian have lived in close neighborhood on this continent since 1492, and the result has been the extinction of the Indian.

The Papuan and the Malay have lived side by side for ages in the tropical regions of the Pacific, and have maintained every possible divergence of tribal life, of blood, government, and religion, down to the present, and yet have remained perpetually and yet peacefully separate and distinct.†

These facts, circling deep historic ages, show that we can find no definite historical precedent or principle applicable to the race-problem in America.

Nevertheless we are not entirely at sea with regard to this problem. There are certain tendencies, seen for over 200 years in our population, which indicate settled, determinate proclivities, and which show, if I mistake not, the destiny of races.

What, then, are the probabilities of the future? Do the indications point to amalgamation or to absorption as the outcome of race-life in America? Are we to have the intermingling of our peoples into one common blood or the perpetuity of our diverse stocks, with the abiding integrity of race, blood, and character?

* "Duties of Higher toward Lower Races." Canon Rawlinson, Princeton Review, Nov., 1878.
† See "Physics and Politics," by Bagehot, pp. 84, 85.

I might meet the theory which anticipates amalgamation by the great principle manifested in every sphere, viz: "That nature is constantly departing from the simple to the complex; starting off in new lines from the homogeneous to the heterogeneous"; striking out in divers ways into variety; and hence we are hedged in, in the aim after blood-unity, by a law of nature which is universal, and which excludes the notion of amalgamation.

But I turn from the abstract to history. It is now about 268 years since the tides of immigration began to beat upon our shores. This may be called a brief period, but 268 years is long enough to fix a new type of man. Has such a new type sprung up here to life? Has a new commingled race, the result of our diverse elements, come forth from the crucible of our heterogeneous nationality?

We will indulge in no speculation upon this subject. We will exclude even the faintest tinge of the imagination. The facts alone shall speak for themselves.

First of all is the history of the Anglo-Saxon race in America. In many respects it has been the foremost element in the American population; in largeness of numbers, in civil polity and power, in educational impress, and in religious influence. What has become of this element of our population? Has it been lost in the current of the divergent streams of life which have been spreading abroad throughout the land?

Why, every one knows that in New England, in Virginia, in the Far West, along the Atlantic Seaboard, that fully three-fifths of the whole American population are the offspring of this same hardy, plodding, common-sense people that they were centuries ago, when their fathers pressed through the forests of Jamestown or planted their feet upon the sterile soil of Plymouth.

Some of you may remember the remark of Mr. Lowell, on his return in 1885 from his mission to England. He said that when English people spoke to him of Americans as a people different from themselves, he always told them that in blood he was just as much an Englishman as they were; and Mr. Lowell in this remark was the spokesman of not less than thirty-six millions of men of as direct Anglo-Saxon descent as the men of Kent or the people of Yorkshire.

The Celtic element came to America in two separate columns. The French entered Canada in 1607. They came with all that glow, fervor, gallantry, social aptitudes, and religious loyalty which, for centuries, have characterized the Gallic blood, and which are still conspicuous features on both sides of the Atlantic.

The other section of the Celtic family began their immigration about 1640; and they have almost depopulated Ireland to populate America; and their numbers now are millions.

One or two facts are observable concerning the French and Irish, viz: (1) That, although kindred in blood, temperament, and religion, they have avoided both neighborhood of locality and marital alliance; and (2) so great has been the increase of the Hibernian family that in Church life and political importance they form a vast solidarity in the nation.

The German, like the Celtic family, came over in two sections. The Batavian stock came first from Holland in 1608, and made New York, New Jersey, and Pennsylvania their habitat. The Germans proper, or High Germans, have been streaming into the Republic since 1680, bringing with them that steadiness and sturdiness, that thrift and acquisitiveness, that art and learning, that genius and acumen, which have given an elastic spring to American culture, depth to philosophy, and inspiration to music and to art.

And here they are in great colonies in the Middle and Western States, and in vast sections of our great cities. And yet where can one discover any decline in the purity of German blood, or the likelihood of its ultimate loss in the veins of alien people?

The Negro contingent was one of the earliest contributions to the American population. The black man came quickly on the heel of the Cavalier at Jamestown, and before the arrival of the Puritan in the east. "That fatal, that perfidious bark" of Sir John Hawkins, that "ferried the slave captive o'er the sea" from Africa, preceded the Mayflower one year and five months.

From that small cargo and its after arrivals have arisen the large black population, variously estimated from 8 to 10,000,000. It is mostly, especially in the wide rural areas of the South, a purely Negro population. In the large cities there is a wide intermixture of blood. This, by some writers, is taken as the indication of ultimate and entire amalgamation. But the past in this incident is no sign of the future. The gross and violent intermingling of the blood of the southern white man cannot be taken as an index of the future of the black race.

Amalgamation in its exact sense means the approach of affinities. The word applied to human beings implies will, and the consent of two parties. In *this* sense there has been no amalgamation of the two races; for the Negro in this land has ever been the truest of men, in marital allegiance, to his own race.

Intermixture of blood there has been—not by the amalgamation, which implies consent, but through the victimizing of the helpless black woman. But even this has been limited in extent. Out of 4,500,000 of this race in the census of 1861, 400,000 were set down as of mixed blood. Thousands of these were the legitimate offspring of colored parents; and the probability is that not more than 150,000 had white fathers. Since emancipation the black woman has gained possession of her own person, and it is the testimony of Dr. Haygood and other eminent Southerners that the base process of intermixture has had a wide and sudden decline, and that the likelihood of the so-called amalgamation of the future is fast dying out.

And now, after this survey of race tides and race life during 268 years, I repeat the question: "Has a *new* race, the product of our diverse elements, sprung up here in America? Or, is there any such a probability for the future?"

Let me answer this question by a recent and striking reference.

Dr. Strong, in his able, startling, striking Tractate, entitled *"Our Country,"* speaks, in ch. 4, p. 44, of the Helvetian settlement in southern Wisconsin. He deprecates the preservation of its race, its language, its worship, and its customs in their integrity. In this, you see, he forgets the old Roman adage that "though men cross the seas they do not change their nature." He then protests (and rightly, too) against the perpetuation of race antipathies, and closes his criticism with the suggestion, similar to that of Canon Rawlinson, of Oxford, viz., that the American people should seek the solution of the race-problem by universal assimilation of blood.

Dr. Strong evidently forgets that the principle of race is one of the most persistent of all things in the constitution of man. It is one of those structural facts in our nature which abide with a fixed, vital, and reproductive power.

Races, like families, are the organisms and the ordinance of God; and race feeling, like the family feeling, is of divine origin. The extinction of race feeling is just as possible as the extinction of family feeling. Indeed, a race *is* a family. The principle of continuity is as masterful in races as it is in families—as it is in nations.

History is filled with the attempts of kings and mighty generals and great statesmen to extinguish this instinct. But their failures are as numerous as their futile attempts; for this sentiment, alike subtle and spontaneous, has both pervaded and stimulated society in every quarter. Indeed, as Lord Beaconsfield says, "race is the key to history." When once the race-type gets fixed as a new variety, then it acts precisely as the family life; for, 1st, it propagates itself by that divine instinct of reproduction, vital in all living creatures, and next, 2nd, it has a growth as a "seed after its own kind and in itself," whereby the race-type becomes a perpetuity, with its own distinctive form, constitution, features, and structure. Heredity is just as true a fact in races as in families, as it is in individuals.

Nay, we see, not seldom, a special persistency in the race life. We see families and tribes and clans swept out of existence, while race "goes on forever." Yea, even nations suffer the same fate. Take, for instance, the unification of States now constantly occurring. One small nation after another is swallowed up by another to magnify its strength and importance, and thus the great empires of the world become colossal powers. But it is observable that the process of unification leaves untouched the vitality and the persistency of race. You have only to turn to Great Britain and to Austria to verify this statement. In both nations we see the intensity of race cohesion, and at the same time the process of unification. Indeed, on all sides, in Europe, we see the consolidation of States; and at the same time the integration of race: Nature and Providence thus developing that principle of unity which binds the universe, and yet at the same time manifesting that conserving power which tends everywhere to fixity of type. And this reminds us of the lines of Tennyson:

> That nature lends such evil dreams?
> Are God and nature, then, at strife,
>   So careful of the type she seems,
>   So careless of the single life.

Hence, when a race once seats itself permanently in a land it is almost as impossible to get rid of it as it is to extirpate a plant that is indigenous to its soil. You can drive out a family from a community. You can rid yourself of a clan or a single tribe by expulsion. You can swallow up by amalgamation a simple emigrant people.

But when a RACE, *i. e.*, a compact, homogeneous population of one blood, ancestry, and lineage—numbering, perchance, some eight or ten millions—once enters a land and settles therein as its home and heritage, then occurs an event as fixed and abiding as the rooting of the Pyrenees in Spain or the Alps in Italy.

The race-problem, it will thus be seen, cannot be settled by extinction of race. No amalgamating process can eliminate it. It is not a carnal question—a problem of breeds, or blood, or lineage.

And even if it were, amalgamation would be an impossibility. How can any one persuade seven or eight millions of people to forget the ties of race? No one could *force* them into the arms of another race. And even then it would take generations upon generations to make the American people homogeneous in blood and essential qualities. Thus take one single case: There are thirty millions of Negroes on the American *continent* (eight or more millions in the United States of America), and constantly increasing at an immense ratio. Nothing but the sheerest, haziest imagination can anticipate the future dissolution of this race and its final loss; and so, too, of the other races of men in America.

Indeed, the race-problem is a moral one. It is a question entirely of ideas. Its solution will come especially from the domain of principles. Like all the other great battles of humanity, it is to be fought out with the weapons of truth. The race-problem is a question of organic life, and it must be dealt with as an ethical matter by the laws of the Christian system. "As diseases of the mind are invisible, so must their remedies be."

And this brings me to the one vast question that still lingers, *i. e.*, the question of AMITY. Race-life is a permanent element in our system. Can it be maintained in peace? Can these races give the world the show of brotherhood and fraternity? Is there a moral remedy in this problem?

Such a state of concord is, we must admit, a rare sight, even in christendom. There is great friction between Celt and Saxon in Britain. We see the violence of both Russ and German against the Jew. The bitterness is a mutual one between Russia on the one hand and Bulgaria and the neighboring dependent principalities on the other, and France and Germany stand facing one another like great fighting cocks.

All this is by no means assuring, and hence we cannot dismiss this question in an off-hand and careless manner.

The current, however, does not set all one way. There is another aspect to this question.

Thus, the Norman and the Frank have lived together harmoniously for centuries; the Welsh, English, and Scotch in England; the Indian, the Spaniard, and Negro in Brazil, and people of very divergent lineage in Spain.

And now the question arises: What are the probabilities of amity in a land where exists such wide divergence of race as the Saxon on the one hand and the Negro on the other?

First of all, let me say that the social idea is to be entirely excluded from consideration. It is absolutely a personal matter, regulated by taste, condition, or either by racial or family affinities; and there it must remain undisturbed forever. The Jews in this land are sufficient for themselves. So are the Germans, the Italians, the Irish, and so are the Negroes. Civil and political freedom trench in no way upon the domestic state or social relations.

Besides, there is something ignoble in any man, any class, any race of men whining and crying because they cannot move in spheres where they are not wanted.

But, beyond the social range there should be no compromise; and this country should be agitated and even convulsed till the battle of liberty is won, and every man in the land is guaranteed fully every civil and political right and prerogative.

The question of equality pertains entirely to the two domains of civil and political life and prerogative.

Now, I wish to show that the probabilities tend toward the complete and entire civil and political equality of all the peoples of this land.

1st. Observe that this is the age of civil freedom. It has not as yet gained its fullest triumphs; neither yet has Christianity.

But it is to be observed in the history of man that, in due time, certain principles get their set in human society, and there is no such thing as successfully resisting them. Their rise is not a matter of chance or haphazard. It is God's hand in history. It is the providence of the Almighty, and no earthly power can stay it.

Such, pre-eminently, was the entrance of Christianity in the centre of the world's civilization, and the planting of the idea of human brotherhood amid the ideas in the laws and legislation of great nations. *That* was the seed from which have sprung all the great revolutions in thought and governmental policies during the Christian era. Its work has been slow, but it has been certain and unfailing. I cannot pause to narrate all its early victories. We will take a limited period. We will begin at the dawn of modern civilization, and note the grand achievements of the idea of Christian brotherhood.

It struck at the doctrine of the Divine Right of Kings, and mortally wounded it. It demanded the extinction of Feudalism, and it got it. It demanded the abolition of the Slave Trade, and it got it. It demanded the abolition of Russian Serfage, and it got it. It demanded the education of the masses, and it got it.

In the early part of the eighteenth century this principle of brotherhood sprouted forth into a grander and more consummate growth, and generated the spirit of democracy.

When I speak of the spirit of democracy I have no reference to that spurious, blustering, self-sufficient spirit which derides God and authority on the one hand, and crushes the weak and helpless on the other. The democratic spirit I am speaking of is that which upholds the doctrine of human rights; which demands honor to all men; which recognizes manhood in all conditions; which uses the State as the means and agency for the unlimited progress of humanity. This principle has its root in the Scriptures of God, and it has come forth in political society to stay! In the hands of man it has indeed suffered harm. It has been both distorted and exaggerated, and without doubt it needs to be chastised, regulated, and sanctified. But the democratic principle in its essence is of God, and in its normal state it is the consummate flower of Christianity, and is irresistible because it is the mighty breath of God.

It is democracy which has demanded the people's participation in government and the extension of suffrage, and it got it. It has demanded a higher wage for labor, and it has got it, and will get more. It has demanded the abolition of Negro slavery, and it has got it. Its present demand is the equality of man in the State, irrespective of race, condition, or lineage. The answer to this demand is the solution of the race-problem.

In this land the crucial test in the race-problem is the civil and political rights of the black man. The only question now remaining among us for the full triumph of Christian democracy is the equality of the Negro.

Nay, I take back my own words. It is NOT the case of the Negro in this land. It is the nation which is on trial. The Negro is only the touch-stone. By this black man she stands or falls.

If the black man cannot be free in this land, if he cannot tread with firmness every pathway to preferment and superiority, neither can the white man. "A bridge is never stronger than its weakest point."

> In nature's chain, whatever link you strike,
> Tenth or ten-thousandth, breaks the chain alike.

So compact a thing is humanity that the despoiling of an individual is an injury to society.

This nation has staked her existence on this principle of democracy in her every fundamental political dogma, and in every organic State document. The democratic idea is neither Anglo-Saxonism, nor Germanism, nor Hibernianism, but HUMANITY, and humanity can live when Anglo-Saxonism or any class of the race of man has perished. Humanity anticipated all human varieties by thousands of years, and rides above them all, and outlives them all, and swallows up them all!

If this nation is not truly democratic then she must die! Nothing is more destructive to a nation than an organic falsehood! This nation cannot live—this nation does not deserve to live—on the basis of a lie!

Her fundamental idea is democracy; and if this nation will not submit herself to the domination of this idea—if she refuses to live in the spirit of this creed—then she is already doomed, and she will certainly be damned.

But neither calamity, I ween, is her destiny.

The democratic spirit is of itself a prophecy of its own fulfillment. Its disasters are trivialities; its repulses only temporary. In this nation the Negro has been the test for over 200 years. But see how far the Negro has traveled this time.

In less than the lifetime of such a man as the great George Bancroft, observe the transformation in the status of the Negro in this land. When *he* was a child the Negro was a marketable commodity, a beast of the field, a chattel in the shambles, outside of the pale of the law, and ignorant as a pagan.

Nay, when I was a boy of 13, I heard the utterance fresh from the lips of the great J. C. Calhoun, to wit, that if he could find a Negro who knew the Greek syntax he would then believe that the Negro was a human being and should be treated as a man.

If he were living to-day he would come across scores of Negroes, not only versed in the Greek syntax, but doctors, lawyers, college students, clergymen, some learned professors, and *one* the author of a new Greek Grammar.

But just here the caste spirit interferes in this race-problem and declares: "You Negroes may get learning; you may get property; you may have churches and religion; but this is your limit! This is a white man's Government! No matter how many millions you may number, we Anglo-Saxons are to rule!" This is the edict constantly hissed in the Negro's ear, in one vast section of the land.

Let me tell you of a similar edict in another land:

Some sixty years ago there was a young nobleman, an undergraduate at Oxford University, a youth of much talent, learning, and political ambition; but, at the same time, he was *then* a foolish youth! His patrician spirit rose in bitter protest against the Reform Bill of that day, which lessened the power of the British aristocracy and increased the suffrages of the Commons. He was a clever young fellow, and he wrote a brilliant poem in defense of his order, notable, as you will see, for its rhythm, melody, and withal for its—silliness! Here are two lines from it:

> Let Laws and Letters, Arts and Learning die;
> But give us still our old Nobility.

Yes, let everything go to smash! Let civilization itself go to the dogs, if only an oligarchy may rule, flourish, and dominate!

We have a blatant provincialism in our own country, whose only solution of the race-problem is the eternal subjection of the Negro, and the endless domination of a lawless and self-created aristocracy.

Such men forget that the democratic spirit rejects the factious barriers of caste, and stimulates the lowest of the kind to the very noblest ambitions of life. They forget that nations are no longer governed by races, but by ideas. They forget that the triumphant spirit of democracy has bred an individualism which brooks not the restraints of classes and aristocracies. They forget that, regardless of "Pope, Consul, King," or oligarchy, this same spirit of democracy lifts up to place and power her own agents for the rule of the world; and brings to the front, now a Dane as King of Greece, and now a Frenchman as King of Sweden; now a Jewish D'Israeli as Prime Minister of England, and now a Gallatin and a Schurz as cabinet ministers in America. They forget that a Wamba and a Gurth in one generation, whispering angry discontent in secret places, become, by the inspiration of democracy, the outspoken Hampdens and Sydneys of another. They forget that, as letters ripen and education spreads, the "Sambos" and "Pompeys" of to-day will surely develop into the Touissants and the Christophes, the Wards and the Garnets of the morrow, champions of their race and vindicators of their rights. They forget that democracy, to use the words of De Tocqueville, "has severed every link of the chain" by which aristocracy had fixed every member of the community, "from the peasant to the king."*

They forget that the Church of God is in the world; that her mission is, by the Holy Ghost, "to take the weak things of the world to confound the mighty," "to put down the mighty from their seats, and to exalt them of low degree"; that now, as in all the ages, she will, by the Gospel, break up tyrannies and useless dynasties, and lift up the masses to nobleness of life, and exalt the humblest of men to excellence and superiority.

Above all things, they forget that "the King invisible, immortal, eternal" is upon the throne of the universe; that thither caste, and bigotry, and race-hate can never reach; that He is everlastingly committed to the interests of the oppressed; that He is constantly sending forth succors and assistances for the rescue of the wronged and injured; that He brings all the forces of the universe to grind to powder all the enormities of earth,

---

* *Democracy in America*, B. 2, Ch. 2.

and to rectify all the ills of humanity, and so hasten on the day of universal brotherhood.

By the presence and the power of that Divine Being all the alienations and disseverances of men shall be healed; all the race-problems of this land easily be solved; and love and peace prevail among men—1888.

AFRICAN CIVILIZATION SOCIETY

Founded in 1858 with Henry Highland Garnet as president, to establish a center for Negro nationality, this organization is of chief interest insofar as it was the object of an attack by Frederick Douglass.

CONSTITUTION

PREAMBLE

It has pleased Almighty God to permit the interior of Africa to be made known to us during the last few years, by the efforts of missionaries and explorers, to an extent hitherto deemed almost impossible. The facts which have become public concerning its climate, soil, productions, minerals, and vast capabilities for improvements, are such, that we can no longer mistake the intention of the Divine Mind towards Africa.

It is evident that the prophecy that "Ethiopia shall soon stretch out her hands unto God," is on the point of fulfillment, and that the work, when commenced, shall be "soon" accomplished, when compared with the apparently slow progress of the Gospel in the other grand divisions of the globe. In order, therefore, to aid in this great work, and promote the civilization and christianization of Africa, as well as the welfare of her children in all lands, we have formed ourselves into an Association, to be known as the African Civilization Society, and we severally agree to be governed by the following.

CONSTITUTION

ARTICLE I

This Society shall be called the "African Civilization Society," and shall act in harmony with all other societies, whose objects are similar to those of this Association.

ARTICLE II

The object of this Society shall be the civilization and christianization of Africa, and of the descendants of African ancestors in any portion of the earth, wherever dispersed. Also, the destruction of the African Slave-trade, by the introduction of lawful commerce and trade into Africa: the promotion of the growth of cotton and other products there, whereby the natives may become industrious producers as well as consumers of articles of commerce: and generally, the elevation of the condition of the colored population of our country, and of other lands.

ARTICLE III

No one shall be sent out under the auspices of this Society, either as a religious teacher, agent, or settler, who shall uphold doctrines which shall justify or aid in perpetuating any system of slavery or involuntary servitude.

ARTICLE IV

The donation or subscription of not less than one dollar annually, shall constitute any individual of good moral character a member of this Society; and the payment at one time of twenty-five dollars shall make any person a life-member.

ARTICLE V

The officers of this Society shall be a President, Vice-President, a Board of twenty Directors, a Recording Secretary, a Corresponding Secretary, and a Treasurer, who shall hold office for one year, and until their successors are regularly chosen.

ARTICLE VI

The members of this Society may be distinguished as either active, corresponding, or honorary members.

ARTICLE VII

The President shall preside at all meetings of the Society, and in the event of his absence, one of the Vice-Presidents shall discharge his duties. The Recording Secretary shall keep a regular and distinct account of the transactions of the Society. The Corresponding Secretary shall conduct the correspondence of the Society, and also act as its General Agent, under the direction, and with the consent of the Board of Directors.

The Treasurer shall keep the accounts, and have charge of the funds of the Society, holding them subject to the control of the Board of Directors.

ARTICLE VIII

The President, Vice-Presidents, Secretaries, and Treasurer shall be ex-officio members and officers of the Board of Directors.

The Board of Directors shall manage and regulate the affairs of the Society, and shall have power to make By-Laws for its own government, so as to fully control the business and funds of the Society.

Five members of the Board of Directors, when regularly convened, shall constitute a quorum for the transaction of business.

ARTICLE IX

The Board of Directors shall have power to form special committees from among their own number, and to fill any vacancy occurring among the officers, for any time intervening before the regular election.

ARTICLE X

The Society shall hold an annual meeting during the month of May, on any day the Board of Directors may designate, to elect officers, receive reports, and transact its official business, not otherwise delegated to the Board of Directors.

Special meetings may be held at other times, as the Board of Directors may designate.

ARTICLE XI

The Annual Meeting shall consist of the regular officers and members of the Society at the time of such meeting, and of delegates from other cooperating Societies, each Society being entitled to one representative.

ARTICLE XII

This Constitution shall be altered only at an annual meeting of the Society, by vote of two thirds of the members present, upon a proposal to that effect transmitted to the Corresponding Secretary, and published in the City of New York at least two months prior to the annual meeting.

SPECIAL MEETING OF THE AFRICAN CIVILIZATION SOCIETY

November 4th, 1861

A special meeting of the African Civilization Society was called at the Bible House, November 4th, 1861, to hold a Conference with Dr. Martin R. Delany, as the representative and exponent of the African movement, as understood by the emigrationists and others, among the colored people of America, to effect and complete a oneness and harmony of sentiment and action, that their white friends, as aiders and assistants, may have a true and definite point as a datum before them.

The following gentlemen composed the Conference:—Messrs. Rev. John Carey, J. W. Alston, R. H. Cain, B. W. Wilkins, Tunis G. Campbell, A. A. Constantine, Robert Hamilton, Dr. M. R. Delany, and Rev. H. M. Wilson. Mr. Hamilton was called to the chair, and Rev. H. M. Wilson, Secretary. Prayer by Rev. R. H. Cain.

After deeply interesting speeches by Messrs. Campbell, Alston, Wilson, Wilkins, Constantine, the Chairman, and Dr. Delany, the following resolutions were adopted:

Resolved, That a Committee be appointed to draw up a basis as a fundamental principle by which the African Civilization Society shall be governed, and its objects and designs defined.

Resolved, That Rev. R. H. Cain, T. G. Campbell, John Carey, Mr. Robert Hamilton, and Dr. M. R. Delany, be that Committee, to report to a General Committee, at 26 Bible House, at 4 o'clock, Thursday, the 7th inst.

Resolved, That having listened with deep interest to Dr. M. R. Delany, we heartily tender him our thanks for his instructing and practical address. Adjourned.

BIBLE HOUSE, NEW YORK,
Nov. 7th, 1861.

General Committee met, pursuant to adjournment. Present—Messrs. R. H. Cain, Charles H. Thompson, Benjamin W. Wilkins, Alfred A. Constantine, Isaac T. Smith, Robert Hamilton, Henry M. Wilson, Martin R. Delany; H. M. Wilson, Chairman, A. A. Constantine, Secretary.

Dr. Delany, on behalf of the Chairman, Rev. R. H. Cain, made the following report, which was taken up and adopted *seriatim:*

SUPPLEMENT TO THE CONSTITUTION OF THE
AFRICAN CIVILIZATION SOCIETY

In order the better to make the origin and objects of the African Civilization Society known, and to define its designs, intentions, and true position, and to secure that harmony and coöperation originally designed with other similar institutions previously established by the colored people of the United States and Canada, as well as that by the friends of the African race in Great Britain, to aid these movements, *Resolved,* That the succeeding Articles be added as an essential and fundamental part of the Constitution:

ARTICLE I

The Society is not designed to encourage general emigration, but will aid only such persons as may be practically qualified and suited to promote the development of Christianity, morality, education, mechanical arts, agriculture, commerce, and general improvement; who must always be carefully selected and well recommended, that the progress of civilization may not be obstructed.

ARTICLE II

The basis of the Society, and ulterior objects in encouraging emigration, shall be—Self-Reliance and Self-Government, on the principle of an African Nationality, the African race being the ruling element of the nation, controlling and directing their own affairs.

ARTICLE III

All agents employed by this Society must act under instructions, and consistently with the fundamental principles of the construction.

REV. RICHARD H. CAIN,
Pastor of Bridge Street Church, Brooklyn, Chairman.

REV. TUNIS G. CAMPBELL,
REV. JOHN CAREY,
ROBERT HAMILTON,
REV. DAVID STEVENS, *Pastor of Zion Church,*
REV. HENRY M. WILSON, *Pastor of 7th Avenue Church,*
REV. C. H. THOMPSON, *Pastor of Siloam Church, Brooklyn,*
REV. B. W. WILKINS,
REV. E. J. ADAMS, *Pastor of Plane Street Church, Newark,*
Rev J. W. C. Pennington, D.D.,*
MR. JERH. W. BOWERS,
MR. HENRY MONTGOMERY,
MR. CHRISTOPHER BROWN,
MR. ABRAM ROBERTS,
MR. HENRY W. BOGERT.

M. R. DELANY, *Secretary.*

On motion, *Resolved,* That the Committee have power to add to their own number.

On motion, *Resolved,* That these proceedings be published in the ANGLO-AFRICAN, and all other papers friendly to the movement be respectfully requested to copy.

HENRY M. WILSON, *Chairman.*
ALFRED A. CONSTANTINE, *Secretary.*

OFFICERS.

REV. H. H. GARNETT, *President,* 174 West 30th St.
R. L. MURRAY, Esq., *Treasurer,* 35 Broadway.
REV. A. A. CONSTANTINE, *Cor. Secretary,* 26 Bible House.
REV. H. M. WILSON, *Assis't Secretary,* 8 Morton St.
ISAAC T. SMITH, *Chairman of the Finance Committee,*
No: 1, 3d Avenue, Mariners' Savings Bank.

Vice Presidents.

D. STEVENS,	R. DUNLAP,	ALBERT BARNES,
JEREMIAH ASHER,	WM. WHIPPER,	A. N. FREEMAN,
D. A. PAYNE,	JOHN CARY,	J. J. MYERS,
D. PARISH,	M. R. DELANY,	J. H. JACKSON,
BENJAMIN COATES,	FRANCIS WAYLAND,	J. T. CRANE,
DUNCAN DUNBAR,	JOSHUA R. GIDDINGS,	THEODORE L. CUYLER,
ASA D. SMITH,	J. P. THOMPSON,	WM. HAGUE.

* Added on motion of Dr. Delany.

Persons wishing to coöperate with this Society may address the President or Corresponding Secretary, at the office, 26 Bible House, New York—1861.

PART II

Assimilation

HENRY HIGHLAND GARNET

(1815–1881)

A radical abolitionist who urged the slaves to rise, Henry Highland Garnet became interested in emigration and became the founder of the African Civilization Society. His writings include An Address to the Slaves of the United States of America, 1843, and The Past and the Present Condition and the Destiny of the Colored Race, 1848.

THE PAST AND THE PRESENT CONDITION, AND THE DESTINY OF THE COLORED RACE

Who is there, after looking at these facts, will question the probability of the assumption, that this republic, and this continent, are to be the theatre in which the grand drama of our triumphant Destiny is to be enacted.

The Red men of North America are retreating from the approach of the white man. They have fallen like trees on the ground in which they first took root, and on the soil which their foliage once shaded. But the Colored race, although they have been transplanted in a foreign land, have clung to and grown with their oppressors, as the wild ivy entwines around the trees of the forest, nor can they be torn thence. At this moment when so much feigned hatred is manifested toward us, our blood is mixed with every tribe from Cape Horn to the Frozen Ocean. Skillful men have set themselves to work at analyzation, and yet in many cases they are perplexed in deciding where to draw the line between the Negro and the Anglo-Saxon. Whatever our colorless brethren say of themselves, so far do they proclaim our future position. Do they say in proud exultation,

> No pent up Utica contracts our powers,
> The whole boundless continent is ours,

in this they bespeak our destiny.

There are those who, either from good or evil motives, plead for the utopian plan of the Colonization of a whole race to the shores of Africa. We are now colonized. We are planted here, and we cannot as a whole people, be re-colonized back to our fatherland. It is too late to make a

successful attempt to separate the black and white people in the New
World. They love one another too much to endure a separation. Where
one is, there will the other be also. Ruth, of the Old Testament, puts the
resolve of our destiny in our mouths, which we will repeat to those who
would expatriate us: "Entreat me not to leave thee nor return from following after thee, for whither thou goest I will go, and where thou lodgest
I will lodge; thy people shall be my people, and thy God shall be my
God. Where thou diest there will I die, and there will I be buried. The
Lord do so to me, and more; if aught but death part thee and me".

This western world is destined to be filled with a mixed race. Statesmen,
distinguished for their forecast, have gravely said that the blacks must
either be removed, or such as I have stated will be the result. It is a stubborn fact that it is impossible to separate the pale man and the man of
color, and therefore the result which to them is so fearful, is inevitable. All
this the wiser portion of the Colonizationists see, and they labor to hinder
it. It matters not whether we abhor or desire such a consummation, it is
now too late to change the decree of nature and circumstances. As well
might we attempt to shake the Alleghanies with our hands, or to burst the
rock of Gibralter with our fists. If the colored people should all consent to
leave this country, on the day of their departure there would be sore lamen-
tations, the like of which the world has not heard since Rachel wept for her
children, and would not be comforted, because they were not. We would
insist upon taking all who have our generous and prolific blood in their
veins. In such an event, the American church and state would be bereaved.
The Reverend Francis L. Hawks, D.D., of the Protestant Episcopal
Church, a man who is receiving the largest salary of any divine in the
country, would be called upon to make the sacrifice of leaving a good
living, and to share the fate of his brethren according to the flesh. The
Reverend Dr. Murphy, of Herkimer, New York, a Presbyterian, would be
compelled to leave his beloved flock; and how could they endure the loss
of a shepherd so eloquent, so faithful and so kind. We should be burdened with that *renegade Negro* of the United States Senate, Mr. Yulee, of
Florida. We should take *one* of the wives of Senator Samuel Houston. The
consort,—the beautiful Cleopatra of his Excellency, R. M. Johnson, late
Democratic Vice President of this great nation,—would be the foremost
in the vast company of exiles. After we all should return to tread the
golden sands of Africa, whether we would add to the morality of our
kindred across the deep waters future generations would decide. One thing
I am certain of, and that is, many of the slaveholders and lynchers of the
South are not very moral now. Our cousins of the tribe of Shem are welcome to our deserters. If they are enriched by them they may be assured
that we are not impoverished.

On the other continent, the destiny of the colored people will be similar
to that of the people among whom they are scattered. Colorphobia is confined almost entirely to the United States and the Canadas. We speak of

prejudice against color, but in fact, nothing of the kind exists. The prejudice is against the condition alone. Were not this the case the American
feeling would pervade the whole earth.

Many things that were intended for evil to us, will result, I trust, in
good. The tyrants have debarred us from the wealth accruing from trade
and commerce. This is an evil. But may it not be hoped that we are their
juniors in the art of cheating? We have among us some arrant cheats, but
it is presumed that but a few will doubt that our white brothers bear off
the palm in this department of human depravity. The besetting sins of the
Anglo-Saxon race are, the love of gain and the love of power. In many
instances, while our services could be dispensed with, we have not been
permitted to join the army, and of course have not been killed in the wars.
We have been driven from the sanctuaries where our oppressors worship,
and it may be that we are not quite as hypocritical as their practices have
made them. When the great national account shall be rendered before the
tribunal of Justice, the guilt of course must be borne by those who might
have had, or who have used the power of the government. There may,
therefore, be some good that may come out of this evil. But no thanks to
the evil doers. Their works are evil still, the good comes in spite of them.

The old doctrine of the natural inferiority of the colored race, propa-
gated in America by Mr. Thomas Jefferson, has long since been refuted by
Dr. John Mason Goode, and numerous respectable witnesses from among
the slandered, both living and dead: Pushkin in Russia, Dumas in France,
Toussaint in Hayti, Banaker, Theodore Sedgwick Wright, and a host in
America, and a brilliant galaxy in Ancient History.

There are blessings in store for our patient, suffering race,—there is
light and glory. The star of our hope is slowly and steadily rising above
the horizon. As a land that has long been covered by storms and clouds,
and shaken by thunder, when the storms and clouds had passed away, and
the thunder was succeeded by a calm, like that which cheered the first glad
morning, and flower and shrub smiled as they looked up to God, and the
mountains, plains and valleys rung with joy,—so shall this race come
forth and re-occupy their station of renown.

But how shall we hasten on that period? How shall we acquit ourselves
on the field where the great battle is to be fought? By following after
peace and temperance, industry and frugality, and love to God, and to all
men, and by resisting tyranny in the name of Eternal Justice. We must
also become acquainted with the arts and sciences, and agricultural pursuits. These will elevate any people and sever any chain.

We must also cherish and maintain a national and patriotic sentiment
and attachment. Some people of color say that they have no home, no
country. I am not among that number. It is empty declamation. It is unwise. It is not logical—it is false. Of all the people in this wide earth,
among the countless hordes of misery, there is not one so poor as to be
without a home and a country. America is my home, my country, and I

have no other. I love whatever good there may be in her institutions. I hate her sins. I loathe her slavery, and I pray Heaven that ere long she may wash away her guilt in tears of repentance. I love the green-hills which my eyes first beheld in my infancy. I love every inch of soil which my feet pressed in my youth, and I mourn because the accursed shade of slavery rests upon it. I love my country's flag, and I hope that soon it will be cleansed of its stains, and be hailed by all nations as the emblem of freedom and independence.

FREDERICK DOUGLASS
(1817–1895)

Escaping from slavery in 1838, Frederick Douglass made his way to New Bedford, Massachusetts, where he was drawn into the ranks of the abolition cause. In 1841 he became an agent of the Massachusetts Anti-Slavery Society and lectured in the North and in England. While on a lecturing tour in England in 1845, English friends bought his freedom for him. In 1847 he founded The North Star (*later changed to* Frederick Douglass' Paper), *a Rochester weekly, which he edited and published. During these years, he had a close association with William Lloyd Garrison. But in 1851 he broke with him when he refused to accept Garrison's view that politics was futile in the antislavery struggle. During the Civil War, he was active in the recruitment of Negro soldiers. After the war, he resided in Washington where he edited the* New National Era *until 1872. In 1877 he was United States Marshal for the District of Columbia and in 1889 Minister to Haiti. His writings include* Life and Times of Frederick Douglass, 1892, *and Philip Foner, ed.,* The Life and Writings of Frederick Douglass (4 vols.), 1950, *a comprehensive collection of his speeches and newspaper articles.*

WHAT ARE THE COLORED PEOPLE DOING FOR THEMSELVES?

The present is a time when every colored man in the land should bring this important question home to his own heart. It is not enough to know that white men and women are nobly devoting themselves to our cause; we should know what is being done among ourselves. That our white friends have done, and are still doing, a great and good work for us, is a fact which ought to excite in us sentiments of the profoundest gratitude; but it must never be forgotten that when they have exerted all their energies, devised every scheme, and done all they can do in asserting our rights, proclaiming our wrongs, and rebuking our foes, their labor is lost —yea, worse than lost, unless we are found in the faithful discharge of our anti-slavery duties. If there be one evil spirit among us, for the casting out of which we pray more earnestly than another, it is that lazy, mean and cowardly spirit, that robs us of all manly self-reliance, and teaches us to depend upon others for the accomplishment of that which we should achieve with our own hands. Our white friends can and are rapidly removing the barriers to our improvement, which themselves have set up; but

the main work must be commenced, carried on, and concluded by ourselves. While in no circumstances should we undervalue or fail to appreciate the self-sacrificing efforts of our friends, it should never be lost sight
of, that our destiny, for good or for evil, for time and for eternity, is, by an
all-wise God, committed to us; and that all the helps or hindrances with
which we may meet on earth, can never release us from this high and
heaven-imposed responsibility. It is evident that we can be improved and
elevated only just so fast and far as we shall improve and elevate ourselves. We must rise or fall, succeed or fail, by our own merits. If we are
careless and unconcerned about our own rights and interests, it is not
within the power of all the earth combined to raise us from our present
degraded condition.

> Hereditary bondmen, know ye not
> Who would be free, themselves must strike the blow?

We say the present is a time when every colored man should ask himself the question, What am I doing to elevate and improve my condition,
and that of my brethren at large? While the oppressed of the old world
are making efforts, by holding public meetings, putting forth addresses,
passing resolutions, and in various other ways making their wishes known
to the world, and the working men of our own country are pressing their
cause upon popular attention, it is a shame that we, who are enduring
wrongs far more grievous than any other portion of the great family of
man, are comparatively idle and indifferent about our welfare. We confess, with the deepest mortification, that out of the five hundred thousand
free colored people in this country, not more than two thousand can be
supposed to take any special interest in measures for our own elevation;
and probably not more than fifteen hundred take, read and pay for an anti-
slavery paper. We say this in sorrow, not in anger. It cannot be said that
we are too poor to patronize our own press to any greater extent than we
now do; for in popular demonstrations of odd-fellowship, free-masonry
and the like, we expend annually from ten to twelve thousand dollars. If
we put forth a call for a National Convention, for the purpose of considering our wrongs, and asserting our rights, and adopting measures for our
mutual elevation and the emancipation of our enslaved fellow-countrymen, we shall bring together about *fifty;* but if we call a grand celebration of odd-fellowship, or free-masonry, we shall assemble, as was the case
a few days ago in New York, from *four to five thousand*—the expense of
which alone would be from seventeen to twenty thousand dollars, a sum
sufficient to maintain four or five efficient presses, devoted to our elevation
and improvement. We should not say this of odd-fellowship and free-
masonry, but that it is swallowing up the best energies of many of our best
men, contenting them with the glittering follies of artificial display, and
indisposing them to seek for solid and important realities. The enemies of

our people see this tendency in us, and encourage it. The same persons who would puff such demonstrations in the newspapers, would mob us if we met to adopt measures for obtaining our just rights. They see our weak points, and avail themselves of them to crush us. We are imitating the inferior qualities and examples of white men, and neglecting superior ones. We do not pretend that all the members of odd-fellow societies and masonic lodges are indifferent to their rights and the means of obtaining them; for we know the fact to be otherwise. Some of the best and brightest among us are numbered with those societies; and it is on this account that we make these remarks. We desire to see these noble men expending their time, talents and strength for higher and nobler objects than any that can be attained by the weak and glittering follies of odd-fellowship and free-masonry.

We speak plainly on this point, for we feel deeply. We have dedicated ourself, heart and soul, without reserve, to the elevation and improvement of our race, and have resolved to sink or swim with them. Our inmost soul is fired with a sense of the various forms of injustice to which we are daily subjected, and we must and will speak out against anything, within ourselves or our guilty oppressors, which may tend to prolong this reign of injustice. To be faithful to our oppressors, we must be faithful to ourselves; and shame on any colored man who would have us do otherwise. For this very purpose the *North Star* was established—that it might be as faithful to ourselves as to our oppressors. In this respect, we intend that it shall be different from most of its predecessors, and if it cannot be sustained in its high position, its death will be welcomed by us. But to return.

It is a doctrine held by many good men, in Europe as well as in America, that every oppressed people will gain their rights just as soon as they prove themselves worthy of them; and although we may justly object to the extent to which this doctrine is carried, especially in reference to ourselves as a people, it must still be evident to all that there is a great truth in it.

One of the first things necessary to prove the colored man worthy of equal freedom, is an earnest and persevering effort on his part to gain it. We deserve no earthly or heavenly blessing, for which we are unwilling to labor. For our part, we despise a freedom and equality obtained for us by others, and for which we have been unwilling to labor. A man who will not labor to gain his rights, is a man who would not, if he had them, prize and defend them. What is the use of standing a man on his feet, if, when we let him go, his head is again brought to the pavement? Look out for ourselves as we will—beg and pray to our white friends for assistance as much as we will—and that assistance may come, and come at the needed time; but unless we, the colored people of America, shall set about the work of our own regeneration and improvement, we are doomed to drag on in our present miserable and degraded condition for ages. Would that we could speak to every colored man, woman and child in the land,

and, with the help of Heaven, we would thunder into their ears their duties and responsibilities, until a spirit should be roused among them, never to be lulled till the last chain is broken.—But here we are mortified to think that we are now speaking to tens where we ought to speak to thousands. Unfortunately, those who have the ear of our people on Sundays, have little sympathy with the anti-slavery cause, or the cause of progress in any of its phases. They are too frequently disposed to follow the beaten paths of their fathers.—The most they aim at, is to get to heaven when they die. They reason thus: Our fathers got along pretty well through the world without learning and without meddling with abolitionism, and we can do the same.—We have in our minds three pulpits among the colored people in the North, which have the power to produce a revolution in the condition of the colored people in this country in three years.

First among these, we may mention the great Bethel Church in Philadelphia. That church is the largest colored church in this Union, and from two to three thousand persons worship there every Sabbath. It has its branches in nearly all parts of the North and West, and a few in the South. It is surrounded by numerous little congregations in Philadelphia. Its ministers and bishops travel in all directions, and vast numbers of colored people belong to its branches all over the country. The Bethel pulpit in Philadelphia may be said to give tone to the entire denomination—"as goes large Bethel, so go the small Bethels throughout the Union." Here is concentrated the talent of the church, and here is the central and ruling power.—Now, if that pulpit would but speak the right word— the word for progress—the word for mental culture—encourage reading, and would occasionally take up contributions to aid those who are laboring for their elevation, as the white churches do to aid the colonization society to send us out of the country—there is no telling the good that would result from such labors. An entire change might soon take place in that denomination; loftier views of truth and duty would be presented; a nobler destiny would be opened up to them, and a deeper happiness would at once be enjoyed through all the ramifications of that church.

Similarly situated is the "Zion Church" in New York. That church exerts a controlling influence over the next largest colored denomination in this country. It, too, is a unit—has its branches in all directions in the North rather than in the South. Its ministers are zealous men, and some of them powerful preachers. There is no estimating the good these men might do, if they would only encourage their congregations to take an interest in the subject of reform.

The next church in importance, is St. Phillip's, in New York. This church is more important on account of the talent and respectability which it comprises, than for its numbers. Now, could the influence of these churches be enlisted in exciting our people to a constant and persevering effort at self-elevation, a joyful change would soon come over us.

What we, the colored people, want, is *character,* and this nobody can give us. It is a thing we must get for ourselves. We must labor for it. It is gained by toil—hard toil. Neither the sympathy nor the generosity of our friends can give it to us. It is attainable—yes, thank God, it is attainable. "There is gold in the earth, but we must dig it"—so with character. It is attainable; but we must attain it, and attain it each for himself. I cannot for you, and you cannot for me.—What matters it to the mass of colored people of this country that they are able to point to their Peningtons, Garnets, Remonds, Wards, Purvises, Smiths, Whippers, Sandersons, and a respectable list of other men of character, which we might name, while our general ignorance makes these men exceptions to our race? Their talents can do little to give us character in the eyes of the world. We must get character for ourselves, as a people. A change in our political condition would do very little for us without this. Character is the important thing, and without it we must continue to be marked for degradation and stamped with the brand of inferiority. With character, we shall be powerful. Nothing can harm us long when we get character.—There are certain great elements of character in us which may be hated, but never despised. Industry, sobriety, honesty, combined with intelligence and a due self-respect, find them where you will, among black or white, must be *looked up to*—can never be *looked down upon.* In their presence, prejudice is abashed, confused and mortified. Encountering this solid mass of living character, our vile oppressors are ground to atoms. In its presence, the sneers of a caricaturing press, the taunts of natural inferiority, the mischievous assertions of Clay, and fine-spun sophisms of Calhoun, are innoxious, powerless and unavailing. In answer to these men and the sneers of the multitude, there is nothing in the wide world half so effective as the presentation of a character precisely the opposite of all their representations. We have it in our power to convert the weapons intended for our injury into positive blessings. That we may sustain temporary injury from gross and general misrepresentation, is most true; but the injury is but temporary, and must disappear at the approach of light, like mist from the vale. The offensive traits of character imputed to us, can only be injurious while they are true of us. For a man to say that sweet is bitter—that right is wrong—that light is darkness—is not to injure the truth, but to stamp himself a liar; and the like is true when they impute to us that of which we are not guilty. We have the power of making our enemies slanderers, and this we must do by showing ourselves worthy and respectable men.

We are not insensible to the various obstacles that throng the colored man's pathway to respectability. Embarrassments and perplexities, unknown to other men, are common to us. Though born on American soil, we have fewer privileges than aliens. The school-house, the work-shop, counting-house, attorney's office, and various professions, are opened to them, but closed to us. This, and much more, is true. A general and withering prejudice—a malignant and active hate, pursues us even in the best parts of this country. But a few days ago, one of our best and most talented men—and he a *lame man,* having lost an important limb—was furiously hurled from a car on the Niagara & Buffalo Railroad, by a band of white ruffians, who claim impunity for their atrocious outrage on the plea that New York law does not protect the rights of colored against a company of white men, and the sequel has proved them right; for the case, it appears, was brought before the grand jury, but that jury found no bill. We cannot at this time dwell on this aspect of the subject.

The fact that we are limited and circumscribed, ought rather to incite us to a more vigorous and persevering use of the elevating means within our reach, than to dishearten us. The means of education, though not so free and open to us as to white persons, are nevertheless at our command to such an extent as to make education possible; and these, thank God, are increasing. Let us educate our children, even though it should us subject to a coarser and scantier diet, and disrobe us of our few fine garments. "For the want of knowledge we are killed all the day." Get wisdom—get understanding, is a peculiarly valuable exhortation to us, and the compliance with it is our only hope in this land.—It is idle, a hollow mockery, for us to pray to God to break the oppressor's power, while we neglect the means of knowledge which will give us the ability to break this power.—God will help us when we help ourselves. Our oppressors have divested us of many valuable blessings and facilities for improvement and elevation; but, thank heaven, they have not yet been able to take from us the privilege of being honest, industrious, sober and intelligent. We may read and understand—we may speak and write—we may expose our wrongs—we may appeal to the sense of justice yet alive in the public mind, and by an honest, upright life, we may at last wring from a reluctant public the all-important confession, that we are men, worthy men, good citizens, good Christians, and ought to be treated as such.—July 14, 1848.

AN ADDRESS TO THE COLORED PEOPLE
OF THE UNITED STATES

Under a solemn sense of duty, inspired by our relation to you as fellow sufferers under the multiplied and grievous wrongs to which we as a people are universally subjected,—we, a portion of your brethren, assembled in National Convention, at Cleveland, Ohio, take the liberty to address you on the subject of our mutual improvement and social elevation.

The condition of our variety of the human family, has long been cheerless, if not hopeless, in this country. The doctrine perseveringly proclaimed in high places in church and state, that it is impossible for colored men to rise from ignorance and debasement, to intelligence and respectability in this country, has made a deep impression upon the public mind generally, and is not without its effect upon us. Under this gloomy doctrine, many of us have sunk under the pall of despondency, and are making no effort to relieve ourselves, and have no heart to assist others. It is from this despond that we would deliver you. It is from this slumber we would rouse you. The present, is a period of activity and hope. The heavens above us are bright, and much of the darkness that overshadowed us has passed away. We can deal in the language of brilliant encouragement, and speak of success with certainty. That our condition has been gradually improving, is evident to all, and that we shall yet stand on a common platform with our fellow countrymen, in respect to political and social rights, is certain. The spirit of the age—the voice of inspiration—the deep longings of the human soul—the conflict of right with wrong—the upward tendency of the oppressed throughout the world, abound with evidence complete and ample, of the final triumph of right over wrong, of freedom over slavery, and equality over caste. To doubt this, is to forget the past, and blind our eyes to the present, as well as to deny and oppose the great law of progress, written out by the hand of God on the human soul.

Great changes for the better have taken place and are still taking place. The last ten years have witnessed a mighty change in the estimate in which we as a people are regarded, both in this and other lands. England has given liberty to nearly one million, and France has emancipated three hundred thousand of our brethren, and our own country shakes with the agitation of our rights. Ten or twelve years ago, an educated colored man was regarded as a curiosity, and the thought of a colored man as an author, editor, lawyer or doctor, had scarce been conceived. Such, thank Heaven, is no longer the case. There are now those among us, whom we are not ashamed to regard as gentlemen and scholars, and who are acknowledged to be such, by many of the most learned and respectable in our land. Mountains of prejudice have been removed, and truth and light are dispelling the error and darkness of ages. The time was, when we trembled in the presence of a white man, and dared not assert, or even ask for our rights, but would be guided, directed, and governed, in any way we were demanded, without ever stopping to enquire whether we were right or wrong. We were not only slaves, but our ignorance made us willing slaves. Many of us uttered complaints against the faithful abolitionists, for the broad assertion of our rights; thought they went too far, and were only making our condition worse. This sentiment has nearly ceased to reign in the dark abodes of our hearts; we begin to see our wrongs as clearly, and comprehend our rights as fully, and as well as our white countrymen. This is a sign of progress; and evidence which cannot be gainsayed. It would be easy to present in this connection, a glowing comparison of our past with our present condition, showing that while the former was dark and dreary, the present is full of light and hope. It would be easy to draw a picture of our present achievements, and erect upon it a glorious future.

But, fellow countrymen, it is not so much our purpose to cheer you by the progress we have already made, as it is to stimulate you to still higher attainments. We have done much, but there is much more to be done.— While we have undoubtedly great cause to thank God, and take courage for the hopeful changes which have taken place in our condition, we are not without cause to mourn over the sad condition which we yet occupy. We are yet the most oppressed people in the world. In the Southern states of this Union, we are held as slaves. All over that wide region our paths are marked with blood. Our backs are yet scarred by the lash, and our souls are yet dark under the pall of slavery.—Our sisters are sold for purposes of pollution, and our brethren are sold in the market, with beasts of burden. Shut up in the prison-house of bondage—denied all rights, and deprived of all privileges, we are blotted from the page of human existence, and placed beyond the limits of human regard. Death, moral death, has palsied our souls in that quarter, and we are a murdered people.

In the Northern states, we are not slaves to individuals, not personal slaves, yet in many respects we are the slaves of the community. We are, however, far enough removed from the actual condition of the slave, to make us largely responsible for their continued enslavement, or their speedy deliverance from chains. For in the proportion which we shall rise in the scale of human improvement, in that proportion do we augment the probabilities of a speedy emancipation of our enslaved fellow-countrymen. It is more than a mere figure of speech to say, that we are as a people, chained together. We are one people—one in general complexion, one in a common degradation, one in popular estimation. As one rises, all must rise, and as one falls all must fall. Having now, our feet on the rock of freedom, we must drag our brethren from the slimy depths of slavery, ignorance, and ruin. Every one of us should be ashamed to consider himself free, while his brother is a slave.—The wrongs of our brethren, should be our constant theme. There should be no time too precious, no calling too holy, no place too sacred, to make room for this cause. We should not only feel it to be the cause of humanity, but the cause of christianity, and fit work for men and angels. We ask you to devote yourselves to this cause, as one of the first, and most successful means of self improvement. In the careful study of it, you will learn your own rights, and comprehend your own responsibilities, and, scan through the vista of coming time, your high, and God-appointed destiny. Many of the brightest and best of our number, have become such by their devotion to this cause, and the society of white abolitionists. The latter have been willing to make themselves of no reputation for our sake, and in return, let us show ourselves worthy of their zeal and devotion. Attend anti-slavery meetings, show that you are interested in the subject, that you hate slavery, and love those who are laboring for its overthrow.—Act with white Abolition societies wherever you can, and where you cannot, get up societies among yourselves, but without exclusiveness. It will be a long time before we gain all our rights; and although it may seem to conflict with our views of human brotherhood, we shall undoubtedly for many years be compelled to have institutions of a complexional character, in order to attain this very idea of human brotherhood. We would, however, advise our brethren to occupy memberships and stations among white persons, and in white institutions, just so fast as our rights are secured to us.

Never refuse to act with a white society or institution because it is white, or a black one, because it is black. But act with all men without distinction of color. By so acting, we shall find many opportunities for removing prejudices and establishing the rights of all men. We say avail yourselves of *white* institutions, not because they are white, but because they afford a more convenient means of improvement. But we pass from these suggestions, to others which may be deemed more important. In the Convention that now addresses you, there has been much said on the subject of labor, and especially those departments of it, with which we as a class have been long identified. You will see by the resolutions there adopted on that subject, that the Convention regarded those employments though right in themselves, as being nevertheless, degrading to us as a class, and therefore, counsel you to abandon them as speedily as possible, and to seek what are called the more respectable employments. While the Convention do not inculcate the doctrine that any kind of needful toil is in itself dishonorable, or that colored persons are to be exempt from what are called menial employments, they do mean to say that such employments have been so long and universally filled by colored men, as to become a badge of degradation, in that it has established the conviction that colored men are only fit for such employments. We therefore, advise you by all means, to cease from such employments, as far as practicable, by pressing into others. Try to get your sons into mechanical trades; press them into the blacksmith's shop, the machine shop, the joiner's shop, the wheelwright's shop, the cooper's shop, and the tailor's shop.

Every blow of the sledge hammer, wielded by a sable arm, is a powerful blow in support of our cause. Every colored mechanic, is by virtue of circumstances, an elevator of his race. Every house built by black men, is a strong tower against the allied hosts of prejudice. It is impossible for us to attach too much importance to this aspect of the subject. Trades are important. Wherever a man may be thrown by misfortune, if he has in his hands a useful trade, he is useful to his fellow man, and will be esteemed accordingly; and of all men in the world who need trades we are the most needy.

Understand this, that independence is an essential condition of respectability. To be dependent, is to be degraded. Men may indeed pity us, but they cannot respect us. We do not mean that we can become entirely

independent of all men; that would be absurd and impossible, in the social state. But we mean that we must become equally independent with
other members of the community. That other members of the community
shall be as dependent upon us, as we upon them.—That such is not now
the case, is too plain to need an argument. The houses we live in are built
by white men—the clothes we wear are made by white tailors—the hats
on our heads are made by white hatters, and the shoes on our feet are
made by white shoe-makers, and the food that we eat, is raised and cultivated by white men. Now it is impossible that we should ever be respected
as a people, while we are so universally and completely dependent upon
white men for the necessaries of life. We must make white persons as
dependent upon us, as we are upon them. This cannot be done while we
are found only in two or three kinds of employments, and those employments have their foundation chiefly, if not entirely, in the pride and indolence of the white people. Sterner necessities, will bring higher respect.

The fact is, we must not merely make the white man dependent upon
us to shave him but to feed him; not merely dependent upon us to black
his boots, but to make them. A man is only in a small degree dependent
on us when he only needs his boots blacked, or his carpet bag carried; as a
little less pride, and a little more industry on his part, may enable him to
dispense with our services entirely. As wise men it becomes us to look
forward to a state of things, which appears inevitable. The time will come,
when those menial employments will afford less means of living than they
now do. What shall a large class of our fellow countrymen do, when
white men find it economical to black their own boots, and shave themselves. What will they do when white men learn to wait on themselves?
We warn you brethren, to seek other and more enduring vocations.

Let us entreat you to turn your attention to agriculture. Go to farming.
Be tillers of the soil. On this point we could say much, but the time and
space will not permit. Our cities are overrun with menial laborers, while
the country is eloquently pleading for the hand of industry to till her soil,
and reap the reward of honest labor. We beg and intreat you, to save your
money—live economically—dispense with finery, and the gaities which
have rendered us proverbial, and save your money. Not for the senseless
purpose of being better off than your neighbor, but that you may be able
to educate your children, and render your share to the common stock of
prosperity and happiness around you. It is plain that the equality which we
aim to accomplish, can only be achieved by us, when we can do for others,
just what others can do for us. We should therefore, press into all the
trades, professions and callings, into which honorable white men press.

We would in this connection, direct your attention to the means by
which we have been oppressed and degraded. Chief among those means,
we may mention the press. This engine has brought to the aid of prejudice,
a thousand stings. Wit, ridicule, false philosophy, and an impure theology,
with a flood of low black-guardism, come through this channel into the

public mind; constantly feeding and keeping alive against us, the bitterest hate. The pulpit too, has been arrayed against us. Men with sanctimonious face, have talked of our being descendants of Ham—that we are under a curse, and to try to improve our condition, is virtually to counteract the purposes of God!

It is easy to see that the means which have been used to destroy us, must be used to save us. The press must be used in our behalf: aye! we must use it ourselves; we must take and read newspapers; we must read books, improve our minds, and put to silence and to shame, our opposers. . .
—September 29, 1848.

PREJUDICE NOT NATURAL

. . . It is because the American Colonization Society cherishes and fosters this feeling of hatred against the black man, that I am opposed to it. And I am especially disposed to speak out my opposition to this colonization scheme to-night, because not only of the renewed interest excited in the colonization scheme by the efforts of Henry Clay and others, but because there is a lecturer in the shape of the Rev. Mr. Miller, of New Jersey, now in England, soliciting funds for our expatriation from this country, and going about trying to organize a society, and to create an impression in favor of removing us from this country. I would ask you, my friends, if this is not mean and impudent in the extreme, for one class of Americans to ask for the removal of another class? I feel, sir, I have as much right in this country as any other man. I feel that the black man in this land has as much right to stay in this land as the white man. Consider the matter in the light of possession in this country. Our connection with this country is contemporaneous with your own. From the beginning of the existence of this people, as a people, the colored man has had a place upon the American soil. To be sure, he was not driven from his home in pursuit of a greater liberty than he enjoyed at home, like the Pilgrim fathers; but in the same year that the Pilgrims were landing in this State, slaves were landing on the James River, in Virginia. We feel on this score, then, that we have as much right here as any other class of people.

We have other claims to being regarded and treated as American citizens. Some of our number have fought and bled for this country, and we only ask to be treated as well as those who have fought against it. We are lovers of this country, and we only ask to be treated as well as the haters of it. We are not only told by Americans to go out of our native land to Africa, and there enjoy our freedom—for we must go there in order to enjoy it—but Irishmen newly landed on our soil, who know nothing of our institutions, nor of the history of our country, whose toil has not been mixed with the soil of the country as ours—have the audacity to propose our removal from this, the land of our birth. For my part, I mean, for one, to stay in this country; I have made up my mind to live among you. I had a kind offer, when I was in England, of a little house and lot, and the free use of it, on the banks of the river Eden. I could easily have stayed there, if I had sought for ease, undisturbed, unannoyed by American skin-aristocracy; for it is an aristocracy of skin—those passengers on board the *Alida* only got their dinners that day in virtue of color; if their skins had been of my color, they would have had to fast all day. Whatever denunciations England may be entitled to on account of her treatment of Ireland and her own poor, one thing can be said of her, that no man in that country, or in any of her dominions, is treated as less than a man on account of his complexion. I could have lived there; but when I remembered this prejudice against color, as it is called, and slavery, and saw the many wrongs inflicted on my people at the North that ought to be combated and put down, I felt a disposition to lay aside ease, to turn my back on the kind offer of my friends, and to return among you—deeming it more noble to suffer along with my colored brethren, and meet these prejudices, than to live at ease, undisturbed, on the other side of the Atlantic. I had rather be here now, encountering this feeling, bearing my testimony against it, setting it at defiance, than to remain in England undisturbed. I have made up my mind wherever I go, I shall go as a man, and not as a slave. When I go on board of your steamboats, I shall always aim to be courteous and mild in my deportment towards all with whom I come in contact, at the same time firmly and constantly endeavoring to assert my equal right as a man and a brother.

But the Colonization Society says this prejudice can never be overcome —that it is natural—God has implanted it. Some say so; others declare that it can only be removed by removing the cause, that is, by removing us to Liberia. I know this is false, from my own experience in this country. I remember that, but a few years ago, upon the railroads from New Bedford and Salem and in all parts of Massachusetts, a most unrighteous and proscriptive rule prevailed, by which colored men and women were subjected to all manner of indignity in the use of those conveyances. Anti-slavery men, however, lifted up their testimony against this principle from year to year; and from year to year, he whose name cannot be mentioned without receiving a round of applause, Wendell Phillips went abroad, exposing this proscription in the light of justice. What is the result? Not a single railroad can be found in any part of Massachusetts, where a colored man is treated and esteemed in any other light than that of a man and a traveller. Prejudice has given way and must give way. The fact that it is giving way proves that this prejudice is not invincible. The time was when it was expected that a colored man, when he entered a church in Boston, would go into the Jim Crow pew—and I believe such is the case now, to a large extent; but then there were those who would defend the custom. But you can scarcely get a defender of this proscription in New England now.

The history of the repeal of the intermarriage law shows that the prejudice against color is not invincible. The general manner in which white persons sit with colored persons shows plainly that the prejudice against color is not invincible. When I first came here, I felt the greatest possible diffidence of sitting with whites. I used to come up from the shipyard, where I worked, with my hands hardened with toil, rough and uncomely, and my movements awkward (for I was unacquainted with the rules of politeness), I would shrink back, and would not have taken my meals with the whites had they not pressed me to do so. Our president, in his earlier intercourse with me, taught me, by example, his abhorrence of this prejudice. He has, in my presence, stated to those who visited him, that if they did not like to sit at the table with me, they could have a separate one for themselves.

The time was, when I walked through the streets of Boston, I was liable to insult if in company with a white person. To-day I have passed in company with my white friends, leaning on their arm and they on mine, and yet the first word from any quarter on account of the color of my skin I have not heard. It is all false, this talk about the invincibility of prejudice against color. If any of you have it, and no doubt some of you have, I will tell you how to get rid of it. Commence to do something to elevate and improve and enlighten the colored man, and your prejudice will begin to vanish. The more you try to make a man of the black man, the more you will begin to think him a man. . .—June 8, 1849.

THE NATURE OF SLAVERY

More than twenty years of my life were consumed in a state of slavery. My childhood was environed by the baneful peculiarities of the slave system. I grew up to manhood in the presence of this hydra-headed monster—not as a master—not as an idle spectator—not as the guest of the slaveholder —but as A SLAVE, eating the bread and drinking the cup of slavery with the most degraded of my brother-bondmen, and sharing with them all the painful conditions of their wretched lot. In consideration of these facts, I feel that I have a right to speak, and to speak *strongly*. Yet, my friends, I feel bound to speak truly.

Goading as have been the cruelties to which I have been subjected— bitter as have been the trials through which I have passed—exasperating as have been, and still are, the indignities offered to my manhood—I find in them no excuse for the slightest departure from truth in dealing with any branch of this subject.

First of all, I will state, as well as I can, the legal and social relation of master and slave. A master is one—to speak in the vocabulary of the southern states—who claims and exercises a right of property in the person of a fellow-man. This he does with the force of the law and the sanction of southern religion. The law gives the master absolute power over the slave. He may work him, flog him, hire him out, sell him, and, in certain contingencies, *kill* him, with perfect impunity. The slave is a human being, divested of all rights—reduced to the level of a brute—a mere "chattel" in the eye of the law—placed beyond the circle of human brotherhood—cut off from his kind—his name, which the "recording angel" may have enrolled in heaven, among the blest, is impiously inserted in a *master's ledger,* with horses, sheep, and swine. In law, the slave has no wife, no children, no country, and no home. He can own nothing, possess nothing, acquire nothing, but what must belong to another. To eat the fruit of his own toil, to clothe his person with the work of his own hands, is considered stealing. He toils that another may reap the fruit; he is industrious that another may live in idleness; he eats unbolted meal that another may eat the bread of fine flour; he labors in chains at home, under a burning sun and biting lash, that another may ride in ease and splendor abroad; he lives in ignorance that another may be educated; he is abused that another may be exalted; he rests his toil-worn limbs on the cold, damp ground that another may repose on the softest pillow; he is clad in coarse and tattered raiment that another may be arrayed in purple and fine linen; he is sheltered only by the wretched hovel that a master may dwell in a magnificent mansion; and to this condition he is bound down as by an arm of iron.

From this monstrous relation there springs an unceasing stream of most revolting cruelties. The very accompaniments of the slave system stamp it as the offspring of hell itself. To ensure good behavior, the slaveholder relies on the whip; to induce proper humility, he relies on the whip; to rebuke what he is pleased to term insolence, he relies on the whip; to supply the place of wages as an incentive to toil, he relies on the whip; to bind down the spirit of the slave, to imbrute and destroy his manhood, he relies on the whip, the chain, the gag, the thumb-screw, the pillory, the bowie-knife, the pistol, and the blood-hound. These are the necessary and unvarying accompaniments of the system. Wherever slavery is found, these horrid instruments are also found. Whether on the coast of Africa, among the savage tribes, or in South Carolina, among the refined and civilized, slavery is the same, and its accompaniments one and the same. It makes no difference whether the slaveholder worships the God of the christians, or is a follower of Mahomet, he is the minister of the same cruelty, and the author of the same misery. *Slavery* is always *slavery;* always the same foul, haggard, and damning scourge, whether found in the eastern or in the western hemisphere.

There is a still deeper shade to be given to this picture. The physical cruelties are indeed sufficiently harassing and revolting; but they are as a few grains of sand on the sea shore, or a few drops of water in the great ocean, compared with the stupendous wrongs which it inflicts upon the mental, moral, and religious nature of its hapless victims. It is only when we contemplate the slave as a moral and intellectual being, that we can adequately comprehend the unparalleled enormity of slavery, and the intense criminality of the slaveholder. I have said that the slave was a man. "What a piece of work is man! How noble in reason! How infinite in faculties! In form and moving how express and admirable! In action how like an angel! In apprehension how like a God! the beauty of the world! the paragon of animals!"

The slave is a man, "the image of God," but "a little lower than the angels"; possessing a soul, eternal and indestructible; capable of endless happiness, or immeasurable woe; a creature of hopes and fears, of affections and passions, of joys and sorrows, and he is endowed with those mysterious powers by which man soars above the things of time and sense, and grasps, with undying tenacity, the elevating and sublimely glorious idea of a God. It is *such* a being that is smitten and blasted. The first work of slavery is to mar and deface those characteristics of its victims which distinguish *men* from *things,* and *persons* from *property.* Its first aim is to destroy all sense of high moral and religious responsibility. It reduces man to a mere machine. It cuts him off from his Maker, it hides from him the laws of God, and leaves him to grope his way from time to eternity in the dark, under the arbitrary and despotic control of a frail, depraved, and sinful fellow-man. As the serpent-charmer of India is compelled to extract the deadly teeth of his venomous prey before he is able to handle him with impunity, so the slaveholder must strike down the conscience of the slave before he can obtain the entire mastery over his victim.

It is, then, the first business of the enslaver of men to blunt, deaden, and destroy the central principle of human responsibility. Conscience is, to the individual soul, and to society, what the law of gravitation is to the universe. It holds society together; it is the basis of all trust and confidence; it is the pillar of all moral rectitude. Without it, suspicion would take the place of trust; vice would be more than a match for virtue; men would prey upon each other, like the wild beasts of the desert; and earth would become a *hell.*

Nor is slavery more adverse to the conscience than it is to the mind. This is shown by the fact, that in every state of the American Union, where slavery exists, except the state of Kentucky, there are laws absolutely prohibitory of education among the slaves. The crime of teaching a slave to read is punishable with severe fines and imprisonment, and, in some instances, with *death itself.*

Nor are the laws respecting this matter a dead letter. Cases may occur in which they are disregarded, and a few instances may be found where slaves may have learned to read; but such are isolated cases, and only prove the rule. The great mass of slaveholders look upon education among the slaves as utterly subversive of the slave system. I well remember when my mistress first announced to my master that she had discovered that I could read. His face colored at once with surprise and chagrin. He said that "I was ruined, and my value as a slave destroyed; that a slave should know nothing but to obey his master; that to give a Negro an inch would lead him to take an ell; that having learned how to read, I would soon want to know how to write; and that by-and-by I would be running away." I think my audience will bear witness to the correctness of this philosophy, and to the literal fulfillment of this prophecy.

It is perfectly well understood at the south, that to educate a slave is to make him discontented with slavery, and to invest him with a power which shall open to him the treasures of freedom; and since the object of the slaveholder is to maintain complete authority over his slave, his constant vigilance is exercised to prevent everything which militates against, or endangers, the stability of his authority. Education being among the menacing influences, and, perhaps, the most dangerous, is, therefore, the most cautiously guarded against.

It is true that we do not often hear of the enforcement of the law, punishing as a crime the teaching of slaves to read, but this is not because of a want of disposition to enforce it. The true reason or explanation of the matter is this: there is the greatest unanimity of opinion among the white population in the south in favor of the policy of keeping the slave in ignorance. There is, perhaps, another reason why the law against education is so seldom violated. The slave is too poor to be able to offer a temptation sufficiently strong to induce a white man to violate it; and it is not to be supposed that in a community where the moral and religious sentiment is in favor of slavery, many martyrs will be found sacrificing their liberty and lives by violating those prohibitory enactments.

As a general rule, then, darkness reigns over the abodes of the enslaved, and "how great is that darkness!"

We are sometimes told of the contentment of the slaves, and are entertained with vivid pictures of their happiness. We are told that they often dance and sing; that their masters frequently give them wherewith to make merry; in fine, that they have little of which to complain. I admit that the slave does sometimes sing, dance, and appear to be merry. But what does this prove? It only proves to my mind, that though slavery is armed with a thousand stings, it is not able entirely to kill the elastic spirit of the bondman. That spirit will rise and walk abroad, despite of whips and chains, and extract from the cup of nature occasional drops of joy and gladness. No thanks to the slaveholder, nor to slavery, that the vivacious captive may sometimes dance in his chains; his very mirth in such circumstances stands before God as an accusing angel against his enslaver.

It is often said, by the opponents of the anti-slavery cause, that the condition of the people of Ireland is more deplorable than that of the American slaves. Far be it from me to underrate the sufferings of the Irish people. They have been long oppressed; and the same heart that prompts me to plead the cause of the American bondman, makes it impossible for me not to sympathize with the oppressed of all lands. Yet I must say that there is no analogy between the two cases. The Irishman is poor, but he is not a slave. He may be in rags, but he is not a slave. He is still the master of his own body, and can say with the poet, "The hand of Douglass is his own." "The world is all before him, where to choose"; and poor as may be my opinion of the British parliament, I cannot believe that it will ever sink to such a depth of infamy as to pass a law for the recapture of fugitive Irishmen! The shame and scandal of kidnapping will long remain wholly monopolized by the American congress. The Irishman has not only the liberty to emigrate from his country, but he has liberty at home. He can write, and speak, and coöperate for the attainment of his rights and the redress of his wrongs.

The multitude can assemble upon all the green hills and fertile plains of the Emerald Isle; they can pour out their grievances, and proclaim their wants without molestation; and the press, that "swift-winged messenger," can bear the tidings of their doings to the extreme bounds of the civilized world. They have their "Conciliation Hall," on the banks of the Liffey, their reform clubs, and their newspapers; they pass resolutions, send forth addresses, and enjoy the right of petition. But how is it with the American slave? Where may he assemble? Where is his Conciliation Hall? Where are his newspapers? Where is his right of petition? Where is his freedom of speech? his liberty of the press? and his right of locomotion? He is said to be happy; happy men can speak. But ask the slave what is his condition—what his state of mind—what he thinks of enslavement? and you had as well address your inquiries to the *silent dead*. There comes no *voice* from the enslaved. We are left to gather his feelings by imagining what ours would be, were our souls in his soul's stead.

If there were no other fact descriptive of slavery, than that the slave is dumb, this alone would be sufficient to mark the slave system as a grand aggregation of human horrors.

Most who are present, will have observed that leading men in this country have been putting forth their skill to secure quiet to the nation. A system of measures to promote this object was adopted a few months ago in congress. The result of those measures is known. Instead of quiet, they have produced alarm; instead of peace, they have brought us war; and so it must ever be.

While this nation is guilty of the enslavement of three millions of innocent men and women, it is as idle to think of having a sound and lasting peace, as it is to think there is no God to take cognizance of the affairs of men. There can be no peace to the wicked while slavery continues in the land. It will be condemned; and while it is condemned there will be agitation. Nature must cease to be nature; men must become monsters; humanity must be transformed; christianity must be exterminated; all ideas of justice and the laws of eternal goodness must be utterly blotted out from the human soul,—ere a system so foul and infernal can escape condemnation, or this guilty republic can have a sound, enduring peace—**December 1, 1850.**

LETTER TO HARRIET BEECHER STOWE

You kindly informed me, when at your house, a fortnight ago, that you designed to do something which should permanently contribute to the improvement and elevation of the free colored people in the United States. You especially expressed an interest in such of this class as had become free by their own exertions, and desired most of all to be of service to them. In what manner, and by what means, you can assist this class most successfully, is the subject upon which you have done me the honor to ask my opinion.

Begging you to excuse the unavoidable delay, I will now most gladly comply with your request, but before doing so, I desire to express, dear Madam, my deep sense of the value of the services which you have already rendered my afflicted and persecuted people, by the publication of your inimitable book on the subject of slavery. That contribution to our bleeding cause, alone, involves us in a debt of gratitude which cannot be measured; and your resolution to make other exertions on our behalf excites in me emotions and sentiments, which I scarcely need try to give forth in words. Suffice it to say, that I believe you to have the blessings of your enslaved countrymen and countrywomen; and the still higher reward which comes to the soul in the smiles of our merciful Heavenly father, whose ear is ever open to the cries of the oppressed.

With such sentiments, dear Madam, I will at once proceed to lay before you, in as few words as the nature of the case will allow, my humble views in the premises. First of all, let me briefly state the nature of the disease, before I undertake to prescribe the remedy. Three things are notoriously true of us as a people. These are POVERTY, IGNORANCE AND DEGRADATION. Of course there are exceptions to this general statement; but these are so few as only to prove its essential truthfulness. I shall not stop here to inquire minutely into the causes which have produced our present condition; nor to denounce those whom I believe to be responsible for these causes. It is enough that we shall agree upon the character of the evil, whose existence we deplore, and upon some plan for its removal.

I assert then, that *poverty, ignorance* and *degradation* are the combined evil or, in other words, these constitute the social disease of the Free Colored people in the United States.

To deliver them from this triple malady, is to improve and elevate them, by which I mean simply to put them on an equal footing with their white fellow-countrymen in the sacred right to "*Life, Liberty* and the pur-

suit of happiness." I am for no fancied or artificial elevation, but only ask
fair play. How shall this be obtained? I answer, first, not by establishing
for our use high schools and colleges. Such institutions are, in my
judgment, beyond our immediate occasions, and are not adapted to our
present most pressing wants. High schools and colleges are excellent institutions, and will, in due season, be greatly subservient to our progress; but
they are the result, as well as they are the demand of a point of progress,
which we, as a people, have not yet attained. Accustomed, as we have
been, to the rougher and harder modes of living, and of gaining a livelihood, we cannot, and we ought not to hope that, in a single leap from our
low condition, we can reach that of *Ministers, Lawyers, Doctors, Editors,
Merchants,* &c. These will, doubtless, be attained by us; but this will only
be, when we have patiently and laboriously, and I may add successfully,
mastered and passed through the intermediate gradations of agriculture
and the mechanic arts. Besides, there are (and perhaps this is a better
reason for my view of the case) numerous institutions of learning in this
country, already thrown open to colored youth. To my thinking, there are
quite as many facilities now afforded to the colored people, as they can
spare the time, from the sterner duties of life, to avail themselves of. In
their present condition of poverty, they cannot spare their sons and daughters two or three years at boarding schools or colleges, to say nothing of
finding the means to sustain them while at such institutions. I take it,
therefore, that we are well provided for in this respect; and that it may be
fairly inferred from the past that the facilities for our education, so far as
schools and colleges in the Free States are concerned, will increase quite in
proportion with our future wants. Colleges have been open to colored
youth in this country during the last dozen years. Yet few, comparatively,
have acquired a classical education; and even this few have found themselves educated far above a living condition, there being no methods by
which they could turn their learning to account. Several of this latter class
have entered the ministry; but you need not be told that an educated people is needed to sustain an educated ministry. There must be a certain
amount of cultivation among the people to sustain such a ministry. At
present, we have not that cultivation amongst us; and therefore, we value,
in the preacher, strong lungs, rather than high learning. I do not say that
educated ministers are not needed amongst us.—Far from it! I wish there
were more of them; but to increase their number is *not* the largest benefit
you can bestow upon us.

You, dear Madam, can help the masses. You can do something for the
thousands; and by lifting these from the depths of poverty and ignorance,
you can make an educated ministry and an educated class possible. In the
present circumstances, prejudice is a bar to the educated black minister
among the whites; and ignorance is a bar to him among the blacks.

We have now two or three colored lawyers in this country; and I rejoice
in the fact; for it affords very gratifying evidence of our progress. Yet it

must be confessed that, in point of success, our lawyers are as great failures as are our ministers. White people will not employ them to the obvious embarrassment of their causes, and the blacks, taking their *cue* from the whites, have not sufficient confidence in their abilities to employ them. Hence, educated colored men, among the colored people, are at a very great discount. It would seem that education and emigration go together with us; for as soon as a man rises amongst us, capable, by his genius and learning, to do us great service, just so soon he finds that he can serve himself better by going elsewhere. In proof of this, I might instance the Russwurms—the Garnetts—the Wards—the Crummells and others—all men of superior ability and attainments, and capable of removing mountains of prejudice against their race, by their simple presence in the country; but these gentlemen, finding themselves embarrassed here by the peculiar disadvantages to which I have referred—disadvantages in part growing out of their education—being repelled by ignorance on the one hand, and prejudice on the other, and having no taste to continue a contest against such odds, they have sought more congenial climes, where they can live more peaceable and quiet lives. I regret their election—but I cannot blame them; for, with an equal amount of education, and the hard lot which was theirs, I might follow their example.

But, again, it has been said that the colored people must become farmers—that they must go on the land, in order to their elevation. Hence, many benevolent people are contributing the necessary funds to purchase land in Canada, and elsewhere, for them. That prince of good men, Gerrit Smith, has given away thousands of acres to colored men in this State, thinking, doubtless, that in so doing he was conferring a blessing upon them. Now, while I do not undervalue the efforts which have been made, and are still being made in this direction, yet I must say that I have far less confidence in such efforts, than I have in the benevolence which prompts them. Agricultural pursuits are not, as I think, suited to our condition. The reason of this is not to be found so much in the occupation, (for it is a noble and ennobling one,) as in the people themselves. That is only a remedy, which can be applied to the case; and the difficulty in agricultural pursuits, as a remedy for the evils of poverty and ignorance amongst us, is that it cannot, for various reasons, be applied.

We cannot apply it, because it is almost impossible to get colored men to go on the land. From some cause or other, (perhaps the adage that misery loves company will explain,) colored people will congregate in the large towns and cities; and they will endure any amount of hardship and privation, rather than separate, and go into the country. Again, very few have the means to set up for themselves, or to get where they could do so.

Another consideration against expending energy in this direction is our want of self-reliance. Slavery more than all things else, robs its victims of self-reliance. To go into the western wilderness, and there to lay the foundation of future society, requires more of that important quality than a life of slavery has left us. This may sound strange to you, coming as it does from a colored man; but I am dealing with facts, and these never accommodate themselves to the feelings or wishes of any. They don't *ask,* but *take leave to be.* It is a fact then, and not less so because I wish it were otherwise, that the colored people are wanting in self-reliance—too fond of society—too eager for immediate results—and too little skilled in mechanics or husbandry to attempt to overcome the wilderness; at least, until they have overcome obstacles less formidable. Therefore, I look to other means than agricultural pursuits for the elevation and improvement of colored people. Of course, I allege this of the many. There are exceptions. Individuals among us, with commendable zeal, industry, perseverance and self-reliance, have found, and are finding, in agricultural pursuits, the means of supporting, improving and educating their families.

The plan which I contemplate will, (if carried into effect,) greatly increase the number of this class—since it will prepare others to meet the rugged duties which a pioneer agricultural condition must impose upon all who take it upon them. What I propose is intended simply to prepare men for the work of getting an honest living—not out of dishonest men —but out of an honest earth.

Again, there is little reason to hope that any considerable number of the free colored people will ever be induced to leave this country, even if such a thing were desirable. This black man—*un*like the Indian—loves civilization. He does not make very great progress in civilization himself but he likes to be in the midst of it, and prefers to share its most galling evils, to encountering barbarism. Then the love of the country, the dread of isolation, the lack of adventurous spirit, and the thought of seeming to desert their "brethren in bonds," are a powerful check upon all schemes of colonization which look to the removal of the colored people, without the slaves. The truth is, dear madam, we are *here,* and here we are likely to remain. Individuals emigrate—nations never. We have grown up with this republic, and I see nothing in her character, or even in the character of the American people as yet, which compels the belief that we must leave the United States. If then, we are to remain here, the question for the wise and good is precisely that you have submitted to me—namely: What can be done to improve the condition of the free people of color in the United States? The plan which I humbly submit in answer to this inquiry—and in the hope that it may find favor with you, and with many friends of humanity who honor, love and co-operate with you—is the establishment in Rochester, N.Y., or in some other part of the United States equally favorable to such an enterprise, of an INDUSTRIAL COLLEGE in which shall be taught several important branches of the mechanical arts. This college is to be opened to colored youth. I will pass over, for the present, the details of such an institution as I propose. It is not worth while that I should dwell upon these at all. Once convinced that something of the sort is needed, and the organizing power will be forthcoming. It is the peculiarity of your favored race that they can always do what they think necessary to be done. I can safely trust all details to yourself, and the wise and good people whom you represent the interest you take in my oppressed fellow-countrymen.

Never having had a day's schooling in all my life I may not be expected to map out the details of a plan so comprehensive as that involved in the idea of a college. I repeat, then, I leave the organization and administration to the superior wisdom of yourself and the friends who second your noble efforts. The argument in favor of an Industrial College—a college to be conducted by the best men—and the best workmen which the mechanical arts can afford; a college where colored youth can be instructed to use their hands, as well as their heads; where they can be put into possession of the means of getting a living whether their lot in after life may be cast among civilized or uncivilized men; whether they choose to stay here, or prefer to return to the land of their fathers—is briefly this: Prejudice against the free colored people in the United States has shown itself nowhere so invincible as among mechanics. The farmer and the professional man cherish no feeling so bitter as that cherished by these. The latter would starve us out of the country entirely. At this moment I can more easily get my son into a lawyer's office to learn law than I can into a blacksmith's shop to blow the bellows and to wield the sledge-hammer. Denied the means of learning useful trades we are pressed into the narrowest limits to obtain a livelihood. In times past we have been the hewers of wood and the drawers of water for American society, and we once enjoyed a monopoly in the menial enjoyments, but this is so no longer. Even these enjoyments are rapidly passing away out of our hands. The fact is—every day begins with the lesson, and ends with the lesson—the colored men must learn trades; and must find new employment; new modes of usefulness to society, or that they must decay under the pressing wants to which their condition is rapidly bringing them.

We must become mechanics; we must build as well as live in houses; we must make as well as use furniture; we must construct bridges as well as pass over them, before we can properly live or be respected by our fellow men. We need mechanics as well as ministers. We need workers in iron, clay, and leather. We have orators, authors, and other professional men, but these reach only a certain class, and get respect for our race in certain select circles. To live here as we ought we must fasten ourselves to our countrymen through their every day cardinal wants. We must not only be able to *black* boots, but to *make* them. At present we are unknown in the Northern States as mechanics. We give no proof of genius or skill at the county, State, or national fairs. We are unknown at any of the great exhibitions of the industry of our fellow-citizens, and being unknown we are unconsidered.

The fact that we make no show of our ability is held conclusive of our inability to make any, hence all the indifference and contempt with which incapacity is regarded, fall upon us, and that too, when we have had no means of disproving the infamous opinion of our natural inferiority. I have during the last dozen years denied before the Americans that we are an inferior race; but this has been done by arguments based upon admitted principles rather than by the presentation of facts. Now, firmly believing, as I do, that there are skill, invention, power, industry, and real mechanical genius, among the colored people, which will bear favorable testimony for them, and which only need the means to develop them, I am decidedly in favor of the establishment of such a college as I have mentioned. The benefits of such an institution would not be confined to the Northern States, nor to the free colored people. They would extend over the whole Union. The slave not less than the freeman would be benefited by such an institution. It must be confessed that the most powerful argument now used by the Southern slaveholder, and the one most soothing to his conscience, is that derived from the low condition of the free colored people of the North. I have long felt that too little attention has been given by our truest friends in this country to removing this stumbling block out of the way of the slave's liberation.

The most telling, the most killing refutation of slavery, is the presentation of an industrious, enterprising, thrifty, and intelligent free black population. Such a population I believe would rise in the Northern States under the fostering care of such a college as that supposed.

To show that we are capable of becoming mechanics I might adduce any amount of testimony; dear madam, I need not ring the changes on such a proposition. There is no question in the mind of any unprejudiced person that the Negro is capable of making a good mechanic. Indeed, even those who cherish the bitterest feelings towards us have admitted that the apprehension that Negroes might be employed in their stead, dictated the policy of excluding them from trades altogether. But I will not dwell upon this point as I fear I have already trespassed too long upon your precious time, and written more than I ought to expect to read. Allow me to say in conclusion, that I believe every intelligent colored man in America will approve and rejoice at the establishment of some such institution as that now suggested. There are many respectable colored men, fathers of large families, having boys nearly grown up, whose minds are tossed by day and by night with the anxious enquiry, "what shall I do with my boys?" Such an institution would meet the wants of such persons. Then, too, the establishment of such an institution would be in character with the eminently practical philanthropy of your trans-Atlantic friends. America could scarce object to it as an attempt to agitate the public mind on the subject of slavery, or to *dissolve the Union*. It could not be tortured into a cause for hard words by the American people, but the noble and good of all classes, would see in the effort an excellent motive, a benevolent object, temperately, wisely, and practically manifested—March 8, 1853.

THE CLAIMS OF THE NEGRO
ETHNOLOGICALLY CONSIDERED

I propose to submit to you a few thoughts on the subject of the Claims of the Negro, suggested by ethnological science, or the natural history of man. But before entering upon that subject, I trust you will allow me to make a remark or two, somewhat personal to myself. The relation between me and this occasion may justify what, in others, might seem an offence against good taste.

This occasion is to me one of no ordinary interest, for many reasons; and the honor you have done me, in selecting me as your speaker, is as grateful to my heart, as it is novel in the history of American Collegiate or Literary Institutions. Surprised as I am, the public are no less surprised, at the spirit of independence, and the moral courage displayed by the gentlemen at whose call I am here. There is felt to be a principle in the matter, placing it far above egotism or personal vanity; a principle which gives to this occasion a general, and I had almost said, an universal interest. I engage to-day, for the first time, in the exercises of any College Commencement. It is a new chapter in my humble experience. The usual course, at such times, I believe, is to call to the platform men of age and distinction, eminent for eloquence, mental ability, and scholarly attainments—men whose high culture, severe training, great experience, large observation, and peculiar aptitude for teaching, qualify them to instruct even the already well instructed, and to impart a glow, a lustre, to the acquirements of those who are passing from the Halls of learning, to the broad theatre of active life. To no such high endeavor as this, is your humble speaker fitted; and it was with much distrust and hesitation that he accepted the invitation, so kindly and perseveringly given, to occupy a portion of your attention here to-day.

I express the hope, then, gentlemen, that this acknowledgment of the novelty of my position, and my unaffected and honest confession of inaptitude, will awaken a sentiment of generous indulgence towards the scattered thoughts I have been able to fling together, with a view to presenting them as my humble contribution to these Commencement Exercises.

Interesting to me, personally, as this occasion is, it is still more interesting to you; especially to such of you as have completed your education, and who (not wholly unlike the gallant ship, newly launched, full rigged, and amply fitted, about to quit the placid waters of the harbor for the boisterous waves of the sea,) are entering upon the active duties and measureless responsibilities incident to the great voyage of life. Before such, the ocean of mind lies outspread more solemn than the sea, studded with difficulties and perils. Thoughts, theories, ideas, and systems, so various, and so opposite, and leading to such diverse results, suggest the wisdom of the utmost precaution, and the most careful survey, at the start. A false light, a defective chart, an imperfect compass, may cause one to drift in endless bewilderment, or to be landed at last amid sharp, destructive rocks.

On the other hand, guided by wisdom, manned with truth, fidelity and industry, the haven of peace, devoutly wished for by all, may be reached in safety by all. The compensation of the preacher is full, when assured that his words have saved even one from error and from ruin. My joy shall be full, if, on this occasion, I shall be able to give a right direction to any one mind, touching the question now to be considered.

Gentlemen, in selecting the Claims of the Negro as the subject of my remarks to-day, I am animated by a desire to bring before you a matter of living importance—a matter upon which action, as well as thought is required. The relation subsisting between the white and black people of this country is the vital question of the age. In the solution of this question, the scholars of America will have to take an important and controlling part. This is the moral battle field to which their country and their God now call them. In the eye of both, the neutral scholar is an ignoble man. Here, a man must be hot, or be accounted cold, or, perchance, something worse than hot or cold. The lukewarm and the cowardly, will be rejected by earnest men on either side of the controversy. The cunning man who avoids it, to gain the favor of both parties, will be rewarded with scorn; and the timid man who shrinks from it, for fear of offending either party, will be despised. To the lawyer, the preacher, the politician, and to the man of letters, there is no neutral ground. He that is not for us, is against us. Gentlemen, I assume at the start, that wherever else I may be required to speak with bated breath, here, at least, I may speak with freedom the thought nearest my heart. This liberty is implied, by the call I have received to be here; and yet I hope to present the subject so that no man can reasonably say, that an outrage has been committed, or that I have abused the privilege with which you have honored me. I shall aim to discuss the claims of the Negro, general and special, in a manner, though not scientific, still sufficiently clear and definite to enable my hearers to form an intelligent judgment respecting them.

The first general claim which may here be set up, respects the manhood of the Negro. This is an elementary claim, simple enough, but not without question. It is fiercely opposed. A respectable public journal, published in Richmond, Va., bases its whole defence of the slave system upon a denial of the Negro's manhood.

The white peasant is free, and if he is a man of will and intellect, can rise in the scale of society; or at least his offspring may. He is not deprived by law of those "inalienable rights," "liberty and the pursuit of happiness," by the use of it. But here is the essence of slavery—that we do declare the Negro destitute of these powers. We bind him by law to the condition of the laboring peasant for ever, without his consent, and we bind his posterity after him. Now, the true question is, have we a right to do this? If we have not, all discussions about his comfortable situation, and the actual condition of free laborers elsewhere, are quite beside the point. If the Negro has the same right to his liberty and the pursuit of his own happiness that the white man has, then we commit the greatest wrong and robbery to hold him a slave—an act at which the sentiment of justice must revolt in every heart—and Negro slavery is an institution which that sentiment must sooner or later blot from the face of the earth.—*Richmond Examiner.*

After stating the question thus, the *Examiner* boldy asserts that the Negro has no such right—BECAUSE HE IS NOT A MAN!

There are three ways to answer this denial. One is by ridicule; a second is by denunciation; and a third is by argument. I hardly know under which of these modes my answer to-day will fall. I feel myself somewhat on trial; and that this is just the point where there is hesitation, if not serious doubt. I cannot, however, argue; I must assert. To know whether a Negro is a man, it must first be known what constitutes a man. Here, as well as elsewhere, I take it, that the "coat must be cut according to the cloth." It is not necessary, in order to establish the manhood of any one making the claim, to prove that such an one equals Clay in eloquence, or Webster and Calhoun in logical force and directness; for, tried by such standards of mental power as these, it is apprehended that very few could claim the high designation of *man.* Yet something like this folly is seen in the arguments directed against the humanity of the Negro. His faculties and powers, uneducated and unimproved, have been contrasted with those of the highest cultivation; and the world has then been called upon to behold the immense and amazing difference between the man admitted, and the man disputed. The fact that these intellects, so powerful and so controlling, are almost, if not quite as exceptional to the general rule of humanity, in one direction, as the specimen Negroes are in the other, is quite overlooked.

Man is distinguished from all other animals, by the possession of certain definite faculties and powers, as well as by physical organization and proportions. He is the only two-handed animal on the earth—the only one that laughs, and nearly the only one that weeps. Men instinctively distinguish between men and brutes. Common sense itself is scarcely needed to detect the absence of manhood in a monkey, or to recognize its presence in a Negro. His speech, his reason, his power to acquire and to retain knowledge, his heaven-erected face, his habitudes, his hopes, his fears, his aspirations, his prophecies, plant between him and the brute creation, a distinction as eternal as it is palpable. Away, therefore, with all the scientific moonshine that would connect men with monkeys; that would have the world believe that humanity, instead of resting on its own characteristic pedestal—gloriously independent—is a sort of sliding scale, making one extreme brother to the ourang-ou-tang, and the other to angels, and all the rest intermediates! Tried by all the usual, and all the *un*usual tests, whether mental, moral, physical, or psychological, the Negro is a MAN— considering him as possessing knowledge, or needing knowledge, his elevation or his degradation, his virtues, or his vices—whichever road you take, you reach the same conclusion, the Negro is a MAN. His good and his bad, his innocence and his guilt, his joys and his sorrows, proclaim his manhood in speech that all mankind practically and readily understand.

A very recondite author says, that "man is distinguished from all other animals, in that he resists as well as adapts himself to his circumstances." He does not take things as he finds them, but goes to work to improve them. Tried by this test, too, the Negro is a man. You may see him yoke the oxen, harness the horse, and hold the plow. He can swim the river; but he prefers to fling over it a bridge. The horse bears him on his back— admits his mastery and dominion. The barnyard fowl know his step, and flock around to receive their morning meal from his sable hand. The dog dances when he comes home, and whines piteously when he is absent. All these know that the Negro is a MAN. Now, presuming that what is evident to beast and to bird, cannot need elaborate argument to be made plain to men, I assume, with this brief statement, that the Negro is a man.

The first claim conceded and settled, let us attend to the second, which is beset with some difficulties, giving rise to many opinions, different from my own, and which opinions I propose to combat.

There was a time when, if you established the point that a particular being is a man, it was considered that such a being, of course, had a common ancestry with the rest of mankind. But it is not so now. This is, you know, an age of science, and science is favorable to division. It must explore and analyze, until all doubt is set at rest. There is, therefore, another proposition to be stated and maintained, separately, which, in other days, (the days before the Notts, the Gliddens, the Agassiz, and Mortons, made their profound discoveries in ethnological science,) might have been included in the first.

It is somewhat remarkable, that, at a time when knowledge is so generally diffused, when the geography of the world is so well understood— when time and space, in the intercourse of nations, are almost annihilated —when oceans have become bridges—the earth a magnificent hall—the hollow sky a dome—under which a common humanity can meet in friendly conclave—when nationalities are being swallowed up—and the ends of the earth brought together—I say it is remarkable—nay, it is strange that there should arise a phalanx of learned men—speaking in the name of *science*—to forbid the magnificent reunion of mankind in one brotherhood. A mortifying proof is here given, that the moral growth of a nation, or an age, does not always keep pace with the increase of knowledge, and suggests the necessity of means to increase human love with human learning.

The proposition to which I allude, and which I mean next to assert, is this, that what are technically called the Negro race, are a part of the human family, and are descended from a common ancestry, with the rest of mankind. The discussion of this point opens a comprehensive field of inquiry. It involves the question of the unity of the human race. Much has and can be said on both sides of that question.

Looking out upon the surface of the Globe, with its varieties of climate, soil, and formations, its elevations and depressions, its rivers, lakes, oceans, islands, continents, and the vast and striking differences which mark and diversify its multitudinous inhabitants, the question has been raised, and pressed with increasing ardor and pertinacity, (especially in modern times,) can all these various tribes, nations, tongues, kindreds, so widely separated, and so strangely dissimilar, have descended from a common ancestry? That is the question, and it has been answered variously by men of learning. Different modes of reasoning have been adopted, but the conclusions reached may be divided into two—the one YES, and the other NO. *Which* of these answers is most in accordance with facts, with reason, with the welfare of the world, and reflects most glory upon the wisdom, power, and goodness of the Author of all existence, is the question for consideration with us? On which side is the weight of the argument, rather than which side is absolutely proved?

It must be admitted at the beginning, that, viewed apart from the authority of the Bible, neither the unity, nor diversity of origin of the human family, can be demonstrated. To use the terse expression of the Rev. Dr. Anderson, who speaking on this point, says; "It is impossible to get far enough back for that." This much, however, can be done. The evidence on both sides, can be accurately weighed, and the truth arrived at with almost absolute certainty.

It would be interesting, did time permit, to give here, some of the most striking features of the various theories, which have, of late, gained attention and respect in many quarters of our country—touching the origin of mankind—but I must pass this by. The argument to-day, is to the unity, as against that theory, which affirms the diversity of human origin.

THE BEARINGS OF THE QUESTION

A moment's reflection must impress all, that few questions have more important and solemn bearings, than the one now under consideration. It is connected with eternal as well as with terrestrial interests. It covers the earth and reaches heaven. The unity of the human race—the brotherhood of man—the reciprocal duties of all to each, and of each to all, are too plainly taught in the Bible to admit of cavil.—The credit of the Bible is at stake—and if it be too much to say, that it must stand or fall, by the decision of this question, *it is* proper to say, that the value of that sacred Book—as a record of the early history of mankind—must be materially affected, by the decision of the question.

For myself I can say, my reason (not less than my feeling, and my faith) welcomes with joy, the declaration of the Inspired Apostle, "that God has made of one blood all nations of men for to dwell upon all the face of the earth." But this grand affirmation of the unity of the human race, and many others like unto it, together with the whole account of the creation, given in the early scriptures, must all get a new interpretation or be overthrown altogether, if a diversity of human origin can be maintained.—Most evidently, this aspect of the question makes it important to those, who rely upon the Bible, as the sheet anchor of their hopes—and the frame work of all religious truth. The young minister must look into this subject and settle it for himself, before he ascends the pulpit, to preach redemption to a fallen race.

The bearing of the question upon Revelation, is not more marked and decided than its relation to the situation of things in our country, at this moment. *One seventh* part of the population of this country is of Negro descent. The land is peopled by what may be called the most dissimilar races on the globe. The black and the white—the Negro and the European—these constitute the American people—and, in all the likelihoods of the case, they will ever remain the principal inhabitants of the United States, in some form or other. The European population are greatly in the ascendant in numbers, wealth and power. They are the rulers of the country—the masters—the Africans, are the slaves—the proscribed portion of the people—and precisely in proportion as the truth of human brotherhood gets recognition, will be the freedom and elevation, in this country, of persons of African descent. In truth, this question is at the bottom of the whole controversy, now going on between the slaveholders on the *one* hand, and the abolitionists on the other. It is the same old question which has divided the selfish, from the philanthropic part of mankind in all ages. It is the question whether the rights, privileges, and immunities enjoyed by some ought not to be shared and enjoyed by all.

It is not quite two hundred years ago, when such was the simplicity (I will not now say the pride and depravity) of the Anglo-Saxon inhabitants of the British West Indies, that the learned and pious Godwin, a missionary to the West Indies, deemed it necessary to write a book, to remove what he conceived to be the injurious belief that it was sinful in the sight of God to baptize Negroes and Indians. The West Indies have made progress since that time.—God's emancipating angel has broken the fetters of slavery in those islands, and the praises of the Almighty are now sung by the sable lips of eight hundred thousand freemen, before deemed only fit for slaves, and to whom even baptismal and burial rights were denied.

The unassuming work of *Godwin* may have had some agency in producing this glorious result. One other remark before entering upon the argument. It may be said, that views and opinions, favoring the unity of the human family, coming from one of lowly condition, are open to the suspicion, that *"the wish is father to the thought,"* and so, indeed, it may be.—But let it be also remembered, that this deduction from the weight of the argument on the one side, is more than counter-balanced by the pride of race and position arrayed on the other. Indeed, ninety-nine out of every hundred of the advocates of a diverse origin of the human family in this country, are among those who hold it to be the privilege of the *Anglo-Saxon* to enslave and oppress the African—and slaveholders, not a few, like the Richmond Examiner to which I have referred, have admitted, that the whole argument in defence of slavery, becomes utterly worthless the moment the African is proved to be equally a man with the Anglo-Saxon. The temptation therefore, to read the Negro out of the human family is exceedingly strong, and may account somewhat for the repeated attempts on the part of Southern pretenders to science, to cast a doubt over the Scriptural account of the origin of mankind. If the origin and motives of most works, opposing the doctrine of the unity of the human race, could be ascertained, it may be doubted whether *one* such work could boast an honest parentage. Pride and selfishness, combined with mental power, never want for a theory to justify them—and when men oppress their fellow-men, the oppressor ever finds, in the character of the oppressed, a full justification for his oppression. Ignorance and depravity, and the inability to rise from degradation to civilization and respectability, are the most usual allegations against the oppressed. The evils most fostered by slavery and oppression, are precisely those which slaveholders and oppressors would transfer from their system to the inherent character of their victims. Thus the very crimes of slavery become slavery's best defence. By making the enslaved a character fit only for slavery, they excuse themselves for refusing to make the slave a freeman. A wholesale method of accomplishing this result, is to overthrow the instinctive consciousness of the common brotherhood of man. For, let it be once granted that the human race are of multitudinous origin, naturally different in their moral, physical, and intellectual capacities, and at once you make plausible a demand for classes, grades and conditions, for different methods of culture, different moral, political, and religious institutions, and a chance is left for slavery, as a necessary institution. The debates in Congress on the Nebraska Bill during the past winter, will show how slaveholders have availed themselves of this doctrine in support of slaveholding. There is no doubt that Messrs. Nott, Glidden, Morton, Smith and Agassiz were duly consulted by our slavery propagating statesmen.

ETHNOLOGICAL UNFAIRNESS TOWARDS THE NEGRO

The lawyers tell us that the credit of a witness is always in order. Ignorance, malice or prejudice, may disqualify a witness, and why not an author? Now, the disposition everywhere evident, among the class of writers alluded to, to separate the Negro race from every intelligent nation and tribe in Africa, may fairly be regarded as one proof, that they have staked out the ground beforehand, and that they have aimed to construct a theory in support of a foregone conclusion. The desirableness of isolating the Negro race, and especially of separating them from the various peoples of Northern Africa, is too plain to need a remark. Such isolation would remove stupendous difficulties in the way of getting the Negro in a favourable attitude for the blows of scientific christendom.

Dr. Samuel George Morton may be referred to as a fair sample of American Ethnologists. His very able work *"Crania Americana,"* published in Philadelphia in 1839, is widely read in this country.—In this great work his contempt for Negroes, is ever conspicuous. I take him as an illustration of what had been alleged as true of his class.

The fact that Egypt was one of the earliest abodes of learning and civilization, is as firmly established as are the everlasting hills, defying, with a calm front the boasted mechanical and architectural skill of the nineteenth century—smiling serenely on the assaults and the mutations of time, there she stands in overshadowing grandeur, riveting the eye and the mind of the modern world—upon her, in silent and dreamy wonder—Greece and Rome—and through them Europe and America have received their civilization from the ancient Egyptians. This fact is not denied by anybody. But Egypt is in Africa. Pity that it had not been in Europe, or in Asia, or better still in America! Another unhappy circumstance is, that the ancient Egyptians were not white people; but were, undoubtedly, just about as dark in complexion as many in this country who are considered genuine Negroes; and that is not all, their hair was far from being of that graceful lankness which adorns the fair Anglo-Saxon head. But the next best thing, after these defects, is a positive unlikeness to the Negro. Accordingly, our learned author enters into an elaborate argument to prove that the ancient Egyptians were totally distinct from the Negroes, and to deny all relationship between. Speaking of the "Copts and Fellahs," whom every body knows are descendants of the Egyptians, he says, *"The Copts, though now remarkably distinct from the people that surround them, derive from their remote ancestors some mixture of Greek, Arabian, and perhaps even Negro blood."* Now, mark the description given of the Egyptians in this same work: *"Complexion brown. The nose is straight, excepting the end, where it is rounded and wide; the lips are rather thick, and the hair black and curly."* This description would certainly seem to make it safe to suppose the presence of *"even* Negro blood." A man, in our day, with brown complexion, "nose rounded and wide, lips thick, hair black and curly," would, I think, have no difficulty in getting himself recognized as a Negro!!

The same authority tells us that the "Copts are supposed by NEIBHUR, DENON and others, to be the descendants of the ancient Egyptians"; and Dr. Morton adds, that it has often been observed that a strong resemblance may be traced between the Coptic visage and that presented in the ancient mummies and statues. Again, he says, the *"Copts can be, at most, but the degenerate remains, both physically and intellectually, of that mighty people who have claimed the admiration of all ages."* Speaking of the Nubians, Dr. Morton says, (page 26,) ——

The hair of the Nubian is thick and black—often curled, either by nature or art, and sometimes *partially frizzled,* but *never woolly.*

Again:——

Although the Nubians occasionally present their national characters unmixed, they generally show traces of their social intercourse with the Arabs, and *even* with the Negroes.

* * *

The repetition of the adverb here *"even,"* is important, as showing the spirit in which our great American Ethnologist pursues his work, and what deductions may be justly made from the value of his researches on that account. In everything touching the Negro, Dr. Morton, in his "Crania Americana," betrays the same spirit. He thinks that the *Sphinx* was not the representative of an Egyptian Deity, but was a shrine, worshiped at by the degraded *Negroes* of Egypt; and this fact he alleges as the secret of the mistake made by Volney, in supposing that the Egyptians were real Negroes. The absurdity of this assertion will be very apparent, in view of the fact that the great Sphinx in question was the chief of a series, full two miles in length. Our author again repels the supposition that the Egyptians were related to Negroes, by saying there is no mention made of *color* by the historian, in relating the marriage of Solomon with Pharaoh's daughter; and with genuine American feeling, he says, such a circumstance as the marrying of an European monarch with the daughter of a Negro would not have been passed over in silence in our day. This is a sample of the reasoning of men who reason from *prejudice* rather than from *facts.* It assumes that a *black skin* in the *East* excites the same prejudice which we see here in the West. Having denied all relationship of the Negro to the ancient Egyptians, with characteristic American assumption, he says, "It is easy to prove, that whatever may have been the hue of their skin, they belong to the same race with ourselves."

Of course, I do not find fault with Dr. Morton, or any other American, for claiming affinity with Egyptians. All that goes in that direction belongs to my side of the question, and is really right.

The leaning here indicated is natural enough, and may be explained by the fact, that an educated man in Ireland ceases to be an Irishman; and an intelligent black man is always supposed to have derived his intelligence from his connection with the white race. To be intelligent is to have one's Negro blood ignored.

There is, however, a very important physiological fact, contradicting this last assumption; and that fact is, that intellect is uniformly derived from the maternal side. Mulattoes, in this country, may almost wholly boast of Anglo Saxon male ancestry.

It is the province of prejudice to blind; and scientific writers, not less than others, write to please, as well as to instruct, and even unconsciously to themselves, (sometimes,) sacrifice what is true to what is popular. Fashion is not confined to dress; but extends to philosophy as well—and it is fashionable now, in our land, to exaggerate the differences between the Negro and the European. If, for instance, a phrenologist, or naturalist undertakes to represent in portraits, the differences between the two races —the Negro and the European—he will invariably present the *highest* type of the European, and the *lowest* type of the Negro.

The European face is drawn in harmony with the highest ideas of beauty, dignity and intellect. Features regular and brow after the Websterian-mold. The Negro, on the other hand, appears with features distorted, lips exaggerated, forehead depressed—and the whole expression of the countenance made to harmonize with the popular idea of Negro imbecility and degradation. I have seen many pictures of Negroes and Europeans, in phrenological and ethnological works; and all, or nearly all, excepting the work of Dr. Prichard, and that other great work, Combs' Constitution of Man, have been more or less open to this objection. I think I have never seen a single picture in an American work, designed to give an idea of the mental endowments of the Negro, which did any thing like justice to the subject; nay, that was not infamously distorted. The heads of A. CRUMMEL, HENRY H. GARNET, SAM'L R. WARD, CHAS. LENOX REMOND, W. J. WILSON, J. W. PENINGTON, J. I. GAINES, M. R. DELANY, J. W. LOGUEN, J. M. WHITFIELD, J. C. HOLLY, and hundreds of others I could mention, are all better formed, and indicate the presence of intellect more than any pictures I have seen in such works; and while it must be admitted that there are Negroes answering the description given by the American ethnologists and others, of the Negro race, I contend that there is every description of head among them, ranging from the highest Indoo Caucasian downward. If the very best type of the European is always presented, I insist that *justice,* in all such works, demands that the very best type of the Negro should also be taken. The importance of this criticism may not be apparent to all;—to the *black* man it is very apparent. He sees the injustice, and writhes under its sting. But to return to Dr. Morton, or rather to the question of the affinity of the Negroes to the Egyptians.

It seems to me that a man might as well deny the affinity of the American to the Englishman, as to deny such affinity between the Negro and the Egyptian. He might make out as many points of difference, in the case of the one as in that of the other. Especially could this be done, if, like ethnologists, in given cases, only typical specimens were resorted to. The lean, slender American, pale and swarthy, if exposed to the sun, wears a very different appearance to the full, round Englishman, of clear, *blonde* complexion. One may trace the progress of this difference in the common portraits of the American Presidents. Just study those faces, beginning with WASHINGTON; and as you come thro' the JEFFERSONS, the ADAMSES, and the MADISONS, you will find an increasing bony and wiry appearance about those portraits, & a greater remove from that serene amplitude which characterises the countenances of the earlier Presidents. I may be mistaken, but I think this is a correct index of the change going on in the nation at large—converting Englishmen, Germans, Irishmen, and Frenchmen, into Americans, and causing them to lose, in a common American character, all traces of their former distinctive national peculiarities.

AUTHORITIES AS TO THE RESEMBLANCE
OF THE EGYPTIANS TO NEGROES

Now, let us see what the best authorities say, as to the personal appearance of the Egyptians. I think it will be at once admitted, that while they differ very strongly from the Negro, debased and enslaved, that difference is not greater than may be observed in other quarters of the globe, among people notoriously belonging to the same variety, the same original stock; in a word, to the same family. If it shall be found that the people of Africa have an African character, as general, as well defined, and as distinct, as have the people of Europe, or the people of Asia, the exceptional differences among them afford no ground for supposing a difference of race; but, on the contrary, it will be inferred that the people of Africa constitute one great branch of the human family, whose origin may be as properly referred to the families of Noah, as can be any other branch of the human family, from whom they differ. Denon, in his *"Travels in Egypt,"* describes the Egyptians, as of full, but "delicate and voluptuous forms, countenances sedate and placid, round and soft features, with eyes long and almond shaped, half shut and languishing and turned up at the outer angles, as if habitually fatigued by the light and heat of the sun; cheeks round; thick lips, full and prominent; mouth large, but cheerful and smiling; complexion dark, ruddy and coppery, and the whole aspect displaying—as one of the most graphic delineators among modern travelers has observed—the genuine African character, of which the *Negro* is the exaggerated and extreme representation." Again, Prichard says, (page 152,)—

Herodotus traveled in Egypt, and was, therefore, well acquainted with the people from personal observation. He does not say anything directly, as to the descriptions of their persons, which were too well known to the Greeks to need such an account, but his indirect testimony is very strongly expressed. After mentioning a tradition, that the people of Colchis were a colony from Egypt, Herodotus says, that "there was one fact strongly in favor of this opinion—the Colchians were *black* in complexion and *woolly* haired.

These are the words by which the complexion and hair of Negroes are described. In another passage, he says that

The pigeon, said to have fled to Dodona, and to have founded the Oracle, was declared to be *black,* and that the meaning of the story was this: The Oracle was, in reality, founded by a female captive from the Thebaid; she was *black,* being an Egyptian. Other Greek writers . . . have expressed themselves in similar terms.

Those who have mentioned the Egyptians as a *swarthy* people, according to Prichard, might as well have applied the term *black* to them, since they were doubtless of a chocolate color. The same author brings together the testimony of Eschylus and others as to the color of the ancient Egyptians, all corresponding, more or less, with the foregoing. Among the most direct testimony educed by Prichard, is, first that of Volney, who, speaking of the modern Copts, says:

They have a puffed visage, swollen eyes, flat nose, and thick lips, and bear much resemblance to mulattoes.

Baron Larrey says, in regard to the same people:

They have projecting cheek bones, dilating nostrils, thick lips, and hair and beard black and *crisp.*

Mr. Ledyard, (whose testimony, says our learned authority, is of the more value, as he had no theory to support,) says:

I suspect the *Copts* to have been the *origin* of the *Negro* race; the nose and lips correspond with those of the Negro; the hair, wherever I can see it among the people here, is curled, *not* like that of the Negroes, but like the mulattoes.

Here I leave our learned authorities, as to the resemblance of the Egyptians to Negroes.

It is not in my power, in a discourse of this sort, to adduce more than a very small part of the testimony in support of a near relationship between the present enslaved and degraded Negroes, and the ancient highly civilized and wonderfully endowed Egyptians. Sufficient has already been adduced, to show a marked similarity in regard to features, hair, color, and I doubt not that the philologist can find equal similarity in the structures of their languages. In view of the foregoing, while it may not be claimed that the ancient Egyptians were Negroes,—viz:—answering, in all respects, to the nations and tribes ranged under the general appellation, Negro; still, it may safely be affirmed, that a strong affinity and a direct relationship may be claimed by the Negro race, to THAT GRANDEST OF ALL THE NATIONS OF ANTIQUITY, THE BUILDERS OF THE PYRAMIDS.

But there are other evidences of this relationship, more decisive than those alleged in a general similarity of personal appearance. Language is held to be very important, by the best ethnologists, in tracing out the remotest affinities of nations, tribes, classes and families. The color of the skin has sometimes been less enduring than the speech of a people. I speak by authority, and follow in the footsteps of some of the most learned writers on the natural and ethnological history of man, when I affirm that one of the most direct and conclusive proofs of the general affinity of Northern African nations, with those of West, East and South Africa, is found in the general similarity of their language. The philologist easily discovers, and is able to point out something like the original source of the multiplied tongues now in use in that yet mysterious quarter of the globe. DR. R. G. LATHAM, F. R. S., corresponding member of the Ethnological Society, New York—in his admirable work, entitled "Man and his Migrations"—says:

In the languages of Abyssinia, the Gheez and Tigre, admitted, as long as they have been known at all, to be *Semitic,* graduate through the Amharic, the Talasha, the Harargi, the Gafat and other languages, which may be well studied in Dr. Beke's valuable comparative tables, into the Agow tongue, unequivocally indigenous to Abyssinia, and through this into the true Negro classes. But, unequivocal as may be the Semitic elements of the Berber, Coptic and Galla, their affinities with the tongues of Western and Southern Africa are more so. I weigh my words when I say, not *equally,* but *more;* changing the expression, for every foot in advance which can be made towards the Semitic tongues in one direction, the African philologist can go a yard towards the Negro ones in the other.

In a note, just below this remarkable statement, Dr. Latham says:

A short table of the Berber and Coptic, as compared with the other African tongues, may be seen in the Classical Museum of the British Association, for 1846. In the Transactions of the Philological Society is a grammatical sketch of the Tumali language, by Dr. S. Tutshek of Munich. The Tumali is a truly Negro language, of Kordufan; whilst, in respect to the extent to which its inflections are formed, by internal changes of vowels and accents, it is fully equal to the Semitic tongues of Palestine and Arabia.

This testimony may not serve prejudice, but to me it seems quite sufficient.

SUPERFICIAL OBJECTIONS

Let us now glance again at the opposition. A volume, on the Natural History of the Human Species, by Charles Hamilton Smith, quite false in many of its facts, and as mischievous as false, has been published recently in this country, and will, doubtless, be widely circulated, especially by those to whom the thought of human brotherhood is abhorrent. This writer says, after mentioning sundry facts touching the dense and spherical structure of the Negro head:

This very structure may influence the erect gait, which occasions the practice common also to the Ethiopian, or mixed nations, of carrying burdens and light weights, even to a tumbler full of water, upon the head.

No doubt this seemed a very sage remark to Mr. Smith, and quite important in fixing a character to the Negro skull, although different to that of Europeans. But if the learned Mr. Smith had stood, previous to writing it, at our door (a few days in succession), he might have seen hundreds of Germans and of Irish people, not bearing burdens of *"light* weight," but of *heavy* weight, upon the same vertical extremity. The carrying of burdens upon the head is as old as Oriental Society; and the man writes himself a blockhead, who attempts to find in the custom a proof of original difference. On page 227, the same writer says:

The voice of the Negroes is feeble and hoarse in the male sex.

The explanation of this mistake in our author, is found in the fact, that an oppressed people, in addressing their superiors—perhaps I ought to say, their oppressors—usually assume a minor tone, as less likely to provoke the charge of intrusiveness. But it is ridiculous to pronounce the voice of the Negro feeble; and the learned ethnologist must be hard pushed, to establish differences, when he refers to this as one. Mr. Smith further declares, that

The typical woolly haired races have never discovered an alphabet, framed a grammatical language, nor made the least step in science or art.

Now, the man is still living (or was but a few years since), among the Mandingoes of the Western coast of Africa, who has framed an alphabet; and while Mr. Smith may be pardoned for his ignorance of that fact, as an ethnologist, he is inexcusable for not knowing that the Mpongwe language, spoken on both sides of the Gaboon River, at Cape Lopez, Cape St. Catharine, and in the interior, to the distance of two or three hundred miles, is as truly a grammatically framed language as any extant. I am indebted, for this fact, to Rev. Dr. M. B. ANDERSON, President of the Rochester University; and by his leave, here is the Grammar—[holding up the Grammar.] Perhaps, of all the attempts ever made to disprove the unity of the human family, and to brand the Negro with natural inferiority, the most compendious and barefaced is the book, entitled *"Types of Mankind,"* by Nott and Glidden. One would be well employed, in a series of Lectures, directed to an exposure of the unsoundness, if not the wickedness of this work.

THE AFRICAN RACE BUT ONE PEOPLE

But I must hasten. Having shown that the people of Africa are, probably, one people; that each tribe bears an intimate relation to other tribes and nations in that quarter of the globe, and that the Egyptians may have flung off the different tribes seen there at different times, as implied by the evident relations of their language, and by other similarities; it can hardly be deemed unreasonable to suppose, that the African branch of the human species—from the once highly civilized Egyptian to the barbarians on the banks of the Niger—may claim brotherhood with the great family of Noah, spreading over the more Northern and Eastern parts of the globe. I will now proceed to consider those physical peculiarities of form, features, hair and color, which are supposed by some men to mark the African, not only as an inferior race, but as a distinct species, naturally and originally different from the rest of mankind, and as really to place him nearer to the brute than to man.

THE EFFECT OF CIRCUMSTANCES UPON
THE PHYSICAL MAN

I may remark, just here, that it is impossible, even were it desirable, in a discourse like this, to attend to the anatomical and physiological argument connected with this part of the subject. I am not equal to that, and if I were, the occasion does not require it. The form of the *Negro*—[I use the term *Negro*, precisely in the sense that you use the term Anglo-Saxon; and I believe, too, that the former will one day be as illustrious as the latter]—has often been the subject of remark. His flat feet, long arms, high cheek bones and retreating forehead, are especially dwelt upon, to his disparagement, and just as if there were no white people with precisely the same peculiarities. I think it will ever be found, that the *well* or *ill* condition of any part of mankind, will leave its mark on the physical as well as on the intellectual part of man. A hundred instances might be cited, of whole families who have degenerated, and others who have improved in personal appearance, by a change of circumstances. A man is worked upon by what *he* works on. He may carve out his circumstances, but his circumstances will carve him out as well. I told a boot maker, in New Castle upon Tyne, that I had been a plantation slave. He said I must pardon him; but he could not believe it; no plantation laborer ever had a high instep. He said he had noticed, that the coal heavers and work people in low condition, had, for the most part, flat feet, and that he could tell, by the shape of the feet, whether a man's parents were in high or low condition. The thing was worth a thought, and I have thought of it, and have looked around me for facts. There is some truth in it; though there are exceptions, in individual cases.

The day I landed in Ireland, nine years ago, I addressed (in company with Father SPRATT, and that good man who has been recently made the subject of bitter attack; I allude to the philanthropic JAMES HAUGHTON, of Dublin) a large meeting of the common people of Ireland, on temperance. Never did human faces tell a sadder tale. More than five thousand were assembled; and I say, with no wish to wound the feelings of any Irishman, that these people lacked only a black skin and woolly hair, to complete their likeness to the plantation Negro. The open, uneducated mouth —the long, gaunt arm—the badly formed foot and ankle—the shuffling gait—the retreating forehead and vacant expression—and, their petty quarrels and fights—all reminded me of the plantation, and my own cruelly abused people. Yet, *that* is the land of GRATTAN, of CURRAN, of O'CONNELL, and of SHERIDAN. Now, while what I have said is true of the common people, the fact is, there are no more really handsome people in the world, than the educated Irish people. The Irishman educated, is a model gentleman; the Irishman ignorant and degraded, compares in form and feature, with the Negro!

I am stating facts. If you go into Southern Indiana, you will see what climate and habit can do, even in one generation. The man may have come from New England, but his hard features, sallow complexion, have left little of New England on his brow. The right arm of the blacksmith is said to be larger and stronger than his left. The ship carpenter is at forty round shouldered. The shoemaker carries the marks of his trade. One locality becomes famous for one thing, another for another. Manchester and Lowell, in America, Manchester and Sheffield, in England, attest this. But what does it all prove? Why, nothing positively, as to the main point; still it raises the inquiry—May not the condition of men explain their various appearances? Need we go behind the vicissitudes of barbarism for an explanation of the gaunt, wiry, ape like appearance of some of the genuine Negroes? Need we look higher than a vertical sun, or lower than the damp, black soil of the Niger, the Gambia, the Senegal, with their heavy and enervating miasma, rising ever from the rank growing and decaying vegetation, for an explanation of the Negro's color? If a cause, full and adequate, can be found here, *why seek further?*

The Eminent Dr. LATHAM, already quoted, says that nine tenths of the white population of the globe are found between 30 and 65 degrees North latitude. Only about one fifth of all the inhabitants of the globe are white; and they are as far from the Adamic complexion as is the Negro. The remainder are—*what?* Ranging all the way from the brunette to jet black. There are the red, the reddish copper color, the yellowish, the dark brown, the chocolate color, and so on, to the jet black. On the mountains on the North of Africa, where water freezes in winter at times, branches of the same people who are *black* in the valley are *white* on the mountains. The Nubian, with his beautiful curly hair, finds it becoming frizzled, crisped, and even woolly, as he approaches the great Sahara. The Portuguese, white in Europe, is brown in Asia. The Jews, who are to be found in all countries, never intermarrying, are white in Europe, brown in Asia, and black in Africa. Again, what does it all prove? Nothing, absolutely; nothing which places the question beyond dispute; but it *does* justify the conjecture before referred to, that outward circumstances *may* have something to do with modifying the various phases of humanity; and that color itself is at the control of the world's climate and its various concomitants. It is the sun that paints the peach—and may it not be, that he paints the *man* as well? My reading, on this point, however, as well as my own observation, have convinced me, that from the beginning the Almighty, within certain limits, endowed mankind with organizations capable of countless variations in form, feature and color, without having it necessary to begin a new creation for every new variety.

A powerful argument in the favor of the oneness of the human family, is afforded in the fact that nations, however dissimilar, may be united in one social state, not only without detriment to each other, but, most clearly, to the advancement of human welfare, happiness and perfection. While it is clearly proved, on the other hand, that those nations freest from foreign elements, present the most evident marks of deterioration. Dr. JAMES MCCUNE SMITH, himself a colored man, a gentleman and scholar, alleges —and not without excellent reason—that this, our own great nation, so distinguished for industry and enterprise, is largely indebted to its composite character. We all know, at any rate, that now, what constitutes the very heart of the civilized world—(I allude to England)—has only risen from barbarism to its present lofty eminence, through successive invasions and alliances with her people. The Medes and Persians constituted one of the mightiest empires that ever rocked the globe. The most terrible nation which now threatens the peace of the world, to make its will the law of Europe, is a grand piece of Mosaic work, in which almost every nation has its characteristic feature, from the wild Tartar to the refined Pole.

But, gentlemen, the time fails me, and I must bring these remarks to a close. My argument has swelled beyond its appointed measure. What I intended to make special, has become, in its progress, somewhat general. I meant to speak here to-day, for the lonely and the despised ones, with whom I was cradled, and with whom I have suffered; and now, gentlemen, in conclusion, what if all this reasoning be unsound? What if the Negro may not be able to prove his relationship to Nubians, Abyssinians and Egyptians? What if ingenious men are able to find plausible objections to all arguments maintaining the oneness of the human race? What, after all, if they are able to show very good reasons for believing the Negro to have been created precisely as we find him on the Gold Coast—along the Senegal and the Niger—I say, what of all this?—*"A man's a man for a' that."* I sincerely believe, that the weight of the argument is in favor of the unity of origin of the human race, or species—that the arguments on the other side are partial, superficial, utterly subversive of the happiness of man, and insulting to the wisdom of God. Yet, what if we grant they are not so? What, if we grant that the case, on our part, is not made out? Does it follow, that the Negro should be held in contempt? Does it follow, that to enslave and imbrute him is either *just* or *wise?* I think not. Human rights stand upon a common basis; and by all the reason that they are supported, maintained and defended, for one variety of the human family, they are supported, maintained and defended for *all* the human family; because all mankind have the same wants, arising out of a common nature. A diverse origin does not disprove a common nature, nor does it disprove a united destiny. The essential characteristics of humanity are everywhere the same. In the language of the eloquent CURRAN, "No matter what complexion, whether an Indian or an African sun has burnt upon him," his title deed to freedom, his claim to life and to liberty, to knowledge and to civilization, to society and to Christianity, are just and perfect. It is registered in the Courts of Heaven, and is enforced by the eloquence of the God of all the earth.

I have said that the Negro and white man are likely ever to remain the principal inhabitants of this country. I repeat the statement now, to submit the reasons that support it. The blacks can disappear from the face of the country by three ways. They may be colonized,—they may be exterminated,—or, they may die out. Colonization is out of the question; for I know not what hardships the laws of the land can impose, which can induce the colored citizen to leave his native soil. He was here in its infancy; he is here in its age. Two hundred years have passed over him, his tears and blood have been mixed with the soil, and his attachment to the place of his birth is stronger than iron. It is not probable that he will be exterminated; two considerations must prevent a crime so stupendous as that—the influence of Christianity on the one hand, and the power of self interest on the other; and, in regard to their dying out, the statistics of the country afford no encouragement for such a conjecture. The history of the Negro race proves them to be wonderfully adapted to all countries, all climates, and all conditions. Their tenacity of life, their powers of endurance, their malleable toughness, would almost imply especial interposition on their behalf. The ten thousand horrors of slavery, striking hard upon the sensitive soul, have bruised, and battered, and stung, but have not killed. The poor bondman lifts a smiling face above the surface of a sea of agonies, *hoping on, hoping ever.* His tawny brother, the Indian, dies, under the flashing glance of the Anglo Saxon. *Not* so the Negro; civilization cannot kill him. He accepts it—becomes a part of it. In the Church, he is an Uncle Tom, in the State, he is the most abused and least offensive. All the facts in his history mark out for him a destiny, united to America and Americans. Now, whether this population shall, by FREEDOM, INDUSTRY, VIRTUE AND INTELLIGENCE, be made a blessing to the country and the world, or whether their multiplied wrongs shall kindle the vengeance of an offended God, will depend upon the conduct of no class of men so much as upon the Scholars of the country. The future public opinion of the land,

whether anti-slavery or pro-slavery, whether just or unjust, whether magnanimous or mean, must redound to the honor of the Scholars of the
country or cover them with shame. There is but one safe road for nations
or for individuals. The fate of a wicked man and of a wicked nation is the
same. The flaming sword of offended justice falls as certainly upon the
nation as upon the man. God has no children whose rights may be safely
trampled upon. The sparrow may not fall to the ground without the notice
of His eye, and men are more than sparrows.

Now, gentlemen, I have done. The subject is before you. I shall not
undertake to make the application. I speak as unto wise men. I stand in
the presence of Scholars. We have met here to-day from vastly different
points in the world's condition. I have reached here—if you will pardon
the egotism—by little short of a miracle; at any rate, by dint of some
application and perseverance. Born, as I was, in obscurity, a stranger to
the halls of learning, environed by ignorance, degradation, and their concomitants, from birth to manhood, I do not feel at liberty to mark out,
with any degree of confidence, or dogmatism, what is the precise vocation
of the Scholar. Yet, this I *can* say, as a denizen of the world, and as a
citizen of a country rolling in the sin and shame of Slavery, the most
flagrant and scandalous that ever saw the sun, "Whatsoever things are
true, whatsoever things are honest, whatsoever things are just, whatsoever
things are pure, whatsoever things are lovely, whatsoever things are of
good report, if there be any virtue, and if there be any praise, think on
these things"—July 12, 1854.

THE DOOM OF THE BLACK POWER

The days of the Black Power are numbered. Its course, indeed, is onward,
but with the swiftness of an arrow, it rushes to the tomb. While crushing
its millions, it is also crushing itself.—The sword of Retribution, sus-
pended by a single hair, hangs over it. That sword must fall. Liberty must
triumph. It possesses an inherent vitality, a recuperative energy, to which
its opposite is a stranger. It may to human appearances be dead, the enemy
may rejoice at its grave, and sing its funeral requiem, but in the midst of
the triumphal shout, it leaps from its well guarded sepulchre, asserts the
divinity of its origin, flashes its indignant eye upon the affrighted enemy,
and bids him prepare *for the last battle, and the grave.*

We were never more hopeful, than at the present time, of the final
triumph of the great Principles which underlie the Abolition movement.
We rest our hopes upon a consciousness of their inherent Righteousness.
Truth is mighty, and will prevail. This is a maxim, which we do not regard as a mere rhetorical flourish. We are conscious that there is a black
side to our picture. The developments of the Slave Power, are anything

but pleasant to contemplate. The Present, with its inflexible realities, seems to be but an echo of the terribleness of the Past. We have lived through the one, we are now grappling with the other. We should not, as an oppressed People, grow despondent. Fear and despondency prevent us from working for the overthrow of our common enemy, with that hopeful spirit which causes us to keep our head above the waters, despite the raging of the elements. If we can at the present crisis, catch but one soft, low whisper of peace to our troubled souls, let us cling to it. Let us rejoice in Hope. The arm of the enemy will yet be paralyzed, and *with our withered arm made whole,* we'll rise in all the majesty and might of *Freemen,* and crush the crushers of the dangerous element of Abolitionism.

Whoever will contemplate the diversified phases of the Abolition Movement, from its inception to the present, will readily discern, that at no period of its history, has it presented so favorable an aspect as at the present. Truth is progressive. It ever has been; it always will be. Retrogression cannot be written on its brow. To the gaze of the world, error may appear, robed in the habiliments of gladness, and riding upon the wings of the wind. Truth may seemingly lag behind, and stop to rest upon the weeping willow. But the progress of the latter is sure and steady. The race is not to the swift; Error will soon lie down and die, but Truth will live forever. Let these reflections continually inspire us while battling with the oppressor.

Again: we should rejoice that the People are beginning to read, mark, and inwardly digest the truth. The attention of the masses is being directed to the enormity, the crushing cruelty, the ever-grasping cupidity of Slavery.—They begin to feel and know that Slavery is as relentless as the greedy grave, that its thirst for human blood can only be satiated for the time being; even a gift of nearly a half a million square miles only cools, *pro tempore,* the ardor of its ferocity. They have found out to their hearts' content, the utter inutility of attempting to compromise, or enter into any kind of contract with it, that so soon as compromises and contracts cease to conduce to its own aggrandizement, it spurns the compromise, and those who were gulled by it, and tramples on the contract. They have also found out that the Slavery question is one in which white men, as well as black men, are immediately interested, that Slavery invades the rights of man, irrespective of color and condition. They now begin to realize as Truth, that which a short time ago, they were wont to regard as the freak of disordered imaginations. Hence, the wolfish cry of *"fanaticism,"* has lost its potency; indeed the *"fanatics"* are looked upon as a pretty respectable body of People. Some consolation can be deduced from this reflection.

Another thought: we regard the present developments of the Slave Power as precipitating the era of its disastrous doom. It has overreached itself, in its efforts to abolish Freedom in the United States, and erect its black standard upon every hill-top and valley in the land. It never wore an aspect so repulsive, as it does to-day. It has made such a frightful noise of late, that the attention of the world is directed toward it. The passage of the Fugitive Slave Act, and the Nebraska Bill; the recent marauding movements of the oligarchy in Kansas, all the ebullitions of its pent-up wrath, are fatal stabs in the monster side. The Anti-Slavery sentiment of the North has been strengthened and increased by these developments; indeed, the Abolitionists have now a most potent ally in the Slave Power. Slaveholders are unconsciously performing good service in the cause of Liberty, by demonstrating in their conduct, the truthfulness of the sentiments advanced and advocated by Abolitionists. The Anti-Slavery men of the land have faithfully admonished the whole country, and held up the Slave Power, as an Oligarchy determined on swaying the sceptre of universal dominion. But they have been regarded fanatics, and enthusiasts, crying wolf, when there was no wolf, inciting peaceful citizens to Rebellion, turning the country upside down, striving to destroy the Union. These and a host of similar allegations have been brought against them.

But now the great masses of the People find out by experience, that the wolf is indeed among them. They see his red, glaring eyes, and they cry out, *"kill the wolf;* he must not be permitted to go any farther in his depredations; our eyes have been opened." Thanks to the Fugitive Slave and Nebraska Bills. They have sealed the doom of the Black Power.

Lastly, we behold that doom written in unmistakable characters, by the great Republican Movement, which is sweeping like a whirlwind over the Free States. We rejoice in this demonstration. It evinces the fact of a growing determination on the part of the North, to redeem *itself* from bondage, to bury party affinities, and predilections, and also the political leaders who have hitherto controlled them; to unite in one grand phalanx, and go forth, and whip the enemy. *We* cannot join this party, because we think it lacks vitality; it does not go far enough in the right direction; it gives aid and comfort to the Slaveholder, by its concessions, and its willingness to "let Slavery alone where it is"—This is the very place where it should be attacked. We cannot attack it very well where it is not. But we have in former articles commented at length on the inconsistency and absurdity of that phase of Anti-Slavery sentiment and action, denominated Free-Soilism. We are, however, hopeful that this Republican Party as it grows in numbers, will also grow *"in the knowledge of the Truth."* A few more pro-Slavery demonstrations, a few more presses thrown into the river, a few more northern ministers driven from the South and West, a few more recaptures of Fugitives, near Bunker Hill, and Plymouth Rock, causing the People to see the system in all its native ugliness, and hate it with indescribable intenseness, and all will be well. We have no fears of ultimate success. Let each man do his duty. Let him continue to *agitate* in the circle in which he moves. Let him not lose sight of his individual responsibility, for this gives tone and vigor to associated action. The Slave's complaint must be heard at the fireside, in the street, in the counting house, in the prayer meeting, in the conference room, from the pulpit, in synods, and associations, and conferences, and especially *at the Polls.* We must follow the oppressor whithersoever he goeth, irrespective of the form in which he may develop himself, or the habiliments he may assume. Use the proper means, fight with the right weapons, let there be no cessation of the warfare, no diversion from the *real cause of the battle,* and we shall yet witness the *end of the Black Power in America*—July 27, 1855.

SPEECH ON THE DRED SCOTT DECISION

While four millions of our fellow countrymen are in chains—while men, women, and children are bought and sold on the auction-block with horses, sheep, and swine—while the remorseless slave-whip draws the warm blood of our common humanity—it is meet that we assemble as we have done to-day, and lift up our hearts and voices in earnest denunciation of the vile and shocking abomination. It is not for us to be governed by our hopes or our fears in this great work; yet it is natural on occasions like this, to survey the position of the great struggle which is going on between slavery and freedom, and to dwell upon such signs of encouragement as may have been lately developed, and the state of feeling these signs or events have occasioned in us and among the people generally. It is a fitting time to take an observation to ascertain where we are, and what our prospects are.

To many, the prospects of the struggle against slavery seem far from cheering. Eminent men, North and South, in Church and State, tell us that the omens are all against us. Emancipation, they tell us, is a wild, delusive idea; the price of human flesh was never higher than now; slavery was never more closely entwined about the hearts and affections of the southern people than now; that whatever of conscientious scruple, religious conviction, or public policy, which opposed the system of slavery forty or fifty years ago, has subsided; and that slavery never reposed upon a firmer basis than now. Completing this picture of the happy and prosperous condition of this system of wickedness, they tell us that this state of things is to be set to our account. Abolition agitation has done it all. How deep is the misfortune of my poor, bleeding people, if this be so! How lost their condition, if even the efforts of their friends but sink them deeper in ruin!

Without assenting to this strong representation of the increasing strength and stability of slavery, without denouncing what of untruth pervades it, I own myself not insensible to the many difficulties and discouragements that beset us on every hand. They fling their broad and gloomy shadows across the pathway of every thoughtful colored man in this country. For one, I see them clearly, and feel them sadly. With an earnest, aching heart, I have long looked for the realization of the hope of my people. Standing, as it were, barefoot, and treading upon the sharp and flinty rocks of the present, and looking out upon the boundless sea of the future, I have sought, in my humble way, to penetrate the intervening mists and clouds, and, perchance, to descry, in the dim and shadowy distance, the white flag of freedom, the precise speck of time at which the cruel bondage of my people should end, and the long entombed millions rise from the foul grave of slavery and death. But of that time I can know nothing, and you can know nothing. All is uncertain at that point. One thing, however, is certain; slaveholders are in earnest, and mean to cling to their slaves as long as they can, and to the bitter end. They show no sign of a wish to quit their iron grasp upon the sable throats of their victims. Their motto is, "a firmer hold and a tighter grip" for every new effort that is made to break their cruel power. The case is one of life or death with them, and they will give up only when they must do that or do worse.

In one view the slaveholders have a decided advantage over all opposition. It is well to notice this advantage—the advantage of complete organization. They are organized; and yet were not at the pains of creating their organizations. The State governments, where the system of slavery exists, are complete slavery organizations. The church organizations in those States are equally at the service of slavery; while the Federal Government, with its army and navy, from the chief magistracy in Washington, to the Supreme Court, and thence to the chief marshalship at New York, is pledged to support, defend, and propagate the crying curse of human bondage. The pen, the purse, and the sword, are united against the simple truth, preached by humble men in obscure places.

This is one view. It is, thank God, only one view; there is another, and a brighter view. David, you know, looked small and insignificant when going to meet Goliath, but looked larger when he had slain his foe. The Malakoff was, to the eye of the world, impregnable, till the hour it fell before the shot and shell of the allied army. Thus hath it ever been. Oppression, organized as ours is, will appear invincible up to the very hour of its fall. Sir, let us look at the other side, and see if there are not some things to cheer our heart and nerve us up anew in the good work of emancipation.

Take this fact—for it is a fact—the anti-slavery movement has, from first to last, suffered no abatement. It has gone forth in all directions, and is now felt in the remotest extremities of the Republic.

It started small, and was without capital either in men or money. The odds were all against it. It literally had nothing to lose, and everything to gain. There was ignorance to be enlightened, error to be combatted, conscience to be awakened, prejudice to be overcome, apathy to be aroused, the right of speech to be secured, mob violence to be subdued, and a deep, radical change to be inwrought in the mind and heart of the whole nation. This great work, under God, has gone on, and gone on gloriously.

Amid all changes, fluctuations, assaults, and adverses of every kind, it has remained firm in its purpose, steady in its aim, onward and upward, defying all opposition, and never losing a single battle. Our strength is in the growth of anti-slavery conviction, and this has never halted.

There is a significant vitality about this abolition movement. It has taken a deeper, broader, and more lasting hold upon the national heart than ordinary reform movements. Other subjects of much interest come and go, expand and contract, blaze and vanish, but the huge question of American Slavery, comprehending, as it does, not merely the weal or the woe of four millions, and their countless posterity, but the weal or the woe of this entire nation, must increase in magnitude and in majesty with every hour of its history. From a cloud not bigger than a man's hand, it has overspread the heavens. It has risen from a grain not bigger than a mustard seed. Yet see the fowls of the air, how they crowd its branches.

Politicians who cursed it, now defend it; ministers, once dumb, now speak in its praise; and presses, which once flamed with hot denunciations against it, now surround the sacred cause as by a wall of living fire. Politicians go with it as a pillar of cloud by day, and the press as a pillar of fire by night. With these ancient tokens of success, I, for one, will not despair of our cause.

Those who have undertaken to suppress and crush out this agitation for Liberty and humanity, have been most woefully disappointed. Many who have engaged to put it down, have found themselves put down. The agitation has pursued them in all their meanderings, broken in upon their seclusion, and, at the very moment of fancied security, it has settled down upon them like a mantle of unquenchable fire. Clay, Calhoun, and Webster each tried his hand at suppressing the agitation; and they went to their graves disappointed and defeated.

Loud and exultingly have we been told that the slavery question is settled, and settled forever. You remember it was settled thirty-seven years ago, when Missouri was admitted into the Union with a slaveholding constitution, and slavery prohibited in all territory north of thirty-six degrees of north latitude. Just fifteen years afterwards, it was settled again by voting down the right of petition, and gagging down free discussion in Congress. Ten years after this it was settled again by the annexation of Texas, and with it the war with Mexico. In 1850 it was again settled. This was called a final settlement. By it slavery was virtually declared to be the equal of Liberty, and should come into the Union on the same terms. By it the right and the power to hunt down men, women, and children, in every part of this country, was conceded to our southern brethren, in order to keep them in the Union. Four years after this settlement, the whole question was once more settled, and settled by a settlement which unsettled all the former settlements.

The fact is, the more the question has been settled, the more it has needed settling. The space between the different settlements has been strikingly on the decrease. The first stood longer than any of its successors.

This last settlement must be called the Taney settlement. We are now —the second, ten years—the third, five years—the fourth stood four years —and the fifth has stood the brief space of two years.

This last settlement must be called the Taney settlement. We are now told, in tones of lofty exultation, that the day is lost—all lost—and that we might as well give up the struggle. The highest authority has spoken. The voice of the Supreme Court has gone out over the troubled waves of the National Conscience, saying peace, be still.

This infamous decision of the Slaveholding wing of the Supreme Court maintains that slaves are within the contemplation of the Constitution of the United States, property; that slaves are property in the same sense that horses, sheep, and swine are property; that the old doctrine that slavery is a creature of local law is false; that the right of the slaveholder to his slave does not depend upon the local law, but is secured wherever the Constitution of the United States extends; that Congress has no right to prohibit slavery anywhere; that slavery may go in safety anywhere under the star-spangled banner; that colored persons of African descent have no rights that white men are bound to respect; that colored men of African descent are not and cannot be citizens of the United States.

You will readily ask me how I am affected by this devilish decision— this judicial incarnation of wolfishness? My answer is, and no thanks to the slaveholding wing of the Supreme Court, my hopes were never brighter than now.

I have no fear that the National Conscience will be put to sleep by such an open, glaring, and scandalous tissue of lies as that decision is, and has been, over and over, shown to be.

The Supreme Court of the United States is not the only power in this world. It is very great, but the Supreme Court of the Almighty is greater. Judge Taney can do many things, but he cannot perform impossibilities. He cannot bale out the ocean, annihilate the firm old earth, or pluck the silvery star of liberty from our Northern sky. He may decide, and decide again; but he cannot reverse the decision of the Most High. He cannot change the essential nature of things—making evil good, and good evil.

Happily for the whole human family, their rights have been defined, declared, and decided in a court higher than the Supreme Court. "There is a law," says Brougham, "above all the enactments of human codes, and by that law, unchangeable and eternal, man cannot hold property in man."

Your fathers have said that man's right to liberty is self-evident. There is no need of argument to make it clear. The voices of nature, of conscience, of reason, and of revelation, proclaim it as the right of all rights, the foundation of all trust, and of all responsibility. Man was born with it. It was his before he comprehended it. The *deed* conveying it to him is written in the center of his soul, and is recorded in Heaven. The sun in the sky is not more palpable to the sight than man's right to liberty is to the moral vision. To decide against this right in the person of Dred Scott, or the humblest and most whip-scarred bondman in the land, is to decide against God. It is an open rebellion against God's government. It is an attempt to undo what God has done, to blot out the broad distinction instituted by the *Allwise* between men and things, and to change the image and superscription of the everliving God into a speechless piece of merchandise.

Such a decision cannot stand. God will be true though every man be a liar. We can appeal from this hell-black judgment of the Supreme Court, to the court of common sense and common humanity. We can appeal from man to God. If there is no justice on earth, there is yet justice in heaven. You may close your Supreme Court against the black man's cry for justice, but you cannot, thank God, close against him the ear of a sympathising world, nor shut up the Court of Heaven. All that is merciful and just, on earth and in Heaven, will execrate and despise this edict of Taney.

If it were at all likely that the people of these free States would tamely submit to this demoniacal judgment, I might feel gloomy and sad over it, and possibly it might be necessary for my people to look for a home in some other country. But as the case stands, we have nothing to fear.

In one point of view, we, the abolitionists and colored people, should meet this decision, unlooked for and monstrous as it appears, in a cheerful spirit. This very attempt to blot out forever the hopes of an enslaved people may be one necessary link in the chain of events preparatory to the downfall and complete overthrow of the whole slave system.

The whole history of the anti-slavery movement is studded with proof that all measures devised and executed with a view to ally and diminish the anti-slavery agitation, have only served to increase, intensify, and embolden that agitation. This wisdom of the crafty has been confounded, and the counsels of the ungodly brought to nought. It was so with the Fugitive Slave Bill. It was so with the Kansas-Nebraska Bill; and it will be so with this last and most shocking of all pro-slavery devices, this Taney decision.

When great transactions are involved, where the fate of millions is concerned, where a long enslaved and suffering people are to be delivered, I am superstitious enough to believe that the finger of the Almighty may be seen bringing good out of evil, and making the wrath of man redound to his honor, hastening the triumph of righteousness.

The American people have been called upon, in a most striking manner, to abolish and put away forever the system of slavery. The subject has been pressed upon their attention in all earnestness and sincerity. The cries of the slave have gone forth to the world, and up to the throne of God. This decision, in my view, is a means of keeping the nation awake on the subject. It is another proof that God does not mean that we shall go to sleep, and forget that we are a slaveholding nation.

Step by step we have seen the slave power advancing; poisoning, corrupting, and perverting the institutions of the country; growing more and more haughty, imperious, and exacting. The white man's liberty has been marked out for the same grave with the black man's.

The ballot box is desecrated, God's law set at nought, armed legislators stalk the halls of Congress, freedom of speech is beaten down in the Senate. The rivers and highways are infested by border ruffians, and white men are made to feel the iron heel of slavery. This ought to arouse us to kill off the hateful thing. They are solemn warnings to which the white people, as well as the black people, should take heed.

If these shall fail, judgment, more fierce or terrible, may come. The lightning, whirlwind, and earthquake may come. Jefferson said that he trembled for his country when he reflected that God is just, and his justice cannot sleep forever. The time may come when even the crushed worm may turn under the tyrant's feet. Goaded by cruelty, stung by a burning sense of wrong, in an awful moment of depression and desperation, the bondman and bondwoman at the south may rush to one wild and deadly struggle for freedom. Already slaveholders go to bed with bowie knives, and apprehend death at their dinners. Those who enslave, rob, and torment their cooks, may well expect to find death in their dinner-pots.

The world is full of violence and fraud, and it would be strange if the slave, the constant victim of both fraud and violence, should escape the contagion. He, too, may learn to fight the devil with fire, and for one, I am in no frame of mind to pray that this may be long deferred.

Two remarkable occurrences have followed the presidential election; one was the unaccountable sickness traced to the National Hotel at Washington, and the other was the discovery of a plan among the slaves, in different localities, to slay their oppressors. Twenty or thirty of the suspected were put to death. Some were shot, some hanged, some burned, and some died under the lash. One brave man owned himself well acquainted with the conspiracy, but said he would rather die than disclose the facts. He received seven hundred and fifty lashes, and his noble spirit went away to the God who gave it. The name of this hero has been by the meanness of tyrants suppressed. Such a man redeems his race. He is worthy to be mentioned with the Hoffers and Tells, the noblest heroes of history. These insurrectionary movements have been put down, but they may break out at any time, under the guidance of higher intelligence, and with a more invincible spirit.

> The fire thus kindled, may be revived again;
> The flames are extinguished, but the embers remain;
> One terrible blast may produce an ignition,
> Which shall wrap the whole South in wild conflagration.

> The pathway of tyrants lies over volcanoes
> The very air they breathe is heavy with sorrows;
> Agonizing heart-throbs convulse them while sleeping,
> And the wind whispers Death as over them sweeping.

By all the laws of nature, civilization, and of progress, slavery is a doomed system. Not all the skill of politicians, North and South, not all the sophistries of Judges, not all the fulminations of a corrupt press, not all the hypocritical prayers, or the hypocritical refusals to pray of a hollow-hearted priesthood, not all the devices of sin and Satan, can save the vile thing from extermination.

Already a gleam of hope breaks upon us from the southwest. One Southern city has grieved and astonished the whole South by a preference for freedom. The wedge has entered. Dred Scott, of Missouri, goes into slavery, but St. Louis declares for freedom. The judgment of Taney is not the judgment of St. Louis.

It may be said that this demonstration in St. Louis is not to be taken as an evidence of sympathy with the slave; that it is purely a white man's victory. I admit it. Yet I am glad that white men, bad as they generally are, should gain a victory over slavery. I am willing to accept a judgment against slavery, whether supported by white or black reasons—though I would much rather have it supported by both. He that is not against us, is on our part.

Come what will, I hold it to be morally certain that, sooner or later, by fair means or foul means, in quiet or in tumult, in peace or in blood, in judgment or in mercy, slavery is doomed to cease out of this otherwise goodly land, and liberty is destined to become the settled law of this Republic.

I base my sense of the certain overthrow of slavery, in part, upon the nature of the American Government, the Constitution, the tendencies of the age, and the character of the American people; and this, notwithstanding the important decision of Judge Taney.

I know of no soil better adapted to the growth of reform than American soil. I know of no country where the conditions for affecting great changes in the settled order of things, for the development of right ideas of liberty and humanity, are more favorable than here in these United States.

The very groundwork of this government is a good repository of Christian civilization. The Constitution, as well as the Declaration of Independence, and the sentiments of the founders of the Republic, give us a platform broad enough, and strong enough, to support the most comprehensive plans for the freedom and elevation of all the people of this country, without regard to color, class, or clime.

There is nothing in the present aspect of the anti-slavery question which should drive us into the extravagance and nonsense of advocating a dissolution of the American Union as a means of overthrowing slavery, or freeing the North from the malign influence of slavery upon the morals of the Northern people. While the press is at liberty, and speech is free, and the ballot-box is open to the people of the sixteen free States; while the slaveholders are but four hundred thousand in number, and we are fourteen millions; while the mental and moral power of the nation is with us; while we are really the strong and they are the weak, it would look worse than cowardly to retreat from the Union.

If the people of the North have not the power to cope with these four hundred thousand slaveholders inside the Union, I see not how they could get out of the Union. The strength necessary to move the Union must ever be less than is required to break it up. If we have got to conquer the slave power to get out of the Union, I for one would much rather conquer, and stay in the Union. The latter, it strikes me, is the far more rational mode of action.

I make these remarks in no servile spirit, nor in any superstitious reverence for a mere human arrangement. If I felt the Union to be a curse, I should not be far behind the very chiefest of the disunion Abolitionists in denouncing it. But the evil to be met and abolished is not in the Union. The power arrayed against us is not a parchment.

It is not in changing the dead form of the Union, that slavery is to be abolished in this country. We have to do not with the dead, but the living; not with the past, but the living present.

Those who seek slavery in the Union, and who are everlastingly dealing blows upon the Union, in the belief that they are killing slavery, are most woefully mistaken. They are fighting a dead form instead of a living and powerful reality. It is clearly not because of the peculiar character of our Constitution that we have slavery, but the wicked pride, love of power, and selfish perverseness of the American people. Slavery lives in this country not because of any paper Constitution, but in the moral blindness of the American people, who persuade themselves that they are safe, though the rights of others may be struck down.

Besides, I think it would be difficult to hit upon any plan less likely to abolish slavery than the dissolution of the Union. The most devoted advocates of slavery, those who make the interests of slavery their constant study, seek a dissolution of the Union as their final plan for preserving slavery from Abolition, and their ground is well taken. Slavery lives and flourishes best in the absence of civilization; a dissolution of the Union would shut up the system in its own congenial barbarism.

The dissolution of the Union would not give the North one single additional advantage over slavery to the people of the North, but would manifestly take from them many which they now certainly possess.

Within the Union we have a firm basis of anti-slavery operation. National welfare, national prosperity, national reputation and honor, and national scrutiny; common rights, common duties, and common country, are so many bridges over which we can march to the destruction of slavery. To fling away these advantages because James Buchanan is President or Judge Taney gives a lying decision in favor of slavery, does not enter into my notion of common sense.

Mr. Garrison and his friends have been telling us that, while in the Union, we are responsible for slavery; and in so telling us, he and they have told us the truth. But in telling us that we shall cease to be responsible for slavery by dissolving the Union, he and they have not told us the truth.

There now, clearly, is no freedom from responsibility for slavery, but in the Abolition of slavery. We have gone too far in this business now to sum up our whole duty in the cant phrase of "no Union with slaveholders."

To desert the family hearth may place the recreant husband out of the sight of his hungry children, but it cannot free him from responsibility. Though he should roll the waters of three oceans between him and them, he could not roll from his soul the burden of his responsibility to them; and, as with the private family, so in this instance with the national family. To leave the slave in his chains, in the hands of cruel masters who are too strong for him, is not to free ourselves from responsibility. Again: If I were on board of a pirate ship, with a company of men and women whose lives and liberties I had put in jeopardy, I would not clear my soul of their blood by jumping in the long boat, and singing out no union with pirates. My business would be to remain on board, and while I never would perform a single act of piracy again, I should exhaust every means given me by my position, to save the lives and liberties of those against whom I had committed piracy. In like manner, I hold it is our duty to remain inside this Union, and use all the power to restore to enslaved millions their precious and God-given rights. The more we have done by our voice and our votes, in times past, to rivet their galling fetters, the more clearly and solemnly comes the sense of duty to remain, to undo what we have done. Where, I ask, could the slave look for release from slavery if the Union were dissolved? I have an abiding conviction founded upon long and careful study of the certain effects of slavery upon the moral sense of slaveholding communities, that if the slaves are ever delivered from bondage, the power will emanate from the free States. All hope that the slaveholders will be self-moved to this great act of justice, is groundless and delusive. Now, as of old, the Redeemer must come from above, not from beneath. To dissolve the Union would be to withdraw the emancipating power from the field.

But I am told this is the argument of expediency. I admit it, and am prepared to show that what is expedient in this instance is right. "Do justice, though the heavens fall." Yes, that is a good motto, but I deny that it would be doing justice to the slave to dissolve the Union and leave the slave in his chains to get out by the clemency of his master, or the strength of his arms. Justice to the slave is to break his chains, and going out of the union is to leave him in his chains, and without any probable chance of getting out of them.

But I come now to the great question as to the constitutionality of slavery. The recent slaveholding decision, as well as the teachings of anti-slavery men, make this a fit time to discuss the constitutional pretensions of slavery.

The people of the North are a law abiding people. They love order and respect the means to that end. This sentiment has sometimes led them to the folly and wickedness of trampling upon the very life of law, to uphold its dead form. This was so in the execution of that thrice accursed Fugitive Slave Bill. Burns and Simms were sent back to the hell of slavery after they had looked upon Bunker Hill, and heard liberty thunder in Faneuil Hall. The people permitted this outrage in obedience to the popular sentiment of reverence for law. While men thus respect law, it becomes a serious matter so to interpret the law as to make it operate against liberty. I have a quarrel with those who fling the Supreme Law of this land between the slave and freedom. It is a serious matter to fling the weight of the Constitution against the cause of human liberty, and those who do it, take upon them a heavy responsibility. Nothing but absolute necessity, shall, or ought to drive me to such a concession to slavery.

When I admit that slavery is constitutional, I must see slavery recognized in the Constitution. I must see that it is there plainly stated that one man of a certain description has a right of property in the body and soul of another man of a certain description. There must be no room for a doubt. In a matter so important as the loss of liberty, everything must be proved beyond all reasonable doubt.

The well known rules of legal interpretation bear me out in this stubborn refusal to see slavery where slavery is not, and only to see slavery where it is.

The Supreme Court has, in its day, done something better than make slaveholding decisions. It has laid down rules of interpretation which are in harmony with the true idea and object of law and liberty.

It has told us that the intention of legal instruments must prevail; and that this must be collected from its words. It has told us that language must be construed strictly in favor of liberty and justice.

It has told us where rights are infringed, where fundamental principles are overthrown, where the general system of the law is departed from, the Legislative intention must be expressed with irresistible clearness, to induce a court of justice to suppose a design to effect such objects.

These rules are as old as law. They rise out of the very elements of law. It is to protect human rights, and promote human welfare. Law is in its nature opposed to wrong, and must everywhere be presumed to be in favor of the right. The pound of flesh, but not one drop of blood, is a sound rule of legal interpretation.

Besides there is another rule of law as well of common sense, which requires us to look to the ends for which a law is made, and to construe its details in harmony with the ends sought.

Now let us approach the Constitution from the standpoint thus indicated, and instead of finding in it a warrant for the stupendous system of robbery, comprehended in the term slavery, we shall find it strongly against that system.

"We, the people of the United States, in order to form a more perfect Union, establish justice, insure domestic tranquility, provide for the common defence, promote the general welfare, and secure the blessings of liberty to ourselves and our posterity, do ordain and establish this constitution for the United States of America."

Such are the objects announced by the instrument itself, and they are in harmony with the Declaration of Independence, and the principles of human well-being.

Six objects are here declared, "Union," "defence," "welfare," "tranquility," and "justice," and "liberty."

Neither in the preamble nor in the body of the Constitution is there a single mention of the term *slave* or *slave holder, slave master* or *slave state,* neither is there any reference to the color, or the physical peculiarities of any part of the people of the United States. Neither is there anything in the Constitution standing alone, which would imply the existence of slavery in this country.

"We, the people"—not we, the white people—not we, the citizens, or the legal voters—not we, the privileged class, and excluding all other classes but we, the people; not we, the horses and cattle, but we the people —the men and women, the human inhabitants of the United States, do ordain and establish this Constitution, &c.

I ask, then, any man to read the Constitution, and tell me where, if he can, in what particular that instrument affords the slightest sanction of slavery?

Where will he find a guarantee for slavery? Will he find it in the declaration that no person shall be deprived of life, liberty, or property, without due process of law? Will he find it in the declaration that the Constitution was established to secure the blessing of liberty? Will he find it in the right of the people to be secure in their persons and papers, and houses, and effects? Will he find it in the clause prohibiting the enactment by any State of a bill of attainder?

These all strike at the root of slavery, and any one of them, but faithfully carried out, would put an end to slavery in every State in the American Union.

Take, for example, the prohibition of a bill of attainder. That is a law entailing on the child the misfortunes of the parent. This principle would destroy slavery in every State of the Union.

The law of slavery is a law of attainder. The child is property because its parent was property, and suffers as a slave because its parent suffered as a slave.

Thus the very essence of the whole slave code is in open violation of a fundamental provision of the Constitution, and is in open and flagrant violation of all the objects set forth in the Constitution.

While this and much more can be said, and has been said, and much better said, by Lysander Spooner, William Goodell, Beriah Green, and Gerrit Smith, in favor of the entire unconstitutionality of slavery, what have we on the other side?

How is the constitutionality of slavery made out, or attempted to be made out?

First, by discrediting and casting away as worthless the most beneficent rules of legal interpretation; by disregarding the plain and common sense reading of the instrument itself; by showing that the Constitution does not mean what it says, and says what it does not mean, by assuming that the written Constitution is to be interpreted in the light of a secret and un-written understanding of its framers, which understanding is declared to be in favor of slavery. It is in this mean, contemptible, underhand method that the Constitution is pressed into the service of slavery.

They do not point us to the Constitution itself, for the reason that there is nothing sufficiently explicit for their purpose; but they delight in sup-posed intentions—intentions nowhere expressed in the Constitution, and everywhere contradicted in the Constitution.

Judge Taney lays down this system of interpreting in this wise:

"The general words above quoted would seem to embrace the whole human family, and, if they were used in a similar instrument at this day, would be so understood. But it is too clear for dispute that the enslaved African race were not intended to be included, and formed no part of the people who framed and adopted this declaration; for if the language, as understood in that day, would embrace them, the conduct of the distin-guished men who framed the Declaration of Independence would have been utterly and flagrantly inconsistent with the principles they asserted; and instead of the sympathy of mankind, to which they appealed, they would have deserved and received universal rebuke and reprobation.

"It is difficult, at this day, to realize the state of public opinion respect-ing that unfortunate class with the civilized and enlightened portion of the world at the time of the Declaration of Independence and the adop-tion of the Constitution; but history shows they had, for more than a century, been regarded as beings of an inferior order, and unfit associates for the white race, either socially or politically, and had no rights which white men are bound to respect; and the black man might be reduced to slavery, bought and sold, and treated as an ordinary article of merchan-dise. This opinion, at that time, was fixed and universal with the civilized portion of the white race. It was regarded as an axiom of morals, which no one thought of disputing, and everyone habitually acted upon it, without doubting, for a moment, the correctness of the opinion. And in no nation was this opinion more fixed, and generally acted upon, than in England;

the subjects of which government not only seized them on the coast of Africa, but took them, as ordinary merchandise, to where they could make a profit on them. The opinion, thus entertained, was universally maintained on the colonies this side of the Atlantic; accordingly, Negroes of the African race were regarded by them as property, and held and bought and sold as such in every one of the thirteen colonies, which united in the Declaration of Independence, and afterwards formed the Constitution."

The argument here is, that the Constitution comes down to us from a slaveholding period and a slaveholding people; and that, therefore, we are bound to suppose that the Constitution recognizes colored persons of African descent, the victims of slavery at that time, as debarred forever from all participation in the benefit of the Constitution and the Declaration of Independence, although the plain reading of both includes them in their beneficent range.

As a man, an American, a citizen, a colored man of both Anglo-Saxon and African descent, I denounce this representation as a most scandalous and devilish perversion of the Constitution, and a brazen misstatement of the facts of history.

But I will not content myself with mere denunciation; I invite attention to the facts.

It is a fact, a great historic fact, that at the time of the adoption of the Constitution, the leading religious denominations in this land were anti-slavery, and were laboring for the emancipation of the colored people of African descent.

The church of a country is often a better index of the state of opinion and feeling than is even the government itself.

The Methodists, Baptists, Presbyterians, and the denomination of Friends, were actively opposing slavery, denouncing the system of bondage, with language as burning and sweeping as we employ at this day.

Take the Methodists. In 1780, that denomination said: "The Conference acknowledges that slavery is contrary to the laws of God, man, and nature, and hurtful to society—contrary to the dictates of conscience and true religion, and doing to others that we would not do unto us." In 1784, the same church declared, "that those who buy, sell, or give slaves away, except for the purpose to free them, shall be expelled immediately." In 1785, it spoke even more stringently on the subject. It then said: "We hold in the deepest abhorrence the practice of slavery, and shall not cease to seek its destruction by all wise and proper means."

So much for the position of the Methodist Church in the early history of the Republic, in those days of darkness to which Judge Taney refers.

Let us now see how slavery was regarded by the Presbyterian Church at that early date.

In 1794, the General Assembly of that body pronounced the following judgment in respect to slavery, slaveholders, and slaveholding.

"1st Timothy, 1st chapter, 10th verse: The law was made for man-stealers.' 'This crime among the Jews exposed the perpetrators of it to capital punishment.' Exodus, xxi, 15.—And the apostle here classes them with sinners of the first rank. The word he uses in its original import, comprehends all who are concerned in bringing any of the human race into slavery, or in retaining them in it. Stealers of men are all those who bring off slaves or freemen, and keep, sell, or buy them. 'To steal a freeman,' says Grotius, 'is the highest kind of theft.' In other instances, we only steal human property, but when we steal or retain men in slavery, we seize those who, in common with ourselves, are constituted, by the original grant, lords of the earth."

I might quote, at length, from the sayings of the Baptist Church and the sayings of eminent divines at this early period, showing that Judge Taney has grossly falsified history, but will not detain you with these quotations.

The testimony of the church, and the testimony of the founders of this Republic, from the declaration downward, prove Judge Taney false; as false to history as he is to law.

Washington and Jefferson, and Adams, and Jay, and Franklin, and Rush, and Hamilton, and a host of others, held no such degrading views on the subject of slavery as are imputed by Judge Taney to the Fathers of the Republic.

All, at that time, looked for the gradual but certain abolition of slavery, and shaped the constitution with a view to this grand result.

George Washington can never be claimed as a fanatic, or as the representative of fanatics. The slaveholders impudently use his name for the base purpose of giving respectability to slavery. Yet, in a letter to Robert Morris, Washington uses this language—language which, at this day, would make him a terror of the slaveholders, and the natural representative of the Republican party.

"There is not a man living, who wishes more sincerely than I do, to see some plan adopted for the abolition of slavery; but there is only one proper and effectual mode by which it can be accomplished, and that is by Legislative authority; and this, as far as my suffrage will go, shall not be wanting."

Washington only spoke the sentiment of his times. There were, at that time, Abolition societies in the slave States—Abolition societies in Virginia, in North Carolina, in Maryland, in Pennsylvania, and in Georgia—all slaveholding States. Slavery was so weak, and liberty so strong, that free speech could attack the monster to its teeth. Men were not mobbed and driven out of the presence of slavery, merely because they condemned the slave system. The system was then on its knees imploring to be spared, until it could get itself decently out of the world.

In the light of these facts, the Constitution was framed, and framed in conformity to it.

It may, however, be asked, if the Constitution were so framed that the rights of all the people were naturally protected by it, how happens it that a large part of the people have been held in slavery ever since its adoption? Have the people mistaken the requirements of their own Constitution?

The answer is ready. The Constitution is one thing, its administration is another, and, in this instance, a very different and opposite thing. I am here to vindicate the law, not the administration of the law. It is the written Constitution, not the unwritten Constitution, that is now before us. If, in the whole range of the Constitution, you can find no warrant for slavery, then we may properly claim it for liberty.

Good and wholesome laws are often found dead on the statute book. We may condemn the practice under them and against them, but never the law itself. To condemn the good law with the wicked practice, is to weaken, not to strengthen our testimony.

It is no evidence that the Bible is a bad book, because those who profess to believe the Bible are bad. The slaveholders of the South, and many of their wicked allies at the North, claim the Bible for slavery; shall we, therefore, fling the Bible away as a pro-slavery book? It would be as reasonable to do so as it would be to fling away the Constitution.

We are not the only people who have illustrated the truth, that a people may have excellent law, and detestable practices. Our Savior denounces the Jews, because they made void the law by their traditions. We have been guilty of the same sin.

The American people have made void our Constitution by just such traditions as Judge Taney and Mr. Garrison have been giving to the world of late, as the true light in which to view the Constitution of the United States. I shall follow neither. It is not what Moses allowed for the hardness of heart, but what God requires, ought to be the rule.

It may be said that it is quite true that the Constitution was designed to secure the blessings of liberty and justice to the people who made it, and to the posterity of the people who made it, but was never designed to do any such thing for the colored people of African descent.

This is Judge Taney's argument, and it is Mr. Garrison's argument, but it is not the argument of the Constitution. The Constitution imposes no such mean and satanic limitations upon its own beneficent operation. And, if the Constitution makes none, I beg to know what right has anybody, outside of the Constitution, for the special accommodation of slaveholding villainy, to impose such a construction upon the Constitution?

The Constitution knows all the human inhabitants of this country as "the people." It makes, as I have said before, no discrimination in favor of, or against, any class of the people, but is fitted to protect and preserve the rights of all, without reference to color, size, or any physical peculiarities. Besides, it has been shown by William Goodell and others, that in eleven out of the old thirteen States, colored men were legal voters at the time of the adoption of the Constitution.

In conclusion, let me say, all I ask of the American people is, that they live up to the Constitution, adopt its principles, imbibe its spirit, and enforce its provisions.

When this is done, the wounds of my bleeding people will be healed, the chain will no longer rust on their ankles, their backs will no longer be torn by the bloody lash, and liberty, the glorious birthright of our common humanity, will become the inheritance of all the inhabitants of this highly favored country—May 1857.

AFRICAN CIVILIZATION SOCIETY

"But I entreated you to tell your readers what your objections are to the civilization and christianization of Africa. What objection have you to colored men in this country engaging in agriculture, lawful trade, and commerce in the land of my forefathers? What objection have you to an organization that shall endeavor to check and destroy the African slave-trade, and that desires to co-operate with anti-slavery men and women of every grade in our own land, and to toil with them for the overthrow of American slavery?—Tell us, I pray you, tell us in your clear and manly style. 'Gird up thy loins, and answer thou me, if thou canst.' "—Letter from Henry Highland Garnet.

Hitherto we have allowed ourselves but little space for discussing the claims of this new scheme for the civilization of Africa, doing little more than indicating our dissent from the new movement, yet leaving our columns as free to its friends as to its opponents. We shall not depart from this course, while the various writers bring good temper and ability to the discussion, and shall keep themselves within reasonable limits. We hope the same impartiality will be shown in the management of the *Provincial Freeman,* the adopted organ of the African Civilization Society. We need discussion among ourselves, discussion to rouse our souls to intenser life and activity.—"Communipaw" did capital service when he gave the subtle brain of Wm. Whipper a little work to do, and our readers the pleasure of seeing it done. Anything to promote earnest thinking among our people may be held as a good thing in itself, whether we assent to or dissent from the proposition which calls it forth.

We say this much before entering upon a compliance with the request of our friend Garnet, lest any should infer that the discussion now going on is distasteful to us, or that we desire to avoid it. The letter in question from Mr. Garnet is well calculated to make that impression. He evidently enjoys a wholesome confidence, not only in the goodness of his own cause, but in his own ability to defend it.—Sallying out before us, as if in "complete steel," he entreats us to appear "in manly style," to *"gird up our loins,"* as if the contest were one requiring all our strength and activity. "Answer thou me if thou canst?"—As if an answer were impossible. Not content with this, he reminds us of his former similar entreaties, thus making it our duty to reply to him, if for no better reason than respect and courtesy towards himself.

The first question put to us by Mr. Garnet is a strange and almost preposterous one. He asks for our "objections to the civilization and christianization of Africa." The answer we have to make here is very easy and very ready, and can be given without even taking the trouble to observe the generous advice to "gird up our loins." We have not, dear brother, the least possible objection either to the civilization or to the christianization of Africa, and the question is just about as absurd and ridiculous as if you had asked us to "gird up our loins," and tell the world what objection Frederick Douglass has to the abolition of slavery, or the elevation of the free people of color in the United States! We not only have no objection to the civilization and christianization of Africa, but rejoice to know that through the instrumentality of commerce, and the labors of faithful missionaries, those very desirable blessings are already being realized in the land of my fathers Africa.

Brother Garnet is a prudent man, and we admire his tact and address in presenting the issue before us, while we cannot assent entirely to its fairness. *"I did not ask you for a statement of your preference of America to Africa."* That is very aptly said, but is it impartially said? Does brother Garnet think such a preference, in view of all the circumstances, a wise and proper one? Or is he wholly indifferent as to the preference or the other? He seems to think that our preferences have nothing to do with the question between us and the African Civilization Society, while we think that this preference touches the very bone of contention. The African Civilization Society says to us, go to Africa, raise cotton, civilize the natives, become planters, merchants, compete with the slave States in the Liverpool cotton market, and thus break down American slavery. To which we simply and briefly reply, "we prefer to remain in America"; and we do insist upon it, in very face of our respected friend, that that is both a direct and candid answer. There is no dodging, no equivocation, but so far as we are concerned, the whole matter is ended. *You* go there, *we* stay here, is just the difference between us and the African Civilization Society, and the true issue upon which co-operation with it or opposition to it must turn.

Brother Garnet will pardon us for thinking it somewhat cool in him to ask us to give our objections to this new scheme. Our objections to it have been stated in substance, repeatedly. It has been no fault of ours if he has not read them.

As long ago as last September, we gave our views at large on this subject, in answer to an eloquent letter from Benjamin Coates, Esq., the real, but not the ostensible head of the African Civilization movement.

Meanwhile we will state briefly, for the benefit of friend Garnet, seven considerations, which prevent our co-operation with the African Civilization Society.

1. No one idea has given rise to more oppression and persecution toward the colored people of this country, than that which makes Africa, not America, their home. It is that wolfish idea that elbows us off the side walk, and denies us the rights of citizenship. The life and soul of this abominable idea would have been thrashed out of it long ago, but for the jesuitical and persistent teaching of the American Colonization Society. The natural and unfailing tendency of the African Civilization Society, by sending *"around the hat"* in all our towns and cities for money to send colored men to Africa, will be to keep life and power in this narrow, bitter and persecuting idea, that Africa, not America, is the Negro's true home.

2. The abolition of American slavery, and the moral, mental and social improvement of our people, are objects of immediate, pressing and transcendent importance, involving a direct and positive issue with the pride and selfishness of the American people. The prosecution of this grand issue against all the principalities and powers of church and state, furnishes ample occupation for all our time and talents; and we instinctively shrink from any movement which involves a substitution of a doubtful and indirect issue, for one which is direct and certain, for we believe that the demand for the abolition of slavery now made in the name of humanity, and according to the law of the Living God, though long delayed, will, if faithfully pressed, certainly triumph.—The African Civilization Society proposes to plant its guns too far from the battlements of slavery for us. Its doctrines and measures are those of doubt and retreat, and it must land just where the American Colonization movement landed, upon the lying assumption, that white and black people can never live in the same land on terms of equality. Detesting this heresy as we do, and believing it to be full of all "deceivableness" of unrighteousness, we shun the paths that lead to it, no matter what taking names they bear, or how excellent the men who bid us to walk in them.

3. Among all the obstacles to the progress of civilization and of christianity in Africa, there is not one so difficult to overcome as the African slave trade. No argument is needed to make this position evident. The African Civilization Society will doubtless assent to its truth. Now, so regarding the slave trade, and believing that the existence of slavery in this country is one of the strongest props of the African slave trade, we hold that the best way to put down the slave trade, and to build up civilization in Africa, is to stand our ground and labor for the abolition of slavery in the U.S. But for slavery here, the slave trade would have been long since swept from the ocean by the united navies of Great Britain, France and the United States. The work, therefore, to which we are naturally and logically conducted, as the one of primary importance, is to abolish slavery. We thus get the example of a great nation on the right side, and break up, so far as America is concerned, a demand for the slave trade. More will have been done. The enlightened conscience of our nation, through

its church and government, and its press, will be let loose against slavery and the slave trade wherever practiced.

4. One of the chief considerations upon which the African Civilization Society is recommended to our favorable regard, is its tendency to break up the slave trade. We have looked at this recommendation, and find no reason to believe that any one man in Africa can do more for the abolition of that trade, while living in Africa, than while living in America. If we cannot make Virginia, with all her enlightenment and christianity, believe that there are better uses for her energies than employing them in breeding slaves for the market, we see not how we can expect to make Guinea, with its ignorance and savage selfishness, adopt our notions of political economy. Depend upon it, the savage chiefs on the western coast of Africa, who for ages have been accustomed to selling their captives into bondage, and pocketing the ready cash for them, will not more readily see and accept our moral and economical ideas, than the slave-traders of Maryland and Virginia. We are, therefore, less inclined to go to Africa to work against the slave-trade, than to stay here to work against it. Especially as the means for accomplishing our object are quite as promising here as there, and more especially since we are here already, with constitutions and habits suited to the country and its climate, and to its better institutions.

5. There are slaves in the United States to the number of four millions. They are stigmatized as an inferior race, fit only for slavery, incapable of improvement, and unable to take care of themselves. Now, it seems plain that here is the place, and we are the people to meet and put down these conclusions concerning our race. Certainly there is no place on the globe where the colored man can speak to a larger audience, either by precept or by example, than in the United States.

6. If slavery depended for its existence upon the cultivation of cotton, and were shut up to that single production, it might even then be fairly questioned whether any amount of cotton culture in Africa would materially affect the price of that article in this country, since demand and supply would go on together. But the case is very different. Slave labor can be employed in raising anything which human labor and the earth can produce. If one does not pay, another will. Christy says "Cotton is King," and our friends of the African Civilization movement are singing the same tune; but clearly enough it must appear to common sense, that "King Cotton" in America has nothing to fear from King Cotton in Africa.

7. We object to enrolling ourselves among the friends of that new Colonization scheme, because we believe that our people should be let alone, and given a fair chance to work out their own destiny where they are. We are perpetually kept, with wandering eyes and open mouths, looking out for some mighty revolution in our affairs here, which is to remove us from this country. The consequence is, that we do not take a firm hold

upon the advantages and opportunities about us. Permanent location is a mighty element of civilization. In a savage state men roam about, having no continued abiding place. They are *"going, going, going."* Towns and cities, houses and homes, are only built up by men who halt long enough to build them. There is a powerful motive for the cultivation of an honorable character, in the fact that we have a country, a neighborhood, a home. The full effect of this motive has not hitherto been experienced by our people. When in slavery, we were liable to perpetual sales, transfers and removals; and now that we are free, we are doomed to be constantly harassed with schemes to get us out of the country. We are quite tired of all this, and wish no more of it.

To all this it will be said that Douglass is opposed to our following the example of white men. They are pushing East, West, North and South. They are going to Oregon, Central America, Australia, South Africa and all over the world. Why should we not have the same right to better our condition that other men have and exercise? Any man who says that we deny this right, or even object to its exercise, only deceives the ignorant by such representations.

If colored men are convinced that they can better their condition by going to Africa, or anywhere else, we shall respect them if they will go, just as we respect others who have gone to California, Fraser Island, Oregon and the West Indies. They are self-moved, self-sustained, and their success or failure is their own individual concern. But widely different is the case, when men combine, in societies, under taking titles, send out agents to collect money, and call upon us to help them travel from continent to continent to promote some selfish or benevolent end. In the one case, it is none of our business where our people go.—They are of age, and can act for themselves.—But when they ask the public to go, or for money, sympathy, aid, or co-operation, or attempt to make it appear anybody's duty to go, the case ceases to be a private individual affair, and becomes a public question, and he who believes that he can make a better use of his time, talents, and influence, than such a movement proposes for him, may very properly say so, without in any measure calling in question the equal right of out people to migrate.

Again it may be said that we are opposed to sending the Gospel to benighted Africa; but this is not the case. The *American Missionary Society,* in its rooms at 48 Beekman Street, has never had occasion to complain of any such opposition, nor will it have such cause. But we will not anticipate the objections which may be brought to the foregoing views. They seem to us sober, rational, and true; but if otherwise, we shall be glad to have them honestly criticised—**February 1859.**

THE PRESENT AND FUTURE OF THE
COLORED RACE IN AMERICA

I think that most of you will agree with me in respect to the surpassing importance of the subject we are here to consider this evening though you may differ from me in other respects. It seems to me that the relation subsisting between the white and colored people of this country, is of all other questions, the great, paramount, imperative, and all commanding question for this age and nation to solve.

All the circumstances of the hour plead with an eloquence, equaled by no human tongue, for the immediate solution of this vital problem. 200,-000 graves.— A distracted and bleeding country plead for this solution. It cannot be denied, nobody now even attempts to deny, that the question, what shall be done with the Negro, is the one grand cause of the tremendous war now upon us, and likely to continue upon us, until the country is united upon some wise policy concerning it. When the country was at peace and all appeared prosperous, there was something like a plausible argument in favor of leaving things to their own course. No such policy avails now. The question now stands before us as one of life and death. We are encompassed by it as by a wall of fire. The flames singe and burn us on all sides, becoming hotter every hour.

Men sneer at it as the "n—r question," endeavoring to degrade it by misspelling it. But they degrade nothing but themselves. They would much rather talk about the Constitution as it is, and the Union as it was, or about the Crittenden, or some other impossible compromise, but the Negro peeps out at every flash of their rhetorical pyrotechnics and utterly refuses to be hid by either fire, dust or smoke. The term, Negro, is at this hour the most pregnant word in the English language. The destiny of the nation has the Negro for its pivot, and turns upon the question as to what shall be done with him. Peace and war, union and disunion, salvation and ruin, glory and shame all crowd upon our thoughts the moment this vital word is pronounced.

You and I have witnessed many attempts to put this Negro question out of the pale of popular thought and discussion, and have seen the utter vanity of all such attempts.—It has baffled all the subtle contrivances of an ease loving and selfish priesthood, and has constantly refused to be smothered under the soft cushions of a canting and heartless religion. It has mocked and defied the compromising cunning of so called statesmen, who would have gladly postponed our present troubles beyond our allotted space of life and bequeath them as a legacy of sorrow to our children. But this wisdom of the crafty is confounded and their counsels brought to naught. A divine energy, omniscient and omnipotent, acting through the silent, solemn and all pervading laws of the universe, irresistible, unalterable and eternal, has ever more forced this mighty question of the Negro upon the attention of the country and the world.

What shall be done with the Negro? meets us not only in the street, in the Church, in the Senate, and in our State Legislatures; but in our diplomatic correspondence with foreign nations, and even on the field of battle, where our brave sons and brothers are striking for Liberty and country, or for honored graves.

This question met us before the war; it meets us during the war, and will certainly meet us after the war, unless we shall have the wisdom, the courage, and the nobleness of soul to settle the status of the Negro, on the solid and immovable bases of Eternal justice.

I stand here tonight therefore, to advocate what I conceive to be such a solid basis, one that shall fix our peace upon a rock. Putting aside all the hay, wood and stubble of expediency, I shall advocate for the Negro, his most full and complete adoption into the great national family of America. I shall demand for him the most perfect civil and political equality, and that he shall enjoy all the rights, privileges and immunities enjoyed by any other members of the body politic. I weigh my words and I mean all I say, when I contend as I do contend, that this is the *only solid, and final solution* of the problem before us. It is demanded not less by the terrible exigencies of the nation, than by the Negro himself for the Negro and the nation, are to rise or fall, be killed or cured, saved or lost together. Save the Negro and you save the nation, destroy the Negro and you destroy the nation, and to save both you must have but one great law of Liberty, Equality and Fraternity for all Americans without respect to color.

Already I am charged with treating this question, in the light of abstract ideas. I admit the charge, and would to heaven that this whole nation could now be brought to view it in the same calm, clear light. The failure so to view it is the one great national mistake. Our wise men and statesmen have insisted upon viewing the whole subject of the Negro upon what they are pleased to call practical and common sense principles, and behold the results of their so called practical wisdom and common sense! Behold, how all to the mocker has gone.

Under this so called practical wisdom and statesmanship, we have had sixty years of compromising servility on the part of the North to the slave power of the South. We have dishonored our manhood and lied in our throats to defend the monstrous abomination. Yet this greedy slave power, with every day of his shameless truckling on our part became more and more exacting, unreasonable, arrogant and domineering, until it has plunged the country into a war such as the world never saw before, and I hope never will see again.

Having now tried, with fearful results, the wisdom of reputed wise men, it is now quite time that the American people began to view this question in the light of other ideas than the cold and selfish ones which have hitherto enjoyed the reputation of being wise and practicable, but which are now proved to be entirely and absolutely impracticable.

The progress of the nation downward has been rapid as all steps downward are apt to be.

First. We found the Golden Rule impracticable.

Second. We found the Declaration of Independence very broadly impracticable.

Third. We found the Constitution of the United States, requiring that the majority shall rule, is impracticable.

Fourth. We found that the union was impracticable.

The golden rule did not hold the slave tight enough. The Constitution did not hold the slave tight enough. The Declaration of Independence did not hold the slave at all, and the union was a loose affair and altogether impracticable. Even the Democratic party bowed and squatted lower than all other parties, became at last weak and impracticable, and the slaveholders broke it up as they would an abolition meeting. Nevertheless: I am aware that there are such things as practicable and impracticable, and I will not ignore the objections, which may be raised against the policy which I would have the nation adopt and carry out toward my enslaved and oppressed fellow countrymen.

There are at least four answers, other than mine, floating about in the public mind, to the question what shall be done with the Negro.

First. It is said that the white race can, if they will, reduce the whole colored population to slavery, and at once make all the laws and institutions of the country harmonize with that state of facts and thus abolish at a blow, all distinctions and antagonisms. But this mode of settling the question, simple as it is, would not work well. It would create a class of tyrants in whose presence no man's Liberty, not even the white man's Liberty would be safe. The slaveholder would then be the only really free man of the country.—All the rest would be either slaves, or be poor white trash, to be kept from between the wind and our slaveholding nobility. The non-slaveholder would be the patrol, the miserable watch dog of the slave plantation.

Second. The next and best defined solution of our difficulties about the Negro, is colonization, which proposes to send the Negro back to Africa where his ancestors came from.—This is a singularly pleasing dream. But as was found in the case of sending missionaries to the moon, it was much easier to show that they might be useful there, than to show how they could be got there. It would take a larger sum of money than we shall have to spare at the close of this war, to send five millions of American born people, five thousand miles across the sea.

It may be safely affirmed that we shall hardly be in a condition at the close of this war to afford the money for such costly transportation, even if we could consent to the folly of sending away the only efficient producers in the largest half of the American union.

Third. It may be said as another mode of escaping the claims of absolute justice, the white people may Emancipate the slaves in form yet retain them as slaves in fact just as General Banks is now said to be doing in Louisiana, or then may free them from individual masters, only to make them slaves to the community. They can make of them a degraded caste. But this would be about the worst thing that could be done. It would make pestilence and pauperism, ignorance and crime, a part of American Institutions. It would be dooming the colored race to a condition indescribably wretched and the dreadful contagion of their vices and crimes would fly like cholera and small pox through all classes. Woe, woe! to this land, when it strips five millions of its people of all motives for cultivating an upright character. Such would be the effect of abolishing slavery, without conferring equal rights. It would be to lacerate and depress the spirit of the Negro, and make him a scourge and a curse to the country. Do anything else with us, but plunge us not into this hopeless pit.

Fourth. The white people of the country may trump up some cause of war against the colored people, and wage that terrible war of races which some men even now venture to predict, if not to desire, and exterminate the black race entirely. They would spare neither age nor sex.

But is there not some chosen curse, some secret thunder in the stores of heaven red with uncommon wrath to blast the men who harbor this bloody solution? The very thought is more worthy of demons than of men. Such a war would indeed remove the colored race from the country. —But it would also remove justice, innocence and humanity from the country. It would fill the land with violence and crime, and make the very name of America a stench in the nostrils of mankind. It would give you hell for a country and fiends for your countrymen.

Now, I hold that there is but one way of wisely disposing of the colored race, and that is to do them right and justice. It is not only to break the chains of their bondage and accord to them personal liberty, but it is to admit them to the full and complete enjoyment of civil and political Equality.

The mere abolition of slavery is not the end of the law for the black man, or for the white man. To emancipate the bondman from the laws that make him a chattel, and yet subject him to laws and deprivations which will inevitably break down his spirit, destroy his patriotism and convert him into a social pest, will be little gain to him and less gain to the country. One of the most plausible arguments ever made for slavery, is that which assumes that those who argue for the freedom of the Negro, do not themselves propose to treat him as an equal fellow citizen. The true course is to look this matter squarely in the face and determine to grant the entire claims of justice and liberty keeping back no part of the price.

But the question comes not only from those who hate the colored race, but from some who are distinguished for their philanthropy: can this thing be done? can the white and colored people of America ever be blended into a common nationality under a system of equal Laws?

Mark, I state the question broadly and fairly. It respects civil and political equality, in its fullest and best sense: can such equality ever be practically enjoyed?

The question is not can there be social equality? That does not exist anywhere.—There have been arguments to show that no one man should own more property than another. But no satisfactory conclusion has been reached. So there are those who talk about social Equality, but nothing better on that subject than *"pursuit,"* the right of pursuit has been attained.

The question is not whether the colored man is mentally equal to his white brother, for in this respect there is no equality among white men themselves.

The question is not whether colored men will be likely to reach the Presidential chair. I have no trouble here: for a man may live quite a tolerable life without ever breathing the air of Washington.

But the question is: Can the white and colored people of this country be blended into a common nationality, and enjoy together, in the same country, under the same flag, the inestimable blessings of life, liberty and the pursuit of happiness, as neighborly citizens of a common country?

I answer most unhesitatingly, I believe they can. In saying this I am not blind to the past. I know it well. As a people we have moved about among you like dwarfs among giants—too small to be seen. We were morally, politically and socially dead. To the eye of doubt and selfishness we were far beyond the resurrection trump. All the more because I know the past. All the more, because I know the terrible experience of the slave, and the depressing power of oppression, do I believe in the possibility of a better future for the colored people of America.

Let me give a few of the reasons for the hope that is within me.

The first is, despite all theories and all disparagements, the Negro is a man. By every fact, by every argument, by every rule of measurement, mental, moral or spiritual, by everything in the heavens above and in the earth beneath which vindicates the humanity of any class of beings, the Negro's humanity is equally vindicated. The lines which separate him from the brute creation are as broad, distinct and palpable, as those which define and establish the very best specimens of the Indo-Caucasian race. I will not stop here to prove the manhood of the Negro. His virtues and his vices, his courage and his cowardice, his beauties and his deformities, his wisdom and his folly, everything connected with him, attests his manhood.

If the Negro were a horse or an ox, the question as to whether he can become a party to the American government, and member of the nation, could never have been raised. The very questions raised against him confirm the truth of what they are raised to disprove. We have laws forbidding the Negro to learn to read, others forbidding his owning a dog, others punishing him for using fire arms, and our Congress came near passing a law that a Negro should in no case be superior to a white man, thus admitting the very possibility of what they were attempting to deny.

The foundation of all governments and all codes of laws is in the fact that man is a rational creature, and is capable of guiding his conduct by ideas of right and wrong, of good and evil, by hope of reward and fear of punishment. Can any man doubt that the Negro answers this description? Do not all the laws ever passed concerning him imply that he is just such a creature? I defy the most malignant accuser to prove that there is a more law abiding people anywhere than are the colored people. I claim for the colored man that he possesses all the natural conditions and attributes essential to the character of a good citizen. He can understand the requirements of the law and the reason of the law. He can obey the law, and with his arm and life defend and execute the law. The preservation of society, the protection of persons and property are the simple and primary objects for which governments are instituted among men.

There certainly is nothing in the ends sought, nor in the character of the means by which they are to be attained, which necessarily excludes colored men. I see no reason why we may not, in time, co-operate with our white fellow-countrymen in all the labors and duties of upholding a common government, and sharing with them in all the advantages and glory of a common nationality.

That the interests of all the people would be promoted by the full participation of colored men in the affairs of government seems very plain to me. The American government rests for support, more than any other government in the world, upon the loyalty and patriotism of all its people. The friendship and affection of her black sons and daughters, as they increase in virtue and knowledge, will be an element of strength to the Republic too obvious to be neglected and repelled. I predict, therefore, that under an enlightened public sentiment, the American people will cultivate the friendship, increase the usefulness and otherwise advance the interests of the colored race. They will be as eager to extend the rights and dignity of citizenship as they have hitherto been eager to deny those rights.

But a word as to objections. The constitution is interposed. It always is.

Let me tell you something. Do you know that you have been deceived and cheated? You have been told that this government was intended from the beginning for white men, and for white men exclusively; that the men who formed the Union and framed the Constitution designed the permanent exclusion of the colored people from the benefits of those institutions. Davis, Taney and Yancey, traitors at the south, have propagated this statement, while their copperhead echoes at the north have repeated the same. There never was a bolder or more wicked perversion of the truth of history. So far from this purpose was the mind and heart of your fathers, that they desired and expected the abolition of slavery. They framed the

Constitution plainly with a view to the speedy downfall of slavery. They carefully excluded from the Constitution any and every word which could lead to the belief that they meant it for persons of only one complexion.

The Constitution, in its language and in its spirit, welcomes the black man to all the rights which it was intended to guarantee to any class of the American people. Its preamble tells us for whom and for what it was made.

But I am told that the ruling class in America being white, it is impossible for men of color ever to become a part of the "body politic." With some men this seems a final statement, a final argument, which it is utterly impossible to answer. It conveys the idea that the body politic is a rather fastidious body, from which everything offensive is necessarily excluded. I, myself, once had some high notions about this body politic and its high requirements, and of the kind of men fit to enter it and share its privileges. But a day's experience at the polls convinced me that the "body politic" is not more immaculate than many other bodies. That in fact it is a very mixed affair. I saw ignorance enter, unable to read the vote it cast. I saw the convicted swindler enter and deposit his vote. I saw the gambler, the horse jockey, the pugilist, the miserable drunkard just lifted from the gutter, covered with filth, enter and deposit his vote. I saw Pat, fresh from the Emerald Isle, requiring two sober men to keep him on his legs, enter and deposit his vote for the Democratic candidate amid the loud hurrahs of his fellow-citizens. The sight of these things went far to moderate my ideas about the exalted character of what is called the body politic, and convinced me that it could not suffer in its composition even should it admit a few sober, industrious and intelligent colored voters.

It is a fact, moreover, that colored men did at the beginning of our national history, form a part of the body politic, not only in what are now the free states, but also in the slave states. Mr. Wm. Goodell, to whom the cause of liberty in America is as much indebted as to any other one American citizen, has demonstrated that colored men formerly voted in eleven out of the thirteen original states.

The war upon the colored voters, and the war upon the Union, originated with the same parties, at the same time, and for the same guilty purpose of rendering slavery perpetual, universal and all controlling in the affairs of the nation.

Let this object be defeated and abandoned, let the country be brought back to the benign objects set forth in the preamble of the Constitution, and the colored man will easily find his way into the body politic, and be welcome in the jury box as well as at the ballot box. I know that prejudice largely prevails, and will prevail to some extent long after slavery shall be abolished in this country, but the power of prejudice will be broken when slavery is once abolished. There is not a black law on the statute book of a single free state that has not been placed there in deference to slavery existing in the slave states.

But it is said that the Negro belongs to an inferior race. Inferior race! This is the apology, the philosophical and ethnological apology for all the hell-black crimes ever committed by the white race against the blacks and the warrant for the repetition of those crimes through all times. Inferior race! It is an old argument. All nations have been compelled to meet it in some form or other since mankind have been divided into strong and weak, oppressors and oppressed. Whenever and wherever men have been oppressed and enslaved, their oppressors and enslavers have in every instance found a warrant for such oppression and enslavement in the alleged character of their victims. The very vices and crimes which slavery generates are usually charged as the peculiar characteristic of the race enslaved. When the Normans conquered the Saxons, the Saxons were a coarse, unrefined, inferior race. When the United States wants to possess herself of Mexican territory, the Mexicans are an inferior race. When Russia wants a share of the Ottoman Empire, the Turks are an inferior race, the sick man of Europe. So, too, when England wishes to impose some new burden on Ireland, or excuse herself for refusing to remove some old one, the Irish are denounced as an inferior race. But this is a monstrous argument. Now, suppose it were true that the Negro is inferior instead of being an apology for oppression and proscription, it is an appeal to all that is noble and magnanimous in the human soul against both. When used in the service of oppression, it is as if one should say, "that man is weak; I am strong, therefore I will knock him down, and as far as I can I will keep him down. Yonder is an ignorant man. I am instructed, therefore I will do what I can to prevent his being instructed and to withhold from him the means of education. There is another who is low in his associations, rude in his manners, coarse and brutal in his appetites, therefore I will see to it that his degradation shall be permanent, and that society shall hold out to him no motives or incitements to a more elevated character." I will not stop here to denounce this monstrous excuse for oppression. That men can resort to it shows that when the human mind is once completely under the dominion of pride and selfishness, the reasoning faculties are inverted if not subverted.

I should like to know what constitutes inferiority and the standard of superiority. Must a man be as wise as Socrates, as learned as Humbolt, as profound as Bacon, or as eloquent as Charles Sumner, before he can be reckoned among superior men? Alas! if this were so, few even of the most cultivated of the white race could stand the test. Webster was white and had a large head, but all white men have not large heads. The Negro is black and has a small head, but all Negroes have not small heads. What rule shall we apply to all these heads? Why this: Give all an equal chance to grow.

But I am told that the Irish element in this country is exceedingly strong, and that that element will never allow colored men to stand upon an equal political footing with white men. I am pointed to the terrible outrages committed from time to time by Irishmen upon Negroes. The mobs at Detroit, Chicago, Cincinnati, and New York, are cited as proving the unconquerable aversion of the Irish towards the colored race.

Well, my friends, I admit that the Irish people are among our bitterest persecutors. In one sense it is strange, passing strange, that they should be such, but in another sense it is quite easily accounted for. It is said that a Negro always makes the most cruel Negro driver, a northern slaveholder the most rigorous master, and the poor man suddenly made rich becomes the most haughty insufferable of all purse-proud fools.

Daniel O'Connell once said that the history of Ireland might be traced like a wounded man through a crowd—by the blood. The Irishman has been persecuted for his religion about as rigorously as the black man has been for his color. The Irishman has outlived his persecution, and I believe that the Negro will survive his.

But there is something quite revolting in the idea of a people lately oppressed suddenly becoming oppressors, that the persecuted can so suddenly become the persecutors.

Let us see a small sample of the laws by which our Celtic brothers have in other days been oppressed. Religion, not color, was the apology for this oppression, and the one apology is about as good as the other.

The following summary is by that life-long friend of the Irish—Sydney Smith:

In 1695, the Catholics were deprived of all means of educating their children, at home or abroad, and of all the privileges of being guardians to their own or to other persons' children. Then all the Catholics were disarmed, and then all the priests banished. After this (probably by way of joke) an act was passed to *confirm* the treaty of Limerick, the great and glorious King William, totally forgetting the contract he had entered into of recommending the religious liberties of the Catholics to the attention of Parliament.

On the 4th of March, 1704, it was enacted that any son of a Catholic who would turn Protestant should succeed to the family estate, which from that moment could no longer be sold, as charged with debt and legacy.

On the same day, Popish fathers were debarred, by a penalty of five hundred pounds, from being guardians to their own children. If the child, however young, declared himself a Protestant, he was to be delivered immediately to the custody of some Protestant relation.

No Protestant to marry a Papist. No Papist to purchase land or take a lease of land for more than thirty-one years. If the profits of the land so leased by the Catholic amounted to above a certain rate, settled by the act, *farm to belong to the first Protestant who made the discovery.* No Papist to be in a line of entail, but the estate to pass on to the next Protesant heir, as if the Papist were dead. If a Papist dies intestate, and no Protestant heir can be found, property to be equally divided among all the sons; or, if he has none, among all the daughters. By the 16th clause of this bill, no Papist to hold any office, civil or military. Not to dwell in Limerick or Galway, except on certain conditions. Not to vote at elections.

In 1709, Papists were prevented from holding an annuity for life. If any son of a Papist chose to turn Protestant and enroll the certificate of his conversion in the Court of Chancery, that court is empowered to compel his father to state the value of his property upon oath, and to make out of that property a competent allowance to the son, at their own discretion, not only for his present maintenance, but for his future portion after the death of his father. An increase of jointure to be enjoyed by Papist wives upon their conversion. Papists keeping schools to be prosecuted as convicts. Popish priests who are converted, to receive thirty pounds per annum.

Rewards are given by the same act for the discovery of Popish clergy— fifty pounds for discovering a Popish bishop, twenty pounds for a common Popish clergy, ten pounds for a Popish usher! Two justices of the peace can compel any Papists above 18 years of age to disclose every particular which has come to his knowledge respecting Popish priests, celebration of mass, or Papist schools. Imprisonment for a year if he refuses to answer. Nobody can hold property in trust for a Catholic. Juries in all trials growing out of these statutes to be Protestants. No Papist to take more than two apprentices, except in the linen trade. All the Catholic clergy to give in their names and places of abode at the quarter sessions, and to keep no curates. Catholics not to serve on grand juries. In any trial upon statutes for strengthening the Protestant interest, a Papist juror may be peremptorily challenged.

In the next reign, Popish horses were attached and allowed to be seized for the militia. Papists cannot be either high or petty constables. No Papists to vote at elections. Papists in towns to provide Protestant watchmen, and not to vote at vestries.

In the reign of George second, Papists were prohibited from being barristers. Barristers and solicitors marrying Papists, considered to be Papists, and subjected to all penalties as such. Persons robbed by privateers, during a war with a Popish Prince, to be indemnified by grand jury presentments, and the money to be levied on the *Catholics* only. No Papist to marry a Protestant; any priest celebrating such marriage *to be hanged.*

A full acount of the laws here referred to may be found in a book entitled, "History of the penal Laws against Irish Catholics," by Henry Parnell, member of Parliament.—They are about as harsh and oppressive, as some of the laws against the colored people in border and Western States.

These barbarous and inhuman laws were all swept away by the act of Catholic Emancipation, and the present barbarous laws against the free colored people, must share the same fate.

There are signs of this good time coming all around us. Slavery has overleapt itself.—Having taken the sword it is destined to perish by the sword, and the long despised Negro is to bear an honorable part in the salvation of himself and the country by the same blow. It has taken two years to convince the Washington Government, of the wisdom of calling the black man to participate in the gigantic effort now making to save the country. Even now they have not fully learned it—but learn it they will, and learn it they must before this tremendous war shall be ended.—Massachusetts, glorious old Massachusetts, has called the black man to the honor of bearing arms, and a thousand are already enrolled.

Now what will be the effect? Suppose colored men are allowed to fight the battles of the Republic. Suppose they do fight and win victories as I am sure they will, what will be the effect upon themselves? Will not the country rejoice in such victories? and will it not extend to the colored man the praise due to his bravery? Will not the colored man himself soon begin to take a more hopeful view of his own destiny?

The fact is, my friends, we are opening a new account with the American people and with the whole human family.

Hitherto we have been viewed and have viewed ourselves, as an impotent and spiritless race, having only a mission of folly and degradation before us. Tonight we stand at the portals of a new world, a new life and a new destiny.

We have passed through the furnace and have not been consumed. During more than two centuries and a half, we have survived contact with the white race. We have risen from the small number of twenty, to the large number of five millions, living and increasing, where other tribes are decreasing and dying. We have illustrated the fact, that the two most opposite races of men known to ethnological science, can live in the same latitudes, longitudes, and altitudes, and that so far as natural causes are concerned there is reason to believe that we may permanently live under the same skies, brave the same climates, and enjoy Liberty, equality and fraternity in a common country—June 1863.

WHAT THE BLACK MAN WANTS

I came here, as I come always to the meetings in New England, as a listener, and not as a speaker; and one of the reasons why I have not been more frequently to the meetings of this society, has been because of the disposition on the part of some of my friends to call me out upon the platform, even when they knew that there was some difference of opinion and of feeling between those who rightfully belong to this platform and myself; and for fear of being misconstrued, as desiring to interrupt or disturb the proceedings of these meetings, I have usually kept away, and have thus been deprived of that educating influence, which I am always free to confess is of the highest order, descending from this platform. I have felt, since I have lived out West, that in going there I parted from a great deal that was valuable; and I feel, every time I come to these meetings, that I have lost a great deal by making my home west of Boston, west of Massachusetts; for, if anywhere in the country there is to be found the highest sense of justice, or the truest demands for my race, I look for it in the East, I look for it here. The ablest discussions of the whole question of our rights occur here, and to be deprived of the privilege of listening to those discussions is a great deprivation.

I do not know, from what has been said, that there is any difference of opinion as to the duty of abolitionists, at the present moment. How can we get up any difference at this point, or any point, where we are so united, so agreed? I went especially, however, with that word of Mr. Phillips, which is the criticism of Gen. Banks and Gen. Banks' policy. I hold that that policy is our chief danger at the present moment; that it practically enslaves the Negro, and makes the Proclamation of 1863 a mockery and delusion. What is freedom? It is the right to choose one's own employment. Certainly it means that, if it means anything; and when any individual or combination of individuals undertakes to decide for any man when he shall work, where he shall work, at what he shall work, and for what he shall work, he or they practically reduce him to slavery. He is a slave. That I understand Gen. Banks to do—to determine for the so-called freedman, when, and where, and at what, and for how much he shall work, when he shall be punished, and by whom punished. It is absolute slavery. It defeats the beneficent intention of the Government, if it has beneficent intentions, in regards to the freedom of our people.

I have had but one idea for the last three years to present to the American people, and the phraseology in which I clothe it is the old abolition phraseology. I am for the "immediate, unconditional, and universal" enfranchisement of the black man, in every State in the Union. Without this, his liberty is a mockery; without this, you might as well almost retain the old name of slavery for his condition; for in fact, if he is not the slave of the individual master, he is the slave of society, and holds his liberty as a privilege, not as a right. He is at the mercy of the mob, and has no means of protecting himself.

It may be objected, however, that this pressing of the Negro's right to suffrage is premature. Let us have slavery abolished, it may be said, let us have labor organized, and then, in the natural course of events, the right of suffrage will be extended to the Negro. I do not agree with this. The constitution of the human mind is such, that if it once disregards the conviction forced upon it by a revelation of truth, it requires the exercise of a higher power to produce the same conviction afterwards. The American people are now in tears. The Shenandoah has run blood—the best blood of the North. All around Richmond, the blood of New England and of the North has been shed—of your sons, your brothers and your fathers.

We all feel, in the existence of this Rebellion, that judgments terrible, wide-spread, far-reaching, overwhelming, are abroad in the land; and we feel, in view of these judgments, just now, a disposition to learn righteousness. This is the hour. Our streets are in mourning, tears are falling at every fireside, and under the chastisement of this Rebellion we have almost come up to the point of conceding this great, this all-important right of suffrage. I fear that if we fail to do it now, if abolitionists fail to press it now, we may not see, for centuries to come, the same disposition that exists at this moment. Hence, I say, now is the time to press this right.

It may be asked, "Why do you want it? Some men have got along very well without it. Women have not this right." Shall we justify one wrong by another? This is a sufficient answer. Shall we at this moment justify the deprivation of the Negro of the right to vote, because some one else is deprived of that privilege? I hold that women, as well as men, have the right to vote, and my heart and my voice go with the movement to extend suffrage to woman; but that question rests upon another basis than that on which our right rests. We may be asked, I say, why we want it. I will tell you why we want it. We want it because it is our *right,* first of all. No class of men can, without insulting their own nature, be content with any deprivation of their rights. We want it again, as a means for educating our race. Men are so constituted that they derive their conviction of their own possibilities largely from the estimate formed of them by others. If nothing is expected of a people, that people will find it difficult to contradict that expectation. By depriving us of suffrage, you affirm our incapacity to form an intelligent judgment respecting public men and public measures; you declare before the world that we are unfit to exercise the elective franchise, and by this means lead us to undervalue ourselves, to put a low estimate upon ourselves, and to feel that we have no possibilities like other men. Again, I want the elective franchise, for one, as a colored man, because ours is a peculiar government, based upon a peculiar idea, and that idea is universal suffrage. If I were in a monarchial government, or an autocratic or aristocratic government, where the few bore rule and the many were subject, there would be no special stigma resting upon me, because I did not exercise the elective franchise. It would do me no great violence. Mingling with the mass I should partake of the strength of the mass; I should be supported by the mass, and I should have the same incentives to endeavor with the mass of my fellow-men; it would be no particular burden, no particular deprivation; but here where universal suffrage is the rule, where that is the fundamental idea of the Government, to rule us out is to make us an exception, to brand us with the stigma of inferiority, and to invite to our heads the missiles of those about us; therefore, I want the franchise for the black man.

There are, however, other reasons, not derived from any consideration merely of our rights, but arising out of the conditions of the South, and of the country—considerations which have already been referred to by Mr.

Phillips—considerations which must arrest the attention of statesmen. I believe that when the tall heads of this Rebellion shall have been swept down, as they will be swept down, when the Davises and Toombses and Stephenses, and others who are leading this Rebellion shall have been blotted out, there will be this rank undergrowth of treason, to which reference has been made, growing up there, and interfering with, and thwarting the quiet operation of the Federal Government in those States. You will see those traitors, handing down, from sire to son, the same malignant spirit which they have manifested, and which they are now exhibiting, with malicious hearts, broad blades, and bloody hands in the field, against our sons and brothers. That spirit will still remain; and whoever sees the Federal Government extended over those Southern States will see that Government in a strange land, and not only in a strange land, but in an enemy's land. A post-master of the United States in the South will find himself surrounded by a hostile spirit; a collector in a Southern port will find himself surrounded by a hostile spirit; a United States marshal or United States judge will be surrounded there by a hostile element. That enmity will not die out in a year, will not die out in an age. The Federal Government will be looked upon in those States precisely as the Governments of Austria and France are looked upon in Italy at the present moment. They will endeavor to circumvent, they will endeavor to destroy, the peaceful operation of this Government. Now, where will you find the strength to counterbalance this spirit, if you do not find it in the Negroes of the South? They are your friends, and have always been your friends. They were your friends even when the Government did not regard them as such. They comprehended the genius of this war before you did. It is a significant fact, it is a marvellous fact, it seems almost to imply a direct interposition of Providence, that this war, which began in the interest of slavery on both sides, bids fair to end in the interest of liberty on both sides. It was begun, I say, in the interest of slavery on both sides. The South was fighting to take slavery out of the Union, and the North fighting to keep it in the Union; the South fighting to get it beyond the limits of the United States Constitution, and the North fighting to retain it within those limits; the South fighting for new guarantees, and the North fighting for the old guarantees;—both despising the Negro, both insulting the Negro. Yet, the Negro, apparently endowed with wisdom from on high, saw more clearly the end from the beginning than we did. When Seward said the status of no man in the country would be changed by the war, the Negro did not believe him. When our generals sent their underlings in shoulder-straps to hunt the flying Negro back from our lines into the jaws of slavery, from which he had escaped, the Negroes thought that a mistake had been made, and that the intentions of the Government had not been rightly understood by our officers in shoulder-straps, and they continued to come into our lines, threading their way through bogs and fens, over briers and thorns, fording streams, swimming rivers, bringing us tidings as to the safe path to march, and pointing out the dangers that threatened us. They are our only friends in the South, and we should be true to them in this their trial hour, and see to it that they have the elective franchise.

I know that we are inferior to you in some things—virtually inferior. We walk about among you like dwarfs among giants. Our heads are scarcely seen above the great sea of humanity. The Germans are superior to us; the Irish are superior to us; the Yankees are superior to us; they can do what we cannot, that is, what we have not hitherto been allowed to do. But while I make this admission, I utterly deny, that we are originally, or naturally, or practically, or in any way, or in any important sense, inferior to anybody on this globe. This charge of inferiority is an old dodge. It has been made available for oppression on many occasions. It is only about six centuries since the blue-eyed and fair-haired Anglo-Saxons were considered inferior by the haughty Normans, who once trampled upon them. If you read the history of the Norman Conquest, you will find that this proud Anglo-Saxon was once looked upon as of coarser clay than his Norman master, and might be found in the highways and byways of old England laboring with a brass collar on his neck, and the name of his master marked upon it. *You* were down then! You are up now. I am glad you are up, and I want you to be glad to help us up also.

The story of our inferiority is an old dodge, as I have said; for wherever men oppress their fellows, wherever they enslave them, they will endeavor to find the needed apology for such enslavement and oppression in the character of the people oppressed and enslaved. When we wanted, a few years ago, a slice of Mexico, it was hinted that the Mexicans were an inferior race, that the old Castilian blood had become so weak that it would scarcely run down hill, and that Mexico needed the long, strong and beneficent arm of the Anglo-Saxon care extended over it. We said that it was necessary to its salvation, and a part of the "manifest destiny" of this Republic, to extend our arm over that dilapidated government. So, too, when Russia wanted to take possession of a part of the Ottoman Empire, the Turks were "an inferior race." So, too, when England wants to set the heel of her power more firmly in the quivering heart of old Ireland, the Celts are an "inferior race." So, too, the Negro, when he is to be robbed of any right which is justly his, is an "inferior man." It is said that we are ignorant; I admit it. But if we know enough to be hung, we know enough to vote. If the Negro knows enough to pay taxes to support the government, he knows enough to vote; taxation and representation should go together. If he knows enough to shoulder a musket and fight for the flag, fight for the government, he knows enough to vote. If he knows as much when he is sober as an Irishman knows when drunk, he knows enough to vote, on good American principles.

But I was saying that you needed a counterpoise in the persons of the slaves to the enmity that would exist at the South after the Rebellion is put down. I hold that the American people are bound, not only in self-defence, to extend this right to the freedmen of the South, but they are bound by their love of country, and by all their regard for the future safety of those Southern States, to do this—to do it as a measure essential to the preservation of peace there. But I will not dwell upon this. I put it to the American sense of honor. The honor of a nation is an important thing. It is said in the Scriptures, "What doth it profit a man if he gain the whole world, and lose his own soul?" It may be said, also, What doth it profit a nation if it gain the whole world, but lose its honor? I hold that the American government has taken upon itself a solemn obligation of honor, to see that this war—let it be long or let it be short, let it cost much or let it cost little—that this war shall not cease until every freedman at the South has the right to vote. It has bound itself to it. What have you asked the black men of the South, the black men of the whole country, to do? Why, you have asked them to incur the deadly enmity of their masters, in order to befriend you and to befriend this Government. You have asked us to call down, not only upon ourselves, but upon our children's children, the deadly hate of the entire Southern people. You have called upon us to turn our backs upon our masters, to abandon their cause and espouse yours; to turn against the South and in favor of the North; to shoot down the Confederacy and uphold the flag—the American flag. You have called upon us to expose ourselves to all the subtle machinations of their malignity for all time. And now, what do you propose to do when you come to make peace? To reward your enemies, and trample in the dust your friends? Do you intend to sacrifice the very men who have come to the rescue of your banner in the South, and incurred the lasting displeasure of their masters thereby? Do you intend to sacrifice them and reward your enemies? Do you mean to give your enemies the right to vote, and take it away from your friends? Is that wise policy? Is that honorable? Could American honor withstand such a blow? I do not believe you will do it. I think you will see to it that we have the right to vote. There is something too mean in looking upon the Negro, when you are in trouble, as a citizen, and when you are free from trouble, as an alien. When this nation was in trouble, in its early struggles, it looked upon the Negro as a citizen. In 1776 he was a citizen. At the time of the formation of the Constitution the Negro had the right to vote in eleven States out of the old thirteen. In your trouble you have made us citizens. In 1812 Gen. Jackson addressed us as citizens—"fellow-citizens." He wanted us to fight. We were citizens then! And now, when you come to frame a conscription bill, the Negro is a citizen again. He has been a citizen just three times in the history of this government, and it has always been in time of trouble. In time of trouble we are citizens. Shall we be citizens in war, and aliens in peace? Would that be just?

I ask my friends who are apologizing for not insisting upon this right, where can the black man look, in this country, for the assertion of his right, if he may not look to the Massachusetts Anti-Slavery Society? Where under the whole heavens can he look for sympathy, in asserting this right, if he may not look to this platform? Have you lifted us up to a certain height to see that we are men, and then are any disposed to leave us there, without seeing that we are put in possession of all our rights? We look naturally to this platform for the assertion of all our rights, and for this one especially. I understand the anti-slavery societies of this country to be based on two principles,—first, the freedom of the blacks of this country; and, second, the elevation of them. Let me not be misunderstood here. I am not asking for sympathy at the hands of abolitionists, sympathy at the hands of any. I think the American people are disposed often to be generous rather than just. I look over this country at the present time, and I see Educational Societies, Sanitary Commissions, Freedmen's Associations, and the like,—all very good: but in regard to the colored people there is always more that is benevolent, I perceive, than just, manifested towards us. What I ask for the Negro is not benevolence, not pity, not sympathy, but simply *justice*. The American people have always been anxious to know what they shall do with us. Gen. Banks was distressed with solicitude as to what he should do with the Negro. Everybody has asked the question, and they learned to ask it early of the abolitionists, "What shall we do with the Negro?" I have had but one answer from the beginning. Do nothing with us! Your doing with us has already played the mischief with us. Do nothing with us! If the apples will not remain on the tree of their own strength, if they are wormeaten at the core, if they are early ripe and disposed to fall, let them fall! I am not for tying or fastening them on the tree in any way, except by nature's plan, and if they will not stay there, let them fall. And if the Negro cannot stand on his own legs, let him fall also. All I ask is, give him a chance to stand on his own legs! Let him alone! If you see him on his way to school, let him alone, don't disturb him! If you see him going to the dinner-table at a hotel, let him go! If you see him going to the ballot-box, let him alone, don't disturb him! If you see him going into a work-shop, just let him alone,—your interference is doing him a positive injury. Gen. Banks' "preparation" is of a piece with this attempt to prop up the Negro. Let him fall if he cannot stand alone! If the Negro cannot live by the line of eternal justice, so beautifully pictured to you in the illustration used by Mr. Phillips, the fault will not be yours, it will be his who made the Negro, and established that line for his government. Let him live or die by that. If you will only untie his hands, and give him a chance, I think he will live. He will work as readily for himself as the white man. A great many delusions have been swept away by this war. One was, that the Negro would not work; he has proved his ability to work. Another was, that the Negro would not fight; that he possessed only the most sheepish attributes of humanity; was a perfect lamb, or an "Uncle Tom;" disposed to take off his coat whenever required, fold his hands, and be whipped by anybody who wanted to whip him. But the war has proved that there is a great deal of human nature in the Negro, and that "he will fight," as Mr. Quincy, our President, said, in earlier days than these, "when there is a reasonable probability of his whipping anybody"—**1865.**

ADDRESS BEFORE THE TENNESSEE COLORED AGRICULTURAL AND MECHANICAL ASSOCIATION

When I had the honor to receive your kind and unexpected invitation to visit Nashville, a city famous for its elegance and refinement, and the scene of so many thrilling events and patriotic associations during the late struggle for Union and liberty, I was naturally enough very much pleased with the prospect of being present on this occasion; but when I was informed that my visit was not to be either for pleasure or observation, but to make an address, and that the said address must be of a character appropriate to this your third annual agricultural exhibition, my joy and enthusiasm received a very decided check; the "native hue of resolution was sicklied over with the pale cast of thought." The fact is—and I am not ashamed to admit it—I felt very much as some of our Generals did when called upon to face the enemy on the open field of battle. I would have gladly been relieved of the command, and to have allowed the imposing task assigned me to fall into other and more competent hands. But your committee was composed of earnest and resolute men. They were men from Tennessee, and as willful as old Hickory himself. They made no account of any modest distrusts of my ability, would hear none of my excuses, and in short would be satisfied with nothing less than my presence and speech on this occasion. Well, gentlemen, these willful men have succeeded; they have got me here, but I beg you to remember the old saying, which must have originated with farmers, for the best things always have originated with them, that "one man may carry a horse to water, but twenty cannot make him drink."

The ground of my hesitation about coming here was not the cholera, for Nashville is now tolerably healthy; it was not the distance I would have to travel to get here, for your railway communications are nearly equal to any in the country, but the trouble was the address, the *appropriate* address. There was the rub. It was the rub then and it is the rub now, and instead of disappearing on my approach it is all the more perplexing when I look out upon this expectant multitude, and remember the high-sounding praises heaped upon me in anticipation of my coming.

Gentlemen, this is an agricultural and mechanical industrial fair. I am surrounded today by industrious mechanics and farmers, and you have got me up here to tell you what I know about farming. Now, I am neither a farmer nor a mechanic. During the last thirty-five years I have been actively employed in a work which left me no time to study either the theory or the practice of farming. I could far more easily tell you what I don't know about farming than what I do know, though the former would take more time to tell than the latter. Well, gentlemen, I do not mean to censure your excellent committee for paying me in advance and insisting upon my coming, thus buying a pig in a bag, not knowing what kind of animal would come forth at the opening, but I am bold to say that they violated in that act one of the very first rules of successful farming, which is to see that the tools are always placed in the hands that can use them best. There are, undoubtedly, hundreds of colored men in the vicinity of Nashville, practical farmers and mechanics, who could address you upon the subjects of this occasion far more appropriately and effectively than I can do. This suggestion may seem rather late, but it may serve you a good turn when the business of selecting a speaker shall come around again.

But, gentlemen, there is a sunnier side to this distressing picture. Since I am now here, and there is no possible way of escape, I may at least employ the device of the boy who whistled in the graveyard to keep up his courage. Several considerations serve in some measure to reconcile me to my task. One of these is the fact that being a public speaker, I have often found myself in just such embarrassing situations at other times and places. If you will pardon me a little autobiography, and, perhaps, a little egotism as well, I will tell you, that like many other men, I have been all my life long doing extraordinary things for the first time, some of which had been better undone. I have been constantly required to undertake the performance of works which came upon me as a surprise, and for which I had no previous training or preparation, and while my work has generally been rather unskillfully and imperfectly done, I have always had a thoughtful and generous people for my judges, who have measured and estimated my achievements not by the rule of intrinsic excellence, but by the rule of my disadvantages, and have thus often accorded me higher praise than I could possibly claim on the score of merit.

Besides this, there is encouragement in the subject itself. Agriculture is one of the very oldest themes and one upon which only a genius can be expected to say anything either new or striking. Originality is out of the question. The knowledge already accumulated and recorded on this subject is vast and minute, and the man who can give you but a glimpse of one of the many sides of this vast accumulation of knowledge does not speak in vain.

In few things perhaps, more than in farming, does one find that there is nothing new under the sun. The sages of today do but reiterate the wisdom of the sages of antiquity. The perception of truth may be new or old, but the truth itself is neither old nor new, but eternal as the Universe. The discovery of the fundamental principles of agriculture reach far beyond the limits of authentic history, for men tilled the soil long before they wrote books, and would have never written books if they had not tilled the soil. All the present rests upon all the past. The very best that any in my circumstances can do is to teach and preach the discoveries made by other men and at other times.

There are doubtless many great truths which yet remain to be discovered and applied to Agriculture, as well as to many other matters of human welfare. It was a favorite saying of Theodore Parker, that "all the space between man's mind and God's mind is crowded with truths which wait to be discovered and organized into law for the practice of men."

But mankind is so nearly on a level of equality that no one man may claim the exclusive merit of original discovery. Truth, like the gentle light of heaven, usually dawns upon more than one mind at the same time, so that there is seldom a discovery which has not more than one to claim the honor of it.

Gentlemen, I find still another source of encouragement. It is in terms you employ in announcing my subject today. I am to speak to you of the importance of agricultural and mechanical industry and of united effort on the part of our people to improve their physical, moral and social condition. Upon a subject so broad and comprehensive and deeply interesting it would be almost impossible to speak without saying something capable of being turned to use by sensible people.

Now, gentlemen, having looked out for myself, always an important lesson, and one which farmers readily learn, let me attend to you. I give you my warmest congratulations, first of all, upon the attitude you have assumed before the American people this day. I especially congratulate you upon the noble example you have set for our whole race. You have gone to work like earnest men, fully believing in the future of your people. You have wisely availed yourselves of a well known power, the power of association, organization, mutual counsel and cooperation. You have dared to organize an Agricultural and Mechanical Association for the State of Tennessee. You propose to avail yourselves of whatever knowledge or wisdom there may be in this State, which can assist you in the work of your general improvement. You have dared to open here in the city of Nashville a State Agricultural Fair, to display the rich fruits of your industry, and to ask your fellow-countrymen of all conditions and colors to view and inspect them. This is an act, on your part as brave as it is wise. It proves that you are not ashamed of your achievements. It proves that you, like the great Oliver Cromwell and all other brave men, want to be painted as you are, and to receive no other or higher credit than that which you honestly win by open and fair competition.

The organization of your State Agricultural Society and this third annual exhibition demonstrate that you appreciate the new order of things which has dawned upon the country. By these two signs you advertise and inform the world of your *farewell,* your departure forever from the moral and intellectual stagnation of a by-gone condition, and have taken up your line of march under the banner of liberty with the more advanced peoples of the earth to higher plains of civilization, culture and refinement.

I congratulate you again, gentlemen, upon the point in time at which you begin your public career of agricultural industry. In this respect the conditions of success are nearly perfect. You have taken the tide at its flood. You start in the full blaze of the accumulated wisdom of ages. No fifty years of human life and exertion have been so crowded with discovery and invention as the first half of this nineteenth century. You may now walk by sight where others only walked by faith. You have not to feel your way in the dark or to hew out any new road to fortune. The very elements around you have been fighting on your side, and, like a fortunate general, you came upon the field of action at exactly the right moment to secure an easy and brilliant victory. Agricultural implements of world-approved materials and of world-approved patterns are ready to your hand. The toil and drudgery of ancient farming have been banished from the field. The heavy cradle which wore out your manhood, and the sickle which bent your bodies in pain, belong to a by-gone age. The old-fashioned hoe, broad, heavy, and cumbrous; and the wooden plow, with its miserable mold-board, and its so-called steel point, that kept you always running to the blacksmith's shop, have followed the sickle and the cradle to their common resting place. Science, the noblest and grandest artificer of human fortune and well-being, the source and explanation of all progress, has patiently unfolded the nature and composition of plants, and made us acquainted with the properties of the common earth, wherever they grow. The quality of soil, best suited to a given class of plants, has been accurately ascertained. The chemical properties of various kinds of manure have been thoroughly investigated. Even the weather, hitherto supposed to be hidden in the inscrutable bosom of infinity, and only known to God, has been compelled to give up its mystery. Instead of being governed by any supposed supreme will, or controlled by the wishes and prayers of men, it is subject to and acts in accordance with eternal and irreversible laws. "Old Probabilities," as the commissioner of this department of knowledge is called, with his nerves of wire, extending all over the country, is able to tell us daily and in advance what storms are in the skies, and when and where they may be expected to descend. There is light everywhere and darkness nowhere. We have only to open our eyes and to behold all around us the essential conditions of successful exertion.

I have spoken of the impossibility of presenting anything original upon this subject. In reading the works of modern writers, it is surprising to find how much and how far we have been anticipated by those who have gone before us in the field of thought and discovery. Most that we have done in modern times has been, after all, to find new applications of old principles. The plow, though vastly improved, is the same implement known by that name thousands of years ago. Deep plowing and draining, and a thorough pulverization of the soil, so earnestly and eloquently insisted upon nowadays, and very wisely so, though now better accomplished by means of our better tools than at any previous time, especially in England, were well known to the cultivators of the soil in China and Egypt centuries ago. The Egyptians even deified Osiris, the inventor of the plow. The small farm theory, by which a man may double the number of his acres, by skillful and thorough cultivation, and one which has been so eloquently and persistently advocated by the lamented Horace Greeley, was by no means a new idea, or in any sense original with him. Cato, two thousand years ago, held and advocated precisely the same idea. The wisdom of the theory may be appropriately commended on this occasion. The principle underlying the small farm theory is very easily comprehended. Everybody knows that distance is an element to be considered in farming and in much other work. As much time and labor are required to walk, plow, or drive over one acre of poor ground as over one acre of rich ground, while the poor acre will give you only half the production of the rich one, and that an article of inferior quality. In the one case you are but half paid for your toil, while in the other you reap an abundant reward both in quantity and in quality.

The same principle, as I have said, operates elsewhere. Talking with Mr. William Whipper, a successful lumber merchant in the city of Philadelphia, he told me, he could not afford to keep a single piece of inferior lumber in his yard, and the reason he assigned for keeping only the very best quality of lumber, was that land was too dear and rents too high, to be occupied by anything of inferior quality. Besides, said he, a poor stick of timber will occupy as much space, and require as many hands and as much labor to handle it, as would a superior article, while it would only command half the price. I came to the conclusion in listening to this reasoning, that I had met in Mr. Whipper a wise man as well as a successful man, one who practically carried out the idea that whatever was worth doing at all is worth being done well.

Gentlemen, I would like to make a speech today of the orthodox agricultural pattern. I would like to tell you of the wise things done and said in respect to ancient and modern tillage. Neither you nor I can afford to be ignorant of the facts of this history, for knowledge is power, here and elsewhere, and there is no danger that we shall know too much about any useful employment. There is for us in the agricultural history of the world a special cause for complacency. If to the race to which we belong mankind can ascribe any glory, the achievements upon which it is founded stretch far away into the past. It is pleasant to know that in color, form, and features, we are related to the first successful tillers of the soil; to the people who taught the world agriculture; that the civilization which made Greece, Rome, and Western Europe illustrious, and even now makes our own land glorious, sprung forth from the bosom of Africa. For, while this vast continent was yet undiscovered by civilized men; while the Briton

and Gallic races wandered like beasts of prey in the forests, the people of
Egypt and Ethiopia rejoiced in well cultivated fields and abundance of
corn. I follow only the father of history when I say that the ancient Egyptians
were black and their hair woolly. However this may be disputed
now, there is no denying that these people more nearly resembled the
African type than the Caucasian.

I would like to dwell here on the progress of agriculture, and note the
causes which have led to its rapid development in this country; to show
how diversified labor produces a home market for the productions of our
soil; how the prosecution of internal improvements of rivers and harbors,
of canals, railroads and steam navigation have stimulated agricultural industry;
how science, observation and experiment have assisted in its general
development; and especially would it be pleasant to comply with the
letter as well as the spirit of your invitation, dwell upon the general importance
of this branch of industry; picture to you the midnight gloom
and destitution which would fall upon the world if its wheels should cease
to revolve, and the earth refuse food for man and beast; how commerce
would languish, how mechanical machinery would gradually become silent;
how the iron horse would stand still on the track; how the fire would
die out on the hearth, the gaunt and withered arms of the mother hang
down in despair; the wan babe in the cradle sleep its last sleep, and the
busy, hopeful, courageous and joyful world would sink back again into the
depths and darkness of barbarism. It would be well enough, too, if there
were time, to give you the testimony of poets, scholars, statesmen and
philosophers of all countries and ages in favor of country life; to follow,
especially, the retiring statesman, when worn and broken by the storms of
public life, or when covered with its honors, to the old farm of his birth,
and paint the scene of peace and sweet content in which he spends his
declining years, and, at last, sinks to rest forever; to dwell at large upon
the soothing charms of nature, the honest affection and trust of well-
treated domestic animals, to prove that among the truly beautiful and
healthful scenes of this world, there is none more beautiful than a well-
managed farm.

But gentlemen, this is an opportunity too unusual, an occasion too peculiar, and my relation to you too singular to make such a disposition of
your time justifiable.

Mine, to-day, is a rare privilege. No man perhaps was ever called upon
to address so vast a concourse of newly-emancipated people; a people wide
awake and just starting in the race of mental, moral and social progress; a
people of whom, heretofore, no reckoning was made; a people recognized
as standing outside of the circle, and ranked by the laws of the land with
horses, sheep, and swine, and like these to be held and bought and sold.

Gentlemen, since this is our first meeting since the revolution, in your
situation and mine, I feel less like dwelling on agriculture in general than
calling upon you to join me in loud, earnest, joyous and long-continued

cheers over our newly-gained freedom. Agricultural industry to-day has an interest for me mainly in respect to the new order of things upon which we have now fairly entered. How it can be made to serve us, as a particular class, is the commanding question of the hour.

If we look abroad over our country and observe the condition of the colored people, we shall find that their greatest want to be regular and lucrative employments for their energies. They have secured their freedom, it is true, but not the friendship and favor of the people around them. The sentiment that greeted them all over the South, when their fetters were broken, was: let the Negro starve! Happily to-day that sentiment is seldom heard, but though seldom heard—I am sorry to say it—it is still felt, and is active in a thousand ways to our hurt. It keeps back the wages of the black laborer by fraud; it refuses to rent and sell land; it excludes them from printers' unions and other mechanical associations; it refuses to teach them trades, and shuts them out from all respectable employments, and consoles itself with the theory that the Negroes—like the Indians—will ultimately die out.

The effect of this ruling in the American mind has driven the Negroes in great numbers from the country into the large cities, and into menial positions, where they easily learn to imitate the vices and follies of the least exemplary whites, and they perish as a consequence. "Let the Negroes starve!" thus executes itself.

In these circumstances, I hail agriculture as a refuge for the oppressed. The grand old earth has no prejudices against race, color, or previous condition of servitude, but flings open her ample breast to all who will come to her for succor and relief. Agriculture is simply the act of cultivating the ground so as to secure its largest and best product for sustaining life and health. There are special and pressing reasons why we, of all the people of the United States, should master this great art. It is our last resort, and if we fail here I see not how we can succeed elsewhere. We are not like the Irish, an organized political power, welded together by a common faith. We are not shrewd like the Hebrew, capable of making fortunes by buying and selling old clothes. We are not like the Germans, who can spend half their time in lager beer saloons and still get rich; but we are just what we are: a laborious, joyous, thoughtless, improvident people, just released from our thraldom, and with just such necessities as agricultural life will secure.

I have already referred generally to the favorable conditions afforded to successful agriculture on our part. Besides land, labor, and skill, there must be heat, moisture, and manure. While man is required to eat bread in the sweat of his brow, nature must give us warmth and moisture, or there is no bread. In the farthest North, where cold, ice, and snow are perpetual, and in the far South, under a vertical sun, where the fierce heat drinks up all of the moisture and leaves the land a sandy desert, agriculture, of course, in such lands and latitudes is impossible.

Happily for us, we have no such heat and no such cold to contend with here. In this respect there is no country in the world more highly favored than the United States, and it would be hard to point to any State more favorable to farming than your own Tennessee. You have mountain, valley, river, and plain, heat and moisture, and a beautifully temperate climate, where, with knowledge, skill and industry, you may obtain the highest agricultural results.

Some of your old citizens, no doubt, continue to regret the change which has taken place in the relations of the people of Tennessee. In the loss of slavery the State, in their estimation, has parted with the source of its happiness and prosperity. To my mind it would be hard to find a greater mistake than this. Emancipation in this State was not only a triumph of justice, but a triumph of agricultural industry. It was not merely a blessing to the slave, but a blessing to the master. I put to the common sense of all who hear me: what possible motive had the slave for a careful, successful cultivation of the soil? What concern could he have for increasing the wealth of the master, or for improving and beautifying the land? The wealth of the master did not attach to the slave, but the reverse. The natural tendency of wealth was to deepen the chasm between the master and the slave, and to break up all sympathy between them. The small slave owners went to the field with their few bondmen and worked side by side with them. Humane and kindly relations sprang up between them; common toils, and common privations made them, in some sense, friends. But the reverse was the case with the rich and great masters. Their hands were unused to toil. They could afford to leave their slaves in the hands of soulless overseers and drivers, who had no motives of kindness or goodwill. Thus it was for the interest of the slave to make the rich man poor and the poor man poorer. To reduce as far as possible the difference between themselves and others, and since they themselves could not be masters, they had a direct and powerful motive for reducing their masters to the poverty of slaves.

This, however, was not the worst element of the situation. The very soil of your State was cursed with a burning sense of injustice. Slavery was the parent of anger and hate. Your fields could not be lovingly planted nor faithfully cultivated in its presence. The eye of the overseer could not be everywhere, and cornhills could be covered with clods in preference to soft and pulverized soil in their absence, for the hand that planted cared nothing for the harvest. Thus you will see that emancipation has liberated the land as well as the people.

In contemplating the successful husbandry of the British Islands, abounding as they do, with fertile fields and the most perfectly formed and best developed cattle, a distinguished Frenchman was led to exclaim: "It is not fertility but liberty that cultivates a country." The State of Tennessee is now to be cultivated by liberty; by knowledge which comes of liberty; by the respectability of labor; by the motive of general welfare, and by the sense of patriotism confined to no particular class, and I predict for her a fast and general increase of happiness and prosperity in the new era which has dawned upon her.

Gentlemen, if this prophecy of prosperity to your State shall prove slow of fulfillment, or be defeated, the fault will not be due to the new order of liberty, but to the old order to slavery. It will not be in the emancipated slave, but in the discontented master. It will not be due to any inherent defect of the principle of liberty, but to the inherent disposition of despotic power, to supplant freedom. A dog will scratch his neck long after his collar is removed. The illusion is kept up when its cause has departed. Neither the slave nor his master can abandon all at once the deeply intrenched errors and habits of centuries.

I take it that one part of the mission of this State Agricultural Association is the speedy and radical extinction of the evils inherited by the emancipated class from their former condition, and that, therefore, it is appropriate on this occasion, to point out some of the palpable of those errors for condemnation and banishment, and inculcate in their stead the wiser and better ideas, suggested by the condition upon which we have entered.

TREATMENT OF ANIMALS

There is no denying that slavery had a direct and positive tendency to produce coarseness and brutality in the treatment and management of domestic animals, especially those most useful to agricultural industry. Not only the slave, but the horse, the ox and the mule shared the general feeling of indifference to rights naturally engendered by a state of slavery. The master blamed the overseer; the overseer the slave, and the slave the horses, oxen and mules, and violence and brutality fell upon the animals as a consequence. Now, there is no successful farming without well-trained and well-treated horses and oxen, and one of the greatest pleasures connected with agricultural life may be found in the pleasant relations capable of subsisting between the farmer and his four-legged companions; for they are company as well as helpers in his toil. I have seen men spend valuable hours of the best part of the day, chasing horse and mule in the open field, which but for the abuses heaped upon them when in harness, would have come instantly upon the call of their master. The loss arising from this source is twofold. Both man and beast have been wearied by this chase, and the tempter of both has been rendered unfavorable to calm and steady exertion. It should be the study of every farmer to make his horse his companion and friend, and to do this, there is but one rule, and that is, uniform sympathy and kindness. All loud and boisterous commands, a brutal flogging should be banished from the field, and only words of cheer and encouragement should be tolerated. A horse is in many respects like a man. He has the five senses, and has memory, affection, and reason to a limited degree. When young, untrained and untamed, he has unbounded faith in his strength and fleetness. He runs, jumps and plays in the pride of his perfections. But convince him that he is a creature of law as well as of freedom by a judicious and kindly application of your superior power, and he will conform his conduct to that law, far better than you most law-abiding citizen.

CARE OF AGRICULTURAL IMPLEMENTS

Gentlemen, in farming, as everywhere else, time is money; and one-tenth of all time of some farmers is lost to useful labor in searching for and mending tools carelessly flung down anywhere and everywhere and left forgotten to rust, decay, and ruin. I have seen in some of our Western States, amid the snows and rains of winter, costly plows, harrows, and mowing machines exposed to all the destructive forces of the elements. Of course, men who farm thus bring no honor to agriculture, but are a disgrace to that vocation. The loss of time, labor, and money, as in the other cases, are not the only evils of this style of practical farming. The loss of temper, the mental confusion to which this one evil gives rise, will rack a man's constitution more than the heaviest, steadiest strokes of well-directed exertion.

THE WELL AND THE WOODPILE

Life is said to be made up of little things, and small annoyances are often more distressing to the temper than large ones. There can be no happy and successful farming when there is no peace at home. When the wife smiles and the children are happy and gleeful, the toil and burdens of the husbandman are light and easily borne. Everything, therefore, which tends to make home happy is in the line of a wise economy, both of time and labor. Where a woman must go half a mile in the woods to tote brush or rotten bark to make a fire, or a quarter of a mile to the spring to fetch water, it is impossible that household affairs can go on either regularly or pleasantly. Such economy is unworthy of the sense of a Hottentot or a Bushman. If you come up tired and hungry from the field; if your house is not neat, sweet and in order; if the eyes of your wife and daughter are red with smoke and tears; if your children are fretting and crying, and you yourself suffer from loss of temper, you have in fact only yourself to blame. You have neglected to supply your woodshed with an ample quantity of sound and well-seasoned wood, and to put down a well of pure water at your door, and have thus omitted the primary conditions of peace, purity and order in your household. By all means, be sure of your water and wood!

MANURES

Successful farming does not entirely depend upon good plowing, harrowing, and hoeing, nor prompt attention to seedtime and harvest. Every crop gathered from the field takes something valuable from the soil upon which it is grown, and the richest land in the world can be made poor if we take everything from it and give it nothing in return. While providing for ourselves, our next best thought should be given to the question as to how we shall provide for the wants of the soil out of which comes our own living. All flesh is grass, and the amount of vegetable matter we obtain from the earth will be the measure of the life and happiness of the men and animals who subsist upon it. Now, there need be no such thing in the world as wornout land. The same soil has been cultivated in China during the space of two thousand years, and the land is as rich to-day as when the plow and the spade first turned it to the light and heat of the sun. The explanation of this prolonged fertility is manure. The Chinaman knows its value and puts his knowledge in practice. He knows how to make, save, and apply it. My advice to you is to go and do likewise. Your first maxim should be: let nothing be wasted! Nothing that will rot in the ground is useless, and nothing should be allowed to decay unused. The very water and soap employed in washing your hands and clothes should find their way to your trimly arranged bed of compost. The bones from your table should also be made to do double duty. The soil of England is richer and yields better crops to-day than two hundred years ago, and the reason is the same there as in China. They attend to the wants of the soil as well as to their own. Feed the land and it will feed you! Starve the land and it will starve you!

AGRICULTURAL BOOKS AND PAPERS

Knowledge is power. There is no work that men are required to do, which they cannot better or more economically do with education than without it. The trouble with us as a people has been to work without a knowledge of the theory of work. We could build ships if some one would draft them. We could build a house if someone would draw the plan. All that we have done has been by rote. We have farmed without a knowledge of the philosophy of farming. We have used our muscles but not our minds. Under the old *regime* we were not expected to think, but only to do as we were told. We were not allowed to profit even by our own experience, and to do things in the easiest and best way which our practical knowledge might suggest. The master and the overseer directed every stroke, and we were but living machines. All is changed now. The machine must begin to think, and in this, the reading of agricultural books and papers will materially assist. It used to be said, if you want to keep a secret from a Negro, put it in a book or a newspaper. This must be said no longer. Every col-

ored farmer and mechanic should take and read one or more of the many
excellent mechanic and agricultural journals. If you cannot read yourself,
let your son or daughter read to you. Depend upon it, an hour spent in this
way, will do more for you than the labor of any other hour in the day.
Muscle is mighty, but mind is mightier, and there is no better field for the
exercise of the mind than is found in the cultivation of the soil.

THE FARMER'S NATURAL ENEMIES

I shall attempt no solution of the origin of evil in the world. Whether it
came by the fall of Adam or the fall of anybody else, I neither know nor
care, for it does not matter. It is enough to know that we have it, and it is
in abundance, and that the best use we can make of it is to resist and
destroy it as far as we can. All nature teems with it, and the life of a
farmer is a constant battle. He not only has to contend with the elements,
but with all manner of destructive insects. Flies, bugs, worms, caterpillars,
grasshoppers and locusts spring out of the ground like armed warriors and
endeavor to flank and defeat him. He must fight or die. His foes will
neither treat nor compromise. It is "kill or be killed." Not an hour is to be
lost. Time gives strength to the enemy and weakness to the farmer. This
insect host must be met and stamped out without delay. The advantage of
a single hour will sometimes enable the caterpillar to ruin your fruit crop.
Prevention is better than cure, and it is better to destroy those enemies in
their eggs than to wait until they are full of life and activity. The warrior
uses the telescope to discover his enemy. The farmer should use the micro-
scope. With a little experience in its use, he can anticipate his foe. Indeed,
you should go a step further than this. You should not only make war
upon the enemy, but upon the conditions of his existence. Like most of the
enemies of human life and welfare, they originate in darkness and in all
manner of unclean and unsightly places. Break up the nest of weed, brier,
and thorns in your fence corners. Take away your old, rotten and wormeaten ground rail. Put a sound one in its place. Let in the bright sunlight
and pure air. Summon fire and water, if it need be, to clean out these
breeders of vermin to prey upon your crops. For when you have done all
in your power, you will still see more to do, but you will at least be rewarded by abundant returns for your wisdom, courage, vigilance and
industry.

UNION AND IMPROVEMENT

Gentlemen, I approach this subject with less confidence of meeting your
approval than at other points. As a race, we have suffered from two very
opposite causes. Disparagement on the one hand, and undue praises on the
other. I propose to err on neither side. This question of improvement or
non-improvement involves the whole subject of our destiny as a part of

the American people. In other words, it is the question whether we shall advance or recede, rise or fall, survive or perish; for one or the other of these things must necessarily happen to us. To stand still is utterly impossible. If we even could hold our own, and stand where we now are, the effect of improvement in all around us would make our standing still retrogression. Of course, gentlemen, we stand to-day in point of civilization far in the rear of our white fellow-citizens. We are, in fact, wearing the old clothes left by a by-gone generation. The books we read, the sermons we hear, the prayers we repeat, are all obtained from the white race. We have neither made books, sermons, prayers, nor hymns. We have no science nor philosophy of our own. We have neither history nor poetry. As Andrew Jackson used to say of Congress: "We are hanging on the verge" of the white man's civilization. It is painful to make such an admission as this; but nothing is gained by concealing the truth either from ourselves or from others.

The question which the future has to answer, is: Whether the Negro is what he is to-day because of his mental and moral constitution, or because he has been enslaved and degraded for centuries. If it shall be found, after the lapse of twenty-five years of freedom, that the colored people of this country have made no improvement in their social condition, it will confirm the opinion that the Negro is, by his very nature, limited to a servile condition. But, if, on the other hand, we supply the world with the proof of our advancement to a plane, even a little above that on which slavery left us, we shall prove that, like all other man, we are capable of civilization, where its conditions are accessible to us. Still further, to simplify the question, which the present is pressing upon us, It is: Whether the black man will prove a better master to himself than his white master was to him.

This, then, is the work to which we have to address ourselves as a race. We are to prove that we can better our own condition and that by the development of our own self-contained qualities. I need not stop here to point out the particular modes of action by which this can be accomplished. I will only indicate one.

ACCUMULATE PROPERTY

Yes, accumulate property. This may sound to you like a new gospel. You have been accustomed to hear that money is the root of all evil; that it is hard for the rich to enter the kingdom of Heaven; that this world is of no account; that we should take no thought for tomorrow, and much more of the same sort. In answer to all which I say: that no people can ever make any social or mental improvement whose exertions are thus limited. Poverty is our greatest calamity. It draws down upon us the very condition which makes us a helpless, hopeless, dependent, and dispirited people, the target for the contempt and scorn of all around us. On the other hand, property, money, if you please, will purchase for us the only condition upon which any people can rise to the dignity of genuine manhood; for, without property, there can be no leisure. Without leisure, there can be no thought. Without thought, there can be no invention. Without invention, there can be no progress.

But how shall we get money? Work for it, save it when you get it. I have spoken of slavery as our enemy. I have nothing to take back at that point. It has robbed us of education. It has robbed us of the care due us by our mothers. It has written its ugliness in our countenance, deformed our feet, and twisted our limbs out of shape; and yet this same slavery has been, in some sense, our best friend. It has trained us to regular industry, and hardened our muscles to toil, and thus has left in our hands the staff of all accomplishments. We can work, and the grateful earth yields as readily and as bountifully to the touch of black industry as of white. We can work, and by this means we can retrieve all our losses. Knowledge, wisdom, culture, refinement, manners, are all founded on work, and the wealth which work brings.

As I already said: we must save as well as work. This cannot be done by travelling from place to place in search of new homes. Rolling stones gather no moss. Emerson says that the men who made Rome worth going to see stayed there. In nine cases out of ten a man's condition is worse by changing his location. You had far better endeavor to remove the evil from your door than to remove and leave it there. "It is better to endure the ills you have than to fly to others you know not of." If you have got a few acres stick by them. The sweat and toil you put into them will add their value and enable you to buy more. Every new beginning you make will have its peculiar troubles. Infancy is the time of special dangers to measures as well as to men. Every baby must have the whooping cough and measles. Life is too short, time is too valuable to be wasted in the experiment of seeking new homes. People are about as good in your neighborhood as anywhere else in the world, and may need you to make them better.

But gentlemen, I have detained you too long already. Our destiny is in our own hands. We are no longer slaves, but freemen. We are no longer property, but persons. We are not aliens, but citizens. We are not only men, but men among men. If any people may have a future, a prosperous and happy future, such a future is possible to us, and I hope it will be the business of every man who hears my voice to-day, to contribute his full share to the sum of the common welfare of our race—September 18, 1873.

THE CIVIL RIGHTS CASE

I have only a very few words to say to you this evening, and in order that those few words shall be well-chosen, and not liable to be misunderstood, distorted, or misrepresented, I have been at the pains of writing them out in full. It may be, after all, that the hour calls more loudly for silence than for speech. Later on in this discussion, when we shall have the full text of the recent decision of the Supreme Court before us, and the dissenting opinion of Judge Harlan, who must have weighty reasons for separating from all his associates, and incurring thereby, as he must, an amount of criticism from which even the bravest man might shrink, we may be in better frame of mind, better supplied with facts, and better prepared to speak calmly, correctly, and wisely, than now. The temptation at this time, is of course, to speak more from feeling than reason, more from impulse than reflection.

We have been, as a class, grievously wounded, wounded in the house of our friends, and this wound is too deep and too painful for ordinary measured speech.

> When a deed is done for Freedom,
> Through the broad earth's aching breast
> Runs a thrill of joy prophetic,
> Trembling on from east to west.

But when a deed is done from slavery, caste and oppression, and a blow is struck at human progress, whether so intended or not, the heart of humanity sickens in sorrow and writhes in pain. It makes us feel as if some one were stamping upon the graves of our mothers, or desecrating our sacred temples of worship. Only base men and oppressors can rejoice in a triumph of injustice over the weak and defenceless, for weakness ought itself to protect from assaults of pride, prejudice and power.

The cause which has brought us here to-night is neither common nor trivial. Few events in our national history have surpassed it in magnitude, importance and significance. It has swept over the land like a moral cyclone, leaving moral desolation in its track.

We feel it, as we felt the furious attempt, years ago, to force the accursed system of slavery upon the soil of Kansas, the enactment of the Fugitive Slave Bill, the repeal of the Missouri Compromise, the Dred Scott decision. I look upon it as one more shocking development of that moral weakness in high places which has attended the conflict between the spirit of liberty and the spirit of slavery from the beginning, and I venture to predict that it will be so regarded by after-coming generations.

Far down the ages, when men shall wish to inform themselves as the real state of liberty, law, religion and civilization in the United States at this juncture of our history, they will overhaul the proceedings of the Supreme Court, and read the decision declaring the Civil Rights Bill unconstitutional and void.

From this they will learn more than from many volumes, how far we have advanced, in this year of grace, from barbarism toward civilization.

Fellow-citizens: Among the great evils which now stalk abroad in our land, the one, I think, which most threatens to undermine and destroy the foundations of our free institutions, is the great and apparently increasing want of respect entertained for those to whom are committed the responsibility and the duty of administering our government. On this point, I think all good men must agree, and against this evil I trust you feel, and we feel, the deepest repugnance, and that we will, neither here nor elsewhere, give it the least breath of sympathy or encouragement. We should never forget, that, whatever may be the incidental mistakes or misconduct of rulers, government is better than anarchy, and patient reform is better than violent revolution.

But while I would increase this feeling, and give it the emphasis of a voice from heaven, it must not be allowed to interfere with free speech, honest expression, and fair criticism. To give up this would be to give up liberty, to give up progress, and to consign the nation to moral stagnation, putrefaction, and death.

In the matter of respect for dignitaries, it should never be forgotten, however, that duties are reciprocal, and while the people should frown down every manifestation of levity and contempt for those in power, it is the duty of the possessors of power so to use it as to deserve and to insure respect and reverence.

To come a little nearer to the case now before us. The Supreme Court of the United States, in the exercise of its high and vast constitutional power, has suddenly and unexpectedly decided that the law intended to secure to colored people the civil rights guaranteed to them by the following provision of the Constitution of the United States, is unconstitutional and void. Here it is:

"No State," says the 14th Amendment, "shall make or enforce any law which shall abridge the privileges or immunities of citizens of the United States; nor shall any State deprive any person of life, liberty, or property without due process of law; nor deny any person within its jurisdiction the equal protection of the laws."

Now, when a bill has been discussed for weeks and months, and even years, in the press and on the platform, in Congress and out of Congress; when it has been calmly debated by the clearest heads, and the most skillful and learned lawyers in the land; when every argument against it has been over and over again carefully considered and fairly answered; when its constitutionality has been especially discussed, pro and con; when it has passed the United States House of Representatives, and has been solemnly enacted by the United States Senate, perhaps the most imposing legislative body in the world; when such a bill has been submitted to the Cabinet of the Nation, composed of the ablest men in the land; when it has passed under the scrutinizing eye of the Attorney-General of the United States; when the Executive of the Nation has given to it his name and formal approval; when it has taken its place upon the statute-book, and has remained there for nearly a decade, and the country has largely assented to it, you will agree with me that the reasons for declaring such a law unconstitutional and void, should be strong, irresistible and absolutely conclusive.

Inasmuch as the law in question is a law in favor of liberty and justice, it ought to have had the benefit of any doubt which could arise as to its strict constitutionality. This, I believe, will be the view taken of it, not only by laymen like myself, but by eminent lawyers as well.

All men who have given any thought to the machinery, the structure, and practical operation of our Government, must have recognized the importance of absolute harmony between its various departments of powers and duties. They must have seen clearly the mischievous tendency and danger to the body politic of any antagonisms between its various branches. To feel the force of this thought, we have only to remember the administration of President Johnson, and the conflict which then took place between the National Executive and the National Congress, when the will of the people was again and again met by the Executive veto, and when the country seemed upon the verge of another revolution. No patriot, however bold, can wish for his country a repetition of those gloomy days.

Now let me say here, before I go on a step further in this discussion, if any man has come here to-night with his breast heaving with passion, his heart flooded with acrimony, wishing and expecting to hear violent denunciation of the Supreme Court, on account of this decision, he has mistaken the object of this meeting, and the character of the men by whom it is called.

We neither come to bury Caesar, nor to praise him. The Supreme Court is the autocratic point in our National Government. No monarch in Europe has a power more absolute over the laws, lives, and liberties. Its Judges live, and ought to live, an eagle's flight beyond the reach of fear or favor, praise or blame, profit or loss. No vulgar prejudice should touch the members of that Court, anywhere. Their decisions should come down to us like the calm, clear light of Infinite justice. We should be able to think of them and to speak of them with profoundest respect for their wisdom, and deepest reverence for their virtue; for what His Holiness, the Pope, is to the Roman Catholic church, the Supreme Court is to the American State. Its members are men, to be sure, and may not claim infallibility, like the Pope, but they are the Supreme power of the Nation, and their decisions are law.

What will be said here to-night, will be spoken, I trust, more in sorrow than in anger, more in a tone of regret than of bitterness.

We cannot, however, overlook the fact that though not so intended, this decision has inflicted a heavy calamity upon seven millions of the people of this country, and left them naked and defenceless against the action of a malignant, vulgar, and pitiless prejudice.

It presents the United States before the world as a Nation utterly destitute of power to protect the rights of its own citizens upon its own soil.

It can claim service and allegiance, loyalty and life, of them, but it cannot protect them against the most palpable violation of the rights of human nature, rights to secure which, governments are established. It can tax their bread and tax their blood, but has no protecting power for their persons. Its National power extends only to the District of Columbia, and the Territories—where the people have no votes—and where the land has no people. All else is subject to the States. In the name of common sense, I ask, what right have we to call ourselves a Nation, in view of this decision, and this utter destitution of power?

In humiliating the colored people of this country, this decision has humbled the Nation. It gives to a South Carolina, or a Mississippi, Railroad Conductor, more power than it gives to the National Government. He may order the wife of the Chief Justice of the United States into a smoking-car full of hirsute men and compel her to go and listen to the coarse jests of a vulgar crowd. It gives to a hotel-keeper who may, from a prejudice born of the rebellion, wish to turn her out at midnight into the darkness of the storm, power to compel her to go. In such a case, according to this decision of the Supreme Court, the National Government has no right to interfere. She must take her claim for protection and redress, not to the Nation, but to the State, and when the State, as I understand it, declares there is upon its Statute book, no law for her protection, the function and power of the National Government is exhausted, and she is utterly without redress.

Bad, therefore, as our case is under this decision, the evil principle affirmed by the court is not wholly confined to or spent upon persons of color. The wife of Chief Justice Waite—I speak of respectfully—is protected to-day, not by law, but solely by the accident of her color. So far as the law of the land is concerned, she is in the same condition as that of the humblest colored woman in the Republic. The difference between colored and white, here, is, that the one, by reason of color, needs legal protection, and the other, by reason of color, does not need protection. It is nevertheless true, that manhood is insulted, in both cases. No man can put a chain about the ankle of his fellow man, without at last finding the other end of it fastened about his own neck.

The lesson of all the ages on this point is, that a wrong done to one man, is a wrong done to all men. It may not be felt at the moment, and the evil day may be long delayed, but so sure as there is a moral government of the universe, so sure will the harvest of evil come.

Color prejudice is not the only prejudice against which a Republic like ours should guard. The spirit of caste is dangerous everywhere. There is the prejudice of the rich against the poor, the pride and prejudice of the idle dandy against the hard handed working man. There is, worst of all, religious prejudice; a prejudice which has stained a whole continent with blood. It is, in fact, a spirit infernal, against which every enlightened man should wage perpetual war. Perhaps no class of our fellow citizens has carried this prejudice against color to a point more extreme and dangerous than have our Catholic Irish fellow citizens, and yet no people on the face of the earth have been more relentlessly persecuted and oppressed on account of race and religion, than the Irish people.

But in Ireland, persecution has at last reached a point where it reacts terribly upon her persecutors. England to-day is reaping the bitter consequences of her injustice and oppression. Ask any man of intelligence to-day, "What is the chief source of England's weakness?" "What has reduced her to the rank of a second-class power?" and the answer will be *"Ireland!"* Poor, ragged, hungry, starving and oppressed as she is, she is strong enough to be a standing menace to the power and glory of England.

Fellow-citizens! We want no black Ireland in America. We want no aggrieved class in America. Strong as we are without the Negro, we are stronger with him than without him. The power and friendship of seven millions of people scattered all over the country, however humble, are not to be despised.

To-day, our Republic sits as a Queen among the nations of the earth. Peace is within her walls of plenteousness within her palaces, but he is a bolder and a far more hopeful man than I am, who will affirm that this peace and prosperity will always last. History repeats itself. What has happened once may happen again.

The Negro, in the Revolution, fought for us and with us. In the war of 1812 Gen. Jackson, at New Orleans, found it necessary to call upon the colored people to assist in its defence against England. Abraham Lincoln found it necessary to call upon the Negro to defend the Union against rebellion, and the Negro responded gallantly in all cases.

Our legislators, our Presidents, and our judges should have a care, lest, by forcing these people outside of law, they destroy that love of country which is needful to the Nation's defense in the day of trouble.

I am not here, in this presence, to discuss the constitutionality or unconstitutionality of this decision of the Supreme Court. The decision may or may not be constitutional. That is a question for lawyers, and not for laymen, and there are lawyers on this platform as learned, able, and eloquent as any who have appeared in this case before the Supreme Court, or as any in the land. To these I leave the exposition of the Constitution; but

I claim the right to remark upon a strange and glaring inconsistency with former decisions, in the action of the court on this Civil Rights Bill. It is a new departure, entirely out of the line of the precedents and decisions of the Supreme Court at other times and in other directions where the rights of colored men were concerned. It has utterly ignored and rejected the force and application of object and intention as a rule of interpretation. It has construed the Constitution in defiant disregard of what was the object and intention of the adoption of the Fourteenth Amendment. It has made no account whatever of the intention and purpose of Congress and the President in putting the Civil Rights Bill upon the Statute Book of the Nation. It has seen fit in this case, affecting a weak and much-persecuted people, to be guided by the narrowest and most restricted rules of legal interpretation. It has viewed both the Constitution and the law with a strict regard to their letter, but without any generous recognition of their broad and liberal spirit. Upon those narrow principles the decision is logical and legal, of course. But what I complain of, and what every lover of liberty in the United States has a right to complain of, is this sudden and causeless reversal of all the great rules of legal interpretation by which this Court was governed in other days, in the construction of the Constitution and of laws respecting colored people.

In the dark day of slavery, this Court, on all occasions, gave the greatest importance to *intention* as a guide to interpretation. The object and *intention* of the law, it was said, must prevail. Everything in favor of slavery and against the Negro was settled by this object and *intention.* The Constitution was construed according to its *intention.* We were over and over again referred to what the framers *meant,* and plain language was sacrificed that the so affirmed *intention* of these framers might be positively asserted. When we said in behalf of the Negro that the Constitution of the United States was intended to establish justice and to secure the blessings of liberty to ourselves and our posterity, we were told that the words said so but that that was obviously not its *intention;* that it was intended to apply only to white people, and that the *intention* must govern.

When we came to that clause of the Constitution which declares that the immigration or importation of such persons as any of the States may see fit to admit shall not be prohibited, and the friends of liberty declared that that provision of the Constitution did not describe the slave-trade, they were told that while its language applied not to slaves, but to persons, still the object and *intention* of that clause of the Constitution was plainly to protect the slave-trade and that that *intention* was the law. When we came to that clause of the Constitution which declares that "No person held to service or labor in one State, under the laws thereof, escaping into another, shall in consequence of any law or regulation therein be discharged from such service or labor, but shall be delivered up on claim of the party to whom such service or labor may be due," we insisted that it neither described nor applied to slaves; that it applied only to persons owing service and labor; that slaves did not and could not owe service and labor; that this clause of the Constitution said nothing of slaves or the masters of slaves; that it was silent as to slave States or free States; that it was simply a provision to enforce a contract; to discharge an obligation between two persons capable of making a contract, and not to force any man into slavery, for the slave could not owe service or make a contract.

We affirmed that it gave no warrant for what was called the "Fugitive Slave Bill," and we contended that that bill was therefore unconstitutional; but our arguments were laughed to scorn by that Court. We were told that the *intention* of the Constitution was to enable masters to recapture their slaves, and that the law of Ninety-three and the Fugitive Slave Law of 1850 were constitutional.

Fellow-citizens! While slavery was the base line of American society, while it ruled the church and the state, while it was the interpreter of our law and the exponent of our religion, it admitted no quibbling, no narrow rules of legal or scriptural interpretations of Bible or Constitution. It sternly demanded its pound of flesh, no matter how much blood was shed in the taking of it. It was enough for it to be able to show the *intention* to get all it asked in the Courts or out of the Courts. But now slavery is abolished. Its reign was long, dark and bloody. Liberty *now,* is the base line of the Republic. Liberty has supplanted slavery, but I fear it has not supplanted the spirit or power of slavery. Where slavery was strong, liberty is now weak.

O for a Supreme Court of the United States which shall be as true to the claims of humanity as the Supreme Court formerly was to the demands of slavery! When that day comes, as come it will, a Civil Rights Bill will not be declared unconstitutional and void, in utter and flagrant disregard of the objects and *intentions* of the National legislature by which it was enacted, and of the rights plainly secured by the Constitution.

This decision of the Supreme Court admits that the Fourteenth Amendment is a prohibition on the States. It admits that a State shall not abridge the privileges or immunities of citizens of the United States, but commits the seeming absurdity of allowing the people of a State to do what it prohibits the State itself from doing.

It used to be thought that the whole was more than a part; that the greater included the less, and that what was unconstitutional for a State to do was equally unconstitutional for an individual member of a State to do. What is a State, in the absence of the people who compose it? Land, air and water. That is all. As individuals, the people of the State of South Carolina may stamp out the rights of the Negro wherever they please, so long as they do not do so as a State. All the parts can violate the Constitution, but the whole cannot. It is not the act itself, according to this decision, that is unconstitutional. The unconstitutionality of the case depends wholly upon the party committing the act. If the State commits it, it is wrong, if the citizen of the State commits it, it is right.

O consistency, thou art indeed a jewel! What does it matter to a colored citizen that a State may not insult and outrage him, if a citizen of a State may? The effect upon him is the same, and it was just this effect that the framers of the Fourteenth Amendment plainly intended by that article to prevent.

It was the act, not the instrument, which was prohibited. It meant to protect the newly enfranchised citizen from injustice and wrong, not merely from a State, but from the individual members of a State. It meant to give him the protection to which his citizenship, his loyalty, his allegiance, and his services entitled him, and this meaning, and this purpose, and this intention, is now declared unconstitutional and void, by the Supreme Court of the United States.

I say again, fellow-citizens, O for a Supreme Court which shall be as true, as vigilant, as active, and exacting in maintaining laws enacted for the protection of human rights as in other days was that Court for the destruction of human rights!

It is said that this decision will make no difference in the treatment of colored people; that the Civil Rights Bill was a dead letter, and could not be enforced. There is some truth in all this, but it is not the whole truth. That bill, like all advance legislation, was a banner on the outer wall of American liberty, a noble moral standard, uplifted for the education of the American people. There are tongues in trees, books, in the running brooks,—sermons in stones. This law, though dead, did speak. It expressed the sentiment of justice and fair play, common to every honest heart. Its voice was against popular prejudice and meanness. It appealed to all the noble and patriotic instincts of the American people. It told the American people that they were all equal before the law; that they belonged to a common country and were equal citizens. The Supreme Court has hauled down this flag of liberty in open day, and before all the people, and has thereby given joy to the heart of every man in the land who wishes to deny to others what he claims for himself. It is a concession to race pride, selfishness and meanness, and will be received with joy by every upholder of caste in the land, and for this I deplore and denounce that decision.

It is a frequent and favorite device of an indefensible cause to misstate and pervert the views of those who advocate a good cause, and I have never seen this device more generally resorted to than in the case of the late decision on the Civil Rights Bill. When we dissent from the opinion of the Supreme Court, and give the reasons why we think that opinion unsound, we are straightway charged in the papers with denouncing the Court itself, and thus put in the attitude of bad citizens. Now, I utterly deny that there has ever been any denunciation of the Supreme Court on this platform, and I defy any man to point out one sentence or one syllable of any speech of mine in denunciation of that Court.

Another illustration of this tendency to put opponents in a false position, is seen in the persistent effort to stigmatize the "Civil Rights Bill" as a "Social Rights Bill." Now, nowhere under the whole heavens, outside of the United States, could any such perversion of truth have any chance of success. No man in Europe would ever dream that because he has a right to ride on a railway, or stop at a hotel, he therefore has the right to enter into social relations with anybody. No one has a right to speak to another without that other's permission. Social equality and civil equality rest upon an entirely different basis, and well enough the American people know it; yet to inflame a popular prejudice, respectable papers like the New York *Times* and the Chicago *Tribune,* persist in describing the Civil Rights Bill as a Social Rights Bill.

When a colored man is in the same room or in the same carriage with white people, as a servant, there is no talk of social equality, but if he is there as a man and a gentleman, he is an offence. What makes the difference? It is not color, for his color is unchanged. The whole essence of the thing is a studied purpose to degrade and stamp out the liberties of a race. It is the old spirit of slavery, and nothing else. To say that because a man rides in the same car with another, he is therefore socially equal, is one of the wildest absurdities.

When I was in England, some years ago, I rode upon highways, byways, steamboats, stage coaches, omnibuses; I was in the House of Commons, in the House of Lords, in the British Museum, in the Coliseum, in the National Gallery, everywhere; sleeping sometimes in rooms where lords and dukes had slept; sitting at tables where lords and dukes were sitting; but I never thought that those circumstances made me socially the equal of lords and dukes. I hardly think that some of our Democratic friends would be regarded among those lords as their equals. If riding in the same car makes one equal, I think that the little poodle I saw sitting in the lap of a lady was made equal by riding in the same car. Equality, social equality, is a matter between individuals. It is a reciprocal understanding. I don't think when I ride with an educated polished rascal, that he is thereby made my equal, or when I ride with a numbskull that it makes me his equal, or makes him my equal. Social equality does not necessarily follow from civil equality, and yet for the purpose of a hell black and damning prejudice, our papers still insist that the Civil Rights Bill is a Bill to establish social equality.

If it is a Bill for social equality, so is the Declaration of Independence, which declares that all men have equal rights; so is the Sermon on the Mount, so is the Golden Rule, that commands us to do to others as we would that others should do to us; so is the Apostolic teaching, that of one blood God has made all nations to dwell on all the face of the earth; so is the Constitution of the United States, and so are the laws and customs of every civilized country in the world; for no where, outside of the United States, is any man denied civil rights on account of his color—**October 22, 1883.**

THE FUTURE OF THE NEGRO

It would require the ken of a statesman and the vision of a prophet combined to tell with certainty what will be the ultimate future of the colored people of the United States, and to neither of these qualifications can I lay claim. We have known the colored man long as a slave, but we have not known him long as a freeman and as an American citizen. What he was as a slave we know; what he will be in his new relation to his fellowmen, time and events will make clear. One thing, however, may safely be laid down as probable, and that is, that the Negro, in one form and complexion or another, may be counted upon as a permanent element of the population of the United States. He is now seven millions, has doubled his number in thirty years, and is increasing more rapidly than the more favored population of the South. The idea of his becoming extinct finds no support in this fact. But will he emigrate? No! Individuals may, but the masses will not. Dust will fly, but the earth will remain. The expense of removal to a foreign land, the difficulty of finding a country where the conditions of existence are more favorable than here, attachment to native land, gradual improvement in moral surroundings, increasing hope of a better future, improvement in character and value by education, impossibility of finding any part of the globe free from the presence of white men,—all conspire to keep the Negro here, and compel him to adjust himself to American civilization.

In the face of history I do not deny that a darker future than I have indicated may await the black man. Contact of weak races with strong has not always been beneficent. The weak have been oppressed, persecuted, driven out, and destroyed. The Hebrews in Egypt, the Moors in Spain, the Caribs in the West Indies, the Picts in Scotland, the Indians and Chinese in our own country, show what may happen to the Negro. But happily he has a moral and political hold upon this country, deep and firm, one which in some measure destroys the analogy between him and other weak peoples and classes. His religion and civilization are in harmony with those of the people among whom he lives. He worships with them in a common temple and at a common altar, and to drag him away is to destroy the temple and tear down the altar. Drive out the Negro and you drive out Christ, the Bible, and American liberty with him. The thought of setting apart a State or Territory and confining the Negro within its borders is a delusion. If the North and South could not live separately in peace, and without bloody and barbarous border wars, the white and black cannot. If the Negro could be bottled up, who could or would bottle up the irrepressible white man? What barrier has been strong enough to confine him? Plainly enough, migration is no policy for the Negro. He would invite the fate of the Indian, and be pushed away before the white man's bayonet.

Nor do I think that the Negro will become more distinct as a class. Ignorant, degraded, and repulsive as he was during his two hundred years of slavery, he was sufficiently attractive to make possible an intermediate race of a million, more or less. If this has taken place in the face of those odious barriers, what is likely to occur when the colored man puts away his ignorance and degradation and becomes educated and prosperous? The tendency of the age is unification, not isolation; not to clans and classes, but to human brotherhood. It was once degradation intensified for a Norman to associate with a Saxon; but time and events have swept down the barriers between them, and Norman and Saxon have become Englishmen. The Jew was once despised and hated in Europe, and is so still in some parts of that continent; but he has risen, and is rising to higher consideration, and no man is now degraded by association with him anywhere. In like manner the Negro will rise in social scale. For a time the social and political privileges of the colored people may decrease. This, however, will be apparent rather than real. An abnormal condition, born of war, carried him to an altitude unsuited to his attainments. He could not sustain himself there. He will now rise naturally and gradually, and hold on to what he gets, and will not drop from dizziness. He will gain both by concession and by self-assertion. Shrinking cowardice wins nothing from either meanness or magnanimity. Manly self-assertion and eternal vigilance are essential to Negro liberty, not less than to that of the white man—July 1884.

THE FUTURE OF THE COLORED RACE

It is quite impossible, at this early date, to say with any decided emphasis what the future of the colored people will be. Speculations of that kind, thus far, have only reflected the mental bias and education of the many who have essayed to solve the problem.

We all know what the Negro has been as a slave. In this relation we have his experience of two hundred and fifty years before us, and can easily know the character and qualities he has developed and exhibited during this long and severe ordeal. In his new relation to his environment, we see him only in the twilight of twenty years of semi-freedom; for he has scarcely been free long enough to outgrow the marks of the lash on his back and the fetters on his limbs. He stands before us, to-day, physically, a maimed and mutilated man. His mother was lashed to agony before the birth of her babe, and the bitter anguish of the mother is seen in the countenance of her offspring. Slavery has twisted his limbs, shattered his feet, deformed his body and distorted his features. He remains black, but no longer comely. Sleeping on the dirt floor of the slave cabin in infancy, cold on one side and warm on the other, a forced circulation of blood on the one side and chilled and retarded circulation on the other, it has come to pass that he has not the vertical bearing of a perfect man. His lack of symmetry, caused by no fault of his own, creates a resistance to his progress which cannot well be overestimated, and should be taken into account, when measuring his speed in the new race of life upon which he has now entered. As I have often said before, we should not measure the Negro from the heights which the white race has attained, but from the depths from which he has come. You will not find Burke, Grattan, Curran and O'Connell among the oppressed and famished poor of the famine-stricken districts of Ireland. Such men come of comfortable antecedents and sound parents.

Laying aside all prejudice in favor of or against race, looking at the Negro as politically and socially related to the American people generally, and measuring the forces arrayed against him, I do not see how he can survive and flourish in this country as a distinct and separate race, nor do I see how he can be removed from the country either by annihilation or expatriation.

Sometimes I have feared that, in some wild paroxysm of rage, the white race, forgetful of the claims of humanity and the precepts of the Christian religion, will proceed to slaughter the Negro in wholesale, as some of that race have attempted to slaughter Chinamen, and as it has been done in detail in some districts of the Southern States. The grounds of this fear, however, have in some measure decreased since the Negro has largely disappeared from the arena of Southern politics, and has betaken himself to industrial pursuits and the acquisition of wealth and education, though even here, if over-prosperous, he is likely to excite a dangerous antagonism; for the white people do not easily tolerate the presence among them of a race more prosperous than themselves. The Negro as a poor ignorant creature does not contradict the race pride of the white race. He is more a source of amusement to that race than an object of resentment. Malignant resistance is augmented as he approaches the plane occupied by the white race, and yet I think that that resistance will gradually yield to the pressure of wealth, education, and high character.

My strongest conviction as to the future of the Negro therefore is, that he will not be expatriated nor annihilated, nor will he forever remain a separate and distinct race from the people around him, but that he will be absorbed, assimilated, and will only appear finally, as the Phoenicians now appear on the shores of the Shannon, in the features of a blended race. I cannot give at length my reasons for this conclusion, and perhaps the reader may think that the wish is father to the thought, and may in his wrath denounce my conclusion as utterly impossible. To such I would say, tarry a little, and look at the facts. Two hundred years ago there were two distinct and separate streams of human life running through this country.

They stood at opposite extremes of ethnological classification: all black on the one side, all white on the other. Now, between these two extremes, an intermediate race has arisen, which is neither white nor black, neither Caucasian nor Ethiopian, and this intermediate race is constantly increasing. I know it is said that marital alliance between these races is unnatural, abhorrent and impossible; but exclamations of this kind only shake the air. They prove nothing against a stubborn fact like that which confronts us daily and which is open to the observation of all. If this blending of the two races were impossible we should not have at least one-fourth of our colored population composed of persons of mixed blood, ranging all the way from a dark-brown color to the point where there is no visible admixture. Besides, it is obvious to common sense that there is no need of the passage of laws, or the adoption of other devices, to prevent what is in itself impossible.

Of course this result will not be reached by any hurried or forced process. It will not arise out of any theory of the wisdom of such blending of the two races. If it comes at all, it will come without shock or noise or violence of any kind, and only in the fullness of time, and it will be so adjusted to surrounding conditions as hardly to be observed. I would not be understood as advocating intermarriage between the two races. I am not a propagandist, but a prophet. I do not say that what I say *should* come to pass, but what I think is likely to come to pass, and what is inevitable. While I would not be understood as advocating the desirability of such a result, I would not be understood as deprecating it. Races and varieties of the human family appear and disappear, but humanity remains and will remain forever. The American people will one day be truer to this idea than now, and will say with Scotia's inspired son:

A man's a man for a' that.

When that day shall come, they will not pervert and sin against the verity of language as they now do by calling a man of mixed blood, a Negro; they will tell the truth. It is only prejudice against the Negro which calls everyone, however nearly connected with the white race, and however remotely connected with the Negro race, a Negro. The motive is not a desire to elevate the Negro, but to humiliate and degrade those of mixed blood; not a desire to bring the Negro up, but to cast the mulatto and the quadroon down by forcing him below an arbitrary and hated color line. Men of mixed blood in this country apply the name "Negro" to themselves, not because it is a correct ethnological description, but to seem especially devoted to the black side of their parentage. Hence in some cases they are more noisily opposed to the conclusion to which I have come, than either the white or the honestly black race. The opposition to amalgamation, of which we hear so much on the part of colored people, is for most part the merest affectation, and will never form an impassable barrier to the union of the two varieties—May 1886.

THE NATION'S PROBLEM

I congratulate you upon this the twenty-seventh anniversary of the abolition of slavery in the District of Columbia, and I gratefully acknowledge the compliment implied in calling upon me to assist in expressing the thoughts and sentiments natural to this and other similar occasions.

For reasons which will become apparent in the course of my address, I respond to your call with more than my usual diffidence.

Our cause, like many other good causes, has its ebbs and flows, successes and failures, joyous hopes and saddening fears. I cannot forget on this occasion that Lewis Hayden, a brave and wise counselor in the cause of our people, a moral hero, has just laid down his armor, filled up the measure of his days, completed his work on earth, and left a mournful void in our ranks. I am reminded, also, that John Bright, the Quaker statesman of England, the man of matchless eloquence, whose roof sheltered me when a stranger and a sojourner, and whose friendship for this republic was only equaled by his sympathy for the oppressed of all lands and nations, has passed away. The death of such a man is not a loss only to his own country and people, but to the oppressed in every quarter of the globe. We do not stand to-day where we stood one year ago, and my speech will be colored by the altered condition of our surroundings.

It has been our custom to hail the anniversary of our emancipation as a joyous event. We have observed it with every manifestation of gratitude. During the years immediately succeeding the abolition of slavery, our speeches and addresses on such occasions naturally overflowed with joy, gratitude, and praise. We remembered with veneration and love the great men by whose moral testimonies, statesmanship, and philanthrophy was brought about the long delayed and long prayed for deliverance of our people.

The great names of Garrison, Whittier, Sumner, Phillips, Stevens, Lincoln and others were gratefully and lovingly repeated. We shouted the praises of these great men as God-inspired benefactors. At that time, too, it was well enough and easy enough to blow aloud our brazen trumpets, call out the crowd, throng the streets with gay processions, and to shout aloud and make a joyful noise over the event, for since the great exodus of the Hebrews from Egyptian bondage no people had had greater cause for such joyous demonstrations. But the time for such demonstrations is now over. It is not the past but the present and the future that most concern us to-day. Our past was slavery. We cannot recur to it with any sense of complacency or composure. The history of it is a record of stripes, a revelation of agony. It is written in characters of blood. Its breath is a sigh, its voice a groan, and we turn from it with a shudder. The duty of to-day is to meet the questions that confront us with intelligence and courage.

Without the least desire to awaken undue alarm, I declare to you that, in my judgment, at no period since the abolition of slavery in the District of Columbia, have the moral, social and political surroundings of the colored people of this country been more solemn and foreboding than they are this day. If this statement is startling it is only because the facts are startling. I speak of the things I do know, and testify of the things I have seen. Nature has given me a buoyant disposition. I like to look upon the bright and hopeful side of affairs. No man can see the silver lining of a black cloud more joyfully than I. But he is a more hopeful man than I am who will tell you that the rights and liberties of the colored people in this country have passed beyond the danger line.

Mark, if you please, the fact, for it is a fact, an ominous fact, that at no time in the history of the conflict between slavery and freedom in this country has the character of the Negro as a man been made the subject of a fiercer and more serious discussion in all the avenues of debate than during the past and present year. Against him have been marshalled the whole artillery of science, philosophy, and history. We are not only confronted by open foes, but we are assailed in the guise of sympathy and friendship and presented as objects of pity.

The strong point made against him and his cause is the statement, widely circulated and greatly relied upon, that no two people so different in race and color can live together in the same country on a level of equal, civil and political rights and powers; that nature herself has ordained that the relations of two such races must be that of domination on the one hand and subjugation on the other. This old slaveholding Calhoun and McDuffy doctrine, which we long ago thought dead and buried, is revived in unexpected quarters, and confronts us to-day as sternly and bitterly as it did forty years ago. Then it was employed as the sure defence of slavery. Now it is employed as a justification of the fraud and violence by which colored men are divested of their citizenship, and robbed of their constitutional rights in the solid South.

To those who are hopefully assuming that there is no cause of apprehension, that we are secure in the possession of all that has been gained by the war and by reconstruction I ask: What means this universal and palpable concern manifested through all the avenues of public sentiment as to the future of the Negro in this country? For this question meets us now at every turn. Letters fairly pour upon me burdened with this inquiry. Whence this solicitude, or apparent solicitude? To me the matter was a sinister meaning. It is prompted not so much by concern for the welfare of the Negro as by consideration of how his relation to the American government may ultimately affect the welfare and happiness of the American people. The Negro is now a member of the body politic. This talk about him implies that he is regarded as a diseased member. It is wisely said by physicians that any member of the human body is in a healthy condition when it gives no occasion to think of it. The fact that the American people of the Caucasian race are continually thinking of the Negro, and never cease to call attention to him, shows that his relation to them is felt to be abnormal and unhealthy.

I want the colored people of this country to understand the true character of the great race which rules, and must rule and determine the destiny of this republic. Justice and magnanimity are elements of American character. They may do much for us. But we are in no condition to depend upon these qualities exclusively. Depend upon it, whenever the American people shall become convinced that they have gone too far in recognizing the rights of the Negro, they will find some way to abridge those rights. The Negro is great, but the welfare of the nation will be considered greater. They will forget the Negro's service in the late war. They may forget his loyalty to the republic. They may forget the enmity of the old slaveholding class to the government. They may forget their solemn obligations of friendship to the Negro, and press to their bosoms the white enemies of the nation, while they give the cold shoulder to the black friends of the nation. Be not deceived. History repeats itself. The black man fought for American independence. The Negro's blood mingled with the white man's blood at Bunker Hill, and in State Street, Boston. But this sacrifice on his part won for him only temporary applause. He was returned to his former condition. He fought bravely under Gen. Jackson at New Orleans, but his reward was only slavery and chains. These facts speak, trumpet-tongued, of the kind of people with whom we have to deal, and through them we may contemplate the sternest possibilities of the future.

I have said that at no time has the character of the Negro been so generally, seriously and unfavorably discussed as now. I do not regard discussion as an evil in itself. On the contrary I regard it not as an enemy, but as a friend. It has served us well at other times in our history, and I hope it may serve us well hereafter. Controversy, whether of words or blows, whether in the forum or on the battle field, may help us, if we but make the right use of it. We are not, however, to be like dumb driven cattle in this discussion, in this war of words and conflicting theories. Our business is to answer back wisely, modestly, and yet grandly.

While I do not regard discussion as an enemy in itself, I cannot but deem it in this instance as out of place and unfortunate. It comes to us as a surprise and a bitter disappointment. It implies a deplorable unrest and unsoundness in the public mind. It shows that the reconstruction of our national institutions upon a basis of liberty, justice and equality is not yet honestly accepted as a final and irrevocable settlement of the Negro's relation to the government, and of his membership in the body politic. There seems to be in it a lurking disposition, a looking around for some plausible excuse for dispossessing the Negro of some part of his inheritance conceded to him in the generous spirit of the new departure of our government. We seem to be trying how not to do it.

Going back to the early days of the anti-slavery movement, I cannot but remark, and I call upon you to remark, the striking contrast between the disposition which then existed to utterly ignore the Negro and the present disposition to make him a topic of universal interest and deepest concern. When the Negro was a slave and stood outside the government, nobody but a few so-called abolition fanatics thought him worthy of the smallest attention. He was almost as completely outside of the nation's thought as he was outside of the nation's law and the nation's religion. But now all is changed. His freedom makes him discussed on every hand. The platform, the pulpit, the press and the legislative hall regard him and struggle with him as a great and difficult problem, one that requires almost divine wisdom to solve. Men are praying over it. It is always a dangerous symptom when men pray to know what is their duty.

Now it is to this gigantic representation to which I object. I deny that the Negro is correctly represented by it. The statement of it is a prejudice to the Negro's cause. It denotes the presence of the death-dealing shadow of an ancient curse. We had fondly hoped, and had reason to hope, that when the Negro ceased to be a slave, when he ceased to be a thing and became a man, when he ceased to be an alien and became a citizen, when the constitution of the United States ceased to be the charter of slavery and became the charter of liberty, the Negro problem was solved and settled forever. The whole contention now raised over him is an anachronism, a misnomer, a false pretense, a delusion and a sham, a crafty substitution of a false issue for the true one.

I deny and utterly scout the idea that there is now, properly speaking, any such thing as a Negro problem now before the American people. It is not the Negro, educated or illiterate, intelligent or ignorant, who is on trial or whose qualities are giving trouble to the nation. The real problem lies in the other direction. It is not so much what the Negro is, what he has been, or what he may be that constitutes the problem. Here, as elsewhere, the lesser is included in the greater. The Negro's significance is dwarfed by a factor vastly larger than himself. The real question, the all-commanding question, is whether American justice, American liberty, American civilization, American law and American Christianity can be made to include and protect alike and forever all American citizens in the rights which, in a generous moment in the nation's life, have been guaranteed to them by the organic and fundamental law of the land. It is whether this great nation shall conquer its prejudices, rise to the dignity of its professions, and proceed in the sublime course of truth and liberty marked out for itself since the late war, or shall swing back to its ancient moorings of slavery and barbarism. The Negro is of inferior activity and power in the solution of this problem. He is the clay, the nation is the potter. He is the subject, the nation is the sovereign. It is not what he shall be or do, but what the nation shall be and do, which is to solve this great national problem.

Speaking for him, I can commend him upon every ground. He is loyal and patriotic; service is the badge of all his tribe. He has proved it before, and will prove it again. The country has never called upon him in vain. What he has been in the past in this respect that he will be in the future. All he asks now, all he has ever asked, all he will ever ask, is that the nation shall fulfill toward him its own recognized and self-imposed obligations. When he asks for bread he will not accept a stone. When he asks for fish he will not accept a serpent. His protest now is against being cheated by cunningly-devised judicial decisions, by frauds upon the ballot box, or by brutal violence of red-shirted rebels. He only asks the American people to adjust the practice to the justice and wisdom of their laws, and he holds that this is first, midst, and last, and the only problem to be solved.

While, however, the Negro may very properly protest against the popular statement of the question, and while he may insist that the one just stated is the proper one, and the only one; while he may hold that primarily and fundamentally it is an American problem and not a Negro problem, he may materially assist in its solution. He can assume an attitude, develop a character, improve his condition, and, in a measure, compel the respect and esteem of his fellow-men.

In order to do this we have, first of all, to learn and to understand thoroughly the nature of the social, moral, and political forces that surround us, and how to shape our ends and wisely determine our destiny. We should endeavor to discover the true sources of our danger—whether they be within ourselves or in circumstances external to ourselves. If I am here for any useful purpose, it is in some measure to answer the question, "What of the night?"

For the present I have seemed to forget that this is an occasion of joy. I have thus far spoken mainly in sorrow rather than in gladness; in grief rather than in gratitude. Like the resolution of Hamlet, my outlook has been sicklied o'er with the pale cast of thought. I must go on in the same line.

Now, what of the night? What of the night? Is it cheered by the beams of celestial light and hope, or is it saddened by ominous clouds, darkness and distant thunder? The latter, and not the former, is the true answer. You and I should be brave enough to look the facts fairly and firmly in the face.

I profoundly wish I could make a different response to this inquiry. But the omens are against me. I am compelled to say that while we have no longer to contend with the physical wrongs and abominations of slavery; while we have no longer to chill the blood of our hearers by talking of whips, chains, branding irons and blood-hounds; we have, as already intimated, to contend with a foe, which, though less palpable, is still a fierce and formidable foe. It is the ghost of a by-gone, dead and buried institution. It loads the very air with a malignant prejudice of race. It has poisoned the fountains of justice, and defiled the altars of religion. It acts upon the body politic as the leprous distillment acted upon the blood and body of the murdered king of Denmark. In ante-bellum times it was the standing defense of slavery. In our own times it is employed in defense of oppression and proscription. Until this foe is conquered and driven from the breasts of the American people, our relations will be unhappy, our progress slow, our lives embittered, our freedom a mockery, and our citizenship a delusion.

The work before us is to meet and combat this prejudice by lives and acquirements which contradict and put to shame this narrow and malignant feeling. We have errors of our own to abandon, habits to reform, manners to improve, ignorance to dispel, and character to build up. This is something which no power on earth can do for us, and which no power on earth can prevent our doing for ourselves, if we will.

In pointing out errors and mistakes common among ourselves, I shall run the risk of incurring displeasure; for no people with whom I am acquainted are less tolerant of criticism than ourselves, especially from one of our own number. We have been so long in the habit of tracing our failures and misfortunes to the views and acts of others that we seem, in some measure, to have lost the talent and disposition of seeing our own faults, or of "seeing ourselves as others see us." And yet no man can do a better service to another man than to correct his mistakes, point out his hurtful errors, show him the path of truth, duty and safety.

One of the few errors to which we are clinging most persistently and, as I think, most mischievously has come into great prominence of late. It is the cultivation and stimulation amongst us of a sentiment which we are pleased to call race pride. I find it in all our books, papers and speeches. For my part I see no superiority or inferiority in race or color. Neither the one nor the other is a proper source of pride or complacency. Our race and color are not of our own choosing. We have no volition in the case one way or another. The only excuse for pride in individuals or races is in the fact of their own achievements. Our color is the gift of the Almighty. We should neither be proud of it nor ashamed of it. But we may well enough be proud or ashamed when we have ourselves achieved success or have, by our faults, failed of success. If the sun has curled our hair and tanned our skin let the sun be proud of its achievement, for we have done nothing for it one way or the other. I see no benefit to be derived from this everlasting exhortation by speakers and writers among us to the cultivation of race pride. On the contrary, I see in it a positive evil. It is building on a false foundation. Besides, what is the thing we are fighting against, and what are we fighting for in this country? What is the mountain devil, the lion in the way of our progress? What is it, but American race pride; an assumption of superiority upon the ground of race and color? Do we not know that every argument we make, and every pretension we set up in favor of race pride is giving the enemy a stick to break our own heads?

But it may be said that we shall put down race pride in the white people by cultivating race pride among ourselves. The answers to this is that the devils are not cast out by Beelzebub, the prince of devils. The poorest and meanest white man, drunk or sober, when he has nothing else to commend him, says: "I am a white man, I am." We can all see the low extremity reached by that sort of race pride, and yet we encourage it when we pride ourselves upon the fact of our color. I heard a Negro say: "I am a Negro, I am." Let us away with this supercilious nonsense. If we are proud let it be because we have had some agency in producing that of which we can properly be proud. Do not let us be proud of what we can neither help nor hinder. The Bible puts us in the condition in this respect of the leopard, and says that we can no more change our skin than the leopard his spots. If we are unfortunate in being placed among a people with which our color is a badge of inferiority, there is no need of our making ourselves ridiculous by forever, in words, affecting to be proud of a circumstance due to no virtue in us, and over which we have no control.

You will, perhaps, think this criticism uncalled for. My answer is that truth is never uncalled for. Right thinking is essential to right acting, and I hope that we shall hereafter see the wisdom of basing our pride and complacency upon substantial results accomplished by the race.

The question here raised is not merely theoretical, but is of practical significance. In some of our colored public journals, with a view to crippling my humble influence with the colored race, I have seen myself charged with a lack of race pride. I am not ashamed of that charge. I have no apology or vindication to offer. If fifty years of uncompromising devotion to the cause of the colored man in this country does not vindicate me, I am content to live without vindication.

While I have no more reason to be proud of one race than another, I dare say, and I fear no contradiction, that there is no other man in the United States prouder than myself of any great achievement, mental or mechanical, of which any colored man or woman is the author. This is not because I am a colored man, but because I am a man, and because color is a misfortune, and is treated as a crime by the American people. My sentiments at this point originate not in my color, but in a sense of justice common to all right-minded men. It is not because I am a Negro, but because I am a man. It is that which gives the sympathy of the crowd to the underdog, no matter what may be his color. When a colored man is charged with a want of race pride, he may well ask, What race? for a large percentage of the colored race are related in some degree to more than one race. But the whole assumption of race pride is ridiculous. Let us have done with complexional superiorities or inferiorities, complexional pride or shame. I want no better basis for my activities and affinities than the broad foundation laid by the Bible itself, that "God has made of one blood all nations of men to dwell on all the face of the earth." This comprehends the Fatherhood of God and the brotherhood of man.

I have another criticism to make of a position which, I think, often invites unfavorable comparison and positive disparagement. It is our noisy assertion of equality with the Caucasian race. There are two kinds of equality, one potential and the other actual, one theoretical and the other practical. We should not be satisfied by merely quoting the doctrine of potential equality as laid down in the Declaration of Independence, but we should give it practical illustration. We have to do as well as to be. If we had built great ships, sailed around the world, taught the science of navigation, discovered far-off islands, capes, and continents, enlarged the boundaries of human knowledge, improved the conditions of man's existence, brought valuable contributions to art, science and literature, revealed great truths, organized great States, administered great governments, defined the laws of the universe, formulated systems of mental and moral philosophy, invented railroads, steam engines, mowing machines, sewing machines, taught the sun to take pictures, the lightning to carry messages, we then might claim, not only potential and theoretical equality, but actual and practical equality. Nothing is gained to our cause by claiming for ourselves more than of right we can establish belongs to us. Manly self-assertion, I know, is a power, and I would have that power employed within the bounds of truth and sobriety. We should never forget, in our relations with our fellows, that modesty is also a power.

When it is manifested without any touch of servility it is as sure to win respect as unfounded pretension is sure to provoke and receive contempt. We should give our critics no advantage at this point, either by word or by conduct. Our battle with popular prejudice requires on our part the utmost circumspection in word and in deed. Our men should be gentlemen and our women ladies, and we can be neither without a modest reserve in mind and in manners.

Were I not speaking to the most cultivated class of our people, for the Bethel Literary Society comprises that class, I might hesitate to employ this course of remark. You, I am quite sure, will not misapprehend my statements or my motives.

There is one other point worthy of animadversion—it is the error that union among ourselves is an essential element of success in our relations to the white race. This, in my judgment, is a very serious mistake. I can hardly point out one more pregnant with peril. It is contended that we are now eight millions; that we hold the balance of power between the two great political parties of the country, and that, if we were only united in one body, under wise and powerful leaders, we could shape the policy of both political parties, make and unmake parties, control the destiny of the republic, and secure for ourselves a desirable and happy future. They say that in union there is strength; that united we stand and divided we fall, and much else of the same sort.

My position is the reverse of all this. I hold that our union is our weakness. In quoting these wise sayings, colored men seem to forget that there are exceptions to all general rules, and that our position in this country is an exceptional position.

The rule for us is the exception. There are times and places when separation and division are better than union, when to stand apart is wiser than standing together. There are buildings which will hold a few, but which will break down under the weight of a crowd; the ice of the river may be strong enough to bear a man, but would break through under the weight of an elephant. The ice under us in this country is very thin, and is made very weak by the warm fogs of prejudice. A few colored people scattered among large white communities are easily accepted by such communities, and a larger measure of liberty is accorded to the few than would be to the many. The trouble is that when we assemble in great numbers anywhere we are apt to form communities by ourselves, and our occupation of any part of a town or city, apart from the people surrounding us, brings us into separate schools, separate churches, separate benevolent and literary societies, and the result is the adoption of a scale of manners, morals and customs peculiar to our condition and to our antecedents as an oppressed people. When we thus isolate ourselves we say to those around us: "We have nothing in common with you," and, very naturally, the reply of our neighbors is in the same tone and to the same effect; for when a people care for nobody, nobody will care for them. When we isolate ourselves we lose, in a large measure, the common benefit of association with those whose advantages have been superior to ours.

The foundation upon which we stand in this country is not strong enough to make it safe to stand together. A nation within a nation is an anomaly. There can be but one American nation under the American government, and we are Americans. The constitution of the country makes us such, and our lines of activity should accord with our citizenship. Circumstances now compel us in certain directions to maintain separate neighborhoods and separate institutions. But these circumstances should only be yielded to when they are irresistible. A Negro neighborhood depreciates the market value of property. We should distribute ourselves among the people, build our houses where if they take fire other houses will be in danger. Common dangers will create common safeguards.

Our policy should be to unite with the great mass of the American people in all their activities, and resolve to fall or flourish with our common country. We cannot afford to draw the color line in politics, trade, education, manners, religion, fashion, or civilization. Especially, we cannot afford to draw the color line in politics. No folly could be greater. A party acting upon that basis would be not merely a misfortune but a dire calamity to our people. The rule of the majority is the fundamental principle of the American government, and it may be safely affirmed that the American people will never permit, tolerate, or submit to the success of any political device or strategy calculated to circumvent and defeat the just application and operation of this fundamental principle of our government.

It is also fair to state that no part of the American people—Irish, Scotch, Italian, or German—could attempt any such political jugglery with less success than ourselves.

Another popular error flaunted in our faces at every turn, and for most part by very weak and impracticable editors, is the alleged duty of colored men to patronize colored newspapers, and this simply because they happen to be edited and published by colored men, and not because of their intrinsic value. Anybody that can find means to issue a paper with a patent back and hang out a colored flag at the head of its columns, demands support on the ground that it is a colored newspaper. For one, I am not disposed to yield to this demand. A colored newspaper maker has no higher claim upon us for patronage than a colored carpenter, a colored shoemaker, or a colored bricklayer. Whether he should be supported should depend upon the character of the man and the quality of his work. Our people should not be required to buy an inferior article offered by a colored man, when for the same money they can purchase a superior article from a white man. We need, and ought to have, the best supply of mental food that the American market affords.

In saying this I do not forget that an able, sound and decent journal, conducted in a spirit of justice and not made a vehicle of malice or personal favoritism, edited and published by colored men is a powerful lever for the elevation and advancement of the colored race. Such a paper has special claims upon all who desire to raise colored people in the estimation of themselves and their surroundings. But while this is true, it is also true that in the same proportion that an able and influential public journal tends to remove popular prejudice and elevate us in the judgment of those whose good opinion is worth having, a feeble, ungrammatical, indecent and wretchedly conducted public journal tends to lower us in the opinion of good men, besides has a debasing influence upon the minds of its readers. Character and quality should rule here as well as elsewhere.

But I leave this aspect of our relations and duties to make a few remarks upon the changed political condition of our country since we last met.

Four years ago we assembled to celebrate the abolition of slavery in the District of Columbia, under a dark and portentous cloud.

The honorable Grover Cleveland, the approved leader and representative of the Democratic party, had, only a few weeks before, been duly inaugurated President of the United States. The fact of his election had carried alarm and consternation into every black man's cabin in the southern States. For the moment it must have seemed to them that the sun of freedom had gone down, and the night of slavery had succeeded. The terror was dismal and heartbreaking enough, and although it turned out to be groundless, it was not altogether unnatural. The Democratic party had, in its day, done much well calculated to create a dread of its return to power.

In the old time it was the ever-faithful ally of the slaveholders, and the inflexible defender of slavery. In the new time, it has been distinguished as the party of the shot-gun, the cart-whip, and the solid South.

While Mr. Cleveland's election brought dreadful forebodings to the cabins of the South, it brought pleasing anticipations to the mansions of the South. The joy of the oppressor was the sorrow of the oppressed. It required very positive assurances from President Cleveland and his friends to allay the apprehensions of the freedmen. The impression made by the election of Gen. Harrison was in striking contrast. It had precisely the opposite effect to that of Mr. Cleveland. The alarm was transferred from the cabin to the mansion—from the former slave to the former master. In the freedmen's breasts confidence took the place of doubt, hope the place of fear, and a sense of relief the place of anxiety. Without the utterance of a single word, without the performance of a single act, the simple fact of the election of a Republican President carried with it the assurance of protection from the power of the oppressor. No higher eulogium could be bestowed upon the Republican party than this faith in its justice and beneficence, by the simple, uneducated and oppressed laborers of the South. Great, too, will be the sorrow and disappointment if some measure shall not be devised under this Republican administration to arrest the arm of lawless violence and prove to these simple people that there is a difference between the Republican party and the Democratic party.

Some of you may remember that in my celebration address four years ago I took occasion to express my satisfaction with the inaugural utterances of Hon. Grover Cleveland, and, although I have been much criticised for what I then said, I have no word of that commendation to retract or qualify. I thought well of Mr. Cleveland's words then and I think well of them now. What I said was this, "No better words have dropped from the east portico of the Capitol since the days of Abraham Lincoln and Ulyssess S. Grant." I did not say, as some of my lying critics found it necessary to allege, that Mr. Cleveland had uttered better words than either Lincoln or Grant. You will also remember that, while I commended the language of Mr. Cleveland, I strongly doubted his ability to live up to the sentiments he then and there expressed, and that doubt has been fully and sadly justified. During all the four years of his administration, after having solemnly sworn to support and enforce the constitution of the United States, he said no word and did no act, expressed no desire to arrest the hand of violence, to stay the effusion of innocent blood, or vindicate in any manner the Negro's constitutional right to vote. He could almost hazard a war with England to protect our fishermen; he could send two ships of war to Hayti to protect an American filibuster, but not one word or blow to protect colored citizens against Southern assassins and murderers.

While I commended the words of Mr. Cleveland, I knew the party and not Mr. Cleveland would determine the character of his administration.

Well, now the American people have returned the Republican party to power, and the question is, what will it do? It has a great prestige, a glorious record. It is the party that carried on the war against treason and rebellion. It is the party that saved the Union, abolished slavery, amended the constitution, made the colored man a soldier, a citizen, and a legal voter. In view of this splendid record there ought to be no doubt or fear as to the course of the present administration. But past experience make us thoughtful. For a dozen years or more the Republican party has seemed in a measure paralyzed in the presence of high-handed fraud and brutal violence toward its newly-made citizens. The question now is, will it regain its former health, activity and power? Will it be as true to its friends in the South as the Democratic party has been to its friends in that section, or will it sacrifice its friends to conciliate its enemies? I have seen this last alternative suggested as the possible outcome of this administration, but I stamp with unmitigated scorn and contempt all such intimations. I know Gen. Harrison, and I believe in Gen. Harrison. I know his Cabinet and believe in its members, and no power can make me believe that this administration will not step to the verge of its constitutional power to protect the rights guaranteed by the Constitution. Not only the Negro, but all honest men, north and south, must hold the Republican party in contempt if it fails to do its whole duty at this point. The Republican party has made the colored man free and the Republican party must make him secure in his freedom, or abandon its pretensions.

As a matter of fact the South has always been able to outwit the North in politics. It cannot be denied that it is now resorting to its old tactics. It is endeavoring to compromise and destroy our Republican President as it has before compromised and destroyed other great northern statesmen. Its plan is modeled after that of Satan's. It takes men up into a high mountain and makes the most extravagant promises to them, but never fulfills one of them. It took Daniel Webster up on high and promised him the Presidency on condition that he would support the Fugitive Slave Bill. He yielded and the fiend grinned with delight at his fall. It took Stephen A. Douglas by the hand and showed him the Missouri Compromise and said it would make him President if he would blot out that line. He stooped to the infamy and was cheated of his reward. It took Horace Greeley, one of the best of men, held up before him the bauble of the Presidency, told him that the South had repented, and deceived the good old man. As soon as it thought that President Hayes was elected it overwhelmed him with letters assuring him that his political fortune would be made by a conciliatory policy. It further assured him that unaccounted thousands were ready to break away from the Democratic party if he would only take a rebel into his cabinet, withdraw the army, and let the South manage its own affairs. He listened and was lost. He trusted to what is called Southern honor and was deceived. The South is playing the same game to-day, and it remains to be seen what the result will be. I am cultivating that charity that hopeth all things.

It was once said by Abraham Lincoln that this republic could not long endure half slave and half free, and the same may be said with even more truth of the black citizens of this country. They cannot remain half slave and half free. They must be one thing or the other.

And this brings me to consider the alternative now presented between slavery and freedom in this country. From my outlook I am free to affirm that I see nothing for the Negro of the South but a condition of absolute freedom or of absolute slavery. I see no half-way place for him. One or the other of these conditions is to solve the so-called Negro problem. There are forces at work in each of these directions, and for the present, that which aims at the re-enslavement of the Negro seems to have the advantage. Let it be remembered that the labor of the Negro is his only capital. Take this from him and he dies from starvation. The present mode of obtaining his labor in the South gives the old master-class a complete mastery over him. I showed this in my last annual celebration address, and I need not go into it here. The payment of the Negro by orders on stores, where the storekeeper controls price, quality and quantity, and is subject to no competition, so that the Negro must buy there and nowhere else—an arrangement by which the Negro never has a dollar to lay by, and can be kept in debt to his employer year in and year out, puts him completely at the mercy of the old master-class. He who could say to the Negro, when a slave, you shall work for me or be whipped to death, can now say to him with equal emphasis, you shall work for me or I will starve you to death. This the plain, matter-of-fact and unexaggerated condition of the plantation Negro in the Southern States to-day.

Do you ask me why the Negro does not emigrate? Why he does not seek a home where he would fare better? I will tell you. He has not a cent of money to emigrate with, and if he had, and desired to exercise that right, he would be arrested for debt, for non-fulfillment of contract, or be shot down like a dog in his tracks. When Southern Senators tell you that they want to be rid of the Negro, and would be glad to have them all clear out, you know and I know and they know that they are speaking falsely, and simply with a view to mislead the North. Only a few days ago armed resistance was made in North Carolina to colored emigration from that State, and the first exodus to Kansas was arrested by the old master-class with shotguns and Winchester rifles. The desire to get rid of the Negro is a hollow sham. His labor is wanted to-day in the South just as it was wanted in the old times when he was hunted by two-legged and four-legged blood-hounds.

Now, when a man is in one place and held there by the force of many or few, and cannot get out of it, he is not far from a condition of slavery. But these old slave-holders have their allies, and one is strong drink.

Whisky makes the Negro drunk, and drunkenness makes him a criminal as well as a pauper, and when he is made both a pauper and criminal the law steps in for satisfaction. It does not send him to prison to work for the State, but, as in the old times, puts him on the auction block and sells him to the highest bidder to work for a planter, where all the manhood he ever had is worked or whipped out of him. What is all this but slavery in another form?

I know that it will be said that I am here exaggerating the danger that impends over the Negro. It will be said that slavery can never exist by law in the South, and that without legislation slavery cannot be revived in the South. This is a stupendous error.

My answer to this argument is, that slavery can as really exist without law as with it, and in some instances more securely, because less likely to be interfered with in the absence of law than in its presence. No man can point to any law in the United States by which slavery was originally established. The fact of slavery always precedes enactments making it legal. Men first make slaves and then make laws affirming the right of slavery.

What they have done in the past they may also do in the future. We must not forget that there is nothing in Southern morals, manners, or religion, against the re-establishment of slavery. A genuine Southern man looks at a Negro simply as an article of property, capable of being exchanged for rice, cotton, sugar and tobacco.

Now, with such a conscience, armed with whisky, armed with ignorance, and the payment of labor with orders on stores, the old master class has the landless colored laborer literally by the throat, and is naturally dragging him back to the house of bondage.

Another and still more important step already taken in the direction of slavery is the precaution to deprive the Negro of all means of defense and protection. In the exercise of their power, acquired by long mastery over the Negro, they have forced him to surrender all arms and ammunition found in his log cabin. No lamb was ever more completely within the power of the wolf than the plantation Negro of to-day is within the hands of the old master class. The old masters know it, and the Negroes know it, and the fact makes the one haughty, domineering and defiant, and the other spiritless, servile and submissive. One is armed and the other defenseless. It is nothing against the courage of the Negro that he does not fight his way to the ballot box, instead of waiting for the government to protect him, as it is its duty to do, for even a brave man, unarmed, will stand and deliver at the mouth of a Winchester rifle or the blade of a Bowie-knife. To the mass of mankind life is more than liberty, for with it there ever remains the hope of liberty.

Now, when you remember that the Negro is taught to believe that the government may be against him; when it is remembered that he is denied the power to keep and bear arms; that he has not recovered from his enforced ignorance of two hundred years; that no adequate means of education has been provided for him; that his vote avails him nothing; that emigration is impossible; that there is neither religion nor conscience in the South to take his part; that he, of all men, is easiest convicted of crime; that he does not see or receive a dollar in payment of wages; that, labor as he will, he is brought in debt to the landed proprietor at the end of the year; that he can lay up nothing for a rainy day; that by the opinion of the Supreme Court of the United States the Fourteenth Amendment affords him no protection against individuals of the State—I say, when you remember all this, you may realize something of the perilous condition of the Negro citizens of the South.

Then, again, the fate of John M. Clayton and of Mr. Phillips, of Arkansas, one of them shot down while peaceably seeking the proofs of his election to Congress, brutally assassinated, and the other kicked and shot to death in open daylight, and neither the murderers in the one case nor the assassinators in the other have been made to answer for their crimes, admonish us that neither the Negro nor the friends of the Negro have yet any standing before the law or in the public opinion of the old slave States.

Now I point to these facts tending toward the re-establishment of Negro slavery in the South, not because I believe slavery will finally be established there, but because they are features of the situation and should be exposed in order that the end at which they aim may not be realized—forewarned, forearmed, the price of liberty is eternal vigilance. I bring this aspect before you upon the principle that an illustrious lawyer adopted, namely, always to try a cause first against his client.

It is easy to indulge in the illusions of hope and to rejoice over what we have gained, and it is always more or less painful to contemplate the possibility of misfortune and disaster. But a brave man will not shrink from looking truth squarely in the face, no matter what may be the consequences, and you and I, and all of us, know that if slavery is not re-established in the Southern States, it will not be because there is any power inside those States, at present, to prevent this practice and return to barbarism.

From every view I have been able to take of the present situation in relation to the colored people of the United States I am forced to the conclusion that the irrepressible conflict of which we heard so much before the war of the rebellion and during the war, and which we supposed was ended by the war, is still in progress. It is still the battle between two opposite civilizations—the one created and sustained by slavery, and the other framed and fashioned in the spirit of liberty and humanity, and this conflict will not be ended until one or the other shall be completely adopted in every section of our common country.

The South is still the South, and under the doctrine of local self-government it shelters the vicious idea that it can defy the Constitution and the Laws of the United States, especially those laws which respect the enfranchisement of colored citizens. This idea of self-government destroyed the Freedman's bureau, drove United States soliders out of the South, expelled Northern immigrants, excluded Negro citizens from State Legislatures, and gave all power to the Southern slave-masters. Such is the situation to-day, and it remains to be seen whether it is to be permanent or transient. In my opinion this state of things cannot be permanent.

While revolutions may for a time seem to roll backwards; while reactionary tendencies and forces may arrest the wheels of progress, and while the colored man of the South may still have to suffer the lash and sting of a by-gone condition, there are forces and influences silently and yet powerfully working out his deliverance. The individual Southern States are great, but the nation is greater. Justice, honor, liberty and fidelity to the Constitution and Laws may seem to sleep, but they are not dead. They are alive and had much more to do with bringing our Republican President into the Presidential chair than is sometimes supposed. The red-shirted rifle companies of Carolina and Mississippi may rule for a time, but only for a time. They may rob the Negro of his vote to-day, but the Negro will have his vote to-morrow. The spirit of the age is with him. Slavery is vanishing from even the darkest corners of the earth. The schoolmaster is abroad—even in the South. The Negro of the plantation may be ignorant, but the Negro of the town and the city will be intelligent. The light of education which has illuminated the one will, in time, illuminate the other.

But there is another force to be relied upon. It is the fact that the representatives of the best civilization of our times are compelled, in self-defense, to extirpate the illegal, unconstitutional barbarism of the late slave-holding States.

There is yet good reason to believe in the virtue of the loyal American people. They hate fraud, loathe rapine, and despise meanness. It was no reckless freak or madness that made them pour out their blood and their treasure in the late war, and there was a deep moral and patriotic purpose at the bottom of that sacrifice; a purpose that is not extinct, and will not be easily abandoned. If the Republican party shall fail to carry out this purpose, God will raise up another party which will be faithful. They resented secession and fought to make a free, strong and united nation. It was the aim of good men then, and it is the aim of good men now, and the effort to gain it will continue till that end shall be obtained. They may be patient and long-suffering. They have been patient and long-suffering. But patience itself will cease to be a virtue.

Do you ask me what can be done? I answer, we can at least purify the ballot box by requiring that no man shall hold a seat in Congress who reaches it by fraud, violence and intimidation; by requiring that every man from the South and from the North and from everywhere else shall come into that body by means uncorrupted by fraud and unstained by blood. They will yet see to it that murder and assassination shall not be the passport to a seat in the councils of the nation. There is to-day a man in that body who holds his place because assassination has stepped between him and an honest contestant. White men may make light of the murder of a score of Negroes, they may shut their eyes and ridicule all enunciations of murder, when committed against defenseless Negroes, but they will not always be deaf to the white man's blood when it cries from the ground for vengeance. The advantage of the black man's cause is that the white man cannot help himself without helping him. Law and order for the one will ultimately be law and order for the other.

There is still another ground of hope for the freedom of the southern States. It is that the good citizens of these States cannot afford, and will not consent always, to lag far behind the old free States in all the elements of civilization. They want population, capital, invention and enterprise. They have rich resources to be developed, and they want both men and money to develop them and enhance their prosperity. The wise and loyal people in these States know very well that they can never be prosperous; that they can never have their share of immigration, from at home or abroad, while they are known and distinguished for intolerance, fraud, violence and Lynch law. They know that while this character attaches to them capital will hold aloof from them, and population will shun them as it would shun a land blasted by pestilence and death. They know that their rich mines and fertile soil will fail to attract immigrants from any country unblasted by slavery. They know that industrious and enterprising men, searching for homes, will turn their backs upon the South and make their way to the West and North, where they can hold and express their opinions without fear of the Bowie-knife and shot-gun of the assassin.

Thus the self-interest of the people of these States will yet teach them justice, humanity and civilization. For the present, the better element at the South is terror-stricken and silent, but encouraged by the trend of the nation to higher and better conditions of existence, it will not always remain dumb and inactive, but will assert itself as Missouri is already doing, and as Arkansas will yet do. I was in this latter State only a few days after the assassination of John M. Clayton. I saw the wholesome horror manifested by the intelligent and worthy citizens of that State, at this dastardly political murder. They were anxious for the good name of Arkansas, and asked me how the good people of the North would regard them. I had to tell them, in sadness, that the outside world would look at them through the warm red blood of John M. Clayton, and the State of Arkansas would be held rigidly responsible till the arrest, trial, conviction and punishment of the assassin and his instigators.

In conclusion, while I have plainly portrayed the sources of danger to our people, while I have described the reactionary forces with which we have to contend, I have no fears as to the character of the final result. The American people are governed, not only by laws and selfish interests, but by large ideas of moral and material civilization.

The spirit of justice, liberty and fair play is abroad in the land; it is in the air. It animates men of all stations, of all professions and callings, and can neither be silenced nor extirpated. It has an agent in every bar of railroad iron, a servant in every electric wire, a missionary in every traveler. It not only tunnels the mountains, fills up the valleys, and sheds upon us the light of science, but it will ultimately destroy the unnumbered wrongs inherited by both races from the system of slavery and barbarism. In this direction is the trend of the nation. States may lag, parties may hesitate, leaders may halt, but to this complexion it must come at last. States, parties and leaders must and will, in the end, adjust themselves to this overwhelming and irresistible tendency. It will make parties and unmake parties, will make rulers and unmake rulers, until it shall become the fixed, universal and irreversible law of the land. For fifty years it has made progress against all contradictions. It stemmed the current of opposition in Church and State. It has removed many proscriptions. It has opened the gates of knowledge. It has abolished slavery. It has saved the Union. It has reconstructed the Government upon a basis of justice and liberty, and it will see to it that the last vestige of fraud and violence on the ballot box shall disappear, and there shall be one country, one law, one liberty for all the people of the United States—April 16, 1889.

THE FOLLY OF COLONIZATION

But I now come to another proposition, held up as a solution of the race problem, and this I consider equally unworthy with the one just disposed of. The two belong to the same low-bred family of ideas.

It is the proposition to colonize the coloured people of America in Africa, or somewhere else. Happily this scheme will be defeated, both by its impolicy and its impracticability. It is all nonsense to talk about the removal of eight millions of the American people from their homes in America to Africa. The expense and hardships, to say nothing of the cruelty attending such a measure, would make success impossible. The American people are wicked, but they are not fools; they will hardly be disposed to incur the expense, to say nothing of the injustice which this measure demands. Nevertheless, this colonizing scheme, unworthy as it is of American statesmanship, and American honour, and though full of mischief to the coloured people, seems to have a strong hold on the public mind, and at times has shown much life and vigor.

The bad thing about it is, that it has, of late, owing to persecution, begun to be advocated by coloured men of acknowledged ability and

learning, and every little while some white statesman becomes its advocate. Those gentlemen will doubtless have their opinion of me; I certainly
have mine of them. My opinion is, that if they are sensible, they are insin-
cere; and if they are sincere, they are not sensible. They know, or they
ought to know that it would take more money than the cost of the late
war, to transport even one half of the coloured people of the United States
to Africa. Whether intentionally or not, they are, as I think, simply trifling
with an afflicted people. They urge them to look for relief where they
ought to know that relief is impossible. The only excuse they can make for
the measure is that there is no hope for the Negro here, and that the
coloured people in America owe something to Africa.

This last sentimental idea makes colonization very fascinating to the
dreamers of both colours. But there is really no foundation for it.

They tell us that we owe something to our native land. This sounds
well. But when the fact is brought to view, which should never be forgotten, that a man can only have one native land and that is the land in
which he is born, the bottom falls entirely out of this sentimental argument.

Africa, according to her colonization advocates, is by no means modest
in her demands upon us. She calls upon us to send her only our best men.
She does not want our riff-raff, but our best men. But these are just the men
who are valuable and who are wanted at home. It is true that we have a
few preachers and laymen with a missionary turn of mind whom we
might easily spare. Some who would possibly do as much good by going
there as by staying here. By this is not the colonization idea. Its advocates
want not only the best, but millions of the best. Better still, they want the
United States Government to vote the money to send them there. They do
not seem to see that if the Government votes money to send the Negro to
Africa, that the Government may employ means to complete the arrangement and compel us to go.

Now I hold that the American Negro owes no more to the Negroes in
Africa than he owes to the Negroes in America. There are millions of
needy people over there, but there are also millions of needy people over
here as well, and the millions in America need intellient men of their
number to help them, as much as intelligent men are needed in Africa to
help her people. Besides, we have a fight on our hands right here, a fight
for the redemption of the whole race, and a blow struck successfully for
the Negro in America, is a blow struck for the Negro in Africa. For, until
the Negro is respected in America, he need not expect consideration elsewhere. All this native land talk, however, is nonsense. The native land of
the American Negro is America. His bones, his muscles, his sinews, are all
American. His ancestors for two hundred and seventy years have lived and
laboured and died, on American soil, and millions of his posterity have
inherited Caucasian blood.

It is pertinent, therefore, to ask, in view of this admixture, as well as in view of other facts, where the people of this mixed race are to go, for their ancestors are white and black, and it will be difficult to find their native land anywhere outside of the United States.

But the worst thing, perhaps, about this colonization nonsense is, that it tends to throw over the Negro a mantle of despair. It leads him to doubt the possibility of his progress as an American citizen. It also encourages popular prejudice with the hope that by persecution or by persuasion the Negro can finally be dislodged and driven from his natural home, while in the nature of the case he must stay here and will stay here, if for no other reason than because he cannot well get away.

I object to the colonization scheme, because it tends to weaken the Negro's hold on one country, while it can give him no rational hope of another. Its tendency is to make him despondent and doubtful, where he should feel assured and confident. It forces upon him the idea that he is forever doomed to be a stranger and a sojourner in the land of his birth, and that he has no permanent abiding place here.

All this is hurtful; with such ideas constantly flaunted before him, he cannot easily set himself to work to better his condition in such ways as are open to him here. It sets him to groping everlastingly after the impossible.

Every man who thinks at all, must know that home is the fountain head, the inspiration, the foundation and main support, not only of all social virtue but of all motives to human progress, and that no people can prosper, or amount to much, unless they have a home, or the hope of a home. A man who has not such an object, either in possession or in prospect, is a nobody and will never be anything else. To have a home, the Negro must have a country, and he is an enemy to the moral progress of the Negro, whether he knows it or not, who calls upon him to break up his home in this country, for an uncertain home in Africa.

But the agitation on this subject has a darker side still. It has already been given out that if we do not go of our own accord, we may be forced to go, at the point of the bayonet. I cannot say that we shall not have to face this hardship, but badly as I think of the tendency of our times, I do not think that American sentiment will ever reach a condition which will make the expulsion of the Negro from the United States by any such means, possible.

Yet, the way to make it possible is to predict it. There are people in the world who know how to bring their own prophecies to pass. The best way to get up a mob, is to say there will be one, and this is what is being done. Colonization is no solution, but an evasion. It is not repentance but putting the wronged ones out of our presence. It is not atonement, but banishment. It is not love, but hate. Its reiteration and agitation only serves to fan the flame of popular prejudice and to add insult to injury.

The righteous judgment of mankind will say if the American people could endure the Negro's presence while a slave, they certainly can and ought to endure his presence as a free man.

If they could tolerate him when he was a heathen, they might bear with him now that he is a Christian. If they could bear with him when ignorant and degraded, they should bear with him now that he is a gentleman and a scholar.

But even the Southern whites have an interest in this question. Woe to the South when it no longer has the strong arm of the Negro to till its soil, "and woe to the nation when it shall employ the sword to drive the Negro from his native land."

Such a crime against justice, such a crime against gratitude, should it ever be attempted, would certainly bring a national punishment which would cause the earth to shudder. It would bring a stain upon the nation's honor, like the blood on Lady Macbeth's hand. The waters of all the oceans would not suffice to wash out the infamy. But the nation will commit no such crime. But in regard to this point of our future, my mind is easy. We are here and are here to stay. It is well for us and well for the American people to rest upon this as final—**January 9, 1894.**

T. THOMAS FORTUNE

(1856–1928)

A journalist who was the editor of the New York Age *and New York* World, *Fortune was an advocate of Negro independence in politics. He also supported the unionization of Negro labor and elementary and industrial education for the Negro. In 1900 he joined with Booker T. Washington in the formation of the National Negro Business League. His most important works include* Black and White: Land, and Labor and Politics in the South, *1884, from which the following sections are taken, and* The Negro in Politics, *1885.*

EDUCATION

. . . Let us now look at the system of education as it has been operated among the colored people of the South.

It cannot be denied that much of the fabulous sums of money lavishly given for the education of the Freedmen of the South, has been squandered upon experiments, which common sense should have dictated were altogether impracticable. Perhaps this was sequential in the early stages of the work, when the instructor was ignorant of the topography of the country, the temper of the people among whom he was to labor, and, more important still, when he was totally ignorant of the particular class upon whom he was to operate—ignorant of their temperament, receptive capacity and peculiar, aye, unique, idiosyncrasies. Thus thousands upon thousands of dollars were expended upon the erection and endowment of "colleges" in many localities where ordinary common schools were unknown. Each college was, therefore, necessarily provided with a primary department, where the child of ten years and the adult of forty struggled in the same classes with the first elements of rudimentary education. The child and the adult each felt keenly his position in the college, and a course of cramming was pursued, injurious to all concerned, to lessen the number in the primary and to increase the number in the college departments. No man can estimate the injury thus inflicted upon not only the student but the cause of education. Even unto to-day there are colleges in localities in the South which run all the year while the common school only runs from three to eight months.

Indeed, the multiplication of colleges and academies for the "higher education of colored youth" is one of the most striking phenomena of the times: as if theology and the classics were the things best suited to and

332

most urgently needed by a class of persons unprepared in rudimentary education, and whose immediate aim must be that of the mechanic and the farmer—to whom the classics, theology and the sciences, in their extremely impecunious state, are unequivocable abstractions. There will be those who will denounce me for taking this view of collegiate and professional preparation; but I maintain that any education is false which is unsuited to the condition and the prospects of the student. To educate him for a lawyer when there are no clients, for medicine when the patients, although numerous, are too poor to give him a living income, to fill his head with Latin and Greek as a teacher when the people he is to teach are to be instructed in the *a b c's*—such education is a waste of time and a senseless expenditure of money.

I do not inveigh against higher education; I simply maintain that the sort of education the colored people of the South stand most in need of is *elementary and industrial.* They should be instructed for the work to be done. Many a colored farmer boy or mechanic has been spoiled to make a foppish gambler or loafer, a swaggering pedagogue or a cranky homiletician. Men may be spoiled by education, even as they are spoiled by illiteracy. Education is the preparation for a future work; hence men should be educated with special reference to that work.

If left to themselves men usually select intuitively the course of preparation best suited to their tastes and capacities. But the colored youth of the South have been allured and seduced from their natural inclination by the premiums placed upon theological, classical and professional training for the purpose of sustaining the reputation and continuance of "colleges" and their professorships.

I do not hesitate to say that if the vast sums of money already expended and now being spent in the equipment and maintenance of colleges and universities for the so called "higher education" of colored youth had been expended in the establishment and maintenance of primary schools and schools of applied science, the race would have profited vastly more than it has, both mentally and materially, while the results would have operated far more advantageously to the State, and satisfactorily to the munificent benefactors.

Since writing the above, I find in a very recent number of Judge Tourgèe's magazine, *The Continent,* the following reflections upon the subject, contributed to that excellent periodical by Prof. George F. Magoun of Iowa College. Mr. Magoun says:

May I offer one suggestion which observation a few years since among the freedmen and much reflection, with comparisons made in foreign countries, have impressed upon me? It is this, that the key of the future for the black men of the South is *industrial* education. The laboring men of other lands cannot hold their own in skilled labor save as they receive such education, and this of a constantly advancing type. The English House of Commons moved two years since for a Royal Commission to study the technical schools of the continent, and the report respecting France made by this commission has been republished at Washington by the United States Commissioner of Education. In our two leading northwestern cities, St. Louis and Chicago, splendid manual training-schools have been formed, and east and west the question of elementary manual training in public schools is up for discussion and decision. All this for *white* laboring men. As long ago as December, 1879, the Legislature of Tennessee authorized a brief manual of the Elementary Principles of Agriculture to be "taught in the public schools of the State," for the benefit of *white* farmers again. The Professor of Chemistry in the Vanderbilt University, Nashville, prepared the book—107 pages. Where in all this is here anything for the educational improvement of the black laborer just where he needs education most? The labor of the South is subject in these years to a marvelous revolution. The only opportunity the freedman has to rise is by furnishing such skilled labor as the great changes going on in that splendid section of the land require. How can he furnish it, unless the education given him is chiefly industrial and technical? Some very pertinent statements of the situation are made in the *Princeton Review* for May. They confirm all that you have said.* As to the various bills before Congress, the writer says: "Immediate assistance should be rendered to the ex-slave States in the development of an education suited to their political and *industrial* needs." Can this be an education in Latin and Greek? (The writer contends earnestly for retaining these studies in classical college and academy courses for students of all colors.) Can it be anything else than training in elementary industry, such as is now demanded for our Northern common-schools? If the denominational freedmen's schools find this a necessity, is it anything less for the Southern public schools act which is contemplated in the bills before Congress?

Mr. Magoun reasons wisely. If the colored men of the South are to continue their grip as the wage-workers and wealth-producers of that section they must bring to their employments common intelligence and skill; and these are to be obtained in the South as in the North, by apprenticeship and in schools specially provided for the purpose. Instead of spending three to seven years in mastering higher education, which presupposes favorable conditions, colored youth should spend those years in acquiring a "common school education," and in mastering some trade by which to make an honest livelihood when they step forth into the world of fierce competition.

Some may ask: Shall we, then, not have some scholars, men learned in all that higher education gives? Of course; and we should have them. Men fitted by nature for special pursuits in life will make preparation for that work. Water will find its level. Genius cannot be repressed. It will find an audience, even though the singer be Robert Burns at his plow in the remoteness of Ayr, or the philosophic Æsop in the humble garb of a Greek pedant's slave. Genius will take care of itself; it is the mass of mankind that must be led by the hand as we lead a small boy. It is therefore that I

* Judge Tourgee has for years been urgently and admirably writing in advocacy of National Aid in Southern Education.

plead, that the masses of the colored race should receive such preparation for the fierce competition of every day life that the odds shall not be against them. I do not plead for the few, who will take care of themselves, but for the many who must be guided and protected lest they fall a prey to the more hardy or unscrupulous.

Mr. Magoun follows out his train of thought in the following logical deductions:

Plainly, if this opportunity for furnishing the skilled labor of the South hereafter (as he has furnished the unskilled heretofore) slips away from the black man, he can never rise. In the race for property, influence, and all success in life, the industrially educated white man—whatever may be said of Southern white men "hating to work"—will outstrip him. Before an ecclesiastical body of representative colored men at Memphis, in the autumn of 1880, I urged this consideration, when asked to advise them about education, as the one most germane to their interests; and preachers and laymen, and their white teachers, approved every word, and gave me most hearty thanks. I counseled aspiring young men to abstain from unsuitable attempts at merely literary training; from overlooking the intermediate links of culture in striving after something "beyond their measure"; from expecting any more to be shot up into the United States Senatorships, etc., by a revolution which had already wellnigh spent its first exceptional force (as a few extraordinary persons are thrown up into extraordinary distinction in the beginning of revolutions); from ambitious rejection of the steady, thorough, toilsome methods of fitting themselves for immediate practical duties and nearer spheres, by which alone any class is really and healthfully elevated. To shirk elementary preparation and aspire after the results of scholarship without its painstaking processes is THE *temptation of colored students,* as I know by having taught them daily in college classes. I rejoice in every such student who really climbs the heights of learning with exceeding joy. But a far greater proportion than has thus far submitted to thorough-going preparation for skilled labor must do so, or there is no great future for them in this land as a race.

But already the absurdity of beginning at the apex of the educational fabric instead of at the base is being perceived by those who have in hand the education of colored youth. A large number of colleges are adding industrial to their other features, and with much success, and a larger number of educators are agitating the wisdom of such feature.

Perhaps no educational institution in the Union has done more for the industrial education of the colored people of the South than the Hampton (Virginia) Normal and Agricultural Institute under the management of General S. C. Armstrong. The success of this one institution in industrial education, and the favor with which it is regarded by the public, augurs well for the future of such institutions. That they may multiply is the fervent wish of every man who apprehends the necessities of the colored people. . . .

Money contributed for eleemosynary purposes is a sacred trust, and should so be applied as to net the greatest good not only to the beneficiary but the donor. The primary object of educational effort among the colored people thus far has been to purify their perverted moral nature and to indoctrinate in them correcter ideas of religion and its obligations; and the effort has not been in vain. Yet I am constrained to say, the inculcation of these principles has been altogether a too predominant idea. Material possibilities are rightly predicated upon correct moral and spiritual bases; but a morally and spiritually sound training must be sustained by such preparation for the actual work of life, as we find it in the machine shop, the grain field, and the commercial pursuits. The moralist and missionary are no equals for the man whose ideas of honest toil are supplemented by a common school training and an educated hand. This is exemplified every day in the ready demand for foreign-born skilled labor over our own people, usually educated as gentlemen without means, as if they were to be kid-gloved fellows, not men who must contend for subsistence with horny-handed men who have graduated from the machine shops and factories and the schools of applied sciences of Europe. Indeed, the absence of the old-time apprentices among the white youth of the North, as a force in our industrial organization to draw upon, can be accounted for upon no other ground than that the supply of foreign-born skilled help so readily fills the demand that employers find it a useless expenditure of means to graduate the American boy. Thus may we account for the "grand rush" young men make for the lighter employments and the professions, creating year after year an idle floating population of miseducated men, and reducing the compensation for clerical work below that received by hod-carriers. This is not a fancy picture; it is an arraignment of the American system of education, which proceeds upon the assumption that boys are all "born with a silver spoon in their mouths" and are destined to reach—not the poor-house, but the Senate House or the White House.

The American system of education proceeds upon a false and pernicious assumption; and, while I protest against its application generally, I protest, in this connection, against its application in the case of the colored youth in particular. What the colored boy, what all boys of the country need, is *industrial not ornamental* education; shall they have it? Let the State and the philanthropists answer.

POLITICAL INDEPENDENCE OF THE NEGRO

In addressing myself to a consideration of the subject: "The colored man as an Independent Force in our Politics," I come at once to one of the vital principles underlying American citizenship and the citizenship of the colored man in a peculiar manner. Upon this question hang all the conditions of man as a free moral agent, as an intelligent reasoning being; as a man thoughtful for the best interests of his country, of his individual interests, and of the interests of those who must take up the work of republican government when the present generation has passed away. When I say that this question is of a most complex and perplexing nature, I only assert what is known of all men.

I would not forget that the arguments for and against independent action on our part are based upon two parties or sets of principles. Principles are inherent in government by the people, and parties are engines created by the people through which to voice the principles they espouse. Parties have divided on one line in this country from the beginning of our national existence to the present time. All other issues merge into two distinct ones—the question of a strong Federal Government, as enunciated by Alexander Hamilton, and maintained by the present Republican party, and the question of the rights and powers of the States, as enunciated by Thomas Jefferson, and as maintained by the present Democratic party,—called the "party of the people," but in fact the party of oligarchy, bloodshed, violence and oppression. The Republican party won its first great victory on the inherent weakness of the Democratic party on the question of Human Rights and the right of the Federal Government to protect itself from the assumption, the aggression, the attempted usurpation, of the States, and it has maintained its supremacy for so long a time as to lead to the supposition that it will rule until such time as it shall fall to pieces of itself because of internal decay and exterior cancers. There does not appear to exist sufficient vitality outside of the Republican party to keep its members loyal to the people or honest to the government. The loyal legislation which would be occasioned by dread of loss of power, and the administration of the government in the most economical form, are wanting, because of the absence of an honest, healthy opposing party.

But it is not my purpose to dwell upon the mechanism of parties, but rather to show why colored Americans should be independent voters, independent citizens, independent men. To this end I am led to lay it down: (1.) That an independent voter must be intelligent, must comprehend the science of government, and be versed in the history of governments and of men; (2.) That an independent voter must be not only a citizen versed in government, but one loyal to his country, and generous and forbearing with his fellow-citizens, not looking always to the word and the act, but looking sometimes to the undercurrent which actuates these—to the presence of immediate interest, which is always strong in human nature, to the love of race, and to the love of section, which comes next to the love of country.

Our country is great not only in mineral and cereal resources, in numbers, and in accumulated wealth, but great in extent of territory, and in multiplicity of interests, out-growing from peculiarities of locality, race, and education of the people. Thus the people of the North and East and West are given to farming, manufacturing, and speculation, making politics a subordinate, not a leading interest; they are consequently wealthy, thrifty and contented: while the people of the South, still in the shadow of defeat in the bloodiest and most tremendous conflict since the Napoleonic wars, are divided sharply into two classes, and given almost exclusively to the pursuits of agriculture and hatred of one another. The existence of this state of things is most disastrous in its nature, and deplorable in its results. It is a barrier against the progress of that section and alien to the spirit and subversive of the principles of our free institutions.

It is in the South that the largest number of our people live; it is there that they encounter the greatest hardships; it is there the problem of their future usefulness as American citizens must have full and satisfactory, or disastrous and disheartening demonstration. Consequently, the colored statesman and the colored editor must turn their attention to the South and make that field the center of speculation, deduction and practical application. We all understand the conditions of society in that section and the causes which have produced them, and, while not forgetting the causes, it is a common purpose to alter the existing conditions, so that they may conform to the logic of the great Rebellion and the spirit and letter of the Federal Constitution. It is not surprising, therefore, that, as an humble worker in the interest of my race and the common good, I have decided views as to the course best to be pursued by our people in that section, and the fruits likely to spring from a consistent advocacy of such views.

I may stand alone in the opinion that the best interests of the race and the best interests of the country will be conserved by building up a bond of union between the white people and the Negroes of the South—advocating the doctrine that the interests of the white and the interests of the colored people are one and the same; that the legislation which affects the one will affect the other; that the good which comes to the one should come to the other, and that, as one people, the evils which blight the hopes of the one blight the hopes of the other; I say, I may stand alone among colored men in the belief that harmony of sentiment between the blacks and whites of the country, in so far forth as it tends to honest division and healthy opposition, is natural and necessary, but I speak that which is a conviction as strong as the Stalwart idea of diversity between Black and White, which has so crystallized the opinion of the race.

It is not safe in a republican form of government that clannishness should exist, either by compulsory or voluntary reason; it is not good for the government, it is not good for the individual. A government like ours is like unto a household. Difference of opinion on non-essentials is wholesome and natural, but upon the fundamental idea incorporated in the Declaration of Independence and re-affirmed in the Federal Constitution the utmost unanimity should prevail. That all men are born equal, so far as the benefits of government extend; that each and every man is justly entitled to the enjoyment of life, liberty and the pursuit of happiness, so long as these benign benefits be not forfeited by infraction upon the rights of others; that freedom of thought and unmolested expression of honest conviction and the right to make these effective through the sacred medium of a fair vote and an honest count, are God-given and not to be curtailed—these are the foundations of republican government; these are the foundations of our institutions; these are the birthright of every American citizen; these are the guarantees which make men free and independent and great.

The colored man must rise to a full conception of his citizenship before he can make his citizenship effective. It is a fatality to create or foster clannishness in a government like ours. Assimilation of sentiment must be the property of the German, the Irish, the English, the Anglo-African, and all other racial elements that contribute to the formation of the American type of citizen. The moment you create a caste standard, the moment you recognize the existence of such, that moment republican government stands beneath the sword of Damocles, the vitality of its being becomes vitiated and endangered. If this be true, the American people have grave cause for apprehension. The Anglo-African element of our population is classed off by popular sentiment, and kept so. It is for the thoughtful, the honest, the calm but resolute men of the race to mould the sentiment of the masses, lift them up into the broad sunlight of freedom. Ignorance, superstition, prejudice, and intolerance are elements in our nature born of the malign institution of servitude. No fiat of government can eradicate these. As they were the slow growth, the gradual development of long years of inhuman conditions, so they must be eliminated by the slow growth of years of favorable conditions. Let us recognize these facts as facts, and labor honestly to supplant them with more wholesome, more cheering realities. The Independent colored man, like the Independent white man, is an American citizen who does his own thinking. When some one else thinks for him he ceases to be an intelligent citizen and becomes a dangerous dupe—dangerous to himself, dangerous to the State.

It is not to be expected now that the colored voters will continue to maintain that unanimity of idea and action characteristic of them when the legislative halls of States resounded with the clamor of law-makers of their creation, and when their breath flooded or depleted State treasuries. The conditions are different now. They find themselves citizens without a voice in the shapement of legislation; tax-payers without representation; men without leadership masterful enough to force respect from inferior numbers in some States, or to hold the balance of power in others. They find themselves at the mercy of a relentless public opinion which tolerates but does not respect their existence as a voting force; but which, on the contrary, while recognizing their right to the free exercise of the suffrage, forbids such exercise at the point of the shotgun of the assassin, whom it not only nerves but shields in the perpetration of his lawless and infamous crimes. And why is this? Why is it that the one hundred and twenty thousand black voters of South Carolina allow the eighty thousand white voters of that State to grind the life out of them by laws more odious, more infamous, more tyrannical and subversive of manhood than any which depopulate the governments of the old world? Is it because the white man is the created viceregent of government? The Scriptures affirm that all are sprung from one parental stem. Is it because he is the constitutionally invested oligarch of government? The Magna Charta of our liberties affirms that "all men are created equal." Is it because the law of the land reserves unto him the dominance of power? The preamble of the Federal Constitution declares that "We" and not "I," constitute "the people of the United States." If the law of God and the law of man agree in the equality of right of man, explain to me the cause which keeps a superior force in subjection to a minority. Look to the misgovernment of the Reconstruction period for the answer—misgovernment by white men and black men who were lifted into a "little brief authority" by a mighty but unwieldy voting force. That black man who connived at and shared in the corruption in the South which resulted in the subversion of the majority rule, is a traitor to his race and his country, wherever he may now be eking out a precarious and inglorious existence, and I have nothing to heap upon his head but the curses, the execrations of an injured people. Like Benedict Arnold he should seek a garret in the desert of population, living unnoticed and without respect, where he might die without arousing the contempt of his people.

The love of Liberty carries with it the courage to preserve it from encroachments from without and from contempt from within. A people in whom the love of Liberty is in-born cannot be enslaved, though they may be exterminated by superior force and intelligence, as in the case of the poor Indian of our own land—a people who, two hundred years ago, spread their untamed hordes from the icebergs of Maine to the balmy sunland of Florida. But to-day where are they? Their love of freedom and valorous defense of priority of ownership of our domain have caused them to be swept from the face of the earth. Had they possessed intelligence with their more than Spartan courage, the wave of extermination could never have rolled over them forever. As a man I admire the unconquerable heroism and fortitude of the Indian. So brave a race of people were worthy a nobler and a happier destiny. As an American citizen, I feel it born in my nature to share in fullest measure all that is American. I sympathize in all the hopes, aspirations and fruitions of my country. There is no pulsation in the animated frame of my native land which does not thrill my nature. There is no height of glory we may reach as a government in which I should not feel myself individually lifted; and there is no depth of degradation to which we may fall to which I should not feel myself individually dragged. In a word, I am an American citizen. I have a heritage in each and every provision incorporated in the Constitution of my country, and should this heritage be attempted to be filched from me by any man or body of men, I should deem the provocation sufficiently grievous to stake even life in defense of it. I would plant every colored man in this country on a platform of this nature—to think for himself, to speak for himself, to act for himself. This is the ideal citizen of an ideal government such as ours is modelled to become. This is my conception of the colored man as an independent force in our politics. To aid in lifting our people to this standard, is one of the missions which I have mapped out for my life-work. I may be sowing the seed that will ripen into disastrous results, but I don't think so. My conception of republican government does not lead me to a conclusion so inconsistent with my hopes, my love of my country and of my race.

I look upon my race in the South and I see that they are helplessly at the mercy of a popular prejudice outgrowing from a previous condition of servitude; I find them clothed in the garments of citizenship by the Federal Government and opposed in the enjoyment of it by their equals, not their superiors, in the benefits of government; I find that the government which conferred the right of citizenship is powerless, or indisposed, to force respect for its own enactments; I find that these people, left to the mercy of their enemies, alone and defenseless, and without judicious leadership, are urged to preserve themselves loyal to the men and to the party which have shown themselves unable to extend to them substantial protection; I find that these people, alone in their struggles of doubt and of prejudice, are surrounded by a public opinion powerful to create and powerful to destroy; I find them poor in culture and poor in worldly substance, and dependent for the bread they eat upon those they antagonize politically. As a consequence, though having magnificent majorities, they have no voice in shaping the legislation which is too often made an engine to oppress them; though performing the greatest amount of labor, they suffer from overwork and insufficient remuneration; though having the greater number of children, the facilities of education are not as ample or as good as those provided for the whites out of the common fund, nor have they means to supply from private avenues the benefits of education denied them by the State. Now, what is the solution of this manifold and grievous state of things? Will it come by standing solidly opposed to the sentiment, the culture, the statesmanship, and the possession of the soil and wealth of the South? Let the history of the past be spread before the eyes of a candid and thoughtful people; let the bulky roll of misgovernment, incompetence, and blind folly be enrolled on the one hand, and then turn to the terrors of the midnight assassin and the lawless deeds which desecrate the sunlight of noontide, walking abroad as a phantom armed with the desperation of the damned!

I maintain the idea that the preservation of our liberties, the consummation of our citizenship, must be conserved and matured, not by standing alone and apart, sullen as the melancholy Dane, but by imbibing all that is American, entering into the life and spirit of our institutions, spreading abroad in sentiment, feeling the full force of the fact that while we are classed as Africans, just as the Germans are classed as Germans, we are in all things American citizens, American freemen. Since we have tried the idea of political unanimity let us now try other ideas, ideas more in consonance with the spirit of our institution. There is no strength in a union that enfeebles. Assimilation, a melting into the corporate body, having no distinction from others, equally the recipients of government—this it is to be the independent man, be his skin tanned by the torrid heat of Africa, or bleached by the eternal snows of the Caucasus. To preach the independence of the colored man is to preach his Americanization. The shackles of slavery have been torn from his limbs by the stern arbitrament of arms; the shackles of political enslavement, of ignorance, and of popular prejudice must be broken on the wheels of ceaseless study and the facility with which he becomes absorbed into the body of the people. To aid himself is his first duty if he believes that he is here to stay, and not a probationer for the land of his forefathers—a land upon which he has no other claim than one of sentiment.

What vital principle affecting our citizenship is championed by the National Republican party of to-day? Is it a fair vote and an honest count? Measure our strength in the South and gaze upon the solitary expression of our citizenship in the halls of the National Legislature. The fair vote which we cast for Rutherford B. Hayes seemed to have incurred the enmity of that chief Executive, and he and his advisers turned the colored voters of the South over to the bloodthirsty minority of that section.

The Republican party has degenerated into an ignoble scramble for place and power. It has forgotten the principles for which Sumner contended, and for which Lincoln died. It betrayed the cause for which Douglass, Garrison and others labored, in the blind policy it pursued in reconstructing the rebellious States. It made slaves freemen and freemen slaves in the same breath by conferring the franchise and withholding the guarantees to insure its exercise; it betrayed its trust in permitting thousands of innocent men to be slaughtered without declaring the South in rebellion, and in pardoning murderers, whom tardy justice had consigned to a felon's dungeon. It is even now powerless to insure an honest expression of the vote of the colored citizen. For these things, I do not deem it binding upon colored men further to support the Republican party when other more advantageous affiliations can be formed. And what of the Bourbon Democratic party? There has not been, there is not now, nor will there ever be, any good thing in it for the colored man. Bourbon Democracy is a curse to our land. Any party is a curse which arrays itself in opposition to human freedom, to the universal brotherhood of man. No colored man can ever claim truthfully to be a Bourbon Democrat. It is a fundamental impossibility. But he can be an independent, a progressive Democrat.

The hour has arrived when thoughtful colored men should cease to put their faith upon broken straws; when they should cease to be the willing tools of a treacherous and corrupt party; when they should cease to support men and measures which do not benefit them or the race; when they should cease to be duped by one faction and shot by the other. The time has fully arrived when they should have their position in parties more fully defined, and when, by the ballot which they hold, they should force more respect for the rights of life and property.

To do this, they must adjust themselves to the altered condition which surrounds them. They must make for themselves a place to stand. In the politics of the country the colored vote must be made as uncertain a quantity as the German and Irish vote. The color of their skin must cease to be an index to their political creed. They must think less of "the party" and more of themselves; give less heed to a name and more heed to principles.

The black men and white men of the South have a common destiny. Circumstances have brought them together and so interwoven their interests that nothing but a miracle can dissolve the link that binds them. It is, therefore, to their mutual disadvantage that anything but sympathy and good will should prevail. A reign of terror means a stagnation of all the energies of the people and a corruption of the fountains of law and justice.

The colored men of the South must cultivate more cordial relations with the white men of the South. They must, by a wise policy, hasten the day when politics shall cease to be the shibboleth that creates perpetual warfare. The citizen of a State is far more sovereign than the citizen of the United States. The State is a real, tangible reality; a thing of life and power; while the United States is, purely, an abstraction—a thing that no man has successfully defined, although many, wise in their way and in their own conceit, have philosophized upon it to their own satisfaction. The metaphysical polemics of men learned in the science of republican government, covering volume upon volume of "debates," the legislation of ignoramuses, styled statesmen, and the "strict" and "liberal" construction placed upon their work by the judicial *magi,* together with a long and disastrous rebellion, to the cruel arbitrament of which the question had been, as was finally hoped, in the last resort, submitted, have failed, all and each, to define that visionary thing the so-called Federal government, and its just rights and powers. As Alexander Hamilton and Thomas Jefferson left it, so it is to-day, a bone of contention, a red flag in the hands of the political matadors of one party to infuriate those of the other parties.

No: it is time that the colored voter learned to leave his powerless "protectors" and take care of himself. Let every one read, listen, think, reform his own ideas of affairs in his own locality; let him be less interested in the continual wars of national politics than in the interests of his own town and county and state; let him make friends of the mammon of unrighteousness of his own neighborhood, so far as to take an intelligent part among his neighbors, white and black, and vote for the men and for the party that will do the best for him and his race, and best conserve the interest of his vicinity. Let there be no aim of *solidifying* the colored vote;

the massing of black means the massing of white by contrast. Individual colored men—and many of them—have done wonders in self-elevation; but there can be no general elevation of the colored men of the South until they use their voting power in independent local affairs with some discrimination more reasonable than an obstinate clinging to a party name. When the colored voters differ among themselves and are to be found on *both sides* of local political contests, they will begin to find themselves of some political importance; their votes will be sought, cast, *and counted.*

And this is the key to the whole situation; let them make themselves a part of the people. It will take time, patience, intelligence, courage; but it can be done: and until it is done their path will lie in darkness and perhaps in blood.

SOLUTION OF THE POLITICAL PROBLEM

I have no faith in parties. In monarchical and imperial governments they are always manipulated by royal boobies, who are in turn manipulated by their empty-pated favorites and their women of soporific virtue; while in republics they are always manipulated by demagogues, tricksters, and corruptionists, who figure in the newspapers as "bosses," "heelers" and "sluggers," and in history as statesmen, senators and representatives. These gentlemen, who *rule* our government and *ruin* our people, comprise what Mr. Matthew Arnold recently termed the "remnant" which should be permitted to run things to suit themselves, the people, the great mass, being incapable of taking care of themselves and the complex machinery of government. Of course, Mr. Arnold, who is necessarily very British in his ideas of government, intended that the "remnant" he had in his "mind's eye," should comprise men of the most exalted character and intelligence, the very things which keep them out of the gutters of politics. Men of exalted character are expected in our country to attend to their own concerns, not the concerns of the people, and to give the "boys" a chance; while the men of exalted intelligence are, by reason of the great industry and seclusiveness necessary to their work, too much wedded to their books and their quiet modes of life to rush into ward meetings and contend for political preferment with the "Mikes" and "Jakes" who make their bread and butter out of the spoils and peculations of office. A Clay or Webster, a Seward or Sumner, sometimes gets into politics, but it is by accident. There is not enough money in our politics to cause honest men to make it an object, while the corruption frequently necessary to maintain a political position, is so disgusting as to deter honest men from making it a business.

A love of power easily degenerates from patriotism into treason or tyranny, or both. As it is easier to fall from virtue to vice than it is to rise from vice to virtue, so it is easier to fall from patriotism than to rise to it.

Before the war the men of the South engaged, at first, in politics as an elegant pastime. They had plenty of leisure and plenty of money. They did not take to literature and science, because these pursuits require severe work and more or less of a strong bias, for a thorough exposition of their profound penetralia. It may be, too, that their assumed patrician sensitiveness shrank from entering into competition with the plebeian fellows who had to study hard and write voluminously for a few pennies to keep soul and body together. And your Southern grandees, before the war, were not compelled to drudge for a subsistence; they had to take little thought for the morrow. Their vast landed estates and black slaves were things that did not fluctuate; under the effective supervision of the viperous slave-driver the black Samson rose before the coming of the sun, and the land, nature's own flower garden and man's inalienable heritage, brought forth golden corn and snowy cotton in their season. Southern intelligence expended its odors in the avenues where brilliance, not profundity, was the passport to popularity. Hence, Southern hospitality (giving to others that which had been deliberately stolen) became almost as proverbial in the *polite* circles of America and Europe as the long established suavity and condescension of the French. And even unto the present time the hospitality of the South, shorn of its profuseness and grandiloquence, is frequently the theme of newspaper hacks and magazine penny-a-liners. But the shadow alone remains; the substance has departed—"There are no birds in last year's nest."

If the literary reputation of the United States had been rated, up to the close of the Rebellion, on the contributions of Southern men—fiction, prose and poetry, science, art, and invention—the polite nations of the world would have regarded us as a nation of semi-barbarians. But, happily, the rugged genius of New England made up then and makes up now for the poverty of literary effort on the part of the South. True, a few men since the war have placed the South in a better light; but even their work, as an index of Southern genius, is regarded as highly precocious and tentative.

The South has yet to demonstrate that she has capacity for high literary effort. In the process of that demonstration, I am fully persuaded that the Anglo-African—with his brilliant wit and humor, his highly imaginative disposition and his innate fondness for literary pursuits—will contribute largely to give the South an enviable and honorable position.

What the South lacked in literary effort before the war she made up in a magnificent galaxy of meteoric statesmen, who rushed into politics with the instinct of ducks taking to the water, and who were forgotten, in the majority of cases, before they had run out their ephemeral career. A few names have survived the earthquake, and are remembered for their cleverness rather than their depth. A few more decades, and they will be re-

membered only by the curious student who plods his weary way through
the labyrinth of Congressional records and the musty archives of States,
seeking for data of times which long ago passed into the hazy vista of
history and romance. Before the war the Southern man of leisure took to
politics more as a pastime than as a serious business. But as the pastime
was agreeable, and as it gave additional weight and distinction, all those
who could, strived to make it appear that they were men of importance in
the Nation. They were largely a nation of politicians,—always brilliant,
shallow, bellicose and dogmatic, as ready to decide an argument with the
shot gun or saber as with reason and logic.

This was the temper of the people who rushed into the war with the
confidence of a schoolboy and who limped out like a man overtaken in his
gymnastic exercise by a paralytic stroke. The war taught the South a very
useful lesson, but did not sufficiently convince it that it was preëminently
a supercilious, arrogant people, who did not and do not possess all the
virtue, intelligence, and courage of the country; that its stock of these
prime elements is woefully small considering the long years it had posed
as America's own patrician class.

But when the war was over, and the Southern nobility turned its
thoughts once more to social arrogance and political dominion, it found
that Othello's occupation was entirely gone. A revolution had swept over
the country more iconoclastic and merciless than that which followed in
the wake of the French revolution nearly a hundred years before. The
bottom rail had been violently placed upon the top; industrial adjustments
had been so completely metamorphosed as to defy detection; while the
basis and the method of political representation and administration had
been so altered as to confound both the old and the new forces.

Aside from the ignorance of the black citizens and the insatiate greed
and unscrupulousness of their carpet-bag leaders—a band of vultures
more voracious and depraved than any which ever before imposed upon
and abused the confidence of a credulous people—the white men of the
South had been educated to regard themselves as, naturally, the factors of
power and the colored people as, naturally, the subject class, no factor at
all. It was these two things which produced that exhibition of barbarity
on the part of the South and impotence on the part of the government
which makes us go to Roumania and the Byzantine court for fit parallel.

But, as I have said, a love of power easily degenerates into treason. If
we may not call the violence, the assassinations, which have disgraced the
South, *treason,* by what fitter name, pray, shall we call it? If the nullification of the letter and spirit of the amendments of the Federal Constitution
by the conquered South was not renewed *treason,* what was it? What is
it?

The white men of the South, to the "manor born," having shown their
superiority in the superlative excellencies of murder, usurpation and robbery (and I maintain they have gone further in the execution of these

infamies than was true of the Negro-Carpet-bag *bacchanalia*); having made majorities dwindle into iotas and vaulted themselves into power at the point of the shot gun and dagger (regular bandit style); having made laws which discriminate odiously against one class while giving the utmost immunity to the other; having, after doing these things, modeled the government they rule upon the pro-slavery doctrine that it is a "white man's government"—having had time to become sobered, the white men of the South should be open to reason, if not to conviction.

The black men of the South know full well that they were disfranchised by illegal and violent methods; they know that laws are purposely framed to defraud and to oppress them. This is dangerous knowledge, dangerous to the black and the white man. It will be decided by one of two courses—wise and judicious statesmanship or bloody and disastrous insurrection. When men are wronged they appeal either to the arbitrament of reason or of violence. No man who loves his country would sanction violence in the adjudication of rights save as a last resort. Reason is the safest tribunal before which to arraign injustice and wrong; but it is not always possible to reach this tribunal.

The black and white citizens of the South must alter the lines which have divided them since the close of the war. They are, essentially, one people, and should be mutual aids instead of mutual hindrances to each other. By "one people" I don't wish to be understood as implying that the white and black man are one in an ethnological, but a generic sense, having a common origin. Living in the same communities, pursuing identical avocations, and subject to the same fundamental laws, however these may differ in construction and application in the several States, it is as much, if not even more, the interest of the white man that the black should be given every possible opportunity to better his mental, material and civil condition. Society is not corrupted from the apex but from the base. It is not the pure rain that falls from the heavens, but the stagnant waters of the pool, that breed disease and death. The corruption of the ballot by white men of the South is more pernicious than the misuse of it by black men; the perversion of the law in the apprehension and punishment of criminals, by being wielded almost exclusively against colored men, not only brings law into contempt of colored men but encourages crime among white men. Thus the entire society is corrupted. Mob law is the most forcible expression of an abnormal public opinion; it shows that society is rotten to the core. When men find that laws are purposely framed to oppress and defraud them they become desperate and reckless; and mob law, by usurping the rightful functions of the judiciary, makes criminals of honest men. As Alexander Pope expressed it:

> Vice is a monster of such frightful mien,
> That to be hated needs but to be seen;
> Yet, seen too oft, familiar with his face,
> We first endure, then pity, then embrace.

The South has nothing to gain and everything to lose in attempting to repress the energies and ambition of the colored man. It is to the safety as well as to the highest efficiency of society that all its members should be allowed the same opportunities for moral, intellectual and material development. "Do unto others as you would have them do unto you." "Thou shalt love thy neighbor as thyself." There is no escape from the law of God. You either deal justly or suffer the evil effects of wrong-doing. The disorders which have made the South a seething cauldron for fifteen years have produced the most widespread contempt of lawful authority not only on the part of the lawless whites but the law-abiding blacks, who have suffered patiently the infliction of all manner of wrong *because they were a generation of slaves, suddenly made freemen.* They permitted themselves to be shot because they had been educated to bare their backs at the command of the white oligarch. But that sort of pusillanimous cowardice cannot be expected to last always. Men in a state of freedom instinctively question the right of others to impose unequal burdens upon them, or to deny to them equal and exact protection of the laws. When oppressed people begin to murmur, grow restless and discontented, the opposer had better change his tactics, or lock himself up, as does the cowardly tyrant of Russia.

A new generation of men has come upon the stage of action in the South. They know little or nothing of the regulations or the horrors of the slave régime. They know they are freemen; they know they are cruelly and unjustly defrauded; and they *question the right* of their equals to oppose and defraud them. A large number of these people have enjoyed the advantage of common school education, and not a few of academic and collegiate education, and a large number have "put money in their purse." The entire race has so changed that they are almost a different people from what they were when the exigencies of war made their manumission imperative. Yet there has been but little change in the attitude of the white men towards this people. They still strenuously deny their right to participate in the administration of justice or to share equally in the blessings of that justice.

There must be a change of policy. The progress of the black man demands it; the interest of the white man compels it. The South cannot hope to share in the industrious emigration constantly flowing into our ports as long as it is scattered over the world that mob law and race distractions constantly interrupt the industry of the people, and put life and property in jeopardy of eminent disturbance; and she cannot hope to encourage the investment of large capital in the development of her industries or the extension of her national system. Capital is timid. It will only seek investment where it is sure of being let alone. Again, while the present state continues, no Southern statesman, however capable he may be, can hope to enjoy the confidence of the country or attain to high official position. Thoughtful, sober people will not entrust power to men who sanction

mob law, and who rise to high honor by conniving at or participating in
assassination and murder. They have too much self-respect to do it.

Only a few weeks since, a narrow-minded senator from the State of
Alabama, speaking upon the question of "National Aid to Education,"
said he would rather vote for an appropriation to place the Southern States
in direct communication with the Congo than to vote money to educate
the blacks. There is no ingrate more execrable than the one who lifts up
his hand or his voice to wrong the man he has betrayed. This senator from
Alabama does not represent the majority of the people of his state. Take
away the shot gun and mob law and he would be compelled to crawl back
into the obscurity out of which he was dragged by his accomplices in
roguery.

The colored man is in the South to stay there. He will not leave it voluntarily and he cannot be driven out. He had no voice in being carried into
the South, but he will have a very loud voice in any attempt to put him
out. The expatriation of 5,000,000 to 6,000,000 people to an alien country needs only to be suggested to create mirth and ridicule. The white men
of the South had better make up their minds that the black men will
remain in the South just as long as corn will tassel and cotton will bloom
into whiteness. The talk about the black people being brought to this
country to prepare themselves to evangelize Africa is so much religious
nonsense boiled down to a sycophantic platitude. The Lord, who is eminently just, had no hand in their forcible coming here; it was preëminently the work of the devil. Africa will have to be evangelized *from
within*, not *from without*. The Colonization society has spent mints of
money and tons of human blood in the selfish attempt to plant an Anglo-
African colony on the West Coast of Africa. The money has been thrown
away and the human lives have been sacrificed in vain. The black people
of this county are Americans, not Africans; and any wholesale expatriation of them is altogether out of the question.

The white men of the South should not deceive themselves: the blacks
are with them to remain. Whether they like it or not, it is a fact that will
not be rubbed out.

If this be true, what should be the policy of the whites towards the
blacks? The question should need no answer at my hands. If it were not
for the unexampled obtuseness of the editors, preachers and politicians of
that section, I should close this chapter here.

The white men and women of the South should get down from the
delectable mountain of delusive superiority which they have climbed; and,
recognizing that "of one blood God made all the children of men," take
hold of the missionary work God has placed under their nose.

Instead of railing at the black man, let them take hold of him in a
Christian spirit and assist him in correcting those moral abscesses and that
mental enervation which they did so awfully much to infuse into him;
they should first take the elephant out of their own eyes before digging at

the gnat in their neighbor's eyes. They should encourage him in his efforts at moral and religious improvement, not by standing off and clapping their hands, but by going into his churches and into his pulpits, showing him the "light and the way" not only by precept but example as well. Can't do it, do you say? Then take your religion and cast it to the dogs, for it is a living lie; it comes not from God but from Beelzebub the Prince of Darkness. A religion that divides Christians is unadulterated paganism; a minister that will not preach the Gospel to sinners, be they black or white, is a hypocrite, who "steals the livery of Heaven to serve the Devil in." They should make liberal provision for the schools set apart for the colored people, and they should visit these schools, not only to mark the progress made, and to encourage teacher and pupil, but to show to the young minds blossoming into maturity and usefulness that they are friends and deeply interested in the progress made. In public, they should seek first to inspire the confidence of colored men by just laws and friendly overtures and by encouraging the capable, honest and ambitious few by placing them in positions of honor and trust. They should show to colored men that they accept the Constitution as amended, and are earnestly solicitous that they should prosper in the world, and become useful and respected citizens. You can't make a friend and partisan of a man by shooting him; you can't make a sober, industrious, honest man by robbing and outraging him. These tactics will not work to the uplifting of a people. "A soft answer turns away wrath." Even a dog caresses the hand that pats him on the head.

The South must spend less money on penitentiaries and more money on schools; she must use less powder and buckshot and more law and equity; she must pay less attention to politics and more attention to the development of her magnificent resources; she must get off the "race line" hobby and pay more attention to the common man; she must wake up to the fact that—

> Worth makes the man, and want of it the fellow,

and that it is to her best interest to place all men upon the same footing before the law; mete out the same punishment to the white scamp that is inexorably meted out to the black scamp, for a scamp is a scamp any way you twist it; a social pest that should be put where he will be unable to harm any one. In an honest acceptance of the new conditions and responsibilities God has placed upon them, and in mutual forebearance, toleration and assistance, the South will find that panacea for which she has sought in vain down to this time.

BOOKER T. WASHINGTON

(1856–1915)

*Born into slavery, the most formative experience of his life was his attend-
ance at Hampton Institute in 1872, an industrial school for Negroes that had
been founded after the Civil War. He was later asked to head a school in Tuskegee, Alabama, which was to be modeled after Hampton Institute. Washington opened the Tuskegee Normal and Agricultural Institute on July 4, 1881,
with a shanty for a schoolhouse and thirty students. The ideas behind Tuskegee were not original nor were they unique to Washington among the Negroes of his time. What was distinctive in his career is the force with which
he applied them in the locality of Tuskegee, ultimately receiving national
recognition in his advocacy of the necessity for industrial education for Negroes. He was the founder and first president of the National Negro Business
League, organized in 1899–1900, and was in fact the leader of the Negro race
during his lifetime. He was influential in the politics of the Republican party
in matters concerning the South, although he never held political office. His
most famous work is his autobiography* Up from Slavery. *In addition to the
works in this anthology his important writings include* The Future of the
Negro, *1902;* The Story of the Negro, *1909;* The Man Farthest Down, *1912.*

THE EDUCATIONAL OUTLOOK IN THE SOUTH

Fourteen years ago it is said that Northern teachers, in the South for the
purpose of teaching in colored schools, were frightened away by the
whites from the town of Tuskegee, Alabama. Four years ago the Democratic members of the Alabama legislature from Tuskegee voluntarily
offered and had passed by the General Assembly a bill, appropriating
$2,000 annually to pay the salaries of teachers in a colored normal school
to be located at Tuskegee. At the end of the first session of the school the
legislature almost unanimously passed a second bill appropriating an additional $1,000 annually, for the same purpose. About one month ago one
of the white citizens of Tuskegee who had at first looked on the school in a
cold, distant kind of a way said to me, "I have just been telling the white
people that the Negroes are more interested in education than we, and are
making more sacrifices to educate themselves." At the end of our first
year's work, some of the whites said, "We are glad that the Normal School
is here because it draws people and makes labor plentiful." At the close of
the second year, several said that the Normal School was beneficial be-

cause it increased trade, and at the close of the last session more than one said that the Normal School is a good institution, it is making the colored people in this state better citizens. From the opening of the school to the present, the white citizens of Tuskegee have been among its warmest friends. They have not only given of their money but they are ever ready to suggest and devise plans to build up the institution. When the school was making an effort to start a brick yard, but was without means, one of the merchants donated an outfit of tools. Every white minister in the town has visited the school and given encouraging remarks. When the school was raising money to build our present hall, it occurred to one of the teachers that it would be a good idea to call on the white ladies for contributions in the way of cakes, etc., toward a fair. The result was that almost every lady, called on, gave something and the fair was made up almost entirely of articles given by these friends. A former slaveholder working on a Negro normal school building under a Negro master carpenter is a picture that the last few years have made possible.

Any movement for the elevation of the Southern Negro, in order to be successful, must have to a certain extent the coöperation of the Southern whites. They control government and own the property—whatever benefits the black man benefits the white man. The proper education of all the whites will benefit the Negro as much as the education of the Negro will benefit the whites. The Governor of Alabama would probably count it no disgrace to ride in the same railroad coach with a colored man, but the ignorant white man who curries the Governor's horse would turn up his nose in disgust. The president of a white college in Tuskegee makes a special effort to furnish our young men work that they may be able to remain in school, while the miserable unlettered "brother in white" would say, "You can't learn a nigger anything." Brains, property, and character for the Negro will settle the question of civil rights. The best course to pursue in regard to the civil rights bill in the South is to let it alone; let it alone and it will settle itself. Good school teachers and plenty of money to pay them will be more potent in settling the race question than many civil rights bills and investigating committees. A young colored physician went into the city of Montgomery, Alabama, a few months ago to practise his profession—he was the first to professionally enter the ex-Confederate capital. When his white brother physicians found out by a six days' examination that he had brains enough to pass a better examination, as one of them said, than many of the whites had passed, they gave him a hearty welcome and offered their services to aid him in consultation or in any other way possible—and they are standing manfully up to their promise. Let there be in a community a Negro who by virtue of his superior knowledge of the chemistry of the soil, his acquaintance with the most improved tools and best breeds of stock, can raise fifty bushels of corn to the acre while his white neighbor only raises thirty, and the white man will come to the black man to learn. Further, they will sit down on the same train, in the same coach and on the same seat, to talk about it. Harmony will come in proportion as the black man gets something that the white man wants, whether it be of brains or of material. Some of the county whites looked at first with disfavor on the establishing of a normal school in Tuskegee. It turned out that there was no brick yard in the county; merchants and farmers wanted to build, but bricks must be brought from a distance or they must wait for one house to burn down before building another. The Normal School with student labor started a brick yard. Several kilns of bricks were burned; the whites came from miles around for bricks. From examining bricks they were led to examine the workings of the school. From the discussion of the brick yard came the discussion of Negro education—and thus many of the "old masters" have been led to see and become interested in Negro education. In Tuskegee a Negro mechanic manufactures the best tinware, the best harness, the best boots and shoes, and it is common to see his store crowded with white customers from all over the county. His word or note goes as far as that of the whitest man.

I repeat for emphasis that any work looking towards the permanent improvement of the Negro South must have for one of its aims the fitting of him to live friendly and peaceably with his white neighbors both socially and politically. In spite of all talks of exodus, the Negro's home is permanently in the South: for coming to the bread-and-meat side of the question, the white man needs the Negro, and the Negro needs the white man. His home being permanently in the South, it is our duty to help him prepare himself to live there an independent, educated citizen.

In order that there may be the broadest development of the colored man and that he may have an unbounded field in which to labor, the two races must be brought to have faith in each other. The teachings of the Negro in various ways for the last twenty years have been rather too much to array him against his white brother than to put the two races in coöperation with each other. Thus Massachusetts supports the Republican party, because the Republican party supports Massachusetts with a protective tariff, but the Negro supports the Republican party simply because Massachusetts does. When the colored man is educated up to the point of reasoning that Massachusetts and Alabama are a long way apart and the conditions of life are very different, and if free trade enables my white neighbor across the street to buy his plows at a cheaper rate it will enable me to do the same thing, then will he be consulted in governmental questions. More than once have I noticed that when the whites were in favor of prohibition the blacks, led even by sober upright ministers, voted against it simply because the whites were in favor of it, and for that reason the blacks said that they knew it was a "Democratic trick." If the whites vote to levy a tax to build a schoolhouse, it is a signal for the blacks to oppose the measure, simply because the whites favor it. I venture the assertion that the sooner the colored man South learns that one political party is not composed of all angels and the other of all devils, and that all his enemies do not live in his own town or neighborhood, and all his friends in some distant section of the country, the sooner will his educational advantages be enhanced many fold. But matters are gradually changing in this respect. The black man is beginning to find out that there are those even among the Southern whites who desire his elevation. The Negro's new faith in the white man is being reciprocated in proportion as the Negro is rightly educated. The white brother is beginning to learn by degrees that all Negroes are not liars and chicken thieves. A former owner of seventy-five or one hundred slaves and now a large planter and merchant said to me a few days ago, "I can see every day the change that is coming about. I have on one of my plantations a colored man who can read and write and he is the most valuable man on the farm. In the first place I can trust him to keep the time of the others or with anything else. If a new style of plow or cotton planter is taken on the place, he can understand its construction in half the time that any of the others can."

My faith is that reforms in the South are to come from within. Southern people have a good deal of human nature. They like to receive the praise of doing good deeds, and they don't like to obey orders that come from Washington telling them that they must lay aside at once customs that they have followed for centuries, and henceforth there must be but one railroad coach, one hotel, and one schoolhouse for ex-master and ex-slave. In proof of my first assertion, the railroads in Alabama required colored passengers to pay the same fare as the whites, and then compelled the colored to ride in the smoking car. A committee of leading colored people laid the injustice of the matter before the railroad commissioners of Alabama, who at once ordered that within thirty days every railroad in the State should provide equal but separate accommodations for both races. Every prominent newspaper in the State pronounced it a just decision. Alabama gives $9,000 annually towards the support of colored normal schools. The last legislature increased the annual appropriation for free schools by $100,000, making the total annual appropriation over $500,-000, and nearly half of this amount goes to colored schools, and I have for the first time to hear of any distinction being made between the races by any state officer in the distribution of this fund. Why, my friends, more pippins are growing in the South than crab apples, more roses than thorns.

Now, in regard to what I have said about the relations of the two races, there should be no unmanly cowering or stooping to satisfy unreasonable whims of Southern white men, but it is charity and wisdom to keep in mind the two hundred years' schooling in prejudice against the Negro which the ex-slaveholders are called upon to conquer. A certain class of whites South object to the general education of the colored man on the ground that when he is educated he ceases to do manual labor, and there is no evading the fact that much aid is withheld from Negro education in the South by the states on these grounds. Just here the great mission of industrial education coupled with the mental comes in. It "kills two birds with one stone," viz.: secures the coöperation of the whites, and does the best possible thing for the black man. An old colored man in a cotton field in the middle of July lifted his eyes toward heaven and said, "De cotton is so grassy, de work is so hard, and de sun am so hot, I believe this darkey am called to preach." This old man, no doubt, stated the true reason why not a few enter school. Educate the black man, mentally and industrially, and there will be no doubt of his prosperity; for a race who has lived at all, and paid, for the last twenty years, twenty-five and thirty per cent interest on the dollar advanced for food, with almost no education, can certainly take care of itself when educated mentally and industrially.

The Tuskegee Normal School, located in the black belt of Alabama, with an ignorant, degraded Negro population of twenty-five thousand within a radius of twenty miles, has a good chance to see the direct needs of the people; and to get a correct idea of their condition one must leave the towns and go far out into the country, miles from any railroad, where the majority of the people live. They need teachers with not only trained heads and hearts, but with trained hands. Schoolhouses are needed in every township and country. The present wrecks of log cabins and bush harbors, where many of the schools are now taught, must be replaced by comfortable, decent houses. In many schoolhouses rails are used for seats, and often the fire is on the outside of the house, while teacher and scholars are on the inside. Add to this a teacher who can scarcely write his name, and who is as weak mentally as morally, and you then have but a faint idea of the educational condition of many parts of the South. It is the work of Tuskegee, not to send into these places teachers who will stand off and tell the people what to do, or what ought to be done, but to send those who can take hold and show the people *how* to do. The blacksmiths, carpenters, brickmasons, and tinners, who learned their trades in slavery, are dying out, and slavery having taught the colored boy that labor is a disgrace, few of their places are being filled. The Negro now has a monopoly of the trades in the South, but he can't hold it unless the young men are taught trades while in school. The large number of educated loafers to be seen around the streets of our large cities furnishes another reason in favor of industrial education. Then the proud fop with his beaver hat, kid gloves, and walking cane, who has done no little to injure the cause of education South, by industrial training, would be brought down to something practical and useful. The Tuskegee Normal School, with a farm of five hundred acres, carpenter's shop, printing office, blacksmith's shop, and brick yard for boys, and a sewing department, laundry, flower gardening, and practical housekeeping for girls, is trying to do its part towards furnishing industrial training. We ask help for nothing that we can do for ourselves; nothing is bought that the students can produce. The boys raise the vegetables, have done the painting, made the brick, the chairs, the tables, the desks; have built a stable, a carpenter's shop, and a blacksmith's shop. The girls do the entire housekeeping, including the mending, ironing, and washing of the boys' clothes; besides they make many garments to sell.

The majority of the students are poor and able to pay but little cash for board; consequently the school keeps three points before it: first, to give the student the best mental training; secondly, to furnish him with labor that will be valuable to the school, and that will enable the student to learn something from the labor *per se;* thirdly, to teach the dignity of labor. A *chance* to help himself is what we want to give to every student; this is the chance that was given me ten years ago when I entered the Hampton Institute with but fifty cents in my pocket, and it is my only ambition in life to do my part in giving it to every other poor but worthy young man and woman.

As to morals, the Negro is slowly but surely improving. In this he has had no standard by which to shape his character. The masses in too many cases have been judged by their so-called leaders, who are as a rule ignorant, immoral preachers or selfish politicians. The number of these preachers is legion. One church near Tuskegee has a total membership of two hundred, and nineteen of these are preachers.

Poverty and ignorance have affected the black man just as they affect the white man. They have made him untruthful, intemperate, selfish, caused him to steal, to be cheated, and made the outcast of society, and he has aspired to positions which he was not mentally and morally capable of filling. But the day is breaking, and education will bring the complete light. The scales of prejudice are beginning to drop from the eyes of the dominant classes South, and through their clearer and more intelligent vision they are beginning to see and recognize the mighty truth that wealth, happiness, and permanent prosperity will only come in proportion as the hand, head, and heart of both races are educated and Christianized—July 16, 1884.

ATLANTA EXPOSITION ADDRESS

One third of the population of the South is of the Negro race. No enterprise seeking the material, civil, or moral welfare of this section can disregard this element of our population and reach the highest success. I but convey to you, Mr. President and Directors, the sentiment of the masses of my race when I say that in no way have the value and manhood of the American Negro been more fittingly and generously recognized than by the managers of this magnificent exposition at every stage of its progress. It is a recognition that will do more to cement the friendship of the two races than any occurrence since the dawn of our freedom.

Not only this, but the opportunity here afforded will awaken among us a new era of industrial progress. Ignorant and inexperienced, it is not

strange that in the first years of our new life we began at the top instead of
at the bottom; that a seat in Congress or the State Legislature was more
sought than real estate or industrial skill; that the political convention or
stump-speaking had more attraction than starting a dairy farm or truck
garden.

A ship lost at sea for many days suddenly sighted a friendly vessel.
From the mast of the unfortunate vessel was seen a signal: "Water, water;
we die of thirst!" The answer from the friendly vessel at once came back:
"Cast down your bucket where you are." A second time the signal, "Water, water; send us water!" ran up from the distressed vessel, and was
answered: "Cast down your bucket where you are." And a third and
fourth signal for water was answered, "Cast down your bucket where you
are." The captain of the distressed vessel, at last heeding the injunction,
cast down his bucket, and it came up full of fresh, sparkling water from
the mouth of the Amazon River. To those of my race who depend upon
bettering their condition in a foreign land, or who underestimate the importance of cultivating friendly relations with the Southern white man
who is their next-door neighbor, I would say: "Cast down your bucket
where you are"—cast it down in making friends, in every manly way, of
the people of all races by whom we are surrounded.

Cast it down in agriculture, mechanics, in commerce, in domestic service, and in the professions. And in this connection it is well to bear in
mind that whatever other sins the South may be called to bear, when it
comes to business, pure and simple, it is in the South that the Negro is
given a man's chance in the commercial world, and in nothing is this
Exposition more eloquent than in emphasizing this chance. Our greatest
danger is that in the great leap from slavery to freedom we may overlook
the fact that the masses of us are to live by the productions of our hands,
and fail to keep in mind that we shall prosper in proportion as we learn to
dignify and glorify common labor, and put brains and skill into the common occupations of life; shall prosper in proportion as we learn to draw
the line between the superficial and the substantial, the ornamental gew-
gaws of life and the useful. No race can prosper till it learns that there is
as much dignity in tilling a field as in writing a poem. It is at the bottom
of life we must begin, and not at the top. Nor should we permit our
grievances to overshadow our opportunities.

To those of the white race who look to the incoming of those of foreign
birth and strange tongue and habits for the prosperity of the South, were I
permitted, I would repeat what I say to my own race, "Cast down your
bucket where you are." Cast it down among the eight million Negroes
whose habits you know, whose fidelity and love you have tested in days
when to have proved treacherous meant the ruin of your firesides. Cast
down your bucket among these people who have without strikes and labor
wars tilled your fields, cleared your forests, builded your railroads and
cities, brought forth treasures from the bowels of the earth, and helped

make possible this magnificent representation of the progress of the South. Casting down your bucket among my people, helping and encouraging them as you are doing on these grounds, and, with education of head, hand, and heart, you will find that they will buy your surplus land, make blossom the waste places in your fields, and run your factories. While doing this, you can be sure in the future, as in the past, that you and your families will be surrounded by the most patient, faithful, law-abiding, and unresentful people that the world has seen. As we have proved our loyalty to you in the past, in nursing your children, watching by the sick bed of your mothers and fathers, and often following them with tear-dimmed eyes to their graves, so in the future, in our humble way, we shall stand by you with a devotion that no foreigner can approach, ready to lay down our lives, if need be, in defense of yours, interlacing our industrial, commercial, civil, and religious life with yours in a way that shall make the interests of both races one. In all things that are purely social we can be as separate as the fingers, yet one as the hand in all things essential to mutual progress.

There is no defense or security for any of us except in the highest intelligence and development of all. If anywhere there are efforts tending to curtail the fullest growth of the Negro, let these efforts be turned into stimulating, encouraging, and making him the most useful and intelligent citizen. Effort or means so invested will pay a thousand per cent interest. These efforts will be twice blessed—"Blessing him that gives and him that takes."

There is no escape through law of man or God from the inevitable:

> The laws of changeless justice bind
> Oppressor with oppressed;
> And close as sin and suffering joined
> We march to fare abreast.

Nearly sixteen millions of hands will aid you in pulling the load upward, or they will pull, against you, the load downward. We shall constitute one third and more of the ignorance and crime of the South, or one third its intelligence and progress; we shall contribute one third to the business and industrial prosperity of the South, or we shall prove a veritable body of death, stagnating, depressing, retarding every effort to advance the body politic.

Gentlemen of the Exposition, as we present to you our humble effort at an exhibition of our progress, you must not expect overmuch. Starting thirty years ago with ownership here and there in a few quilts and pumpkins and chickens (gathered from miscellaneous sources), remember, the path that has led from these to the inventions and production of agricultural implements, buggies, steam engines, newspapers, books, statuary carving, paintings, the management of drugstores and banks, has not been trodden without contact with thorns and thistles. While we take pride in what we exhibit as a result of our independent efforts, we do not for a moment forget that our part in this exhibition would fall far short of your expectations but for the constant help that has come to our educational life, not only from the Southern states, but especially from Northern philanthropists, who have made their gifts a constant stream of blessing and encouragement.

The wisest among my race understand that the agitation of questions of social equality is the extremest folly, and that progress in the enjoyment of all the privileges that will come to us must be the result of severe and constant struggle rather than of artificial forcing. No race that has anything to contribute to the markets of the world is long, in any degree, ostracized. It is important and right that all privileges of the law be ours, but it is vastly more important that we be prepared for the exercise of those privileges. The opportunity to earn a dollar in a factory just now is worth infinitely more than the opportunity to spend a dollar in an opera house.

In conclusion, may I repeat that nothing in thirty years has given us more hope and encouragement, and drawn us so near to you of the white race, as this opportunity offered by the Exposition; and here bending, as it were, over the altar that represents the results of the struggles of your race and mine, both starting practically empty-handed three decades ago, I pledge that, in your effort to work out the great and intricate problem which God has laid at the doors of the South, you shall have at all times the patient, sympathetic help of my race; only let this be constantly in mind, that while, from representations in these buildings of the product of field, of forest, of mine, of factory, letters, and art, much good will come, yet far above and beyond material benefits will be that higher good, that, let us pray God, will come in a blotting out of sectional differences and racial animosities and suspicions, in a determination to administer absolute justice, in a willing obedience among all classes to the mandates of law. This, coupled with our material prosperity, will bring into our beloved South a new heaven and a new earth—**September 18, 1895.**

OUR NEW CITIZEN

From whence came our new citizen? Who is he? And what is his mission? It is interesting to note that the Negro is the only citizen of this country who came here by special invitation and by reason of special provision. The Caucasian came here against the protest of the leading citizens of this country in 1492. We were so important to the prosperity of this country that special vessels were sent to convey us hither.

Shall we be less important in the future than in the past? The Negroes are one eighth of your population. Our race is larger than the population

of the Argentine Republic, larger than Chile, larger than Peru and Vene-
zuela combined—nearly as large as Mexico.

Whether the call has come for us to clear the forests of your country, to
make your cotton, rice, and sugar cane, build houses or railroads, or to
shoulder arms in defense of our country, have we not answered that call?
When the call has come to educate our children, to teach them thrift,
habits of industry, have we not filled every school that has been opened
for us? When with others there have been labor wars, strikes, and destruction of property, have we not set the world an example in each one quietly
attending to his own business? When, even here in the North, the shop,
the factory, the trades have closed against us, have we not patiently, faithfully gone on taking advantage of our disadvantages, and through it all
have we not continued to rise, to increase in numbers and prosperity? If in
the past we have thus proven our right to your respect and confidence,
shall it be less so in the future? If in proportion as we contribute, by the
exercise of the higher virtues, by the product of brain and skilled hand, to
the common prosperity of our country, shall we not receive all the privileges of any other citizen, whether born out of this country or under the
Stars and Stripes?

You of the great and prosperous North still owe a serious and uncompleted duty to your less fortunate brothers of the white race South who
suffered and are still suffering the consequences of American slavery.
What was the task you asked them to perform? Returning to their destitute homes after years of war, to face blasted hopes, devastation, a shattered industrial system, you asked them to add to their burdens that of
preparing in education, politics, and economics, in a few short years, for
citizenship four or five millions of former slaves. That the South, staggering under the burden, made blunders, that in some measure there has been
disappointment, no one need be surprised.

And yet, taking it all in all, we may, I think, safely challenge history to
find a case where two races, but yesterday master and slave, today citizen
and citizen, have made such marvelous progress in the adjustment of
themselves to new conditions, where each has traveled so fast in the divine
science of forgetting and forgiving; and yet do not misunderstand me that
all is done or that there are not serious wrongs yet to be blotted out.

In making these observations I do not, I cannot, forget as an humble
representative of my race the vacant seat, the empty sleeve, the lives
offered up on Southern battlefields, that we might have a united country
and that our flag should shelter none save freemen, nor do I forget the
millions of dollars that have gone into the South from the hands of philanthropic individuals and religious organizations.

Nor are we of the black race leaving the work alone to your race in the
North or your race in the South—mark what this new citizen is doing. Go
with me tonight to the Tuskegee Institute in the Black Belt of Alabama,

in an old slave plantation where a few years ago my people were bought and sold, and I will show you an industrial village, which is an example of others, with nearly eight hundred young men and women working with head and hand by night and by day, preparing themselves, in literature, in science, in agriculture, in dairying, in fruit-growing, in stock-raising, in brick-making, in brick masonry, in woodwork, in ironwork, in tinwork, in leatherwork, in cloth, in cooking, in laundrying, in printing, in household science—in the duties of Christian citizenship—preparing themselves that they may prepare thousands of others of our race that they may contribute their full quota of virtue, of thrift and intelligence to the prosperity of our beloved country. It is said that we will be hewers of wood and drawers of water, but we shall be more, we shall turn the wood into houses, into machinery, into implements of commerce and civilization. We shall turn the water into steam, into electricity, into dairy and agricultural products, into food and raiment—and thus wind our life about yours, thus knit our civil and commercial interests into yours in a way that shall make us all realize anew that "of one blood hath God made all men to dwell and prosper on the face of the earth."

But when all this is said, I repeat, gentlemen of the club, that you of this generation owe to the South, not less than to yourselves, an unfulfilled duty. Surely, surely, if the Negro, with all that is behind him, can forget the past, you ought to rise above him in this regard. When the South is poor you are poor, when the South commits crime you commit crime, when the South prospers you prosper. There is no power that can separate our destiny. Let us ascend in this matter above color or race or party or sectionalism into the region of duty of man to man, American to American, Christian to Christian. If the Negro who has been oppressed, ostracized, denied rights in a Christian land, can help you, North and South, to rise, can be the medium of your rising to these sublime heights of unselfishness and self-forgetfulness, who may say that the Negro, this new citizen, will not see in it a recompense for all that he has suffered and will have performed a mission that will be placed beside that of the lowly Nazarine?

Let the Negro, the North, and the South do their duty with a new spirit and a new determination during this, the dawning of a new century, and at the end of fifty years a picture will be painted—what is it? A race dragged from its native land in chains, three hundred years of slavery, years of fratricidal war, thousands of lives laid down, freedom for the slave, reconstruction, blunders, bitterness between North and South. The South staggers under the burden; the North forgets the past and comes to the rescue; the Negro, in the midst, teaching North and South patience, forbearance, long-suffering, obedience to law, developing in intellect, character and property, skill and habits of industry. The North and South, joining hands with the Negro, take him whom they have wronged, help him, encourage him, stimulate him in self-help, give him the rights of man, and, in lifting up the Negro, lift themselves up into that atmosphere where there is a new North, a new South—a new citizen—a new republic—January 31, 1896.

DEMOCRACY AND EDUCATION

It is said that the strongest chain is no stronger than its weakest link. In the Southern part of our country there are twenty-two millions of your brethren who are bound to you by ties which you cannot tear asunder if you would. The most intelligent man in your community has his intelligence darkened by the ignorance of a fellow citizen in the Mississippi bottoms. The most wealthy in your city would be more wealthy but for the poverty of a fellow being in the Carolina rice swamps. The most moral and religious among you has his religion and morality modified by the degradation of the man in the South whose religion is a mere matter of form or emotionalism.

The vote in your state that is cast for the highest and purest form of government is largely neutralized by the vote of the man in Louisiana whose ballot is stolen or cast in ignorance. When the South is poor, you are poor; when the South commits crime, you commit crime. My friends, there is no mistake; you must help us to raise the character of our civilization or yours will be lowered. No member of your race in any part of our country can harm the weakest and meanest member of mine without the proudest and bluest blood in the city of Brooklyn being degraded. The central ideal which I wish you to help me consider is the reaching and lifting up of the lowest, most unfortunate, negative element that occupies so large a proportion of our territory and composes so large a percentage of our population. It seems to me that there never was a time in the history of our country when those interested in education should more earnestly consider to what extent the mere acquiring of a knowledge of literature and science makes producers, lovers of labor, independent, honest, unselfish, and, above all, supremely good. Call education by what name you please, and if it fails to bring about these results among the masses it falls short of its highest end. The science, the art, the literature that fails to reach down and bring the humblest up to the fullest enjoyment of the blessings of our government is weak, no matter how costly the buildings or apparatus used, or how modern the methods in instruction employed. The study of arithmetic that does not result in making someone more honest and self-reliant is defective. The study of history that does not result in making men conscientious in receiving and counting the ballots of their fellow men is most faulty. The study of art that does not result in making the strong less willing to oppress the weak means little. How I wish that from the most humble log cabin schoolhouse in Alabama we could burn it, as it were, into the hearts and heads of all, that usefulness, service to our brother, is the supreme end of education. Putting the thought more directly as it applies to conditions in the South: Can you make your intelligence affect us in the same ratio that our ignorance affects you? Let us put a not improbable case. A great national question is to be decided, one that involves peace or war, the honor or dishonor of our nation—yea, the very existence of the government. The North and West are divided. There are five million votes to be cast in the South, and of this number one half are ignorant. Not only are one half the voters ignorant, but, because of this ignorant vote, corruption, dishonesty in a dozen forms have crept into the exercise of the political franchise, to the extent that the conscience of the intelligent class is soured in its attempts to defeat the will of the ignorant voters. Here, then, on the one hand you have an ignorant vote, and on the other hand an intelligent vote minus a conscience. The time may not be far off when to this kind of jury we shall have to look for the verdict that is to decide the course of our democratic institutions.

When a great national calamity stares us in the face, we are, I fear, too much given to depending on a short campaign of education to do on the hustings what should have been accomplished in the schoolroom. With this preliminary survey, let us examine with more care the work to be done in the South before all classes will be fit for the highest duties of citizenship. In reference to my own race I am confronted with some embarrassment at the outset because of the various and conflicting opinions as to what is to be its final place in our economic and political life. Within the last thirty years—and, I might add, within the last three months—it has been proven by eminent authority that the Negro is increasing in numbers so fast that it is only a question of a few years before he will far outnumber the white race in the South, and it has also been proven that the Negro is fast dying out and it is only a question of a few years before he will have completely disappeared. It has also been proven that crime among us is on the increase and that crime is on the decrease; that education helps the Negro, that education also hurts him; that he is fast leaving the South and taking up his residence in the North and West, and that the tendency of the Negro is to drift to the lowlands of the Mississippi bottoms. It has been proven that as a slave laborer he produced less cotton than a free man. It has been proven that education unfits the Negro for work, and that education also makes him more valuable as a laborer; that he is our greatest criminal and that he is our most law-abiding citizen. In the midst of these opinions, in the words of a modern statesman, "I hardly know where I am at." I hardly know whether I am myself or the other fellow. But in the midst of this confusion there are a few things of which I feel certain that furnish a basis for thought and action. I know that, whether we are increasing or decreasing, whether we are growing better or worse, whether we are valuable or valueless, a few years ago fourteen of us were brought into this country and now there are eight million of us. I know that, whether in slavery or freedom, we have always been loyal to the Stars and Stripes, that no schoolhouse has been opened for us that has not been filled; that 1,500,000 ballots that we have the right to cast are as potent for weal and woe as the ballot cast by the whitest and most influential man in your commonwealth. I know that wherever our life touches yours we help or hinder; that wherever your life touches ours you make us stronger or weaker. Further I know that almost every other race that tried to look the white man in the face has disappeared. With all the conflicting opinions, and with the full knowledge of all our weaknesses, I know that only a few centuries ago in this country we went into slavery pagans: we came out Christians; we went into slavery pieces of property: we came out American citizens; we went into slavery without a language: we came out speaking the proud Anglo-Saxon tongue; we went into slavery with the slave chains clanking about our wrists: we came out with the American ballot in our hands. My friends, I submit it to your sober and candid judgment, if a race that is capable of such a test, such a transformation, is not worth saving and making a part, in reality as well as in name, of our democratic government. It is with an ignorant race as it is with a child: it craves at first the superficial, the ornamental, the signs of progress rather than the reality. The ignorant race is tempted to jump, at one bound, to the position that it has required years of hard struggle for others to reach. It seems to me that the temptation in education and missionary work is to do for a people a thousand miles away without always making a careful study of the needs and conditions of the people whom we are trying to help. The temptation is to run all people through a certain educational mold regardless of the condition of the subject or the end to be accomplished. Unfortunately for us as a race, our education was begun, just after the war, too nearly where New England education ended. We seemed to overlook the fact that we were dealing with a race that has little love for labor in their native land and consequently brought little love for labor with them to America. Added to this was the fact that they had been forced for two hundred and fifty years to labor without compensation under circumstances that were calculated to do anything but teach them the dignity, beauty, and civilizing power of intelligent labor. We forgot the industrial education that was given the Pilgrim Fathers of New England in clearing and planting its cold, bleak, and snowy hills and valleys, in providing shelter, founding the small mills and factories, in supplying themselves with home-made products, thus laying the foundation of an industrial life that now keeps going a large part of the colleges and missionary effort of the world. May I be tempted one step further in showing how prone we are to make our education formal, technical, instead of making it meet the needs of conditions regardless of formality and technicality? At least eighty per cent of my pupils in the South are found in the rural districts, and they are dependent on agriculture in some form for their support. Notwithstanding in this instance we have a whole race depending upon agriculture, and notwithstanding thirty years have passed since our freedom, aside from what we have done at Hampton and Tuskegee and one or two other institutions, not a thing has been attempted by state or philanthropy in the way of educating the race in this industry on which their very existence depends. Boys have been taken from the farms and educated in law, theology, Hebrew, and Greek—educated in everything else but the very subject they should know the most about. I question whether or not among all the educated colored people in the United States you can find six, if we except the institutions named, that have received anything like a thorough training in agriculture. It would have seemed, since self-support and industrial independence are the first conditions for lifting up any race, that education in theoretical and practical agriculture, horticulture, dairying, and stock-raising should have occupied the first place in our system. Some time ago when we decided to make tailoring a part of our training at the Tuskegee Institute, I was amazed to find that it was almost impossible to find in the whole country an educated colored man who could teach the making of clothing. I could find them by the score who could teach astronomy, theology, Greek, or Latin, but almost none who could instruct in the making of clothing, something that has to be used by every one of us every day in the year. How often has my heart been made to sink as I have gone through the South and into the homes of the people and found women who could converse intelligently on Grecian history, who had studied geometry, could analyze the most complex sentences, and yet could not analyze the poorly cooked and still more poorly served bread and fat meat that they and their families were eating three times a day. It is little trouble to find girls who can locate Pekin and the Desert of Sahara on an artificial globe; but seldom can you find one who can locate on an actual dinner table the proper place for the carving knife and fork or the meat and vegetables. A short time ago, in one of our Southern cities, a colored man died who had received training as a skilled mechanic during the days of slavery. By his skill and industry he had built up a great business as a house contractor and builder. In this same city there are thirty-five thousand colored people, among them young men who have been well educated in languages and literature, but not a single one could be found who had been trained in architectural and mechanical drawing that could carry on the business which this ex-slave had built up, and so it was soon scattered to the wind. Aside from the work done in the institutions that I have mentioned, you will find no colored men who have been trained in the principles of architecture, notwithstanding the vast majority of the race is without homes. Here, then, are the three prime conditions for growth, for civilization—food, clothing, shelter—yet we have been the slaves of form and custom to such an extent that we have failed in a large measure to look matters squarely in the face and meet actual needs. You cannot graft a fifteenth-century civilization onto a twentieth-century civilization by the mere performance of mental gymnastics. Understand, I speak in no fault-finding spirit, but with a feeling of deep regret for what has been done; but the future must be an improvement on the past.

I have endeavored to speak plainly in regard to the past, because I fear that the wisest and most interested have not fully comprehended the task which American slavery has laid at the doors of the Republic. Few, I fear, realize what is to be done before the seven million of my people in the South can be made a safe, helpful, progressive part of our institutions. The South, in proportion to its ability, has done well, but this does not change facts. Let me illustrate what I mean by a single example. In spite of all that has been done, I was in a county in Alabama a few days ago where there are some thirty thousand colored people and about seven thousand whites; in this county not a single public school for Negroes has been open this year longer than three months, not a single colored teacher has been paid more than fifteen dollars a month for his teaching. Not one of these schools was taught in a building worthy of the name of schoolhouse. In this county the state or public authorities do not own a dollar's worth of school property—not a schoolhouse, a blackboard, or a piece of crayon. Each colored child had spent on him this year for his education about fifty cents, while one of your children had spent on him this year for education not far from twenty dollars. And yet each citizen of this county is expected to share the burdens and privileges of our democratic form of government just as intelligently and conscientiously as the citizens of your beloved Kings County. A vote in this county means as much to the nation as a vote in the city of Boston. Crime in this country is as truly an arrow aimed at the heart of the government as crime committed in your own streets. Do you know that a single schoolhouse built this year in a town near Boston to shelter about three hundred students has cost more for building alone than will be spent for the education, including buildings, apparatus, teachers, of the whole colored school population of Alabama? The commissioner of education for the state of Georgia recently reported to the state legislature that in the state there were two hundred thousand children that had entered no school the past year, and one hundred thousand more who were in school but a few days, making practically three hundred thousand children between six and sixteen years of age that are growing up in ignorance in one Southern state. The same report states that outside of the cities and towns, while the average number of schoolhouses in a county is sixty, all of these sixty schoolhouses are worth in a lump sum less than $2,000, and the report further adds that many of the schoolhouses in Georgia are not fit for horse stables. These illustrations, my friends, as far as concerns the Gulf states, are not exceptional cases or overdrawn.

I have referred to industrial education as a means of fitting the millions of my people in the South for the duties of citizenship. Until there is industrial independence it is hardly possible to have a pure ballot. In the country districts of the Gulf states it is safe to say that not more than one black man in twenty owns the land he cultivates. Where so large a proportion of the people are dependent, live in other people's houses, eat other people's food, and wear clothes they have not paid for, it is a pretty hard thing to tell how they are going to vote. My remarks thus far have referred mainly to my own race. But there is another side. The longer I live and the more I study the question, the more I am convinced that it is not so much a problem as to what you will do with the Negro as what the Negro will do with you and your civilization. In considering this side of the subject, I thank God that I have grown to the point where I can sympathize with a white man as much as I can sympathize with a black man. I have grown to the point where I can sympathize with a Southern white man as much as I can sympathize with a Northern white man. To me "a man's a man for a' that and a' that." As bearing upon democracy and education, what of your white brethren in the South, those who suffered and are still suffering the consequences of American slavery for which both you and they are responsible? You of the great and prosperous North still owe to your unfortunate brethren of the Caucasian race in the South, not less than to yourselves, a serious and uncompleted duty. What was the task you asked them to perform? Returning to their destitute homes after years of war to face blasted hopes, devastation, a shattered industrial system, you asked them to add to their own burdens that of preparing in education, politics, and economics in a few short years, for citizenship, four millions of former slaves. That the South, staggering under the burden, made blunders, and that in a measure there has been disappointment, no one need be surprised.

The educators, the statesmen, the philanthropists have never comprehended their duty toward the millions of poor whites in the South who were buffeted for two hundred years between slavery and freedom, between civilization and degradation, who were disregarded by both master and slave. It needs no prophet to tell the character of our future civilization when the poor white boy in the country districts of the South receives one dollar's worth of education and your boy twenty dollars' worth, when one never enters a library or reading room and the other has libraries and reading rooms in every ward and town. When one hears lectures and sermons once in two months and the other can hear a lecture or sermon every day in the year. When you help the South you help yourselves. Mere abuse will not bring the remedy. The time has come, it seems to me, when in this matter we should rise above party or race or sectionalism into the region of duty of man to man, citizen to citizen, Christian to Christian, and if the Negro who has been oppressed and denied rights in a Christian land can help you North and South to rise, can be the medium of your rising into this atmosphere of generous Christian brotherhood and self-forgetfulness, he will see in it a recompense for all that he has suffered in the past. Not very long ago a white citizen of the South boastingly expressed himself in public to this effect: "I am now forty-six years of age, but have never polished my own boots, have never saddled my own horse, have never built a fire in my own room, have never hitched a horse." He was asked a short time since by a lame man to hitch his horse, but refused and told him to get a Negro to do it. Our state law requires that a voter is required to read the constitution before voting, but the last clause of the constitution is in Latin and the Negroes cannot read Latin, and so they are asked to read the Latin clause and are thus disfranchised, while the whites are permitted to read the English portion of the constitution. I do not quote these statements for the purpose of condemning the individual or the South, for though myself a member of a despised and unfortunate race, I pity from the bottom of my heart any of God's creatures whence such a statement can emanate. Evidently here is a man who, as far as mere book training is concerned, is educated, for he boasts of his knowledge of Latin, but, so far as the real purpose of education is concerned—the making of men useful, honest, and liberal—this man has never been touched. Here is a citizen in the midst of our republic, clothed in a white skin, with all the technical signs of education, but who is as little fitted for the highest purpose of life as any creature found in Central Africa. My friends, can we make our education reach down far enough to touch and help this man? Can we so control science, art, and literature as to make them to such an extent a means rather than an end; that the lowest and most unfortunate of God's creatures shall be lifted up, ennobled and glorified; shall be a freeman instead of a slave of narrow sympathies and wrong customs? Some years ago a bright young man of my race succeeded in passing a competitive examination for a cadetship at the United States naval academy at Annapolis. Says the young man, Mr. Henry Baker, in describing his stay at this institution: "I was several times attacked with stones and was forced finally to appeal to the officers, when a marine was detailed to accompany me across the campus and from the mess hall at meal times. My books were mutilated, my clothes were cut and in some instances destroyed, and all the petty annoyances which ingenuity could devise were inflicted upon me daily, and during seamanship practice aboard the *Dale* attempts were often made to do me personal injury while I would be aloft in the rigging. No one ever addressed me by name. I was called the Moke usually, the Nigger for variety. I was shunned as if I were a veritable leper and received curses and blows as the only method my persecutors had of relieving the monotony." Not once during the two years, with one exception, did any one of the more than four hundred cadets enrolled ever come to him with a word of advice, counsel, sympathy, or information, and he never held conversation with any one of them for as much as five minutes during the whole course of his experience at the academy, except on occasions when he was defending himself against their assaults. The one exception where the departure from the rule was made was in the case of a Pennsylvania boy, who stealthily brought him a piece of his birthday cake at twelve o'clock one night. The act so surprised Baker that his suspicions were aroused, but these were dispelled by the donor, who read to him a letter which he had received from his mother, from whom the cake came, in which she requested that a slice be given to the colored cadet who was without friends. I recite this incident and not for the purpose merely of condemning the wrong done a member of my race; no, no, not that. I mention the case, not for the one cadet, but for the sake of the four hundred cadets, for the sake of the four hundred American families, the four hundred American communities whose civilization and Christianity these cadets represented. Here were four hundred and more picked young men representing the flower of our country, who had passed through our common schools and were preparing themselves at public expense to defend the honor of our country. And yet, with grammar, reading, and arithmetic in the public schools, and with lessons in the arts of war, the principles of physical courage at Annapolis, both systems seemed to have utterly failed to prepare a single one of these young men for real life, that he could be brave enough, Christian enough, American enough, to take this poor defenseless black boy by the hand in open daylight and let the world know that he was his friend. Education, whether of black man or white man, that gives one physical courage to stand in front of the cannon and fails to give him moral courage to stand up in defense of right and justice is a failure. With all that the Brooklyn Institute of Arts and Sciences stands for in its equipment, its endowment, its wealth and culture, its instructors, can it produce a mother that will produce a boy that will not be ashamed to have the world know that he is a friend to the most unfortunate of God's creatures? Not long ago a mother, a black mother, who lived in one of your Northern states, had heard it whispered around in her community for years that the Negro was lazy, shiftless, and would not work. So when her boy grew to sufficient size, at considerable expense and great self-sacrifice, she had her boy thoroughly taught the machinist's trade. A job was secured in a neighboring shop. With dinner bucket in hand and spurred on by the prayers of the now happy mother, the boy entered the shop to begin his first day's work. What happened? Had any one of the twenty white Americans been so educated that he gave this stranger a welcome into their midst? No, not this. Every one of the twenty white men threw down his tools and deliberately walked out, swearing that he would not give a black man an opportunity to earn an honest living. Another shop was tried, with the same result, and still another and the same. Today this promising and ambitious black man is a wreck—a confirmed drunkard, with no hope, no ambition. My friends, who blasted the life of this young man? On whose hands does his blood rest? Our system of education, or want of education, is responsible. Can our public schools and colleges turn out a set of men that will throw open the doors of industry to all men everywhere, regardless of color, so all shall have the same opportunity to earn a dollar that they now have to spend a dollar? I know a good many species of cowardice and prejudice, but I know none equal to this. I know not who is the worst, the ex-slaveholder who perforce compelled his slave to work without compensation, or the man who perforce compels the Negro to refrain from working for compensation. My friends, we are one in this country. The question of the highest citizenship and the complete education of all concerns nearly ten million of my own people and over sixty million of yours. We rise as you rise; when we fall you fall. When you are strong we are strong; when we are weak you are weak. There is no power that can separate our destiny. The Negro can afford to be wronged; the white man cannot afford to wrong him. Unjust laws or customs that exist in many places regarding the races injure the white man and inconvenience the Negro. No race can wrong another race simply because it has the power to do so without being permanently injured in morals. The Negro can endure the temporary inconvenience, but the injury to the white man is permanent. It is for the white man to save himself from his degradation that I plead. If a white man steals a Negro's ballot it is the white man who is permanently injured. Physical death comes to the one Negro lynched in a county, but death of the morals—death of the soul—comes to the thousands responsible for the lynching. We are a patient, humble people. We can afford to work and wait. There is plenty in this country for us to do. Away up in the atmosphere of goodness, forbearance, patience, long-suffering, and forgiveness the workers are not many or overcrowded. If others would be little we can be great. If others would be mean we can be good. If others would push us down we can help push them up. Character, not circumstances, makes the man. It is more important that we be prepared for voting than that we vote, more important that we be prepared to hold office than that we hold office, more important that we be prepared for the highest recognition than that we be recognized. Those who fought and died on the battlefield performed their duty heroically and well, but a duty remains for you and me. The mere fiat of law could not make an ignorant voter an intelligent voter; could not make one citizen respect another; these results come to the Negro, as to all races, by beginning at the bottom and working up to the highest civilization and accomplishment. In the economy of God, there can be but one standard by which an individual can succeed—there is but one for a race. This country demands that every race measure itself by the American standard. By it a race must rise or fall, succeed or fail, and in the last analysis mere sentiment counts but little. During the next half-century and more my race must continue passing through the severe American crucible.

We are to be tested in our patience, in our forbearance, our power to endure wrong, to withstand temptation, to succeed, to acquire and use skill, our ability to complete, to succeed in commerce; to disregard the superficial for the real, the appearance for the substance; to be great and yet the servant of all. This, this is the passport to all that is best in the life of our republic, and the Negro must possess it or be debarred. In working out our destiny, while the main burden and center of activity must be with us, we shall need in a large measure the help, the encouragement, the guidance that the strong can give the weak. Thus helped, we of both races in the South shall soon throw off the shackles of racial and sectional prejudice and rise above the clouds of ignorance, narrowness, and selfishness into that atmosphere, that pure sunshine, where it will be our highest ambition to serve man, our brother, regardless of race or past conditions—September 30, 1896.

ADDRESS DELIVERED AT HAMPTON INSTITUTE

Few, if any, occasions within the past thirty years have meant more to the Negro race than that which calls us here. The Negro has been a laborer in this country nearly three hundred years, but with few exceptions he has been a forced laborer, an unskilled laborer, or an ignorant laborer; but here at the mouth of the James, but a few miles distant from where we entered this country as slaves, we have inaugurated today the largest and most complete attempt in this country to make the Negro an intelligent, conscientious, skillful producer, and to have him appreciate the dignity, beauty, and civilizing power that there is in labor. For this magnificent opportunity, not only the Hampton Institute but the Negro race bows in thanks to Mr. Morris K. Jesup, the generous helper, who has made what we see here possible; Dr. J. L. M. Curry, the farseeing agent of the John F. Slater Fund; as well as all the trustees and generous friends who have united in the opening of this new door. Coming as it does on the heels of the decision of the great American Jury, that our own country is to go forward and not backward in its business and commercial life, this enterprise means much, not alone to the Negro, but to the entire nation. Within the two decades it will be decided whether the Negro, by discarding ante-bellum ideas and methods, by putting brains and skill into the common occupations that lie at his door, will be able to lift labor out of toil, drudgery, and degradation into that which is dignified, beautiful, and glorified. Further, it will be decided within this time whether the Negro is to be replaced, crushed out as a helpful industrial factor by the fast-spreading trades unions, in connection with thousands of foreign skilled laborers, that even now press hard and fast upon his heels and seem to press him into the very death. This question is for such unselfish members of the Anglo-Saxon race as are gathered here to help decide—and in deciding, not alone for the Negro, but whether you will have eight million people in this country, a nation within a nation, that will be a burden, a menace to your civilization and commercial life.

The Negro in slavery was tied to the white man through the bill of sale.

In freedom he must tie himself to the white man through the bonds of commerce and the cultivation of the sympathetic good will of his white neighbor. When a black man has the best farm to be found in his county, every white man will respect him. A white man knows the Negro that lives in a two-story brick house whether he wants to or not. When a black man is the largest taxpayer in a community, his neighbors will not object very long to his voting and having his vote honestly counted. In the future there must be a more vital and practical connection between the Negro's educated brain and his means of earning a living.

But what has all this to do with the higher interests—the moral and religious side? I answer: Show me a race that is living on the outer edges of the industrial world, on the skimmed milk of business, and I will show you a race that is the football for political parties, and a race that cannot be what it should be in morals, and religion. I may be accused of wrong interpretation, but when the Bible says, "Work out your salvation with fear and trembling," I am tempted to believe that it means what it says. In the past we have had the fear and trembling. As a race I believe we are to work out our salvation, work it out with pen and ink, work it out with rule and compass, work it out with horsepower and steam power, work it out on the farm, in the shop, schoolroom, sewing room, the office, and in all life's callings. Here on these consecrated grounds I believe that we have a movement today that means the salvation of the Negro race, and as my people are taught in these classrooms, in these shops, on this farm from year to year to mix up with their religion zeal and habits of thrift, economy, carpentry, and blacksmithing with farming and sewing, with printing and house-building, and then as this influence penetrates the hills and valleys, the rice swamps, the Virginia tobacco fields, the Louisiana sugar bottoms, every hamlet and city, we shall agree that it is most possible for a race as for an individual to actually work out its salvation.

In attempting to elevate a race that has been in the position of the Negro race, nothing is so hard to avoid as extremes. It is not always easy to make a race, as well as its friends, see that on growth and development must we hang the line of certain well-defined and natural laws; that when there is artificial forcing, we have the superficial and deceptive signs of progress, but the real and permanent growth is wanting. The past history and present environment of the Negro lead him too often to imitate the white man at certain superficial points without stopping to count the steps, the years that it has taken the white man to reach his present position, or to note the foundations upon which his progress rests. Here at Hampton we have not alone the signs of progress but the reality. There is no position, however high, in science, or letters, or politics, that I would withhold from any race, but I would have the foundation sure—**November 18, 1895.**

LETTER TO THE LOUISIANA STATE CONSTITUTIONAL CONVENTION

In addressing you this letter, I know that I am running the risk of appearing to meddle with something that does not concern me. But since I know that nothing but sincere love for our beautiful Southland, which I hold as near to my heart as any of you can, and a sincere love for every black and white man within her borders, is the only thing actuating me to write. I am willing to be misjudged, if need be, if I can accomplish a little good.

But I do not believe that you, gentlemen of the Convention, will misinterpret my motives. What I say will, I believe, be considered in the same earnest spirit in which I write.

I am no politician; on the other hand, I have always advised my race to give attention to acquiring property, intelligence and character, as the necessary bases of good citizenship, rather than to mere political agitation. But the question upon which I write is out of the region of ordinary politics; it affects the civilization of two races, not for a day alone, but for a very long time to come; it is up in the region of duty of man to man, of Christian to Christian.

Since the war, no State has had such an opportunity to settle for all time the race question, so far as it concerns politics, as is now given in Louisiana. Will your Convention set an example to the world in this respect? Will Louisiana take such high and just grounds in respect to the Negro that no one can doubt that the South is as good a friend to the Negro as he possesses elsewhere? In all this, gentlemen of the Convention, I am not pleading for the Negro alone, but for the morals, the higher life of the white man as well. For the more I study this question, the more I am convinced that it is not so much a question as to what the white man will do with the Negro, as to what the Negro will do with the white man's civilization.

The Negro agrees with you that it is necessary to the salvation of the South that restriction be put upon the ballot. I know that you have two serious problems before you; ignorant and corrupt government on the one hand, and on the other, a way to restrict the ballot so that control will be in the hands of the intelligent, without regard to race. With the sincerest sympathy with you in your efforts to find a way out of the difficulty, I want to suggest that no State in the South can make a law that will provide an opportunity or temptation for an ignorant white man to vote and withhold the same opportunity from an ignorant colored man, without injuring both men. No State can make a law that can thus be executed, without dwarfing for all time the morals of the white man in the South. Any law controlling the ballot, that is not absolutely just and fair to both races, will work more permanent injury to the whites than to the blacks.

The Negro does not object to an educational or property test, but let the law be so clear that no one clothed with State authority will be tempted to perjure and degrade himself, by putting one interpretation upon it for the white man and another for the black man. Study the history of the South, and you will find that where there has been the most dishonesty in the matter of voting, there you will find to-day the lowest moral condition of both races. First, there was the temptation to act wrongly with the Negro's ballot. From this it was an easy step to dishonesty with the white man's ballot, to the carrying of concealed weapons, to the murder of a Negro, and then to the murder of a white man, and then to lynching. I entreat you not to pass such a law as will prove an eternal millstone about the neck of your children.

No man can have respect for government and officers of the law, when he knows, deep down in his heart, that the exercise of the franchise is tainted with fraud.

The road that the South has been compelled to travel during the last thirty years has been strewn with thorns and thistles. It has been as one groping through long darkness into the light. The time is not distant when the world will begin to appreciate the real character of the burden that was imposed upon the South when 4,500,000 ex-slaves, ignorant and impoverished, were given the franchise. No people had ever been given such a problem to solve. History had blazed no path through the wilderness that could be followed. For thirty years, we wandered in the wilderness. We are beginning to get out. But there is but one road out, and all makeshifts, expedients, "profit and loss calculations," but lead into the swamps, quicksands, quagmires and jungles. There is a highway that will lead both races out into the pure, beautiful sunshine, where there will be nothing to hide and nothing to explain, where both races can grow strong and true and useful in every fibre of their being. I believe that your Convention will find this highway; that it will enact a fundamental law which will be absolutely just and fair to white and black alike.

I beg of you, further, that in the degree that you close the ballot-box against the ignorant, that you open the school house. More than one half of the people of your State are Negroes. No State can long prosper when a large percentage of its citizenship is in ignorance and poverty, and has no interest in government. I beg of you that you do not treat us as alien people. We are not aliens. You know us; you know that we have cleared your forests, tilled your fields, nursed your children and protected your families. There is an attachment between us that few understand. While I do not presume to be able to advise you, yet it is in my heart to say that if your Convention would do something that would prevent, for all time, strained relations between the two races, and would permanently settle the matter of political relations in our Southern States, at least, let the very best educational opportunities be provided for both races: and add to this the enactment of an election law that shall be incapable of unjust discrimination, at the same time providing that in proportion as the ignorant secure education, property and character, they will be given the right of citizenship. Any other course will take from one-half your citizens interest in the State, and hope and ambition to become intelligent producers and taxpayers—to become useful and virtuous citizens. Any other course will tie the white citizens of Louisiana to a body of death.

The Negroes are not unmindful of the fact that the white people of your State pay the greater proportion of the school taxes, and that the poverty of the State prevents it from doing all that it desires for public education; yet I believe you will agree with me, that ignorance is more costly to the State than education; that it will cost Louisiana more not to educate her Negroes than it will cost to educate them. In connection with a generous provision for public schools, I believe that nothing will so help my own people in your State as provision at some institution for the highest academic and normal training, in connection with thorough training in agriculture, mechanics and domestic economy. The fact is that 90 per cent. of our people depend upon the common occupations for their living, and outside of the cities 85 per cent. depend upon agriculture for support. Notwithstanding this, our people have been educated since the war in everything else but the very thing that most of them live by. First-class training in agriculture, horticulture, dairying, stock-raising, the mechanical arts and domestic economy, will make us intelligent producers, and not only help us to contribute our proportion as tax-payers, but will result in retaining much money in the State that now goes outside for that which can be produced in the State. An institution that will give this training of the hand, along with the highest mental culture, will soon convince our people that their salvation is in the ownership of property, industrial and business development, rather than in mere political agitation.

The highest test of the civilization of any race is in its willingness to extend a helping hand to the less fortunate. A race, like an individual, lifts itself up by lifting others up. Surely no people ever had a greater chance to exhibit the highest Christian fortitude and magnanimity than is now presented to the people of Louisiana. It requires little wisdom or statesmanship to repress, to crush out, to retard the hopes and aspirations of a people, but the highest and most profound statesmanship is shown in guiding and stimulating a people so that every fibre in the body, mind and soul shall be made to contribute in the highest degree to the usefulness and nobility of the State. It is along this line that I pray God the thoughts and activities of your Convention be guided—**February 19, 1898.**

AN INTERVIEW ON THE HARDWICK BILL

The Hardwick Bill was a measure introduced in the Georgia Legislature for the purpose of disfranchising the colored people. While this Bill was before the Legislature, Principal Booker T. Washington gave the following interview to The Atlanta Constitution. The Bill was defeated in the Legislature, receiving only 3 votes in its favor in the Lower House where it was introduced, 137 votes being cast against it.

Professor Booker T. Washington, the head of the famous industrial school for colored youths at Tuskegee, and probably the foremost man of his race to-day, gave his views on the question of franchise restriction to a representative of The Constitution yesterday. Professor Washington spent the day in the city, having come here on business. When asked for an expression on the Hardwick Bill, he said that he did not care to discuss that or any other specific measure, but on the subject of an educational qualification restricting the ballot to the intelligence of the country, he had very decided views. "I dread the idea of seeming to intrude my views too often upon the public," said Professor Washington, "but I feel that I can speak very frankly upon the subject, because I am speaking to the South and Southern people. It has been my experience that when our Southern people are convinced that one speaks from the heart and tries to speak that which he feels is for the permanent good of both races, he is always accorded a respectful hearing. No possible influence could tempt me to say that which I thought would tend merely to stir up strife or to induce my own people to return to the old time methods of political agitation, rather than give their time, as most of them are now doing, to the more fundamental principles of citizenship, education, industry and prosperity.

DECISION LEFT TO THE SOUTH

"The question of the rights and elevation of the Negro is now left almost wholly to the South, as it has been long pleaded should be done," added Professor Washington. "The South has over and over said to the North and her representatives have repeated it in Congress, that if the North and the Federal Government would 'hands off,' the South would deal justly and fairly with the Negro. The prayer of the South has been almost wholly answered. The world is watching the South as it has never done before. Not only have the North and the Federal Congress practically agreed to leave the matter of the Negro's citizenship in the hands of the South, but many conservative and intelligent Negroes in recent years have advised the Negro to cast his lot more closely with the Southern white man, and to cease a continued senseless opposition to his interests. This policy has gained ground to such an extent that the white man controls practically every State and every county and township in the South.

VARIOUS ELECTION LAWS

"There is a feeling of friendship and mutual confidence growing between the two races that is most encouraging. But in the midst of this condition of things, one is surprised and almost astounded at the measures being introduced and passed by the various law-making bodies of the Southern States. What is the object of the election laws? Since there is white domination throughout the South, there can be but one object in the passing of these laws—to disfranchise the Negro. At the present time the South has a great opportunity as well as responsibility. Will she shirk this opportunity or will she look matters in the face and grapple with it bravely, taking the Negro by the hand and seeking to lift him up to the point where he will be prepared for citizenship? None of the laws passed by any Southern State, or that are now pending, will do this. These new laws will simply change the form of the present bad election system and widen the breach between the two races, when we might, by doing right, cement the friendship between them.

DANGEROUS ALL AROUND

"To pass an election law with an 'understanding' clause, simply means that some individual will be tempted to perjure his soul and degrade his whole life by deciding in too many cases that the Negro does not 'understand' the constitution and that a white man, even though he be an ignorant white foreigner with recently acquired citizenship, does 'understand' it. In a recent article President Hadley, of Yale University, covers the whole truth when he says: 'We cannot make a law which shall allow the right exercise of a discretionary power and prohibit its wrong use. The 'understanding' clause may serve to keep Negroes from voting, but the time will come when it will also be used to keep white men from voting, if any number of them disagree with the election officer who holds the discretionary power. While discussing this matter, it would be unfair to the white people of the South and to my own race, if I were not perfectly frank. What interpretation does the outside world and the Negro put upon these 'understanding' clauses? Either that they are meant to leave a loophole so that the ignorant white man can vote, or to prevent the educated Negro from voting. If this interpretation is correct in either case, the law is unjust. It is unjust to the white man because it takes away from him the incentive to prepare himself to become an intelligent voter. It is unjust to the Negro because it makes him feel that no matter how well he prepares himself in education for voting, he will be refused a vote through the operation of the 'understanding' clause.

IN A FALSE POSITION

"And what is worse, this treatment will keep alive in the Negro's breast the feeling that he is being wrongfully treated by the Southern white man, and therefore he ought to vote against him, whereas, with just treatment the years will not be many before a large portion of the colored people will be willing to vote with the Southern white people. Then again, I believe that such laws put our Southern white people in a false position. I cannot think that there is any large number of white people in the South who are so ignorant or so poor that they cannot get education and property enough that will enable them to stand the test by the side of the Negro in these respects. I do not believe that these white people want it continually advertised to the world that some special law must be passed by which they will seem to be given an unfair advantage over the Negro by reason of their ignorance or poverty. It is unfair to blame the Negro for not preparing himself for citizenship by acquiring intelligence, and then when he does get education and property, to pass a law that can be so operated as to prevent him from being a citizen, even though he may be a large tax-payer. The Southern white people have reached the point where they can afford to be just and generous; where there will be nothing to hide and nothing to explain. It is an easy matter, requiring little thought, generosity or statesmanship to push a weak man down when he is struggling to get up. Any one can do that. Greatness, generosity, statesmanship are shown in stimulating, encouraging every individual in the body politic to make of himself the most useful, intelligent and patriotic citizen possible. Take from the Negro all incentive to make himself and children useful property-holding citizens, and can any one blame him for becoming a beast capable of committing any crime?

REPRESSION WILL FAIL

"I have the greatest sympathy with the South in its efforts to find a way out of present difficulties, but I do not want to see the South tie itself to a body of death. No form of repression will help matters. Spain tried that for 400 years and was the loser. There is one, and but one way out of our present difficulties, and that is the right way. All else but right will fail. We must face the fact that the tendency of the world is forward, and not backward. That all civilized countries are growing in the direction of giving liberty to their citizens, not withholding it. Slavery ceased because it was opposed to the progress of both races, and so all forms of repression will fail—must fail—in the long run. Whenever a change is thought necessary to be made in the fundamental law of the States, as Governor Candler says in his recent message: 'The man who is virtuous and intelligent, however poor or humble; or of whatever race or color, may be safely intrusted with the ballot.' And as the recent industrial convention at

Huntsville, Ala., composed of the best brains of the white South, puts it: 'To move the race problem from the domain of politics, where it has so long and seriously vexed the industrial progress of the South, we recommend to the several States of the South the adoption of an intelligent standard of citizenship THAT WILL EQUALLY APPLY TO BLACK AND WHITE ALIKE.' We must depend upon the mental, industrial and moral elevation of all the people to bring relief. The history of the world proves that there is no other safe cure. We may find a way to stop the Negro from selling his vote, but what about the conscience of the man who buys his vote? We must go to the bottom of the evil.

SHOULD BE EQUALITY OF TREATMENT

"Our Southern States cannot afford to have suspicion of evil intention resting upon them. It not only will hurt them morally, but financially. In conclusion, let me add that the Southern States owe it to themselves not to pass unfair election laws, because it is against the constitution of the United States, and each State is under a solemn obligation that every citizen, regardless of color, shall be given the full protection of the laws. No State can make a law that can be so interpreted to mean one thing when applied to the black man and another when applied to the white man, without disregarding the constitution of the United States. In the second place, unfair election laws in the long run, I repeat, will injure the white man more than the Negro; such laws will not only disfranchise the Negro, but the white man as well. The history of the country shows that in those States where the election laws are most just, there you will find the most wealth, the most intelligence and the smallest percentage of crime. The best element of white people in the South are not in favor of oppressing the Negro, they want to help him up, but they are sometimes mistaken as to the best method of doing this. While I have spoken very plainly, I do not believe that any one will misinterpret my motives. I am not in politics per se, nor do I intend to be, neither would I encourage my people to become mere politicians, but the question I have been discussing strikes at the very fundamental principles of citizenship"—1900.

ON MAKING OUR RACE LIFE
COUNT IN THE LIFE OF THE NATION

In the Bible one finds over and over again the words "a peculiar people." Reference is made to the Jews as "a peculiar people,"—a people differing in thought and temperament and mode of life from others by whom they were surrounded. Now the race to which Americans of African lineage belong is often described as "a peculiar people," having had, as we know, a peculiar history. They differ in color and in appearance, and in a very large degree their temperament and thought differ from that of the people about them. Now the Jews because they were different from the peoples by whom they were surrounded, because of their peculiar religious bent, were able to give to the world the doctrine of the unity and Fatherhood of God, and Christianity, the finest flower of Jewry. It is then, I think, not too much to hope that the very qualities which make the Negro different from the peoples by whom he is surrounded will enable him, in the fulness of time, to make a peculiar contribution to the nation of which he forms a part.

What that contribution is to be no man can now tell, but we must keep in mind that the race is made of individuals and

> every man God made
> Is different, has some deed to do,
> Some work to work. Be undismayed.
> Though thine be humble, do it, too.

As with an individual, so with a race. When you and I and all the other individuals that go to make up our race shall have learned to do well our own peculiar work, we shall be able to determine the bent of the race. It must fall upon you and me, who have had opportunity to work out in some measure our own individual problems, to give direction to the race. It is for us, therefore, to bring to the enrichment of our lives, as individuals, every quality which we are capable of cultivating.

There is in the New Testament a passage which I like to refer to and to think of; it reads something like this: "He that overcometh shall be clothed in white raiment." The expression "He that overcometh" occurs several times in the New Testament. I am anxious that the Tuskegee students shall get the idea firmly fixed in their minds that there are definite rewards coming to the individual or to the race that overcomes obstacles and succeeds in spite of seemingly insurmountable difficulties. The palms of victory are not for the race that merely complains and frets and rails. I do not mean to say that there is not a place for race loyalty and enthusiasm. There is a proper and vital place for protests against the wrongs that are inflicted without cause or reason. Every race, like every individual, should be swift to protest against injustice and wrongs, but no race must be content with mere protests. Every race must show to the world by tangible, visible, indisputable evidence that it can do more than merely call attention to the wrongs inflicted upon it. The reward of life is for those who choose the good where evil calls out on every hand. That reward is moral character. The more temptations resisted—the more difficult the struggle—the more robust the character. The wholly innocent person is much less praiseworthy than is he who has faced temptation and has come out of it unscarred. The virtues of foresight and thrift and frugality, brought bravely to the front, will bring large material possessions which if properly used will refine and enrich life.

I am constrained to refer once more to that "peculiar people," the Jews, —a race that has been handicapped in very much the same way as the colored people. Their opportunities have been limited in many directions. In Russia to-day they are in many cases debarred from schools and from entrance into the professions. And, notwithstanding the barriers in this country, one of the most noted banking firms in the United States is composed of Jews. Members of a despised race, they made up their minds that in spite of difficulties they would not stop to complain, but would compel recognition by making a real contribution to the country of which they formed a part. The Japanese race is a convincing example of the respect which the world gives to a race that can put brains and commercial activity into the development of the resources of a country. What material difficulties the thrifty Hollanders have had to overcome in the development of their country! But the battle against water and wind has developed not only a country, but an energetic, thrifty people. The Netherlands have literally been made by these sturdy Hollanders, who because they overcame are looked upon as a great and happy people.

There is, then, opportunity for the colored people to enrich the material life of their adopted country by doing what their hands find to do, minor duties though they be, so well that nobody else of any race can do them better. This is the aim that the Tuskegee student should keep steadily before him. If he remembers that all service, however lowly, is true service, an important step will have been taken in the solution of what we term "the race problem."

For it must be remembered that no individual of any race can contribute to the solution of any general problem until he has first worked out his own peculiar problem. Some months ago I met a former schoolmate whom I had not seen for a number of years. I was naturally interested to hear about his progress, and began to question him. I asked him where he lived, and he said he had no abiding-place, in fact he had lived in a half dozen places since we parted. In answer to other questions, I found that he had no special trade, no special business, no bank account. I asked then what he had been doing in the intervening years, and he answered he had been travelling about over the country, doing his best to solve the race problem. That man should rather have been at work at the solution of his own individual problem. An individual circumstanced as he was could not solve anybody's problem. It is important to have one's own dooryard clean before calling attention to the imperfection in the neighbor's yard. Each Negro can put much into the life of his race by making his own individual life present a model in purity and patience, in industry and courage, in showing the world how to get strength out of difficulties. The late President Garfield once said that no person ever drowned, no matter how many times he was thrown overboard, who was worth saving, and that remark, with a few modifications, might be applied to a race. No race is ever lost that is worth saving, and no race need be lost that wants to save itself. The world is full of little people who through lack of wisdom and patience and perseverance merely add to the world's burdens. The despised Negro has the chance to show to the world that charity which suffereth long and is kind and which never faileth. In the face of discouragements and difficulties the Negro must ever remember that nobody can degrade him. Nobody can degrade a big race or a big man. No one can degrade a single member of any race. The individual himself is the only one who can inflict that punishment. Frederick Douglass was on one occasion compelled to ride for several hours in a portion of a freight car. A friend went into the freight car to console him and said to him that he hated to see a man of his intelligence in so humiliating a position. "I am ashamed that they have thus degraded you." But Douglass, straightening himself up in his seat, looked the friend in the face and said, "They cannot degrade Frederick Douglass." And so they cannot degrade a single individual who does not want to be degraded. Injustice cannot work harm upon the oppressed without injuring the oppressor. The Negro people must live the precepts taught by the Christ. They must go on multiplying, day by day, deeds of worthiness, piling them up mountain high. And just as you and I, as individuals, are called upon to serve the race of which we are a part, so let us as a race recognize the fact that we are a part of a great nation which we are bound to serve—1906.

EARLY PROBLEMS OF FREEDOM

The close of the Civil War left many of the agencies of emancipation without a cause. The anti-slavery publications, the state and national anti-slavery societies, "vigilance committees," and the vast Underground Railroad system, saw their purposes accomplished in the terms of peace. The American Anti-Slavery Society, which had been the longest in existence, and which, under the leadership of William Lloyd Garrison, had done more for freedom than any other single agency, was now ready to wind up its affairs. When a proposition was made for its dissolution, Frederick Douglass opposed it, giving his reasons in these words: "I felt that the work of the society was not done, that it had not fulfilled its mission, which was not merely to emancipate but to elevate the enslaved class . . . that the Negro still had a cause and that he needed my pen and voice to plead for it."

In taking this position, he showed that he had a clear and far-reaching comprehension of the many and serious problems and obligations that would in time result from the enforced emancipation of his people. He clearly foresaw that these problems were of a kind which had never before come within the range and scope of our national experience, and that if the country were to make the most of the good results of the war, and minimize its evils, the machinery of liberation and destruction must somehow be converted to the service of peace and construction. Two great questions had been settled, that the United States was to remain an indivisible nation, and that slavery was henceforth impossible in this nation.

The problems growing out of these achievements are still difficult. Before the Civil War, the people of the United States might have been classified as non-slave-holding and slave-holding white people; enslaved and free Negroes. Now, two of these classes, the slave-holders and the enslaved Negroes, disappeared and in the latter's stead, a new element was injected into the population, the freedmen, 4,000,000 souls, utterly destitute, without learning, without experience, and without traditions; dependent for their guidance, and almost for bare existence, upon the direction and good-will of the older elements. If, after the war, the South and the North could have united to repair the damages and solve the problems the conflict had left behind it, the history of the colored people in America, as well as their present condition, might have been different from what it is.

In facing the problems of reconstruction, the people of the North had no precedents and little knowledge of the Negro's character to guide them. The men who had the responsibility of providing for the present and future, of rehabilitating the South on the basis of freedom, were trained to treat every question, social and political, from the standpoint of party politics. But reconstruction needed the services of the sociologist more than of the party leader. There were but few in public life capable of treating these matters in a non-partisan, a non-sectional, and a scientific spirit. Men could not so quickly overcome the animosities engendered by the Civil War. Abraham Lincoln, who alone seemed to have a spirit large enough to be the President of all the people, even to the least of them, was gone, and there was none in the public service to take his place. While others acted in the spirit of war, he acted in the spirit of peace. In managing large questions, he had a wonderful insight into the things that would aggravate conditions and a fine courage in avoiding them, until they had spent their force with as little harm as possible. His penetrative powers, the contagion of his kindly spirit, his unswerving love for what was just, were needed quite as much after as before and during the civil strife. Had Mr. Lincoln lived, his clear vision, it is safe to say, would have avoided many of the evils to which the country has since fallen heir. As it was, however much the white people in slavery's former domain may have suffered, the Negro has borne the brunt of every mistake of the period of Reconstruction.

The Southern people had lost (so it seemed at the time at least) everything that was worth having and fighting for,—their "cause," their property in slaves, their prestige, and their political supremacy. Their homes were devastated and their plantations ravaged by the conquering Yankees. Their task was not to build up what had been destroyed, but to begin anew. It is asking too much to expect that they could have faced these conditions with a cheerful spirit. The slaves, as property, were now free, and this freedom was regarded as a punishment visited upon their former masters.

Free labor was new, and apart from this there was none of it to take the place of that of the liberated slaves. Furthermore, the white people had little or no faith in their possible usefulness. They feared that the Negro as a free man would not work, would not honor his contracts, and would use his liberty to commit all sorts of crimes against society. They could not, at once, rid themselves of the feeling that physical compulsion was the only way to keep the Negro within the bounds of law and labor. Carl Schurz, who, under the authority of the President, made a very thorough and statesman-like investigation of conditions, issued an official report of his findings, and it is clear from this paper that, if the Southern people could have overcome their fears of Negro freedom, the work of reconstruction would have been greatly simplified. They, however, were in no frame of mind to accept and honor any program for reconstruction emanating from the Negro and what was best to be done for him and with him.

Between the North and the South, stood the ex-slave, free and that was all. His situation was anomalous. As Mr. Douglass aptly says, "He was free from individual masters, but the slave of society." Yet, because of his long service to the country, either as a slave or a freeman, he deserved more than he could possibly have been paid in terms of law, defining and defending his rights. He was without power and, as Mr. Douglass in describing him, said, "a man without force, is without the essential dignity of human nature."

In this almost totally helpless condition, the North expected too much of him and the ex-masters too little. It required more than the shock of four years of internecine war to change the solidarity of slavery into a society of organized self-helpfulness. A people who had been so long enslaved could not help being slavish in habits and instincts. They had little family life, no society, no institution except the church, a rudimentary conception of common interests, and very few traditions and ideals. No race ever came into the domain of freedom, independence, and democracy so little furnished with the elements of self-protection and self-determining purpose, as did the emancipated slaves forty years ago. Yet there were everywhere in the South important exceptions to this condition of race helplessness. Many free colored people, especially in the cities, were not hopelessly behind in the procession of progress. They fully understood the meaning of the war and its results. When the last gun was fired and they saw emancipation as a reality, their joy was unbounded. In many of the Southern cities, thousands of them gathered in the open streets and commons, where they shouted and prayed with full hearts, voicing in songs of jubilee and thanksgiving their gratitude for their great deliverance. There has been nothing like these demonstrations in the history of American liberty. No one who saw them could have any doubt whatever as to the Negro's appreciation of his freedom. It is a notable fact that in none of them was ever heard a word of hatred or revenge toward those who had been responsible for their long enslavement. Their gratitude was too great to leave room for resentment. God, Lincoln, and Freedom formed a mysterious trinity in the new awakening of these emancipated people.

All this was perfectly natural and hopeful, so far as it went, but it was not long before exultation gave way to the consciousness that this dearly bought liberty was a serious thing. The Negro capacity for happiness was large, but he could not live and sustain himself by this alone. Owning nothing, he had no place to live. Having nothing, he could get nothing. In addition to the ex-slaves, who were still fastened to the places where slavery left them and freedom found them, a great multitude, known as refugees, after emancipation made their way into the Union lines. When the war closed these were still with the Union army and dependent upon it for rations. It soon became apparent to those in authority, that something must be done in a large way by the Federal government itself to provide for this unorganized horde. To meet this serious condition, Congress, in the spring of 1865, passed an act establishing the "Freedmen's Bureau for the Relief of Freedmen and Refugees." Its main provisions were as follows:

> The Bureau was to have supervision and management of abandoned lands.
> It was to look after all subjects relating to refugees and freedmen.
> It was to be under the control of a commission appointed by the President and to continue its labors for one year after the close of the war.
> The Secretary of War was given authority to issue provisions, clothing, and fuel for the immediate and temporary needs of freedmen and their wives and children.
> The War Department was to set apart for the use of loyal refugees and freedmen abandoned lands under the control of the United States Army and assign to such freedmen, not more than forty acres of land, and to protect such persons in the possession of such land for at least three years at an annual rent, not to exceed six per cent. upon the appraised value of the land. At the end of that time, the tenant was allowed to purchase it and receive therefor from the government a certificate of purchase.

In addition to these provisions, the Freedmen's Bureau was intended to be a "friendly intermediary" between the ex-masters and ex-slaves. Nothing could have been done more surely to smooth the way for a kindly relationship between the two parties in question, if such a relationship had been possible. General O. O. Howard was the first commissioner of that Bureau. He had made a record as a soldier in the Union Army, but, better still, he was a man of humane impulses, without sectional bias, and of exalted Christian character. The value of his services in the work of Reconstruction can be easily seen by a glance at some of his reports made to Congress in 1865–1870.

In these five years of work on the part of the Bureau to bring order out of chaos, there had been established over 4,000 schools, employing 9,000 teachers and giving instruction to about a quarter of a million pupils of all ages. In 1870 the school attendance in the old slave-states amounted to nearly eighty per cent. of the enrollment. The demand for learning on the part of the colored people, as shown by the Bureau's work, was amazing, and afforded a gratifying evidence of their sense of responsibility as freedmen. The Negroes themselves made a good showing of what they were able to do by their own efforts in creating the means for their instruction. They sustained over 1,300 schools and built over 500 school buildings, contributing more than $200,000 out of their earnings to further the cause of education.

The value of the Freedmen's Bureau in thus stimulating an interest in this important subject and in developing a serious sense of responsibility on the part of the freedmen cannot well be overestimated. Carl Schurz in his report says:

"The Freedmen's Bureau would have been an institution of the greatest value, under competent leadership, had not its organization, to some extent, been invaded by mentally and morally unfit persons. . . . Nothing was needed at this time so much as an acknowledged authority, standing guard between the master and the ex-slave, commanding and possessing the confidence and respect of both, to aid the emancipated black man to make the best possible use of his unaccustomed freedom, and to aid the white man to whom free Negro labor was a well-nigh incurable idea, in meeting the difficulties, partly real and partly conjured up by the white man's prejudiced imagination."

The lack of fit men, in sufficient numbers, to continue the good work inaugurated by the Freedmen's Bureau was the cause, in great part, of the failure of Reconstruction methods of helpfulness. There were employed men of partisan spirit whose vision was clouded by political aspirations, and thus the future well-being of both races in the South was not kept paramount. The cause of most of the evils that in a few years followed and overwhelmed the colored people in the South, was lack of men strong in character, patriotism, justice, and understanding for the work in hand. This is true, in spite of the fact that there were those who were equal to the occasion, but who alone had not the power to perform the tasks set for them. No greater injury has been done the colored people of this country than that which resulted from putting them in a position of political antagonism to their former masters.

But the purposes of this biography do not require a full statement of the causes that led to the overthrow of the temporary supremacy held by the freedmen and their Northern allies. A careful reading of the history of the Southern states since the adoption of the Thirteenth Amendment to the Constitution of the United States in 1865, must convince the impartial reader that the Negroes were less the instigators than the victims of the mistakes of Reconstruction. Many of those who played the false rôle of friends and leaders left the freedmen to bear the brunt of the punishment which they have since suffered patiently, heroically, and alone. The Negroes of the South during the Reconstruction period were always amenable to wise direction. Those who were on hand to guide them, easily won their favor. There seems to be no reason to doubt that, had it been offered, the freedmen would have followed the leadership of the best elements in the South as willingly, if not more willingly, than that which they did accept.

The difficulty was that the Southern people could not in a day, or in a decade, change their inborn conviction that emancipation was forced upon them as a punishment. They accepted this punishment in a spirit in which injured pride, the sense of loss of property, loss of "cause," and revenge were elements. But with all these losses and defeats, the imperious temper of the Southern people suffered no impairment, and they were in no mood to take hold of the work of Reconstruction in the spirit of the victorious North.

The South hesitated to act, and the ex-slave had no power to do so. As a result, the responsibility for movements for the protection of the Negroes fell to the North. It sought to accomplish this object by giving freedmen all the rights of citizenship. Under the presuppositions upon which our government was founded, this step was logical, even though it may have been, and indeed seems to have been, at that time unwise.

What has been said in the foregoing pages indicates what may be called the new field of labor for Frederick Douglass after emancipation. When the great war came to an end and the object for which he had so long labored was indeed an accomplished fact, he confessed that his great joy was somewhat tinged with a feeling of sadness. He said, "I felt that I had reached the end of the noblest part of my life." He was still in his prime, and all his faculties were clear and ready for action. He had no occupation, no business, no profession. His training and associations, during the previous thirty years, had unfitted him for manual labor, and he had no fortune that would enable him to live without exertion of some kind. But thoughts and feelings of this sort were soon swept aside by new interests and anxieties of the most absorbing character.

In the first place, fresh evidences of his popularity began to manifest themselves. His struggle for emancipation had been so conspicuous, his eloquence so stirring, and his participation in all the great questions of the day so earnest and compelling, that his vogue continued as before.

In the great diversity of distinguished men and women who figured in the history of the quarter of a century immediately preceding the Civil

War, Frederick Douglass was in the fullest sense of the word, a "self-made man." All kinds of persons were interested in him. His authority on every matter that concerned the Negro, North or South, was seldom questioned. His leadership, up to this time, was not often disputed. The American people manifested greater desire to hear him than ever before and invitations to lecture began to pour in upon him from colleges, lyceums, literary societies, and churches. It is scarcely too much to say that he was one of the most popular men on the lecture platform, and at a time when such illustrious personages as Henry Ward Beecher, Wendell Phillips, Theodore Tilton, Anna Dickinson, and Mary A. Livermore gave to the American lyceum its highest distinction. His themes were no longer anti-slavery in character. His new lectures bore such titles as, "Self-made Men," "The Races of Men," "William, the Silent," "John Brown," etc., all of which showed a wide reading, and a mastery of the art of eloquence. In addition to these lectures, he was called upon from every direction for informal talks on an almost endless variety of subjects.

But whatever might be the theme or the occasion, he could not get away from the Negro problem. As he said, "I never rise to speak before any American audience, without a feeling that my failure or success will bring harm or benefit to my whole race." When the all-important question of reconstruction came to be considered, Mr. Douglass was found to be fully conversant with the progress of events, prepared to say his word, and play his part. While other men were uncertain, confused, and timid, Douglass's stand was bold, direct, and fearless. When it was time for him to speak and act, his words attracted wide attention and many persons in and out of Congress were willing to follow his leading. He had always been frank, honorable, and resourceful on the question of just treatment for his race and he was so far in advance of most of the men who had it in their power to make and unmake the laws, that it would have been a decided misfortune for the colored people to have been without his guidance. He had a wide acquaintance among men in public life. No other Negro in this country, at the time, knew political leaders in and out of Congress so intimately. His qualities of prudence and sagacity, as well as his great personal charm, made him welcome in the councils of his party. He was the soul of honor. Being thus gifted, Douglass was able to be as much for his people in a personal as in a public capacity. He had a way of getting close to the men in power and of reaching their hearts and enlisting their sympathies for the objects in whose service he was engaged. This was most fortunate. His race was without official connection with the government, without experience, and with no clearly defined status as citizens. If ever the colored people needed a strong man capable in every way to represent them, it was now, when the war was over and the question, what to do with the free Negro, must be answered in definite terms of law and governmental policy. Aside from his commanding abilities, and his personal attractiveness to men, Mr. Douglass had lived through the very experiences that fitted him to know and feel what the Negro needed and ought to have. He had been a slave, a fugitive slave, and a freedman, at a time, too, when Negro freedom was most despaired of. No white man could appreciate, as he could and did, the sweetness of the terms, Freedom and Liberty. One of his earliest utterances on this subject indicates his feeling at this period. "I saw no chance," he said, "of bettering the condition of the freedman, until he should cease to be merely a freedman and should become a citizen, and that there was no safety for him or for anybody else in America, outside of the American government."

At the time when Mr. Douglass publicly took this position, he was far more radical than some of the most ardent of his anti-slavery associates. This declaration was then regarded as a challenge to the sense of justice of the American people. Many earnest friends of the Negro thought it was asking too much, even though the race deserved the franchise. Others argued that the Negro was unfit for the suffrage and that it would aggravate the already strained relations between the two races in the South. Opposition was expected by Mr. Douglass and he was ready to meet it. No one understood better than he that his people had had no training for citizenship, but he was accustomed to say, that "if the Negro knows enough to fight for his country, he knows enough to vote; if he knows enough to pay taxes to support the government, he knows enough to vote; if he knows as much when sober as an Irishman knows when he is drunk, he knows enough to vote." He anticipated the evils that would follow the enfranchisement of the ex-slaves, but insisted that such evils would be temporary and that the good would be permanent. He further insisted that it was worth all the suffering endured by his race to have that principle established; that the right of suffrage would be an incentive to arouse the latent energies of the Negro to become worthy of full citizenship, and that such impulse was imperatively needed. He always declared that political equality was a widely different thing from social equality. He vigorously protested that the right of suffrage did not mean Negro domination in the slave states, if the best white people would wisely assume the leadership of the blacks. He believed in the domination of the fittest, and insisted that the white people of the South, because of their superiority in intelligence and in all the forces that make for supremacy, were in no danger of being overwhelmed by the new voters. He believed in the rule of the competent and that in the long run intelligent supremacy would be tempered with justice and the true spirit of democracy. He believed that those who were strong enough, either to help the ex-slave to get upon his feet or to crush him in his efforts to rise, would choose the more generous course.

At any rate, he deemed the time ripe to claim for the freedmen full citizenship and equality before the law. When the question came forward for discussion, the people of the North were filled with enthusiasm over the results of the war and for the great objects they believed to have been achieved by it. It was the occasion to make a hero of every one who had taken part in the civil contest on the side of the Union. Even the Negro, for the first time, became the recipient of more than respectful considera- tion. The people of the North were as proud of his freedom as he was himself. If to give the Negro the franchise, and laws to protect him in the exercise of it as a citizen, would make more lasting the results of the war, the North was now in a mood to grant it to him, since it seemed to add to the significance of the great struggle which had just been so victoriously concluded. Douglass took advantage of this condition of things to advo- cate suffrage for his people. By speech and print and personal appeals to the leaders of public opinion, he urged this cause upon them in and out of season. There was no lack of evidence that it was gaining in every direc- tion. The number of those who thought the suffrage ought to be granted, because it was right; those who thought it a good thing from a partisan standpoint, and those who thought the results of the war would be lost unless the Negro were given the privilege, increased rapidly.

What Douglass calls one of the first steps in the direction of popular favor for universal suffrage, was an interview that he had with President Johnson on the 7th of March, 1866. He headed a delegation of prominent colored men, including George T. Downing, Lewis H. Douglass, William E. Matthews, John Jones, John F. Cook, Joseph E. Otis, A. W. Ross, Wil- liam Whipper, John M. Brown, and Alexander Dunlop. The visit of these black men to the President for the purpose of urging upon the govern- ment the policy of the franchise for the freedmen, attracted the attention of the entire nation. Nothing better could have been devised to bring the whole question before the people and obtain a hearing for it.

The delegation soon found that Mr. Johnson was not in sympathy with their plans for Negro enfranchisement. The President had evidently antic- ipated their purpose in calling upon him and he was fully prepared to answer their arguments. He spoke to them at great length and left no ground for them to doubt his position in the matter. He also gave them no opportunity to reply. On returning from the White House, his colleagues empowered Mr. Douglass to prepare an address to the public, to be printed simultaneously with Mr. Johnson's address to them. Mr. Doug- lass's paper was in the form of a reply to the President's arguments against the suffrage proposition, and was as follows:

Mr. President:—In consideration of a delicate sense of propriety as well as of your own repeated intimations of indisposition to discuss or listen to a reply to the views and opinions you were pleased to express to us in your elaborate speech to-day, the undersigned would respectfully take this method of replying thereto.

Believing as we do that the views and opinions you expressed in that address are entirely unsound and prejudicial to the highest interest of our race, as well as to our country at large, we cannot do other than expose the same and, as far as may be in our power, arrest their dangerous influence. It is not necessary at this time to call attention to more than two or three features of your remarkable address. The first point to which we feel especially bound to take exceptions, is your attempt to found a policy opposed to our enfranchisement, upon the alleged ground of an existing hostility on the part of the former slaves to the poor white people of the South. We admit the existence of this hostility, and hold that it is entirely reciprocal. But you obviously commit an error by drawing an argument from an incident of slavery, and making it a basis for a policy adapted to a state of freedom. The hostility between the whites and blacks of the South is easily explained. It has its root and sap in the relation of slavery, and was incited on both sides by the cunning of the slave-masters. These masters secured their ascendancy over both the poor whites and blacks by putting enmity between them.

They divided both to conquer each. There was no earthly reason why the blacks should not hate and dread the poor whites when in a state of slavery, for it was from this class that their masters received their slave-catchers and slave-drivers and overseers. They were the men called in upon all occasions by the masters whenever any fiendish outrage was to be committed upon the slaves. Now, sir, you cannot but perceive that, the cause of this hatred removed, the effect must be removed also. Slavery is abolished. The cause of this antagonism is removed, and you must see that it is altogether illogical to legislate from slave-holding and slave-driving premises for a people, whom you have repeatedly declared it your purpose to maintain in freedom.

Besides, if it were true, as you allege, that the hostility of the blacks toward the whites must necessarily project itself into a state of freedom, and that this enmity between the two races is even more intense in a state of freedom than in a state of slavery, in the name of Heaven, we reverently ask, how can you, in view of your proffered desire to promote the welfare of the black man, deprive him of all means of defense, and clothe him, whom you regard as his enemy, in the panoply of political power? Can it be that you recommend a policy which would arm the strong and cast down the defenseless? Can you, by any possibility of reasoning, regard this as just, fair, or wise? Experience proves that those are most abused who can be abused with the greatest impunity. Men are whipped oftenest who are whipped easiest. Peace between races is not to be secured by degrading one race and exalting another, by giving power to one and withholding from another, but by maintaining a state of equal justice between all classes. First pure, then peaceable.

On the colonization theory you were pleased to broach, very much could be said. It is impossible to suppose, in view of the usefulness of the black man in time of peace as a laborer in the South and in time of war as a soldier in the North, and a growing respect for his rights among the people and his increasing adaptation to a high state of civilization in his native land, that there can ever come a time when he can be removed from this country without a terrible shock to its prosperity and peace. Besides, the worst enemy of the nation could not cast upon its fair name a greater infamy than to admit that Negroes could be tolerated among them in a state of the most degrading slavery and oppression, and must be cast away, driven to exile, for no other cause than having been freed from their chains.

When the question reached Congress, the Negro was not lacking in friends who were willing to go the full length of the Frederick Douglass program of Reconstruction. The first step taken was a report made to the Senate by a committee having the subject in charge. This report in effect provided that the whole matter of franchise be left to the option of the several states concerned. Mr. Douglass believed he saw in this proposition the continued political enslavement of his people, and he was on his guard. The following communication written and sent to the Senate by the delegation which had visited President Johnson speaks for itself:

To the Honorable, the Senate of the United States:—The undersigned, being a delegation representing the colored people of the several states, and now sojourning in Washington, charged with the duty to look after the best interests of the recently emancipated, would most respectfully, but earnestly, pray your honorable body to favor no amendment of the Constitution of the United States which will grant any one or all of the states of this Union to disfranchise any class of citizens on the ground of race or color, for any consideration whatever. They would further respectfully represent that the Constitution as adopted by the Fathers of this Republic in 1789 evidently contemplated the result which has now happened, to wit, the abolition of slavery. The men who framed it, and those who adopted it, framed and adopted it for the people, and the whole people, colored men being at the time legal voters in most of the states. In that instrument as it now stands, there is not a sentence or a syllable conveying any shadow of right or authority by which any State may make color or race a disqualification for the exercise of the right of suffrage, and the undersigned will regard as a real calamity the introduction of any words expressly or by implication, giving any state or states such power; and we respectfully submit that if the amendment now pending before your honorable body shall be adopted, it will enable any state to deprive any class of citizens of the elective franchise, notwithstanding it was obviously framed with a view to affect the question of Negro suffrage only.

For these and other reasons the undersigned respectfully pray that the amendment to the Constitution recently passed by the House and now before your body, be not adopted. And as in duty bound, etc.

In addition to this letter addressed to the United States Senate, Mr. Douglass and his associates saw and argued the matter with every member of that body who would grant them an audience. The "Option Measure" was defeated and to a considerable extent through Mr. Douglass's influence. By this time the question of Negro suffrage had become a leading issue. For the purpose of obtaining the sense of the country on this subject, there was arranged what was known at the time as the "National Loyalists' Convention," to be held at Philadelphia in September, 1866. It was made up of delegates from all parts of the Union, including many influential men in and out of public life. Rochester elected Mr. Douglass as its sole representative, which was a great tribute to him, giving new recognition to the Negro race. The entire country was quick to take notice of the city's action, in so important a gathering, and there was not only objection but open opposition to Mr. Douglass's taking a seat in the convention. Some of the leading delegates united in an effort to persuade him not to go.

Speaking of the situation, Mr. Douglass says that at Harrisburg, there was attached to his train cars loaded with representatives from some of the western states.

When my presence became known to these gentlemen, he continues, a consultation was immediately held among them upon the question of what was best to be done with me. It seems strange, in view of all the progress which had been made, that such a question should arise. But the circumstances of the times made me the Jonah of the Republican ship, and responsible for the contrary winds and misbehaving weather. I was duly waited upon by a committee of my brother delegates to represent to me the undesirableness of my attendance upon the National Loyalists' Convention. The spokesman of these sub-delegates was a gentleman from New Orleans. . . . He began by telling me that he knew my history and my works and that he entertained no very slight degree of respect for me; that both himself and the gentlemen who sent him, as well as those who accompanied him, regarded me with admiration; that there was not among them the remotest objection to sitting in the convention with me, but their personal wishes in the matter they felt should be set aside for the sake of our common cause; that whether I should or should not go in the convention was purely a matter of expediency; that I must know that there was a very strong and bitter prejudice against my race in the North as well as in the South and that the cry of social and political equality would not fail to be raised against the Republican party if I should attend this loyal National convention. . . . I listened very attentively to the address, uttering no word during its delivery; but when it was finished, I said to the speaker and the committee, with all the emphasis I could throw into my voice and manner, "Gentlemen, with all respect, you might as well ask me to put a loaded pistol to my head and blow my brains out, as to ask me to keep out of this convention to which I have been duly elected. Then, gentlemen, what would you gain by the exclusion? Would not the charge of cowardice, certain to be brought against you, prove more damaging than that of amalgamation; would you not be branded all over the land as dastardly hypocrites, professing principles which you have no wish or intention of carrying out? As a matter of policy or expediency, you will be wise to let me in. Everybody knows that I have been duly elected as a delegate by the city of Rochester. This fact has been broadly announced and commented upon all over the country. If I am not admitted, the public will ask, 'Where is Douglass? Why is he not seen in the convention?' and you would find that inquiry more difficult to answer than any charge brought against you for favoring political or social equality; but ignoring the question of policy altogether and looking at it as one of right and wrong, I am bound to go into that convention; not to do so would be to contradict the principles and practice of my life."

The delegates withdrew from the car in which Mr. Douglass was riding without accomplishing their purpose. It was soon made evident to him that his argument had not changed the prejudices of his visitors. When he reached Philadelphia and learned of the plans of the convention, he easily detected a concerted scheme to ignore him altogether. "I was," he says, "the ugly and deformed child of the family and to be kept out of sight as much as possible, while there was company in the house."

It had been arranged that the delegates should assemble at Independence Hall and from there march in a body through the streets to the building where the convention was to be held. Mr. Douglass was present at Independence Hall at the appointed time, but he at once realized the situation. Only a few of the delegates, like General B. F. Butler, had the courage even to greet him. He was not only snubbed generally, but it was hinted to him that if he attempted to walk in the procession through the streets of a city where but a few years ago Negroes had been assaulted and their houses and schools burned down, he would be jeered at, insulted, and perhaps mobbed. It required no little courage to act in the face of these conditions, but Douglass never wavered. He was strong enough not to falter even at the desertion of men whom he had a right to regard as his friends.

When the procession was formed, the delegates were to march two abreast. By this arrangement, the man who would have the hardihood to walk beside the only Negro in line would be an easy mark for scorn and contempt if not bodily attack. It was believed that no white man, under these conditions, would dare to march with Douglass. One delegate after another, those who had formerly taken counsel with him, passed him by. But to use his own words: "There was one man present who was broad enough to take in the whole situation and brave enough to meet the duty of the hour; one who was neither afraid nor ashamed to own me as a man and a brother. One man of the purest Caucasian type, a poet, a scholar, brilliant as a writer, eloquent as a speaker, and holding a high influential position, the editor of a weekly journal having the largest circulation of any weekly paper in the state of New York, and that man was Theodore Tilton. He came to me in my isolation, seized me by the hand in a most brotherly way, and proposed to walk with me in the procession."

The delegates marching through the streets of Philadelphia met with a great ovation, and Mr. Douglass was singled out for special marks of favor. Along the entire way he was loudly cheered, applauded, and congratulated by the multitude. Those who had misjudged the sentiments of the Philadelphians were ashamed of themselves when they saw that he was apparently the most popular man in the procession.

A very pleasing incident occurred on the line of march that day which served to call special attention to him. As his eyes caught a glimpse of a beautiful young woman among the spectators, he was seen suddenly to leave his place and fervently greet her. She was a member of the Auld family, and Mr. Douglass, recognizing her at once, paid her homage publicly. It appears that she had come to Philadelphia from her home in Baltimore when she heard that the ex-slave was to be there and walk in the procession as one of the great men of the occasion, and had been following the line for over an hour with the hope of catching a view of the man who, but for his desire for freedom, might still have been a servant in her family. The newspapers made much of the incident, and described it as one of the most dramatic features of the day.

By the time the marchers had reached the hall, the fear of Mr. Douglass's presence, as a delegate, had given way to a feeling of respect, pride, and comradeship. He threw off all restraint, and went in to win from this body a resolution in favor of the franchise for his people. He delivered one of those powerful and convincing addresses that he was well able to make when aroused. As a result, he quite captured and controlled the sentiment of the convention in favor of his resolution, and when it adjourned Mr. Douglass was congratulated for having achieved a personal triumph that was remarkable for its completeness.

After the adoption of the Thirteenth, Fourteenth, and Fifteenth Amendments, there was some curious speculation as to what place Frederick Douglass would take in this larger world of citizenship that he had helped to create. A number of his friends and admirers thought that he had led his people so successfully out of the wilderness of slavery that he should now put himself into a position where he could guide them further in the proper use of their rights and privileges as citizens of the republic. Many urged that the South was the right place for one of his power and standing. No colored man in this country had such training for large responsibilities as Mr. Douglass had had, during the previous thirty years of service. It was also feared that, without such leadership as he could bring to the South, small men, of mere political training and of partisan methods and ambitions, would assume the direction of the newly-made citizens, and, by their selfishness and greed, bring down upon these poor people more miseries than could be cured in many generations. Everything seemed to invite Frederick Douglass to these new duties and new responsibilities. It was pointed out to him how easily he could become a pioneer by being elected to the House of Representatives, or even to the Senate, from some of the reconstructed states of the South.

He thought long and seriously over the project, but finally concluded not to change his habitation for the sake of gaining political power. He expressed his conclusions on the matter as follows:

That I did not yield to this temptation was not entirely due to my age, but the idea did not entirely square well with my better judgment and sense of propriety. The thought of going to live among a people in order to gain their votes and acquire official honors was repugnant to my sense of self-respect, and I had not lived long enough in the political atmosphere of Washington to have this feeling blunted so as to make me indifferent to its suggestions. . . . I had small faith in my aptitude as a politician, and could not hope to cope with rival aspirants. My life and labors in the North had in a measure unfitted me for such work, and I could not have readily adapted myself to that peculiar oratory found to be most effective with the newly enfranchised class. Upon the whole, I have never regretted that I did not enter the arena of Congressional honors to which I was invited. Outside of mere personal considerations, I saw, or thought I saw, that, in the nature of the case, the sceptre of power had passed from the old slave-states to the free and loyal states, and that hereafter, at least for some time to come, the loyal North, with its advanced civilization, must dictate the policy and control of the destiny of the republic. I had an audience ready made in the free-states, one which the labors of thirty years had prepared for me, and before this audience the freedmen needed an advocate as much as they needed a member in Congress. I think that in this I was right, for thus far our colored members in Congress have not largely made themselves felt in the legislation of this country, and I have little reason to think that I could have done better than they—1907.

PROGRESS OF THE AMERICAN NEGRO

During the past twenty-five years the Southern Negro has made substantial progress in many directions, has responded unmistakably to the demands of American civilization. Some measure of this progress is to be found in the answers to these questions:

1. Has the Negro, succumbing to a competition too severe, exhibited tendencies to die out, as has, for example, the Maori population of New Zealand?
2. Has the Negro, with reasonable rapidity, become more intelligent?
3. To what extent has the Negro bought homes?
4. In his occupations is the Negro advancing to higher levels?

The facts show pretty plainly that, severe to him as is competition with many races which centuries have made more efficient, the Negro holds his own with dogged persistence. In 1880 there were 6,580,789 Negroes in this country; twenty years later we find this number increased to 8,840,-789 an increase of 2,259,996 souls, or 34.3 per cent. Certainly a new born race that can merely maintain its numbers in the face of the severest competition the world can boast, deserves praise; but what shall be said of my race? It has not merely maintained its numbers, but has actually grown 34.3 per cent. in twenty years. Of course the Africanization of this republic is not imminent. It is true that in Arkansas, Oklahoma, Mississippi, Alabama, Florida, West Virginia, the Negro element has actually increased faster than the native whites of native parents; but despite this fact, in the South Atlantic states as a whole—Delaware, Maryland, District of Columbia, Virginia, West Virginia, North Carolina, South Carolina, Georgia, and Florida—the native whites of native parentage increased 29.2 as against 19.9 per cent. for the Negro element. As an element in the total population of the country, the Negro race has steadily decreased since the first census—1790. (The only real exception to this statement is the year

1810, in which the population of Negroes was larger than in 1800 owing to the large importations of slaves, before the restriction of the slave trade in 1808.) Thus in 1880 the Negro element was 13.1 per cent. of the total population, but in 1900 only 11.6 per cent. In the matter of numbers this is clearly "a white man's country," and yet the Negro race is steadily advancing, and in two decades has increased in number 34.3 per cent. The Red Indian of America and the Maori of New Zealand are not precedents for the Negro of the United States. Neither death nor deportation will benevolently assimilate the Negro into non-existence; the Negro is here in America, and here to stay. His well being and continued progress are essential to the welfare of the republic.

This solidarity of interest has been splendidly recognized by the white people of the South. I believe that the Southern white people realize more and more clearly the fundamental idea of the American common school —that all of the property of the state should educate impartially all the children of all the people. It is not merely the man who enters the tax office who really pays the taxes; the laborers, each of whom pays one quarter cent more to the pound for a commodity because of a license tax, really pay the license tax, however indirect the payment. The moral idea that underlies the American common school and the actual incident of taxation—these two things are winning increasing recognition in every one of the Southern States. Moreover the value of land is largely determined by the relative intelligence and consequent efficiency of the laboring population; and the Negro constitutes a very large percentage of the South's labor. Since 1880 $105,807,930 have been spent for the Negro schools in the former slave states. In the school year, 1879–80, $2,120,-485 were spent for colored schools, and in 1900–01, $6,035,550—an increase of $3,915,065, or almost 285 per cent. In 1879–80 the expenditure per capita of the school population for the colored was $1.01, but 1900–01, $2.21. It is true that in the latter year the white child received $4.92 or considerably more than twice the amount received by the colored child. I believe, nevertheless, that the whole South is interested in the spread of Negro education.

Negro illiteracy is a stain that the schools are rapidly washing away. Though constituting only 13.1 per cent. of the total population in 1880, the colored population bore the burden of 51.6 per cent. of the illiteracy. Though 70 per cent. of the colored population were illiterate in 1880, only 45.5 per cent. were illiterate in 1900—a magnificent progress for the South and the Negro. It is true for the whole country that only 4.6 per cent. of the native white population were illiterate in 1900, as against 44.5 per cent. of the colored, but the South is determined to lessen this immense handicap upon the Negro just as rapidly as possible. During my efforts toward the uplift of some part of my race, I have had reason again and again to recognize that the mere ability to read and write is not all an American citizen must have; he must be and he must have sound moral character. Too often members of my race have been content with merely being "smart." I am glad to say that in many schools in the South carpentry and gardening have been emboldened to stand erect in company with reading, writing and arithmetic. But aside from these matters, the Negro has progressed since 1880 in literacy in the most gratifying way; to appreciable extent progress in literacy indicates progress in intelligence, in character, in general efficiency.

The schools have greatly aided the Negro in the buying and proper maintenance of homes. The white or black man, by the sweat of whose brow a home has been bought, is, by virtue of that fact, an infinitely better citizen. Under authority of a special act of Congress, investigation concerning the proprietorship of homes was first made in 1890.

In 1860 the Negro was without a home of his own, without capital, without thrift, with nothing like proper appreciation of the value of a home. And yet in 1890, of the homes occupied by Negro heads of families, 18.7 per cent. were owned—an immense advance in civilization, and all in thirty years. Moreover, of the homes thus owned 88.8 were owned absolutely free of all encumbrance. The significance of this fact is rendered more clearly when you consider that only 71.2 per cent. of the homes occupied by white heads of families in that year were owned. In the decade 1890 to 1900, the Negro heads of families increased their ownership of homes to 21.8 per cent. and of this increased number, 74.2 per cent. were owned as against 68 per cent. for white heads of families. I am unaware that history records such an example of substantial progress in civilization in a time so short. Here is the unique fact that from a penniless population, just out of slavery, that placed a premium upon thriftlessness, 372,414 owners of homes have emerged, and of these, 255,156 are known to own their homes absolutely free of encumbrance. In these heads of Negro families lie the pledge of my race to American civilization.

In the occupations in which the Negroes are engaged, are they advancing to higher levels? Of the wage-earners in the whole country in 1900, 14.3 per cent. were colored. As compared with the other elements the colored element has the largest proportion engaged in agricultural pursuits and in domestic and personal service; and the smallest proportion in professional service, trade and transportation, and manufacturing and mechanical pursuits. The census of 1900 shows that about 34 per cent. of the Negro wage earners of the United States are agricultural laborers; this is a fact fundamental in any solution of the race problem. About 19 per cent. of the Negro wage-earners are farmers, planters and overseers; and about 14 per cent. are laborers (not specified): about 12 per cent. were servants and waiters; about 6 per cent. laundresses and launderers; and every other class of Negro wage-earners constitutes less than 2½ per cent. of the total. From this rather detailed statement it is clear that the Negro is chiefly represented in agricultural labor—34 per cent. of the Negro wage-earners were, in 1900, agricultural laborers and 19 per cent. were farmers, planters, and overseers; these two groups thus accounting for 53 per cent. of the total wage-earners. An examination of the Negro in agriculture will therefore be an examination of the great masses of the race.

In the United States as a whole in 1900, 746,717 farms were operated by Negroes; 27.2 per cent. of the farms in the South Central division and 30 per cent. of the farms in the South Atlantic division were operated by Negroes; 33 per cent. of the farms in Florida; 39.9 per cent. of the farms in Georgia; 42.1 per cent. of the farms in Alabama; 50.2 per cent. of the farms in Louisiana; 27.2 per cent. of the farms in Mississippi were, in 1900, operated by Negroes. The Negro, therefore, is of fundamental importance in American agriculture. Of the Negro farmers in the United States 70.5 per cent. derived their principal income from cotton, 12.4 per cent. from miscellaneous products, 6.9 per cent. from hay and grain, 4.1 per cent. from live stock, and 2.6 per cent. from tobacco. In the South the Negro farmers were almost wholly occupied with growing cotton and corn. An investigation of the black farmers and laborers in the cotton belt of the South is an investigation of the great mass of the Negro people in America.

For many reasons it is most convenient to compare conditions in 1860 rather than in 1880 with conditions in 1900.

The census for 1900 contains a considerable body of evidence that I might use for testing the progress of the Southern Negro in agriculture. Thus, in 1900 about 34 per cent. of the Negro wage-earners in the United States were merely agricultural laborers, and about 19 per cent. of the Negro wage-earners were farmers, planters and overseers. These farmers, planters and overseers have simply lifted themselves by their boot straps! They have risen from a low to a higher level in their occupations and in American civilization.

I might show how the Negro agricultural laborer of exceptional ability has become share tenant, then cash tenant, then part owner, and finally owner—all with almost lightning rapidity and against fearful odds. Moreover I might cite in proof of the progress of the Negro in agriculture the value of his farm products not fed to live stock. Thus in the South Atlantic States 35.5 [per cent.] of the number of farms operated by Negro farmers in 1900 had products in 1899, not fed to live stock, worth $100 and under $235; and 30.4 per cent. had products worth $250 and under $500. And in the South Central States 31.6 per cent. of the number of farms operated by Negro farmers had products in 1899 not fed to live stock worth $100 and under $250; and 36.7 per cent. had products worth $250 and under $500. This is an enormous advance for the Negro since 1860.

But I propose to test the progress of the Negro in agriculture by the severest test—not a comparison with European peasantry, but with native whites with native parents in the Southern States. Certainly no fair-minded man could wish a test more severe; certainly we should be surprised if these native whites of purest stock did not immensely outstrip the

Negro. Let us, however, inquire how these two classes compare (1) with respect to the amount of cotton produced to the acre; and (2) with respect to the relative number of owners added since 1860.

The advance of the Negro as an independent factor in the production of cotton is well illustrated by the comparison of results obtained, especially under the two forms of land tenure in which each race exercises, to the same degree, individual judgment in the cultivation of its crops, as cash tenants and as owners. In 1899 the average yield of cotton was 0.397 bale for the white owner and 0.368 bale for the Negro owner; 0.403 bale for the white cash tenant, and 0.381 bale for the Negro cash tenant. In each form of tenure the Negro produced only from two or three one-hundredths of a bale less than the white man, and received only 60 cents to $1 less income. In Arkansas colored farmers for all three tenures had a greater production per acre than the white. Mississippi showed a greater production for colored cash tenants. Three other cotton states agree with these in crediting a higher production to colored share tenants. "Considering the fact that he emerged from slavery only one-third of a century ago," says the wholly dispassionate census report, "and considering also his comparative lack of means for procuring the best lands or getting the best results from what he has, this near approach to the standard attained by the white man's experience for more than a century denotes remarkable progress."

Practically all of the Negro owners of farms have become owners since 1860; in that year the Negro was landless. In the South Central States since 1860 Negro farmers have come to operate as owners and managers 95,624 farms and as tenants 348,805. The farms operated by owners or managers are thus 21.5 per cent. of the total. The per cent. of gain in ownership is about half that made by the white farmers since 1860. These facts spell progress unmistakably. In the South Atlantic States in 1860 there were 301,940 farms, practically all operated by white farm-owners and managers. In 1900 there were 673,354 farms operated by white farmers; and of these 450,541 were conducted either by farmers who owned the whole or a part of their land, or by hired white managers, and 222,813 by cash or share tenants. In forty years the number of farms operated by white farmers increased 371,414 and of that number 148,-601 or 40 per cent. were those of owners or managers and 222,813 or 60 per cent. those of tenants. At the same time 287,933 Negroes had acquired control of farm land in these states of whom 202,578 or 70.4 per cent. were tenants and 85,355 or 29.6 per cent. were owners or managers. In these eventful forty years the relative number of owners among the Negro farmers of the South Atlantic States has grown from absolutely nothing, three-fourths as rapidly as the relative number of owners among the whites, who in 1860 owned every acre of the land. In both the South Central States and South Atlantic States the Negroes have thus compassed a magnificent achievement.

In the short space at my disposal I have simply attempted to indicate some of the ways in which the Negro of the South has made substantial progress, and responded to the demands of American civilization—1907.

THE NEGRO AND THE LABOR PROBLEM OF THE SOUTH

Recent industrial changes bring into prominence two facts, first, that the South is likely for all times to be the cotton center of the world, and second, that the continued increase in the use of cotton goods among all nations will give to every acre of land in the South a value that it has not heretofore possessed. With these facts in mind a natural inquiry is, what can the Negro do to help forward the interest of the South, and what can the white man do to help the Negro and himself?

I shall hope to suggest an answer to both these questions. A few days ago I spent a day in the rural district of one of the counties of Georgia, and heard a great deal of discussion about the scarcity of efficient farm labor. After spending the day in the country, I returned to Atlanta for the night. Between 10 and 11 o'clock I made a tour through Decatur street and several streets in that vicinity. I think I do not exaggerate when I say that I found in and near Decatur street enough people who were not regularly employed to operate successfully fifty of the largest plantations in the State of Georgia. This single example would mean little except that it represents a condition more or less prevalent in practically all of our larger cities and all of our Southern States.

As an economic problem, we have on the one hand a surplus of idle labor in the cities and on the other much vacant land, unpicked cotton and a scarcity of farm labor; it is a tremendously difficult situation. The problem of changing these conditions confronts not only the South, but the North as well, and it is not by any means confined to my race. For the present, I desire to deal with it mainly as it affects my race and the land-owners of the South, be that land-owner white or black.

In order that what I may say on this subject shall be of any value to the white man or to my own race, I shall have to ask the privilege of perfect frankness. The many subjects affecting the interest of both races require perfect frankness on both sides. My readers will agree with me, I think, when I say that it is possible for a Negro to know more of the feelings and motives of colored people than a white man can possibly know.

In my recent visit to Atlanta, I did that which I have often done in large cities of the South wherever I have found a floating class of colored people. I made individual inquiry as to why they preferred an uncertain existence in the city to a life of comparative prosperity upon a farm, either as owners, renters, or laborers. While I shall not attempt to use their exact words, I sum up the reasons they gave me in a few sentences.

Just now,—at the time I write—the South is in the midst of the season when land-holders are making plans for another year's crop. Some of the matters that were brought out I shall try to discuss a little fully and maybe with profit to land-owners. In the South as elsewhere, there are two classes, those whom labor seeks and those who have to seek labor. The first group is comparatively small, but such a class exists; but it can and ought to be increased. There are, in my opinion, two classes of faults as between white farmers and black labor. One, on the part of the white people, the other on the part of the black people. To find and state faults, however, is easy. To suggest a remedy, one that shall promote the prosperity and happiness of both races is the aim of this chapter.

To return to the main complaints of the colored people as they have stated them to me time and time again: These people who have talked may be right, they may be wrong, they may state facts, or they may state untruths, but this I know, they represent the attitude of a large class of the colored people, who give the following as chief reasons for leaving the farms:

Poor dwelling-houses, loss of earnings each year because of unscrupulous employers, high-priced provisions, poor school-houses, short school terms, poor school teachers, bad treatment generally, lynchings and white-capping, fear of the practice of peonage, and general lack of police protection and want of encouragement.

Let us assume that these conditions do exist in some sections, and with certain individual planters. As a mere matter of dollars and cents, if for no higher reason, I believe that it will pay every owner of a plantation throughout the South to see to it that the houses of the tenants are not only made comfortable but attractive in a degree. The land-owner who thinks that he can secure the best class of colored people when he provides only a broken-down, one-room cabin for them to live in will find himself mistaken. The chances are that the planter who provides comfortable houses for his tenants will keep them much longer and will have a more reliable service. The matter of being cheated out of his earnings at the end of the year is, of course, a complaint that is very hard to discuss, and I know is likely to involve much exaggeration, and the more ignorant the aggrieved person is, the more given is he to such complaints and exaggeration, but I must not conceal the fact that such feeling is deep and widespread, and I ought to make the same statement regarding the high prices charged during the year for provisions, etc., supplied.

Some of the colored people who have migrated into the cities give as their reason for leaving the country the poor school facilities in the rural communities. In practically every large city in the South, the colored man is enabled by public missionary and private schools, to keep his child in school eight or nine months of the year. Not only is this true, but the school-houses are comfortable and the teachers are efficient. In many of the rural communities, the location of the school-house is far from the home of the child, the building is uncomfortable, the term lasts but four or five months, the teacher's salary is so small that it generally invites a most inefficient class of teachers. I know one community that has had great trouble this year in getting cotton pickers and other laborers, and inquiry reveals the fact that the Negro children were in school last year only four months, and the teacher received from the public fund but $11 per month for his services. Under such conditions, who can blame a large number of colored people for leaving the plantations of the country districts?

Purely as an economic proposition, I believe that it will not only pay the land-owners of the South, either as individuals or by united effort to see that good school-houses are provided on or near these plantations, that the schools are kept open six or eight months in a year, and there is a good teacher regularly employed; where the school fund is not large enough to supply a good school-house, they should extend the school term and provide a first-class, moral teacher. Further, it will pay to lead the way in seeing that reasonable facilities are also provided.

This, I repeat, will lead to demand for land, and increase of efficiency of the labor force. Financially, there will soon be a great difference in the price of land when there are tenants bidding for opportunities instead of going to cities as now. Wherever it is practicable, I would urge that a primary course in agriculture be given in every county school. This would lead to a love of farm work and country life.

Again, many are not on the farm as they say, because they have not been treated fairly. To illustrate: I recall that some years ago a certain white farmer asked me to secure for him a young colored man to work about the house and to work in the field. The young man was secured, a bargain was entered into to the effect that he was to be paid a certain sum of money and his board and lodging furnished as well. At the end of the colored boy's first day on the farm he returned. I asked the reason and he said that after working all of the afternoon he was handed a buttered biscuit for his supper, and no place was provided for him to sleep.

At night he was told he could find a place to sleep in the fodder loft. This white farmer, whom I know well, is not a cruel man and seeks generally to do the right thing, but in this case he simply overlooked the fact that it would have paid him better in dollars and cents to give some thought and attention to the comfort of his helper. This case is more or less typical. Had this boy been well cared for, he would have so advertised the place that others would have sought work there.

It is too well known that in a few counties of several of our Southern States there has been such a reign of lawlessness led by the whitecappers and lynchers that many of our best colored people have been driven from their homes and have sought in large cities safety and police protection. In too many cases the colored people who have been molested have been those who by their thrift and diligence have secured homes and other property. These colored people have been oppressed in most instances, not by property-holding intelligent white people, but by the worst and most shiftless element of whites. Have the higher class of whites escaped the responsibility for letting their affairs be controlled by the worst element? The practice of peonage in a few counties of the South has also caused a fear among an element of the colored people that prevents their going into, or remaining in the country districts that they may be forced to labor involuntarily and without proper remuneration. I have said that such lawless conditions exists in only a "few" counties in the South, and I use the word advisedly. In the majority of the counties of the South, life and property are just as safe as anywhere in the United States, but the harm comes because of the widespread notoriety that a few lawless communities and countries have given the South, and this serves to spread the idea pretty generally among the colored people that if they want police protection when they are charged with crime or under suspicion, they must hastily seek the confines of a city. I repeat that fear has stripped some counties of this most valuable colored labor, and left the dregs of that population. In the matter of law and order, my constant appeal is that there be hearty co-operation between the best whites and best blacks.

Nothing is clearer than that crime is rarely committed by the colored man who has education and owns property. I have not failed either to say to the colored people on not more than one occasion, "We shall see to it that crime in all its phases is condemned by the race, and a public sentiment kept alive that will make it impossible for a criminal to be shielded or protected by any member of the race, at any time or in any place."

Few white people realize how far a little encouragement goes in helping to make better and more useful citizens of the colored people. Some months ago, I recall that I listened for an hour to a white man in the South who was making a political speech. He was in a state where a revised constitution had disfranchised nineteen-twentieths of the colored voters and there was not the slightest chance of any political "uprising," or even opposition on the part of the colored people. Yet two-thirds of this man's address was devoted to ridicule and abuse of the colored people. The sad feature of such an address lies in the fact that in many parts of the country such a speech is taken seriously. To most of those who heard it and those who knew the man in that community, it did no especial harm for the people knew that his talk did not tally with his actions, but he had become so accustomed to making that kind of speech that he repeated it by force of habit. This man had drawn his first life's sustenance from the breast of a colored woman, had been reared by one, and at that moment had dozens of the best colored people of that section on his plantation, any one of whom would have laid down his life for him, and the man himself would have fought to the death in the defense of these colored servants of his.

Every year these land-holders were making him richer by their patient, faithful labor, and he would trust them with all that he possessed. In this community the Negroes had never made an unavailing appeal to this man for aid in building churches or school-houses, or in supporting a school. Few white men anywhere in the world in their actual daily practice had done more to help the black man. Yet, such a speech read in the newspapers at a distance would give the impression to a thousand colored laborers that the county in which the speaker lived was for them absolutely unsafe. Such a speech was not calculated to gain a single vote, but it was calculated in my opinion, to lose to the community a good many bales of cotton. I repeat that few understand how much good can be accomplished in the way of helping the colored people to lead law-abiding and useful lives if more white people would take occasion, both in private and public, to praise their good qualities instead of reviling and ridiculing them.

In regard to the duties and obligations of my own people, I would say that unless they realize fully the opportunities that are before them in the South and seize every chance to improve their method of labor, the time will come when Italians and other foreigners will attempt to displace them in the labor work of the South, just as the Chinese are displacing the Negroes in South Africa.

One charge frequently brought against us is that we cannot be depended upon for constant and uninterrupted labor; that an excursion or other excitement will take laborers from every place where their services are most needed. The complaint is frequently made that if paid on Saturday night, the laborers will probably not return to work until all the cash received has been expended and that on the plantations, the colored tenant takes but little interest in caring for the property of the landlord. These things our people should change.

The South, I believe, is on the eve of a season of prosperity, such as it has never before experienced, and by mutual understanding and sympathetic cooperation each of these two races of the South can help forward the interests of the other, and thus cement a friendship between them that shall be an object lesson for all the world. To help toward this end is my apology for speaking so plainly and in such detail—**1907.**

THE FRUITS OF INDUSTRIAL TRAINING

The political, educational, social and economic evolution through which the South passed during, say, the first fifteen or twenty years after the close of the Civil War, furnished one of the most interesting periods that any country has passed through.

A large share of the thought and activity of the white South, of the black South and that section of the North especially interested in my race was directed during the years of the reconstruction period towards politics, or towards matters bearing upon what were termed civil or social rights. The work of education was rather slow and covered a large section of the South; still I think I am justified in saying that in the public mind the Negro's relation to politics overshadowed nearly every other interest. The education of the race was conducted quietly, and attracted comparatively little attention just as is true at the present time. The appointment of one Negro postmaster at a third or fourth rate post-office will be given wider publicity through the daily press than the founding of a school, or some important discovery in science.

With reference to the black man's political relation to the state and Federal Governments, I think I am safe in saying that for many years after the Civil War, there were sharp and antagonistic views between the North and the South, as well as between the White South and the Black South. At practically every point where there was a political question to be decided in the South the blacks would array themselves on one side, and the whites on the other. I remember that very soon after I began teaching school in Alabama, an old colored man came to me just prior to an election. He said: "You can read de newspaper and most of us can't, but dar is one thing dat we knows dat you don't, and dat is how to vote down here; and we wants you to vote as we does." He added, "I tell you how we does, we watches de white man; we keeps watching de white man; de nearer it gets to 'lection time de more we watches de white man. We watches him till we finds out which way he gwine to vote. After we find out which way he gwine'r vote, den we votes 'zactly de other way; den we knows we's right."

Stories on the other side might be given showing that a certain class of white people, both at the polls and in the Legislatures voted just as unreasonably in opposing politically what they thought the Negro or the North wanted, no matter how much benefit might ensue from a contrary action. Unfortunately such antagonism did not end with matters political, but in many cases, affected the relation of the races in nearly every walk of life. Aside from political strife, there was naturally deep feeling between the North and the South on account of the war. On nearly every question growing out of the war, which was debated in Congress, or in political campaigns, there was the keenest difference and often the deepest feeling. There was almost no question of even a semi-political nature, or having a remote connection with the Negro upon which there was not sharp and often bitter division between the North and the South. It is needless to say that in many cases the Negro was the sufferer. He was being ground between the upper and nether millstones. Even to this day, it is well nigh impossible, largely by reason of the force of habit in certain states to prevent state and even local campaigns from being centered in some form upon the black man. In states like Mississippi, for example, where the Negro ceased nearly a score of years ago, by operation of law, to be a determining factor in politics, he forms in some way the principal fuel for compaign discussion at nearly every election. The sad feature of this is, as I have indicated in a previous chapter, to prevent the presentation before the masses of the people of matters pertaining to local and state improvement, and to great national issues like finance, tariff, or foreign policies. It prevents the masses from receiving the broad and helpful education which every political campaign should furnish, and, what is equally unfortunate, it prevents the youth from seeing and hearing on the platform the great political leaders of the two national parties. During a national campaign, few of the great Democratic leaders debate national questions in the South, because it is felt that the old antagonism to the Negro politically will keep the South voting one way. Few of the great Republican leaders appear on Southern platforms, because they feel that nothing will be gained.

But this is somewhat aside from my purpose, which is, I repeat, to make plain that in all political matters, there was for years after the war no meeting grounds of agreement for the two races, or for the North and South. Upon the question of the Negro's civil rights as embodied in what was called the Civil Rights Bill there was almost the same sharp line of division between the races, and, in theory, at least, between the Northern and Southern whites, largely because the former were supposed to be giving the blacks social recognition and encouraging intermingling between the races. The white teachers who came from the North to work in missionary schools, received for years little recognition or encouragement from the rank and file of their own race. The lines were so sharply drawn that in cities where native Southern white women taught Negro children in the public schools, they would have no dealings with the Northern white woman, who, perhaps, taught Negro children from the same family in a missionary school.

I want to call attention here to a phase of Reconstruction policy which is often overlooked. All now agree that there was much in Reconstruction that was unwise and unfortunate. However, we may regard that policy, and much as we may regret mistakes, the fact is too often overlooked that it was during the Reconstruction Period that a public school system for the education of all the people of the South was first established in most of

the states. Much that was done by those in charge of Reconstruction legislation has been overturned, but the public school system still remains.
True, it has been modified and improved, but the system remains, and is
every day growing in popularity and strength.

As to the difference of opinion between the North and the South regarding Negro education, I find that many people, especially in the North,
have the wrong conception of the attitude of the Southern white people. It
is and has been very generally thought that what is termed "Higher Education" of the Negro, has been from the first opposed by the white South.
This opinion is far from being correct. I remember that in 1881, when I
began the work of establishing the Tuskegee Institute in Alabama, practically all the white people who talked to me on the subject took it for
granted that instruction in the Greek, Latin, and modern languages would
be one of the main features of our curriculum. I heard no one oppose what
he thought our course of study was to embrace. In fact, there are many
white people in the South at the present time who do not know that instruction in the dead languages is not given at the Tuskegee Institute. In
further proof of what I have said, if one would go through the catalogs
maintained by the states for Negro people, and managed by Southern
white people, he will find in almost every case that instruction in the
higher branches is given with the consent and approval of white officials.
This was true as far back as 1880. It is not unusual to meet at this time
Southern white people who are as emphatic in their belief in the value of
classical education as a certain element of colored people themselves. In
matters relating to political and civil rights, the breach was broad, and
without apparent hope of being bridged; even in the matter of religion,
practically all the denominations had split on the subject of the Negro,
though I should add that there is now, and always has been, a closer touch,
and more co-operation in matters of religion between the white and colored people in the South than is generally known. But the breach between
the white churches in the South and North remains.

In matters of education the difference was much less sharp. The truth is
that a large element in the South had little faith in the efficacy of the
higher or any other kind of education of the Negro. They were indifferent,
but did not openly oppose: on the other hand, there has always been a
potent element of white people in all the Southern States who have stood
out openly and bravely for the education of all the people, regardless of
race. This element has thus far been successful in shaping and leading
public opinion, and I think that it will continue to do so more and more.
This statement must not be taken to mean that there is yet an equitable
division of the school funds raised by common taxation, between the two
races in many sections of the South, though the Southern States deserve
much credit for what has been done.

I wish, however, to emphasize the fact that while there was either open
antagonism or indifference in the directions I have named, it was the in-

troduction of industrial training into the Negro's education that seemed to furnish the first basis for anything like united and sympathetic interest and action between the two races in the South, and between the whites in the North and those in the South. Aside from its direct benefit to the black race, industrial education has furnished a basis for mutual faith and co-operation, which has meant more to the South, and to the work of education than has been realized.

This was, at the least, something in the way of construction. Many people, I think, fail to appreciate the difference between the problems now before us and those that existed previous to the civil war. Slavery presented a problem of destruction; freedom presents a problem of construction.

From its first inception the white people of the South had faith in the theory of industrial education, because they had noted, what was not unnatural, that a large element of the colored people at first interpreted freedom to mean freedom from work with the hands. They naturally had not learned to appreciate the fact that they had been worked, and that one of the great lessons for freemen to learn is to work. They had not learned the vast difference between working and being worked. The white people saw in the movement to teach the Negro youth the dignity, beauty and civilizing power of all honorable labor with the hands, something that would lead the Negro into his new life of freedom gradually and sensibly, and prevent his going from one extreme of life to the other too suddenly. Furthermore, industrial education appealed directly to the individual and community interest of the white people. They saw at once that intelligence coupled with skill would add wealth to the community and to the state, in which both races would have an added share. Crude labor in the days of slavery, they believed could be handled and made in a degree profitable, but ignorant and unskilled in a state of freedom could not be made so. Practically every white man in the South was interested in agricultural or in mechanical or in some form of manual labor; every white man was interested in all that related to the home life,—the cooking and serving of food, laundering, dairying, poultry-raising and house keeping in general. There was no family whose interest in intelligent and skillful nursing was not now and then quickened by the presence of a trained nurse. As already stated, there was general appreciation of the fact that industrial education of the black people had direct, vital and practical bearing upon the life of each white family in the South; while there was no such appreciation of the results of mere literary training. If a black man became a lawyer, a doctor, a minister, or an ordinary teacher, his professional duties would not ordinarily bring him in touch with the life of the white portion of the community, but rather confine him almost exclusively to his own race. While purely literary or professional education was not opposed by the white population, it was something in which they found little or no interest, beyond a confused hope that it would result in producing a higher and better type of Negro manhood. The minute it was seen that through industrial education the Negro youth was not only studying chemistry, but also how to apply the knowledge of chemistry to the enrichment of the soil, or to cooking, or to dairying, and that the student was being taught not only geometry and physics, but their application to blacksmithing, brickmaking, farming, and what not, then there began to appear for the first time a common bond between the two races and co-operation between the North and South.

One of the most interesting and valuable instances of the kind that I know of is presented in the case of Mr. George W. Carver, one of our instructors in agriculture at Tuskegee Institute. For some time it has been his custom to prepare articles containing information concerning the conditions of local crops, and warning the farmers against the ravages of certain insects and diseases. The local white papers are always glad to publish these articles, and they are read by white and colored farmers.

Some months ago a white land-holder in Montgomery County asked Mr. Carver to go through his farm with him for the purpose of inspecting it. While doing so Mr. Carver discovered traces of what he thought was a valuable mineral deposit, used in making a certain kind of paint. The interest of the land-owner and the agricultural instructor at once became mutual. Specimens of the deposits were taken to the laboratories of the Tuskegee Institute and analyzed by Mr. Carver. In due time the land-owner received a report of the analysis, together with a statement showing the commercial value and application of the mineral. I shall not go through the whole interesting story, except to say that a stock company, composed of some of the best white people in Alabama, has been organized and is now preparing to build a factory for the purpose of putting their product on the market. I hardly need add that Mr. Carver has been freely consulted at every step, and his services generously recognized in the organization of the concern. When the company was being formed, the following testimonial among others was embodied in the printed copy of the circular:—

"George W. Carver, Director of the Department of Agriculture, Tuskegee, Alabama, says:—

" 'The pigment is an ochreous clay. Its value as a paint is due to the presence of ferric oxide, of which it contains more than any of the French, Australian, American, Irish, or Welsh ochres. Ferric oxides have long been recognized as the essential constituents of such paints as Venetian red, Turkish red, oxide red, Indian red, and scarlet. They are most durable, being quite permanent when exposed to light and air. As a stain they are most valuable.' "

In further proof of what I wish to emphasize, I think I am safe in saying that the work of the Hampton Normal and Agricultural Institute, under the late General S. C. Armstrong, was the first to receive any kind of recognition and hearty sympathy from the Southern white people, and General Armstrong was, perhaps, the first Northern educator of Negroes who won the confidence and co-operation of the white South. The effects of General Armstrong's introduction of industrial education at Hampton, and its extension to the Tuskegee Institute in the far South, are now actively and helpfully apparent in the splendid work being accomplished for the whole South by the Southern Education Board, with Mr. Robert C. Ogden at its head, and by the General Education Board which was organized with Mr. William H. Baldwin, Jr., as its president. Mr. Baldwin has since died and Mr. Ogden has been elected president. Without the introduction of manual training it is doubtful whether such work as is now being wrought through these two boards for both races in the South, could have been possible within a quarter of a century to come. Later on in the history of our country it will be recognized and appreciated that the far-reaching and statesmanlike efforts of these two boards for general education in the South, and with the co-operation and assistance of such men as Mr. George Foster Peabody, Dr. Wallace Buttrick, Mr. John D. Rockefeller of the North, and Mr. Edgar Gardner Murphy, Chancellor Hill, Dr. Alderman, Dr. McIver, Dr. Dabney, and others of the South, will have furnished the material for one of the brightest and most encouraging chapters in the history of our country. The fact that we have reached the point where men and women who were so far apart twenty years ago can meet in the South and discuss freely from the same platform questions relating to the industrial, educational, political, moral, and religious development of the two races, marks a great step in advance. It is true, however, that as yet the Negro has not been invited to share in these discussions.

Aside from the reasons I have given showing why the South favored industrial education, coupled with intellectual and moral training, many of the whites saw, for example, that the Negroes who were master carpenters and contractors, under the guidance of their owners, could become still greater factors in the development of the South if their children were not suddenly removed from the atmosphere and occupations of their fathers, and if they could be taught to use the thing in hand as a foundation for higher growth. Many of the white people were wise enough to see that such education would enable some of the Negro youths to become more skillful carpenters and contractors, and that if they laid an economic foundation in this way in their generation, they would be laying a foundation for a more abstract education of their children in the future.

Again, a large element of people in the South favored manual training for the Negro because they were wise enough to see that the South was largely free from the restrictive influences of the Northern trades unions, and that such organizations would secure little hold in the South so long as the Negro kept abreast in intelligence and skill with the same class of people elsewhere. Many realized that the South would be tying itself to a body of death if it did not help the Negro up. In this connection I want to call attention to the fact that the official records show that within one year about one million foreigners came into the United States. Notwithstanding this number, practically none went into the Southern States; to be more exact, the records show that in 1892 only 2,278 all told went into the states of Alabama, Arkansas, Georgia, Kentucky, Mississippi, North Carolina, South Carolina, Tennessee, and Virginia. One ship sometimes brings as many to New York. Various reasons are given to explain why these foreigners systematically avoid the South. One is that the climate is so hot; and another is that they do not like the restrictions thrown about the ballot; and still another is the presence of the Negro in so large numbers. Whatever the true reason is, the fact remains that foreigners avoid the South, and the South is more and more realizing that it cannot keep pace with the progress being made in other parts of the country if a third of its population is ignorant and without skill.

The South must frankly face this truth, that for a long period it must depend upon the black man to do for it what the foreigner is now doing for the great West. If, by reason of his skill and knowledge, one man in Iowa learns to produce as much corn in a season as four men can produce in Alabama, it requires little reasoning to see that Alabama will buy most of her corn from Iowa.

Another interesting result of the introduction of industrial education for the Negro has been its influence upon the white people of the South; and, I believe, upon the whites of the North, as well. This phase of it has proved of interest in making hand training a conciliatory element between the races.

In 1883 I was delivering an address on industrial education before the Colored State Teachers' Association of one of our Southern States. When I had finished, some of the teachers began to ask the State Superintendent of Education, who was on the program, some questions about the subject. He politely but firmly stopped the questions by stating that he knew absolutely nothing about industrial training, and had never heard it discussed before. At that time there was no such education being given at any white institution in that state. With one or two exceptions, this case will illustrate what was true of all the Southern States. A careful investigation of the subject will show that it was not until after industrial education was started among the colored people, and its value proved, that it was taken up by the Southern white people.

Manual training or industrial and technical schools for the whites have, for the most part, been established under state auspices, and are at this time chiefly maintained by the states. An investigation would also show that in securing money from the state legislatures for the purpose of introducing hand work, one of the main arguments used was the existence and success of industrial training among the Negroes. It was often argued that the white boys and girls would be left behind unless they had the opportunities for securing the same kind of training that was being given the colored people.

Although it is, I think, not generally known, it is a fact that since the idea of industrial or technical education for white people took root within the last few years, much more money is spent annually for such education for the whites than for the colored people. Anyone who has not looked into the subject will be surprised to find how thorough and high grade the work is. Take, for example, the State of Georgia, and it will be found that several times as much is being spent at the Industrial College for white girls at Milledgeville, and at the technical schools for whites at Atlanta, as is being spent in the whole state for the industrial education of the Negro youths. I have met no Southern white educators who have not been generous in their praise of the Negro schools for taking the initiative in hand training. This fact has again served to create in matters relating to education a bond of sympathy between the two races in the South. Referring again to the influence of industrial training for the Negro in education, in the Northern States, I find, while writing this article, the following announcement in the advertisement of what is perhaps the most high-priced and exclusive girls' seminary in Massachusetts:—

In planning a system of education for young ladies with the view of fitting them for the greatest usefulness in life, the idea was conceived of supplementing the purely intellectual work by practical training in the art of home management and its related subjects.

It was the first school of high literary grade to introduce courses in Domestic Science into the regular curriculum.

The results were so gratifying as to lead to the equipment of Experiment Hall, a special building, fitted for the purpose of studying the principles of Applied Housekeeping. Here the girls do the actual work of cooking, marketing, arranging menus, and attend to all the affairs of a well-arranged household.

Courses are arranged also in sewing, dressmaking, and millinery; they are conducted on a similar practical basis, and equip the student with a thorough knowledge of the subject.

A dozen years ago I do not believe that any such announcement would have been made.

Beginning with the year 1877, the Negro in the South lost practically all political control; that is to say, as early as 1885 the Negro scarcely had any members of his race in the National Congress or state legislatures, and long before this date had ceased to hold state offices. This was true, notwithstanding the protests and fervent oratory of such strong race leaders as Frederick Douglass, B. K. Bruce, John R. Lynch, P. B. S. Pinchback, and John M. Langston, with a host of others. When Frederick Douglass, the greatest man that the race has produced, died in 1895, it is safe to say that the Negro in the Southern States, with here and there a few exceptions, had practically no political control, or political influence, except in sending delegates to national conventions, or in holding by appointment a few federal positions. It became evident to many of the wise Negroes that the race would have to depend for its success in the future less upon political agitation and the opportunity for holding office, and more upon something more tangible and substantial. It was at this period in the Negro's development, when the distance between the races was greatest, and the spirit and ambition of the colored people most depressed, that the idea of industrial or business development was introduced and began to be made prominent. It did not take the more level-headed members of the race long to see that while the Negro in the South was surrounded by many difficulties, there was practically no line drawn and little race discrimination in the world of commerce, banking, storekeeping, manufacturing, and the skilled trades, and in agriculture; and in this lay his great opportunity. They understood that while the whites might object to a Negro's being postmaster, they would not object to his being the president of a bank, and in the latter occupation they would give him assistance and encouragement. The colored people were quick to see that while the Negro would not be invited as a rule to attend the white man's prayer-meeting, he would be invited every time to attend the stockholder's meeting of a business concern in which he had an interest, and that he could buy property in practically any portion of the South where the white man could buy it. The white citizens were all the more willing to encourage the Negro in this economic or industrial development, because they saw that the prosperity of the Negro meant also the prosperity of the white man. They say, too, that when a Negro became the owner of a home and was a taxpayer, having a regular trade or other occupation, he at once became a conservative and safe citizen and voter; one who would consider the interests of his whole community before casting his ballot; and, further, one whose ballot could not be purchased.

One case in point is that of the twenty-eight teachers at our school at Tuskegee who applied for life-voting certificates under the new constitution of Alabama, not one was refused registration, and if I may be forgiven a personal reference, in my own case, the Board of Registers were kind enough to send me a special request to the effect that they wished me not to fail to register as a life voter. I do not wish to convey the impression that all worthy colored people have been registered in Alabama, because there have been many inexcusable and unlawful omissions; but, with few exceptions, the 2,700 who have been registered represent the best Negroes in the state.

Though in some parts of the country he is now misunderstood, I believe that the time is going to come when matters can be weighed soberly and when the whole people are going to see that President Roosevelt is, and has been from the first, in line with this policy, that of encouraging the colored people who by industry and economy have won their way into the confidence and respect of their neighbors. Both before and since he became President I have had many conversations with him, and at all times I have found him most enthusiastic in his desire to help all the people of the South.

The growth of the race in industrial and business directions within the last few years cannot perhaps be better illustrated than by what is now the largest secular national organization among the colored people, the National Negro Business League. This organization brings together annually, as I have elsewhere described, hundreds of men and women who have worked their way up from the bottom to the point where they are now in some cases bankers, merchants, manufacturers, planters, etc. The sight of this body of men and women would surprise a large part of American citizens, who do not know the better side of Negro life.

It ought to be stated frankly here that at first, and for several years after the introduction of industrial training at such educational centers as Hampton and Tuskegee, there was opposition from colored people and from portions of those Northern white people engaged in educational and missionary work among the colored people in the South. Most of those who manifested such opposition were, I believe, actuated by the highest and most honest motives. From the first the rank and file of the blacks were quick to see the advantages of industrial training, as is shown by the fact that industrial schools have always been overcrowded. Opposition to industrial training was based largely on the old and narrow ground that it was something that the Southern white people favored, and therefore must be against the interests of the Negro. Again, others opposed it because they feared that it meant the abandonment of all political privileges, and the higher or classical education of the race. They feared that the final outcome would be the "materialization" of the Negro and the smothering of his spiritual and aesthetic nature. Others felt that industrial education had for its object the limitation of the Negro's development, and the branding him for all time as a special hand-working class.

Now that enough time has elapsed for those who opposed it to see that it meant none of these things, opposition, except from a very few of the colored people living in one or two Northern cities away from the problem has ceased, and this system has the enthusiastic support of the Negroes and of most of the whites who formerly opposed it. All are beginning to see that it was never meant that all Negro youths should secure industrial education, any more than it is meant that all white youths should pass through the Massachusetts Institute of Technology, or the Amherst Agricultural College, to the exclusion of such training as is given at Harvard, Yale or Dartmouth; but that in a peculiar sense a large proportion of the Negro youths needed to have that education which would enable them to secure an economic foundation, without which no people can succeed in any of the higher walks of life.

It is because of the fact that the Tuskegee Institute began at the bottom, with work in the soil, in wood, in iron, in leather, that it has now developed to the point where it is able to furnish employment as teachers to twenty-eight Negro college graduates of the best colleges in the country. This is about three times as many Negro college graduates as any other institution in the United States for the education of colored people employs, the total number of officers and instructors at Tuskegee being about one hundred and ten, and excluding clerks, stenographers and helpers of various kinds.

Those who once opposed this, see now that while the Negro youth who becomes skilled in agriculture and a successful farmer may not be able himself to pass through a purely literary college, he is laying the foundation for his children and grandchildren to do it if desirable. Industrial education in this generation is contributing in the highest degree to make what is called higher education a success. It is now realized that in so far as the race has intelligent and skillful producers, the greater will be the success of the minister, lawyer, doctor, and teacher. Opposition has melted away, too, because all men now see that it will take a long time to "materialize" a race, millions of which hold neither houses nor railroads, nor bank stock, nor factories, nor coal and gold mines.

Another reason for the growth of a better understanding of the objects and influence of industrial training, is the fact, as before stated, that it has been taken up with much interest and activity by the Southern whites, and that it has been established at such universities as Cornell in the East, and in practically all of the state colleges of the Great West.

It is now seen that the result of such education will be to help the black man to make for himself an independent place in our great American life. It was largely the poverty of the Negro that made him the prey of the designing politicians immediately after the war; and wherever poverty and lack of industry exist to-day, one does not find in him that deep spiritual life which the race must in the future possess in a higher degree.

To those who still express the fear that perhaps too much stress is put upon industrial education for the Negro, I would add that I should emphasize the same kind of training for any people, whether black or white, in the same stage of development as the masses of the colored people.

For a number of years this country has looked to Germany for much in the way of education, and a large number of America's brightest men and women are sent there each year. The official reports show that in Saxony, Germany, alone, there are 287 industrial schools, or one such school to every 14,641 people. This is true of a people who have back of them centuries of wealth and culture. In the South I am safe in saying that there is not more than one effective industrial school for every 400,000 colored people.

A recent dispatch from Germany says that the German Emperor has had a kitchen fitted up in the palace for the single purpose of having his daughter taught cooking. If all classes and nationalities, who are in most cases thousands of years ahead of the Negro in the arts of civilization, continue their interest in industrial training, I cannot understand how any reasonable person can object to such education for a large part of a people who are in the poverty-stricken condition that is true of a large element of my race, especially when such hand training is combined, as it should be, with the best education of head and heart—1907.

THE AMERICAN NEGRO AND
HIS ECONOMIC VALUE

Within the last two years and more I have had letters from the Sandwich Islands, Cuba, and South America, all asking that American Negroes be induced to go to these places as laborers. In each case there would seem to be abundant labor already in the places named. It is there, but it seems to be not of the quality and value of that of the Negro in the United States.

These letters have led me to think a good deal about the Negro as an industrial factor in our country.

To begin with we must bear in mind that when the first twenty slaves were landed at Jamestown, Virginia, in 1619, it was this economic value which caused them to be brought to this country. At the same time that these slaves were being brought to the shores of Virginia from their native land, Africa, the woods of Virginia were swarming with thousands of another dark-skinned race. The question naturally arises: Why did the importers of Negro slaves go to the trouble and expense of going thousands of miles for a dark-skinned people to hew wood and draw water for the whites, when they had right about them a people of another race who could have answered this purpose? The answer is, that the Indian was tried and found wanting in the commercial qualities which the Negro seemed to possess. The Indian would not submit to slavery as a race, and in those instances where he was tried as a slave his labor was not profitable and he was found to be unable to stand the physical strain of slavery. As a slave the Indian died in large numbers. This was true in San Domingo and in other parts of the American continent.

The two races, the Indian and the Negro, have often been compared to the disadvantage of the Negro. It has been more than once stated that the Indian proved himself the superior race by not submitting to slavery. We shall see about this. In this respect it may be that the Indian secured a temporary advantage in so far as race feeling or prejudice is concerned; I mean by this that he escaped the badge of servitude which has fastened itself upon the Negro, and not only upon the Negro in America, for the known commercial value of the Negro has made him a subject of traffic in other portions of the globe during many centuries. Even to this day, portions of Africa continue to be the stamping ground of the slave-trader.

The Indian refused to submit to bondage and learn the white man's ways. The result is that the greater portion of the American Indians have disappeared, the greater portion of those who remain are not civilized.

The Negro, wiser and more enduring than the Indian, patiently endured slavery; and contact with the white man has given the Negro in America a civilization vastly superior to that of the Indian.

The Indian and the Negro met on the American continent for the first time at Jamestown, in 1619. Both were in the darkest barbarism. There were twenty Negroes and thousands of Indians. At the present time there are between nine and ten millions of Negroes and less than sixty-five thousand Indians. Not only has the Indian decreased in numbers, but he is an annual tax upon the government for food and clothing to the extent of $12,784,676 (1899), to say nothing of the large amount that is annually spent in policing him. The one in this case not only decreased in numbers and failed to add anything to the economic value of his country, but has actually proven a charge upon it.

Let me see how it is with the other. For a long time our National laws bearing upon immigration have been framed so as to prevent the influx into this country of any classes or races that might prove a burden upon the tax-payers, because of their poverty and inability to sustain themselves, as well as their low standards of life which would enable them to underbid the American laborer. The effect has been, then, to keep out certain races and classes. For two centuries or more it was the policy of the United States to bring in the Negro at almost any cost. This country has two hundred and fifty years in which to judge the economic value of the black man, and the verdict at the end was that he was constantly increasing in value, especially in the Southern part of the United States.

Would any individual, or any country, have gone to the expense during so many years to import a people that had no economic value?

The Negro seems to be about the only race that has been able to look the white man in the face during the long period of years and live, not only live but multiply. The Negro has not only done this, but he has had the good sense to get something from the white man at every point he has touched him—something that has made for a stronger and better race.

As compared with the Malay race, the Negro has proven his superiority as an economic factor in civilization. Take for example the Malays in the Sandwich Islands. Before the Sandwich Islanders came in contact with the white race, they had a civilization that was about equal to that of the twenty Negroes who came to Jamestown in 1619. Since their contact with the white man they have constantly decreased in numbers, and have so utterly failed to prove of economic value that practically all the industries of the Islands are kept in motion by other races, and a strong effort has recently been made, as I have noted, to induce a large number of black Americans to go to these Islands as laborers.

The industries that gave the South its power, prominence, and wealth prior to the Civil War, were mainly cotton, sugar-cane, rice and tobacco.

Before the way could be prepared for the proper growing and marketing of these crops, forests had to be cleared, houses to be built, public roads and railroads to be constructed. In all of this no one will deny that the Negro was the chief dependence.

The Negro was not only valuable as a common workman, but reached a degree of skill and intelligence in mechanics that added a large per cent. to his money value. Indeed, many of the most complicated structures at the South to-day stand as monuments to the skill and ability of the Negro mechanic of ante-bellum days.

In the planting, cultivating, and marketing of the cotton, rice, sugar-cane and tobacco crops, the black man was about the sole dependence, especially in the lower tier of the Southern States. In the manufacture of tobacco, he became a skilled and proficient workman, and at the present time, in the South, holds the lead in this respect in the large tobacco manufactories.

Not only did the black man prove his worth in the way of skilled and common labor, but there were thousands of Negroes who demonstrated that they possessed executive ability of a high order. Many of the large plantations had Negro overseers, to whom the whole financial interests of the masters were largely intrusted. To be able to plan months ahead for planting and harvesting of the crop, to reckon upon the influence of weather conditions, and to map out profitable work for scores of men, women, and children, required an executive ability of no mean order. In very few instances did the black manager prove false to his trust.

Without the part the Negro played in the physical development of the South, it is safe to say that it would be as undeveloped as much of the territory in the far West.

The most valuable testimony that I have seen upon the subject that this article covers is from the pen of Prof. N. S. Shaler, Dean of the Scientific School of Harvard University, which appeared recently in Appleton's Popular Science Monthly. My readers, I am sure, will forgive me for using a rather long quotation from Prof. Shaler's article. I do it for the reason that Prof. Shaler is not only a recognized scientist, but for the further reason that he is a Southern man, and has had abundant opportunity to secure valuable testimony. Prof. Shaler says:

"The Negroes who came to North America had to undergo as complete a transition as ever fell to the lot of man, without the least chance to undergo an acclimatizing process. They were brought from the hottest part of the earth to the region where the winter's cold is of almost arctic severity; from an exceedingly humid to a very dry air. They came to service under alien taskmasters, strange to them in speech and purpose. They had to betake themselves to unaccustomed food and to clothing such as they had never worn before. Rarely could one of the creatures find about him a familiar face, or friend, parent, or child, or any object that recalled his past life to him. It was an appalling change. Only those who know

how the Negro cleaves to all the dear, familiar things of life, how fond
he is of warmth and friendliness, can conceive the physical and mental
shock that this introduction to new things meant to him. To people of our
own race it would have meant death. But these wonderful folk appear to
have withstood the trials of their deportation in a marvelous way. They
showed no peculiar liability for disease. Their longevity or period of usefulness was not diminished, or their fecundity obviously impaired. So far
as I have been able to learn, nostalgia was not a source of mortality, as it
would have been with any Aryan population. The price they brought in
the market and the satisfaction of their purchasers with their qualities
show that they were from the first almost ideal laborers.

"If we compare the Algonquin Indian, in appearance a sturdy fellow,
with these Negroes, we see of what stuff the blacks are made. A touch of
housework and of honest toil took the breath of the aborigines away, but
these tropical exotics fell to their tasks and trials far better than the men
of our own kind could have done. . . . Moreover, the production of good
tobacco requires much care, which extends over about a year from the
time the seed is planted. Some parts of the work demand a measure of
judgment such as intelligent Negroes readily acquire. They are, indeed,
better fitted for the task than white men, for they are commonly more
interested in their tasks than whites of the laboring class. The result was
that before the period of the Revolutionary War slavery was firmly established in the tobacco planting colonies of Maryland, Virginia, and North
Carolina; it was already the foundation of their only considerable industry. . . . This industry (cotton), even more than that of raising tobacco
called for abundant labor, which could be absolutely commanded and severely tasked in the season of extreme heat. For this work the Negro
proved to be the only fit man, for while the whites can do this work, they
prefer other employment. Thus it came about that the power of slavery in this country became rooted in its soil. The facts show that, based on
an ample foundation of experience, the judgment of the Southern people
was to the effect that this creature of the tropics was a better laborer in
their fields than the men of their own race.

"Much has been said about the dislike of the white man for work in
association with Negroes. The failure of the whites to have a larger share
in the agriculture of the South has been attributed to this cause. This
seems to be clearly an error. The dislike to the association of races, in
labor is, in the slaveholding States, less than in the North. There can be
no question that if the Southern folk could have made white laborers
profitable they would have preferred to employ them, for the reason that
they would have required less fixed capital for their operation. The fact
was and is, that the Negro is there a better laboring man in the field than
the white. Under the conditions, he is more enduring, more contented, and
more trustworthy than the men of our own race."

So much for the Negro as a financial factor in American life before the Civil War. What of his value as a free man?

There were not a few who predicted that as soon as the Negro became a free man he would not only cease to support himself and others but would become a tax upon the community.

Few people in any part of our country have ever seen a black hand reach out from a street corner asking for charity. In our Northern communities a large amount of money is spent by individuals and municipalities in caring for the sick, the poor, and other classes of unfortunates. In the South, with very few exceptions, the Negro takes care of himself and of the unfortunate members of his race. This is usually done by a combination of individual members of the race, or through the churches or fraternal organizations.

The fact is often referred to that the Negro pays a very small proportion of the taxes that support his own schools. As to whether or not this is true depends a good deal on the theory of political economy that we follow, as I have sought to point out. . . . Some of the highest authorities on political economy contend that it is the man who rents the house that pays the taxes on it, rather than the man who simply holds the title to it. Certain it is that without the Negro to produce the raw material in the South, from which a large proportion of taxes are paid, there would not be a very large tax paid by any one.

Reliable statistics concerning the economic progress of the Negro are difficult to be obtained, owing to the fact that few of these states keep a record separating the property owned by Negroes from that owned by white people. The State of Virginia and one or two Southern States do keep such a record. Taking the mater of taxes as a basis for indicating the Negro's value, Prof. J. W. Cromwell, of Washington, D.C., gave the following statistics bearing upon the colored people of the State of Virginia, at a recent conference held at the Hampton Institute:—

The colored people contributed in 1898 directly to the expenses of the state government the sum of $9,576.76, and for schools $3,239.41 from their personal property, a total of $12,816.17; while from their real estate for the purposes of their commonwealth there were paid by them $34,303.53, and for schools, $11,357.22, or a total of $45,760.75; a grand total of $58,576.92.

The report for the same year shows them to own 978,118 acres of land, valued at $3,800,459, improved by buildings valued at $2,056,490, a total of $5,856,949. In the towns and cities they own lots assessed at $2,154,331, improved by buildings valued at $3,400,636, a total of $5,554,967 for town property and a grand total of $11,411,916 of their property of all kinds in the commonwealth. A comparative statement for different years would doubtless show a general upward tendency.

The counties of Accomac, Essex, King and Queen, Middlesex, Mathews, Northampton, Northumberland, Richmond, Westmoreland, Gloucester, Prin-

ASSIMILATION

cess Anne and Lancaster, all agricultural, show an aggregate of 114,197 acres held by Negroes in 1897, against 108,824 held in the previous year, an increase of 5,379, or nearly five per cent. The total valuation of lands, owned by Negroes in the same counties for 1897, is $547,800 against $196,385 for the year next preceding, a gain of $51,150, or more than ten per cent. Their personal property, as assessed in 1897, was $517,560, in 1896, $527,688, a loss of $10,128. Combining the real and personal property of 1897, we have $1,409,059 against $1,320,504 for 1896, a net gain of $88,555, an increase of six and one-half per cent.

The greatest excitement and anxiety was recently created among the white people in two counties of Georgia because of the fact that a large proportion of the colored people decided to leave. No stone has been left upturned to induce the colored people to remain in the county and prevent financial ruin to many white farmers.

Any one who has followed the testimony given before the United States Industrial Commission will see that several white men from the South have stated, in the most emphatic language, that the Negro is the best laborer that the South has ever had, and is the best that the South is likely to get in the future. Not the least part of the Negro's worth at the present time (and this is going to be more apparent in the future than now) is that he presents a conservative, reliable factor in relation to "strikes" and "lockouts." The Negro is not given to "strikes." His policy is to leave each individual free to work when, where, and for whom he pleases.

What I have thus far stated relates mainly to the common Negro laborer before and, since the war. But what about the educated Negro?

Reference is often made to the large proportion of criminal and idle colored men in the large cities. I admit that this class is much larger than it should be, and in some cities it is beginning to present a rather serious problem. Two things however should be kept in mind when considering the younger generation of colored people: First, that the transition from slavery to freedom was a tremendous one; that the Negro's idea of freedom for generations had been that it meant freedom from restraint and work; that the Negro mother and father had little opportunity during slavery to learn how to train children; and that the family life was practically unknown to the Negro until about thirty years ago. Secondly, the figures relating to criminality among all races in all countries show that it is the younger people—those between the ages of sixteen and thirty-five—that are given to crime and idleness.

Notwithstanding these facts, I want to present some testimony showing that the young, educated Negro is not failing to prove his worth.

Some time ago I sent letters to a few hundred white men, scattered throughout the Southern States, in which these three questions were asked:

1. Has education made the Negro a more useful citizen?

2. Has it made him more economical and more inclined to acquire wealth?

3. Has it made him a more valuable workman, especially where thought and skill are required?

Answers came from three hundred of my correspondents, and nine-tenths of them answered the questions emphatically in the affirmative. A few expressed doubts, and only one answered the question with an unmodified "No."

In each case I was careful to ask my correspondents to base their answers upon the conditions existing in their own neighborhood.

The greatest thing that can be done for the Negro at the present time is to make him the most useful and indispensable man in his community. This can be done by thorough education of hand, head, and, especially, by constantly distilling into every fibre of his being the thought that labor is ennobling and that idleness, all forms of it, is a disgrace—1907.

THE INTELLECTUALS AND
THE BOSTON MOB

It makes a great deal of difference in the life of a race, as it does in the life of an individual, whether the world expects much or little of that individual or of that race. I suppose that every boy and every girl born in poverty have felt at some time in their lives the weight of the world against them. What the people in the communities did not expect them to do it was hard for them to convince themselves that they could do.

After I got so that I could read a little, I used to take a great deal of satisfaction in the lives of men who had risen by their own efforts from poverty to success. It is a great thing for a boy to be able to read books of that kind. It not only inspires him with the desire to do something and make something of his life, but it teaches him that success depends upon his ability to do something useful, to perform some kind of service that the world wants.

The trouble in my case, as in that of other coloured boys of any age, was that the stories we read in school were all concerned with the success and achievements of white boys and men. Occasionally I spoke to some of my schoolmates in regard to the characters of whom I had read, but they invariably reminded me that the stories I had been reading had to do with the members of another race. Sometimes I tried to argue the matter with them, saying that what others had done some of us might also be able to do, and that the lack of a past in our race was no reason why it should not have a future.

They replied that our case was entirely different. They said, in effect, that because of our colour and because we carried in our faces the brand of a race that had been in slavery, white people did not want us to succeed.

In the end I usually wound up the discussion by recalling the life of Frederick Douglass, reminding them of the high position which he had reached and of the great service which he had performed for his own race and for the cause of human freedom in the long anti-slavery struggle.

Even before I had learned to read books or newspapers, I remember hearing my mother and other coloured people in our part of the country speak about Frederick Douglass's wonderful life and achievements. I heard so much about Douglass when I was a boy that one of the reasons why I wanted to go to school and learn to read was that I might read for myself what he had written and said. In fact, one of the first books that I remember reading was his own story of his life, which Mr. Douglass published under the title of "My Life and Times." This book made a deep impression upon me, and I read it many times.

After I became a student at Hampton, under Gen. Samuel C. Armstrong, I heard a great deal more about Frederick Douglass, and I followed all his movements with intense interest. At the same time I began to learn something about other prominent and successful coloured men who were at that time the leaders of my race in the United States. These were such men as Congressman John M. Langston, of Virginia; United States Senator Blanche K. Bruce, of Mississippi; Lieut.-Gov. P. B. S. Pinchback, of Louisiana; Congressman John R. Lynch, of Mississippi; and others whose names were household words among the masses of the coloured people at that time. I read with the greatest eagerness everything I could get hold of regarding the prominent Negro characters of that period, and was a faithful student of their lives and deeds. Later on I had the privilege of meeting and knowing all of these men, but at that time I little thought that it would ever be my fortune to meet and know any of them.

On one occasion, when I happened to be in Washington, I heard that Frederick Douglass was going to make a speech in a near-by town. I had never seen him nor heard him speak, so I took advantage of the opportunity. I was profoundly impressed both by the man and by the address, but I did not dare approach even to shake hands with him. Some three or four years after I had organized the Tuskegee Institute I invited Mr. Douglass to make a visit to the school and to speak at the commencement exercises of the school. He came and spoke to a great audience, many of whom had driven thirty or forty miles to hear the great orator and leader of the race. In the course of time I invited all of the prominent coloured men whose names I have mentioned, as well as others, to come to Tuskegee and speak to our students and to the coloured people in our community.

As a matter of course, the speeches (as well as the writings) of most of these men were concerned for the most part with the past history, or with the present and future political problems, of the Negro race. Mr. Douglass's great life-work had been in the political agitation that led to the destruction of slavery. He had been the great defender of the race, and in the struggle to win from Congress and from the country at large the recognition of the Negro's rights as a man and a citizen he had played an important part. But the long and bitter political struggle in which he had engaged against slavery had not prepared Mr. Douglass to take up the equally difficult task of fitting the Negro for the opportunities and responsibilities of freedom. The same was true to a large extent of other Negro leaders. At the time when I met these men and heard them speak I was invariably impressed, though young and inexperienced, that there was something lacking in their public utterances. I felt that the millions of Negroes needed something more than to be reminded of their sufferings and of their political rights; that they needed to do something more than merely to defend themselves.

Frederick Douglass died in February, 1895. In September of the same year I delivered an address in Atlanta at the Cotton States Exposition.

I spoke in Atlanta to an audience composed of leading Southern white people, Northern white people, and members of my own race. This seemed to me to be the time and the place, without condemning what had been done, to emphasize what ought to be done. I felt that we needed a policy, not of destruction, but of construction; not of defense, but of aggression; a policy, not of hostility or surrender, but of friendship and advance. I stated, as vigorously as I was able, that usefulness in the community where we resided was our surest and most potent protection.

One other point which I made plain in this speech was that, in my opinion, the Negro should seek constantly in every manly, straightforward manner to make friends of the white man by whose side he lived, rather than to content himself with seeking the good-will of some man a thousand miles away.

While I was fully convinced, in my own mind, that the policy which I had outlined was the correct one, I was not at all prepared for the widespread interest with which my words were received.

I received telegrams and congratulations from all parts of the country and from many persons whose names I did not know or had heard of only indirectly through the newspapers or otherwise. Very soon invitations began to come to me in large numbers to speak before all kinds of bodies and on all kinds of subjects. In many cases I was offered for my addresses what appeared to me almost fabulous sums. Some of the lecture bureaus offered me as high as $300 and $400 a night for as long a period as I would speak for them. Among other things which came to me was an offer from a prominent Western newspaper of $1000 and all expenses for my services if I would describe for it a famous prize-fight.

I was invited, here and there, to take part in political campaigns, especially in states where the Negro vote was important. Lecture bureaus not only urged upon me the acceptance of their offers through letters, but even sent agents to Tuskegee. Newspapers and magazines made generous offers to me to write special articles for them. I decided, however, to wait until I could get my bearings. Apparently the words which I had spoken at Atlanta, simple and almost commonplace as they were, had touched a deep and responsive chord in the public mind.* This gave me much to think about. In the meantime I determined to stick close to my work at Tuskegee.

One of the most surprising results of my Atlanta speech was the number of letters, telegrams, and newspaper editorials that came pouring in upon me from all parts of the country, demanding that I take the place of "leader of the Negro people," left vacant by Frederick Douglass's death, or assuming that I had already taken this place. Until these suggestions began to pour in upon me, I never had the remotest idea that I should be selected or looked upon, in any such sense as Frederick Douglass had been, as a leader of the Negro people. I was at that time merely a Negro school teacher in a rather obscure industrial school. I had devoted all my time and attention to the work of organizing and bringing into existence the Tuskegee Institute, and I did not know just what the functions and duties of a leader were, or what was expected of him on the part of the coloured people or of the rest of the world. It was not long, however, before I began to find out what was expected of me in the new position into which a sudden newspaper notoriety seemed to have thrust me.

I was not a little embarrassed, when I first began to appear in public, to find myself continually referred to as "the successor of Frederick Douglass." Wherever I spoke—whether in the North or in the South—I found, thanks to the advertising I had received, that large audiences turned out to hear me.

It has been interesting, and sometimes amusing, to note the amount and variety of disinterested advice received by a man whose name is to any

* The following is copied from the official history of the exposition:

Then came Booker T. Washington, who was destined to make a national reputation in the next fifteen minutes. He appeared on the programme by invitation of the directors as the representative of the Negro race. This would appear to have been a natural arrangement, if not a matter of course, and it seems strange now that there should have been any doubt as to the wisdom or propriety of giving the Negro a place in the opening exercises. Nevertheless, there was, and the question was carefully, even anxiously, considered before it was decided. There were apprehensions that the matter would encourage social equality and prove offensive to the white people, and in the end unsatisfactory to the coloured race. But the discussion satisfied the board that this course was right, and they resolved to risk the expediency of doing right. The sequel showed the wisdom of their decision. The orator himself touched upon the subject with great tact, and the recognition that was given has greatly tended to promote good feeling between the races, while the wide and self-respecting course of the Negroes on that occasion has raised them greatly in the estimation of their white fellow-citizens.

In introducing the speaker, Governor Bullock said: "We have with us to-day the representative of Negro enterprise and Negro civilization. I have the honour to introduce to you Prof. Booker T. Washington, principal of the Tuskegee Normal and Industrial College, who will formally present the Negro exhibit."

Professor Washington was greeted with applause, and his speech received marked attention.

extent before the public. During the time that my Atlanta address was, so to speak, under discussion, and almost every day since, I have received one or more letters advising me and directing my course in regard to matters of public interest.

One day I receive a letter, or my attention is called to some newspaper editorial, in which I am advised to stick to my work at Tuskegee and put aside every other interest that I may have in the advancement of my race. A day or two later I may receive a letter, or read an editorial in a newspaper, saying that I am making a mistake in confining my attention entirely to Tuskegee, to Negro education, or even to the Negro in the United States. It has been frequently urged upon me, for example, that I ought, in some way or other, to extend the work that we are trying to do at Tuskegee to Africa or to the West Indies, where Negroes are a larger part of the population than in this country.

There has been a small number of white people and an equally small number of coloured people who felt, after my Atlanta speech, that I ought to branch out and discuss political questions, putting emphasis upon the importance of political activity and success for the members of my race. Others, who thought it quite natural that, while I was in the South, I should not say anything that would be offensive, expected that I would cut loose in the North and denounce the Southern people in a way to keep alive and intensify the sectional differences which had sprung up as a result of slavery and the Civil War. Still others thought that there was something lacking in my style of defending the Negro. I went too much into the facts and did not say enough about the Rights of Man and the Declaration of Independence.

When these people found that I did not change my policy as a result of my Atlanta speech, but stuck to my old line of argument, urging the importance of education of the hand, the head, and the heart, they were thoroughly disappointed. So far as my addresses made it appear that the race troubles in the South could be solved by education rather than by political measures, they felt that I was putting the emphasis in the wrong place.

I confess that all these criticisms and suggestions were not without effect upon my mind. But, after thinking the matter all over, I decided that, pleasant as it might be to follow the programme that was laid out for me, I should be compelled to stick to my original job and work out my salvation along the lines that I had originally laid down for myself.

My determination to stand by the programme which I had worked out during the years that I had been at Tuskegee and which I had expressed in my Atlanta speech, soon brought me into conflict with a small group of coloured people who sometimes styled themselves "The Intellectuals," at other times "The Talented Tenth." As most of these men were graduates of Northern colleges and made their homes for the most part in the North, it was natural enough, I suppose, that they should feel that leadership in all race matters should remain, as heretofore, in the North. At any rate, they were opposed to any change from the policy of uncompromising and relentless antagonism to the South so long as there seemed to them to be anything in Southern conditions wrong or unjust to the Negro.

My life in the South and years of study and effort in connection with actual and concrete problems of Southern life had given me a different notion, and I believed that I had gained some knowledge and some insight which the college graduates that I have referred to were naturally the from the study of books.

The first thing to which they objected was my plan for the industrial education of the Negro. It seemed to them that in teaching coloured people to work with the hands I was making too great a concession to public opinion in the South. Some of them thought, probably, that I did not really believe in industrial education myself; but in any case they were opposed to any "concession," no matter whether industrial education was good or bad.

According to their way of looking at the matter, the Southern white man was the natural enemy of the Negro, and any attempt, no matter for what purpose, to gain his sympathy or support must be regarded as a kind of treason to the race.

All these matters furnished fruitful subjects for controversy, in all of which the college graduates that I have referred to were naturally the leaders. The first thing that such a young man was tempted to do after leaving college was, it seems, to start out on a lecturing tour, travelling about from one town to another for the purpose of discussing what are known as "race" subjects.

I remember one young man in particular who graduated from Yale University and afterward took a post-graduate course at Harvard, and who began his career by delivering a series of lectures on "The Mistakes of Booker T. Washington." It was not long, however, before he found that he could not live continuously on my mistakes. Then he discovered that in all his long schooling he had not fitted himself to perform any kind of useful and productive labour. After he had failed in several other directions he appealed to me, and I tried to find something for him to do. It is pretty hard, however, to help a young man who has started wrong. Once he gets the idea that—because he has crammed his head full with mere book knowledge—the world owes him a living, it is hard for him to change. The last I heard of the young man in question, he was trying to eke out a miserable existence as a book agent while he was looking about for a position somewhere with the Government as a janitor or for some other equally humble occupation.

When I meet cases, as I frequently do, of such unfortunate and misguided young men as I have described, I cannot but feel the most profound sympathy for them, because I know that they are not wholly to blame for their condition. I know that, in nine cases out of ten, they have gained the idea at some point in their career that, because they are Negroes, they are entitled to the special sympathy of the world, and they have thus got into the habit of relying on this sympathy rather than on their own efforts to make their way.

In college they gave little thought or attention to preparing for any definite task in the world, but started out with the idea of preparing themselves to solve the race problem. They learned in college a great deal about the history of New England freedom; their minds were filled with the traditions of the anti-slavery struggle; and they came out of college with the idea that the only thing necessary to solve at once every problem in the South was to apply the principles of the Declaration of Independence and the Bill of Rights. They had learned in their studies little of the actual present-day conditions in the South and had not considered the profound difference between the political problem and the educational problem, between the work of destruction and of construction, as it applies to the task of race building.

Among the most trying class of people with whom I come in contact are the persons who have been educated in books to the extent that they are able, upon every occasion, to quote a phrase or a sentiment from Shakespeare, Milton, Cicero, or some other great writer. Every time any problem arises they are on the spot with a phrase or a quotation. No problem is so difficult that they are not able, with a definition or abstraction of some kind, to solve it. I like phrases, and I frequently find them useful and convenient in conversation, but I have not found in them a solution for many of the actual problems of life.

In college they studied problems and solved them on paper. But these problems had already been solved by some one else, and all that they had to do was to learn the answers. They had never faced any unsolved problems in college, and all that they had learned had not taught them the patience and persistence which alone solve real problems.

I remember hearing this fact illustrated in a very apt way by a coloured minister some years ago. After great sacrifice and effort he had constructed in the South a building to be used for the purpose of sheltering orphans and aged coloured women. After this minister had succeeded in getting his building constructed and paid for, a young coloured man came to inspect it and at once began pointing out the defects in the building. The minister listened patiently for some time and then, turning to the young man, he said: "My friend, you have an advantage over me." Then he paused and looked at the young man, and the young man looked inquiringly at the minister, who continued: "I am not able to find fault with any building which you have constructed."

Perhaps I ought to add, in order that my statements may not be misleading, that I do not mean to say that the type of college man that I have described is confined to the members of my own race. Every kind of life produces its own peculiar kind of failures, and they are not confined to one race. It would be quite as wrong for me to give the impression that the description which I have given applies to all coloured graduates of New England or other colleges and to none others. As a matter of fact, almost from the beginning we have had men from these colleges at Tuskegee; I have come into contact with others at work in various institutions of the South; and I have found that some of the sanest and most useful workers were those who had graduated at Harvard and other New England colleges. Those to whom I have referred are the exception rather than the rule.

There is another class of coloured people who make a business of keeping the troubles, the wrongs, and the hardships of the Negro race before the public. Having learned that they are able to make a living out of their troubles, they have grown into the settled habit of advertising their wrongs—partly because they want sympathy and partly because it pays. Some of these people do not want the Negro to lose his grievances, because they do not want to lose their jobs.

A story told me by a coloured man in South Carolina will illustrate how people sometimes get into situations where they do not like to part with their grievances. In a certain community there was a coloured doctor of the old school, who knew little about modern ideas of medicine, but who in some way had gained the confidence of the people and had made considerable money by his own peculiar methods of treatment. In this community there was an old lady who happened to be pretty well provided with this world's goods and who thought that she had a cancer. For twenty years she had enjoyed the luxury of having this old doctor treat her for that cancer. As the old doctor became—thanks to the cancer and to other practice—pretty well-to-do, he decided to send one of his boys to a medical college. After graduating from the medical school, the young man returned home, and his father took a vacation. During this time the old lady who was afflicted with the "cancer" called in the young man, who treated her; within a few weeks the cancer (or what was supposed to be the cancer) disappeared, and the old lady declared herself well.

When the father of the boy returned and found the patient on her feet and perfectly well, he was outraged. He called the young man before him and said: "My son, I find that you have cured that cancer case of mine. Now, son, let me tell you something. I educated you on that cancer. I put you through high school, through college, and finally through the medical school on that cancer. And now you, with your new ideas of practising medicine, have come here and cured that cancer. Let me tell you, son, you have started all wrong. How do you expect to make a living practising medicine in that way?"

I am afraid that there is a certain class of race-problem solvers who don't want the patient to get well, because as long as the disease holds out they have not only an easy means of making a living, but also an easy medium through which to make themselves prominent before the public.

My experience is that people who call themselves "The Intellectuals" understand theories, but they do not understand things. I have long been convinced that, if these men could have gone into the South and taken up and become interested in some practical work which would have brought them in touch with people and things, the whole world would have looked very different to them. Bad as conditions might have seemed at first, when they saw that actual progress was being made, they would have taken a more hopeful view of the situation.

But the environment in which they were raised had cast them in another world. For them there was nothing to do but insist on the application of the abstract principles of protest. Indignation meetings in Faneuil Hall, Boston, became at one time so frequent as to be a nuisance. It would not have been so bad if the meetings had been confined to the subjects for which they were proposed; but when "The Intellectuals" found that the Southern people rarely, if ever, heard of their protests and, if they did hear of them, paid no attention to them, they began to attack the persons nearer home. They began to attack the people of Boston because they said that the people of Boston had lost interest in the cause of the Negro. After attacking the friends of the Negro elsewhere, particularly all those who happened to disagree with them as to the exact method of aiding the Negro, they made me a frequent and favourite object of attack—not merely for the reasons which I have already stated, but because they felt that if they attacked me in some particularly violent way it would surprise people and attract attention. There is no satisfaction in holding meetings and formulating protests unless you can get them into the newspapers. I do not really believe that these people think as badly of the person whom they have attacked at different times as their words would indicate. They are merely using them as a sort of sounding-board or megaphone to make their own voices carry farther. The persistence and success with which these men sought this kind of advertising has led the general public to believe the number of my opponents among the Negro masses to be much larger than it actually is.

A few years ago when I was in Boston and the subject of those who were opposing me was under discussion, a coloured friend of mine, who did not belong to the so-called "Talented Tenth," used an illustration which has stuck in my mind. He was originally from the South, although he had lived in Boston for a number of years. He said that he had once lived in Virginia, near a fashionable hotel. One day a bright idea struck him and he went to the proprietor of the hotel and made a bargain to furnish him regularly with a large number of frogs, which were in great demand as a table delicacy. The proprietor asked him how many he could furnish. My friend replied that he felt quite sure that he could furnish him with a cart-load, if necessary, once a week. The bargain was concluded. The man was to deliver at the hotel the following day as large a number of frogs as possible.

When he appeared, my friend had just six frogs. The proprietor looked at the frogs, and then at my friend.

"Where are the others?" he said.

"Well, it is this way," my friend replied; "for months I had heard those bull-frogs in a pond near my house, and they made so much noise that I supposed there were at least a million of them there. When I came to investigate, however, I found that there were only six."

Inspired by their ambition to "make themselves heard," and, as they said, compel the public to pay attention to their grievances, this little group kept up their agitation in various forms and at different places, until their plans culminated one night in Boston in 1903. To convince the public how deep and sincere they were in their peculiar views, and how profoundly opposed they were to every one who had a different opinion, they determined to do something desperate. The coloured citizens of Boston had asked me to deliver an address before them in one of their largest churches. The meeting was widely advertised, and there was a large audience present. Unknown to any of my coloured friends in Boston, this group, who, as I have stated, were mostly graduates of New England colleges, organized a mob to disturb the meeting and to break it up if possible. The presiding officer at the meeting was the Hon. William H. Lewis, a graduate of Amherst College and of the Harvard Law School. Various members of the group were scattered in different parts of the church. In addition to themselves there were present in the audience—and this, better than anything else, shows how far they had been carried in their fanaticism—some of the lowest men and women from vile dens in Boston, whom they had in some way or other induced to come in and help them disturb the meeting.

As soon as I began speaking, the leaders, stationed in various parts of the house, began asking questions. In this and in a number of other ways they tried to make it impossible for me to speak. Naturally the rest of the audience resented this, and eventually it was necessary to call in the police and arrest the disturbers.

Of course, as soon as the disturbance was over, most of those who had participated in it were ashamed of what they had done. Many of those who had classed themselves with "The Intellectuals" before, hastened to disavow any sympathy with the methods of the men who had organized the disturbance. Many who had before been lukewarm in their friendship became my closest friends. Of course the two leaders, who were afterward convicted and compelled to serve a sentence in the Charles Street Jail, remained unrepentant. They tried to convince themselves that they had been made martyrs in a great cause, but they did not get much encouragement in this notion from other coloured people, because it was not possible for them to make clear just what the cause was for which they had suffered.

The masses of coloured people in Boston and in the United States indorsed me by resolution and condemned the disturbers of the meeting. The Negro newspapers as a whole were scathing in their criticism of them. For weeks afterward my mail was filled with letters from coloured people, asking me to visit various sections and speak to the people.

I was intensely interested in observing the results of this disturbance. For one thing I wanted to find out whether a principle in human nature that I had frequently observed elsewhere would prove true in this case.

I have found in my dealings with the Negro race—and I believe that the same is true of all races—that the only way to hold people together is by means of a constructive, progressive programme. It is not argument, nor criticism, nor hatred, but work in constructive effort, that gets hold of men and binds them together in a way to make them rally to the support of a common cause.

Before many weeks had passed, these leaders began to disagree among themselves. Then they began to quarrel, and one by one they began to drop away. The result is that, at the present time, the group has been almost completely dispersed and scattered. Many of "The Intellectuals" to-day do not speak to one another.

The most surprising thing about this disturbance, I confess, is the fact that it was organized by the very people who have been loudest in condemning the Southern white people because they had suppressed the expression of opinion on public questions and denied the Negro the right of free speech.

As a matter of fact, I have talked to audiences in every part of this country; I have talked to coloured audiences in the North and to white audiences in the South; I have talked to audiences of both races in all parts of the South; everywhere I have spoken frankly and, I believe, sincerely on everything that I had in my mind and heart to say. When I had something to say about the white people I said it to the white people; when I had something to say about coloured people I said it to coloured people. In all these years—that is the curious thing about it—no effort has been made, so far as I can remember, to interrupt or to break up a meeting at which I was present until it was attempted by "The Intellectuals" of my own race in Boston.

I have gone to some length to describe this incident because it seems to me to show clearly the defects of that type of mind which the so-called "Intellectuals" of the race represent.

I do not wish to give the impression by what I have said that, behind all the intemperance and extravagance of these men, there is not a vein of genuine feeling and even at times of something like real heroism. The trouble is that all this fervour and intensity is wasted on side issues and trivial matters. It does not connect itself with anything that is helpful and constructive. These crusaders, as nearly as I can see, are fighting windmills.

The truth is, I suspect, as I have already suggested, that "The Intellectuals" live too much in the past. They know books but they do not know men. They know a great deal about the slavery controversy, for example, but they know almost nothing about the Negro. Especially are they ignorant in regard to the actual needs of the masses of the coloured people in the South to-day.

There are some things that one individual can do for another, and there are some things that one race can do for another. But, on the whole, every individual and every race must work out its own salvation. Let me add that if one thing more than another has taught me to have confidence in the masses of my own people it has been their willingness (and even eagerness) to learn and their disposition to help themselves and depend upon themselves as soon as they have learned how to do so—1911.

THE MISTAKES AND THE FUTURE
OF NEGRO EDUCATION

During the thirty years I have been engaged in Negro education in the South my work has brought me into contact with many different kinds of Negro schools. I have visited these schools in every part of the South and have had an opportunity to study their work and learn something of their difficulties as well as of their successes. During the last five years, for example, I have taken time from my other work to make extended trips of observation through eight different states, looking into the condition of the schools and saying a word, wherever I went, in their interest. I have had opportunities, as I went about, to note not merely the progress that has been made inside the school houses, but to observe, also, the effects which the different types of schools have had upon the homes and in the communities by which they are surrounded.

Considering all that I have seen and learned of Negro education in the way I have described, it has occurred to me that I could not do better in the concluding reminiscences of my own larger education than give some sort of summary statement, not only of what has been accomplished, but what seems to be the present needs and prospects of Negro education in general for the Southern States. In view also of the fact that I have gained the larger part of my own larger education in what I have been able to do for this cause, the statement may not seem out of place here. Let me then, first of all, say that never in the history of the world has a people, coming so lately out of slavery, made such efforts to catch up with and attain the highest and best in the civilization about them; never has such a people made the same amount of progress in the same time as in the case of the Negro people of America.

At the same time, I ought to add, also, that never in the history of the world has there been a more generous effort on the part of one race to help civilize and build up another than has been true of the American white man and the Negro. I say this because it should be remembered that, if the white man in America was responsible for bringing the Negro here and holding him in slavery, the white man in America was equally responsible for giving him his freedom and the opportunities by which he has been able to make the tremendous progress of the last forty-eight years.

In spite of this fact, in looking over and considering conditions of Negro education in the South to-day, not so much with reference to the past as to the future, I am impressed with the imperfect, incomplete, and unsatisfactory condition in which that education now is. I fear that there is much misconception, both in the North and in the South, in regard to the actual opportunities for education which the Negro has.

In the first place, in spite of all that has been said about it, the mass of the Negro people has never had, either in the common schools or in the Negro colleges in the South, an education in the same sense as the white people in the Northern States have had an education. Without going into details, let me give a few facts in regard to the Negro schools of so-called higher learning in the South. There are twenty-five Negro schools which are ordinarily classed as colleges in the South. They have, altogether, property and endowments, according to the report of the United States commissioner of education, of $7,993,028. There are eleven single institutions of higher learning in the Northern States, each of which has property and endowment equal to or greater than all the Negro colleges in the South. There are, for instance, five colleges or universities in the North every one of which has property and endowments amounting to more than $20,000,000; there are three universities which together have property and endowments amounting to nearly $100,000,000.

The combined annual income of twenty-four principal Negro colleges is $1,048,317. There are fifteen white schools that have a yearly income of from one million to five million dollars each. In fact, there is one single institution of learning in the North which, in the year of 1909, had an income, nearly twice as large as the combined income of the one hundred and twenty-three Negro colleges, industrial schools, and other private institutions of learning of which the commissioner of education has any report. These facts indicate, I think, that however numerous the Negro institutions of higher learning may be, the ten million Negroes in the United States are not getting from them, either in quality or in quantity, an education such as they ought to have.

Let me speak, however, of conditions as I have found them in some of the more backward Negro communities. In my own state, for example, there are communities in which Negro teachers are now being paid not more than from fifteen dollars to seventeen dollars a month for services covering a period of three or four months in the year. As I stated in a recent open letter to the Montgomery *Advertiser,* more money is paid for

Negro convicts than for Negro teachers. About forty-six dollars a month is now being paid for first-class, able-bodied Negro convicts, thirty-six dollars for second-class, and twenty-six dollars for third-class, and this is for twelve months in the year. This will, perhaps, at least suggest the conditions that exist in some of the Negro rural schools.

I do not mean to say that conditions are as bad everywhere as these that I refer to. Nevertheless, when one speaks "of the results of Negro education" it should be remembered that, so far as concerns the masses of the Negro people, education has never yet been really tried.

One of the troubles with Negro education at the present time is that there are no definite standards of education among the different Negro schools. It is not possible to tell, for instance, from the name of an institution, whether it is teaching the ordinary common school branches, Greek and Latin, or carpentry, blacksmithing, and sewing. More than that, there is no accepted standard as to the methods or efficiency of the teaching in these schools. A student may be getting a mere smattering, not even learning sufficient reading and writing to be able to read with comfort a book or a newspaper. He may be getting a very good training in one subject and almost nothing in some other. A boy entering such a school does not know what he is going for, and, nine times out of ten, he will come away without knowing what he got. In many cases, the diploma that the student carries home with him at the conclusion of his course is nothing less than a gold brick. It has made him believe that he has gotten an education, when he has actually never had an opportunity to find out what an education is.

I have in mind a young man who came to us from one of those little colleges to which I have referred where he had studied Greek, Latin, German, astronomy, and, among other things, stenography. He found that he could not use his Greek and Latin and that he had not learned enough German to be able to use the language, so he came to us as a stenographer. Unfortunately, he was not much better in stenography and in English than he was in German. After he had failed as a stenographer, he tried several other things, but because he had gone through a college and had a diploma, he could never bring himself to the point of fitting himself to do well any one thing. The consequence was that he went wandering about the country, always dissatisfied and unhappy, never giving satisfaction to himself or to his employers.

Although this young man was not able to write a letter in English without making grammatical errors or errors of some kind or other, the last time I heard of him he was employed as a teacher of business, in fact, he was at the head of the business department in one of the little colleges to which I have referred. He was not able to use his stenography in a well-equipped office, but he was able to teach stenography sufficiently well to meet the demands of the business course as given in the kind of Negro college of which there are, unfortunately, too many in the South.

Now, there was nothing the matter with this young man—excepting his education. He was industrious, ambitious, absolutely trustworthy, and, if he had been able to stick at any one position long enough to learn to do the work required of him well, he would have made, in my opinion, a very valuable man. As it was, his higher education spoiled him. In going through college he had been taught that he was getting an education when, as a matter of fact, he really had no education worth the mention.

One of the mistakes that Negro schools have frequently made has been the effort to cover, in some sort of way, the whole school curriculum from the primary, through the college, taking their students, as a friend of mine once said, "from the cradle to the grave." The result is that many of the Negro colleges have so burdened themselves with the work of an elementary grade that they are actually doing no college work at all, although they still keep up the forms and their students still speak of themselves as "college students."

In this way nearly every little school calling itself a college has attempted to set up a complete school system of its own, reaching from the primary grade up through the university. These schools, having set themselves an impossible task, particularly in view of the small means that they have at their command, it is no wonder that their work is often badly done.

I remember visiting one of these institutions in the backwoods district of one of the Southern States. The school was carried on in an old ramshackle building, which had been erected by the students and the teachers, although it was evident that not one of them had more than the most primitive notion of how to handle a saw or a square.

The wind blew through the building from end to end. Heaps of Bibles, which had been presented to the school by some friends, were piled up on the floor in one corner of the building. The dormitory was in the most disorderly condition one could possibly imagine. Half of the building had been burned away and had never been rebuilt. Broken beds and old mattresses were piled helter-skelter about in the rooms. What showed as well as anything the total incompetency of everybody connected with the school were the futile efforts that had been made to obtain a supply of drinking water. The yard around the school, which they called the "campus," was full of deep and dangerous holes, where some one had attempted at different times to dig a well but failed, because, as was evident enough, he had not the slightest idea of how the work should have been done.

At the time I was there the school was supplied with water from an old swamp in the neighbourhood, but the president of the college explained to me an elaborate plan which he had evolved for creating an artificial lake and this enterprise, he said, had the added advantage of furnishing work for the students.

When I asked this man in regard to his course of study, he handed me a great sheet of paper, about fifteen inches wide and two feet long, filled with statements that he had copied from the curricula of all sorts of different schools, including theological seminaries, universities, and industrial schools. From this sheet, it appeared that he proposed to teach in his school everything from Hebrew to telegraphy. In fact, it would have taken at least two hundred teachers to do all the work that he had laid out.

When I asked him why it was that he did not confine himself within the limits of what the students needed and of what he would be able to teach, he explained to me that he had found that some people wanted one kind of education and some people wanted another. As far as he was concerned, he took a liberal view and was willing to give anybody anything that was wanted. If his students wanted industrial education, theological education, or college education, he proposed to give it to them.

I suggested to him that the plan was liberal enough, but it would be impossible for him to carry it out. "Yes," he replied, "it may be impossible just now, but I believe in aiming high." The pathetic thing about it all was that this man and the people with whom he had surrounded himself were perfectly sincere in what they were trying to do. They simply did not know what an education was or what it was for.

We have in the South, in general, five types of Negro schools. There are (1) the common schools, supported in large part by state funds supplemented in many cases by contributions from the coloured people; (2) academies and so-called colleges, or universities, supported partly by different Negro religious denominations and partly by the contributions of philanthropic persons and organizations; (3) the state normal, mechanical, and agricultural colleges, supported in part by the state and in part by funds provided by the Federal Government; (4) medical schools, which are usually attached to some one or other of the colleges, but really maintain a more or less independent existence; (5) industrial schools, on the model of Hampton and Tuskegee.

Although these schools exist, in many cases, side by side, most of them are attempting to do, more or less, the work of all the others. Because every school is attempting to do the work of every other, the opportunities for coöperation and team work are lost. Instead one finds them frequently quarrelling and competing among themselves both for financial support and for students. The colleges and the academies frequently draw students away from the public schools. The state agricultural schools, supported in part by the National Government, are hardly distinguishable from some of the theological seminaries. Instead of working in coöperation with one another and with the public authorities in building up the public schools, thus bringing the various institutions of learning into some sort of working harmony and system, it not infrequently happens that the different schools are spending time and energy in trying to hamper and injure one another.

We have had some experience at Tuskegee of this lack of coöperation among the different types of Negro schools. For some years we have employed as teachers a large number of graduates, not only from some of the better Negro colleges in the South, but from some of the best colleges in the North as well. In spite of the fact that Tuskegee offers a larger market for the services of these college graduates than they are able to find elsewhere, I have yet to find a single graduate who has come to us from any of these colleges in the South who has made any study of the aims or purposes of industrial education. And this is true, although some of the colleges claim that a large part of their work consists in preparing teachers for work in industrial schools.

Not only has it been true that graduates of these colleges have had no knowledge or preparation which fitted them for teaching in an industrial school, but in many cases, they have come to us with the most distorted notions of what these industrial schools were seeking to do.

Perhaps the larger proportion of the college graduates go, when they leave college, as teachers into the city or rural schools. Nevertheless, there is the same lack of coöperation between the colleges and the public schools that I have described as existing between the colleges and the industrial schools. It is a rare thing, so far as my experience goes, for students in the Negro colleges to have had an opportunity to make any systematic study of the actual condition and needs of the schools or communities in which they are employed after they graduate. Instead of working out and teaching methods of connecting the school with life, thus making it a centre and a source of inspiration that might gradually transform the communities about them, these colleges have too frequently permitted their graduates to go out with the idea that their diploma was a sort of patent of nobility, and that the possessor of it was a superior being who was making a sacrifice in merely bestowing himself or herself as a teacher upon the communities to which he or she was called.

One of the chief hindrances to the progress of Negro education in the public schools in the South is in my opinion due to the fact that the Negro colleges in which so many of the teachers are prepared have not realized the importance of convincing the Southern white people that education makes the same improvement in the Negro that it does in the white man; makes him so much more useful in his labour, so much better a citizen, and so much more dependable in all the relations of life, that it is worth while to spend the money to give him an education. As long as the masses of the Southern white people remain unconvinced by the results of the education which they see about them that education makes the Negro a better man or woman, so long will the masses of the Negro people who are dependent upon the public schools for their instruction remain to a greater or less extent in ignorance.

Some of the schools of the strictly academic type have declared that their purpose in sticking to the old-fashioned scholastic studies was to make of their students Christian gentlemen. Of course, every man and every woman should be a Christian and, if possible, a gentleman or a lady; but it is not necessary to study Greek or Latin to be a Christian. More than that, a school that is content with merely turning out ladies and gentlemen who are not at the same time something else—who are not lawyers, doctors, business men, bankers, carpenters, farmers, teachers, not even housewives, but merely ladies and gentlemen—such a school is bound, in my estimation, to be more or less of a failure. There is no room in this country, and never has been, for the class of people who are merely gentlemen, and, if I may judge from what I have lately seen abroad, the time is coming when there will be no room in any country for the class of people who are merely gentlemen—for people, in other words, who are not fitted to perform some definite service for the country or the community in which they live.

In the majority of cases I have found that the smaller Negro colleges have been modelled on the schools started in the South by the anti-slavery people from the North directly after the war. Perhaps there were too many institutions started at that time for teaching Greek and Latin, considering that the foundation had not yet been laid in a good common-school system. It should be remembered, however, that the people who started these schools had a somewhat different purpose from that for which schools ordinarily exist to-day. They believed that it was necessary to complete the emancipation of the Negro by demonstrating to the world that the black man was just as able to learn from books as the white man, a thing that had been frequently denied during the long anti-slavery controversy.

I think it is safe to say that that has now been demonstrated. What remains to be shown is that the Negro can go as far as the white man in using his education, of whatever kind it may be, to make himself a more useful and valuable member of society. Especially is it necessary to convince the Southern white man that education, in the case of the coloured man, is a necessary step in the progress and upbuilding, not merely of the Negro, but of the South.

It should be remembered in this connection that there are thousands of white men in the South who are perfectly friendly to the Negro and would like to do something to help him, but who have not yet been convinced that education has actually done the Negro any good. Nothing will change their minds but an opportunity to see results for themselves.

The reason more progress has not been made in this direction is that the schools planted in the South by the Northern white people have remained —not always through their own fault to be sure—in a certain sense, alien institutions. They have not considered, in planning their courses of instruction, the actual needs either of the Negro or of the South. Not infrequently young men and women have gotten so out of touch during the time that they were in these schools with the actual conditions and needs of the Negro and the South that it has taken years before they were able to get back to earth and find places where they would be useful and happy in some form or other of necessary and useful labour.

Sometimes it has happened that Negro college students, as a result of the conditions under which they were taught, have yielded to the temptation to become mere agitators, unwilling and unfit to do any kind of useful or constructive work. Naturally under such conditions as teachers, or in any other capacity, they have not been able to be of much use in winning support in the South for Negro education. Nevertheless it is in the public schools of the South that the masses of the Negro people must get their education, if they are to get any education at all.

I have long been of the opinion that the persons in charge of the Negro colleges do not realize the extent to which it is possible to create in every part of the South a friendly sentiment toward Negro education, provided it can be shown that this education has actually benefited and helped in some practical way the masses of the Negro people with whom the white man in the South comes most in contact. We should not forget that as a rule in the South it is not the educated Negro, but the masses of the people, the farmers, labourers, and servants, with whom the white people come in daily contact. If the higher education which is given to the few does not in some way directly or indirectly reach and help the masses very little will be done toward making Negro education popular in the South or toward securing from the different states the means to carry it on.

On the other hand, just so soon as the Southern white man can see for himself the effects of Negro education in the better service he receives from the labourer on the farm or in the shop; just so soon as the white merchant finds that education is giving the Negro not only more wants, but more money with which to satisfy these wants, thus making him a better customer; when the white people generally discover that Negro education lessens crime and disease and makes the Negro in every way a better citizen, then the white taxpayer will not look upon the money spent for Negro education as a mere sop to the Negro race, or perhaps as money entirely thrown away.

I said something like this some years ago to the late Mr. H. H. Rogers and together we devised a plan for giving the matter a fair test. He proposed that we take two or three counties for the purpose of the experiment, give them good schools, and see what would be the result.

We agreed that it would be of no use to build these schools and give them outright to the people, but determined rather to use a certain amount of money to stimulate and encourage the coloured people in these counties to help themselves. The experiment was started first of all in Macon County, Ala., in the fall of 1905. Before it was completed Mr.

Rogers died, but members of his family kindly consented to carry on the work to the end of the term that we had agreed upon—that is to say, to October, 1910.

As a result of this work forty-six new school buildings were erected at an average cost of seven hundred dollars each; school terms were lengthened from three and four to eight and nine months, at an average cost to the people themselves of thirty-six hundred dollars per year. Altogether about twenty thousand dollars was raised by the people in the course of this five-year period. Similar work on a less extensive scale was done in four other counties. As a result we now have in Macon County a model public-school system, supported in part by the county board of education, and in part by the contributions of the people themselves.

As soon as we had begun with the help of the coloured people in the different country communities to erect these model schools throughout the county, C. J. Calloway, who had charge of the experiment, began advertising in coloured papers throughout the South that in Macon County it was possible for a Negro farmer to buy land in small or large tracts near eight-months' schools. Before long the Negro farmers not only from adjoining counties, but from Georgia and the neighbouring states, began to make inquiries. A good many farmers who were not able to buy land but wanted to be near a good school began to move into the county in order to go to work on the farms. Others who already had property in other parts of the South sold out and bought land in Macon County. Mr. Calloway informs me that, during the last five years, he alone has sold land in this country to something like fifty families at a cost of $49,740. He sold during the year 1910, 1450 acres at a cost of $21,335.

I do not think that any of us realized the full value of this immigration into Macon County until the census of 1910 revealed the extent to which the dislocation of the farming population has been going on in other parts of the state. The census shows, for example, that a majority of the Black Belt counties in Alabama instead of increasing have lost population during the last ten years. It is in the Black Belt counties which have no large cities that this decrease has taken place. Macon County, although it has no large cities, is an exception, for instead of losing population it shows an increase of more than ten per cent.

I think that there are two reasons for this: In the first place there is very little Negro crime and no mob violence in Macon County. The liquor law is enforced and there are few Negroes in Macon County who do not coöperate with the officers of the law in the effort to get rid of the criminal element.

In the second place, Macon County is provided not only with the schools that I have described, but with teachers who instruct their pupils in regard to things that will help them and their parents to improve their homes, their stock, and their land, and in other ways to earn a better living.

When the facts brought out by the census were published in Alabama they were the subject of considerable discussion among the large planters and in the public press generally. In the course of this discussion I called attention, in a letter to the Montgomery *Advertiser,* to the facts to which I have referred.

In commenting upon this letter the editor of the *Advertiser* said:

The State of Alabama makes liberal appropriations for education and it is part of the system for the benefit to reach both white and black children. It must be admitted that there are many difficulties in properly spending the money and properly utilizing it which will take time and the legislature to correct. The matter complained of in the Washington letter could be easily remedied by the various county superintendents and it is their duty to see that the causes for such complaint are speedily removed. Negro fathers and mothers have shown intense interest in the education of their children and if they cannot secure what they want at present residences they will as soon as possible seek it elsewhere. We commend Booker Washington's letter on this subject to the careful consideration of all the school officials and to all citizens of Alabama.

The value of the experiment made in Macon County is, in my opinion, less in the actual good that has been done to the twenty-six thousand people, white and black, who live there, than it is in the showing by actual experiment what a proper system of Negro education can do in a country district toward solving the racial problem.

We have no race problem in Macon County; there is no friction between the races; agriculture is improving; the county is growing in wealth. In talking with the sheriff recently he told me that there is so little crime in this county that he scarcely finds enough to keep him busy. Furthermore, I think I am perfectly safe in saying that the white people in this county are convinced that Negro education pays.

What is true of Macon County may, in my opinion, be true of every other county in the South. Much will be accomplished in bringing this about if those schools which are principally engaged in preparing teachers shall turn about and face in the direction of the South, where their work lies. My own experience convinces me that the easiest way to get money for any good work is to show that you are willing and able to perform the work for which the money is given. The best illustration of this is, perhaps, the success, in spite of difficulties and with almost no outside aid, of the best of the Negro medical colleges. These colleges, although very largely dependent upon the fees of their students for support, have been successful because they have prepared their students for a kind of service for which there was a real need.

What convinces me that the same sort of effort outside of Macon County will meet with the same success is that it has in fact met with the same success in the case of Hampton and some other schools that are doing a somewhat similar work. On "the educational campaigns" which I have made from time to time through the different Southern States I have been continually surprised and impressed at the interest taken by the better class of white people in the work that I was trying to do. Everywhere in the course of these trips I have met with a cordial, even an enthusiastic, reception not only from the coloured people but from the white people as well.

For example, during my trip through North Carolina in November of 1910, not only were the suggestions I tried to make for the betterment of the schools and for the improvement of racial relations frequently discussed and favourably commented upon in the daily newspapers, but after my return I received a number of letters and endorsements from distinguished white men in different parts of the state who had heard what I had had to say.

I was asked the other day by a gentleman who has long been interested in the welfare of the coloured people what I thought the Negro needed most after nearly fifty years of freedom. I promptly answered him that the Negro needed now what he needed fifty years ago, namely, education. If I had attempted to be more specific I might have added that what Negro education needed most was not so much more schools or different kinds of schools as an educational policy and a school system.

In the last analysis, the work of building up such a school system as I have suggested must fall upon the industrial normal schools and colleges which prepare the teacher, because it is the success or failure of the teacher which determines the success of the school. In order to make a beginning in the direction which I have indicated, the different schools and colleges will have to spend much less time in the future than they have in the past in quarrelling over the kind of education the Negro ought to have and devote more time and attention to giving him some kind of education.

In order to accomplish this it will be necessary for these schools to obtain very much larger sums of money for education than they are now getting. I believe, however, if the different schools will put the matter to the people in the North and the people in the South "in the right shape," it will be possible to get much larger sums from every source. I believe the state governments in the South are going to see to it that the Negro public schools get a much fairer share of the money raised for education in the future than they have in the past. At the same time I feel that very few people realize the extent to which the coloured people are willing and able to pay, and, in fact, are now paying, for their own education. The higher and normal schools can greatly aid the Negro people in raising among themselves the money necessary to build up the educational system of the South if they will prepare their teachers to give the masses of the people the kind of education which will help them to increase their earnings instead of giving them the kind of education that makes them discontented and unhappy and does not give them the courage or disposition to help themselves.

In spite of all the mistakes and misunderstandings, I believe that the

Negro people, in their struggle to get on their feet intellectually and find the kind of education that would fit their needs, have done much to give the world a broader and more generous conception of what education is and should be than it had before.

Education, in order to do for the Negro the thing he most needed, has had to do more and different things than it was considered possible and fitting for a school to undertake before the problem of educating a newly enfranchised people arose. It has done this by bringing education into contact with men and women in their homes and in their daily work.

The importance of the scheme of education which has been worked out, particularly in industrial schools, is not confined to America or to the Negro race. Wherever in Europe, in Africa, in Asia, or elsewhere great masses are coming for the first time in contact with and under the influence of a higher civilization, the methods of industrial education that have been worked out in the South by, with, and through the Negro schools are steadily gaining recognition and importance.

It seems to me that this is a fact that should not only make the Negro proud of his past, brief as it has been, but, at the same time, hopeful of the future—1911.

IS THE NEGRO HAVING A FAIR CHANCE?

If I were asked the simple, direct question, "Does the Negro in America have a fair chance?" it would be easy to answer simply, "No," and then refer to instances with which every one is familiar to justify this reply. Such a statement would, however, be misleading to any one who was not intimately acquainted with the actual situation. For that reason I have chosen to make my answer not less candid and direct, I hope, but a little more circumstantial.

THE NEGRO TREATED BETTER IN AMERICA
THAN ELSEWHERE

Although I have never visited either Africa or the West Indies to see for myself the condition of the people in these countries, I have had opportunities from time to time, outside of the knowledge I have gained from books, to get some insight into actual conditions there. But I do not intend to assert or even suggest that the condition of the American Negro is satisfactory, nor that he has in all things a fair chance. Nevertheless, from all that I can learn I believe I am safe in saying that nowhere are there ten millions of black people who have greater opportunities or are making greater progress than the Negroes in America.

I know that few native Africans will agree with me in this statement.

For example, we had at Tuskegee a student from the Gold Coast who came to America to study in our Bible Training School and incidentally to learn something of our methods of study and work. He did not approve at all of our course of study. There was not enough theology, and too much work to suit him. As far as he was concerned, he could not see any value in learning to work, and he thought it was a pretty poor sort of country in which the people had to devote so much time to labor. "In my country," he said, "everything grows of itself. We do not have to work. We can devote all our time to the larger life."

LITTLE IMMIGRATION OF NEGROES

In the last ten years the official records show that 37,000 Negroes have left other countries to take residence in the United States. I can find no evidence to show that any considerable number of black people have given up residence in America.

The striking fact is, that Negroes from other countries are constantly coming into the United States, and few are going out. This seems in part to answer the question as to whether the Negro is having a fair chance in America as compared with any other country in which Negroes live in any large numbers.

By far the largest number of Negro immigrants come from the West Indies. Even Haiti, a free Negro republic, furnishes a considerable number of immigrants every year. In all my experience and observation, however, I cannot recall a single instance in which a Negro has left the United States to become a citizen of the Haitian Republic. On the other hand, not a few leaders of thought and action among the Negroes in the United States are those who have given up citizenship in the little Black Republic in order to live under the Stars and Stripes. The majority of the colored people who come from the West Indies do so because of the economic opportunities which the United States offers them. Another large group, however, comes to get education. Here at the Tuskegee Institute in Alabama we usually have not far from one hundred students from South America and the various West Indian Islands. In the matter of opportunity to secure the old-fashioned, abstract book education several of the West Indian Islands give Negroes a better chance than is afforded them in most of our Southern States, but for industrial and technical education they are compelled to come to the United States.

In the matter of political and civil rights; including protection of life and property and even-handed justice in the courts, Negroes in the West Indies have the advantage of Negroes in the United States. In the island of Jamaica, for example, there are about 15,000 white people and 600,000 black people, but of the "race problem," in regard to which there is much agitation in this country, one hears almost nothing there. Jamaica has neither mobs, race riots, lynchings, nor burnings, such as disgrace our civilization. In that country there is likewise no bitterness between white man and black man. One reason for this is that the laws are conceived and executed with exact and absolute justice, without regard to race or color.

UNEQUAL LAWS THE CAUSE OF RACIAL
TROUBLE IN AMERICA

Reduced to its lowest terms, the fact is that a large part of our racial troubles in the United States grow out of some attempt to pass and execute a law that will make and keep one man superior to another, whether he is intrinsically superior or not. No greater harm can be done to any group of people than to let them feel that a statutory enactment can keep them superior to anybody else. No greater injury can be done to any youth than to let him feel that because he belongs to this or that race, or because of his color, he will be advanced in life regardless of his own merits or efforts.

In what I have said I do not mean to suggest that in the West Indian Islands there is any more social intermingling between whites and blacks than there is in the United States. The trouble in most parts of the United States is that mere civil and legal privileges are confused with social intermingling. The fact that two men ride in the same railway coach does not mean in any country in the world that they are socially equal.

The facts seem to show, however, that after the West Indian Negro has carefully weighted his civil and political privileges against the economic and other advantages to be found in the United States, he decides that, all things considered, he has a better chance in the United States than at home. The Negro in Haiti votes, but votes have not made that country happy; or have not even made it free, in any true sense of the word. There is one other fact I might add to this comparison: nearly all the Negro church organizations in the United States have mission churches in the islands, as they have also in Africa.

Does the Negro in our country have a fair chance as compared with the native black man in Africa, the home of the Negro? In the midst of the preparation of this article, I met Bishop Isaiah B. Scott of the Methodist Episcopal Church, one of the strongest and most intelligent colored men that I know. Bishop Scott has spent the greater part of his life in the Southern States, but during the last seven years he has lived in Liberia and traveled extensively on the west coast of Africa, where he has come into contact with all classes of European white people. In answer to my question, Bishop Scott dictated the following sentence, which he authorized me to use:

The fairest white man that I have met in dealing with the colored man is the American white man. He understands the colored man better because of his contact with him, and he has more respect for the colored man who has accomplished something.

Basing my conclusions largely on conversations which I have had with native Africans, with Negro missionaries, and with Negro diplomatic officials who have lived in Africa, especially on the west coast and in South Africa, I am led to the conclusion that, all things considered, the Negro in the United States has a better chance than he has in Africa.

THE NEGRO AS A DEPENDENT RACE

In certain directions the Negro has had greater opportunities in the States in which he served as a slave than he has had in the States in which he has been for a century or more a free man. This statement is borne out by the fact that in the South the Negro rarely has to seek labor, but, on the other hand, labor seeks him. In all my experience in the Southern States, I have rarely seen a Negro man or woman seeking labor who did not find it. In the South the Negro has business opportunities that he does not have elsewhere. While in social matters the lines are strictly drawn, the Negro is less handicapped in business in the South than any other part of the country. He is sought after as a depositor in banks. If he wishes to borrow money, he gets it from the local bank just as quickly as the white man with the same business standing. If the Negro is in the grocery business or in the dry-goods trade, or if he operates a drug store, he gets his goods from the wholesale dealer just as readily and on as good terms as his white competitor. If the Southern white man has a dwelling-house, a storehouse, factory, school, or court-house to erect, it is natural for him to employ a colored man as builder or contractor to perform that work. What is said to be the finest school building in the city of New Orleans was erected by a colored contractor. In the North a colored man who ran a large grocery store would be looked upon as a curiosity. The Southern white man frequently buys his groceries from a Negro merchant.

Fortunately, the greater part of the colored people in the South have remained as farmers on the soil. The late census shows that eighty per cent. of Southern Negroes live on the land.

There are few cases where a black man cannot buy and own a farm in the South. It is as a farmer in the Southern States that the masses of my race have economically and industrially the largest opportunity. No one stops to ask before purchasing a bale of cotton or a bushel of corn if it has been produced by a white hand or a black hand.

The Negro now owns, as near as I can estimate, 15,000 grocery and dry-goods stores, 300 drug stores, and 63 banks. Negroes pay taxes on between $600,000,000 and $700,000,000 of property of various kinds in the United States. Unless he had had a reasonably fair chance in the South, the Negro could not have gained and held this large amount of property, and would not have been able to enter in the commerce of this country to the extent that he has.

SKILLED NEGRO LABOR BETTER TREATED
IN THE SOUTH THAN IN THE NORTH

As a skilled laborer, the Negro has a better opportunity in the South than in the North. I think it will be found generally true in the South as elsewhere that wherever the Negro is strong in numbers and in skill he gets on well with the trades-unions. In these cases the unions seek to get him in, or they leave him alone, and in the latter case do not seek to control him. In the Southern States, where the race enters in large numbers in the trades, the trades-unions have not had any appreciable effect in hindering the progress of the Negro as a skilled laborer or as a worker in special industries, such as coal-mining, iron-mining, etc. In border cities, like St. Louis, Washington, and Baltimore, however, the Negro rarely finds work in such industries as brick-laying and carpentry. One of the saddest examples of this fact that I ever witnessed was in the City of Washington, where on the campus of Howard University, a Negro institution, a large brick building was in process of erection. Every man laying brick on this building was white, every man carrying a hod was a Negro. The white man, in this instance, was willing to erect a building in which Negroes could study Latin, but was not willing to give Negroes a chance to lay the bricks in its walls.

Let us consider for a moment the Negro in the professions in the Southern States. Aside from school teaching and preaching, into which the racial question enters in only a slight degree, there remain law and medicine. All told, there are not more than 700 colored lawyers in the Southern States, while there are perhaps more than 3000 doctors, dentists, and pharmacists. With few exceptions, colored lawyers feel, as they tell me, that they do not have a fair chance before a white jury when a white lawyer is on the other side of the case. Even in communities where Negro lawyers are not discriminated against by juries, their clients feel that there is danger in intrusting cases to a colored lawyer. Mainly for these two reasons, colored lawyers are not numerous in the South; yet, in cases where colored lawyers combine legal practice with trading and real estate, they have in several instances been highly successful.

THE DIFFICULTY OF OBTAINING
UNIFORM TREATMENT

Here again, however, it is difficult to generalize. People speak of the "race question" in the South, overlooking the fact that each one of the 1300 counties in the Southern States is a law unto itself. The result is that there are almost as many race problems as there are counties. The Negro may have a fair chance in one county, and have no chance at all in the adjoining county. The Hon. Josiah T. Settles, for example, has practised both criminal and civil law for thirty years in Memphis. He tells me that he meets with no discrimination on account of his color either from judges, lawyers, or juries. There are other communities, like New Orleans and Little Rock, where Negro lawyers are accorded the same fair treatment, and, I ought to add, that, almost without exception, Negro lawyers tell me they are treated fairly by white judges and white lawyers.

The professional man who is making the greatest success in the South is the Negro doctor, and I should include the pharmacists and dentists with the physicians and surgeons. Except in a few cities, white doctors are always willing to consult with Negro doctors.

The young Negro physician in the South soon finds himself with a large and paying practice, and, as a rule, he makes use of this opportunity to improve the health conditions of his race in the community. Some of the most prosperous men of my race in the South are Negro doctors. Again, the very fact that a Negro cannot buy soda-water in a white drug store makes an opportunity for the colored drug store, which often becomes a sort of social center for the colored population.

From an economic point of view, the Negro in the North, when compared with the white man, does not have a fair chance. This is the feeling not only of the colored people themselves, but of almost every one who has examined into the conditions under which colored men work. But here also one is likely to form a wrong opinion. There is, to begin with, this general difference between the North and the South, that whereas in the South there is, as I have already suggested, a job looking for every idle man, in the North, on the contrary, there are frequently two or three idle men looking for every job. In some of the large cities of the North there are organizations to secure employment for colored people. For a number of years I have kept in pretty close touch with those at the head of these organizations, and they tell me that in many cases they have been led to believe that the Negro has a harder time in finding employment than is actually true. The reason is that those who are out of employment seek these organizations. Those who have steady work, in positions which they have held for years, do not seek them.

As a matter of fact, I have been surprised to find how large a number of colored people there are in Boston, New York, Philadelphia, and Chicago who hold responsible positions in factories, stores, banks, and other places. In regard to these people one hears very little. There is a colored man, for example, in Cleveland who has been for years private secretary to a railway president. In St. Paul there is a colored man who holds a similar position; in Baltimore there is still another colored private secretary to a railway president.

THE SHIFTING OF OCCUPATIONS

In recent years there has been a great shifting of employment between the races. A few years ago all the rough work in the mines, on the railway, and elsewhere was performed by Irish immigrants. Now this work is done by Poles, Hungarians, and Italians. In cities like New York, Chicago, and Pittsburgh one finds to-day fewer colored people employed as hotel waiters, barbers, and porters than twenty years ago. In New York, however, many colored men are employed in the streets and in the subways. In Pittsburgh thousands of colored men are employed in the iron mills. In Chicago Negroes are employed very largely in the packing-houses. Twenty years ago in these cities there were almost no colored people in these industries. In addition to the changes I have mentioned, many colored people have gone into businesses of various kinds on their own account. It should be remembered, also, that, while in some trades and in some places discrimination is made against the Negro, in other trades and in other places this discrimination works in his favor. The case in point is the Pullman-car service. I question whether any white man, however efficient, could secure a job as a Pullman-car porter.

BETTER OPPORTUNITY FOR EDUCATION
IN THE NORTH

In the North, as a rule, the Negro has the same opportunities for education as his white neighbor. When it comes to making use of this education, however, he is frequently driven to a choice between becoming an agitator, who makes his living out of the troubles of his race, or emigrating to the Southern States, where the opportunities for educated colored men are large. One of the greatest sources of bitterness and despondency among colored people in the North grows out of their inability to find a use for their education after they have obtained it. Again, they are seldom sure of just what they may or may not do. If one is a stranger in a city, he does not know in what hotel he will be permitted to stay; he is not certain what seat he may occupy in the theater, or whether he will be able to obtain a meal in a restaurant.

THE UNCERTAINTY OF TREATMENT OF
THE RACE IN THE NORTH

The uncertainty, the constant fear and expectation of rebuff which the colored man experiences in the North, is often more humiliating and more wearing than the frank and impersonal discrimination which he meets in the South. This is all the more true because the colored youth in most of the Northern States, educated as they are in the same schools with white youths, taught by the same teachers, and inspired by the same ideals of American citizenship, are not prepared for the discrimination that meets them when they leave school.

Despite all this, it cannot be denied that the Negro has advantages in the North which are denied him in the South. They are the opportunity to vote and to take part, to some extent, in making and administering the laws by which he is governed, the opportunity to obtain an education, and, what is of still greater importance, fair and unbiased treatment in the courts, the protection of the law.

I have touched upon conditions North and South, which, whether they affect the Negro favorably or adversely, are for the most part so firmly entrenched in custom, prejudice, and human nature that they must perhaps be left to the slow changes of time. There are certain conditions in the South, however, in regard to which colored people feel perhaps more keenly because they believe if they were generally understood they would be remedied. Very frequently the Negro people suffer injury and wrong in the South because they have or believe they have no way of making their grievances known. Not only are they not represented in the legislatures, but it is sometimes hard to get a hearing even in the press. On one of my educational campaigns in the South I was accompanied by a colored newspaper man. He was an enterprising sort of chap and at every public meeting we held he would manage in some way to address the audience on the subject of his paper. On one occasion, after appealing to the colored people for some time, he turned to the white portion of the audience.

"You white folks," he said, "ought to read our colored papers to find out what colored people are doing. You ought to find out what they are doing and what they are thinking. You don't know anything about us," he added. "Don't you know a colored man can't get his name in a white paper unless he commits a crime?"

I do not know whether the colored newspaper man succeeded in getting any subscriptions by this speech or not, but there was much truth in his statement.

THE GREATEST SOURCE OF DISSATISFACTION
TO THE NEGRO IN THE SOUTH

One thing that many Negroes feel keenly, although they do not say much about it to either black or white people, is the conditions of railway travel in the South.

Now and then the Negro is compelled to travel. With few exceptions, the railroads are almost the only great business concerns in the South that pursue the policy of taking just as much money from the black traveler as from the white traveler without feeling that they ought, as a matter of justice and fair play, not as a matter of social equality, to give one man for his money just as much as another man. The failure of most of the roads to do justice to the Negro when he travels is the source of more bitterness than any one other matter of which I have any knowledge.

It is strange that the wide-awake men who control the railroads in the Southern States do not see that, as a matter of dollars and cents, to say nothing of any higher consideration, they ought to encourage, not discourage, the patronage of nine millions of the black race in the South. This is a traveling population that is larger than the whole population of Canada, and yet, with here and there an exception, railway managers do not seem to see that there is any business advantage to them in giving this large portion of the population fair treatment.

What embitters the colored people in regard to railroad travel, I repeat, is not the separation, but the inadequacy of the accommodations. The colored people are given half of a baggage-car or half of a smoking-car. In most cases, the Negro portion of the car is poorly ventilated, poorly lighted, and, above all, rarely kept clean; and then, to add to the colored man's discomfort, no matter how many colored women may be in the colored end of the car, nor how clean or how well educated these colored women may be, this car is made the headquarters for the newsboy. He spreads out his papers, his magazines, his candy, and his cigars over two or three seats. White men are constantly coming into the car and almost invariably light cigars while in the colored coach, so that these women are required to ride in what is virtually a smoking-car.

On some of the roads colored men and colored women are forced to use the same toilet-room. This is not true of every Southern railway. There are some railways in the South, notably the Western Railway of Alabama, which make a special effort to see that the colored people are given every facility in the day coaches that the white people have, and the colored people show in many ways that they appreciate this consideration.

Here is an experience of R. S. Lovinggood, a colored man of Austin, Texas. I know Mr. Lovinggood well. He is neither a bitter nor a foolish man. I will venture to say that there is not a single white man in Austin, Texas, where he lives, who will say that Professor Lovinggood is anything but a conservative, sensible man.

"At one time," he said to me, in speaking of some of his traveling experiences, "I got off at a station almost starved. I begged the keeper of the restaurant to sell me a lunch in a paper and hand it out of the window. He refused, and I had to ride a hundred miles farther before I could get a sandwich.

"At another time I went to a station to purchase my ticket. I was there thirty minutes before the ticket-office was opened. When it did finally open I at once appeared at the window. While the ticket-agent served the white people at one window, I remained there beating the other until the train pulled out. I was compelled to jump aboard the train without my ticket and wire back to get my trunk expressed. Considering the temper of the people, the separate coach law may be the wisest plan for the South, but the statement that the two races have equal accommodations is all bosh. I pay the same money, but I cannot have a chair or a lavatory and rarely a through car. I must crawl out at all times of night, and in all kinds of weather, in order to catch another dirty 'Jim Crow' coach to make my connections. I do not ask to ride with white people. I do ask for equal accommodations for the same money."

LACK OF A "SQUARE DEAL" IN EDUCATION
IN THE SOUTH

In the matter of education, the Negro in the South has not had what Colonel Roosevelt calls a "square deal." In the North, not only the Jew, the Slav, the Italian, many of whom are such recent arrivals that they have not yet become citizens and voters, even under the easy terms granted them by the naturalization laws of the Northern States, have all the advantages of education that are granted to every other portion of the population, but in several States an effort is now being made to give immigrant peoples special opportunities for education over and above those given to the average citizens. In some instances, night schools are started for their special benefit. Frequently schools which run nine months in the winter are continued throughout the summer, whenever a sufficient number of people can be induced to attend them. Sometimes, as for example, in New York State, where large numbers of men are employed in digging the Erie Canal and in excavating the Croton Aqueduct, camp schools are started where the men employed on these public works in the day may have an opportunity to learn the English language at night. In some cases a special kind of text-book, written in two or three different languages, has been prepared for use in these immigrant schools, and frequently teachers are specially employed who can teach in the native languages if necessary.

While in the North all this effort is being made to provide education for these foreign peoples, many of whom are merely sojourners in this country, and will return in a few months to their homes in Europe, it is only natural that the Negro in the South should feel that he is unfairly treated when he has, as is often true in the country districts, either no school at all, or one with a term of no more than four or five months, taught in the wreck of a log-cabin and by a teacher who is paid about half the price of a first-class convict.

This is no mere rhetorical statement. If a Negro steals or commits a murderous assault of some kind, he will be tried and imprisoned, and then, if he is classed as a first-class convict, he will be rented out at the rate of $46 per month for twelve months in the year. The Negro who does not commit a crime, but prepares himself to serve the State as a first-grade teacher, will receive from the State for that service perhaps $30 per month for a period of not more than six months.

Taking the Southern States as a whole, about $10.23 per capita is spent in educating the average white boy or girl, and the sum of $2.82 per capita in educating the average black child.

Let me take as an illustration one of our Southern farming communities, where the colored population largely outnumbers the white. In Wilcox County, Alabama, there are nearly 11,000 black children and 2000 white children of school age. Last year $3569 of the public school fund went for the education of the black children in that county, and $30,294 for the education of the white children, this notwithstanding that there are five times as many Negro children as white. In other words, there was expended for the education of each Negro child in Wilcox County thirty-three cents, and for each white child $15. In the six counties surrounding and touching Wilcox County there are 55,000 Negro children of school age. There was appropriated for their education last year from the public school fund $40,000, while for the 19,622 white children in the same counties there was appropriated from the public fund $199,000.

There are few, if any, intelligent white people in the South or anywhere else who will claim that the Negro is receiving justice in these counties in the matter of the public school fund. Especially will this seem true when it is borne in mind that the Negro is the main dependence for producing the farm products which constitute the chief wealth of that part of Alabama. I say this because I know there are thousands of fair-minded and liberal white men in the South who do not know what is actually going on in their own States.

In the State of Georgia, Negroes represent forty-two per cent. of the farmers of the State, and are largely employed as farm laborers on the plantations. Notwithstanding this fact, Georgia has two agricultural colleges and eleven district agricultural high schools for whites, supported at an annual cost to the State of $140,000, while there is only one school where Negroes have a chance to study agriculture, and to the support of this the State contributes only $8000 a year. When one hears it said that the Negro farmer of Georgia is incompetent and inefficient as compared with the white farmer of Minnesota or Wisconsin, can any one say that this is fair to the Negro?

Not a few Southern white men see what is needed and are not afraid to say so. A. A. Gunby of Louisiana recently said: "Every one competent to speak and honest enough to be candid knows that education benefits and improves the Negro. It makes him a better neighbor and workman, no matter what you put him at."

Every one agrees that a public library in a city tends to make better citizens, keeping people usefully employed instead of spending their time in idleness or in committing crime. Is it fair, as is true of most of the large cities of the South, to take the Negro's money in the form of taxes to support a public library, and then to make no provision for the Negro using any library? I am glad to say that some of the cities, for instance, Louisville, Kentucky, and Jacksonville, Florida, have already provided library facilities for their black citizens or are preparing to do so.

One excuse that is frequently made in the South for not giving the Negro a fair share of the moneys expended for education is that the Negro is poor and does not contribute by his taxes sufficient to support the schools that now exist. True, the Negro is poor; but in the North that would be a reason for giving him more opportunities for education, not fewer, because it is recognized that one of the greatest hindrances to progress is ignorance. As far as I know, only two men have ever given thorough consideration to the question as to the amount the Negro contributes directly or indirectly toward his own education. Both of these are Southern white men. One of them is W. N. Sheats, former Superintendent of Education for the State of Florida. The other is Charles L. Coon, Superintendent of Schools at Wilson, North Carolina, and formerly connected with the Department of Education for that State.

THE NEGRO PAYS MORE THAN HIS SHARE
TO EDUCATION IN THE SOUTH

In his annual report for 1900, Mr. Sheats made a thorough analysis of the sources of the school fund in Florida, and of the way in which it is distributed between the white and Negro schools. In referring to the figures which he obtained, he said:

A glance at the foregoing statistics indicates that the section of the State designated as "Middle Florida" is considerably behind all the rest in all stages of educational progress. The usual plea is that this is due to the intolerable burden of Negro education, and a general discouragement and inactivity is ascribed to this cause. The following figures are given to show that the education of the Negroes of Middle Florida does not cost the white people of that section one cent. Without discussing the American principle that it is the duty of all property to educate every citizen as a means of protection to the State, and with no reference to what taxes that citizen may pay, it is the purpose of this paragraph to show that the backwardness of education of the white people is in no degree due to the presence of the Negro, but that the presence of the Negro has been actually contributing to the sustenance of the white schools.

Mr. Sheats shows that the amount paid for Negro schools from Negro taxes or from a division of other funds to which Negroes contribute indirectly with the whites, amounted to $23,984. The actual cost of Negro schools, including their pro rata for administration expenses, was $19,467.

"If this is a fair calculation," Mr. Sheats concludes, "the schools for Negroes are not only no burden on the white citizens, but $4525 for Negro schools contributed from other sources was in some way diverted to the white schools. A further loss to the Negro schools is due to the fact that so few polls are collected from Negroes by county officials."

Mr. Coon, in an address on "Public Taxation and Negro Schools" before the 1909 Conference for Education in the South, at Atlanta, Georgia, said:

The South is spending $32,068,851 on her public schools, both white and black, but what part of this sum is devoted to Negro public schools, which must serve at least forty per cent. of her school population? It is not possible to answer this question with absolute accuracy, but it is possible from the several State reports to find out the whole amount spent for teachers, and in all the States, except Arkansas, what was spent for white and Negro teachers separately. The aggregate amount now being spent for public teachers of both races in these eleven States is $23,856,914, or 74.4 per cent. of the whole amount expended. Of this sum not more than $3,818,705 was paid to Negro teachers, or twelve per cent. of the total expenditures.

He also brought out the fact that in Virginia, if, in addition to the direct taxes paid by Negroes, they had received their proportion of the taxes on corporate property and other special taxes, such as fertilizers, liquor, etc., there would have been expended on the Negro schools $18,077 more than was expended; that is, they would have received $507,305 instead of $489,228. In North Carolina there would have been expended $26,539 more than was expended, the Negroes receiving $429,197 instead of $402,658. In Georgia there would have been expended on the Negro schools $141,682 more than was expended.

In other words, Superintendent Coon seems to prove that Negro schools in the States referred to are not only no burden to the white taxpayers, but that the colored people do not get back all the money for their schools that they themselves pay in taxes. In each case there is a considerable amount taken from the Negroes' taxes and spent somewhere else or for other purposes.

CONVICT LABOR A GREAT EVIL IN THE SOUTH

It would help mightily toward the higher civilization for both races if more white people would apply their religion to the Negro in their community, and ask themselves how they would like to be treated if they were in the Negro's place. For example, no white man in America would feel that he was being treated with justice if every time he had a case in court, whether civil or criminal, every member of the jury was of some other race. Yet this is true of the Negro in nearly all of the Southern States. There are few white lawyers or judges who will not admit privately that it is almost impossible for a Negro to get justice when he has a case against a white man and all the members of the jury are white. In these circumstances, when a Negro fails to receive justice, the injury to him is temporary, but the injury to the character of the white man on the jury is permanent.

In Alabama eighty-five per cent. of the convicts are Negroes. The official records show that last year Alabama had turned into its treasury $1,085,854 from the labor of its convicts. At least $900,000 of this came from Negro convicts, who were for the most part rented to the coal-mining companies in the northern part of the State. The result of this policy has been to get as many able-bodied convicts as possible into the mines, so that contractors might increase their profits. Alabama, of course, is not the only State that has yielded to the temptation to make money out of human misery. The point is, however, that while $900,000 is turned into the State treasury from Negro-convict labor, to say nothing of Negro taxes, there came out of the State treasury, to pay Negro teachers, only $357,585.

I speak of this matter as much in the interest of the white man as of the black. Whenever and wherever the white man, acting as a court officer, feels that he cannot render absolute justice because of public sentiment, that white man is not free. Injustice in the courts makes slaves of two races in the South, the white and the black.

THE BALLOT TO THE INTELLIGENT NEGRO

No influence could ever make me desire to go back to the conditions of Reconstruction days to secure the ballot for the Negro. That was an order of things that was bad for the Negro and bad for the white man. In most Southern States it is absolutely necessary that some restriction be placed upon the use of the ballot. The actual methods by which this restriction was brought about have been widely advertised, and there is no necessity for me discussing them here. At the time these measures were passed I urged that, whatever law went upon the statute-book in regard to the use of the ballot, it should apply with absolute impartiality to both races. This policy I advocate again in justice to both white man and Negro.

Let me illustrate what I mean. In a certain county of Virginia, where the county board had charge of registering those who were to be voters, a colored man, a graduate of Harvard University, who had long been a resident of the county, a quiet, unassuming man, went before the board to register. He was refused on the ground that he was not intelligent enough to vote. Before this colored man left the room a white man came in who was so intoxicated that he could scarcely tell where he lived. This white man was registered, and by a board of intelligent white men who had taken an oath to deal justly in administering the law.

Will any one say that there is wisdom or statesmanship in such a policy as that? In my opinion it is a fatal mistake to teach the young black man and the young white man that the dominance of the white race in the South rests upon any other basis than absolute justice to the weaker man.

It is a mistake to cultivate in the mind of any individual or group of individuals the feeling and belief that their happiness rests upon the misery of some one else, or that their intelligence is measured by the ignorance of some one else; or their wealth by the poverty of some one else. I do not advocate that the Negro make politics or the holding of office an important thing in his life. I do urge, in the interest of fair play for everybody, that a Negro who prepares himself in property, in intelligence, and in character to cast a ballot, and desires to do so, should have the opportunity.

In these pages I have spoken plainly regarding the South because I love the South as I love no other part of our country, and I want to see her white people equal to any white people on the globe in material wealth, in education, and in intelligence. I am certain, however, that none of these things can be secured and permanently maintained except they are founded on justice.

THE CRIME OF LYNCHING

In most parts of the United States the colored people feel that they suffer more than others as the result of the lynching habit. When he was Governor of Alabama, I heard Governor Jelks say in a public speech that he knew of five cases during his administration of innocent colored people having been lynched. If that many innocent people were known to the governor to have been lynched, it is safe to say that there were other innocent persons lynched whom the governor did not know about. What is true of Alabama in this respect is true of other States. In short, it is safe to say that a large proportion of the colored people lynched are innocent.

A lynching-bee usually has its origin in a report that some crime has been committed. The story flies from mouth to mouth. Excitement spreads. Few take the time to get the facts. A mob forms and fills itself with bad whisky. Some one is captured. In case rape is charged, the culprit is frequently taken before the person said to have been assaulted. In the excitement of the moment, it is natural that the victim should say that the first person brought before her is guilty. Then comes more excitement and more whisky. Then comes the hanging, the shooting, or burning of the body.

Not a few cases have occurred where white people have blackened their faces and committed a crime, knowing that some Negro would be suspected and mobbed for it. In other cases it is known that where Negroes have committed crimes, innocent men have been lynched and the guilty ones have escaped and gone on committing more crimes.

Within the last twelve months there have been seventy-one cases of lynching, nearly all of colored people. Only seventeen were charged with the crime of rape. Perhaps they are wrong to do so, but colored people in the South do not feel that innocence offers them security against lynching.

They do feel, however, that the lynching habit tends to give greater security to the criminal, white or black. When ten millions of people feel that they are not sure of being fairly tried in a court of justice, when charged with crime, is it not natural that they should feel that they have not had a fair chance?

I am aware of the fact that in what I have said in regard to the hardships of the Negro in this country I throw myself open to the criticism of doing what I have all my life condemned and everywhere sought to avoid; namely, laying over-emphasis on matters in which the Negro race in America has been badly treated, and thereby overlooking those matters in which the Negro has been better treated in America than anywhere else in the world.

Despite all any one has said or can say in regard to the injustice and unfair treatment of the people of my race at the hands of the white men in this country, I venture to say that there is no example in history of the people of one race who have had the assistance, the direction, and the sympathy of another race in all its efforts to rise to such an extent as the Negro in the United States.

Notwithstanding all the defects in our system of dealing with him, the Negro in this country owns more property, lives in better houses, is in a larger measure encouraged in business, wears better clothes, eats better food, has more school-houses and churches, more teachers and ministers, than any similar group of Negroes anywhere else in the world.

What has been accomplished in the past years, however, is merely an indication of what can be done in the future.

As white and black learn day by day to adjust, in a spirit of justice and fair play, those interests which are individual and racial, and to see and feel the importance of those fundamental interests which are common, so will both races grow and prosper. In the long run no individual and no race can succeed which sets itself at war against the common good—**November 1912.**

MY VIEW OF SEGREGATION LAWS

In all of my experience I have never yet found a case where the masses of the people of any given city were interested in the matter of the segregation of white and colored people; that is, there has been no spontaneous demand for segregation ordinances. In certain cities politicians have taken the leadership in introducing such segregation ordinances into city councils, and after making an appeal to racial prejudices have succeeded in securing a backing for ordinances which would segregate the Negro people from their white fellow citizens. After such ordinances have been introduced it is always difficult, in the present state of public opinion in the

South, to have any considerable body of white people oppose them, because their attitude is likely to be misrepresented as favoring Negroes against white people. They are, in the main, afraid of the stigma, "Negro-lover."

It is probably useless to discuss the legality of segregation; that is a matter which the courts will finally pass upon. It is reasonably certain, however, that the courts in no section of the country would uphold a case where Negroes sought to segregate white citizens. This is the most convincing argument that segregation is regarded as illegal, when viewed on its merits by the whole body of our white citizens.

Personally I have little faith in the doctrine that it is necessary to segregate the whites from the blacks to prevent race mixture. The whites are the dominant race in the South, they control the courts, the industries and the government in all of the cities, counties and states except in those few communities where the Negroes, seeking some form of self-government, have established a number of experimental towns or communities.

I have never viewed except with amusement the sentiment that white people who live next to Negro populations suffer physically, mentally and morally because of their proximity to colored people. Southern white people who have been brought up in this proximity are not inferior to other white people. The President of the United States was born and reared in the South in close contact with black people. Five members of the present Cabinet were born in the South; and many of them, I am sure, had black "mammies." The Speaker of the House of Representatives is a Southern man, the chairman of leading committees in both the United States Senate and the Lower House of Congress are Southern men. Throughout the country to-day, people occupying the highest positions not only in the government but in education, industry and science, are persons born in the South in close contact with the Negro.

Attempts at legal segregation are unnecessary for the reason that the matter of residence is one which naturally settles itself. Both colored and whites are likely to select a section of the city where they will be surrounded by congenial neighbors. It is unusual to hear of a colored man attempting to live where he is surrounded by white people or where he is not welcome. Where attempts are being made to segregate the races legally, it should be noted that in the matter of business no attempt is made to keep the white man from placing his grocery store, his dry goods store, or other enterprise right in the heart of a Negro district. This is another searching test which challenges the good faith of segregationists.

It is true that the Negro opposes these attempts to restrain him from residing in certain sections of a city or community. He does this not because he wants to mix with the white man socially, but because he feels that such laws are unnecessary. The Negro objects to being segregated because it usually means that he will receive inferior accommodations in return for the taxes he pays. If the Negro is segregated, it will probably mean that the sewerage in his part of the city will be inferior; that the streets and sidewalks will be neglected, that the street lighting will be poor; that his section of the city will not be kept in order by the police and other authorities, and that the "undesirables" of other races will be placed near him, thereby making it difficult for him to rear his family in decency. It should always be kept in mind that while the Negro may not be directly a large taxpayer, he does pay large taxes indirectly. In the last analysis, all will agree that the man who pays house rent pays large taxes, for the price paid for the rent includes payment of the taxes on the property.

Right here in Alabama nobody is thinking or talking about land and home segregation. It is rather remarkable that in the very heart of the Black Belt where the black man is most ignorant the white people should not find him so repulsive as to set him away off to himself. If living side by side is such a menace as some people think, it does seem as if the people who have had the bulk of the race question to handle during the past fifty years would have discovered the danger and adjusted it long ago.

A segregated Negro community is a terrible temptation to many white people. Such a community invariably provides certain types of white men with hiding-places—hiding-places from the law, from decent people of their own race, from their churches and their wives and daughters. In a Negro district in a certain city in the South a house of ill-repute for white men was next door to a Negro denominational school. In another town a similar kind of house is just across the street from the Negro grammar school. In New Orleans the legalized vice section is set in the midst of the Negro section, and near the spot where stood a Negro school and a Negro church, and near the place where the Negro orphanage now operates. Now when a Negro seeks to buy a house in a reputable street he does it not only to get police protection, lights and accommodations, but to remove his children to a locality in which vice is not paraded.

In New Orleans, Atlanta, Birmingham, Memphis—indeed in nearly every large city in the South—I have been in the homes of Negroes who live in white neighborhoods, and I have yet to find any race friction; the Negro goes about his business, the white man about his. Neither the wives nor the children have the slightest trouble.

White people who argue for the segregation of the masses of black people forget the tremendous power of objective teaching. To hedge any set of people off in a corner and sally among them now and then with a lecture or a sermon is merely to add misery to degradation. But put the black man where day by day he sees how the white man keeps his lawns, his windows; how he treats his wife and children, and you will do more real helpful teaching than a whole library of lectures and sermons. Moreover, this will help the white man. If he knows that his life is to be taken as a model, that his hours, dress, manners, are all to be patterns for someone less fortunate, he will deport himself better than he would otherwise. Practically all the real moral uplift the black people have got from the whites—and this has been great indeed—has come from this observation of the white man's conduct. The South to-day is still full of the type of Negro with gentle manners. Where did he get them? From some master or mistress of the same type.

Summarizing the matter in the large, segregation is ill-advised because

1. It is unjust.
2. It invites other unjust measures.
3. It will not be productive of good, because practically every thoughtful Negro resents its injustice and doubts its sincerity. Any race adjustment based on injustice finally defeats itself. The Civil War is the best illustration of what results where it is attempted to make wrong right or seem to be right.
4. It is unnecessary.
5. It is inconsistent. The Negro is segregated from his white neighbor, but white business men are not prevented from doing business in Negro neighborhoods.
6. There has been no case of segregation of Negroes in the United States that has not widened the breach between the two races. Wherever a form of segregation exists it will be found that it has been administered in such a way as to embitter the Negro and harm more or less the moral fibre of the white man. That the Negro does not express this constant sense of wrong is no proof that he does not feel it.

It seems to me that the reasons given above, if carefully considered, should serve to prevent further passage of such segregation ordinances as have been adopted in Norfolk, Richmond, Louisville, Baltimore, and one or two cities in South Carolina.

Finally, as I have said in another place, as white and black learn daily to adjust, in a spirit of justice and fair play, those interests which are individual and racial, and to see and feel the importance of those fundamental interests which are common, so will both races grow and prosper. In the long run no individual and no race can succeed which sets itself at war against the common good; for "in the gain or loss of one race, all the rest have equal claim"—December 4, 1915.

ARCHIBALD H. GRIMKE

(1849–1930)

Graduated from the Harvard Law School in 1874, Archibald H. Grimke be-
gan a law practice in Boston, also writing for the Boston Herald *and the*
Boston Traveller. *In 1894 he was appointed by President Cleveland as consul*
to Santo Domingo. Grimke was president of the American Negro Academy
from 1903 to 1916 and contributed numerous papers of historical and so-
ciological emphasis to the "Occasional Papers" of that organization. He was a
vice president of the N.A.A.C.P. and a crusader against racial discrimination.
His works include William Lloyd Garrison, the Abolitionist, *1891;* Charles
Sumner, the Scholar in Politics, *1892;* Why Disfranchisement Is Bad, *1904;*
The Sex Question and Race Segregation, *1915; and* The Shame of America,
or the Negro's Case against the Republic, *1924.*

MODERN INDUSTRIALISM AND
THE NEGROES OF THE UNITED STATES

What is that tremendous system of production, organization and struggle
known as modern industrialism going to do with the Negroes of the
United States? Passing into its huge hopper and between its upper and
nether millstones, are they to come out grist for the nation, or mere chaff,
doomed like the Indian to ultimate extinction in the raging fire of racial
and industrial rivalry and progress? Sphinx's riddle, say you, which yet
awaits its Oedipus? Perhaps, though an examination of the past may show
us that the riddle is not awaiting its Oedipus so much as his answer, which
he has been writing slowly, word by word, and inexorably, in the social
evolution of the republic for a century, and is writing still. If we succeed
in reading aright what has already been inscribed by that iron pen, may
we not guess the remainder, and so catch from afar the fateful answer?
Possibly. Then let us try.

With unequaled sagacity the founders of the American Republic
reared, without prototype or precedent, its solid walls and stately columns
on the broad basis of human equality, and of certain inalienable rights,
such as life, liberty and the pursuit of happiness, to which they declared all
men entitled. Deep they sunk their foundation piles on the consent of the
governed, and committed fearlessly, sublimely, the new state to the

people. But there was an exception, and on this exception hangs our tale, and turns the dark drama of our national history.

Those founders had to deal with many novel and perplexing problems of construction, but none seemed so difficult to handle as were those which grew out of the presence of African slavery, as an industrial system, in several of the States. At the threshold of national existence these men were constrained by circumstances to make an exception to the primary principles which they had placed at the bottom of their untried and bold experiment in popular government. This sacrifice of fundamental truth carried along with it one of the sternest retributions of history. For it involved the admission on equal footing into the Union of a fundamental error in ethics and economics, with which our new industrial democracy was forced presently to engage in deadly strife for existence and survivorship.

The American fathers were, undoubtedly, aware of the misfortune of admitting under one general government, and on terms of equality, two mutually invasive and destructive social ideas and their corresponding systems of labor. But they were baffled at the time by what appeared to be a political necessity, and so met the grand emergency of the age by concession and a spirit of conciliation. Many of them, indeed, desired on economic as well as on moral grounds the abolition of slavery, and probably felt the more disposed to compromise with the evil in the general confidence with which they regarded its early and ultimate extinction.

This humane expectation of the young republic failed of realization, owing primarily and chiefly, I think, to the potent influence upon the institution of slavery of certain labor-saving inventions and their industrial application in England and America during the last quarter of the eighteenth century. These epoch-making inventions were the spinning jenny of Hargreaves, the spinning machine of Arkwright and the mule of Crompton, in combination with the steam engine, which turned, says John Richard Green, "Lancastershire into a hive of industry." And last, though not least in its direct and indirect effects on slavery, was the cotton gin of Eli Whitney, which formed the other half—the other hand, so to speak—of the spinning frame. The new power loom in England created a growing demand for raw cotton, which the American contrivance enabled the Southern planter to meet with an increased supply of the same. Together these inventions operated naturally to enhance the value of slave labor and slave land, and therein conduced powerfully to the slave revival in the United States, which followed their introduction into the economic world. The slave industrial system, no longer then a declining factor in the life of the young nation, assumed, instead, unexpected importance in it, and started promptly upon a course of extraordinary expansion and prosperity.

Two other circumstances combined with the one just mentioned to produce this unexpected and deplorable result. They were the slave compromises of the Constitution and the early territorial expansion of the republic southward. These compromises gathered the reviving slave system, as it were, under the wings of the general government, and so tempered the adverse forces with which it had to struggle for existence within the Union to its tender condition. They embraced the right to import Negroes into the United States, as slaves, until the year 1808, which operated to satisfy, in part, the rising demand of the South for slave labor; also the right to recover fugitive slaves in any part of the country, which added immensely to the security of this species of property, and the right of the slave-holding States, under the three-fifths rule of representation in the lower house of Congress, to count five slaves as three freemen, which rule, taken in conjunction with the equality of State representation in the upper branch of that body, gave to that section an immediate and controlling influence upon federal policy and legislation.

The territorial expansion of the republic southward coincided curiously in point of time with the territorial needs of the slave system incident to its industrial revival. Increased demand for the products of slave labor in the market of the world had, by the action of natural causes, raised the demand for that labor in the South. This increased demand was satisfied, to a limited extent, by the Constitutional provision relative to the importation of that labor into the United States prior to the year 1808, and to an unlimited extent by the peculiar Southern industry of slave breeding, and the domestic slave trade, which, owing to favorable economic conditions, became presently great and thriving enterprises for the production of wealth. The crop of slaves grew in time to be as valuable as the crop of cotton, and the slave section waxed, in consequence, rich and prosperous apace. But as our expanding slave system was essentially agricultural, it required large and expanding areas within which to operate efficiently. Wherefore there arose early in the slave-holding section an industrial demand for more slave soil. There was a political reason, also, which intensified this demand for more slave soil, but as it was merely incidental to the economic cause, I will leave it undiscussed for the present. This economic demand of the expanding slave system for more land was met by the opportune cession to the United States by Georgia and North Carolina of the southwest region, out of which the States of Alabama, Mississippi and Tennessee were subsequently carved, and by the acquisition of the Louisiana and the Florida territories. So much for the causes, conditions and circumstances in the early history of the republic, which combined to revive slavery, and to make it an immensely important factor in American industrial life, and consequently an immensely important factor in American political life as well.

Just a word in passing regarding the character of Southern labor. It was, as you all know, mainly agricultural. Its enforced ignorance, and its legally and morally degraded condition, incapacitated the slave-holding States from diversifying their single industry and limited them to the tillage of the earth. This feature was economically the fatal defect of the slave industrial system in its rivalry with the free industrial system of the North. There were, of course, other forms of labor employed in the South, such as the house-servant class, while many of the Negroes on plantations and in Southern cities worked as carpenters, bricklayers, blacksmiths, harness-makers, millwrights, wheelwrights, barbers, tailors, stevedores, etc., etc.; but, as labor classes, they were relatively of slight importance in point of numbers, and as wealth producers, in comparison to the field hand.

Unlike the Indian under similar circumstances, the Negro did not succumb to the terrible toil and inhumanity of his environment. He did not decline numerically, nor show any tendency to do so, but exhibited instead extraordinary vitality and reproductive vigor. In physical quality and equipment he was, as a laborer, ideally adapted to the South, and accordingly augmented enormously in social and commercial value to that section, and in numbers, at the same time. He possessed, besides, certain other traits which fitted him peculiarly to his hard lot and task. He was of laborers the most patient, the most submissive, the most faithful, the most cheerful. He was capable of the strongest affection and of making the greatest sacrifices for those to whom he belonged. In his simple and untutored heart there was no desire for vengeance, and in his brave black hands he bore nothing but gifts to the South—gifts of golden leisure, untold wealth, baronial pleasure and splendor, infinite service, and, withal, a phenomenal effacement of himself. Economically weak, yet singularly favored by a fortuitous combination of circumstances, slave labor flourished and expanded until at length it came into rough contact and rivalry with modern industrialism as it leaped into life under the magical influence of free institutions in the non slave-holding half of the Union.

It might be said that modern industrialism in America had its rise in certain causes and circumstances which existed at the beginning of the present century. It is well known how at that time almost the entire commerce of the civilized world outside of Great Britain and her colonial possessions was carried on under the American flag, in American bottoms, and also how among British orders in council, Napoleon's Berlin and Milan decrees and our own embargo and non-intercourse acts, retaliatory measures adopted by our government, this splendid commerce was speedily and effectually destroyed, and how finally this catastrophe produced in turn our first industrial crisis under the Constitution. New England found herself, in consequence, in great and widespread public distress, and her large capital, erstwhile engaged in commercial ventures at vast profit, became suddenly idle and nonproductive. But it is an ill wind which blows no good. So it was in the case of New England at this period. For the ill wind which carried ruin to her commerce and want to hundreds of thousands of people, carried also the seeds and small beginnings of all her subsequent manufacturing greatness and prosperity. With the development of manufactures, which now followed, and the diversifying of American industries in the northern section of the Union, modern industrialism as a tremendously aggressive social factor and system of free labor was thereupon launched upon its long and stormy rivalry and struggle with slave institutions and slave labor for the possession of the republic, and, as a resultant of this conflict, it began to affect also the history and destiny of the Negroes of the United States.

New England, naturally enough, was not at all well disposed toward a government whose acts had inflicted upon her such bitter distress, such ruinous dislocations of her capital and labor. This angry discontent was much aggravated later by the War of 1812, into which, in the opinion of that section, the country was precipitated by reason of Southern domination in national affairs. And thus was, perhaps, awakened in the North for the first time a distinct consciousness of the existence in the peculiar labor and institutions of the South, of interests and forces actively opposed to those of free labor and free institutions.

With the close of this war and the conclusion of peace, the nonslaveholding section took on fresh industrial life and embarked then upon that career of material exploitation and development which has placed it and the wonderful achievements of its diversified industries in the front rank of rivals in the markets of the world. From this period dates the beginning of our national policy of protection of domestic industries, and the rise of a powerful monied class in politics which bore to the new industrial interests similar relations to those sustained by the slave power to Southern labor and institutions. The early policy of a tariff for revenue with incidental encouragement inaugurated by Hamilton, was now readapted to the growing needs of the new industrialism, and the growing demands of its champions. The principle of protection was made as elastic in its practical application to tariff legislation as Northern industrial interests would, from time to time, and in their stages of rapid progress, seem to require.

The labor employed by the new industrialism was free white labor, each unit of which as wage earner and citizen was vitally concerned in whatever made for its safety and prosperity. The universal prevalence of the principle of popular education, and the remarkable educational function exercised upon the mental and moral faculties of the people by a right to a voice in the government, gave to this section in due time the most intelligent, energetic and productive labor in the world. Indeed, it is now well understood that modern industrialism attains its highest efficiency as a system of production in that society where popular education is best provided for, and where participation of the masses in the business of government reaches its fullest and freest expression. The freer and the more intelligent a people, all things else being equal, the more productive will be their labor over that of a rival's who may be wanting in these regards. The early and unexpected revival and expansion of slavery in the South was thus followed and met by a rapid counterexpansion of free industrialism at the North on an extraordinary scale.

This conflictive situation evolved presently industrial complications and disturbances of the gravest national importance. Following the treaty of Ghent, the South fell into financial difficulties, and experienced quite generally an increasing pressure of hard times. Although wealthy and prosperous heretofore, it then began to exhibit symptoms of industrial weakness, and to assume more and more a dependent attitude toward the monied classes of the free States. On the other hand, the free industrialism of those States waxed bolder in demands for national protection with the thing it fed on. Its cry was always for more, and so the tariff of 1816 was followed by that of 1824, and it in turn by the one of 1828, during which period industrial depression reached a crisis in the South, producing widespread distress among its slave-planting interests.

Here is Benton's gloomy picture of that section in 1828: "In place of wealth a universal pressure for money was felt; not enough for common expenses; the price of all property down; the country drooping and languishing; towns and cities decaying, and the frugal habits of the people pushed to the verge of universal self-denial for the preservation of their family estates." What was the cause of all this misfortune and misery? Benton found it, and other Southern leaders also, in the unequal action of federal fiscal legislation. "Under this legislation," he shrewdly remarks, "the exports of the South have been made the basis of the federal revenue. The twenty-odd millions annually levied upon imported goods are deducted out of the price of their cotton, rice and tobacco, either in the diminished prices which they receive for these staples in foreign ports, or in the increased price which they pay for the articles they have to consume at home."

The storm centre of this area of industrial depression passed over Virginia, the Carolinas and Georgia. The very heart of the slave system was thus attacked by the unequal fiscal action of the general government. The South needed for its great staples of cotton, rice and tobacco the freest access to the markets of the world, and unrestricted competition of the world in its own market, and this the principle of protection denied to it. For the grand purpose of the new policy of protection was to occupy and retain as far and as fast as practicable, and in some cases a little farther and faster, a monopoly of the home market for the products of the new industrialism, and therefore to exclude foreign buyers and sellers therefrom on equal terms with their domestic rivals. Owing to the limitations of its peculiar labor the South was disabled from adapting itself, as the North had just done, to changing circumstances and new economic conditions, and so was deprived of participation in the benefits of a high tariff. Its slave system and industrial prosperity were accordingly caught by the free industrialism of the North at a fatal disadvantage and pressed mercilessly to the wall.

And so it happened that the protective tariff which was welcomed as a boon by one set of industrial interests in the Union was by another set at the same time denounced as an abomination. But when the struggle between them grew fierce and threatened to disrupt the sections a compromise was hit upon and a sort of growling truce established for a season whereby the industrial rivals were persuaded that, in spite of the existence of bitter differences and memories, they could nevertheless live in peace and prosperity under the same general government. The soul of the compromise measures of 1833, which provided for the gradual abolishment, during nine years, of the specific features of the high tariff objectionable to the South, failed, however, to reach the real seat of the trouble, namely, the counterexpanding movements of the two systems, with their mutual inclinations during the operation, to encroach the one upon the other, and a natural tendency on the part of the stronger to destroy the weaker in an incessant conflict for survivorship, which would persist with the certainty and constancy of a law of nature, compromise acts by Congress to the contrary notwithstanding. And so the struggle for existence between the two industrial forces went on beneath the surface of things. Meanwhile modern industrialism was gaining steadily over its slave competitor in social strength and political importance and power.

This conflict for industrial domination developed logically in an industrial republic into one for political domination. It was unavoidable, under the circumstances, that the strife between out two opposing systems of labor should gather about the federal government and rage fiercest for its possession as a supreme coign of vantage. The power which was devoted to the protection of slavery and the power which was devoted to the protection of the new industrialism here locked horns in a succession of engagements for position and final mastery. It seems to have been early understood by a sort of national instinct, popular intuition, that as this issue between the contesting systems happened to be decided the Union would thereupon be put in the way of becoming eventually either wholly free or wholly slave, as the case might be. Wherefore the two sections massed in time their opposing forces for the long struggle at this quarter of the field of action.

It has already been noted that certain advantages had accrued to the South from the original distribution of political power under the national Constitution, and from sundry cessions of territory to the general government after the adoption of that instrument. But while the South secured indeed the lion's share of those early advantages, the North got at least two of considerable moment, viz., the Constitutional provision for the abolition of the Africans slave trade, in 1808, which imposed, after that year and from that source, a check upon the numerical increase of slaves within the Union, and, secondly, the Ordinance of 1787, which excluded forever the peculiar labor of the South from spreading into or taking root in the Northwest territory, and, therefore, in that direction placed a limit to its territorial expansion. Together they proved eventually of immense utility to free industrialism in its strife with the slave industrial system, the first operating in its favor negatively, and the second positively in the five populous and prosperous commonwealths which were subsequently organized out of this domain, and in which free labor grew and multiplied apace.

The struggle over the admission of Missouri into the Union terminated in a drawn battle, in which both sides gained and lost. The slave system obtained *in esse* an additional slave State and two others *in posse,* out of the Louisiana terriory, while free industrialism secured the erection of an imaginary fence through this land, to the north of which its slave rival was never to settle. Maine was also admitted to preserve the *status quo* and balance of political forces between the sections. Alas! however, for the foresight of statesmen who build for the present only, and are too much engrossed by the cares and fears of a day to see far into national realities, or to follow beneath the surface of things the action of moral and economic laws and to deduce therefrom the trend of national life. The slave wall of 1820, confidently counted upon by its famous builders to constitute thenceforth a permanent guarantee of peace between the rivals, disappointed these calculations, for it developed ultimately into a fresh source of discord and strife. And in view of the unavoidable conflict of our counterexpanding systems of labor, their constant tendency to encroach the one upon the other in the operation, and the bitter and ever-enduring dread and increasing demands of the weaker, it was impossible for the compromise of 1820 to prove otherwise.

The South, under the leadership of Calhoun, came presently to regard the Missouri arrangement as a capital blunder on its part, and from the standpoint of that section this conclusion seems strictly logical. For the location of a slave line upon the Louisiana territory operated in fact as a decided check to the expansion of slavery as a social rival and a political power at one and the same time, while it added immensely to the potential strength of the rapidly expanding forces of modern industrialism in its contest for social and political supremacy in the Union.

In the growing exigency of the slave industrial system, under these circumstances, the reparation of this blunder was deemed urgent, and so, in casting about to find some solution of its problem, the attempted abrogation of the compromise law itself not being considered wise by Calhoun, the slave power fell upon Texas, struggling for independence. An agitation was consequently started to correct the error of the Missouri compromise by the annexation of a region of country described in the graphic language of Webster to be so vast that "A bird could not fly over it in a week." What the South had lost by the blunder of the slave wall of 36° 30′ was then expected, barring accidents of course, to be restored to it in the new slave States, and in the large augmentation of slave representation in the general government, which would eventually ensue from the act of annexation. But the accident of the Mexican war wrecked completely the deep scheme of the Texan plotters, and neutralized the political advantage which had accrued to the slave power in the admission of Texas into the

Union by the acquisition of California and New Mexico at the close of that war. It was a checkmate by destiny. Chance had at a critical moment aligned itself definitely on the side of modern industrialism in the American republic and given a decisive turn to the long contest with its slave rival.

With the admission of California as a free State the political balance between our two opposing systems of labor was irreparably destroyed. For, while the South possessed Texas, and an expectation of acquiring new slave States therefrom, this expectation amounted practically to bare possibility. For it was found, owing to the inferior colonizing resources of the slave system, far easier to annex this immense domain than to people it, or to organize out of it States for emergent needs. On the other hand, the superior colonizing ability of free labor, taken in conjunction with all that vast, unoccupied territory belonging to it and inviting settlement, promised, in the ordinary course of events, to increase and confirm this preponderance of political power, and so to seal the fate of slavery. Nor do I forget in this connection that the bill, which organized into territories Utah and New Mexico, was, in deference to Southern demand, purged of the Wilmot *proviso*. But this concession on the part of Northern politicians had no real value to the South, for, as Webster pointed out at the time, slave labor was effectually interdicted from competing with free labor for the possession of this land by a power higher than the Wilmot *proviso*, viz., by a law of nature. The failure, however, to re-enact this decree of nature in 1850 prepared the way for the demolition of the slave wall four years later, and thus operated to hasten the grand catastrophe.

The repeal of the Missouri compromise did for the more or less fluid state of anti-slavery sentiment at the North what Goethe says a blow will do for a vessel of water on the verge of freezing—the water is thereby converted instantly into solid ice. So did the agitation produced by the abrogation of that act convert the gradually congealing sentiment of the free States on the subject of slavery into settled opposition to its farther extension to the national territories and into a fixed purpose to confine it within its then existing limits. But to put immovable bounds to the territorial expansion of the slave industrial system was virtually, under the circumstance, to provide for its decline and ultimate extinction, for the beginning of a period of actual and inhibited non-extension of slavery as a rival system of labor in the Union would mark the termination of its period of growth and the commencement of its industrial decay. The peril of the slave system was certainly extreme, and the dread of the slave power was not less so.

The national situation was full of gloom and menace to the industrial rivals. For the passions of the slave power were taking on an ominously violent and reckless energy of expression, which, unless all signs fail, would take on presently a no less violent and reckless energy of action. The crisis was intensified, first, by the repeal on the part of certain free

States of their slave-sojournment laws; second, by the extraordinary activity of the underground railroad; third, by increasing opposition in the North to the execution of the Fugitive Slave law, all of which, acting together, seriously impaired the value and security of slave property in the Union; fourth, by that fierce, obstinate, but futile, struggle of the South to obtain possession of Kansas, and the exposure thereby of its marked inferiority as a colonizer in competition with modern industrialism; fifth, by the growing influence of the abolition movement, and, sixth, by those nameless terrors of slave insurrections, which were evoked by the apparition of John Brown at Harper's Ferry. This acute situation was finally rendered intolerable to the slave power upon the election of Abraham Lincoln on a sectional platform, pledged to a policy of uncompromising resistance to the farther extension of slavery to the territories. Worsted within the Union, it was natural that the South should refuse to yield at this point of the conflict, and that it should make an attempt, as a dernier resort, to secede from it with its peculiar institution for the purpose of continuing the battle for its existence outside of a political system in which it had been overborne and hemmed in upon itself by modern industrialism and so doomed by that inexorable force to slow but absolutely certain extinction.

But the Union, which had developed such deadly industrial peril to the South, had created for the North its immense industrial prosperity, was, in sooth, the origin and mainspring of its powerful and progressive civilization. And so, while the preservation of the peculiar institution and civilization of the former necessitated a rupture of the old Union and the formation of a new one, founded on Negro slavery, every interest and attachment of the latter cried out for the maintenance of the old and the destruction of the new government. The long conflict of the two rival systems of labor culminated in the war to save the old Union on the part of the North and to establish a new one on the part of the South, whose Constitution rested directly upon the doctrine of social unity. Social duality was the great fact in the Constitution of the old Union; social uniformity was to be the great fact in the new. A State divided socially against itself cannot stand. The South learned this supreme lesson in political philosophy well, much more quickly and thoroughly than had the North, whose comprehension of it was painfully slow. And even that part of the grand truth which it did come to apprehend after prolonged wrestlings with bitter experience it reduced to practice in every emergency with moral fears and tremblings.

In the tremendous trial of strength between the sections which followed the rebel shot on Sumter the South was at the end of four years completely overmatched by the North, and by sheer weight of numbers and material resources was borne down at all points and forced back into the old Union, less its system of slave labor. For the destruction of the Southern Confederacy had involved, as a military necessity, the destruction of Negro slavery, which was its chief cornerstone. With the adoption of the Thirteenth Amendment to the Constitution the ancient cause of sectional difference and strife, viz., duality of labor systems, was supposed, quite generally at the North, to have been removed, and that a new era of unity in this respect had thereupon straightway begun. It seems to have been little understood by the North at the time, and since, for that matter, that Negro slavery in the South would die hard, and that it has a fatal gift of metamorphosis (ability to change its form without changing its nature), and that while it had under the well-directed stroke of the national arm disappeared as chattel slavery, it would reappear, unless hindered, as African serfdom throughout the Southern States, and that they would return to the Union much stronger politically than when they seceded, and much better equipped for a renewal of the unquenched strife for industrial existence in 1865 than they were in 1860.

The immediate work of reconstructing civil society in the old slave States to meet the new condition of freedom was now by an egregious executive blunder left wholly to the master class, with the startling result at its close that, whereas Negro slavery had been abolished, Negro serfdom reappeared in every instance as the industrial basis of the reconstructed States, and that a serf power was about to take the place of the slave power in the newly restored Union more dangerous than the old slave power to free industrialism than five is greater than three in federal numbers. For, while according to the old rule of slave representation in the lower house of Congress it took five slaves to nullify the votes of three freemen, under a new rule of apportionment which would probably obtain five serfs would be equivalent politically to five freemen. At this all the ancient hatred and dread of its Protean rival blazed hotly in the heart of the North, and with its passionate fear emerged a no less passionate desire to secure forever the domination of its industrial democracy over the newborn nation.

Actuated by this motive to dominate the republic, the freedmen whom the old master class had by prompt legislation reduced to a condition of serfdom were thereupon raised by the North through Constitutional amendment to the plane of citizenship. And when this act proved inadequate to arrest the threatened Southern revival in the national government, the ballot was next placed in their hands to avert the impending danger. It was under such circumstances that the work of Southern reconstruction was entered upon by Congress, i.e., in reality by the North, the South having had its chance and failed to reconstruct itself upon a basis satisfactory to its victorious rival, and in consonance with its sense of industrial and political security and progress.

I know that it is now the universal vogue to criticize and condemn this stupendous work of Congress as wholly wanting in knowledge of human nature and as woefully deficient in wise statesmanship. I know also that hindsight is at all times attended with less embarrassment to him who uses it than is foresight; and I know, besides, that those historic actors who had not attained unto a position of futurity in respect to their task, but whose task sustained to them that relative place instead, were obliged to do the best they could with whatever quantum of the latter faculty they might have possessed and toward the manful achievement of their duty. And this is what Congress did at this juncture. In view of the long, bitter and disastrous strife between the two sets of industrial ideas and interests in the republic, of the complex and earthquake circumstances and conditions in which they were thrown in relation to each other at the close of the rebellion, together with the imperious urgency for immediate and decisive action on the part of the North, I confess that it is extremely difficult to see even with the aid of hindsight what other practicable course was then open to that section to pursue than the one selected by Congress in the emergency as the best and wisest. And all things considered, it was the best and wisest, which, when the present generation of criticism and reaction has passed, will, I think, be so adjudged by impartial truth.

Congress might at this juncture have led the country by another way out of the perils which threatened afresh its peace and security, by a way dreadful and inhuman, it is true, but which offered nevertheless a radical and permanent cure for the evils which flow naturally from the union under one general government of two mutually invasive and destructive industrial systems, viz., by the forcible deportation of the entire black population of the South, and the introduction into their stead of an equal number of white immigrants. Such a course would have certainly achieved the unification of the sections by the extinguishment and elimination of the weaker of our two rival systems of labor. It was, however, a solution of its Southerm problem, which the nation was in morals, economics and humanity precluded absolutely from adopting, for three simple and sufficient reasons: First, for the sake of the South, which, wasted and bewildered, lay sullen and prostrate amidst the wreck and chaos of civil strife and at its lowest ebb of productive energy and wealth, its sole recuperative chance depending on the labor of its former slaves. To deport this labor, under the circumstances, would have been cruelly to deprive that section of its last vital resource, and to sink it to a state of industrial collapse and misery, by the side of which its condition at the close of the war might have seemed prosperity and paradise. Second, the nation itself could ill sustain the shock incident to such a huge amputation from the body of its productive labor, and which must have, for long and bitter years, affected disastrously its solvency, greatness and progress. Besides, the presence in the lately rebellious States of a mass of loyal people, like the blacks, constituted an immensely important element of strength and security to the newly restored Union. And, third, the blacks themselves had by two centuries of unpaid toil bought the right to remain in a country which had enslaved them, yet for whose defense and preservation against foreign and domestic foes and through three wars they had bared their brave arms and generous breasts and poured out royally and without measure their devotion, their blood and their life.

The general welfare of the reunited nation demanded not only political unification of the States under one supreme government, but their social unification as well on a common industrial basis of free labor. The coexistence under the old Constitution of two contrary systems of labor had given rise to seventy years of strife and rivalry between the sections, and had plunged them finally into one of the fiercest and most destructive wars of modern times. It was clearly recognized at the close of that war that the foundations of the restored Union should be made to rest directly on the enduring bedrock of a uniform system of free labor for both sections, not as formerly on the shifting sands of two conflicting social orders. For as long as our ancient duality of labor system shall continue to exist there will necessarily continue to exist also duality of ideas, interests and institutions. I do not mean mere variety in these regards which operates beneficiently, but profound and abiding social and political differences, engendering profound and abiding social and political antagonisms, naturally and inevitably affecting sometimes more, sometimes less, national stability and security, and leaving everywhere in the subconscious life of the republic a sense of vague uneasiness, rising periodically to the keenest anxiety, like the everpresent dread felt by a city subject to seismic disturbances. For what has once happened, the cause continuing, may happen again.

The Southern soil was at the moment broken up roughly by the hot ploughshare of civil war. It might have been better prepared for the reception of the good seed by the slower process of social evolution. But the guiding spirits of that era had no choice. The tide of an immense historic opportunity had risen. It was at its flood. Then was the accepted hour—then or never it appeared to them—and so they scattered broadcast seed ideas of the equality of all men before the law, their inalienable right to life, liberty, and the pursuit of happiness, and the derivation of the powers of all just governments from the consent of the governed. These revolutionary ideas fell alongside of the uptorn but living roots of other and hostile political principles, and of the ramified and deep-growing prejudices of an old social order, and had forthwith to engage in a life and death struggle against tremendous odds for existence. Many there are who see in the reconstruction period nothing except the asserted incapacity of the Negro for self-government—nothing but carpet-bag rule and its attendant corruption. But bad as those governments were, they were, nevertheless, the actual vehicles which conveyed into the South the seeds of our industrial democracy and of a new social and political order. From that period dates the beginning of an absolutely new epoch for that section. The forces set free then in the old slave States have been gradually unfolding themselves amid giant difficulties ever since. They are, I believe, in the South to stay, and are destined ultimately to conquer every square inch of its mind and matter, and so to produce the perfect unification of the republic, by producing the perfect unification of its immense, heterogeneous population, regardless of race, color or previous condition of servitude, on the broad basis of industrial and political equality and fair play.

The contest of the old industrial rivals has, in consequence of this influx of democratic ideas into the South, and the resultant modification of environment there, taken on fresh and deplorable complications. The struggle between the old and the new which is in progress throughout that section is no longer a simple conflict between the two sets of industrial principles of the Union along sectional lines, as formerly, but along race lines now as well. The self-evident truths of the Declaration of Independence invading the old slave States have divided that house against itself. Their powerful ally, popular education, is creating everywhere moral unrest and discontent with present injustices and a growing desire on the part of the Negro to have what is denied him, but which others enjoy, viz., free and equal opportunities in the rivalry of life. This battle of ideas in the South is, in reality, a battle for the enduring unification of the sections, the permanent pacification of the republic. The labors of the fathers for a more perfect union will have been in vain unless the Negro wins in this irrepressible conflict between the two industrial systems of the country. It is greatly to be lamented that a question of color and difference of race has so completely disabled the nation and the South from seeing things relating to this momentous subject clear, and seeing them straight. Those who see in this problem only a conflict of races in the South see but a little way into its depths, for underlying this conflict of races is a conflict of opposing ideas and interests which have for a century vexed the peace of the nation. The existence of a system of labor in the South distinct from that of the North separated the two halves of the Union industrially, as far as the East is from the West, made of them in truth two hostile nations, although united under one general government. This difference has been the cause of all the division and strife between the sections, and it will continue to operate as such till completely abolished.

The clinging of the South, under the circumstances, to its old social and political ideas and system, or to such fragments of them as now remain, and its persistent attempts to put these broken parts together, and to preserve thereby what so disastrously distinguishes it from the rest of the country, is an economic error of the first magnitude—an error which injuriously affects its own industrial prosperity and greatness by retarding its material development and by infecting at the same time with increasing unrest and discontent its faithful and peaceful black labor. The fight which the South is making along this line is a fight not half so much against the Negro as against its own highest good, and that of the country's for it has in this matter opposed itself ignorantly and madly to the great laws which control the economic world, to the great laws which are the soul of modern industrialism, laws which govern production and exchange, consumption and competition, supply and demand, which determine everywhere, between rival parts of the same country and between rival nations as well, that commercial struggles, industrial rivalries, shall always terminate in the survival of the fittest. If in such a battle the South sow seeds of economic weakness, when it ought to sow seeds of economic strength, it will go down before its rivals, whether those rivals be in this country or in any other country or part of the world. In such a struggle if it would win it will need to avail itself of all the means which God and nature have placed at its disposition.

One of the most important of these means, perhaps the most important single factor in the development and prosperity of the South, is its Negro labor. It is more to it, if viewed aright, than all of its gold, iron and coal mines put together. If properly treated and trained it will mean fabulous wealth and greatness to that section. Lest you say that I exaggerate, I will quote the estimate put upon this labor by the Washington *Post,* which will hardly be accused of enthusiasm touching any matter relating to the Negro, I think. Here it is:

"We hold as between the ignorant of the two races, the Negro is preferable. They are conservative; they are good citizens; they take no stock in social schisms and vagaries; they do not consort with anarchists; they cannot be made the tools and agents of incendiaries; they constitute the solid, worthy, estimable yeomanry of the South. Their influence in government would be infinitely more wholesome than the influence of the white sansculottes, the riff-raff, the idlers, the rowdies and the outlaws. As between the Negro, no matter how illiterate he may be, and the poor white the property owners of the South prefer the former."

The South cannot, economically, eat its cake and have it too. It cannot adopt a policy and a code of laws to degrade its Negro labor, to hedge it about with unequal restrictions and proscriptive legislation, and raise it at the same time to the highest state of productive efficiency. But it must as an economic necessity raise this labor to the highest point of efficiency or suffer inevitable industrial feebleness and inferiority. What are the things which have made free labor at the North the most productive labor in the world and of untold value and wealth to that section? What, but its intelligence, skill, self-reliance and power of initiative? And how have these qualities been put into it? I answer unhesitatingly, by those twin systems of universal education and popular suffrage. One system trains the children, the other the adult population. The same wide diffusion of knowledge, and large and equal freedom and participation in the affairs of government, which have done so much for Northern labor, cannot possibly do less for Southern labor.

For weal or woe the Negro is in the South to stay. He will never leave it voluntarily, and forcible deportation of him is impracticable. And for economic reasons, vital to that section, as we have seen, he must not be oppressed or repressed. All attempts to push him and tie him down to the dead level of an inferior caste, to restrict his activities arbitrarily and permanently to hewing wood and drawing water for the white race, without regard to his possibilities for higher things, is in this age of strenuous industrial competition and struggle an economic blunder, pure and simple, to say nothing of the immorality of such action. Like water, let the Negro find his natural level, if the South would get the best and the most out of him. If nature has designed him to serve the white race forever, never fear. He will not be able to elude nature; he will not escape his destiny. But he must be allowed to act freely; nature does not need our aid here. Depend on it, she will make no mistake. Her inexorable laws provide for the survival of the fittest only. Let the Negro freely find himself, whether in doing so he falls or rises in the scale of life.

With his labor the Negro is in the market of the world. If, all things considered, he has the best article for the price offered, he will sell; otherwise not. But it is of immense value and moment to the South in both respects. If his labor in all departments of industry in which it may be employed be raised by education of head and hand, by the largest freedom and equality of opportunities, to the highest efficiency of which it is capable, who more than the South will reap its resultant benefits? So will the whole country reap the resultant benefits in the diffused well-being and productivity of its laboring classes, and at the same time in the final removal of the ancient cause of difference and discord between its parts. But if the Negro fail by reason of inherent fitness to survive in such a struggle, his failure will be followed by decline in numbers and ultimate extinction, which will involve no violent dislocation of the labor of the republic, but a displacement so gradual that while one race is vanishing another will be silently crowding into the space thus vacated.

The commercial and industrial rivalry of the nations of the world was never so sharp and intense as at the present time, and all signs point to increased competition among them during this century. In this contest the labor of each country is primarily the grand determining factor. It must from sheer necessity and stress of circumstances be brought in each instance to the highest state of economic efficiency by every resource in the possession of the respective world rivals. And this will be attempted in the future by each of these world rivals on a grandeur of scale and with a scientific thoroughness and energy in the use of educational means not yet realized by the most progressive of them. For those nations who succeed best in this respect will prevail over those others which fail to raise their labor to an equally high grade of efficiency. Now, if Negro labor is the best for its climate and needs, the South must seek earnestly, constantly, by every means in its power, to raise that labor to the highest state of economic efficiency of which it is capable. That section must do so in spite of its chimerical fears of Negro domination, in spite of its rooted race prejudices. It must educate and emancipate this labor, all hostile sentiment of whatever nature to the contrary notwithstanding, if it will hold its own in that great cosmic struggle for existence in which it is now engaged with powerful rivals at home and abroad. Nor can the republic be indifferent on this head. No country in this age of strenuous commercial competition can forget with impunity its duty in this regard. Neglect here brings swift retribution to any nation which carries a vast horde of crude and relatively inefficient labor into an industrial struggle with the rest of the world, for the world's labor will henceforth assume more and more the character of vast standing armies engaged in world-wide industrial warfare. Each unit of these industrial armies will be ultimately trained and disciplined to the highest possible efficiency, and will some time form together perfect machines, which will operate with clock-like precision and purpose at any given quarter of the field of action. In obedience to the first law of nature our country in its battle with industrial rivals to retain present advantages and win new ones in world markets, will have to elevate the whole body of its labor regardless of color or race, to the highest state of economic productivity of which that labor is capable in all of its parts. Colossal forces are behind and under the movement which is making for the final emancipation of the Negro, and for his eventual admission on terms of complete equality of rights and opportunities into the arena of that never-ending rivalry and struggle which is the law of progress.

The Negro has proved himself one of the best soldiers in the world; he will prove himself in this country, provided fair play be accorded him, one of the most productive laborers in the world also. He has the capacity for becoming one of the best all-round laborers and artisans in our industrial army of conquest and one of the best all-round citizens of the republic likewise. Overcome, then, your prejudices, ye white men of the South, and ye white men, too, of the North; trust the Negro in peace as ye have trusted him in war, nor forget that the freest and most intelligent labor is ever the best and most productive labor, and that liberal and equal laws and institutions are the one unerring way yet discovered by human experience and wisdom whereby modern industrialism and democracy may reach their highest development and the highest development of humanity at the same time. This is the age of the people, of consolidation and competition. It is the age of industrialism and democracy, aye, industrialism and democracy are destiny. Try ever so hard, we shall not escape our destiny, neither the Negro, nor the South, nor the nation—1908.

PART III

Cultural Nationalism

WILLIAM EDWARD BURGHARDT DU BOIS

(1868–1963)

After graduating from Fisk University in 1888, Du Bois studied at Harvard, with a period abroad at the University of Berlin, and received a Ph.D. degree from Harvard in 1895. His doctoral dissertation, "The Suppression of the Slave Trade," was published in 1896. From 1897 until 1910, he was a professor at Atlanta University where he conducted a number of studies about the social condition of the Negro. In 1910 he left academic work to become director of publicity for the N.A.A.C.P. and editor of its magazine, The Crisis. *In 1932 he returned to Atlanta University to become head of the sociology department where he remained until 1944. Du Bois was the leader of a small band of intellectuals who advocated literary education for the "talented tenth" of Negro society in opposition to Washington. Du Bois also thought that Washington was not militant enough with regard to agitation for civil rights and formed the Niagara Movement in 1905 as a protest against both Washington's leadership and the deteriorating legal situation. This movement was one of the bases for the present-day N.A.A.C.P. He was an influential figure in the Pan-African Movement from the meeting of the very first Pan-African Congress in 1919. Toward the very end of his life he emigrated to Ghana, where he died. He was a prolific writer. His works include* Black Reconstruction, *1935;* Black Folk Then and Now: An Essay in the History and Sociology of the Negro Race, *1939;* Dusk of Dawn: An Essay Toward an Autobiography of a Race Concept, *1940; and* Color and Democracy, *1945.*

THE CONSERVATION OF RACES

The American Negro has always felt an intense personal interest in discussions as to the origins and destinies of races: primarily because back of most discussions of race with which he is familiar, have lurked certain assumptions as to his natural abilities, as to his political, intellectual and moral status, which he felt were wrong. He has, consequently, been led to deprecate and minimize race distinctions, to believe intensely that out of one blood God created all nations, and to speak of human brotherhood as though it were the possibility of an already dawning to-morrow.

Nevertheless, in our calmer moments we must acknowledge that human beings are divided into races; that in this country the two most extreme types of the world's races have met, and the resulting problem as to the future relations of these types is not only of intense and living interest to us, but forms an epoch in the history of mankind.

It is necessary, therefore, in planning our movements, in guiding our future development, that at times we rise above the pressing, but smaller questions of separate schools and cars, wage-discrimination and lynch law, to survey the whole question of race in human philosophy and to lay, on a basis of broad knowledge and careful insight, those large lines of policy and higher ideals which may form our guiding lines and boundaries in the practical difficulties of every day. For it is certain that all human striving must recognize the hard limits of natural law, and that any striving, no matter how intense and earnest, which is against the constitution of the world, is vain. The question, then, which we must seriously consider is this: What is the real meaning of Race; what has, in the past, been the law of race development, and what lessons has the past history of race development to teach the rising Negro people?

When we thus come to inquire into the essential difference of races we find it hard to come at once to any definite conclusion. Many criteria of race differences have in the past been proposed, as color, hair, cranial measurements and language. And manifestly, in each of these respects, human beings differ widely. They vary in color, for instance, from the marble-like pallor of the Scandinavian to the rich, dark brown of the Zulu, passing by the creamy Slav, the yellow Chinese, the light brown Sicilian and the brown Egyptian. Men vary, too, in the texture of hair from the obstinately straight hair of the Chinese to the obstinately tufted and frizzled hair of the Bushman. In measurement of heads, again, men vary; from the broad-headed Tartar to the medium-headed European and the narrow-headed Hottentot; or, again in language, from the highly-inflected Roman tongue to the monosyllabic Chinese. All these physical characteristics are patent enough, and if they agreed with each other it would be very easy to classify mankind. Unfortunately for scientists, however, these criteria of race are most exasperatingly intermingled. Color does not agree with texture of hair, for many of the dark races have straight hair; nor does color agree with the breadth of the head, for the yellow Tartar has a broader head than the German; nor, again, has the science of language as yet succeeded in clearing up the relative authority of these various and contradictory criteria. The final word of science, so far, is that we have at least two, perhaps three, great families of human beings—the whites and Negroes, possibly the yellow race. That other races have arisen from the intermingling of the blood of these two. This broad division of the world's races which men like Huxley and Raetzel have introduced as more nearly true than the old five-race scheme of Blumenbach, is nothing more than an acknowledgment that, so far as purely physical characteristics are concerned, the differences between men do not explain all the differences of their history. It declares, as Darwin himself said, that great as is the physical unlikeness of the various races of men their likenesses are greater, and upon this rests the whole scientific doctrine of Human Brotherhood.

Although the wonderful developments of human history teach that the grosser physical differences of color, hair and bone go but a short way toward explaining the different roles which groups of men have played in Human Progress, yet there are differences—subtle, delicate and elusive, though they may be—which have silently but definitely separated men into groups. While these subtle forces have generally followed the natural cleavage of common blood, descent and physical peculiarities, they have at other times swept across and ignored these. At all times, however, they have divided human beings into races, which, while they perhaps transcend scientific definition, nevertheless, are clearly defined to the eye of the Historian and Sociologist.

If this be true, then the history of the world is the history, not of individuals, but of groups, not of nations, but of races, and he who ignores or seeks to override the race idea in human history ignores and overrides the central thought of all history. What, then, is a race? It is a vast family of human beings, generally of common blood and language, always of common history, traditions and impulses, who are both voluntarily and involuntarily striving together for the accomplishment of certain more or less vividly conceived ideals of life.

Turning to real history, there can be no doubt, first, as to the widespread, nay, universal, prevalence of the race idea, the race spirit, the race ideal, and as to its efficiency as the vastest and most ingenious invention for human progress. We, who have been reared and trained under the individualistic philosophy of the Declaration of Independence and the laisser-faire philosophy of Adam Smith, are loath to see and loath to acknowledge this patent fact of human history. We see the Pharaohs, Caesars, Toussaints and Napoleons of history and forget the vast races of which they were but epitomized expressions. We are apt to think in our American impatience, that while it may have been true in the past that closed race groups made history, that here in conglomerate America *nous avons changer tout cela*—we have changed all that, and have no need of this ancient instrument of progress. This assumption of which the Negro people are especially fond, can not be established by a careful consideration of history.

We find upon the world's stage today eight distinctly differentiated races, in the sense in which History tells us the word must be used. They are, the Slavs of eastern Europe, the Teutons of middle Europe, the English of Great Britain and America, the Romance nations of Southern and Western Europe, the Negroes of Africa and America, the Semitic people of Western Asia and Northern Africa, the Hindoos of Central Asia and the Mongolians of Eastern Asia. There are, of course, other minor race groups, as the American Indians, the Esquimaux and the South Sea Islanders; these larger races, too, are far from homogeneous; the Slav includes the Czech, the Magyar, the Pole and the Russian; the Teuton includes the German, the Scandinavian and the Dutch; the English include the Scotch, the Irish and the conglomerate American. Under Romance nations the widely-differing Frenchman, Italian, Sicilian and Spaniard are comprehended. The term Negro is, perhaps, the most indefinite of all, combining the Mulattoes and Zamboes of America and the Egyptians, Bantus and Bushmen of Africa. Among the Hindoos are traces of widely differing nations, while the great Chinese, Tartar, Corean and Japanese families fall under the one designation—Mongolian.

The question now is: What is the real distinction between these nations? Is it the physical differences of blood, color and cranial measurements? Certainly we must all acknowledge that physical differences play a great part, and that, with wide exceptions and qualifications, these eight great races of to-day follow the cleavage of physical race distinctions; the English and Teuton represent the white variety of mankind; the Mongolian, the yellow; the Negroes, the black. Between these are many crosses and mixtures, where Mongolian and Teuton have blended into the Slav, and other mixtures have produced the Romance nations and the Semites. But while race differences have followed mainly physical race lines, yet no mere physical distinctions would really define or explain the deeper differences—the cohesiveness and continuity of these groups. The deeper differences are spiritual, psychical, differences—undoubtedly based on the physical, but infinitely transcending them. The forces that bind together the Teuton nations are, then, first, their race identity and common blood; secondly, and more important, a common history, common laws and religion, similar habits of thought and a conscious striving together for certain ideals of life. The whole process which has brought about these race differentiations has been a growth, and the great characteristic of this growth has been the differentiation of spiritual and mental differences between great races of mankind and the integration of physical differences.

The age of nomadic tribes of closely related individuals represents the maximum of physical differences. They were practically vast families, and there were as many groups as families. As the families came together to form cities the physical differences lessened, purity of blood was replaced by the requirement of domicile, and all who lived within the city bounds became gradually to be regarded as members of the group; *i. e.,* there was a slight and slow breaking down of physical barriers. This, however, was accompanied by an increase of the spiritual and social differences between cities. This city became husbandmen, this, merchants, another warriors, and so on. The *ideals of life* for which the different cities struggled were different. When at last cities began to coalesce into nations there was another breaking down of barriers which separated groups of men. The larger and broader differences of color, hair and physical proportions were not by any means ignored, but myriads of minor differences disappeared, and the sociological and historical races of men began to approximate the present division of races as indicated by physical researches. At the same time the spiritual and physical differences of race groups which constituted the nations became deep and decisive. The English nation stood for constitutional liberty and commercial freedom; the German nation for science and philosophy; the Romance nations stood for literature and art, and the other race groups are striving, each in its own way, to develop for civilization its particular message, its particular ideal, which shall help to guide the world nearer and nearer that perfection of human life for which we all long, that "one far off Divine event."

This has been the function of race differences up to the present time. What shall be its function in the future? Manifestly some of the great races of today—particularly the Negro race—have not as yet given to civilization the full spiritual message which they are capable of giving. I will not say that the Negro race has as yet given no message to the world, for it is still a mooted question among scientists as to just how far Egyptian civilization was Negro in its origin; if it was not wholly Negro, it was certainly very closely allied. Be that as it may, however the fact still remains that the full, complete Negro message of the whole Negro race has not as yet been given to the world: that the messages and ideal of the yellow race have not been completed, and that the striving of the mighty Slavs has but begun. The question is, then: How shall this message be delivered; how shall these various ideals be realized? The answer is plain: By the development of these race groups, not as individuals, but as races. For the development of Japanese genius, Japanese literature and art, Japanese spirit, only Japanese, bound and welded together, Japanese inspired by one vast ideal, can work out in its fullness the wonderful message which Japan has for the nations of the earth. For the development of Negro genius, of Negro literature and art, of Negro spirit, only Negroes bound and welded together, Negroes inspired by one vast ideal, can work out in its fullness the great message we have for humanity. We cannot reverse history; we are subject to the same natural laws as other races, and if the Negro is ever to be a factor in the world's history—if among the gaily-colored banners that deck the broad ramparts of civilization is to hang one uncompromising black, then it must be placed there by black hands, fashioned by black heads and hallowed by the travail of 200,000,000 black hearts beating in one glad song of jubilee.

For this reason, the advance guard of the Negro people—the 8,000,000 people of Negro blood in the United States of America—must soon come to realize that if they are to take their just place in the van of Pan-Negroism, then their destiny is *not* absorption by the white Americans. That if in America it is to be proven for the first time in the modern world that not only Negroes are capable of evolving individual men like Toussaint, the Saviour, but are a nation stored with wonderful possibilities of culture, then their destiny is not a servile imitation of Anglo-Saxon culture, but a stalwart originality which shall unswervingly follow Negro ideals.

It may, however, be objected here that the situation of our race in America renders this attitude impossible; that our sole hope of salvation lies in our being able to lose our race identity in the commingled blood of the nation; and that any other course would merely increase the friction of races which we call race prejudice, and against which we have so long and so earnestly fought.

Here, then, is the dilemma, and it is a puzzling one, I admit. No Negro who has given earnest thought to the situation of his people in America has failed, at some time in life, to find himself at these cross-roads; has failed to ask himself at some time: What, after all, am I? Am I an American or am I a Negro? Can I be both? Or is it my duty to cease to be a Negro as soon as possible and be an American? If I strive as a Negro, am I not perpetuating the very cleft that threatens and separates Black and White America? Is not my only possible practical aim the subduction of all that is Negro in me to the American? Does my black blood place upon me any more obligation to assert my nationality than German, or Irish or Italian blood would?

It is such incessant self-questioning and the hesitation that arises from it, that is making the present period a time of vacillation and contradiction for the American Negro; combined race action is stifled, race responsibility is shirked, race enterprises languish, and the best blood, the best talent, the best energy of the Negro people cannot be marshalled to do the bidding of the race. They stand back to make room for every rascal and demagogue who chooses to cloak his selfish deviltry under the veil of race pride.

Is this right? Is it rational? Is it good policy? Have we in America a distinct mission as a race—a distinct sphere of action and an opportunity for race development, or is self-obliteration the highest end to which Negro blood dare aspire?

If we carefully consider what race prejudice really is, we find it, historically, to be nothing but the friction between different groups of people; it is the difference in aim, in feeling, in ideals of two different races; if, now, this difference exists touching territory, laws, language, or even religion, it is manifest that these people cannot live in the same territory without fatal collision; but if, on the other hand, there is substantial agreement in laws, language and religion; if there is a satisfactory adjustment of economic life, then there is no reason why, in the same country and on the same street, two or three great national ideals might not thrive and develop, that man of different races might not strive together for their race ideals as well, perhaps even better, than in isolation. Here, it seems to me, is the reading of the riddle that puzzles so many of us. We are Americans, not only by birth and by citizenship, but by our political ideals, our language, our religion. Farther than that, our Americanism does not go. At that point, we are Negroes, members of a vast historic race that from the very dawn of creation has slept, but half awakening in the dark forests of its African fatherland. We are the first fruits of this new nation, the harbinger of that black to-morrow which is yet destined to soften the whiteness of the Teutonic to-day. We are that people whose subtle sense of song has given America its only American music, its only American fairy tales, its only touch of pathos and humor amid its mad money-getting plutocracy. As such, it is our duty to conserve our physical powers, our intellectual endowments, our spiritual ideals; as a race we must strive by race organization, by race solidarity, by race unity to the realization of that broader humanity which freely recognizes differences in men, but sternly deprecates inequality in their opportunities of development.

For the accomplishment of these ends we need race organizations: Negro colleges, Negro newspapers, Negro business organizations, a Negro school of literature and art, and an intellectual clearing house, for all these products of the Negro mind, which we may call a Negro Academy. Not only is all this necessary for positive advance, it is absolutely imperative for negative defense. Let us not deceive ourselves at our situation in this country. Weighted with a heritage of moral iniquity from our past history, hard pressed in the economic world by foreign immigrants and native prejudice, hated here, despised there and pitied everywhere; our one haven of refuge is ourselves, and but one means of advance, our own belief in our great destiny, our own implicit trust in our ability and worth. There is no power under God's high heaven that can stop the advance of eight thousand thousand honest, earnest, inspired and united people. But—and here is the rub—they *must* be honest, fearlessly criticising their own faults, zealously correcting them; they must be *earnest*. No people that laughs at itself, and ridicules itself, and wishes to God it was anything but itself ever wrote its name in history; it *must* be inspired with the Divine faith of our black mothers, that out of the blood and dust of battle will march a victorious host, a mighty nation, a peculiar people, to speak to the nations of earth a Divine truth that shall make them free. And such a people must be united; not merely united for the organized theft of political spoils, not united to disgrace religion with whoremongers and ward-heelers; not united merely to protest and pass resolutions, but united to stop the ravages of consumption among the Negro people, united to keep black boys from loafing, gambling and crime; united to guard the purity of black women and to reduce that vast army of black prostitutes that is today marching to hell; and united in serious organizations, to determine by careful conference and thoughtful interchange of opinion the broad lines of policy and action for the American Negro.

This, is the reason for being which the American Negro Academy has.

It aims at once to be the epitome and expression of the intellect of the black-blooded people of America, the exponent of the race ideals of one of the world's great races. As such, the Academy must, if successful, be

(*a*). Representative in character.

(*b*). Impartial in conduct.

(*c*). Firm in leadership.

It must be representative in character; not in that it represents all interests or all factions, but in that it seeks to comprise something of the *best* thought, the most unselfish striving and the highest ideals. There are scattered in forgotten nooks and corners throughout the land, Negroes of some considerable training, of high minds, and high motives, who are unknown to their fellows, who exert far too little influence. These the Negro Academy should strive to bring into touch with each other and to give them a common mouthpiece.

The Academy should be impartial in conduct; while it aims to exalt the people it should aim to do so by truth—not by lies, by honesty—not by flattery. It should continually impress the fact upon the Negro people that they must not expect to have things done for them—they MUST DO FOR THEMSELVES; that they have on their hands a vast work of self-reformation to do, and that a little less complaint and whining, and a little more dogged work and manly striving would do us more credit and benefit than a thousand Force or Civil Rights bills.

Finally, the American Negro Academy must point out a practical path of advance to the Negro people; there lie before every Negro today hundreds of questions of policy and right which must be settled and which each one settles now, not in accordance with any rule, but by impulse or individual preference; for instance: What should be the attitude of Negroes toward the educational qualification for voters? What should be our attitude toward separate schools? How should we meet discriminations on railways and in hotels? Such questions need not so much specific answers for each part as a general expression of policy, and nobody should be better fitted to announce such a policy than a representative honest Negro Academy.

All this, however, must come in time after careful organization and long conference. The immediate work before us should be practical and have direct bearing upon the situation of the Negro. The historical work of collecting the laws of the United States and of the various States of the Union with regard to the Negro is a work of such magnitude and importance that no body but one like this could think of undertaking it. If we could accomplish that one task we would justify our existence.

In the field of Sociology an appalling work lies before us. First, we must unflinchingly and bravely face the truth, not with apologies, but with solemn earnestness. The Negro Academy ought to sound a note of warning that would echo in every black cabin in the land: *Unless we conquer our present vices they will conquer us;* we are diseased, we are developing criminal tendencies, and an alarmingly large percentage of our men and women are sexually impure. The Negro Academy should stand and proclaim this over the housetops, crying with Garrison: *I will not equivocate, I will not retreat a single inch, and I will be heard.* The Academy should seek to gather about it the talented, unselfish men, the pure and noble-minded women, to fight an army of devils that disgraces our manhood and our womanhood. There does not stand today upon God's earth a race more capable in muscle, in intellect, in morals, than the American Negro, if he will bend his energies in the right direction; if he will

> Burst his birth's invidious bar
> And grasp the skirts of happy chance,
> And breast the blows of circumstance,
> And grapple with his evil star.

In science and morals, I have indicated two fields of work for the Academy. Finally, in practical policy, I wish to suggest the following *Academy Creed:*

1. We believe that the Negro people, as a race, have a contribution to make to civilization and humanity, which no other race can make.

2. We believe it the duty of the Americans of Negro descent, as a body, to maintain their race identity until this mission of the Negro people is accomplished, and the ideal of human brotherhood has become a practical possibility.

3. We believe that, unless modern civilization is a failure, it is entirely feasible and practicable for two races in such essential political, economic and religious harmony as the white and colored people of America, to develop side by side in peace and mutual happiness, the peculiar contribution which each has to make to the culture of their common country.

4. As a means to this end we advocate, not such social equality between these races as would disregard human likes and dislikes, but such a social equilibrium as would, throughout all the complicated relations of life, give due and just consideration to culture, ability, and moral worth, whether they be found under white or black skins.

5. We believe that the first and greatest step toward the settlement of the present friction between the races—commonly called the Negro Problem—lies in the correction of the immorality, crime and laziness among the Negroes themselves, which still remains as a heritage from slavery. We believe that only earnest and long continued efforts on our own part can cure these social ills.

6. We believe that the second great step toward a better adjustment of the relations between the races, should be a more impartial selection of ability in the economic and intellectual world, and a greater respect for personal liberty and worth, regardless of race. We believe that only earnest efforts on the part of the white people of this country will bring much needed reform in these matters.

7. On the basis of the foregoing declaration, and firmly believing in our high destiny, we, as American Negroes, are resolved to strive in every honorable way for the realization of the best and highest aims, for the development of strong manhood and pure womanhood, and for the rearing of a race ideal in America and Africa, to the glory of God and the uplifting of the Negro people—1897.

THE PHILADELPHIA NEGRO

COLOR PREJUDICE

Incidentally throughout this study the prejudice against the Negro has been again and again mentioned. It is time now to reduce this somewhat indefinite term to something tangible. Everybody speaks of the matter, everybody knows that it exists, but in just what form it shows itself or how influential it is few agree. In the Negro's mind, color prejudice in Philadelphia is that widespread feeling of dislike for his blood, which keeps him and his children out of decent employment, from certain public conveniences and amusements, from hiring houses in many sections, and in general, from being recognized as a man. Negroes regard this prejudice as the chief cause of their present unfortunate condition. On the other hand most white people are quite unconscious of any such powerful and vindictive feeling; they regard color prejudice as the easily explicable feeling that intimate social intercourse with a lower race is not only undesirable but impracticable if our present standards of culture are to be maintained; and although they are aware that some people feel the aversion more intensely than others, they cannot see how such a feeling has much influence on the real situation, or alters the social condition of the mass of Negroes.

As a matter of fact, color prejudice in this city is something between these two extreme views: it is not to-day responsible for all, or perhaps the greater part of the Negro problems, or of the disabilities under which the race labors; on the other hand it is a far more powerful social force than most Philadelphians realize. The practical results of the attitude of most of the inhabitants of Philadelphia toward persons of Negro descent are as follows:

1. As to getting work:

No matter how well trained a Negro may be, or how fitted for work of any kind, he cannot in the ordinary course of competition hope to be much more than a menial servant.

He cannot get clerical or supervisory work to do save in exceptional cases.

He cannot teach save in a few of the remaining Negro schools.

He cannot become a mechanic except for small transient jobs, and cannot join a trades union.

A Negro woman has but three careers open to her in this city: domestic service, sewing, or married life.

2. As to keeping work:

The Negro suffers in competition more severely than white men.

Change in fashion is causing him to be replaced by whites in the better paid positions of domestic service.

Whim and accident will cause him to lose a hard-earned place more quickly than the same things would affect a white man.

Being few in number compared with the whites the crime or carelessness of a few of his race is easily imputed to all, and the reputation of the good, industrious and reliable suffer thereby.

Because Negro workmen may not often work side by side with white workmen, the individual black workman is rated not by his own efficiency, but by the efficiency of a whole group of black fellow workmen which may often be low.

Because of these difficulties which virtually increase competition in his case, he is forced to take lower wages for the same work than white workmen.

3. As to entering new lines of work:

Men are used to seeing Negroes in inferior positions; when, therefore, by any chance a Negro gets in a better position, most men immediately conclude that he is not fitted for it, even before he has a chance to show his fitness.

If, therefore, he set up a store, men will not patronize him.

If he is put into public position men will complain.

If he gain a position in the commercial world, men will quietly secure his dismissal or see that a white man succeeds him.

4. As to his expenditure:

The comparative smallness of the patronage of the Negro, and the dislike of other customers makes it usual to increase the charges or difficulties in certain directions in which a Negro must spend money.

He must pay more house-rent for worse houses than most white people pay.

He is sometimes liable to insult or reluctant service in some restaurants, hotels and stores, at public resorts, theatres and places of recreation; and at nearly all barbershops.

5. As to his children:

The Negro finds it extremely difficult to rear children in such an atmosphere and not have them either cringing or impudent: if he impresses upon them patience with their lot, they may grow up satisfied with their condition; if he inspires them with ambition to rise, they may grow to despise their own people, hate the whites and become embittered with the world.

His children are discriminated against, often in public schools.

They are advised when seeking employment to become waiters and maids.

They are liable to species of insult and temptation peculiarly trying to children.

6. As to social intercourse:

In all walks of life the Negro is liable to meet some objection to his presence or some discourteous treatment; and the ties of friendship or memory seldom are strong enough to hold across the color line.

If an invitation is issued to the public for any occasion, the Negro can never know whether he would be welcomed or not; if he goes he is liable to have his feelings hurt and get into unpleasant altercation; if he stays away, he is blamed for indifference.

If he meet a lifelong white friend on the street, he is in a dilemma; if he does not greet the friend he is put down as boorish and impolite; if he does greet the friend he is liable to be flatly snubbed.

If by chance he is introduced to a white woman or man, he expects to be ignored on the next meeting, and usually is.

White friends may call on him, but he is scarcely expected to call on them, save for strictly business matters.

If he gain the affections of a white woman and marry her he may invariably expect that slurs will be thrown on her reputation and on his, and that both his and her race will shun their company.

When he dies he cannot be buried beside white corpses.

7. The result:

Any one of these things happening now and then would not be remarkable or call for especial comment; but when one group of people suffer all these little differences of treatment and discriminations and insults continually, the result is either discouragement, or bitterness, or over-sensitiveness, or recklessness. And a people feeling thus cannot do their best.

Presumably the first impulse of the average Philadelphian would be emphatically to deny any such marked and blighting discrimination as the above against a group of citizens in this metropolis. Every one knows that in the past color prejudice in the city was deep and passionate; living men can remember when a Negro could not sit in a street car or walk many streets in peace. These times have passed, however, and many imagine that active discrimination against the Negro has passed with them. Careful inquiry will convince any such one of his error. To be sure a colored man to-day can walk the streets of Philadelphia without personal insult; he can go to theatres, parks and some places of amusement without meeting more than stares and discourtesy; he can be accommodated at most hotels and restaurants, although his treatment in some would not be pleasant. All this is a vast advance and augurs much for the future. And yet all that has been said of the remaining discrimination is but too true.

During the investigation of 1896 there was collected a number of actual cases, which may illustrate the discriminations spoken of. So far as possible these have been sifted and only those which seem undoubtedly true have been selected.

1. As to getting work:

It is hardly necessary to dwell upon the situation of the Negro in regard to work in the higher walks of life: the white boy may start in the lawyer's office and work himself into a lucrative practice; he may serve a physician as office boy or enter a hospital in a minor position, and have his talent alone between him and affluence and fame; if he is bright in school, he may make his mark in a university, become a tutor with some time and much inspiration for study, and eventually fill a professor's chair. All these careers are at the very outset closed to the Negro on account of his color; what lawyer would give even a minor case to a Negro assistant? or what university would appoint a promising young Negro as tutor? Thus the young white man starts in life knowing that within some limits and barring accidents, talent and application will tell. The young Negro starts knowing that on all sides his advance is made doubly difficult if not wholly shut off, by his color. Let us come, however, to ordinary occupations which concern more nearly the mass of Negroes. Philadelphia is a great industrial and business centre, with thousands of foremen, managers and clerks —the lieutenants of industry, who direct its progress. They are paid for thinking and for skill to direct, and naturally such positions are coveted because they are well paid, well thought-of and carry some authority. To such positions Negro boys and girls may not aspire no matter what their qualifications. Even as teachers and ordinary clerks and stenographers they find almost no openings. Let us note some actual instances:

A young woman who graduated with credit from the Girls' Normal School in 1892, has taught in the kindergarten, acted as substitute, and waited in vain for a permanent position. Once she was allowed to substitute in a school with white teachers; the principal commended her work, but when the permanent appointment was made a white woman got it.

A girl who graduated from a Pennsylvania high school and from a business college sought work in the city as a stenographer and typist. A prominent lawyer undertook to find her a position; he went to friends and said, "Here is a girl that does excellent work and is of good character; can you not give her work?" Several immediately answered yes. "But," said the lawyer, "I will be perfectly frank with you and tell you she is colored"; and not in the whole city could he find a man willing to employ her. It happened, however, that the girl was so light in complexion that few not knowing would have suspected her descent. The lawyer therefore gave her temporary work in his own office until she found a position outside the city. "But," said he, "to this day I have not dared to tell my clerks that they worked beside a Negress." Another woman graduated from the high school and the Palmer College of Shorthand, but all over the city has met with nothing but refusal of work.

Several graduates in pharmacy have sought to get their three years required apprenticeship in the city and in only one case did one succeed, although they offered to work for nothing. One young pharmacist came from Massachusetts and for weeks sought in vain for work here at any price; "I wouldn't have a darky to clean out my store, much less to stand behind the counter," answered one druggist. A colored man answered an advertisement for a clerk in the suburbs. "What do you suppose we'd want of a nigger?" was the plain answer. A graduate of the University of Pennsylvania in mechanical engineering, well recommended, obtained work in the city, through an advertisement, on account of his excellent record. He worked a few hours and then was discharged because he was found to be colored. He is now a waiter at the University Club, where his white fellow graduates dine.* Another young man attended Spring Garden Institute and studied drawing for lithography. He had good references from the institute and elsewhere, but application at the five largest establishments in the city could secure him no work. A telegraph operator has hunted in vain for an opening, and two graduates of the Central High School have sunk to menial labor. "What's the use of an education?" asked one. Mr. A——has elsewhere been employed as a traveling salesman. He applied for a position here by letter and was told he could have one. When they saw him they had no work for him.

Such cases could be multiplied indefinitely. But that is not necessary; one has but to note that notwithstanding the acknowledged ability of many colored men, the Negro is conspicuously absent from all places of honor, trust or emolument, as well as from those of respectable grade in commerce and industry.

Even in the world of skilled labor the Negro is largely excluded. Many would explain the absence of Negroes from higher vocations by saying that while a few may now and then be found competent, the great mass are not fitted for that sort of work and are destined for some time to form a laboring class. In the matter of the trades, however, there can be raised no serious question of ability; for years the Negroes filled satisfactorily the trades of the city, and to-day in many parts of the South they are still prominent. And yet in Philadelphia a determined prejudice, aided by public opinion, has succeeded nearly in driving them from the field:

A——, who works at a bookbinding establishment on Front street, has learned to bind books and often does so for his friends. He is not allowed to work at the trade in the shop, however, but must remain a porter at a porter's wages.

B—— is a brushmaker; he has applied at several establishments, but they would not even examine his testimonials. They simply said: "We do not employ colored people."

* And is, of course, pointed out by some as typifying the educated Negro's success in life.

C—— is a shoemaker; he tried to get work in some of the large department stores. They "had no place" for him.

D—— was a bricklayer, but experienced so much trouble in getting work that he is now a messenger. . . .

Such is the tangible form of Negro prejudice in Philadelphia. Possibly some of the particular cases cited can be proven to have had extenuating circumstances unknown to the investigator; at the same time many not cited would be just as much in point. At any rate no one who has with any diligence studied the situation of the Negro in the city can long doubt but that his opportunities are limited and his ambition circumscribed about as has been shown. There are of course numerous exceptions, but the mass of the Negroes have been so often refused openings and discouraged in efforts to better their condition that many of them say, as one said, "I never apply—I know it is useless." Beside these tangible and measurable forms there are deeper and less easily described results of the attitude of the white population toward the Negroes: a certain manifestation of a real or assumed aversion, a spirit of ridicule or patronage, a vindictive hatred in some, absolute indifference in others; all this of course does not make much difference to the mass of the race, but it deeply wounds the better classes, the very classes who are attaining to that to which we wish the mass to attain. Notwithstanding all this, most Negroes would patiently await the effect of time and commonsense on such prejudice did it not today touch them in matters of life and death; threaten their homes, their food, their children, their hopes. And the result of this is bound to be increased crime, inefficiency and bitterness.

It would, of course, be idle to assert that most of the Negro crime was caused by prejudice; the violent economic and social changes which the last fifty years have brought to the American Negro, the sad social history that preceded these changes, have all contributed to unsettle morals and pervert talents. Nevertheless it is certain that Negro prejudice in cities like Philadelphia has been a vast factor in aiding and abetting all other causes which impel a half-developed race to recklessness and excess. Certainly a great amount of crime can be without doubt traced to the discrimination against Negro boys and girls in the matter of employment. Or to put it differently, Negro prejudice costs the city something.

The connection of crime and prejudice is, on the other hand, neither simple nor direct. The boy who is refused promotion in his job as porter does not go out and snatch somebody's pocketbook. Conversely the loafers at Twelfth and Kater streets, and the thugs in the county prison are not usually graduates of high schools who have been refused work. The connections are much more subtle and dangerous; it is the atmosphere of rebellion and discontent that unrewarded merit and reasonable but unsatisfied ambition make. The social environment of excuse, listless despair, careless indulgence and lack of inspiration to work is the growing force that turns black boys and girls into gamblers, prostitutes and rascals. And this social environment has been built up slowly out of the disappointments of deserving men and the sloth of the unawakened. How long can a city say to a part of its citizens, "It is useless to work; it is fruitless to deserve well of men; education will gain you nothing but disappointment and humiliation?" How long can a city teach its black children that the road to success is to have a white face? How long can a city do this and escape the inevitable penalty?

For thirty years and more Philadelphia has said to its black children: "Honesty, efficiency and talent have little to do with your success; if you work hard, spend little and are good you may earn your bread and butter at those sorts of work which we frankly confess we despise; if you are dishonest and lazy, the State will furnish your bread free." Thus the class of Negroes which the prejudices of the city have distinctly encouraged is that of the criminal, the lazy and the shiftless; for them the city teems with institutions and charities; for them there is succor and sympathy; for them Philadelphians are thinking and planning; but for the educated and industrious young colored man who wants work and not platitudes, wages and not alms, just rewards and not sermons—for such colored men Philadelphia apparently has no use.

What then do such men do? What becomes of the graduates of the many schools of the city? The answer is simple: most of those who amount to anything leave the city, the others take what they can get for a livelihood. Let us for a moment glance at the statistics of three colored schools:*

1. The O. V. Catto Primary School.
2. The Robert Vaux Grammar School.
3. The Institute for Colored Youth.

There attended the Catto school, 1867–97, 5915 pupils. Of these there were promoted from the full course, 653. 129 of the latter are known to be in positions of higher grade; or taking out 93 who are still in school, there remain 36 as follows: 18 teachers, 10 clerks, 2 physicians, 2 engravers, 2 printers, 1 lawyer and 1 mechanic.

The other 524 are for the most part in service, laborers and housewives. Of the 36 more successful ones fully half are at work outside of the city.

Of the Vaux school there were, 1877–89, 76 graduates. Of these there are 16 unaccounted for; the rest are:

Teachers	27	Barbers	4
Musicians	5	Clerks	3
Merchants	3	Physician	1
Mechanic	1	Deceased	8
Clergymen	3	Housewives	5
			60

* Kindly furnished by the principals of these schools.

From one-half to two-thirds of these have been compelled to leave the city in order to find work; one, the artist, Tanner, whom France recently honored, could not in his native land much less in his native city find room for his talents. He taught school in Georgia in order to earn money enough to go abroad.

The Institute of Colored Youth has had 340 graduates, 1856–97; 57 of these are dead. Of the 283 remaining 90 are unaccounted for. The rest are:

Teachers	117	Electrical Engineer	1
Lawyers	4	Professor	1
Physicians	4	Government clerks	5
Musicians	4	Merchants	7
Dentists	2	Mechanics	5
Clergymen	2	Clerks	23
Nurses	2	Teacher of cooking	1
Editor	1	Dressmakers	4
Civil Engineer	1	Students	7
			191

Here, again, nearly three-fourths of the graduates who have amounted to anything have had to leave the city for work. The civil engineer, for instance, tried in vain to get work here and finally had to go to New Jersey to teach.

There have been 9, possibly 11, colored graduates of the Central High School. These are engaged as follows:

Grocer	1	Porter	1
Clerks in service of city	2	Butler	1
Caterer	1	Unknown	3 or 5

It is high time that the best conscience of Philadelphia awakened to her duty; her Negro citizens are here to remain; they can be made good citizens or burdens to the community; if we want them to be sources of wealth and power and not of poverty and weakness then they must be given employment according to their ability and encouraged to train that ability and increase their talents by the hope of reasonable reward. To educate boys and girls and then refuse them work is to train loafers and rogues.*

From another point of view it could be argued with much cogency that the cause of economic stress, and consequently of crime, was the recent inconsiderate rush of Negroes into cities; and that the unpleasant results of this migration, while deplorable, will nevertheless serve to check the movement of Negroes to cities and keep them in the country where their

* Cf. on this point the interesting article of John Stevens Durham in the *Atlantic Monthly*, 1898.

chance for economic development is widest. This argument loses much of its point from the fact that it is the better class of educated Philadelphia-born Negroes who have the most difficulty in obtaining employment. The new immigrant fresh from the South is much more apt to obtain work suitable for him than the black boy born here and trained in efficiency. Nevertheless it is undoubtedly true that the recent migration has both directly and indirectly increased crime and competition. How is this movement to be checked? Much can be done by correcting misrepresentations as to the opportunities of city life made by designing employment bureaus and thoughtless persons; a more strict surveillance of criminals might prevent the influx of undesirable elements. Such efforts, however, would not touch the main stream of immigration. Back of that stream is the worldwide desire to rise in the world, to escape the choking narrowness of the plantation, and the lawless repression of the village, in the South. It is a search for better opportunities of living, and as such it must be discouraged and repressed with great care and delicacy, if at all. The real movement of reform is the raising of economic standards and increase of economic opportunity in the South. Mere land and climate without law and order, capital and skill, will not develop a country. When Negroes in the South have a larger opportunity to work, accumulate property, be protected in life and limb, and encourage pride and self-respect in their children, there will be a diminution in the stream of immigrants to Northern cities. At the same time if those cities practice industrial exclusion against these immigrants to such an extent that they are forced to become paupers, loafers and criminals, they can scarcely complain of conditions in the South. Northern cities should not, of course, seek to encourage and invite a poor quality of labor, with low standards of life and morals. The standards of wages and respectability should be kept up; but when a man reaches those standards in skill, efficiency and decency no question of color should, in a civilized community, debar him from an equal chance with his peers in earning a living. . . .

A FINAL WORD

Two sorts of answers are usually returned to the bewildered American who asks seriously: What is the Negro problem? The one is straightforward and clear: it is simply this, or simply that, and one simple remedy long enough applied will in time cause it to disappear. The other answer is apt to be hopelessly involved and complex—to indicate no simple panacea, and to end in a somewhat hopeless—There it is; what can we do? Both of these sorts of answers have something of truth in them: the Negro problem looked at in one way is but the old world questions of ignorance, poverty, crime, and the dislike of the stranger. On the other hand it is a mistake to think that attacking each of these questions single-handed without reference to the others will settle the matter: a combination of social problems is far more than a matter of mere addition,—the combination itself is a problem. Nevertheless the Negro problems are not more hopelessly complex than many others have been. Their elements despite their bewildering complication can be kept clearly in view: they are after all the same difficulties over which the world has grown gray: the question as to how far human intelligence can be trusted and trained; as to whether we must always have the poor with us; as to whether it is possible for the mass of men to attain righteousness on earth; and then to this is added that question of questions: after all who are Men? Is every featherless biped to be counted a man and brother? Are all races and types to be joint heirs of the new earth that men have striven to raise in thirty centuries and more? Shall we not swamp civilization in barbarism and drown genius in indulgence if we seek a mythical Humanity which shall shadow all men? The answer of the early centuries to this puzzle was clear: those of any nation who can be called Men and endowed with rights are few: they are the privileged classes—the well-born and the accidents of low-birth called up by the King. The rest, the mass of the nation, the *pöbel,* the mob, are fit to follow, to obey, to dig and delve, but not to think or rule or play the gentleman. We who were born to another philosophy hardly realize how deep-seated and plausible this view of human capabilities and powers once was; how utterly incomprehensible this republic would have been to Charlemagne or Charles V. or Charles I. We rather hasten to forget that once the courtiers of English kings looked upon the ancestors of most Americans with far greater contempt than these Americans look upon Negroes—and perhaps, indeed, had more cause. We forget that once French peasants were the "Niggers" of France, and that German princelings once discussed with doubt the brains and humanity of the *bauer.*

Much of this—or at least some of it—has passed and the world has glided by blood and iron into a wider humanity, a wider respect for simple manhood unadorned by ancestors or privilege. Not that we have discovered, as some hoped and some feared, that all men were created free and equal, but rather that the differences in men are not so vast as we had assumed. We still yield the well-born the advantages of birth, we still see that each nation has its dangerous flock of fools and rascals; but we also find most men have brains to be cultivated and souls to be saved.

And still this widening of the idea of common Humanity is of slow growth and to-day but dimly realized. We grant full citizenship in the World-Commonwealth to the "Anglo-Saxon" (whatever that may mean), the Teuton and the Latin; then with just a shade of reluctance we extend it to the Celt and Slav. We half deny it to the yellow races of Asia, admit the brown Indians to an ante-room only on the strength of an undeniable past; but with the Negroes of Africa we come to a full stop, and in its heart the civilized world with one accord denies that these come within the pale of nineteenth century Humanity. This feeling, widespread and deep-seated, is, in America, the vastest of the Negro problems; we have, to be sure, a threatening problem of ignorance but the ancestors of most Americans were far more ignorant than the freedmen's sons; these ex-slaves are poor but not as poor as the Irish peasants used to be; crime is rampant but not more so, if as much, as in Italy; but the difference is that the ancestors of the English and the Irish and the Italians were felt to be worth educating, helping and guiding because they were men and broth-ers, while in America a census which gives a slight indication of the utter disappearance of the American Negro from the earth is greeted with ill-concealed delight.

Other centuries looking back upon the culture of the nineteenth would have a right to suppose that if, in a land of freemen, eight millions of human beings were found to be dying of disease, the nation would cry with one voice, "Heal them!" If they were staggering on in ignorance, it would cry, "Train them!" If they were harming themselves and others by crime, it would cry, "Guide them!" And such cries are heard and have been heard in the land; but it was not one voice and its volume has been ever broken by counter-cries and echoes, "Let them die!" "Train them like slaves!" "Let them stagger downward!"

This is the spirit that enters in and complicates all Negro social prob-lems and this is a problem which only civilization and humanity can suc-cessfully solve. Meantime we have the other problems before us—we have the problems arising from the uniting of so many social questions about one centre. In such a situation we need only to avoid underestimat-ing the difficulties on the one hand and overestimating them on the other. The problems are difficult, extremely difficult, but they are such as the world has conquered before and can conquer again. Moreover the battle involves more than a mere altruistic interest in an alien people. It is a battle for humanity and human culture. If in the hey-day of the greatest of the world's civilizations, it is possible for one people ruthlessly to steal another, drag them helpless across the water, enslave them, debauch them, and then slowly murder them by economic and social exclusion until they disappear from the face of the earth—if the consummation of such a crime be possible in the twentieth century, then our civilization is vain and the republic is a mockery and a farce.

But this will not be; first, even with the terribly adverse circumstances under which Negroes live, there is not the slightest likelihood of their dying out; a nation that has endured the slave-trade, slavery, reconstruc-tion, and present prejudice three hundred years, and under it increased in numbers and efficiency, is not in any immediate danger of extinction. Nor is the thought of voluntary or involuntary emigration more than a dream of men who forget that there are half as many Negroes in the United States as Spaniards in Spain. If this be so then a few plain propositions may be laid down as axiomatic:

 1. The Negro is here to stay.

2. It is to the advantage of all, both black and white, that every Negro should make the best of himself.

3. It is the duty of the Negro to raise himself by every effort to the standards of modern civilization and not to lower those standards in any degree.

4. It is the duty of the white people to guard their civilization against debauchment by themselves or others; but in order to do this it is not necessary to hinder and retard the efforts of an earnest people to rise, simply because they lack faith in the ability of that people.

5. With these duties in mind and with a spirit of self-help, mutual aid and co-operation, the two races should strive side by side to realize the ideals of the republic and make this truly a land of equal opportunity for all men.

The Duty of the Negroes

That the Negro race has an appalling work of social reform before it need hardly be said. Simply because the ancestors of the present white inhabitants of America went out of their way barbarously to mistreat and enslave the ancestors of the present black inhabitants, gives those blacks no right to ask that the civilization and morality of the land be seriously menaced for their benefit. Men have a right to demand that the members of a civilized community be civilized; that the fabric of human culture, so laboriously woven, be not wantonly or ignorantly destroyed. Consequently a nation may rightly demand, even of a people it has consciously and intentionally wronged, not indeed complete civilization in thirty or one hundred years, but at least every effort and sacrifice possible on their part toward making themselves fit members of the community within a reasonable length of time; that thus they may early become a source of strength and help instead of a national burden. Modern society has too many problems of its own, too much proper anxiety as to its own ability to survive under its present organization, for it lightly to shoulder all the burdens of a less advanced people, and it can rightly demand that as far as possible and as rapidly as possible the Negro bend his energy to the solving of his own social problems—contributing to his poor, paying his share of the taxes and supporting the schools and public administration. For the accomplishment of this the Negro has a right to demand freedom for self-development, and no more aid from without than is really helpful for furthering that development. Such aid must of necessity be considerable: it must furnish schools and reformatories, and relief and preventive agencies; but the bulk of the work of raising the Negro must be done by the Negro himself, and the greatest help for him will be not to hinder and curtail and discourage his efforts. Against prejudice, injustice and wrong the Negro ought to protest energetically and continuously, but he must never forget that he protests because those things hinder his own efforts, and that those efforts are the key to his future.

And those efforts must be mighty and comprehensive, persistent, well-aimed and tireless; satisfied with no partial success, lulled to sleep by no colorless victories; and, above all, guided by no low selfish ideals; at the same time they must be tempered by common sense and rational expectation. In Philadelphia those efforts should first be directed toward a lessening of Negro crime; no doubt the amount of crime imputed to the race is exaggerated, no doubt features of the Negro's environment over which he has no control, excuse much that is committed; but beyond all this the amount of crime that can without doubt rightly be laid at the door of the Philadelphia Negro is large and is a menace to a civilized people. Efforts to stop this crime must commence in the Negro homes; they must cease to be, as they often are, breeders of idleness and extravagance and complaint. Work, continuous and intensive; work, although it be menial and poorly rewarded; work, though done in travail of soul and sweat of brow, must be so impressed upon Negro children as the road to salvation, that a child would feel it a greater disgrace to be idle than to do the humblest labor. The homely virtues of honesty, truth and chastity must be instilled in the cradle, and although it is hard to teach self-respect to a people whose million fellow-citizens half-despise them, yet it must be taught as the surest road to gain the respect of others.

It is right and proper that Negro boys and girls should desire to rise as high in the world as their ability and just desert entitle them. They should be ever encouraged and urged to do so, although they should be taught also that idleness and crime are beneath and not above the lowest work. It should be the continual object of Negroes to open up better industrial chances for their sons and daughters. Their success here must of course rest largely with the white people, but not entirely. Proper co-operation among forty or fifty thousand colored people ought to open many chances of employment for their sons and daughters in trades, stores and shops, associations and industrial enterprises.

Further, some rational means of amusement should be furnished young folks. Prayer meetings and church socials have their place, but they cannot compete in attractiveness with the dance halls and gambling dens of the city. There is a legitimate demand for amusement on the part of the young which may be made a means of education, improvement and recreation. A harmless and beautiful amusement like dancing might with proper effort be rescued from its low and unhealthful associations and made a means of health and recreation. The billiard table is no more wedded to the saloon than to the church if good people did not drive it there. If the Negro homes and churches cannot amuse their young people, and if no other efforts are made to satisfy this want, then we cannot complain if the saloons and clubs and bawdy-houses send these children to crime, disease and death.

There is a vast amount of preventive and rescue work which the Negroes themselves might do: keeping little girls off the street at night, stopping the escorting of unchaperoned young ladies to church and elsewhere, showing the dangers of the lodging system, urging the buying of homes and removal from crowded and tainted neighborhoods, giving lectures and tracts on health and habits, exposing the dangers of gambling and policy-playing, and inculcating respect for women. Day-nurseries and sewing-schools, mothers' meetings, the parks and airing places, all these things are little known or appreciated among the masses of Negroes, and their attention should be directed to them.

The spending of money is a matter to which Negroes need to give especial attention. Money is wasted to-day in dress, furniture, elaborate entertainments, costly church edifices, and "insurance" schemes, which ought to go toward buying homes, educating children, giving simple healthful amusement to the young, and accumulating something in the savings bank against a "rainy day." A crusade for the savings bank as against the "insurance" society ought to be started in the Seventh Ward without delay.

Although directly after the war there was great and remarkable enthusiasm for education, there is no doubt but that this enthusiasm has fallen off, and there is to-day much neglect of children among the Negroes, and failure to send them regularly to school. This should be looked into by the Negroes themselves and every effort made to induce full regular attendance.

Above all, the better classes of the Negroes should recognize their duty toward the masses. They should not forget that the spirit of the twentieth century is to be the turning of the high toward the lowly, the bending of Humanity to all that is human; the recognition that in the slums of modern society lie the answers to most of our puzzling problems of organization and life, and that only as we solve those problems is our culture assured and our progress certain. This the Negro is far from recognizing for himself; his social evolution in cities like Philadelphia is approaching a mediaeval stage when the centrifugal forces of repulsion between social classes are becoming more powerful than those of attraction. So hard has been the rise of the better class of Negroes that they fear to fall if now they stoop to lend a hand to their fellows. This feeling is intensified by the blindness of those outsiders who persist even now in confounding the good and bad, the risen and fallen in one mass. Nevertheless the Negro must learn the lesson that other nations learned so laboriously and imperfectly, that his better classes have their chief excuse for being in the work they may do toward lifting the rabble. This is especially true in a city like Philadelphia which has so distinct and creditable a Negro aristocracy; that they do something already to grapple with these social problems of their race is true, but they do not yet do nearly as much as they must, nor do they clearly recognize their responsibility.

Finally, the Negroes must cultivate a spirit of calm, patient persistence in their attitude toward their fellow citizens rather than of loud and intemperate complaint. A man may be wrong, and know he is wrong, and yet some finesse must be used in telling him of it. The white people of Philadelphia are perfectly conscious that their Negro citizens are not treated fairly in all respects, but it will not improve matters to call names or impute unworthy motives to all men. Social reforms move slowly and yet when Right is reinforced by calm but persistent Progress we somehow all feel that in the end it must triumph.

The Duty of the Whites

There is a tendency on the part of many white people to approach the Negro question from the side which just now is of least pressing importance, namely, that of the social intermingling of races. The old query: Would you want your sister to marry a Nigger? still stands as a grim sentinel to stop much rational discussion. And yet few white women have been pained by the addresses of black suitors, and those who have, easily got rid of them. The whole discussion is little less than foolish; perhaps a century from to-day we may find ourselves seriously discussing such questions of social policy, but it is certain that just as long as one group deems it a serious *mésalliance* to marry with another just so long few marriages will take place, and it will need neither law nor argument to guide human choice in such a matter. Certainly the masses of whites would hardly acknowledge that an active propaganda of repression was necessary to ward off intermarriage. Natural pride of race, strong on one side and growing on the other, may be trusted to ward off such mingling as might in this stage of development prove disastrous to both races. All this therefore is a question of the far-off future.

To-day, however, we must face the fact that a natural repugnance to close intermingling with unfortunate ex-slaves has descended to a discrimination that very seriously hinders them from being anything better. It is right and proper to object to ignorance and consequently to ignorant men; but if by our actions we have been responsible for their ignorance and are still actively engaged in keeping them ignorant, the argument loses its moral force. So with the Negroes: men have a right to object to a race so poor and ignorant and inefficient as the mass of the Negroes; but if their policy in the past is parent of much of this condition, and if to-day by shutting black boys and girls out of most avenues of decent employment they are increasing pauperism and vice, then they must hold themselves largely responsible for the deplorable results.

There is no doubt that in Philadelphia the centre and kernel of the Negro problem so far as the white people are concerned is the narrow opportunities afforded Negroes for earning a decent living. Such discrimination is morally wrong, politically dangerous, industrially wasteful, and socially silly. It is the duty of the whites to stop it, and to do so primarily for their own sakes. Industrial freedom of opportunity has by long experience been proven to be generally best for all. Moreover the cost of crime and pauperism, the growth of slums, and the pernicious influences of idleness and lewdness, cost the public far more than would the hurt to the feelings of a carpenter to work beside a black man, or a shop-girl to stand beside a darker mate. This does not contemplate the wholesale replacing of white workmen for Negroes out of sympathy or philanthropy; it does mean that talent should be rewarded, and aptness used in commerce and industry whether its owner be black or white; that the same incentive to good, honest, effective work be placed before a black office boy as before a white one—before a black porter as before a white one; and that unless this is done the city has no right to complain that black boys lose interest in work and drift into idleness and crime. Probably a change in public opinion on this point to-morrow would not make very much difference in the positions occupied by Negroes in the city: some few would be promoted, some few would get new places—the mass would remain as they are; but it would make one vast difference: it would inspire the young to try harder, it would stimulate the idle and discouraged and it would take away from this race the omnipresent excuse for failure: prejudice. Such a moral change would work a revolution in the criminal rate during the next ten years. Even a Negro bootblack could black boots better if he knew he was a menial not because he was a Negro but because he was best fitted for that work.

We need then a radical change in public opinion on this point; it will not and ought not to come suddenly, but instead of thoughtless acquiescence in the continual and steadily encroaching exclusion of Negroes from work in the city, the leaders of industry and opinion ought to be trying here and there to open up new opportunities and give new chances to bright colored boys. The policy of the city to-day simply drives out the best class of young people whom its schools have educated and social opportunities trained, and fills their places with idle and vicious immigrants. It is a paradox of the times that young men and women from some of the best Negro families of the city—families born and reared here and schooled in the best traditions of this municipality have actually had to go to the South to get work, if they wished to be aught but chambermaids and bootblacks. Not that such work may not be honorable and useful, but that it is as wrong to make scullions of engineers as it is to make engineers of scullions. Such a situation is a disgrace to the city—a disgrace to its Christianity, to its spirit of justice, to its common sense; what can be the end of such a policy but increased crime and increased excuse for crime? Increased poverty and more reason to be poor? Increased political serfdom of the mass of black voters to the bosses and rascals who divide the spoils? Surely here lies the first duty of a civilized city.

Secondly, in their efforts for the uplifting of the Negro the people of Philadelphia must recognize the existence of the better class of Negroes and must gain their active aid and co-operation by generous and polite conduct. Social sympathy must exist between what is best in both races and there must no longer be the feeling that the Negro who makes the best of himself is of least account to the city of Philadelphia, while the vagabond is to be helped and pitied. This better class of Negro does not want help or pity, but it does want a generous recognition of its difficulties, and a broad sympathy with the problem of life as it presents itself to them. It is composed of men and women educated and in many cases cultured; with proper co-operation they could be a vast power in the city, and the only power that could successfully cope with many phases of the Negro problems. But their active aid cannot be gained for purely selfish motives, or kept by churlish and ungentle manners; and above all they object to being patronized.

Again, the white people of the city must remember that much of the sorrow and bitterness that surrounds the life of the American Negro comes from the unconscious prejudice and half-conscious actions of men and women who do not intend to wound or annoy. One is not compelled to discuss the Negro question with every Negro one meets or to tell him of a father who was connected with the Underground Railroad; one is not compelled to stare at the solitary black face in the audience as though it were not human; it is not necessary to sneer, or be unkind or boorish, if the Negroes in the room or on the street are not all the best behaved or have not the most elegant manners; it is hardly necessary to strike from the dwindling list of one's boyhood and girlhood acquaintances or school-day friends all those who happen to have Negro blood, simply because one has not the courage now to greet them on the street. The little decencies of daily intercourse can go on, the courtesies of life be exchanged even across the color line without any danger to the supremacy of the Anglo-Saxon or the social ambition of the Negro. Without doubt social differences are facts not fancies and cannot lightly be swept aside; but they hardly need to be looked upon as excuses for downright meanness and incivility.

A polite and sympathetic attitude toward these striving thousands; a delicate avoidance of that which wounds and embitters them; a generous granting of opportunity to them; a seconding of their efforts, and a desire to reward honest success—all this, added to proper striving on their part, will go far even in our day toward making all men, white and black, realize what the great founder of the city meant, when he named it the City of Brotherly Love—1899.

OF MR. BOOKER T. WASHINGTON
AND OTHERS

From birth till death enslaved; in word,
in deed, unmanned!

. . . . . .

Hereditary bondsmen! Know ye not
Who would be free themselves must
strike the blow?

BYRON

Easily the most striking thing in the history of the American Negro since 1876 is the ascendancy of Mr. Booker T. Washington. It began at the time when war memories and ideals were rapidly passing; a day of astonishing commercial development was dawning; a sense of doubt and hesitation overtook the freedmen's sons,—then it was that his leading began. Mr. Washington came, with a simple definite programme, at the psychological moment when the nation was a little ashamed of having bestowed so much sentiment on Negroes, and was concentrating its energies on Dollars. His programme of industrial education, conciliation of the South, and submission and silence as to civil and political rights, was not wholly original; the Free Negroes from 1830 up to war-time had striven to build industrial schools, and the American Missionary Association had from the first taught various trades; and Price and others had sought a way of honorable alliance with the best of the Southerners. But Mr. Washington first indissolubly linked these things; he put enthusiasm, unlimited energy, and perfect faith into this programme, and changed it from a by-path into a veritable Way of Life. And the tale of the methods by which he did this is a fascinating study of human life.

It startled the nation to hear a Negro advocating such a programme after many decades of bitter complaint; it startled and won the applause of the South, it interested and won the admiration of the North; and after a confused murmur of protest, it silenced if it did not convert the Negroes themselves.

To gain the sympathy and coöperation of the various elements comprising the white South was Mr. Washington's first task; and this, at the time Tuskegee was founded, seemed, for a black man, well-nigh impossible. And yet ten years later it was done in the word spoken at Atlanta: "In all things purely social we can be as separate as the five fingers, and yet one as the hand in all things essential to mutual progress." This "Atlanta Compromise" is by all odds the most notable thing in Mr. Washington's career. The South interpreted it in different ways: the radicals received it as a complete surrender of the demand for civil and political equality; the conservatives, as a generously conceived working basis for mutual understanding. So both approved it, and to-day its author is certainly the most distinguished Southerner since Jefferson Davis, and the one with the largest personal following.

Next to this achievement comes Mr. Washington's work in gaining place and consideration in the North. Others less shrewd and tactful had formerly essayed to sit on these two stools and had fallen between them; but as Mr. Washington knew the heart of the South from birth and training, so by singular insight he intuitively grasped the spirit of the age which was dominating the North. And so thoroughly did he learn the speech and thought of triumphant commercialism, and the ideals of material prosperity, that the picture of a lone black boy poring over a French grammar amid the weeds and dirt of a neglected home soon seemed to him the acme of absurdities. One wonders what Socrates and St. Francis of Assisi would say to this.

And yet this very singleness of vision and thorough oneness with his age is a mark of the successful man. It is as though Nature must needs make men narrow in order to give them force. So Mr. Washington's cult has gained unquestioning followers, his work has wonderfully prospered, his friends are legion, and his enemies are confounded. To-day he stands as the one recognized spokesman of his ten million fellows, and one of the most notable figures in a nation of seventy millions. One hesitates, therefore, to criticise a life which, beginning with so little, has done so much. And yet the time is come when one may speak in all sincerity and utter courtesy of the mistakes and shortcomings of Mr. Washington's career, as well as of his triumphs, without being thought captious or envious, and without forgetting that it is easier to do ill than well in the world.

The criticism that has hitherto met Mr. Washington has not always been of this broad character. In the South especially has he had to walk warily to avoid the harshest judgments,—and naturally so, for he is dealing with the one subject of deepest sensitiveness to that section. Twice— once when at the Chicago celebration of the Spanish-American War he alluded to the color-prejudice that is "eating away the vitals of the South," and once when he dined with President Roosevelt—has the resulting Southern criticism been violent enough to threaten seriously his popularity. In the North the feeling has several times forced itself into words, that Mr. Washington's counsels of submission overlooked certain elements of true manhood, and that his educational programme was unnecessarily narrow. Usually, however, such criticism has not found open expression, although, too, the spiritual sons of the Abolitionists have not been prepared to acknowledge that the schools founded before Tuskegee, by men of broad ideals and self-sacrificing spirit, were wholly failures or worthy of ridicule. While, then, criticism has not failed to follow Mr. Washington, yet the prevailing public opinion of the land has been but too willing to deliver the solution of a wearisome problem into his hands, and say, "If that is all you and your race ask, take it."

Among his own people, however, Mr. Washington has encountered the strongest and most lasting opposition, amounting at times to bitterness, and even to-day continuing strong and insistent even though largely silenced in outward expression by the public opinion of the nation. Some of this opposition is, of course, mere envy; the disappointment of displaced demagogues and the spite of narrow minds. But aside from this, there is among educated and thoughtful colored men in all parts of the land a feeling of deep regret, sorrow, and apprehension at the wide currency and ascendancy which some of Mr. Washington's theories have gained. These same men admire his sincerity of purpose, and are willing to forgive much to honest endeavor which is doing something worth the doing. They coöperate with Mr. Washington as far as they conscientiously can; and, indeed, it is no ordinary tribute to this man's tact and power that, steering as he must between so many diverse interests and opinions, he so largely retains the respect of all.

But the hushing of the criticism of honest opponents is a dangerous thing. It leads some of the best of the critics to unfortunate silence and paralysis of effort, and others to burst into speech so passionately and intemperately as to lose listeners. Honest and earnest criticism from those whose interests are most nearly touched,—criticism of writers by readers, of government by those governed, of leaders by those led,—this is the soul of democracy and the safeguard of modern society. If the best of the American Negroes receive by outer pressure a leader whom they had not recognized before, manifestly there is here a certain palpable gain. Yet there is also irreparable loss,—a loss of that peculiarly valuable education which a group receives when by search and criticism it finds and commissions its own leaders. The way in which this is done is at once the most elementary and the nicest problem of social growth. History is but the record of such group-leadership; and yet how infinitely changeful is its type and character! And of all types and kinds, what can be more instructive than the leadership of a group within a group?—that curious double movement where real progress may be negative and actual advance be relative retrogression. All this is the social student's inspiration and despair.

Now in the past the American Negro has had instructive experience in the choosing of group leaders, founding thus a peculiar dynasty which in the light of present conditions is worth while studying. When sticks and stones and beasts form the sole environment of a people, their attitude is largely one of determined opposition to and conquest of natural forces. But when to earth and brute is added an environment of men and ideas, then the attitude of the imprisoned group may take three main forms,—a feeling of revolt and revenge; an attempt to adjust all thought and action to the will of the greater group; or, finally, a determined effort at self-realization and self-development despite environing opinion. The influence of all of these attitudes at various times can be traced in the history of the American Negro, and in the evolution of his successive leaders.

Before 1750, while the fire of African freedom still burned in the veins of the slaves, there was in all leadership or attempted leadership but the one motive of revolt and revenge,—typified in the terrible Maroons, the Danish blacks, and Cato of Stono, and veiling all the Americas in fear of insurrection. The liberalizing tendencies of the latter half of the eighteenth century brought, along with kindlier relations between black and white, thoughts of ultimate adjustment and assimilation. Such aspiration was especially voiced in the earnest songs of Phyllis, in the martyrdom of Attucks, the fighting of Salem and Poor, the intellectual accomplishments of Banneker and Derham, and the political demands of the Cuffes.

Stern financial and social stress after the war cooled much of the previous humanitarian ardor. The disappointment and impatience of the Negroes at the persistence of slavery and serfdom voiced itself in two movements. The slaves in the South, aroused undoubtedly by vague rumors of the Haytian revolt, made three fierce attempts at insurrection,—in 1800 under Gabriel in Virginia, in 1822 under Vesey in Carolina, and in 1831 again in Virginia under the terrible Nat Turner. In the Free States, on the other hand, a new and curious attempt at self-development was made. In Philadelphia and New York color-prescription led to a withdrawal of Negro communicants from white churches and the formation of a peculiar socio-religious institution among the Negroes known as the African Church,—an organization still living and controlling in its various branches over a million of men.

Walker's wild appeal against the trend of the times showed how the world was changing after the coming of the cotton-gin. By 1830 slavery seemed hopelessly fastened on the South, and the slaves thoroughly cowed into submission. The free Negroes of the North, inspired by the mulatto immigrants from the West Indies, began to change the basis of their demands; they recognized the slavery of slaves, but insisted that they themselves were freemen, and sought assimilation and amalgamation with the nation on the same terms with other men. Thus, Forten and Purvis of Philadelphia, Shad of Wilmington, Du Bois of New Haven, Barbadoes of Boston, and others, strove singly and together as men, they said, not as slaves; as "people of color," not as "Negroes." The trend of the times, however, refused them recognition save in individual and exceptional cases, considered them as one with all the despised blacks, and they soon found themselves striving to keep even the rights they formerly had of voting and working and moving as freemen. Schemes of migration and colonization arose among them; but these they refused to entertain, and they eventually turned to the Abolition movement as a final refuge.

Here, led by Remond, Nell, Wells-Brown, and Douglass, a new period of self-assertion and self-development dawned. To be sure, ultimate freedom and assimilation was the ideal before the leaders, but the assertion of the manhood rights of the Negro by himself was the main reliance, and

John Brown's raid was the extreme of its logic. After the war and emancipation, the great form of Frederick Douglass, the greatest of American Negro leaders, still led the host. Self-assertion, especially in political lines, was the main programme, and behind Douglass came Elliot, Bruce, and Langston, and the Reconstruction politicians, and, less conspicuous but of greater social significance Alexander Crummell and Bishop Daniel Payne.

Then came the Revolution of 1876, the suppression of the Negro votes, the changing and shifting of ideals, and the seeking of new lights in the great night. Douglass, in his old age, still bravely stood for the ideals of his early manhood,—ultimate assimilation *through* self-assertion, and on no other terms. For a time Price arose as a new leader, destined, it seemed, not to give up, but to re-state the old ideals in a form less repugnant to the white South. But he passed away in his prime. Then came the new leader. Nearly all the former ones had become leaders by the silent suffrage of their fellows, had sought to lead their own people alone, and were usually, save Douglass, little known outside their race. But Booker T. Washington arose as essentially the leader not of one race but of two,—a compromiser between the South, the North, and the Negro. Naturally the Negroes resented, at first bitterly, signs of compromise which surrendered their civil and political rights, even though this was to be exchanged for larger chances of economic development. The rich and dominating North, however, was not only weary of the race problem, but was investing largely in Southern enterprises, and welcomed any method of peaceful coöperation. Thus, by national opinion, the Negroes began to recognize Mr. Washington's leadership; and the voice of criticism was hushed.

Mr. Washington represents in Negro thought the old attitude of adjustment and submission; but adjustment at such a peculiar time as to make his programme unique. This is an age of unusual economic development, and Mr. Washington's programme naturally takes an economic cast, becoming a gospel of Work and Money to such an extent as apparently almost completely to overshadow the higher aims of life. Moreover, this is an age when the more advanced races are coming in closer contact with the less developed races, and the race-feeling is therefore intensified; and Mr. Washington's programme practically accepts the alleged inferiority of the Negro races. Again, in our own land, the reaction from the sentiment of war time has given impetus to race-prejudice against Negroes, and Mr. Washington withdraws many of the high demands of Negroes as men and American citizens. In other periods of intensified prejudice all the Negro's tendency to self-assertion has been called forth; at this period a policy of submission is advocated. In the history of nearly all other races and peoples the doctrine preached at such crises has been that manly self-respect is worth more than lands and houses, and that a people who voluntarily surrender such respect, or cease striving for it, are not worth civilizing.

In answer to this, it has been claimed that the Negro can survive only through submission. Mr. Washington distinctly asks that black people give up, at least for the present, three things,—

First, political power,

Second, insistence on civil rights,

Third, higher education of Negro youth,—

and concentrate all their energies on industrial education, the accumulation of wealth, and the conciliation of the South. This policy has been courageously and insistently advocated for over fifteen years, and has been triumphant for perhaps ten years. As a result of this tender of the palm-branch, what has been the return? In these years there have occurred:

1. The disfranchisement of the Negro.

2. The legal creation of a distinct status of civil inferiority for the Negro.

3. The steady withdrawal of aid from institutions for the higher training of the Negro.

These movements are not, to be sure, direct results of Mr. Washington's teachings; but his propaganda has, without a shadow of doubt, helped their speedier accomplishment. The question then comes: Is it possible, and probable, that nine millions of men can make effective progress in economic lines if they are deprived of political rights, made a servile caste, and allowed only the most meagre chance for developing their exceptional men? If history and reason give any distinct answer to these questions, it is an emphatic *No*. And Mr. Washington thus faces the triple paradox of his career:

1. He is striving nobly to make Negro artisans business men and property-owners; but it is utterly impossible, under modern competitive methods, for workingmen and property-owners to defend their rights and exist without the right of suffrage.

2. He insists on thrift and self-respect, but at the same time counsels a silent submission to civic inferiority such as is bound to sap the manhood of any race in the long run.

3. He advocates common-school and industrial training, and depreciates institutions of higher learning; but neither the Negro common-schools, nor Tuskegee itself, could remain open a day were it not for teachers trained in Negro colleges, or trained by their graduates.

This triple paradox in Mr. Washington's position is the object of criticism by two classes of colored Americans. One class is spiritually descended from Toussaint the Savior, through Gabriel, Vesey, and Turner, and they represent the attitude of revolt and revenge; they hate the white South blindly and distrust the white race generally, and so far as they agree on definite action, think that the Negro's only hope lies in emigration beyond the borders of the United States. And yet, by the irony of fate, nothing has more effectually made this programme seem hopeless than the recent course of the United States toward weaker and darker peoples in the West Indies, Hawaii, and the Philippines,—for where in the world may we go and be safe from lying and brute force?

The other class of Negroes who cannot agree with Mr. Washington has hitherto said little aloud. They deprecate the sight of scattered counsels, of internal disagreement; and especially they dislike making their just criticism of a useful and earnest man an excuse for a general discharge of venom from small-minded opponents. Nevertheless, the questions involved are so fundamental and serious that it is difficult to see how men like the Grimkes, Kelly Miller, J. W. E. Bowen, and other representatives of this group, can much longer be silent. Such men feel in conscience bound to ask of this nation three things:

1. The right to vote.
2. Civic equality.
3. The education of youth according to ability.

They acknowledge Mr. Washington's invaluable service in counselling patience and courtesy in such demands; they do not ask that ignorant black men vote when ignorant whites are debarred, or that any reasonable restrictions in the suffrage should not be applied; they know that the low social level of the mass of the race is responsible for much discrimination against it, but they also know, and the nation knows, that relentless color-prejudice is more often a cause than a result of the Negro's degradation; they seek the abatement of this relic of barbarism, and not its systematic encouragement and pampering by all agencies of social power from the Associated Press to the Church of Christ. They advocate, with Mr. Washington, a broad system of Negro common schools supplemented by thorough industrial training; but they are surprised that a man of Mr. Washington's insight cannot see that no such educational system ever has rested or can rest on any other basis than that of the well-equipped college and university, and they insist that there is a demand for a few such institutions throughout the South to train the best of the Negro youth as teachers, professional men, and leaders.

This group of men honor Mr. Washington for his attitude of conciliation toward the white South; they accept the "Atlanta Compromise" in its broadest interpretation; they recognize, with him, many signs of promise, many men of high purpose and fair judgment, in this section; they know that no easy task has been laid upon a region already tottering under heavy burdens. But, nevertheless, they insist that the way to truth and right lies in straightforward honesty, not in indiscriminate flattery; in praising those of the South who do well and criticising uncompromisingly those who do ill; in taking advantage of the opportunities at hand and urging their fellows to do the same, but at the same time in remembering that only a firm adherence to their higher ideals and aspirations will ever keep those ideals within the realm of possibility. They do not expect that the free right to vote, to enjoy civic rights, and to be educated, will come in a moment; they do not expect to see the bias and prejudices of years disappear at the blast of a trumpet; but they are absolutely certain that the way for a people to gain their reasonable rights is not by voluntarily throwing them away and insisting that they do not want them; that the way for a people to gain respect is not by continually belittling and ridiculing themselves; that, on the contrary, Negroes must insist continually, in season and out of season, that voting is necessary to modern manhood, that color discrimination is barbarism, and that black boys need education as well as white boys.

In failing thus to state plainly and unequivocally the legitimate demands of their people, even at the cost of opposing an honored leader, the thinking classes of American Negroes would shirk a heavy responsibility, —a responsibility to themselves, a responsibility to the struggling masses, a responsibility to the darker races of men whose future depends so largely on this American experiment, but especially a responsibility to this nation,—this common Fatherland. It is wrong to encourage a man or a people in evil-doing; it is wrong to aid and abet a national crime simply because it is unpopular not to do so. The growing spirit of kindliness and reconciliation between the North and South after the frightful differences of a generation ago ought to be a source of deep congratulation to all, and especially to those whose mistreatment caused the war; but if that reconciliation is to be marked by the industrial slavery and civic death of those same black men, with permanent legislation into a position of inferiority, then those black men, if they are really men, are called upon by every consideration of patriotism and loyalty to oppose such a course by all civilized methods, even though such opposition involves disagreement with Mr. Booker T. Washington. We have no right to sit silently by while the inevitable seeds are sown for a harvest of disaster to our children, black and white.

First, it is the duty of black men to judge the South discriminatingly. The present generation of Southerners are not responsible for the past, and they should not be blindly hated or blamed for it. Furthermore, to no class is the indiscriminate endorsement of the recent course of the South toward Negroes more nauseating than to the best thought of the South. The South is not "solid"; it is a land in the ferment of social change, wherein forces of all kinds are fighting for supremacy; and to praise the ill the South is to-day perpetrating is just as wrong as to condemn the good. Discriminating and broad-minded criticism is what the South needs,— needs it for the sake of her own white sons and daughters, and for the insurance of robust, healthy mental and moral development.

To-day even the attitude of the Southern whites toward the blacks is not, as so many assume, in all cases the same; the ignorant Southerner hates the Negro, the workingmen fear his competition, the money-makers wish to use him as a laborer, some of the educated see a menace in his upward development, while others—usually the sons of the masters—wish to help him to rise. National opinion has enabled this last class to maintain the Negro common schools, and to protect the Negro partially in property, life, and limb. Through the pressure of the money-makers, the Negro is in danger of being reduced to semi-slavery, especially in the country districts; the workingmen, and those of the educated who fear the Negro, have united to disfranchise him, and some have urged his deportation; while the passions of the ignorant are easily aroused to lynch and abuse any black man. To praise this intricate whirl of thought and prejudice is nonsense; to inveigh indiscriminately against "the South" is unjust; but to use the same breath in praising Governor Aycock, exposing Senator Morgan, arguing with Mr. Thomas Nelson Page, and denouncing Senator Ben Tillman, is not only sane, but the imperative duty of thinking black men.

It would be unjust to Mr. Washington not to acknowledge that in several instances he has opposed movements in the South which were unjust to the Negro; he sent memorials to the Louisiana and Alabama constitutional conventions, he has spoken against lynching, and in other ways has openly or silently set his influence against sinister schemes and unfortunate happenings. Notwithstanding this, it is equally true to assert that on the whole the distinct impression left by Mr. Washington's propaganda is, first, that the South is justified in its present attitude toward the Negro because of the Negro's degradation; secondly, that the prime cause of the Negro's failure to rise more quickly is his wrong education in the past; and, thirdly, that his future rise depends primarily on his own efforts. Each of these propositions is a dangerous half-truth. The supplementary truths must never be lost sight of: first, slavery and race-prejudice are potent if not sufficient causes of the Negro's position; second, industrial and common-school training were necessarily slow in planting because they had to await the black teachers trained by higher institutions,—it being extremely doubtful if any essentially different development was possible, and certainly a Tuskegee was unthinkable before 1880; and, third, while it is great truth to say that the Negro must strive and strive *mightily* to help himself, it is equally true that unless his striving be not simply seconded, but rather aroused and encouraged, by the initiative of the richer and wiser environing group, he cannot hope for great success.

In his failure to realize and impress this last point, Mr. Washington is especially to be criticised. His doctrine has tended to make the whites, North and South, shift the burden of the Negro problem to the Negro's shoulders and stand aside as critical and rather pessimistic spectators; when in fact the burden belongs to the nation, and the hands of none of us are clean if we bend not our energies to righting these great wrongs.

The South ought to be led, by candid and honest criticism, to assert her better self and do her full duty to the race she has cruelly wronged and is still wronging. The North—her co-partner in guilt—cannot salve her conscience by plastering it with gold. We cannot settle this problem by diplomacy and suaveness, by "policy" alone. If worse come to worst, can the moral fibre of this country survive the slow throttling and murder of nine millions of men?

The black men of America have a duty to perform, a duty stern and delicate,—a forward movement to oppose a part of the work of their greatest leader. So far as Mr. Washington preaches Thrift, Patience, and Industrial Training for the masses, we must hold up his hands and strive with him, rejoicing in his honors and glorying in the strength of this Joshua called of God and of man to lead the headless host. But so far as Mr. Washington apologizes for injustice, North or South, does not rightly value the privilege and duty of voting, belittles the emasculating effects of caste distinctions, and opposes the higher training and ambition of our brighter minds,—so far as he, the South, or the Nation, does this,—we must unceasingly and firmly oppose them. By every civilized and peaceful method we must strive for the rights which the world accords to men, clinging unwaveringly to those great words which the sons of the Fathers would fain forget: "We hold these truths to be self-evident: That all men are created equal; that they are endowed by their Creator with certain unalienable rights; that among these are life, liberty, and the pursuit of happiness"—1903.

THE TALENTED TENTH

The Negro race, like all races, is going to be saved by its exceptional men. The problem of education, then, among Negroes must first of all deal with the Talented Tenth; it is the problem of developing the Best of this race that they may guide the Mass away from the contamination and death of the Worst, in their own and other races. Now the training of men is a difficult and intricate task. Its technique is a matter for educational experts, but its object is for the vision of seers. If we make money the object of man-training, we shall develop money-makers but not necessarily men; if we make technical skill the object of education, we may possess artisans but not, in nature, men. Men we shall have only as we make manhood the object of the work of the schools—intelligence, broad sympathy, knowledge of the world that was and is, and of the relation of men to it—this is the curriculum of that Higher Education which must underlie true life. On this foundation we may build bread winning, skill of hand and quickness of brain, with never a fear lest the child and man mistake the means of living for the object of life.

If this be true—and who can deny it—three tasks lay before me; first to show from the past that the Talented Tenth as they have risen among American Negroes have been worthy of leadership; secondly, to show

how these men may be educated and developed; and thirdly, to show their relation to the Negro problem.

You misjudge us because you do not know us. From the very first it has been the educated and intelligent of the Negro people that have led and elevated the mass, and the sole obstacles that nullified and retarded their efforts were slavery and race prejudice; for what is slavery but the legalized survival of the unfit and the nullification of the work of natural internal leadership? Negro leadership, therefore, sought from the first to rid the race of this awful incubus that it might make way for natural selection and the survival of the fittest. In colonial days came Phillis Wheatley and Paul Cuffe striving against the bars of prejudice; and Benjamin Banneker, the almanac maker, voiced their longings when he said to Thomas Jefferson, "I freely and cheerfully acknowledge that I am of the African race, and in colour which is natural to them, of the deepest dye; and it is under a sense of the most profound gratitude to the Supreme Ruler of the Universe, that I now confess to you that I am not under that state of tyrannical thraldom and inhuman captivity to which too many of my brethren are doomed, but that I have abundantly tasted of the fruition of those blessings which proceed from that free and unequalled liberty with which you are favored, and which I hope you will willingly allow, you have mercifully received fromm the immediate hand of that Being from whom proceedeth every good and perfect gift.

"Suffer me to recall to your mind that time, in which the arms of the British crown were exerted with every powerful effort, in order to reduce you to a state of servitude; look back, I entreat you, on the variety of dangers to which you were exposed; reflect on that period in which every human aid appeared unavailable, and in which even hope and fortitude wore the aspect of inability to the conflict, and you cannot but be led to a serious and grateful sense of your miraculous and providential preservation, you cannot but acknowledge, that the present freedom and tranquility which you enjoy, you have mercifully received, and that a peculiar blessing of heaven.

"This, sir, was a time when you clearly saw into the injustice of a state of Slavery, and in which you had just apprehensions of the horrors of its condition. It was then that your abhorrence thereof was so excited, that you publicly held forth this true and invaluable doctrine, which is worthy to be recorded and remembered in all succeeding ages: 'We hold these truths to be self-evident, that all men are created equal; that they are endowed with certain inalienable rights, and that among these are life, liberty and the pursuit of happiness.' "

Then came Dr. James Derham, who could tell even the learned Dr. Rush something of medicine, and Lemuel Haynes, to whom Middlebury College gave an honorary A.M. in 1804. These and others we may call the

Revolutionary group of distinguished Negroes—they were persons of marked ability, leaders of a Talented Tenth, standing conspicuously among the best of their time. They strove by word and deed to save the color line from becoming the line between the bond and free, but all they could do was nullified by Eli Whitney and the Curse of Gold. So they passed into forgetfulness.

But their spirit did not wholly die; here and there in the early part of the century came other exceptional men. Some were natural sons of unnatural fathers and were given often a liberal training and thus a race of educated mulattoes sprang up to plead for black men's rights. There was Ira Aldridge, whom all Europe loved to honor; there was that Voice crying in the Wilderness, David Walker, and saying:

"I declare it does appear to me as though some nations think God is asleep, or that he made the Africans for nothing else but to dig their mines and work their farms, or they cannot believe history, sacred or profane. I ask every man who has a heart, and is blessed with the privilege of believing—Is not God a God of justice to all his creatures? Do you say he is? Then if he gives peace and tranquility to tyrants and permits them to keep our fathers, our mothers, ourselves and our children in eternal ignorance and wretchedness to support them and their families, would he be to us a God of Justice? I ask, O, ye Christians, who hold us and our children in the most abject ignorance and degradation that ever a people were afflicted with since the world began—I say if God gives you peace and tranquility, and suffers you thus to go on afflicting us, and our children, who have never given you the least provocation—would He be to us a God of Justice? If you will allow that we are men, who feel for each other, does not the blood of our fathers and of us, their children, cry aloud to the Lord of Sabaoth against you for the cruelties and murders with which you have and do continue to afflict us?"

This was the wild voice that first aroused Southern legislators in 1829 to the terrors of abolitionism.

In 1831 there met that first Negro convention in Philadelphia, at which the world gaped curiously but which bravely attacked the problems of race and slavery, crying out against persecution and declaring that "Laws as cruel in themselves as they were unconstitutional and unjust, have in many places been enacted against our poor, unfriended and unoffending brethren (without a shadow of provocation on our part), at whose bare recital the very savage draws himself up for fear of contagion —looks noble and prides himself because he bears not the name of Christian." Side by side this free Negro movement, and the movement for abolition, strove until they merged into one strong stream. Too little notice has been taken of the work which the Talented Tenth among Negroes took in the great abolition crusade. From the very day that a Philadelphia colored man became the first subscriber to Garrison's "Liberator," to the day when Negro soldiers made the Emancipation Proclamation possible, black leaders worked shoulder to shoulder with white men in a movement, the success of which would have been impossible without them. There was Purvis and Remond, Pennington and Highland Garnett, Sojourner Truth and Alexander Crummel, and above all, Frederick Douglass—what would the abolition movement have been without them? They stood as living examples of the possibilities of the Negro race, their own hard experiences and well wrought culture said silently more than all the drawn periods of orators—they were the men who made American slavery impossible. As Maria Weston Chapman once said, from the school of anti-slavery agitation "a throng of authors, editors, lawyers, orators and accomplished gentlemen of color have taken their degree! It has equally implanted hopes and aspirations, noble thoughts, and sublime purposes, in the hearts of both races. It has prepared the white man for the freedom of the black man, and it has made the black man scorn the thought of enslavement, as does a white man, as far as its influence has extended. Strengthen that noble influence! Before its organization, the country only saw here and there in slavery some faithful Cudjoe or Dinah, whose strong natures blossomed even in bondage, like a fine plant beneath a heavy stone. Now, under the elevating and cherishing influence of the American Anti-slavery Society, the colored race, like the white, furnishes Corinthian capitals for the noblest temples."

Where were these black abolitionists trained? Some, like Frederick Douglass, were self-trained, but yet trained liberally; others, like Alexander Crummell and McCune Smith, graduated from famous foreign universities. Most of them rose up through the colored schools of New York and Philadelphia and Boston, taught by college-bred men like Russworm, of Dartmouth, and college-bred white men like Neau and Benezet.

After emancipation came a new group of educated and gifted leaders: Langston, Bruce and Elliot, Greener, Williams and Payne. Through political organization, historical and polemic writing and moral regeneration, these men strove to uplift their people. It is the fashion of to-day to sneer at them and to say that with freedom Negro leadership should have begun at the plow and not in the Senate—a foolish and mischievous lie; two hundred and fifty years that black serf toiled at the plow and yet that toiling was in vain till the Senate passed the war amendments; and two hundred and fifty years more the half-free serf of to-day may toil at his plow, but unless he have political rights and righteously guarded civic status, he will still remain the poverty-stricken and ignorant plaything of rascals, that he now is. This all sane men know even if they dare not say it.

And so we come to the present—a day of cowardice and vacillation, of strident wide-voiced wrong and faint hearted compromise; of double-faced dallying with Truth and Right. Who are to-day guiding the work of the Negro people? The "exceptions" of course. And yet so sure as this Talented Tenth is pointed out, the blind worshippers of the Average cry

out in alarm: "These are exceptions, look here at death, disease and crime
—these are the happy rule." Of course they are the rule, because a silly
nation made them the rule: Because for three long centuries this people
lynched Negroes who dared to be brave, raped black women who dared to
be virtuous, crushed dark-hued youth who dared to be ambitious, and encouraged and made to flourish servility and lewdness and apathy. But not
even this was able to crush all manhood and chastity and aspiration from
black folk. A saving remnant continually survives and persists, continually aspires, continually shows itself in thrift and ability and character.
Exceptional it is to be sure, but this is its chiefest promise; it shows the
capability of Negro blood, the promise of black men. Do Americans ever
stop to reflect that there are in this land a million men of Negro blood,
well-educated, owners of homes, against the honor of whose womanhood
no breath was ever raised, whose men occupy positions of trust and usefulness, and who, judged by any standard, have reached the full measure of
the best type of modern European culture? Is it fair, is it decent, is it
Christian to ignore these facts of the Negro problem, to belittle such aspiration, to nullify such leadership and seek to crush these people back into
the mass out of which by toil and travail, they and their fathers have
raised themselves?

Can the masses of the Negro people be in any possible way more
quickly raised than by the effort and example of this aristocracy of talent
and character? Was there ever a nation on God's fair earth civilized from
the bottom upward? Never; it is, ever was and ever will be from the top
downward that culture filters. The Talented Tenth rises and pulls all that
are worth the saving up to their vantage ground. This is the history of
human progress; and the two historic mistakes which have hindered that
progress were the thinking first that no more could ever rise save the few
already risen; or second, that it would better the unrisen to pull the risen
down.

How then shall the leaders of a struggling people be trained and the
hands of the risen few strengthened? There can be but one answer: The
best and most capable of their youth must be schooled in the colleges and
universities of the land. We will not quarrel as to just what the university
of the Negro should teach or how it should teach it—I willingly admit
that each soul and each race-soul needs its own peculiar curriculum. But
this is true: A university is a human invention for the transmission of
knowledge and culture from generation to generation, through the training of quick minds and pure hearts, and for this work no other human
invention will suffice, not even trade and industrial schools.

All men cannot go to college but some men must; every isolated group
or nation must have its yeast, must have for the talented few centers of
training where men are not so mystified and befuddled by the hard and
necessary toil of earning a living, as to have no aims higher than their
bellies, and no God greater than Gold. This is true training, and thus in

the beginning were the favored sons of the freedmen trained. Out of the colleges of the North came, after the blood of war, Ware, Cravath, Chase, Andrews, Bumstead and Spence to build the foundations of knowledge and civilization in the black South. Where ought they to have begun to build? At the bottom, of course, quibbles the mole with his eyes in the earth. Aye! truly at the bottom, at the very bottom; at the bottom of knowledge, down in the very depths of knowledge there where the roots of justice strike into the lowest soil of Truth. And so they did begin; they founded colleges, and up from the colleges shot normal schools, and out from the normal schools went teachers, and around the normal teachers clustered other teachers to teach the public schools; the college trained in Greek and Latin and mathematics, 2,000 men; and these men trained full 50,000 others in morals and manners, and they in turn taught thrift and the alphabet to nine millions of men, who to-day hold $300,000,000 of property. It was a miracle—the most wonderful peace-battle of the 19th century, and yet to-day men smile at it, and in fine superiority tell us that it was all a strange mistake; that a proper way to found a system of education is first to gather the children and buy them spelling books and hoes; afterward men may look about for teachers, if haply they may find them; or again they would teach men Work, but as for Life—why, what has Work to do with Life, they ask vacantly.

Was the work of these college founders successful; did it stand the test of time? Did the college graduates, with all their fine theories of life, really live? Are they useful men helping to civilize and elevate their less fortunate fellows? Let us see. Omitting all institutions which have not actually graduated students from a college course, there are to-day in the United States thirty-four institutions giving something above high school training to Negroes and designed especially for this race.

Three of these were established in border States before the War; thirteen were planted by the Freedmen's Bureau in the years 1864–1869; nine were established between 1870 and 1880 by various church bodies; five were established after 1881 by Negro churches, and four are state institutions supported by United States' agricultural funds. In most cases the college departments are small adjuncts to high and common school work. As a matter of fact six institutions—Atlanta, Fisk, Howard, Shaw, Wilberforce and Leland, are the important Negro colleges so far as actual work and number of students are concerned. In all these institutions, seven hundred and fifty Negro college students are enrolled. In grade the best of these colleges are about a year behind the smaller New England colleges and a typical curriculum is that of Atlanta University. Here students from the grammar grades, after a three years' high school course, take a college course of 136 weeks. One-fourth of this time is given to Latin and Greek; one-fifth, to English and modern languages; one-sixth, to history and social science; one-seventh, to natural science; one-eighth to mathematics, and one-eighth to philosophy and pedagogy.

In addition to these students in the South, Negroes have attended Northern colleges for many years. As early as 1826 one was graduated from Bowdoin College, and from that time till to-day nearly every year has seen elsewhere, other such graduates. They have, of course, met much color prejudice. Fifty years ago very few colleges would admit them at all. Even to-day no Negro has ever been admitted to Princeton, and at some other leading institutions they are rather endured than encouraged. Oberlin was the great pioneer in the work of blotting out the color line in colleges, and has more Negro graduates by far than any other Northern college.

The total number of Negro college graduates up to 1899, (several of the graduates of that year not being reported), was as follows:

	Negro Colleges	White Colleges
Before '76	137	75
'75–80	143	22
'80–85	250	31
'85–90	413	43
'90–95	465	66
'95–99	475	88
Class Unknown	57	64
Total	1,914	390

Of these graduates 2,079 were men and 252 were women; 50 per cent. of Northern-born college men come South to work among the masses of their people, at a sacrifice which few people realize; nearly 90 per cent. of the Southern-born graduates instead of seeking that personal freedom and broader intellectual atmosphere which their training has led them, in some degree, to conceive, stay and labor and wait in the midst of their black neighbors and relatives. [The obvious numerical discrepancies present in the table and descriptive paragraph appear in the original text— H.B.]

The most interesting question, and in many respects the crucial question, to be asked concerning college-bred Negroes, is: Do they earn a living? It has been intimated more than once that the higher training of Negroes has resulted in sending into the world of work, men who could find nothing to do suitable to their talents. Now and then there comes a rumor of a colored college man working at menial service, etc. Fortunately, returns as to occupations of college-bred Negroes, gathered by the Atlanta conference, are quite full—nearly sixty per cent. of the total number of graduates.

This enables us to reach fairly certain conclusions as to the occupations of all college-bred Negroes. Of 1,312 persons reported, there were:

Per Cent.

Teachers,	53.4	
Clergymen,	16.8	
Physicians, etc.,	6.3	
Students,	5.6	
Lawyers,	4.7	
In Govt. Service,	4.0	
In Business,	3.6	
Farmers and Artisans,	2.7	
Editors, Secretaries and Clerks,	2.4	
Miscellaneous.	.5	

Over half are teachers, a sixth are preachers, another sixth are students and professional men; over 6 per cent. are farmers, artisans and merchants, and 4 per cent. are in government service. In detail the occupations are as follows:

Occupations of College-Bred Men

Teachers:

Presidents and Deans,	19	
Teachers of Music,	7	
Professors, Principals and Teachers,	675	TOTAL 701

Clergymen:

Bishop,	1	
Chaplains U.S. Army,	2	
Missionaries,	9	
Presiding Elders,	12	
Preachers,	197	TOTAL 221

Physicians:

Doctors of Medicine,	76	
Druggists,	4	
Dentists,	3	TOTAL 83
Students,		74
Lawyers,		62

Civil Service:

U.S. Minister Plenipotentiary,	1	
U.S. Consul,	1	
U.S. Deputy Collector,	1	
U.S. Gauger,	1	
U.S. Postmasters,	2	
U.S. Clerks,	44	
State Civil Service,	2	
City Civil Service,	1	TOTAL 53

Business Men:

Merchants, etc.,	30	
Managers,	13	
Real Estate Dealers,	4	TOTAL 47
Farmers,		26

Clerks and Secretaries:

Secretary of National Societies,	7	
Clerks, etc.,	15	TOTAL 22
Artisans,		9
Editors,		9
Miscellaneous,		5

These figures illustrate vividly the function of the college-bred Negro. He is, as he ought to be, the group leader, the man who sets the ideals of the community where he lives, directs its thoughts and heads its social movements. It need hardly be argued that the Negro people need social leadership more than most groups; that they have no traditions to fall back upon, no long established customs, no strong family ties, no well defined social classes. All these things must be slowly and painfully evolved. The preacher was, even before the war, the group leader of the Negroes, and the church their greatest social institution. Naturally this preacher was ignorant and often immoral, and the problem of replacing the older type by better educated men has been a difficult one. Both by direct work and by direct influence on other preachers, and on congregations, the college-bred preacher has an opportunity for reformatory work and moral inspiration, the value of which cannot be overestimated.

It has, however, been in the furnishing of teachers that the Negro college has found its peculiar function. Few persons realize how vast a work, how mighty a revolution has been thus accomplished. To furnish five millions and more of ignorant people with teachers of their own race and blood, in one generation, was not only a very difficult undertaking, but a very important one, in that, it placed before the eyes of almost every Negro child an attainable ideal. It brought the masses of the blacks in contact with modern civilization, made black men the leaders of their communities and trainers of the new generation. In this work college-bred Negroes were first teachers, and then teachers of teachers. And here it is that the broad culture of college work has been of peculiar value. Knowledge of life and its wider meaning, has been the point of the Negro's deepest ignorance, and the sending out of teachers whose training has not been simply for bread winning, but also for human culture, has been of inestimable value in the training of these men.

In earlier years the two occupations of preacher and teacher were practically the only ones open to the black college graduate. Of later years a larger diversity of life among his people, has opened new avenues of employment. Nor have these college men been paupers and spendthrifts; 557 college-bred Negroes owned in 1899, $1,342,862.50 worth of real estate, (assessed value) or $2,411 per family. The real value of the total accumulations of the whole group is perhaps about $10,000,000, or $5,000 a piece. Pitiful, is it not, beside the fortunes of oil kings and steel trusts, but after all is the fortune of the millionaire the only stamp of true and successful living? Alas! it is, with many, and there's the rub.

The problem of training the Negro is to-day immensely complicated by the fact that the whole question of the efficiency and appropriateness of our present systems of education, for any kind of child, is a matter of active debate, in which final settlement seems still afar off. Consequently it often happens that persons arguing for or against certain systems of education for Negroes, have these controversies in mind and miss the real question at issue. The main question, so far as the Southern Negro is concerned, is: What under the present circumstance, must a system of education do in order to raise the Negro as quickly as possible in the scale of civilization? The answer to this question seems to me clear: It must strengthen the Negro's character, increase his knowledge and teach him to earn a living. Now it goes without saying, that it is hard to do all these things simultaneously or suddenly, and that at the same time it will not do to give all the attention to one and neglect the others; we could give black boys trades, but that alone will not civilize a race of ex-slaves; we might simply increase their knowledge of the world, but this would not necessarily make them wish to use this knowledge honestly; we might seek to strengthen character and purpose, but to what end if this people have nothing to eat or to wear? A system of education is not one thing, nor does it have a single definite object, nor is it a mere matter of schools. Education is that whole system of human training within and without the school house walls, which molds and develops men. If then we start out to train an ignorant and unskilled people with a heritage of bad habits, our system of training must set before itself two great aims—the one dealing with knowledge and character, the other part seeking to give the child the technical knowledge necessary for him to earn a living under the present circumstances. These objects are accomplished in part by the opening of the common schools on the one, and of the industrial schools on the other. But only in part, for there must also be trained those who are to teach these schools—men and women of knowledge and culture and technical skill who understand modern civilization, and have the training and aptitude to impart it to the children under them. There must be teachers, and teachers of teachers, and to attempt to establish any sort of a system of common and industrial school training, without *first* (and I say *first* advisedly) without *first* providing for the higher training of the very best teachers, is simply throwing your money to the winds. School houses do not teach themselves—piles of brick and mortar and machinery do not send out *men*. It is the trained, living human soul, cultivated and strengthened by long study and thought, that breathes the real breath of life into boys and girls and makes them human, whether they be black or white, Greek, Russian or American. Nothing, in these latter days, has so dampened the faith of thinking Negroes in recent educational movements, as the fact that such movements have been accompanied by ridicule and denouncement and decrying of those very institutions of higher training which made the Negro public school possible, and make Negro industrial schools thinkable. It was Fisk, Atlanta, Howard and Straight, those colleges born of the faith and sacrifice of the abolitionists, that placed in the black schools of the South the 30,000 teachers and more, which some, who depreciate the work of these higher schools, are using to teach their own new experiments. If Hampton, Tuskegee and the hundred other industrial schools prove in the future to be as successful as they deserve to be, then their success in training black artisans for the South, will be due primarily to the white colleges of the North and the black colleges of the South, which trained the teachers who to-day conduct these institutions. There was a time when the American people believed pretty devoutly that a log of wood with a boy at one end and Mark Hopkins at the other, represented the highest ideal of human training. But in these eager days it would seem that we have changed all that and think it necessary to add a couple of saw-mills and a hammer to this outfit, and, at a pinch, to dispense with the services of Mark Hopkins.

I would not deny, or for a moment seem to deny, the paramount necessity of teaching the Negro to work, and to work steadily and skillfully; or seem to depreciate in the slightest degree the important part industrial schools must play in the accomplishment of these ends, but I *do* say, and insist upon it, that it is industrialism drunk with its vision of success, to imagine that its own work can be accomplished without providing for the training of broadly cultured men and women to teach its own teachers, and to teach the teachers of the public schools.

But I have already said that human education is not simply a matter of schools; it is much more a matter of family and group life—the training of one's home, of one's daily companions, of one's social class. Now the black boy of the South moves in a black world—a world with its own leaders, its own thoughts, its own ideals. In this world he gets by far the larger part of his life training, and through the eyes of this dark world he peers into the veiled world beyond. Who guides and determines the education which he receives in his world? His teachers here are the group-leaders of the Negro people—the physicians and clergymen, the trained fathers and mothers, the influential and forceful men about him of all kinds; here it is, if at all, that the culture of the surrounding world trickles through and is handed on by the graduates of the higher schools. Can such culture training of group leaders be neglected? Can we afford to ignore it? Do you think that if the leaders of thought among Negroes are not trained and educated thinkers, that they will have no leaders? On the contrary a hundred half-trained demagogues will still hold the places they so largely occupy now, and hundreds of vociferous busy-bodies will multiply. You have no choice; either you must help furnish this race from within its own ranks with thoughtful men of trained leadership, or you must suffer the evil consequences of a headless misguided rabble.

I am an earnest advocate of manual training and trade teaching for black boys, and for white boys, too. I believe that next to the founding of Negro colleges the most valuable addition to Negro education since the war, has been industrial training for black boys. Nevertheless, I insist that the object of all true education is not to make men carpenters, it is to make carpenters men; there are two means of making the carpenter a man, each equally important: the first is to give the group and community in which he works, liberally trained teachers and leaders to teach him and his family what life means; the second is to give him sufficient intelligence and technical skill to make him an efficient workman; the first object demands the Negro college and college-bred men—not a quantity of such colleges, but a few of excellent quality; not too many college-bred men, but enough to leaven the lump, to inspire the masses, to raise the Talented Tenth to leadership; the second object demands a good system of common schools, well-taught, conveniently located and properly equipped.

The Sixth Atlanta Conference truly said in 1901:

We call the attention of the Nation to the fact that less than one million of the three million Negro children of school age, are at present regularly attending school, and these attend a session which lasts only a few months.

We are to-day deliberately rearing millions of our citizens in ignorance, and at the same time limiting the rights of citizenship by educational qualifications. This is unjust. Half the black youth of the land have no opportunities open to them for learning to read, write and cipher. In the discussion as to the proper training of Negro children after they leave the public schools, we have forgotten that they are not yet decently provided with public schools.

Propositions are beginning to be made in the South to reduce the already meagre school facilities of Negroes. We congratulate the South on resisting, as much as it has, this pressure, and on the many millions it has spent on Negro education. But it is only fair to point out that Negro taxes and the Negroes' share of the income from indirect taxes and endowments have fully repaid this expenditure, so that the Negro public school system has not in all probability cost the white taxpayers a single cent since the war.

This is not fair. Negro schools should be a public burden, since they are a public benefit. The Negro has a right to demand good common school training at the hands of the States and the Nation since by their fault he is not in position to pay for this himself.

What is the chief need for the building up of the Negro public school in the South? (The Negro race in the South needs teachers to-day above all else. This is the concurrent testimony of all who know the situation.

For the supply of this great demand two things are needed—institutions of higher education and money for school houses and salaries.) It is usually assumed that a hundred or more institutions for Negro training are to-day turning out so many teachers and college-bred men that the race is threatened with an over-supply. This is sheer nonsense. There are to-day less than 3,000 living Negro college graduates in the United States, and less than 1,000 Negroes in college. Moreover, in the 164 schools for Negroes, 95 per cent. of their students are doing elementary and secondary work, work which should be done in the public schools. Over half the remaining 2,157 students are taking high school studies. The mass of so-called "normal" schools for the Negro, are simply doing elementary common school work, or, at most, high school work, with a little instruction in methods. The Negro colleges and the post-graduate courses at other institutions are the only agencies for the broader and more careful training of teachers. The work of these institutions is hampered for lack of funds. It is getting increasingly difficult to get funds for training teachers in the best modern methods, and yet all over the South, from State Superintendents, county officials, city boards and school principals comes the wail, "We need TEACHERS!" and teachers must be trained. As the fairest minded of all white Southerners, Atticus G. Haygood, once said: "The defects of colored teachers are so great as to create an urgent necessity for training better ones. Their excellencies and their successes are sufficient to justify the best hopes of success in the effort, and to vindicate the judgment of those who make large investments of money and service, to give to colored students opportunity for thoroughly preparing themselves for the work of teaching children of their people."

The truth of this has been strikingly shown in the marked improvement of white teachers in the South. Twenty years ago the rank and file of white public school teachers were not as good as the Negro teachers. But they, by scholarships and good salaries, have been encouraged to thorough normal and collegiate preparation, while the Negro teachers have been discouraged by starvation wages and the idea that any training will do for a black teacher. If carpenters are needed it is well and good to train men as carpenters. But to train men as carpenters, and then set them to teaching is wasteful and criminal; and to train men as teachers and then refuse them living wages, unless they become carpenters, is rank nonsense.

The United States Commissioner of Education says in his report for 1900: "For comparison between the white and colored enrollment in secondary and higher education, I have added together the enrollment in high schools and secondary schools, with the attendance on colleges and universities, not being sure of the actual grade of work done in the colleges and universities. The work done in the secondary schools is reported in such detail in this office, that there can be no doubt of its grade."

He then makes the following comparisons of persons in every million enrolled in secondary and higher education:

	Whole Country	Negroes
1880	4,362	1,289
1900	10,743	2,061

And he concludes: "While the number in colored high schools and colleges had increased somewhat faster than the population, it had not kept pace with the average of the whole country, for it had fallen from 30 per cent to 24 per cent of the average quota. Of all colored pupils, one (1) in one hundred was engaged in secondary and higher work, and that ratio has continued substantially for the past twenty years. If the ratio of colored population in secondary and higher education is to be equal to the average for the whole country, it must be increased to five times its present average." And if this be true of the secondary and higher education, it is safe to say that the Negro has not one-tenth his quota in college studies. How baseless, therefore, is the charge of too much training! We need Negro teachers for the Negro common schools, and we need first-class normal schools and colleges to train them. This is the work of higher Negro education and it must be done.

Further than this, after being provided with group leaders of civilization, and a foundation of intelligence in the public schools, the carpenter, in order to be a man, needs technical skill. This calls for trade schools. Now trade schools are not nearly such simple things as people once thought. The original idea was that the "Industrial" school was to furnish education, practically free, to those willing to work for it; it was to "do" things—i.e.: become a center of productive industry, it was to be partially, if not wholly, self-supporting, and it was to teach trades. Admirable as were some of the ideas underlying this scheme, the whole thing simply would not work in practice; it was found that if you were to use time and material to teach trades thoroughly, you could not at the same time keep the industries on a commercial basis and make them pay. Many schools started out to do this on a large scale and went into virtual bankruptcy. Moreover, it was found also that it was possible to teach a boy a trade mechanically, without giving him the full educative benefit of the process, and, vice versa, that there was a distinctive educative value in teaching a boy to use his hands and eyes in carrying out certain physical processes, even though he did not actually learn a trade. It has happened, therefore, in the last decade, that a noticeable change has come over the industrial schools. In the first place the idea of commercially remunerative industry in a school is being pushed rapidly to the background. There are still schools with shops and farms that bring an income, and schools that use student labor partially for the erection of their buildings and the furnishing of equipment. It is coming to be seen, however, in the education of the Negro, as clearly as it has been seen in the education of the youths the world over, that it is the *boy* and not the material product, that is the true object of education. Consequently the object of the industrial school came to be the thorough training of boys regardless of the cost of the training, so long as it was thoroughly well done.

Even at this point, however, the difficulties were not surmounted. In the first place modern industry has taken great strides since the war, and the teaching of trades is no longer a simple matter. Machinery and long processes of work have greatly changed the work of the carpenter, the iron-worker and the shoemaker. A really efficient workman must be to-day an intelligent man who has had good technical training in addition to thorough common school, and perhaps even higher training. To meet this situation the industrial schools began a further development; they established distinct Trade Schools for the thorough training of better class artisans, and at the same time they sought to preserve for the purposes of general education, such of the simpler processes of elementary trade learning as were best suited therefor. In this differentiation of the Trade School and manual training, the best of the industrial schools simply followed the plain trend of the present educational epoch. A prominent educator tells us that, in Sweden, "In the beginning the economic conception was generally adopted, and everywhere manual training was looked upon as a means of preparing the children of the common people to earn their living. But gradually it came to be recognized that manual training has a more elevated purpose, and one, indeed, more useful in the deeper meaning of the term. It came to be considered as an educative process for the complete moral, physical and intellectual development of the child."

Thus, again, in the manning of trade schools and manual training schools we are thrown back upon the higher training as its source and chief support. There was a time when any aged and wornout carpenter could teach in a trade school. But not so to-day. Indeed the demand for college-bred men by a school like Tuskegee, ought to make Mr. Booker T. Washington the firmest friend of higher training. Here he has as helpers the son of a Negro senator, trained in Greek and the humanities, and graduated at Harvard; the son of a Negro congressman and lawyer, trained in Latin and mathematics, and graduated at Oberlin; he has as his wife, a woman who read Virgil and Homer in the same class room with me; he has as college chaplain, a classical graduate of Atlanta University; as teacher of science, a graduate of Fisk; as teacher of history, a graduate of Smith,—indeed some thirty of his chief teachers are college graduates, and instead of studying French grammars in the midst of weeds, or buying pianos for dirty cabins, they are at Mr. Washington's right hand helping him in a noble work. And yet one of the effects of Mr. Washington's propaganda has been to throw doubt upon the expediency of such training for Negroes, as these persons have had.

Men of America, the problem is plain before you. Here is a race transplanted through the criminal foolishness of your fathers. Whether you like it or not the millions are here, and here they will remain. If you do not lift them up, they will pull you down. Education and work are the levers to uplift a people. Work alone will not do it unless inspired by the right ideals and guided by intelligence. Education must not simply teach work—it must teach Life. The Talented Tenth of the Negro race must be made leaders of thought and missionaries of culture among their people. No others can do this work and Negro colleges must train men for it. The Negro race, like all other races, is going to be saved by its exceptional men—**1903.**

DECLARATION OF PRINCIPLES OF THE NIAGARA MOVEMENT

PROGRESS

The members of the conference, known as the Niagara Movement, assembled in annual meeting in Buffalo, July 11th, 12th and 13th, 1905, congratulate the Negro-Americans on certain undoubted evidences of progress in the last decade, particularly the increase of intelligence, the buying of property, the checking of crime, the uplift in home life, the advance in literature and art, and the demonstration of constructive and executive ability in the conduct of great religious, economic and educational institutions.

SUFFRAGE

At the same time, we believe that this class of American citizens should protest emphatically and continually against the curtailment of their political rights. We believe in manhood suffrage; we believe that no man is so good, intelligent or wealthy as to be entrusted wholly with the welfare of his neighbor.

CIVIL LIBERTY

We believe also in protest against the curtailment of our civil rights. All American citizens have the right to equal treatment in places of public entertainment according to their behavior and deserts.

ECONOMIC OPPORTUNITY

We especially complain against the denial of equal opportunities to us in economic life; in the rural districts of the South this amounts to peonage and virtual slavery; all over the South it tends to crush labor and small business enterprises; and everywhere American prejudice, helped often by iniquitous laws, is making it more difficult for Negro-Americans to earn a decent living.

EDUCATION

Common school education should be free to all American children and compulsory. High school training should be adequately provided for all, and college training should be the monopoly of no class or race in any section of our common country. We believe that, in defense of our own institutions, the United States should aid common school education, particularly in the South, and we especially recommend concerted agitation to this end. We urge an increase in public high school facilities in the South, where the Negro-Americans are almost wholly without such provisions. We favor well-equipped trade and technical schools for the training of artisans, and the need of adequate and liberal endowment for a few institutions of higher education must be patent to sincere well-wishers of the race.

COURTS

We demand upright judges in courts, juries selected without discrimination on account of color and the same measure of punishment and the same efforts at reformation for blacks as well as for white offenders. We need orphanages and farm schools for dependent children, juvenile reformatories for delinquents, and the abolition of the dehumanizing convict-lease system.

PUBLIC OPINION

We note with alarm the evident retrogression in the land of sound public opinion on the subject of manhood rights, republican government and human brotherhood, and we pray God that this nation will not degenerate into a mob of boasters and oppressors, but rather will return to the faith of the fathers, that all men were created free and equal, with certain unalienable rights.

HEALTH

We plead for health—for an opportunity to live in decent houses and localities, for a chance to rear our children in physical and moral cleanliness.

EMPLOYERS AND LABOR UNIONS

We hold up for public execration the conduct of two opposite classes of men: The practice among employers of importing ignorant Negro-American laborers in emergencies, and then affording them neither protection nor permanent employment; and the practice of labor unions in proscribing and boycotting and oppressing thousands of their fellow-toilers, simply because they are black. These methods have accentuated and will accentuate the war of labor and capital, and they are disgraceful to both sides.

PROTEST

We refuse to allow the impression to remain that the Negro-American assents to inferiority, is submissive under oppression and apologetic before insults. Through helplessness we may submit, but the voice of protest of ten million Americans must never cease to assail the ears of their fellows, so long as America is unjust.

COLOR-LINE

Any discrimination based simply on race or color is barbarous, we care not how hallowed it be by custom, expediency, or prejudice. Differences made on account of ignorance, immorality, or disease are legitimate methods of fighting evil, and against them we have no word of protest; but discriminations based simply and solely on physical peculiarities, place of birth, color or skin, are relics of that unreasoning savagery of which the world is and ought to be thoroughly ashamed.

"JIM CROW" CARS

We protest against the "Jim Crow" car, since its effect is and must be to make us pay first-class fare for third-class accomodations, render us open to insults and discomfort and to crucify wantonly our manhood, womanhood and self-respect.

SOLDIERS

We regret that this nation has never seen fit adequately to reward the black soldiers who, in its five wars, have defended their country with their blood, and yet have been systematically denied the promotions which their abilities deserve. And we regard as unjust, the exclusion of black boys from the military and navy training schools.

WAR AMENDMENTS

We urge upon Congress the enactment of appropriate legislation for securing the proper enforcement of those articles of freedom, the thirteenth, fourteenth and fifteenth amendments of the Constitution of the United States.

We repudiate the monstrous doctrine that the oppressor should be the sole authority as to the rights of the oppressed.

OPPRESSION

The Negro race in America stolen, ravished and degraded, struggling up through difficulties and oppression, needs sympathy and receives criticism; needs help, and is given hindrance, needs protection and is given mob-violence, needs justice and is given charity, needs leadership and is given cowardice and apology, needs bread and is given a stone. The nation will never stand justified before God until these things are changed.

THE CHURCH

Especially are we surprised and astonished at the recent attitude of the church of Christ—on the increase of a desire to bow to racial prejudice, to narrow the bounds of human brotherhood, and to segregate black men in some outer sanctuary. This is wrong, unchristian and disgraceful to the twentieth century civilization.

AGITATION

Of the above grievances we do not hesitate to complain, and to complain loudly and insistently. To ignore, overlook, or apologize for these wrongs is to prove ourselves unworthy of freedom. Persistent manly agitation is the way to liberty, and toward this goal the Niagara Movement has started and asks the co-operation of all men of all races.

HELP

At the same time we want to acknowledge with deep thankfulness the help of our fellowmen from the abolitionist down to those who to-day still stand for equal opportunity and who have given and still give of their wealth and of their poverty for our advancement.

DUTIES

And while we are demanding, and ought to demand, and will continue to demand the rights enumerated above, God forbid that we should ever forget to urge corresponding duties upon our people:

The duty to vote
The duty to respect the rights of others
The duty to work
The duty to obey the laws
The duty to be clean and orderly
The duty to send out children to school
The duty to respect ourselves, even as we respect others

This statement, complaint and prayer we do submit to the American people and Almighty God—**1905.**

RESOLUTIONS OF THE NIAGARA MOVEMENT

The men of the Niagara Movement, coming from the toil of the year's hard work, and pausing a moment from the earning of their daily bread, turn toward the nation and again ask in the name of ten million the privilege of a hearing. In the past year the work of the Negro hater has flourished in the land. Step by step the defenders of the rights of American citizens have retreated. The work of stealing the black man's ballot has progressed and the fifty and more representatives of stolen votes still sit in the nation's capital. Discrimination in travel and public accommodation has so spread that some of our weaker brethren are actually afraid to thunder against color discrimination as such and are simply whispering for ordinary decencies.

Against this the Niagara Movement eternally protests. We will not be satisfied to take one jot or tittle less than our full manhood rights. We claim for ourselves every single right that belongs to a freeborn American, political, civil and social; and until we get these rights we will never cease to protest and assail the ears of America. The battle we wage is not for ourselves alone, but for all true Americans. It is a fight for ideals, lest this, our common fatherland, false to its founding, become in truth the land of the Thief and the home of the Slave—a by-word and a hissing among the nations for its sounding pretensions and pitiful accomplishment.

Never before in the modern age has a great and civilized folk threatened to adopt so cowardly a creed in the treatment of its fellow-citizens, born and bred on its soil. Stripped of verbiage and subterfuge and in its naked nastiness, the new American creed says: fear to let black men even try to rise lest they become the equals of the white. And this is the land that professes to follow Jesus Christ. The blasphemy of such a course is only matched by its cowardice.

In detail our demands are clear and unequivocal.

First. We would vote; with the right to vote goes everything: freedom, manhood, the honor of your wives, the chastity of your daughters, the right to work, and the chance to rise; let no man listen to those who deny this.

We want full manhood suffrage, and we want it now, henceforth and forever.

Second. We want discrimination in public accommodation to cease. Separation in railway and street cars, based simply on race and color, is un-American, undemocratic, and silly. We protest against all such discrimination.

Third. We claim the right of freemen to walk, talk and be with them that wish to be with us. No man has the right to choose another man's friends, and to attempt to do so is an impudent interference with the most fundamental human privilege.

Fourth. We want the laws enforced against rich as well as poor; against Capitalist as well as Laborer; against white as well as black. We are not more lawless than the white race, we are more often arrested, convicted and mobbed. We want justice even for criminals and outlaws. We want the Constitution of the country enforced. We want Congress to take charge of the Congressional elections. We want the Fourteenth Amendment carried out to the letter and every State disfranchised in Congress which attempts to disfranchise its rightful voters. We want the Fifteenth Amendment enforced and no State allowed to base its franchise simply on color.

The failure of the Republican Party in Congress at the session just closed to redeem its pledge of 1904 with reference to suffrage conditions at the South seems a plain, deliberate, and premeditated breach of promise, and stamps that party as guilty of obtaining votes under false pretense.

Fifth. We want our children educated. The school system in the country districts of the South is a disgrace and in few towns and cities are the Negro schools what they ought to be. We want the national government to step in and wipe out illiteracy in the South. Either the United States will destroy ignorance or ignorance will destroy the United States.

And when we call for education, we mean real education. We believe in work. We ourselves are workers, but work is not necessarily education. Education is the development of power and ideal. We want our children trained as intelligent human beings should be, and we will fight for all time against any proposal to educate black boys and girls simply as servants and underlings, or simply for the use of other people. They have a right to know, to think, to aspire.

These are some of the chief things which we want. How shall we get them? By voting where we may vote; by persistent, unceasing agitation; by hammering at the truth; by sacrifice and work.

We do not believe in violence, neither in the despised violence of the raid nor the lauded violence of the soldier, nor the barbarous violence of the mob; but we do believe in John Brown, in that incarnate spirit of justice, that hatred of a lie, that willingness to sacrifice money, reputation, and life itself on the altar of right. And here on the scene of John Brown's martyrdom, we reconsecrate ourselves, our honor, our property to the final emancipation of the race for whose freedom John Brown died—**August 15, 1906.**

THE EVOLUTION OF THE RACE PROBLEM

Those who complain that the Negro problem is always with us and apparently insoluble must not forget that under this vague and general designation are gathered many social problems and many phases of the same problem; that these problems and phases have passed through a great evolutionary circle and that to-day especially one may clearly see a repetition, vaster but similar, of the great cycle of the past.

That problem of the past, so far as the black American was concerned, began with caste—a definite place preordained in custom, law and religion where all men of black blood must be thrust. To be sure, this caste idea as applied to blacks was no sudden, full grown conception, for the enslavement of the workers was an idea which America inherited from Europe and was not synonymous for many years with the enslavement of the blacks, although the blacks were the chief workers. Men came to the idea of exclusive black slavery by gradually enslaving the workers, as was the world's long custom, and then gradually conceiving certain sorts of work and certain colors of men as necessarily connected. It was, when once set up definitely in the southern slave system, a logically cohering whole which the simplest social philosopher could easily grasp and state. The difficulty was it was too simple to be either just or true. Human nature is not simple and any classification that roughly divides men into good and bad, superior and inferior, slave and free, is and must ever be ludicrously untrue and universally dangerous as a permanent exhaustive classification. So in the southern slave system the thing that from the first damned it was the free Negro—the Negro legally free, the Negro economically free and the Negro spiritually free.

How was the Negro to be treated and conceived of who was legally free? At first with perfect naturalness he was treated as a man—he voted in Massachusetts and in South Carolina, in New York and Virginia; he intermarried with black and white, he claimed and received his civil rights —all this until the caste of color was so turned as to correspond with the caste of work and enslave not only slaves but black men who were not slaves. Even this system, however, was unable to ensure complete economic dependence on the part of all black men; there were continually artisans, foremen and skilled servants who became economically too valuable to be slaves. In vain were laws hurled at Negro intelligence and responsibility; black men continued to hire their time and to steal some smattering of knowledge, and it was this fact that became the gravest menace to the slave system. But even legal and economic freedom was not so dangerous to slavery as the free spirit which continually cropped out among men fated to be slaves: they thought, they dreamed, they aspired, they resisted. In vain were they beaten, sold south and killed, the ranks were continually filled with others and they either led revolt at home or ran away to the North, and these by showing their human qualities continually gave the lie to the slave assumption. Thus it was the free Negro in these manifold phases of his appearance who hastened the economic crisis which killed slavery and who made it impossible to make the caste of work and the caste of color correspond, and who became at once the promise and excuse of those who forced the critical revolution.

To-day in larger cycle and more intricate detail we are passing through certain phases of a similar evolution. To-day we have the caste idea—again not a sudden full grown conception but one being insidiously but consciously and persistently pressed upon the nation. The steps toward it which are being taken are: first, political disfranchisement, then vocational education with the distinct idea of narrowing to the uttermost of the vocations in view, and finally a curtailment of civil freedom of travel, association, and entertainment, in systematic effort to instill contempt and kill self-respect.

Here then is the new slavery of black men in America—a new attempt to make degradation of social condition correspond with certain physical characteristics—not to be sure fully realized as yet, and probably unable for reasons of social development ever to become as systematized as the economic and physical slavery of the past—and yet realized to an extent almost unbelievable by those who have not taken the pains to study the facts—to an extent which makes the lives of thinking black men in this land a perpetual martyrdom.

But right here as in the past stands in the path of this idea the figure of this same thinking black man—this new freedman. This freedman again as in the past presents himself as free in varying phases: there is the free black voter of the North and border states whose power is far more tremendous than even he dare think so that he is afraid to use it; there is the black man who has accomplished economic freedom and who by working himself into the vast industrial development of the nation is to-day accumulating property at a rate that is simply astounding. And finally there is the small but growing number of black men emerging into spiritual freedom and becoming participators and freemen of the kingdom of culture around which it is so singularly difficult to set metes and bounds, and who in art, science and literature are making their modest but ineffaceable mark.

The question is what is the significance of this group of men for the future of the caste programme and for the future social development of America? In order to answer this question intelligently let us retrace our steps and follow more carefully the details of the proposed programme of renewed caste in America. This programme when one comes to define and state it is elusive. There are even those who deny its existence as a definite consciously conceived plan of action. But, certain it is, there is growing unanimity of a peculiar sort on certain matters. And this unanimity is centering about three propositions:

1. That it was a mistake to give Negroes the ballot.
2. That Negroes are essentially an inferior race.
3. That the only permanent settlement of the race problem will be open and legal recognition of this inferiority.

When now a modern nation condemns ten million of its fellows to such a fate it would be supposed that this conclusion has been reluctantly forced upon them after a careful study and weighing of the facts. This, however, is not the case in the Negro problem. On the contrary there has been manifest a singular reluctance and indisposition carefully to study the Negro problem. Ask the average American: Why should the ballot have been withheld from the Negro, and he will answer: "Because he wasn't fit for it." But that is not a sufficient answer: first, because few newly enfranchised groups of the most successful democracies have been fit for the ballot when it was first given, and secondly, because there were Negroes in the United States fit for the ballot in 1870. Moreover the political philosophy that condemns out of hand the Fifteenth Amendment does not often stop to think that the problem before the American nation 1865–1870 was not a simple problem of fixing the qualifications of voters. It was, on the contrary, the immensely more complicated problem of enforcing a vast social and economic revolution on a people determined not to submit to it. Whenever a moral reform is forced on a people from without there ensue complicated and tremendous problems, whether that reform is the correction of the abuse of alcohol, the abolition of child labor or the emancipation of slaves. The enforcement of such a reform will strain every nerve of the nation and the real question is not: Is it a good thing to strain the framework of the nation but rather: Is slavery so dangerous a thing that sudden enfranchisement of the ex-slaves is too great a price to pay for its abolition?

To be sure there are those who profess to think that the white South of its own initiative after the war, with the whole of the wealth, intelligence and law-making power in its hands, would have freely emancipated its slaves in obedience to a decree from Washington, just as there are those who would entrust the regulation of the whiskey traffic to saloon keepers and the bettering of the conditions of child labor to the employers. It is no attack on the South or on saloon keepers or on employers to say that such a reform from such a source is unthinkable. It is simply human nature that men trained to a social system or condition should be the last to be entirely entrusted with its reformation. It was, then, not the Emancipation Proclamation but the Fifteenth Amendment that made slavery impossible in the United States and those that object to the Fifteenth Amendment have simply this question to answer: Which was best, slavery or ignorant Negro voters? The answer is clear as day: Negro voters never did anything as bad as slavery. If they were guilty of all the crimes charged to them by the wildest enemies, even then what they did was less dangerous, less evil and less cruel than the system of slavery whose death knell they struck. And when in addition to this we remember that the black voters of the South established the public schools, gave the poor whites the ballot, modernized the penal code and put on the statute books of the South page after page of legislation that still stands to-day—when we remember this, we have a right to conclude that the Fifteenth Amendment was a wise and far-sighted piece of statesmanship.

But to-day the men who oppose the right of Negroes to vote are no longer doing so on the ground of ignorance, and with good reason, for to-day a majority and an appreciable majority of the black men of the South twenty-one years of age and over can read and write. In other words, the bottom has been clean knocked out of their ignorance argument and yet the fact has elicited scarcely a loud remark.

Indeed we black men are continually puzzled by the easy almost unconscious way in which our detractors change their ground. Before emancipation it was stated and reiterated with bitter emphasis and absolute confidence that a free Negro would prove to be a shiftless scamp, a barbarian and a cannibal reverting to savagery and doomed to death. We forget to-day that from 1830 to 1860 there was not a statement made by the masters of slaves more often reiterated than this, and more dogmatically and absolutely stated. After emancipation, for twenty years and more, so many people looked for the fulfilment of the prophecy that many actually saw it and we heard and kept hearing and now and then still hear that the Negro to-day is worse off than in slavery days. Then, as this statement grew less and less plausible, its place came to be taken by other assumptions. When a Louisiana senator saw the first Negro school he stopped and said: "This is the climax of foolishness!" The Negro could not be educated—he could imitate like a parrot but real mental development was impossible.

Then, when Negroes did learn some things, it was said that education spoiled them; they can learn but it does them no practical good; the young educated Negroes become criminals—they neither save nor work, they are shiftless and lazy. Now to-day are coming uncomfortable facts for this theory. The generation now working and saving its post-bellum and yet no sooner does it come on the stage than accumulated property goes on at an accelerated pace so far as we have measurements. In Georgia the increase of property among Negroes in the last ten years has been 83%. But no sooner do facts like these come to the fore than again the ground of opposition subtly shifts and this last shifting has been so gradual and so insidious that the Negro and his friends are still answering arguments that are no longer being pushed. The most subtle enemies of democracy and the most persistent advocates of the color line admit almost contemptuously most that their forebears strenuously denied: the Negroes have progressed since slavery, they are accumulating some property, some of them work readily and they are susceptible of elementary training; but, they say, all thought of treating black men like white men must be abandoned. They are an inferior stock of men, limited in attainment by nature. You cannot legislate against nature, and philanthropy is powerless against deficient cerebral development.

To realize the full weight of this argument recall to mind a character like John Brown and contrast his attitude with the attitude of to-day. John Brown loved his neighbor as himself. He could not endure, therefore, to see his neighbor poor, unfortunate or oppressed. This natural sympathy was strengthened by a saturation in Hebrew religion which stressed the personal responsibility of every man's soul to a just God. To this religion of equality and sympathy with misfortune, was added the strong influence of the social doctrines of the French Revolution with its emphasis on freedom and power in political life. And on all this was built John Brown's own inchoate but growing belief in a juster and more equal distribution of property. From all this John Brown concluded—and acted on that conclusion—that all men were created free and equal and that the cost of liberty was less than the price of repression. Up to the time of John Brown's death this doctrine was a growing, conquering social thing. Since then there has come a change and many would rightly find reason for that change in the coincidence that the year John Brown suffered martyrdom was the year that first published the Origin of Species. Since that day tremendous scientific and economic advance has been accompanied by distinct signs of moral change in social philosophy; strong arguments have been made for the fostering of war, the social utility of human degradation and disease, and the inevitable and known inferiority of certain classes and races of men. While such arguments have not stopped the efforts of the advocates of peace, the workers for social uplift and the believers in human brotherhood, they have, it must be confessed, often made their voices falter and tinged their arguments with apology.

Why is this? It is because the splendid scientific work of Darwin, Weissman, Galton and others has been widely and popularly interpreted as meaning that there is such essential and inevitable inequality among men and races of men as no philanthropy can or ought to eliminate; that civilization is a struggle for existence whereby the weaker nations and individuals will gradually succumb and the strong will inherit the earth. With this interpretation has gone the silent assumption that the white European stock represents the strong surviving peoples and that the swarthy, yellow and black peoples are the ones rightly doomed to eventual extinction.

One can easily see what influence such a doctrine would have on the race problem in America. It meant moral revolution in the attitude of the

nation. Those that stepped into the pathway marked by the early abolitionists faltered and large numbers turned back. They said: They were
good men—even great, but they have no message for us to-day—John
Brown was a "belated covenanter," William Lloyd Garrison was an
anachronism in the age of Darwin—men who gave their lives to lift not
the unlifted but the unliftable. We have, consequently, the present reaction—a reaction which says in effect: Keep these black people in their
places, and do not attempt to treat a Negro simply as a white man with a
black face; to do this would mean moral deterioration of the race and
nation—a fate against which a divine racial prejudice is successfully fighting. This is the attitude of the larger portion of the thinking nation to-
day.

It is not, however, an attitude that has brought mental rest or social
peace. On the contrary, it is to-day involving a degree of moral strain and
political and social anomaly that gives the wisest pause. The chief difficulty has been that the natural place in which, by scientific law, the black
race in America should stay cannot easily be determined. To be sure, the
freedmen did not, as the philanthropists of the sixties apparently expected,
step in forty years from slavery to nineteenth century civilization. Neither,
on the other hand, did they, as the ex-masters confidently predicted, retro-
grade and die. Contrary to both these views, they chose a third and apparently quite unawaited way: from the great, sluggish, almost imperceptibly
moving mass they sent off larger and larger numbers of faithful workmen
and artisans, some merchants and professional men, and even men of educational ability and discernment. They developed in a generation no world
geniuses, no millionaires, no captains of industry, no artists of first rank;
but they did in forty years get rid of the larger part of their illiteracy,
accumulate a half billion of property in small homesteads and gained now
and then respectful attention in the world's ears and eyes. It has been
argued that this progress of the black man in America is due to the exceptional men among them and does not measure the ability of the mass.
Such admission is, however, fatal to the whole argument. If the doomed
races of men are going to develop exceptions to the rule of inferiority then
no law, scientific or moral, should or can proscribe the race as such.

To meet this difficulty in racial philosophy a step has been taken in
America fraught with the gravest social consequences to the world and
threatening not simply the political but the moral integrity of the nation:
that step is to deny in the case of black men the validity of those evidences
of culture, ability and decency which are accepted unquestioningly in the
case of other people, and by vague assertion, unprovable assumption, unjust emphasis, and now and then by deliberate untruth, to secure not only
the continued proscription of these people, but by caste distinction to shut
in the faces of their rising classes many of the paths to further advance.

When a social policy based on a supposed scientific sanction leads to
such a moral anomaly it is time to examine rather carefully the logical

foundations of the argument. And so soon as we do this many things are clear. First, assuming that there are certain stocks of human beings whose elimination the best welfare of the world demands; it is certainly questionable if these stocks include the majority of mankind and it is indefensible and monstrous to pretend that we know to-day with any reasonable certainty which these stocks are. We can point to degenerate individuals and families here and there among all races, but there is not the slightest warrant for assuming that there do not exist among the Chinese and Hindus, the African Bantus and American Indians as lofty possibilities of human culture as any European race has ever exhibited. It is, to be sure, puzzling to know why the Soudan should linger a thousand years in culture behind the valley of the Seine, but it is no more puzzling than the fact that the valley of the Thames was miserably backward as compared with the banks of the Tiber. Climate, human contact, facilities of communication, and what we call accident have played great part in the rise of culture among nations: to ignore these and to assert dogmatically that the present distribution of culture is a fair index of the distribution of human ability and desert is to make an assertion for which there is not the slightest scientific warrant.

What the age of Darwin has done is to add to the eighteenth century idea of individual worth the complementary idea of physical immortality of the human race. And this, far from annulling or contracting the idea of human freedom, rather emphasizes its necessity and eternal possibility— the boundlessness and endlessness of possible human achievement. Freedom has come to mean not individual caprice or aberration but social self-realization in an endless chain of selves, and freedom for such development is not the denial but the central assertion of the evolutionary theory. So, too, the doctrine of human equality passed through the fire of scientific inquiry not obliterated but transfigured; not equality of present attainment but equality of opportunity for unbounded future attainment is the rightful demand of mankind.

What now does the present hegemony of the white races threaten? It threatens by the means of brute force a survival of some of the worst stocks of mankind. It attempts to people the best part of the earth and put in absolute authority over the rest not only, and indeed not mainly, the culture of Europe, but its greed and degradation—not only some representatives of the best stocks of the west end of London, upper New York and the Champs Elysées but also, and in as large, if not larger, numbers, the worst stocks of Whitechapel, the East Side and Montmartre; and it attempts to make the slums of white society in all cases and under all circumstances the superior of any colored group, no matter what its ability or culture; it attempts to put the intelligent, property holding, efficient Negroes of the South under the heels and at the absolute mercy of such constituencies as Tillman, Vardaman and Jeff Davis represent.

To be sure, this outrageous programme of wholesale human degenera-

tion is not outspoken yet save in the backward civilizations of the southern
United States, South Africa and Australia. But its enunciation is listened to
with respect and tolerance in England, Germany and the northern states
and nowhere with more equanimity than right here in New York by those
very persons who accuse philanthropy with seeking to degenerate white
blood by an infiltration of colored strains. And the average citizen is voting ships and guns to carry out this programme.

This movement gathered force and strength during the latter half of
the nineteenth century and reached its culmination when France, Germany and England and Russia began the partition of China and the East.
With the sudden self-assertion of Japan its wildest dreams collapsed, but
it is still to-day a living, virile, potent force and motive, and the most
subtle and dangerous enemy of world peace and the dream of human
brotherhood. It has a whole vocabulary of its own: the strong races, superior peoples, race preservation, the struggle for survival and a peculiar use
of the word "white." And by this it means the right of white men of any
kind to club blacks into submission, to make them surrender their wealth
and the use of their women, and to submit to the dictation of white men
without murmur, for the sake of being swept off the fairest portions of the
earth or held there in perpetual serfdom or guardianship. Ignoring the
fact that the era of physical struggle for survival has passed away among
human beings and that there is plenty of room accessible on earth for all,
this theory makes the possession of Krupp guns the main criterion of mental stamina and moral fitness.

Even armed with this morality of the club and every advantage of modern culture, the white races have been unable to possess the earth; many
signs of degeneracy have appeared among them; their birthrate is falling,
their average ability is not increasing, their physical stamina is impaired,
their social condition is not reassuring, and their religion is a growing
mass of transparent and self-confessed hypocrisy. Lacking the physical
ability to take possession of the world, they are to-day fencing in America,
Australia, and South Africa and declaring that no dark race shall occupy
or develop the land which they themselves are unable to use. And all this
on the plea that their stock is threatened with deterioration from without,
when in fact its most dangerous fate is deterioration from within. We are
in fact to-day repeating in our intercourse between races all the former
evils of class injustice, unequal taxation and rigid caste. Individual nations
outgrew these fatal things by breaking down the horizontal barriers between classes. We are bringing them back by seeking to erect vertical
barriers between races. Men were told that abolition of compulsory class
distinction meant leveling down, degradation, disappearance of culture
and genius, and the triumph of the mob. As a matter of fact, it has been
the salvation of European civilization. Some deterioration and leveling
there was, but it was more than balanced by the discovery of new reser-
voirs of ability and strength. So to-day we are told that free racial contact

—or "social equality" as southern *patois* has it—means contamination of blood and lowering of ability and culture. It need mean nothing of the sort. Abolition of class distinction does not mean universal intermarriage of stocks, but rather the survival of the fittest by peaceful personal and social selection, a selection all the more effective because free democracy and equality of opportunity allow the best to rise to their rightful place.

The same is true in racial contact. The abolition of the lines of vertical race distinction and their tearing away involves fewer chances of degradation and greater opportunities of human betterment than in the case of class lines. On the other hand, the persistence in racial distinctions spells disaster sooner or later. The earth is growing smaller and more accessible. Race contact will become in the future increasingly inevitable, not only in America, Asia and Africa, but even in Europe. The color line will mean not simply a return to the absurdities of class as exhibited in the sixteenth and seventeenth centuries, but even to the caste of ancient days. This, however, the Japanese, the Chinese, the East Indian and the Negroes are going to resent in just such proportion as they gain the power; and they are gaining the power, and they cannot be kept from gaining more power. The price of repression will then be hypocrisy and slavery and blood.

This is the problem of to-day, and what is its mighty answer? It is this great word: The cost of liberty is less than the price of repression. The price of repressing the world's darker races is shown in a moral retrogression and economic waste unparalleled since the age of the African slave trade. What would be the cost of liberty? What would be the cost of giving the great stocks of mankind every reasonable help and incentive to self-development—opening the avenues of opportunity freely, spreading knowledge, suppressing war and cheating, and treating men and women as equals the world over whenever and wherever they attain equality? It would cost something. It would cost something in pride and prejudice, for eventually many a white man would be blacking black men's boots; but this cost we may ignore—its greatest cost would be the new problems of racial intercourse and intermarriage which would come to the front. Freedom and equal opportunity in this respect would inevitably bring some intermarriage of whites and yellows and browns and blacks. If such marriages are proven inadvisable how could they be stopped? Easily. We associate with cats and cows but we do not fear intermarriage with them even though they be given all freedom of development. So, too, intelligent human beings can be trained to breed intelligently without the degradation of such of their fellows as they may not wish to breed with. In the southern United States on the contrary it is assumed that unwise marriage can only be stopped by the degradation of the blacks, the classing of their women with prostitutes, the loading the whole race with every badge of public isolation, degradation and contempt and by burning offenders at the stake.

Is this civilization? No. The civilized method of preventing ill-advised marriage lies in the training of mankind in ethics of sex and childbearing. We cannot ensure the survival of the best blood by the public murder and degradation of unworthy suitors, but we can substitute a civilized human selection of husbands and wives which shall ensure the survival of the fittest. Not the methods of the jungle, not even the careless choices of the drawing room, but the thoughtful selection of the schools and laboratory is the ideal of future marriage. This will cost something in ingenuity, self-control, and toleration but it will cost less than forcible repression.

Not only is the cost of repression to-day large—it is a continually increasing cost, because of the fact that furnished the fatal moral anomaly against which physical slavery could not stand—the free Negro—the Negro who in spite of contempt, discouragement, caste and poverty has put himself on a plane where it is simply impossible to deny that he is by every legitimate measurement the equal of his average white neighbor. The former argument was as I have mentioned that no such class existed. This assertion was persisted in until it became ludicrous. To-day the fashion is come to regard this class as exceptional so far as the logic of the Negro problem is concerned, dangerous so far as social peace is concerned, and its existence more than offset by an abnormal number of criminals, degenerates and defectives.

Right here, then, comes the center of the present problem, namely: What is the *truth* about this? What are the real facts? How far is Negro crime due to inherited and growing viciousness and how far to poverty, degradation and systematic oppression?

How far is Negro labor lazy and how far is it the listless victim of systematic theft?

How far is the Negro woman lewd and how far the helpless victim of social custom?

How far are Negro children being educated to-day in the public schools of the South and how far is the effort to curtail that training increasingly successful?

How far are Negroes leaving the farms and rushing to the cities to escape work and how far to escape slavery?

How far is this race designated as Negroes the descendants of African slaves and how far is it descended from the most efficient white blood of the nation?

What does actual physical and social measurement prove as to the status of these descendants of black men?

All these are fundamental questions. Not a single valid conclusion as to the future can be absolutely insisted upon without definite skilful scientific answers to these questions and yet not a single systematic effort to answer these questions on an adequate scale has been made in these United States from 1619 to 1909. Not only this but on all sides opposition ranging from indifference and reluctance to actual force is almost universal when any attempt to study the Negro problem adequately is proposed. Yet in spite of this universal and deliberate ignorance the demand is made that one line of solution, which a number of good men have assumed is safe and sane, shall be accepted by everybody and particularly by thinking black men. The penalty for not accepting this programme is to be dubbed a radical, a busy-body, an impatient dreamer and a dangerous agitator. Yet this programme involves justification of disfranchisement, the personal humiliation of Jim-Crowism, a curtailed and purposely limited system of education and a virtual acknowledgment of the inevitable and universal inferiority of black men. And then in the face of this we are asked to look pleasant and do our very best. I think it is the most cowardly dilemma that a strong people ever thrust upon the weak. And I for one have protested and do protest and shall protest that in my humble opinion the assumption is an outrageous falsehood dictated by selfishness, cowardice and greed and for the righteousness of my cause and the proof of my assertions, I appeal to one arbitrament and one alone and that is: THE TRUTH —1909.

PART IV

❧ ▣ ☙

The Revival of Political Nationalism

MARCUS GARVEY

(1887–1940)

Born in Jamaica, Garvey came to New York in 1917 where he founded the Universal Negro Improvement Association and the Negro World, *a weekly paper that was the vehicle for his views. Garvey envisaged and propagandized for a free Africa to which Negroes might emigrate. He also founded the Negro Factories Corporation and the Black Star Steamship Line. Because of erratic and amateur financing of these organizations Garvey was jailed upon the charge of using the mails to defraud. This broke the movement. After his release in 1927, he was deported to Jamaica. His writings in the* Negro World *have been collected in* Philosophy and Opinions of Marcus Garvey, or Africa for the Africans, *compiled by Amy-Jacques Garvey, 1925.*

RACE ASSIMILATION

Some Negro leaders have advanced the belief that in another few years the white people will make up their minds to assimilate their black populations; thereby sinking all racial prejudice in the welcoming of the black race into the social companionship of the white. Such leaders further believe that by the amalgamation of black and white, a new type will spring up, and that type will become the American and West Indian of the future.

This belief is preposterous. I believe that white men should be white, yellow men should be yellow, and black men should be black in the great panorama of races, until each and every race by its own initiative lifts itself up to the common standard of humanity, as to compel the respect and appreciation of all, and so make it possible for each one to stretch out the hand of welcome without being able to be prejudiced against the other because of any inferior and unfortunate condition.

The white man of America will not, to any organized extent, assimilate the Negro, because in so doing, he feels that he will be committing racial suicide. This he is not prepared to do. It is true he illegitimately carries on a system of assimilation; but such assimilation, as practised, is one that he is not prepared to support because he becomes prejudiced against his own offspring, if that offspring is the product of black and white; hence, to the white man the question of racial differences is eternal. So long as Negroes occupy an inferior position among the races and nations of the world, just so long will others be prejudiced against them, because it will be profitable for them to keep up their system of superiority. But when the Negro by his own initiative lifts himself from his low state to the highest human standard he will be in a position to stop begging and praying, and demand a place that no individual, race or nation will be able to deny him—1922.

THE TRUE SOLUTION OF
THE NEGRO PROBLEM

As far as Negroes are concerned, in America we have the problem of lynching, peonage and dis-franchisement.

In the West Indies, South and Central America we have the problem of peonage, serfdom, industrial and political governmental inequality.

In Africa we have, not only peonage and serfdom, but outright slavery, racial exploitation and alien political monopoly.

We cannot allow a continuation of these crimes against our race. As four hundred million men, women and children, worthy of the existence given us by the Divine Creator, we are determined to solve our own problem, by redeeming our Motherland Africa from the hands of alien exploiters and found there a government, a nation of our own, strong enough to lend protection to the members of our race scattered all over the world, and to compel the respect of the nations and races of the earth.

Do they lynch Englishmen, Frenchmen, Germans or Japanese? No. And Why? Because these people are represented by great governments, mighty nations and empires, strongly organized. Yes, and ever ready to shed the last drop of blood and spend the last penny in the national treasury to protect the honor and integrity of a citizen outraged anywhere.

Until the Negro reaches this point of national independence, all he does as a race will count for naught, because the prejudice that will stand out against him even with his ballot in his hand, with his industrial progress to show, will be of such an overwhelming nature as to perpetuate mob violence and mob rule, from which he will suffer, and which he will not be able to stop with his industrial wealth and with his ballot.

You may argue that he can use his industrial wealth and his ballot to force the government to recognize him, but he must understand that the government is the people. That the majority of the people dictate the policy of governments, and if the majority are against a measure, a thing, or a race, then the government is impotent to protect that measure, thing or race.

If the Negro were to live in this Western Hemisphere for another five hundred years he would still be outnumbered by other races who are prejudiced against him. He cannot resort to the government for protection for government will be in the hands of the majority of the people who are prejudiced against him, hence for the Negro to depend on the ballot and his industrial progress alone, will be hopeless as it does not help him when he is lynched, burned, jim-crowed and segregated. The future of the Negro therefore, outside of Africa, spells ruin and disaster—**1922.**

AN APPEAL TO THE SOUL
OF WHITE AMERICA

> Blessed are the peacemakers; for they
> shall be called the children of God.
> MATT. V. 9.

Surely the soul of liberal, philanthropic, liberty-loving, white America is not dead.

It is true that the glamor of materialism has, to a great degree, destroyed the innocence and purity of the national conscience, but, still, beyond our politics, beyond our soulless industrialism, there is a deep feeling of human sympathy that touches the soul of white America, upon which the unfortunate and sorrowful can always depend for sympathy, help and action.

It is to that feeling that I appeal for four hundred million Negroes of the world, and fifteen millions of America in particular.

There is no real white man in America, who does not desire a solution of the Negro problem. Each thoughtful citizen has probably his own idea of how the vexed question of races should be settled. To some the Negro could be gotten rid of by wholesale butchery, by lynching, by economic starvation, by a return to slavery, and legalized oppression, while others would have the problem solved by seeing the race all herded together and kept somewhere among themselves; but a few—those in whom they have an interest—should be allowed to live around as the wards of a mistaken philanthropy; yet, none so generous as to desire to see the Negro elevated to a standard of real progress and prosperity, welded into a homogeneous whole, creating of themselves a mighty nation, with proper systems of government, civilization and culture, to mark them admissible to the fraternities of nations and races without any disadvantage.

I do not desire to offend the finer feelings and sensibilities of those white friends of the race who really believe that they are kind and considerate to us as a people; but I feel it my duty to make a real appeal to conscience and not to belief. Conscience is solid, convicting and permanently demonstrative; belief is only a matter of opinion, changeable by superior reasoning. Once the belief was that it was fit and proper to hold the Negro as a slave, and in this the bishop, priest and layman agreed. Later on, they changed their belief or opinion, but at all times, the conscience of certain people dictated to them that it was wrong and inhuman to hold human beings as slaves. It is to such a conscience in white America that I am addressing myself.

Negroes are human beings—the peculiar and strange opinions of writers, ethnologists, philosophers, scientists and anthropologists notwithstanding. They have feelings, souls, passions, ambitions, desires, just as other men, hence they must be considered.

Has white America really considered the Negro in the light of permanent human progress? The answer is NO.

Men and women of the white race, do you know what is going to happen if you do not think and act now? One of two things. You are either going to deceive and keep the Negro in your midst until you have perfectly completed your wonderful American civilization with its progress of art, science, industry and politics, and then, jealous of your own success and achievements in those directions, and with the greater jealousy of seeing your race pure and unmixed, cast him off to die in the whirlpool of economic starvation, thus getting rid of another race that was not intelligent enough to live, or, you simply mean by the largeness of your hearts to assimilate fifteen million Negroes into the social fraternity of an American race, that will neither be white nor black! Don't be alarmed! We must prevent both consequences. No real race loving white man wants to destroy the purity of his race, and no real Negro conscious of himself, wants to die, hence there is room for an understanding, and an adjustment. And that is just what we seek.

Let white and black stop deceiving themselves. Let the white race stop thinking that all black men are dogs and not to be considered as human beings. Let foolish Negro agitators and so-called reformers, encouraged by deceptive or unthinking white associates, stop preaching and advocating the doctrine of "social equality," meaning thereby the social intermingling of both races, intermarriages, and general social co-relationship. The two extremes will get us nowhere, other than breeding hate, and encouraging discord, which will eventually end disastrously to the weaker race.

Some Negroes, in the quest of position and honor, have been admitted to the full enjoyment of their constitutional rights. Thus we have some of our men filling high and responsible government positions, others, on their own account, have established themselves in the professions, commerce and industry. This, the casual onlooker, and even the men themselves, will say carries a guarantee and hope of social equality, and permanent racial progress. But this is the mistake. There is no progress of the Negro in America that is permanent, so long as we have with us the monster evil—prejudice.

Prejudice we shall always have between black and white, so long as the latter believes that the former is intruding upon their rights. So long as white laborers believe that black laborers are taking and holding their jobs, so long as white artisans believe that black artisans are performing the work that they should do; so long as white men and women believe that black men and women are filling the positions that they covet; so long as white political leaders and statesmen believe that black politicians and statesmen are seeking the same positions in the nation's government; so long as white men believe that black men want to associate with, and marry white women, then we will ever have prejudice, and not only prejudice, but riots, lynchings, burnings, and God to tell what next will follow!

It is this danger that drives me mad. It must be prevented. We cannot allow white and black to drift along unthinkingly toward this great gulf and danger, that is nationally ahead of us. It is because of this that I speak, and now call upon the soul of great white America to help.

It is no use putting off. The work must be done, and it must be started now.

Some people have misunderstood me. Some don't want to understand me. But I must explain myself for the good of the world and humanity.

Those of the Negro race who preach social equality, and who are working for an American race that will, in complexion, be neither white nor black, have tried to misinterpret me to the white public, and create prejudice against my work. The white public, not stopping to analyze and question the motive behind criticisms and attacks, aimed against new leaders and their movements, condemn without even giving a chance to the criticised, to be heard. Those of my own race who oppose me because I refuse to endorse their program of social arrogance and social equality, gloat over the fact that by their misrepresentation and underhand methods, they were able to have me convicted and imprisoned for crime which they calculate will so discredit me as to destroy the movement that I represent, in opposition to their program of a new American race; but we will not now consider the opposition to a program or a movement, but state the facts as they are, and let deep souled white America pass its own judgment.

In another one hundred years white America will have doubled its population; in another two hundred years it will have trebled itself. The keen student must realize that the centuries ahead will bring us an overcrowded country; opportunities, as the population grows larger, will be fewer; the competition for bread between the people of their own class will become keener, and so much more so will there be no room for two competitive races, the one strong, and the other weak. To imagine Negroes as district attorneys, judges, senators, congressmen, assemblymen, aldermen, government clerks and officials, artisans and laborers at work, while millions of white men starve, is to have before you the bloody picture of wholesale mob violence that I fear, and against which I am working.

No preaching, no praying, no presidential edict will control the passion of hungry unreasoning men of prejudice when the hour comes. It will not come, I pray, in our generation, but it is of the future that I think and for which I work.

A generation of ambitious Negro men and women, out from the best colleges, universities and institutions, capable of filling the highest and best positions in the nation, in industry, commerce, society and politics! Can you keep them back? If you do so they will agitate and throw your constitution in your faces. Can you stand before civilization and deny the truth of your constitution? What are you going to do then? You who are just will open the door of opportunity and say to all and sundry, "Enter in." But, ladies and gentlemen, what about the mob, that starving crowd of your own race? Will they stand by, suffer and starve, and allow an opposite, competitive race to prosper in the midst of their distress? If you can conjure these things up in your mind, then you have the vision of the race problem of the future in America.

There is but one solution, and that is to provide an outlet for Negro energy, ambition, and passion, away from the attractions of white opportunity and surround the race with opportunities of its own. If this is not done, and if the foundation for same is not laid now, then the consequence will be sorrowful for the weaker race, and disgraceful to our ideals of justice, and shocking to our civilization.

The Negro must have a country and a nation of his own. If you laugh at the idea, then you are selfish and wicked, for you and your children do not intend that the Negro shall discommode you in yours. If you do not want him to have a country and a nation of his own; if you do not intend to give him equal opportunities in yours, then it is plain to see that you mean that he must die, even as the Indian, to make room for your generations.

Why should the Negro die? Has he not served America and the world? Has he not borne the burden of civilization in this Western world for three hundred years? Has he not contributed of his best to America? Surely all this stands to his credit. But there will not be enough room and the one answer is "find a place." We have found a place; it is Africa, and as black men for three centuries have helped white men build America, surely generous and grateful white men will help black men build Africa.

And why shouldn't Africa and America travel down the ages as protectors of human rights and guardians of democracy? Why shouldn't black men help white men secure and establish universal peace? We can only have peace when we are just to all mankind; and for that peace, and for the reign of universal love, I now appeal to the soul of white America. Let the Negroes have a government of their own. Don't encourage them to believe that they will become social equals and leaders of the whites in America, without first on their own account proving to the world that they are capable of evolving a civilization of their own. The white race can best help the Negro by telling him the truth and not by flattering him into believing that he is as good as any white man without first proving the racial, national, constructive metal of which he is made.

Stop flattering the Negro about social equality, and tell him to go to work and build for himself. Help him in the direction of doing for himself, and let him know that self-progress brings its own reward.

I appeal to the considerate and thoughtful conscience of white America not to condemn the cry of the Universal Negro Improvement Association for a nation in Africa for Negroes, but to give us a chance to explain ourselves to the world. White America is too big, and when informed and touched, too liberal, to turn down the cry of the awakened Negro for "a place in the sun"—1923.

RACIAL REFORMS AND REFORMERS

Who thinks of the poor but the poor? The rich and self-satisfied are too busily engaged in the enjoyment of their own pleasures, and the patronage of their own class, to halt to any great extent to give the underdogs of human society a thought that would help them rise above their condition.

The missionary work that is being done to lift the unfortunate to the height of a new social order is surrounded with hypocrisy and professionalism; hence, its usefulness is not seen or felt among those to be served.

As in the struggle to lift the unfortunate poor we have no real, honest effort; so, in the struggle of race to find a place in the affairs of the world, we get very little, if any, sympathy and encouragement from the progressive and successful.

There is a vast difference between the white and black races. The two are at extremes. One is dazzlingly prosperous and progressive; the other is abjectly poor and backward.

The fight is to lift the backward and non-progressive to the common standard of progress and civilization; but, apparently, no appreciable number of the prosperous and progressive desire this change. The selfishness of class and monopoly of standing seem to dictate a prejudice of race that creates a barrier to the accepted Christian belief that all men are brothers, and a God is our common Father.

In this conflict of life each human being finds a calling. Some of us are called to be preachers, ministers of the Gospel, politicians, statesmen, industrialists, teachers, philosophers, laborers and reformers. To the reformer, above all, falls the duty or obligation of improving human society, not to the good of the selfish few, but to the benefit of the greatest number. . . .

And it is here that we must call the attention of the white race to the wrong and injury that they are inflicting upon the rest of the world. It is all well for those who revel in their immediate power to turn a deaf ear to the cries of the suffering races, to oppress, exploit, and even murder them, but what of the consequence? . . .

If the great statesmen and religious leaders of the world would only forget the selfishness of their own races, and call their conferences and give out their edicts not from the Anglo-Saxon, Teutonic, Celtic or Anglo-American point of view, but from the view of all humanity considered, then we would indeed come face to face with a new world evolving a new civilization.

Friends, white cannot prosper to the disadvantage of black. Yellow cannot prosper to the disadvantage of brown, for in so doing we but pile up confusion and remorse for our children. This is history; it tells the tales of the past, it will of the future. Then why not make the future right? . . .

There is a fraternity of humanitarians, unknown though it be, that is working for a true solution of our human problems. Wilberforce, Clarkston, Buxton, Lovejoy, John Brown, white though they were, had the vision of the future of men. They worked for the freedom of black humanity, therefore, in the midst of our sorrow and in the racial thought of revenge come up the spirits of such great humanitarians that silence the tongue of evil; as in the white race, so among the blacks, our beautiful spirits stand out, for wasn't there a Douglass, a Washington and even the typical Uncle Tom?

We hope that the humanitarians of today of all races will continue to work in furtherance of that ideal—justice, liberty, freedom and true human independence, knowing thereby no color or no race.

The Negro of the world, and America in particular, needs a national homeland with opportunities and privileges like all other peoples. If we work and fight for this why should others jeer and laugh at us? Why should they say that we are "ignorant" and "benighted"? Was it ignorance to free Britain from the grasp of the invader? Was it ignorance to free America from the heel of the oppressor? Was it ignorance to liberate France from the yoke of the tyrant? Surely not. Then why is it ignorant for Negroes to work for the restoration of their country, Africa?

Broad and liberal-minded white men, although surrounded by the selfishness of a material environment, will not condemn and persecute the work of even black reform, but for justice's sake give unto each and everyone his due—**1923**.

WHO AND WHAT IS A NEGRO?

The New York World under date of January 15, 1923, published a statement of Drs. Clark Wissler and Franz Boaz (the latter a professor of anthropology at Columbia University), confirming the statement of the French that Moroccan and Algerian troops used in the invasion of Germany were not to be classified as Negroes, because they were not of that race. How the French and these gentlemen arrive at such a conclusion is marvelous to understand, but I feel it is the old-time method of depriving the Negro of anything that would tend to make him recognized in any useful occupation or activity.

The custom of these anthropologists is whenever a black man, whether he be Moroccan, Algerian, Senegalese or what not, accomplishes anything of importance, he is no longer a Negro. The question, therefore, suggests itself, "Who and what is a Negro?" The answer is, "A Negro is a person of dark complexion or race, who has not accomplished anything and to whom others are not obligated for any useful service." If the Moroccans and Algerians were not needed by France at this time to augment their occupation of Germany or to save the French nation from extinction, they would have been called Negroes as usual, but now that they have rendered themselves useful to the higher appreciation of France they are no longer members of the Negro race, but can be classified among a higher type as made out by the two professors above mentioned. Whether these professors or France desire to make the Moroccans other than Negroes we are satisfied that their propaganda before has made these people to understand that their destiny is linked up with all other men of color throughout the world, and now that the hundreds of millions of darker peoples are looking toward one common union and destiny through the effort of universal cooperation, we have no fear that the Moroccans and Algerians will take care of the situation in France and Germany peculiar to the interest of Negroes throughout the world.

Let us not be flattered by white anthropologists and statesmen who, from time to time, because of our success here, there or anywhere, try to make out that we are no longer members of the Negro race. If we were Negroes when we were down under the heel of oppression then we will be Negroes when we are up and liberated from such thraldom.

The Moroccans and Algerians have a splendid opportunity of proving the real worth of the Negro in Europe, and who to tell that one day Africa will colonize Europe, even as Europe has been endeavoring to colonize the world for hundreds of years.

NEGROES ROBBED OF THEIR HISTORY

The white world has always tried to rob and discredit us of our history. They tell us that Tut-Ankh-Amen, a King of Egypt, who reigned about the year 1350 B. C. (before Christ), was not a Negro, that the ancient civilization of Egypt and the Pharaohs was not of our race, but that does not make the truth unreal. Every student of history, of impartial mind, knows that the Negro once ruled the world, when white men were savages and barbarians living in caves; that thousands of Negro professors at that time taught in the universities in Alexandria, then the seat of learning; that ancient Egypt gave to the world civilization and that Greece and Rome have robbed Egypt of her arts and letters, and taken all the credit to themselves. It is not surprising, however, that white men should resort to every means to keep Negroes in ignorance of their history, it would be a great shock to their pride to admit to the world today that 3,000 years ago black men excelled in government and were the founders and teachers of art, science and literature. The power and sway we once held passed away, but now in the twentieth century we are about to see a return of it in the rebuilding of Africa; yes, a new civilization, a new culture, shall spring up from among our people, and the Nile shall once more flow through the land of science, of art, and of literature, wherein will live black men of the highest learning and the highest accomplishments.

Professor George A. Kersnor, head of the Harvard-Boston expedition to the Egyptian Soudan, returned to America early in 1923 and, after describing the genius of the Ethiopians and their high culture during the period of 750 B. C. to 350 A. D. in middle Africa, he declared the Ethiopians were not African Negroes. He described them as dark colored races . . . showing a mixture of black blood. Imagine a dark colored man in middle Africa being anything else but a Negro. Some white men, whether they be professors or what not, certainly have a wide stretch of imagination. The above statements of the professors support my contention at all times that the prejudice against us as Negroes is not because of color, but because of our condition. If black men throughout the world as a race will render themselves so independent and useful as to be sought out by other race groups it will simply mean that all the problems of race will be smashed to pieces and the Negro would be regarded like anybody else—a man to be respected and admired—**January 16, 1923.**

AN APPEAL TO THE
CONSCIENCE OF THE BLACK RACE
TO SEE ITSELF

It is said to be a hard and difficult task to organize and keep together large numbers of the Negro race for the common good. Many have tried to congregate us, but have failed, the reason being that our characteristics are such as to keep us more apart than together.

The evil of internal division is wrecking our existence as a people, and if we do not seriously and quickly move in the direction of a readjustment it simply means that our doom becomes imminently conclusive.

For years the Universal Negro Improvement Association has been working for the unification of our race, not on domestic-national lines only, but universally. The success which we have met in the course of our effort is rather encouraging, considering the time consumed and the environment surrounding the object of our concern.

It seems that the whole world of sentiment is against the Negro, and the difficulty of our generation is to extricate ourselves from the prejudice that hides itself beneath, as well as above, the action of an international environment.

Prejudice is conditional on many reasons, and it is apparent that the Negro supplies, consciously or unconsciously, all the reasons by which the world seems to ignore and avoid him. No one cares for a leper, for lepers are infectious persons, and all are afraid of the disease, so, because the Negro keeps himself poor, helpless and undemonstrative, it is natural also that no one wants to be of him or with him.

PROGESS AND HUMANITY

Progress is the attraction that moves humanity, and to whatever people or race this "modern virtue" attaches itself, there will you find the splendor of pride and self-esteem that never fail to win the respect and admiration of all.

It is the progress of the Anglo-Saxons that singles them out for the respect of all the world. When their race had no progress or achievement to its credit, then, like all other inferior peoples, they paid the price in slavery, bondage, as well as through prejudice. We cannot forget the time when even the ancient Briton was regarded as being too dull to make a good Roman slave, yet today the influence of that race rules the world.

It is the industrial and commercial progress of America that causes Europe and the rest of the world to think appreciatively of the Anglo-American race. It is not because one hundred and ten million people live in the United States that the world is attracted to the republic with so much reverence and respect—a reverence and respect not shown to India with its three hundred millions, or to China with its four hundred millions. Progress of and among any people will advance them in the respect and appreciation of the rest of their fellows. It is such a progress that the Negro must attach to himself if he is to rise above the prejudice of the world.

The reliance of our race upon the progress and achievements of others for a consideration in sympathy, justice and rights is like a dependence upon a broken stick, resting upon which will eventually consign you to the ground.

SELF-RELIANCE AND RESPECT

The Universal Negro Improvement Association teaches our race self-help and self-reliance, not only in one essential, but in all those things that contribute to human happiness and well-being. The disposition of the many to depend upon the other races for a kindly and sympathetic consideration of their needs, without making the effort to do for themselves, has been the race's standing disgrace by which we have been judged and through which we have created the strongest prejudice against ourselves.

There is no force like success, and that is why the individual makes all efforts to surround himself throughout life with the evidence of it. As of the individual, so should it be of the race and nation. The glittering success of Rockefeller makes him a power in the American nation; the success of Henry Ford suggests him as an object of universal respect, but no one knows and cares about the bum or hobo who is Rockefeller's or Ford's neighbor. So, also, is the world attracted by the glittering success of races and nations, and pays absolutely no attention to the bum or hobo race that lingers by the wayside.

The Negro must be up and doing if he will break down the prejudice of the rest of the world. Prayer alone is not going to improve our condition, nor the policy of watchful waiting. We must strike out for ourselves in the course of material achievement, and by our own effort and energy present to the world those forces by which the progress of man is judged.

A NATION AND COUNTRY

The Negro needs a nation and a country of his own, where he can best show evidence of his own ability in the art of human progress. Scattered as an unmixed and unrecognized part of alien nations and civilizations is but to demonstrate his imbecility, and point him out as an unworthy derelict, fit neither for the society of Greek, Jew nor Gentile.

It is unfortunate that we should so drift apart, as a race, as not to see that we are but perpetuating our own sorrow and disgrace in failing to appreciate the first great requisite of all peoples—organization.

Organization is a great power in directing the affairs of a race or nation toward a given goal. To properly develop the desires that are uppermost, we must first concentrate through some system or method, and there is none better than organization. Hence, the Universal Negro Improvement Association appeals to each and every Negro to throw in his lot with those of us who, through organization, are working for the universal emancipation of our race and the redemption of our common country, Africa.

No Negro, let him be American, European, West Indian or African, shall be truly respected until the race as a whole has emancipated itself, through self-achievement and progress, from universal prejudice. The Negro will have to build his own government, industry, art, science, literature and culture, before the world will stop to consider him. Until then, we are but wards of a superior race and civilization, and the outcasts of a standard social system.

The race needs workers at this time, not plagiarists, copyists and mere imitators; but men and women who are able to create, to originate and improve, and thus make an independent racial contribution to the world and civilization.

MONKEY APINGS OF "LEADERS"

The unfortunate thing about us is that we take the monkey apings of our "so-called leading men" for progress. There is no progress in aping white people and telling us that they represent the best in the race, for in that respect any dressed monkey would represent the best of its species, irrespective of the creative matter of the monkey instinct. The best in a race is not reflected through or by the action of its apes, but by its ability to create of and by itself. It is such a creation that the Universal Negro Improvement Association seeks.

Let us not try to be the best or worst of others, but let us make the effort to be the best of ourselves. Our own racial critics criticise us as dreamers and "fanatics," and call us "benighted" and "ignorant," because they lack racial backbone. They are unable to see themselves creators of their own needs. The slave instinct has not yet departed from them. They still believe that they can only live or exist through the good graces of their "masters." The good slaves have not yet thrown off their shackles; thus, to them, the Universal Negro Improvement Association is an "impossibility."

It is the slave spirit of dependence that causes our "so-called leading men" (apes) to seek the shelter, leadership, protection and patronage of the "master" in their organization and so-called advancement work. It is the spirit of feeling secured as good servants of the master, rather than as independents, why our modern Uncle Toms take pride in laboring under alien leadership and becoming surprised at the audacity of the Universal Negro Improvement Association in proclaiming for racial liberty and independence.

But the world of white and other men, deep down in their hearts, have much more respect for those of us who work for our racial salvation under the banner of the Universal Negro Improvement Association, than they could ever have in all eternity for a group of helpless apes and beggars who make a monopoly of undermining their own race and belittling themselves in the eyes of self-respecting people, by being "good boys" rather than able men.

Surely there can be no good will between apes, seasoned beggars and independent minded Negroes who will at least make an effort to do for themselves. Surely, the "dependents" and "wards" (and may I not say racial imbeciles?) will rave against and plan the destruction of movements like the Universal Negro Improvement Association that expose them to the liberal white minds of the world as not being representative of the best in the Negro, but, to the contrary, the worst. The best of a race does not live on the patronage and philanthropy of others, but makes an effort to do for itself. The best of the great white race doesn't fawn before and beg black, brown or yellow men; they go out, create for self and thus demonstrate the fitness of the race to survive; and so the white race of

America and the world will be informed that the best in the Negro race is not the class of beggars who send out to other races piteous appeals annually for donations to maintain their coterie, but the groups within us that are honestly striving to do for themselves with the voluntary help and appreciation of that class of other races that is reasonable, just and liberal enough to give to each and every one a fair chance in the promotion of those ideals that tend to greater human progress and human love.

The work of the Universal Negro Improvement Association is clear and clean-cut. It is that of inspiring an unfortunate race with pride in self and with the determination of going ahead in the creation of those ideals that will lift them to the unprejudiced company of races and nations. There is no desire for hate or malice, but every wish to see all mankind linked into a common fraternity of progress and achievement that will wipe away the odor of prejudice, and elevate the human race to the height of real godly love and satisfaction—1923.

THE NEGRO'S PLACE IN
WORLD REORGANIZATION

Gradually we are approaching the time when the Negro peoples of the world will have either to consciously, through their own organization, go forward to the point of destiny as laid out by themselves, or must sit quiescently and see themselves pushed back into the mire of economic serfdom, to be ultimately crushed by the grinding mill of exploitation and be exterminated ultimately by the strong hand of prejudice.

There is no doubt about it that we are living in the age of world reorganization out of which will come a set program for the organized races of mankind that will admit of no sympathy in human affairs, in that we are planning for the great gigantic struggle of the survival of the fittest group. It becomes each and every one engaged in this great race for place and position to use whatsoever influence possible to divert the other fellow's attention from the real object. In our own sphere in America and the western world we find that we are being camouflaged, not so much by those with whom we are competing for our economic, political existence, but by men from within our own race, either as agents of the opposition or as unconscious fools who are endeavoring to flatter us into believing that our future should rest with chance and with Providence, believing that through these agencies will come the solution of the restless problem. Such leadership is but preparing us for the time that is bound to befall us if we do not exert ourselves now toward our own creative purpose. The mission of the Universal Negro Improvement Association is to arouse the sleeping consciousness of Negroes everywhere to the point where we will, as one concerted body, act for our own preservation. By laying the foundation for such we will be able to work toward the glorious realization of an emancipated race and a constructed nation. Nationhood is the strongest security of any people and it is for that the Universal Negro Improvement Association strives at this time. With the clamor of other peoples for a similar purpose, we raise a noise even to high heaven for the admission of the Negro into the plan of autonomy.

BLACK AFRICA

On every side we hear the cry of white supremacy—in America, Canada, Australia, Europe, and even South America. There is no white supremacy beyond the power and strength of the white man to hold himself against the others. The supremacy of any race is not permanent; it is a thing only of the time in which the race finds itself powerful. The whole world of white men is becoming nervous as touching its own future and that of other races. With the desire of self-preservation, which naturally is the first law of nature, they raise the hue and cry that the white race must be first in government and in control. What must the Negro do in the face of such a universal attitude but to align all his forces in the direction of protecting himself from the threatened disaster of race domination and ultimate extermination?

Without a desire to harm anyone, the Universal Negro Improvement Association feels that the Negro should without compromise or any apology appeal to the same spirit of racial pride and love as the great white race is doing for its own preservation, so that while others are raising the cry of a white America, a white Canada, a white Australia, we also without reservation raise the cry of a "Black Africa." The critic asks, "Is this possible?" and the four hundred million courageous Negroes of the world answer, "Yes."

Out of this very reconstruction of world affairs will come the glorious opportunity for Africa's freedom. Out of the present chaos and European confusion will come an opportunity for the Negro never enjoyed in any other age, for the expansion of himself and the consolidation of his manhood in the direction of building himself a national power in Africa.

The germ of European malice, revenge and antagonism is so deeply rooted among certain of the contending powers that in a short while we feel sure they will present to Negroes the opportunity for which we are organized.

DISABLEMENT OF GERMANY NOT PERMANENT

No one believes in the permanent disablement of Germany, but all thoughtful minds realize that France is but laying the foundation through revenge for a greater conflict than has as yet been seen. With such another upheaval, there is absolutely no reason why organized Negro opinion could not be felt and directed in the channel of their own independence in Africa.

To fight for African redemption does not mean that we must give up our domestic fights for political justice and industrial rights. It does not mean that we must become disloyal to any government or to any country wherein we were born. Each and every race outside of its domestic national loyalty has a loyalty to itself; therefore, it is foolish for the Negro to talk about not being interested in his own racial, political, social and industrial destiny. We can be as loyal American citizens or British subjects as the Irishman or the Jew, and yet fight for the redemption of Africa, a complete emancipation of the race.

Fighting for the establishment of Palestine does not make the American Jew disloyal; fighting for the independence of Ireland does not make the Irish-American a bad citizen. Why should fighting for the freedom of Africa make the Afro-American disloyal or a bad citizen?

The Universal Negro Improvement Association teaches loyalty to all governments outside of Africa; but when it comes to Africa, we feel that the Negro has absolutely no obligation to any one but himself.

Out of the unsettled state and condition of the world will come such revolutions that will give each and every race that is oppressed the opportunity to march forward. The last world war brought the opportunity to many heretofore subject races to regain their freedom. The next world war will give Africa the opportunity for which we are preparing. We are going to have wars and rumors of wars. In another twenty or thirty years we will have a changed world, politically, and Africa will not be one of the most backward nations, but African shall be, I feel sure, one of the greatest commonwealths that will once more hold up the torchlight of civilization and bestow the blessings of freedom, liberty and democracy upon all mankind—**March 24, 1923.**

AIMS AND OBJECTS OF MOVEMENT
FOR SOLUTION OF NEGRO PROBLEM

Generally the public is kept misinformed of the truth surrounding new movements of reform. Very seldom, if ever, reformers get the truth told about them and their movements. Because of this natural attitude, the Universal Negro Improvement Association has been greatly handicapped in its work, causing thereby one of the most liberal and helpful human movements of the twentieth century to be held up to ridicule by those who take pride in poking fun at anything not already successfully established.

The white man of America has become the natural leader of the world. He, because of his exalted position, is called upon to help in all human efforts. From nations to individuals the appeal is made to him for aid in all things affecting humanity, so, naturally, there can be no great mass movement or change without first acquainting the leader on whose sympathy and advice the world moves.

It is because of this, and more so because of a desire to be Christian friends with the white race, why I explain the aims and objects of the Universal Negro Improvement Association.

The Universal Negro Improvement Association is an organization among Negroes that is seeking to improve the condition of the race, with the view of establishing a nation in Africa where Negroes will be given the opportunity to develop by themselves, without creating the hatred and animosity that now exist in countries of the white race through Negroes rivaling them for the highest and best positions in government, politics, society and industry. The organization believes in the rights of all men, yellow, white and black. To us, the white race has a right to the peaceful possession and occupation of countries of its own and in like manner the yellow and black races have their rights. It is only by an honest and liberal consideration of such rights can the world be blessed with the peace that is sought by Christian teachers and leaders.

THE SPIRITUAL BROTHERHOOD OF MAN

The following preamble to the constitution of the organization speaks for itself:

"The Universal Negro Improvement Association and African Communities' League is a social, friendly, humanitarian, charitable, educational, institutional, constructive, and expansive society, and is founded by persons, desiring to the utmost to work for the general uplift of the Negro peoples of the world. And the members pledge themselves to do all in their power to conserve the rights of their noble race and to respect the rights of all mankind, believing always in the Brotherhood of Man and the Fatherhood of God. The motto of the organization is: One God! One Aim! One Destiny! Therefore, let justice be done to all mankind, realizing that if the strong oppresses the weak confusion and discontent will ever mark the path of man, but with love, faith and charity toward all the reign of peace and plenty will be heralded into the world and the generation of men shall be called Blessed."

The declared objects of the association are:

"To establish a Universal Confraternity among the race; to promote the spirit of pride and love; to reclaim the fallen; to administer to and assist the needy; to assist in civilizing the backward tribes of Africa; to assist in the development of Independent Negro Nations and Communities; to establish a central nation for the race; to establish Commissaries or Agencies in the principal countries and cities of the world for the representation of all Negroes; to promote a conscientious Spiritual worship among the native tribes of Africa; to establish Universities, Colleges, Academies and Schools for the racial education and culture of the people; to work for better conditions among Negroes everywhere."

SUPPLYING A LONG FELT WANT

The organization of the Universal Negro Improvement Association has supplied among Negroes a long-felt want. Hitherto the other Negro movements in America, with the exception of the Tuskegee effort of Booker T. Washington, sought to teach the Negro to aspire to social equality with the whites, meaning thereby the right to intermarry and fraternize in every social way. This has been the source of much trouble and still some Negro organizations continue to preach this dangerous "race destroying doctrine" added to a program of political agitation and aggression. The Universal Negro Improvement Association on the other hand believes in and teaches the pride and purity of race. We believe that the white race should uphold its racial pride and perpetuate itself, and that the black race should do likewise. We believe that there is room enough in the world for the various race groups to grow and develop by themselves without seeking to destroy the Creator's plan by the constant introduction of mongrel types.

The unfortunate condition of slavery, as imposed upon the Negro, and which caused the mongrelization of the race, should not be legalized and continued now to the harm and detriment of both races.

The time has really come to give the Negro a chance to develop himself to a moral-standard-man, and it is for such an opportunity that the Universal Negro Improvement Association seeks in the creation of an African nation for Negroes, where the greatest latitude would be given to work out this racial ideal.

There are hundreds of thousands of colored people in America who desire race amalgamation and miscegenation as a solution of the race problem. These people are, therefore, opposed to the race pride ideas of black and white; but the thoughtful of both races will naturally ignore the ravings of such persons and honestly work for the solution of a problem that has been forced upon us.

Liberal white America and race loving Negroes are bound to think at this time and thus evolve a program or plan by which there can be a fair and amicable settlement of the question.

We cannot put off the consideration of the matter, for time is pressing on our hands. The educated Negro is making rightful constitutional demands. The great white majority will never grant them, and thus we march on to danger if we do not now stop and adjust the matter.

The time is opportune to regulate the relationship between both races. Let the Negro have a country of his own. Help him to return to his original home, Africa, and there give him the opportunity to climb from the lowest to the highest positions in a state of his own. If not, then the nation will have to hearken to the demand of the aggressive, "social equality" organization, known as the National Association for the Advancement of Colored People, of which W. E. B. Du Bois is leader, which declares vehemently for social and political equality, viz.: Negroes and whites in the same hotels, homes, residential districts, public and private places, a Negro as president, members of the Cabinet, Governors of States, Mayors of cities, and leaders of society in the United States. In this agitation, Du Bois is ably supported by the "Chicago Defender," a colored newspaper published in Chicago. This paper advocated Negroes in the Cabinet and Senate. All these, as everybody knows, are the Negroes' constitutional rights, but reason dictates that the masses of the white race will never stand by the ascendancy of an opposite minority group to the favored positions in a government, society and industry that exist by the will of the majority, hence the demand of the Du Bois group of colored leaders will only lead, ultimately, to further disturbances in riots, lynching and mob rule. The only logical solution therefore, is to supply the Negro with opportunities and environments of his own, and there point him to the fullness of his ambition.

NEGROES WHO SEEK SOCIAL EQUALITY

The Negro who seeks the White House in America could find ample play for his ambition in Africa. The Negro who seeks the office of Secretary of State in America would have a fair chance of demonstrating his diplomacy in Africa. The Negro who seeks a seat in the Senate or of being governor of a State in America, would be provided with a glorious chance for statesmanship in Africa.

The Negro has a claim on American white sympathy that cannot be denied. The Negro has labored for 300 years in contributing to America's greatness. White America will not be unmindful, therefore, of this consideration, but will treat him kindly. Yet it is realized that all human beings have a limit to their humanity. The humanity of white America, we realize, will seek self-protection and self-preservation, and that is why the thoughtful and reasonable Negro sees no hope in America for satisfying the aggressive program of the National Association for the Advancement of Colored People, but advances the reasonable plan of the Universal Negro Improvement Association, that of creating in Africa a nation and government for the Negro race.

This plan when properly undertaken and prosecuted will solve the race problem in America in fifty years. Africa affords a wonderful opportunity at the present time for colonization by the Negroes of the Western world. There is Liberia, already established as an independent Negro government. Let white America assist Afro-Americans to go there and help develop the country. Then, there are the late German colonies; let white sentiment force England and France to turn them over to the American and West Indian Negroes who fought for the Allies in the World's War. Then, France, England and Belgium owe America billions of dollars which they claim they cannot afford to repay immediately. Let them compromise by turning over Sierra Leone and the Ivory Coast on the West Coast of Africa and add them to Liberia and help make Liberia a state worthy of her history.

The Negroes of Africa and America are one in blood. They have sprung from the same common stock. They can work and live together and thus make their own racial contribution to the world.

Will deep thinking and liberal white America help? It is a considerate duty.

It is true that a large number of self-seeking colored agitators and so-called political leaders, who hanker after social equality and fight for the impossible in politics and governments, will rave, but remember that the slave-holder raved, but the North said, "Let the slaves go free"; the British Parliament raved when the Colonists said, "We want a free and American nation"; the Monarchists of France raved when the people declared for a more liberal form of government.

The masses of Negroes think differently from the self-appointed leaders of the race. The majority of Negro leaders are selfish, self-appointed and not elected by the people. The people desire freedom in a land of their own, while the colored politician desires office and social equality for himself in America, and that is why we are asking white America to help the masses to realize their objective. . .—1923.

RACIAL IDEALS

The coming together, all over this country, of fully six million people of Negro blood, to work for the creation of a nation of their own in their motherland, Africa, is no joke.

There is now a world revival of thought and action, which is causing peoples everywhere to bestir themselves towards their own security, through which we hear the cry of Ireland for the Irish, Palestine for the Jew, Egypt for the Egyptian, Asia for the Asiatic, and thus we Negroes raise the cry of Africa for the Africans, those at home and those abroad.

Some people are not disposed to give us credit for having feelings, passions, ambitions and desires like other races; they are satisfied to relegate us to the back-heap of human aspirations; but this is a mistake. The Almighty Creator made us men, not unlike others, but in His own image; hence, as a race, we feel that we, too, are entitled to the rights that are common to humanity.

The cry and desire for liberty is justifiable, and is made holy everywhere. It is sacred and holy to the Anglo-Saxon, Teuton and Latin; to the Anglo-American it precedes that of all religions, and now come the Irish, the Jew, the Egyptian, the Hindoo, and, last but not least, the Negro, clamoring for their share as well as their right to be free.

All men should be free—free to work out their own salvation. Free to create their own destinies. Free to nationally build up themselves for the upbringing and rearing of a culture and civilization of their own. Jewish culture is different from Irish culture. Anglo-Saxon culture is unlike Teutonic culture. Asiatic culture differs greatly from European culture; and, in the same way, the world should be liberal enough to allow the Negro latitude to develop a culture of his own. Why should the Negro be lost among the other races and nations of the world and to himself? Did nature not make of him a son of the soil? Did the Creator not fashion him out of the dust of the earth?—out of that rich soil to which he bears such a wonderful resemblance?—a resemblance that changes not, even though the ages have flown? No, the Ethiopian cannot change his skin; and so we appeal to the conscience of the white world to yield us a place of national freedom among the creatures of present-day temporal materialism.

We Negroes are not asking the white man to turn Europe and America over to us. We are not asking the Asiatic to turn Asia over for the accommodation of the blacks. But we are asking a just and righteous world to restore Africa to her scattered and abused children.

We believe in justice and human love. If our rights are to be respected, then, we, too, must respect the rights of all mankind; hence, we are ever ready and willing to yield to the white man the things that are his, and we feel that he, too, when his conscience is touched, will yield to us the things that are ours.

We should like to see a peaceful, prosperous and progressive white race in America and Europe; a peaceful, prosperous and progressive yellow race in Asia, and, in like manner, we want, and we demand, a peaceful, prosperous and progressive black race in Africa. Is that asking too much? Surely not. Humanity, without any immediate human hope of racial oneness, has drifted apart, and is now divided into separate and distinct groups, each with its own ideals and aspirations. Thus, we cannot expect any one race to hold a monopoly of creation and be able to keep the rest satisfied.

DISTINCT RACIAL GROUP IDEALISM

From our distinct racial group idealism we feel that no black man is good enough to govern the white man, and no white man good enough to rule the black man; and so of all races and peoples. No one feels that the other, alien in race, is good enough to govern or rule to the exclusion of native racial rights. We may as well, therefore, face the question of superior and inferior races. In twentieth century civilization there are no inferior and superior races. There are backward peoples, but that does not make them inferior. As far as humanity goes, all men are equal, and especially where peoples are intelligent enough to know what they want. At this time all peoples know what they want—it is liberty. When a people have sense enough to know that they ought to be free, then they naturally become the equal of all, in the higher calling of man to know and direct himself. It is true that economically and scientifically certain races are more progressive than others; but that does not imply superiority. For the Anglo-Saxon to say that he is superior because he introduced submarines to destroy life, or the Teuton because he compounded liquid gas to outdo in the art of killing, and that the Negro is inferior because he is backward in that direction is to leave one's self open to the retort "Thou shalt not kill," as being the divine law that sets the moral standard of the real man. There is no superiority in the one race economically monopolizing and holding all that would end to the sustenance of life, and thus cause unhappiness and distress to others; for our highest purpose should be to love and care for each other, and share with each other the things that our Heavenly Father has placed at our common disposal; and even in this, the African is unsurpassed, in that he feeds his brother and shares with him the product of the land. The idea of race superiority is questionable; nevertheless, we must admit that from the white man's standard, he is far superior to the rest of us, but that kind of superiority is too inhuman and dangerous to be permanently helpful. Such a superiority was shared and indulged in by other races before, and even by our own, when we boasted of a wonderful civilization on the banks of the Nile, when others were still groping in darkness; but because of our unrighteousness it failed, as all such will. Civilization can only last when we have reached the point where we will be our brother's keeper. That is to say, when we feel it righteous to live and let live.

NO EXCLUSIVE RIGHT TO THE WORLD

Let no black man feel that he has the exclusive right to the world, and other men none, and let no white man feel that way, either. The world is the property of all mankind, and each and every group is entitled to a portion. The black man now wants his, and in terms uncompromising he is asking for it.

The Universal Negro Improvement Association represents the hopes and aspirations of the awakened Negro. Our desire is for a place in the world; not to disturb the tranquillity of other men, but to lay down our burden and rest our weary backs and feet by the banks of the Niger, and sing our songs and chant our hymns to the God of Ethiopia. Yes, we want rest from the toil of centuries, rest of political freedom, rest of economic and industrial liberty, rest to be socially free and unmolested, rest from lynching and burning, rest from discrimination of all kinds.

Out of slavery we have come with our tears and sorrows, and we now lay them at the feet of American white civilization. We cry to the considerate white people for help, because in their midst we can scarce help ourselves. We are strangers in a strange land. We cannot sing, we cannot play on our harps, for our hearts are sad. We are sad because of the tears of our mothers and the cry of our fathers. Have you not heard the plaintive wail? It is your father and my father burning at stake; but, thank God, there is a larger humanity growing among the good and considerate white people of this country, and they are going to help. They will help us to recover our souls.

As children of captivity we look forward to a new day and a new, yet ever old, land of our fathers, the land of refuge, the land of the Prophets, the land of the Saints, and the land of God's crowning glory. We shall gather together our children, our treasures and our loved ones, and, as the children of Israel, by the command of God, faced the promised land, so in time we shall also stretch forth our hands and bless our country.

Good and dear America that has succored us for three hundred years knows our story. We have watered her vegetation with our tears for two hundred and fifty years. We have built her cities and laid the foundation of her imperialism with the mortar of our blood and bones for three centuries, and now we cry to her for help. Help us, America, as we helped you. We helped you in the Revolutionary War. We helped you in the Civil War, and, although Lincoln helped us, the price is not half paid. We helped you in the Spanish-American war. We died nobly and courageously in Mexico, and did we not leave behind us on the stained battlefields of France and Flanders our rich blood to mark the poppies' bloom, and to bring back to you the glory of the flag that never touched the dust? We have no regrets in service to America for three hundred years, but we pray that America will help us for another fifty years until we have solved the troublesome problem that now confronts us. We know and realize that two ambitious and competitive races cannot live permanently side by side, without friction and trouble, and that is why the white race wants a white America and the black race wants and demands a black Africa.

Let white America help us for fifty years honestly, as we have helped her for three hundred years, and before the expiration of many decades there shall be no more race problem. Help us to gradually go home, America. Help us as you have helped the Jews. Help us as you have helped the Irish. Help us as you have helped the Poles, Russians, Germans and Armenians.

The Universal Negro Improvement Association proposes a friendly cooperation with all honest movements seeking intelligently to solve the race problem. We are not seeking social equality; we do not seek intermarriage, nor do we hanker after the impossible. We want the right to have a country of our own, and there foster and re-establish a culture and civilization exclusively ours. Don't say it can't be done. The Pilgrims and colonists did it for America, and the new Negro, with sympathetic help, can do it for Africa.

BACK TO AFRICA

The thoughtful and industrious of our race want to go back to Africa, because we realize it will be our only hope of permanent existence. We cannot all go in a day or year, ten or twenty years. It will take time under the rule of modern economics, to entirely or largely depopulate a country of a people, who have been its residents for centuries, but we feel that, with proper help for fifty years, the problem can be solved. We do not want all the Negroes in Africa. Some are no good here, and naturally will be no good there. The no-good Negro will naturally die in fifty years. The Negro who is wrangling about and fighting for social equality will naturally pass away in fifty years, and yield his place to the progressive Negro who wants a society and country of his own.

Negroes are divided into two groups, the industrious and adventurous, and the lazy and dependent. The industrious and adventurous believe that whatsoever others have done it can do. The Universal Negro Improvement Association belongs to this group, and so you find us working, six million strong, to the goal of an independent nationality. Who will not help? Only the mean and despicable "who never to himself hath said, this is my own, my native land." Africa is the legitimate, moral and righteous home of all Negroes, and now, that the time is coming for all to assemble under their own vine and fig tree, we feel it our duty to arouse every Negro to a consciousness of himself.

White and black will learn to respect each other when they cease to be active competitors in the same countries for the same things in politics and society. Let them have countries of their own, wherein to aspire and climb without rancor. The races can be friendly and helpful to each other, but the laws of nature separate us to the extent of each and every one developing by itself.

We want an atmosphere all our own. We would like to govern and rule ourselves and not be encumbered and restrained. We feel now just as the white race would feel if they were governed and ruled by the Chinese. If we live in our own districts, let us rule and govern those districts. If we have a majority in our communities, let us run those communities. We form a majority in Africa and we should naturally govern ourselves there. No man can govern another's house as well as himself. Let us have fair play. Let us have justice. This is the appeal we make to white America— **1924.**

Sources and Acknowledgments

Martin R. Delany

The Condition, Elevation, Emigration, and Destiny of the Colored People of the United States, "Politically Considered" was originally published in 1852 (Philadelphia: Privately printed). Reprinted are chapters 1–7, 16–the end.

Official Report of the Niger Valley Exploring Party was originally published in 1861 (New York: Thomas Hamilton). Reprinted are sections 11–13.

Edward W. Blyden

"The Call of Providence to the Descendants of Africa in America" is from *Liberia's Offering* (New York: John A. Gray, 1862), pp. 67–91.

"The African Problem and the Method of Its Solution," the annual discourse delivered at the seventy-third anniversary of the American Colonization Society in Washington, D.C., January 19, 1890, was originally published as a pamphlet, Washington, D.C., 1890.

James T. Holly

A Vindication of the Capacity of the Negro Race for Self-Government and Civilized Progress as Demonstrated by Historical Events of the Haytian Revolution, "and the Subsequent Acts of That People since Their National Independence," was originally published in 1857 (New Haven: Afric-American Printing Company).

Alexander Crummell

"The Relations and Duties of Free Colored Men in America to Africa," a letter to Mr. Charles B. Dunbar, M.D., September 1, 1860, is from *Future of Africa* (New York: Charles Scribner, 1862). The selection reprinted is pp. 215–223, 273–281.

"The Race Problem in America" is from *Africa and America: Addresses and Discourses* (Springfield, Mass.: Willey & Co., 1891), pp. 39–57.

African Civilization Society

"Constitution of the African Civilization Society" was originally published as a pamphlet, New Haven, 1861.

Henry Highland Garnet

The Past and the Present Condition, and the Destiny of the Colored Race was originally published in 1848 (Troy, N.Y.; Steam Press of J. C. Kneeland and Co.). The excerpt reprinted is pp. 25–29.

Frederick Douglass

"What Are the Colored People Doing for Themselves?" is from *The North Star,* July 14, 1848.

"An Address to the Colored People of the United States," is from *The North Star,* September 29, 1848.

"Prejudice Not Natural" [title supplied by the editor] is an excerpt from "The American Colonization Society," originally published in the *Liberator,* June 8, 1849.

"The Nature of Slavery," an extract from a lecture delivered at Rochester, December 1, 1850, was published in *My Bondage and My Freedom* (New York and Auburn: Miller, Orton, and Mulligan, 1855), pp. 429–434.

"Letter to Harriet Beecher Stowe" was originally published in *Proceedings of the Colored National Convention, Held in Rochester, July 6th, 7th, and 8th, 1853* (Rochester: Printed at the Office of *Frederick Douglass' Paper*, 1853), pp. 33–38.

"The Claims of the Negro Ethnologically Considered," an address delivered before the literary societies of Western Reserve College at commencement, July 12, 1854, was originally published as a pamphlet (Rochester, 1854).

"The Doom of the Black Power" is from *Frederick Douglass' Paper*, July 27, 1855.

"Speech on the Dred Scott Decision" is from "Two Speeches by Frederick Douglass; one on West India Emancipation, delivered at Canandaigua, August 4th, and the other on the Dred Scott Decision, delivered in New York on the occasion of the Anniversary of the American Abolition Society, May 1857," a pamphlet published in Rochester, 1857.

"African Civilization Society" is from *Douglass' Monthly*, February 1859.

"The Present and Future of the Colored Race in America" is from *Douglass' Monthly*, June 1863.

"What the Black Man Wants" is from William D. Kelley et al., *The Equality of All Men before the Law Claimed and Defended* (Boston: Press of G. C. Rand & Avery, 1865), pp. 36–39.

"Address before the Tennessee Colored Agricultural and Mechanical Association" delivered in Nashville, September 18, 1873, was originally published as a pamphlet (Washington, D.C., 1873).

"The Civil Rights Case" is from "Proceedings of the Civil Rights Mass Meeting Held at Lincoln Hall, October 22, 1883: Speeches of Hon. Frederick Douglass and Robert G. Ingersoll," a pamphlet published in Washington, D.C., 1883.

"The Future of the Negro" is from *The North American Review*, July 1884, pp. 84–86.

"The Future of the Colored Race" is from *The North American Review*, May 1886, pp. 437–440.

"The Nation's Problem," a speech delivered before the Bethel Literary and Historical Society in Washington, D.C., April 16, 1889, was originally published as a pamphlet (Washington, D.C., 1889).

"The Folly of Colonization" [title supplied by the editor] is an excerpt from an address on "The Lessons of the Hour," delivered in Washington, D.C., January 9, 1894, and originally published as a pamphlet (Baltimore, 1894).

T. Thomas Fortune
"Education," "Political Independence of the Negro," and "Solution of the Political Problem" are from *Black and White*, "Land, Labor, and Politics in the South" (New York: Fords, Howard, & Hulbert, 1884), pp. 79–87, 90–92, 112–146.

Booker T. Washington
"The Educational Outlook in the South" is an address delivered to the National Education Association at Madison, Wisconsin, July 16, 1884.

"Atlanta Exposition Address" was deilvered at the opening of the Cotton States and International Exposition at Atlanta, Georgia (September 18, 1865).

"Our New Citizen" is an address delivered before the Hamilton Club, Chicago, Illinois (January 31, 1896).

"Democracy and Education" is an address delivered before the Institute of Arts and Sciences, Brooklyn, New York, September 30, 1896.

"Address Delivered at Hampton Institute" was delivered November 18, 1896.

"Letter to the Louisiana State Constitutional Convention" (February 19, 1898) and "An Interview on the Hardwick Bill," originally published in the Atlanta Constitution, 1900, are in a brochure of the Schomburg Collection of the New York Public Library.

"Early Problems of Freedom" is from *Frederick Douglass* (Philadelphia and London: George W. Jacobs & Company, 1907), pp. 245–272.

"Progress of the American Negro," "The Negro and the Labor Problem of the South," "The Fruits of Industrial Training," and "The American Negro and His Economic Value" are from *The Negro in Business* (Boston and Chicago: Hertel, Jenkins & Co., 1907), chs. 27, 28, 30, 31. "On Making Our Race Life Count in the Life of the Nation" is from *Putting the Most into Life* (New York: T.Y. Crowell & Co., 1906), ch. 6.

"The Intellectuals and the Boston Mob" and "The Mistakes and the Future of Negro Education" are from *My Larger Education,* Garden City, N.Y.; Doubleday, Page & Co., 1911), chs. 5, 12.

"Is the Negro Having a Fair Chance," originally published in *The Century Magazine,* November 1912, pp. 46–55, and "My View of Segregation Laws," originally published in *The New Republic,* December 4, 1915, 113–114, are reprinted with permission of Mrs. Portia Washington Pittman.

Archibald H. Grimke

"Modern Industrialism and the Negroes of the United States" was originally published as The American Negro Academy, *Occasional Papers,* No. 12 (Washington, D.C., 1908).

William Edward Burghardt Du Bois

"The Conservation of Races" was originally published as The American Negro Academy, *Occasional Papers,* No. 2 (Washington, D.C., 1897).

The Philadelphia Negro: A Social Study was originally published in 1899 (Philadelphia: The University of Pennsylvania Press). The excerpt reprinted within is from chs. 16, 18.

"Of Mr. Booker T. Washington and Others" is from *The Souls of Black Folk* (Chicago: McClurg & Co., 1903), ch. 3.

"The Talented Tenth" is from Booker T. Washington et al., *The Negro Problem* (New York: James Pott & Co., 1903), pp. 33–75.

"Declaration of Principles of the Niagara Movement" (1905) and "Resolutions of the Niagara Movement" (August 15, 1906) are brochures in the Schomburg Collection of the New York Public Library.

"The Evolution of the Race Problem is from *Proceedings of the National Negro Conference* (New York, 1909), pp. 142–158.

Marcus Garvey

"Race Assimilation," "The True Solution of the Negro Problem," "An Appeal
to the Soul of White America," "Racial Reforms and Reformers," "Who and What
Is a Negro?" "An Appeal to the Conscience of the Black Race to See Itself," "The
Negro's Place in World Reorganization," "Aims and Objects of Movement for Solution of Negro Problem," and "Racial Ideals" [title supplied by editor; speech delivered at Madison Square Garden, New York City, March 16, 1924] are from Amy
Jacques-Garvey, ed., *Philosophy and Opinions of Marcus Garvey* (New York: Universal Publishing House, 1923 and 1925), 2 vols., and are reprinted with permission
of Mrs. Amy Jacques-Garvey.

Index